Traditional
Oral Epic

Traditional
Oral Epic

The *Odyssey*, *Beowulf*,
and the Serbo-Croatian Return Song

John Miles Foley

UNIVERSITY OF CALIFORNIA PRESS
Berkeley   Los Angeles   Oxford

University of California Press
Berkeley and Los Angeles, California

University of California Press, Ltd.
Oxford, England
©1990 by
The Regents of the University of California

Library of Congress Cataloging-in-Publication Data

Foley, John Miles.
  Traditional oral epic.

  Bibliography: p.
  Includes index.
    1. Epic literature—History and criticism.   2. Oral
tradition.   I. Title.
  PN56.E65F65 1990 809.1′3   88-29596
  ISBN 0-520-06409-7 (alk. paper)

Printed in the United States of America

1   2   3   4   5   6   7   8   9

For my little son,
John Miles Foley, Jr.

How fragile we are

CONTENTS

PREFACE

Since the purpose of a comparative study is to compare, it cannot focus as closely on any single literature or tradition as can a book devoted solely to that literature or tradition. A comparative study makes whatever contribution it can by pointing out similarities and differences that are beyond the natural scope of books on a single area, by complementing more narrowly conceived research and scholarship. The danger in broader studies is self-evident: comparative work can fall victim to overgeneralization, to dilettantism, even to faulty reasoning within any one area. But the risk is occasionally worth taking, and especially in the case of studies in oral tradition, for the comparative work can draw strength from more focused scholarship and, in return, provide a fuller, richer context for investigation within a particular literature or tradition.

Judicious comparison means an honest appraisal of differences as well as similarities. Studies in oral tradition have unfortunately not always heeded this double responsibility, emphasizing continuities or parallels across traditions much more often than idiosyncratic features. This imbalance was no doubt inevitable, however, given the fact that careful discrimination simply was not possible before the establishment of basic congruencies. In any event, the time now seems right for a "tradition-dependent" perspective—a point of view that understands oral traditions (and oral-derived texts) as individual expressions of an enormously large and complex phenomenon.

Within this perspective the present studies concentrate primarily on *structure*—that is, on the tectonics of oral and oral-derived epic from the level of prosody and phraseology through that of narrative pattern—in ancient Greek, Serbo-Croatian, and Old English. The Greek and Yugoslav poems were chosen because of a natural fit in poetic genre: the *Odyssey* and the Serbo-Croatian Return Song follow the same overall sequence of events and are not uncommonly considered to be of the same subgenre. *Beowulf* was included on the grounds that it represents the only surviving epic from the Anglo-Saxon tradition.

The opening chapter sets the tone and prospectus for the book by raising the issue of poetics, and with it the question of comparability among traditions. Chapter 2 expands the idea of tradition-dependence to discrimination among documents, that is, to a consideration of how the actual oral or written records of these oral and oral-derived epics both compare and differ. In the third chapter, the philological foundation of these studies as a whole, I compare the three epic prosodies—as individual instruments and, where possible, as reflexes of Indo-European prosody. Chapters 4 through 6 then extend the investigation from meter to phraseology, chapters 7 through 9 explore the "typical scene" or "theme," and the final chapter focuses on the level of "story-pattern" or tale type.

In its nearly exclusive attention to matters of structure, the present volume attempts to outline a comparative context for studies of phraseology and narrative pattern in various traditions of oral epic. Likewise, I view it as preliminary to a responsible study of traditional aesthetics, a project to follow this one. Bibliographic and historical support for these and other projects is available in two earlier books (Foley 1985, 1988); I have thus intentionally kept such information to a minimum here.

A few technical matters should be mentioned. I have employed the Oxford standard editions of the *Iliad* and *Odyssey*, the Klaeber edition of *Beowulf*, and the *SCHS* (*Serbo-Croatian Heroic Songs*) editions of Parry Collection epics; most of the Serbo-Croatian material is, however, drawn from my own editing of unpublished Parry Collection songs from the region of Stolac in Hercegovina. I am very grateful to Albert Lord, Honorary Curator of the Collection, for the privilege of being allowed to work with these materials, and to David Bynum for his help during the initial editing. Since my aim in the chapter on ancient Greek epic phraseology is to illustrate compositional structure and not to assess the diction quantitatively, I have not included variant Homeric readings in analyses of the *Odyssey* and *Iliad* (though I agree with Mark Edwards [1986] that statistical profiles must always include variant readings). All translations of primary and secondary sources, unless otherwise attributed, are my own. For the sake of convenience, bibliographical citations to "Parry" are meant to refer to Milman Parry; his son, Adam, and son's wife, Anne Amory, are referred to as "A. Parry" and "Amory Parry," respectively. Likewise, "Lord" designates Albert Lord, with his wife Mary Louise cited as "M. Lord."

Over the years during which these studies took shape, three institutions were particularly generous with their support. The American Council of Learned Societies provided me with a fellowship to work at the Parry Collection in 1976-77; the first editing of Stolac texts was accomplished under its auspices. In 1980-81 a Guggenheim fellowship provided the time to complete the prosodic and phraseological analyses and to draft most of the chapters. The University of Missouri's award of a research leave in 1985-86 fostered the completion and revision of the volume as it stands, and a subsequent Research Council grant from the same institution defrayed copyediting charges.

I am also indebted to colleagues in various fields, scholars whose published work or personal discussion (or both) have greatly enhanced my understanding of oral traditional epic. Among them are Patricia Arant, Samuel Armistead, David Bynum, Mishael Caspi, Joseph Duggan, Alan Dundes, Mark Edwards, Donald Fry, Joel Halpern, Eric Havelock (*in memoriam*), Lauri Havrilahti, Edward Irving, Elizabeth and Michael Jeffreys, Werner Kelber, Robert Kellogg, Barbara Kerewsky-Halpern, Svetozar Koljević, Tim Lally, John Miletich, Nada Milošević-Djordjević, Gregory Nagy, Joseph Nagy, Ward Parks, R. Parthasarathy, Svetozar Petrović, Burton Raffel, Karl Reichl, Frederick Turner, and Ruth Webber. For special thanks I single out Robert Creed, Anne Lebeck (*in memoriam*), Albert Lord, Michael Nagler, Walter Ong, and Alain Renoir. Of course, none of these people or institutions is responsible for any errors or infelicities that remain in these studies.

Since the final form of this book was accepted for publication in mid-1987, I have in most cases been unable to take account of scholarship that appeared after 1986.

Colleagues at the University of California Press have been remarkably helpful at all stages, handling a difficult manuscript with patience and real editorial acuity. I especially thank Dan Dixon, guiding light from the outset; Anne Canright, copyeditor extraordinaire; and Rose Vekony, an editor of enormous skill and understanding. For assistance with checking and reading proof, I am greatly indebted to Adam Davis.

Closer to the hearth, I am ever grateful to my family—to Joshua and Lizzie, and also to my aunt and foster parent Frances Foley Kelly, but most of all to Anne-Marie, without whose Penelope-like steadfastness, love, and "intervention" this project would not have been completed. The book thus brought forth is dedicated to my late son John, whose happy, responsive touch his mother and I will always remember.

ONE

Traditional
Oral Poetics

This chapter, like the volume in general, explores some fundamental issues in oral literature research from a comparative point of view. It consists of three parts: (1) a brief examination of certain of the most significant contemporary problems in oral traditional poetics, (2) a "program for reading" traditional texts (as opposed to a poetics intended for literary works), and (3) a sample application of the program to five texts from the Serbo-Croatian, ancient Greek, and Old English poetic canons. While I cannot claim to confront all of the relevant issues in this single chapter, I hope that these initial remarks have meaning for those who aim at an understanding of oral and traditional texts on their own terms. For that is precisely the legacy and challenge of oral literature research to date: namely, to attempt the untried trajectory from structural explanation to a unified poetics for these texts. We cannot, nor in fact do we need to, settle any longer for the comfortable sinecure of a strictly *literary* criticism; we need to strike out, to make bold new hypotheses based on the solid data of recent discoveries about *oral* and *traditional* poetry, for these hypotheses are bound to be closer approximations than those based on strictly post-oral, non-traditional verse. In a preliminary way, then, this opening chapter tries to respond to this need for a new poetics.[1]

CONTEMPORARY ISSUES

The first and foremost area of uncertainty in oral literature research has to do directly with two key words—*oral* and *traditional*—as they were first used

---

1. I shall devote a future study, tentatively titled *Immanent Art*, exclusively to the directions mapped out in section 2 of this first chapter, "A Program for Reading Traditional Texts." Since, however, the implementation of the reading program can proceed only after a firm foundation in the comparative philology of oral epic poetry exists, the present volume will concentrate on the various levels of structure in comparative oral epic.

by the classicist Milman Parry in referring to Homer's *Iliad* and *Odyssey*.[2] To take the latter first, note what Parry wrote in 1928 about the nature of Homeric language:

> To establish in the *Iliad* and the *Odyssey* the existence of an artificial language is to prove that Homeric style, in so far as it makes use of that language, is traditional. For the character of that language reveals that it is a work beyond the powers of a single man, or even of a single generation of poets; consequently we know that we are in the presence of a stylistic element which is the product of a tradition and which every bard of Homer's time must have used. (1928a, in 1971, 6)

Parry is describing a formulaic language,[3] a diction which from our text-centered point of view is repetitive or recurrent, and he is deriving from the existence of that diction a poetic *tradition*. He does not mean by his use of that word what T. S. Eliot meant in his famous essay on what is finally an unrelated topic, nor does he mean (as he has often been accused of meaning) that Homer is trapped or conditioned by his language. The poetic tradition properly understood is not at all a limiting but rather a connotatively explosive medium, a touchstone or nexus of indication and reference wholly different from the medium at the disposal of the "non-traditional" artist, for such a diction and narrative structure have obvious and necessary reference not only to the present poem, poet, and time but also to an enormous number of other poets, poems, and eras. Written diction and tradition, no matter how dense with allusions and inherited figures, can never command this open connotative field of reference.[4]

Scholars reacting to Parry's original writings and to Albert Lord's later and equally masterful scholarship have seldom understood this special sense of *traditional*. They have too often perceived the language and narrative weave of Homeric epic and other such works as closed systems, that is, as fully formed, mechanical complexes which the poet need only activate in order to re-create the poem. Analyses of traditional patterning have, in the great majority of instances, implicitly assumed a synchronic text, one which need merely be formulaically, narratively, or syntactically parsed in order to be explained and faithfully interpreted. What scholars have rarely recognized is

2. In this volume there will be no attempt to refer to a wide or even representative selection of general works on oral literature research. For a historical introduction to the field, see my *Theory of Oral Composition: History and Methodology* (1988); for bibliography through 1982, see Foley 1985, updated annually in *Oral Tradition*.

3. Parry's original definition of the *formula* (1930, in 1971, 272) is "a group of words which is regularly employed under the same metrical conditions to express a given essential idea." Lord's definition of *themes* (1960, 68) is "the groups of ideas regularly used in telling a tale in the formulaic style of traditional song." For references to further work in more than ninety separate language traditions, see Foley 1985 and note 2 above.

4. See further, e.g., Renoir 1981b and Foley 1986a,b.

that a traditional text is not simply a synchronic latticework, but also a dia-chronic document of great age and depth. For tradition is nothing if not dia-chronic: it has roots which reach back into its pre-textual history and which inform the present avatar of its identity. Just as, given the insights of recent literary criticism, we cannot any longer settle for one-dimensional models of *Jane Eyre* or the works of Proust, so we cannot afford to countenance the reductive distortion of a poetic tradition to a closed synchronic system. We must actively affirm the historical and evolutionary nature of oral tradition, for this is a crucial aspect of its context.[5]

The variously construed term *oral* is nearly as important as *traditional* to our grasp of poetics. Should we agree with Parry and Lord in carefully limiting the textual sample to oral epic (usually from the Moslem rather than the Christian tradition) composed by entirely unlettered singers, or should we broaden our perspective—and if so, how much should it be broadened? The spirit of Ruth Finnegan's (1977) extension of the corpus of oral poetry beyond the epics of Yugoslavia, ancient Greece, and elsewhere to the myriad other genres composed and performed orally around the world can only mark a positive—even necessary—development, since we need to understand the larger context of oral poetry as well as the material on which we choose to focus. As I have tried to illustrate elsewhere (Foley 1980a), cross-cultural comparisons can quite usefully be drawn between members of genres other than epic; the Old English and Serbo-Croatian magical charms provide one opportunity for such an examination. What must be observed rigorously in every comparative undertaking, however, is the integrity of genre. One simply cannot expect a cogent analysis to come out of a comparison of, for example, riddles and epics; the generic assumptions implicit in the forms must be at variance, and this variance seriously reduces, if not actually invalidates, the legitimacy of the proposed comparison. If we wish to include a number of genres in our survey of an oral culture, we need to proceed in our analyses along methodological lines which respect the principle of *genre-dependence*.

The term *oral* also begs the question of what is to be included under its heading. Not only various genres but also various kinds of texts present them-selves. Some of these, like the Serbo-Croatian *epske pjesme* recorded by Parry and Lord,[6] are known to be oral in origin and in execution; they contain no ambiguous elements possibly traceable to written composition and can confidently be classed as oral traditional texts in the truest sense of that rubric. Another kind of text, much more common and much more commented upon, is that which has come down to us in manuscript only. We may have a few hints about its recording, but these clues are often undependable or mutually contradictory. Often this second kind of text suffers from further complications,

5. See esp. G. Nagy 1974, 1979; Peabody 1975; Janko 1982.
6. For a description of the collecting, see *SCHS* 1:3–20; Lord 1951b.

such as the idiosyncrasy of its recording or editing (one thinks of the stitched-together *Kalevala* of Finland) or the fragmentary or multilingual nature of its remains (the *Gilgamesh*). In light of the controversy over the formulaic test for orality and its frankly uneven application and results,[7] which of these manuscript texts do we admit to fellowship with known oral material, and which do we exclude?

Again I would recommend making some finer distinctions than are customarily pursued by those on either side of the controversy. The formulaic test *as it has generally been carried out* cannot prove oral provenance,[8] for as long as scholars commit the egregious philological sin of importing models and definitions directly from ancient Greek to other poetries without taking account of necessary differences in prosody and versification, nothing can be proved. By counterposing Homeric phraseology to the diction of Old English, Old French, or whatever other poetry one chooses as comparand, without making adjustment for the individual characteristics of each poetry, one simply calculates the extent to which the compared work is composed of Homeric Greek formulas, obviously a useless index. This simple principle of *tradition-dependence*, that is, of respect for a given literature's linguistic and prosodic integrity, has consistently been ignored by comparatists eager to achieve what may seem like ground-breaking results but which are actually based on flawed assumptions from the start. Along with genre-dependence, this attention to language-dependent features would clear away much of the confusion which presently impedes progress in oral literature research.

If the formulaic test for orality must be abandoned (at least in its present form),[9] then what can we do about categorizing our manuscript texts of uncertain provenance? Again I find the question as contemporarily phrased too exclusive and heavy-handed, too much like the Higher Critical battles of the nineteenth and early twentieth centuries over the riddle of the Homeric Question. If we cannot in the present state of knowledge confidently pronounce a problematic text oral, then why not admit that inability and proceed from there? Scholars have shown us that the *Chanson de Roland* and *Beowulf*, for example, have *oral traditional characteristics*: both texts demonstrate a formulaic phraseology, an inventory of typical scenes, and so on.[10] If that information is not enough to prove beyond doubt their orality in the specific Parry-Lord sense of a *guslar* singing in a *kafana*, then so be it; certainly the demonstration of oral traditional characteristics is not entirely in vain.

---

7. As noted in Bynum 1978, 10–11. For the complex history of formulaic studies in Old English, see Foley 1981b, 27–122; Olsen 1986, 1988.

8. See now Lord's similar view (1986c).

9. See chapter 3 for a detailed exposition of how deep the prosodic differences are among the ancient Greek hexameter, the Serbo-Croatian *deseterac*, and the Old English alliterative line.

10. See J. Duggan 1973; and, in general, Foley 1985. On the controversy over what such elements mean to the provenance of a text, see, e.g., Duggan 1981a,b versus Calin 1981a,b.

But it is precisely this faulty conclusion—that is, that because a specific formula count or a certain kind of narrative recurrency is lacking we can cast a text back into the comfortable confines of a written, non-traditional literature—that constitutes a distortion fully as culpable as the overly ambitious assertion of orality that it seeks to correct. For it does not follow that tradition, even oral tradition, ends with the poet's or culture's first draught of literacy. What does end, unambiguously, is the oral tradition in its Ur-form, together with the possibility of recording the oral text in its Ur-form. What continues, just as unambiguously, even in the hands of a skilled writer of verse drawing on an earlier mode, is some vestige of orality and some vestige of tradition.[11] From this perspective, texts which exhibit undeniably oral traditional features, no matter how uncertain a provenance a fair examination of their known history may produce, cannot be treated as or classed with literary works of a much later time.[12] If we must then leave some of our manuscripts in an intermediate category, let us make sure that we opt for that more accurate (if finally indeterminate) characterization rather than settling for the apparently simple but imprecise model of "oral versus written" texts.

A PROGRAM FOR READING TRADITIONAL TEXTS

In this section I shall gather up some of the points made above and attempt a brief codification. In the process it should be possible to posit a short program for confronting both *unambiguously oral texts*, such as the songs collected by Parry and Lord, and what I call *oral-derived texts*, that is, the manuscript or tablet works of finally uncertain provenance that nonetheless show oral traditional characteristics. This methodology must of course be preliminary and suggestive, for at this relatively early stage in the development of oral literature research no program can claim to offer more than a starting point for the poetics of oral and traditional works. But it can from a general perspective draw a few fundamental distinctions about the ontology of different kinds of texts, distinctions which have not been made and very much need to be made. What is more, even these first few steps can help to point the way toward the controlled, exacting comparison to be attempted in the succeeding chapters of these studies.

First is the matter of the term *text*, a concern purposely left undiscussed in my opening remarks. In using this term I mean to indicate a real, objective, and tangible score, an entity that exists both as a thing in itself and as a directive for its perceivers. In this second sense I take advantage of current

11. See esp. Ong 1967, 1977, also 1982. Recently Lord has presented new findings on the influence of fixed texts and transitional material (1986a,c). Also worthy of note in this regard are Opland 1975, 1983; Stock 1983.

12. Compare the remarks of Renoir 1986 on *Sir Gawain and the Green Knight*, Cynewulf, and the *Hildebrandslied*.

critical notions about the "activity" of a text, the dynamics or chemistry of its parts when brought together and to life by the reader.[13] Both senses of the word are important, as we shall recognize explicitly later on: the text serves as an object and as a libretto for the reader's or listener's personal "performance" of the work.

In addition to the dual nature of the text as objective and subjective, I would also stress its special identity in relation to the oral tradition from which it derives, whatever the exact tenor of that relationship might be. For example, a "pure oral text," as described above, represents only one performance of a given song and song-type by a given singer, so that the generic levels of the performance multiply rapidly as the context is determined (see Lord 1960, chap. 5). These levels of generic form are the lifeblood of the tradition, for they insure its recurrency over time and over place. Using the word and concept *text* allows us to designate the particular object we desire to confront or analyze within this reduplicative series. Likewise, in the case of an oral-derived work, we can again specify the one version of a multiform to be confronted, or, if the manuscript poem in question is too far removed from the tradition to be simply one instance of a multiform, the term *text* can still designate the unitary document which in this case will be comprised of quite different elements. As we shall see, this final instance proves to be a significant one, for when a poem is informed by *both* a traditional *and* a non-traditional, learned aesthetic, there is very often a tendency on the part of critics to eliminate either the one or the other aspect.[14] In an effort to make its poetics more straightforward, these critics would dismiss the vigor of such a hybrid text by miscasting its real nature or by characterizing it pejoratively as a "mixed" work. In this case the label *text* helps to maintain the centrifugal parts of the piece for resolution by a centripetal poetics.

A second step in our reading program would be the determination of whether a given text is actually oral or is in fact oral-derived. In either case, of course, we assume the work in question to be at least in part traditional because it exhibits unambiguously oral traditional characteristics. Further, and this point should be stressed, the minimal assumption of an oral-derived text does not automatically preclude true orality; it merely admits a degree of uncertainty about textual history and adopts a demonstrably valid position in favor of a likely conjecture.

For example, the Milman Parry Collection houses thousands of known oral epics, some of them recorded from *guslari* acoustically while sung, others recorded while spoken without the accompaniment of the single-stringed *gusle*, and still others taken from dictation at a much slower pace. As Lord (1953) has demonstrated, these kinds of texts are somewhat different in extent and

---

13. See, e.g., Foley 1984b and 1986b.
14. Some particularly well conceived exceptions to this rule are Renoir 1986, 1988; Olsen 1984.

detail, though usually not significantly different in general structure. In the nineteenth century, however, before modern acoustical recording apparatus became available, Serbo-Croatian epics were committed to a fossilized textual form exclusively through the agency of a scribe or scribe-editor.[15] In such a case we would want to know as far as possible the scribe's control over the performance and his subsequent or concurrent editing of the manuscript. In short, whatever intervenes between the spoken word and its apotheosis as a written record, whether during the performance or at some later time, contributes to the history of that oral text as part of its context. To settle for the most convenient (because most visible) stage of that process—the printed edition alone—is to misread the oral text.

Should we on the other hand be confronting a manuscript work whose certain orality we cannot prove, many of the same criteria for judgment and meaningful reading still apply. If we know only a few details about the recording or (let us say, in order to avoid ambiguity) the creation of a given text, we must nonetheless take them into account; while these few details may fall short of a complete description, they do contribute to context. In the case of an oral-derived text, many of these features will be paleographical in nature. For example, do the graphemics of the manuscript indicate anything about its character? Or does the codex which contains it offer a reading context of any sort? Perhaps we may be able to unearth some information about the manuscript history of such a text—for instance, about the vexed question of the Alexandrians' treatment of Homer. Again, as in the case of the certainly oral work, the oral-derived text demands as its context all that we can discover about what intervened between its formation as a text and the copy in our hands.

The judgment of either oral or oral-derived tells us in general terms what is to be expected in a given work. In the former case we can expect, with certain qualifications resulting from the circumstances of creation and transmission discussed above, a text whose poetics follow characteristic outlines best determined by an intimate acquaintance with the tradition from which the text takes its meaning. Reading as many works as possible within the tradition— that is, developing what synchronic linguists call a "competence" or ability to understand the "traditional grammar"—provides the most thorough preparation. With a known oral poem and a well-collected oral tradition, one can approach this ideal situation and develop an awareness of a work's traditional context.[16] This experience will go a long way toward the formulation of a poetics for that text and tradition, and it will also provide the best possible

15. For a general survey of this process and its fruits, see Coote 1978. Cf. the insights of the recent study of performance texts by Fine (1985).

16. On using a computerized text-processor to "read" numerous versions of a song concurrently and thereby to gain a sense of the gestalt that is their tradition, see Foley 1981a, 1984a.

preparation for comparative work, especially in that large number of cases in which the literature to be compared is not certainly oral or well collected.

And, of course, not only are many known oral traditions not well collected, but almost all manuscript poetries with oral traditional features are very sparsely recorded.[17] In such cases, in which the most immediate context is lacking, one would do well to supplement the investigation with a comparative context, seeking to elucidate one literature through an analog.[18] This was in the early going Parry's and Lord's basic methodology, turning the observable realities of Serbo-Croatian oral epic back on Homer to illuminate the ancient Greek texts by comparison. In the instance of at least some of the Old English and Old French poems, however, such a comparison would obscure the differences between oral and oral-derived. As a corollary to the Parry-Lord procedure, then, I would suggest that scholars in search of analogs for oral or oral-derived texts look first to possibilities in the respective categories. It may turn out, as in these studies, that the criteria of tradition- and genre-dependence make comparison between and among texts from different categories especially attractive and promising, and that these primary considerations must override the secondary matter of oral versus oral-derived. But no matter what the particular situation, the object remains the most exacting, controlled, and productive comparison possible.

A third procedure in our program of poetics is the observation of the principle earlier termed *genre-dependence*. Many potentially fruitful comparisons have been to some extent qualified by drawing analogies between very different genres, such as between lyric (and non-narrative) panegyric and narrative epic. As a first approximation, genres in two or more literatures should be either narrative or non-narrative; that is, they should be either forms that involve the progress of a tale, such as is found in epic, or the kinds of momentary, brief song-types such as lyric which have no narrative dimension to speak of. More specifically, the works to be compared should be, as far as is feasible in separate poetic traditions, precisely the same genre. Of course, this sort of exact congruency is not always practically achievable, and even when it may seem from formal criteria that we have a close fit, often enough that is not really the case;[19] nevertheless, by aspiring to fulfillment of the criterion of genre-dependence, we engage a given poem in as appropriate a cross-

17. Perhaps the sole Western European exception to this rule of thumb is Old French epic poetry, the *chanson de geste* tradition, on which see esp. J. Duggan 1973.

18. As Renoir (1981b, 439–40) envisions it, such comparative criticism is advantageous in two respects: "The first is that it provides a flexible but *specific* context whose integrity is readily ascertainable and against which we may in turn measure the integrity of a given text, about which we are thus enabled to make reasonably objective statements. The second is that it provides us with the means for understanding certain aspects of ancient texts through legitimate comparison with more modern texts."

19. On this point, see Ben-Amos 1969; Dundes 1962.

traditional comparison as possible. In turn, the appropriateness of the comparison, and therefore of the object poem's comparative context, will help us to formulate its poetics most sensitively and to improve our competence as readers of the poem.

A fourth programmatic principle of approaching an oral or oral-derived text, that of *tradition-dependence*, itself consists of three smaller parts. In general we can say, as was remarked above, that literatures differ significantly from one another, most obviously in their linguistic properties but also, because they are dependent on linguistic realities, in their prosodic properties. A viable poetics must take account of these idiosyncrasies in assembling its textual profile. As principle 1, then, I would set as the first goal of tradition-dependence a close philological mastery of the tradition within which the given text emerges.[20] The rigorous understanding of the text in its own language and its most immediate context would then make principle 2, a meticulous survey of *differences* as well as similarities between or among a text and its analog(s), a credible endeavor. Without both principles 1 and 2 we fall victim to the superficial gesture of the dilettante, uncritically remarking similarities at the expense of a faithful overall perspective. While this kind of rigor is certainly necessary for a successful reading of a known oral text (otherwise a false context is established), it is even more crucial to understanding the poetics of an oral-derived text, where the traditional features to be understood are not as unambiguous, and perhaps not as clear or as frequent, as those in the known oral text.

Principle 3 pertains mostly to the certainly oral work, but may as an abstraction affect the manuscript poem as well. It concerns the place of a given text within what may be called the "local tradition" (as opposed to the national tradition as a whole) and within the repertoire of the given singer. Again the Parry texts provide an illustration. As one becomes more and more acquainted with the Serbo-Croatian tradition, he senses increasingly the truth of Lord's caution that one must read the songs of a given singer and of his fellow performers in order to understand the local tradition and the individual *guslar*'s role in it.[21] Even though the poetic language of any region is multidialectal and "polychronic" (cf. Parry 1932 on Homeric Greek), containing archaisms alongside contemporary diction, it will nonetheless bear the characteristic imprints of its locale and also of its user's idiolect. The epic language at large is like a grand inventory of smaller, specialized sets of local diction, and these

20. Although this might seem the most obvious prerequisite for any sort of study of literature, in fact comparative analysis of oral traditions has suffered from lack of its fulfillment. Those who summon the Serbo-Croatian tradition as an analog without considering anything more than translations are among the most common, and most egregious, offenders.

21. For illustration of the three levels of tradition (the individual or idiolectal, the local or dialectal, and the national), see chapters 5 and 8 on, respectively, formulaic and thematic structure in the Return Song from the Stolac region.

sets are in turn divided into yet more specialized individual sets whose character depends on geography, religious affiliation, repertoire, and the influence of other singers. All of these factors contextualize the text by being aspects of its tradition-dependence.

The fifth and last theorem in our brief program is the question of the confluence or co-existence of synchronic and diachronic forms in the single traditional text. We may speak generally of textual activity on the synchronic level by describing a given text's digest of formulas, themes, sound-patterns, story-patterns, and the like. For the known oral text these elements have their reality in the act of text-making as it is carried on by the poet, the nominal author of the work and the particular author of the text at hand. Further study of his repertoire and of the community of singers in which he functions will create a synchronic context, a profile for the text. But it would be short-sighted to judge the process of contextualization complete with this profile. As indicated in the opening section, a text has also a diachronic context, a historical or evolutionary aspect which extends far back into the pre-textual history of a given work.

We know that tradition preserves what is of value to it from the past, and we also know that that preservation is not a consciously designed undertaking but rather a reflex of the tradition itself.[22] For example, archaeologists have pointed out the chronological strata in Homer (e.g., Snodgrass 1971); however, the poem apparently senses no flaw in what we would see as an anachronistic juxtaposition of elements or beliefs. From another point of view, Gregory Nagy (1974) has shown that the roots of the Homeric formula *kleos aphthiton* are, along with its Sanskrit cognate *śráva(s) ákṣitam*, to be found in Indo-European mythology; again it is diachrony, in this case of great depth, that fills out an important part of the poem's context.[23] In fact, of course, these two examples have reference to materials and ideas that are anachronistic only from our decidedly synchronic perspective of post-oral and post-traditional thinking. Tradition simply finds no discrepancy here; elements from different eras, even vastly different eras, are held together in a diachronic suspension unique to traditional texts. We need to take more careful account of this historical or evolutionary perspective, even when its traces are difficult to interpret either because they exist only as fragments or suggestions or because we must ferret out new information; and we need to look for its contextualizing influence in both oral and oral-derived texts.

APPLICATION OF THE PROGRAM:
APPROACHES TO READING FIVE TRADITIONAL TEXTS

It is time now to put the reading program into action, to test its power to elucidate some actual texts. In doing so I am aware of the objection that a

22. On the "homeostatic" nature of oral tradition, see, variously, Peabody 1975; Turner 1986.
23. For other examples of diachronic approaches, see Hoekstra, e.g. 1964, 1969; Janko 1982.

poetics is not possible until the structure and dynamics of the texts have been established. What I hope to accomplish here is merely a prolegomenon to a subsequent work that will be based on the structural principles with which this volume is concerned. Nevertheless, I do feel that it is important to know where the entire investigation is headed from the start; the applications made below are thus intended simply to indicate some profitable directions for future criticism, and certainly not to exhaust their possibilities.

What I propose to do, then, before turning to the oral and oral-derived epics that are the real subject of these studies, is to try out the reading program on five traditional texts or groups of texts: (1) a Serbo-Croatian epic; (2) the Homeric *Odyssey*; (3) Serbo-Croatian and Old English magical charms; (4) the Old English *Beowulf*; and (5) the shorter Old English poem *The Seafarer*. Our steps may be outlined as follows:

    A. Question of "text"
    B. Oral or oral-derived
    C. Genre-dependence
    D. Tradition-dependence
       1. Original language and philology
       2. Comparison/contrast with other traditions
       3. National, local, idiolectal levels
    E. Synchronic and diachronic contexts

In this way I hope to present by example the outlines of a traditional poetics in an applied form, a poetics flexible enough both to accommodate the various kinds of texts one can and does encounter and at the same time to allow the necessary focus and refinement that each individual tradition, singer, and text requires and deserves.

1. As my first example, a Serbo-Croatian oral epic, I choose an easily accessible published text, *The Captivity of Djulić Ibrahim* (*Ropstvo Djulić Ibrahima*), Parry no. *674* sung by Salih Ugljanin on November 24, 1934, in Novi Pazar and published as no. 4 of the first two volumes of *SCHS* (original-language text and translation, respectively).[24] Because the primary form of the song is that of an acoustic recording, a performed text whose sounds are recoverable, the objective and subjective aspects of the work come as close as possible to superimposition. While we cannot re-create the original setting and audience, we can re-create much of the rest of the performance and, to the extent that we are ourselves acquainted with the tradition, become an audience in an approximate way.[25] So the question of text proves in this way to be an easy

24. I use this particular version of a Return Song because of its ready access in both the original and translation; as documented below, virtually all of the material analyzed in these studies also belongs to the epic subgenre of Return. See esp. chapters 5, 8, and 10. On the standard Parry Collection notation, see n. 51 to chapter 2.

25. Compare the observations on text and audience that are interwoven throughout the essays in Tedlock 1983.

one, as long as we do not confuse the published edition with the performance as preserved on aluminum records; by recognizing the real text as a sung and heard reality informing the edition we read, we can proceed to the next and subsequent steps prepared for comparison. We shall find later that the present working designation of Ugljanin's text—as *Ropstvo*, version no. 4—will bear emendation to identify its context, but at this point the indication of a unitary document is entirely appropriate.

Nor do we need to pause long over the question of oral versus oral-derived: the *Ropstvo* text is a known oral epic and is therefore best contextualized by a thorough knowledge of Serbo-Croatian oral epic tradition. In this particular case such an acquaintance can be readily gained by consulting the resources of the Milman Parry Collection and its many hundreds of epic texts, and secondarily by reference to other collections of Serbo-Croatian oral narrative (e.g., Karadžić, Marjanović, and Hörmann). Most immediately, this text was *sung* to the accompaniment of the *gusle* (rather than spoken for the records or taken from dictation); it will thus relate in certain formal aspects to other sung texts.[26] Furthermore, it was composed by Ugljanin, a considerable part of whose repertoire has been recorded and published in the *Serbo-Croatian Heroic Songs* series. This material forms another sort of context, which may be measured comparatively for various stylistic properties—such as formula, theme, frequency and kind of enjambement, and so forth—and so used to deepen our understanding of *Ropstvo* no. 4. The most obvious analogs in this regard are nos. 5 and 6—recited and dictated versions, respectively, of the *Ropstvo*.[27] Widening the textual circle a bit more, we can then proceed from compositional mode and repertoire to an analysis of the local tradition. Here the comparative method extends the field of inquiry to the songs and repertoires of other singers, with comparisons and contrasts including all characteristics of composition and other performance data through the shape and function of large narrative patterns. The known oral text may thus command a host of contexts, all of which are important to reading the text and thus constitute part of its poetics.

After these determinations we shall want to establish the generic context of *Ropstvo* no. 4, so that worthwhile comments and comparisons can be promoted and unproductive ones avoided. The *Ropstvo* is an example of a relatively well known subspecies of South Slavic and Balkan epic, what Lord has called the "Return Song."[28] To proceed from general to specific, then, the text in question can be classed as "epic," with all the generic connotations that accompany the term in Serbo-Croatian poetic tradition. We may summon for comparison

---

26. See Lord 1953, and chapters 5 and 8 below.

27. See Lord's comparisons in *SCHS* 1:339–58.

28. On the pattern of Return, see esp. Lord 1969; Foley 1978c, 1986b. For a full list of relevant scholarship, see chapter 10 below.

all types of oral epics within the tradition and perhaps also from related and unrelated oral traditions, being careful to weigh the worth of each proposed comparand according to the requirements of the reading program, and thus establish for the object text a wide but finely differentiated context. After that initial step, the specific nature of the Return Song and its various avatars in the Yugoslav and other traditions should be addressed. This process will include relating the *Ropstvo* to the story-pattern of Return, abstracted by Lord (1969) in the form A—D—R—Rt—W, where A = Absence, D = Devastation, R = Return, Rt = Retribution, and W = Wedding. The characteristic form of this kind of epic entails a hero long absent from his homeland (A); while he suffers in captivity, suitors consume his possessions and attempt to marry his fiancée or wife (D); he then returns (R) and takes his revenge (Rt) on all those who have plotted against him; and finally, if he finds her faithful, he remarries or rejoins the wife or fiancée who was left behind (W). This pattern contextualizes many hundreds of Return Songs in the Yugoslav tradition and offers a proven avenue for genre-dependent comparison of a sensitive, exacting kind between Serbo-Croatian and other literatures.[29]

The principle of tradition-dependence can also open pathways to a better understanding of the poetics of *Ropstvo* no. 4. A rigorous philological scrutiny of the text will, for example, yield information about typical prosodic, phonological, and dialectal qualities; preparing a trial edition of a sung text like *Ropstvo* no. 4 is one way to underline those properties. Often something so apparently trivial as the group of sounds that the *guslar* employs as hiatus bridges or the phonological dynamics of an error in inflection can lead to a larger apprehension of the poem's context. Once this scrutiny has been completed, comparisons with texts from other traditions, admitted as comparands in accordance with the other steps in the reading program, can be productively undertaken. As the second principle associated with tradition-dependence, the crucial point is to give each tradition its due: for instance, one cannot speak simply of some archetypal construct called "the formula"; rather, one must describe each verbal pattern in terms of the prosody in symbiosis with which it is made and remade. Comparatists wishing to evaluate the similarities between formulaic structure in *Ropstvo* no. 4 and an Old English poem, for example, must acknowledge the differences between the epic *deseterac* and the Anglo-Saxon alliterative line (see chapter 3). Complementarily, the nature of the theme in *Ropstvo* no. 4 and of that in, for instance, the *Odyssey* or the *Iliad* must be studied in the same tradition-dependent manner. Finally, even a comparison at the most abstract level of story-pattern must take note of differences within traditions in order to make a valuable contribution to context. The remaining aspect of tradition-dependence is that of the relationship

29. See, e.g., Coote's (1981) comparative analysis of Serbo-Croatian, Russian, and Turkish songs of Return.

of a text to its more immediate context, the singer's repertoire and the local tradition, both of which were discussed above.

In applying the last of the principles in our reading program, that of ascertaining both synchronic and diachronic contexts, I would cite first the "historical" demonstration of a cognate for the Return Song in ancient Greek and the deduction that the pattern is thus of Indo-European origin.[30] In the case of the *Ropstvo*, clearly a member of the same epic subgenre, then, we must posit a long pre-textual history to complement any synchronic "dialectology" assembled by reference to the recently recorded tradition. Another diachronically based observation would have to do with the relationship between the Serbo-Croatian *deseterac* and a reconstructed Indo-European verse form.[31] Scholars seem to agree that the epic decasyllable is extraordinarily archaic in certain basic features, apparently preserving many Indo-European characteristics in nearly Ur-form. This aspect of context presents an opportunity for a comparative evolutionary commentary to correspond with a synchronic portrait of formal metrical features in various epic lines.

2. A second type of text, the ancient Greek Return Song, has only one surviving example, the Homeric *Odyssey*. Here the question of text is not as simple as in *Ropstvo* no. 4, for, as we shall see in chapter 2, the manuscript history of the *Odyssey* is very much a piecemeal record. This uncertainty about the text extends to the second principle of our reading program: a final judgment that *this* text is taken directly from oral tradition is not defensible on the basis of the present evidence, and so we must settle for the category of "oral-derived" if the integrity of the reading process is to be observed. As I noted above, however, this does not by any means rule out the application of oral traditional theory.[32] We can and indeed must apply the methods learned from analysis of other oral and oral-derived texts in an effort to recover the traditional character of the *Odyssey*, that aspect of the great poem which depends for its active appreciation on an understanding of the poetic tradition. Because the *Odyssey* is (at least) an oral-derived text, we need to discover the nature of its traditional forms, whether they be formulas, themes, story-patterns, or whatever. In myriad ways, the traditional forms that make up the text condition and even generate meaning by establishing a background or context for the nominal, situation-specific actions and realities of the story.

The criterion of genre-dependence limits the potential comparands for the *Odyssey* to epic songs, and in particular epic songs of Return, for the ancient

30. This is Lord's hypothesis (1969, 19), confirmed by evidence presented by others (e.g., Coote 1981).

31. See esp. Jakobson 1952; also chapter 3 below.

32. Nor, in fact, does it rule out the possibility that the *Odyssey* text is truly oral traditional. In setting the calibration of our reading program, however, we should make only the minimal, ascertainable assumption, thus avoiding an unnecessary and finally unprovable assertion that would weaken the whole process of interpretation.

Greek work also follows the five-part pattern of absence, devastation, return, retribution, and wedding located first in *Ropstvo* no. 4. Within the Homeric tradition the only other fully preserved epic is the *Iliad*, but it is of course quite differently structured from the *Odyssey*. The epic tale of the Trojan adventure has its own story-pattern, a Withdrawal-Devastation-Return sequence, and thus operates on different principles at the level of overall narrative movement.[33] This means in turn that the thematic contents of the *Iliad* and *Odyssey* must vary correspondingly.[34] Formulaic inventories of the two poems will compare more closely, since traditional patterning at the level of the line is not as attached to story-pattern as are larger units, although some scholars feel that poetic diction, in addition to being partially determined by its function in a given storytelling situation, is also conditioned by the dramatis personae themselves.[35] And philologists have long been aware of linguistic differences between the two epics (see Janko 1982). What genre-dependence prescribes, then, is a comparison of the *Odyssey* and the *Iliad* that is carefully weighted to include the discrepancies cited, and also a cross-traditional comparison with Return Songs from another Balkan area.

Our fourth principle, tradition-dependence, helps to insure the validity of the cross-traditional process by leavening the obvious similarities between works with a respect for tradition-dependent characteristics. As remarked above, we shall need in such cases to take a hard look at all comparands in the original languages from an exacting philological perspective. Many of the other problems attendant on consideration of Serbo-Croatian epic are, however, not applicable to the *Odyssey*: we have no firm knowledge of national, local, or idiolectal traditions with which to rationalize the dialect mixture, simply because of the paucity of surviving texts. Accordingly, the synchronic context is limited to the 28,000-line corpus of Homeric epic, with the qualifications already discussed. Diachronically, we may investigate many of the same structures mentioned before in reference to *Ropstvo* no. 4. The evolutionary identity of the Homeric hexameter and its historical relationship to phraseology, for example, have been subjects of fruitful debate (see further chapter 3). The field of comparative Indo-European mythology, at the other end of the spectrum, may eventually offer another aspect of diachronic context.

3. In moving from the Homeric *Odyssey* to the relatively minor poetic genre of the magical charm or spell in Serbo-Croatian and Old English, I take

---

33. On this pattern see Lord 1960, 186–97; Nagler 1974, 131–66.

34. For excellent studies of typical scenes and other structures in the *Iliad* and *Odyssey*, see Fenik 1968, 1974.

35. Thus the long battle over the language of Achilles and the question of whether there is in general the possibility for "literary" manipulation of phraseology to reflect specific characters. See the opening salvo by Adam Parry (1956); contributions to the ensuing discussion include Donlan 1971; Reeve 1973; Claus 1975; Hogan 1976; Friedrich and Redfield 1978, 1981; Duban 1981; Messing 1981; Nimis 1986.

advantage of a chance to demonstrate the range and sensitivity of the reading program. For here the question of text conditions the proceedings in very definite ways from the start. The Old English magical charms, to take the more straightforward case first, are found in various medieval "leechdom" manuscripts of uncertain provenance,[36] and their structure and content are unusual enough to cause a great variety of textual problems for prospective editors and commentators. In addition to what may seem an erratic prosody, scholars have also to deal with charm texts whose diachronic identity stems from an apparent overlay of Christian elements on an earlier Germanic base. Though much of the overlay characteristically takes a prose form, the layers are not always separable, and one can be uncertain of the proper context for explication. The Serbo-Croatian spells, in contrast, generically and collectively known as *bajanje* by those who practice and make use of them, have been sparingly collected by native investigators and then published only in fragments. In 1975, however, a research team of which I was a member made a reasonably extensive recording of magical charms in and around the Serbian village of Orašac in the region of Šumadija south of Belgrade.[37] This collection of texts, which includes many alternate versions of the same spell by the same and different informants, provides an opportunity to study multiformity in a non-narrative genre. In comparing these Yugoslav texts with those drawn from the Anglo-Saxon leechdoms, we must be careful to allow for the inherent variance between recorded oral texts (complete with the expected "blemishes" in syntax and morphology typical of unedited material) and those edited from manuscripts of uncertain provenance.

These observations lead directly to the question of oral versus oral-derived. Only the Yugoslav charms are known oral material; the Anglo-Saxon spells must be placed in the oral-derived category, and the comparison must admit the possible discrepancies. As far as genre-dependence is concerned, we may feel confident that the comparison and contextualization are as exact and fair as possible in the present state of knowledge, especially since certain charms, like the Old English "Nine Herbs" remedy and a Serbo-Croatian spell against the incursion of nine windborne diseases, show marked similarities beyond the formal equivalence of genre.

Tradition-dependence manifests itself most immediately in the prosody that informs each body of material. The Yugoslav poems tend toward a symmetrical octosyllable, as do the lyric or "women's" songs (*ženske pjesme*) also performed

---

36. For a convenient edition, see Grendon 1909.

37. This research was undertaken by an interdisciplinary team of anthropologists and specialists in oral tradition (Robert P. Creed, Barbara Kerewsky Halpern, Joel M. Halpern, and myself) with the support of a grant from the National Endowment for the Humanities. For accounts of the fieldwork and analyses to date, see Kerewsky Halpern and Foley 1978; Foley 1977a, 1980b, 1981c, 1982.

almost exclusively by women,[38] and they demonstrate a bewildering array of sound-patterns, including full- and near-rhyme, assonance, consonance, and phonetic series, as well as formulaic and syntactic frames. The Old English magic tends in its verse component toward the standard alliterative line of Old English poetry, but in this case as well a great many sound-patterns stretch the charm line out of its conventional metric: single half-lines, hypermetric verses, and seemingly faulty units of all kinds are the result.[39] The last step in our reading program, that of formulating a diachronic description to complement synchronic analysis, awaits fulfillment.

4. With the Old English epic *Beowulf* we enter a complex and much-discussed area. The question of text is apparently simple enough: the poem exists uniquely in the Cotton Vitellius A. xv. manuscript. But we do not know how that probably tenth-century copy (most scholars consider it a copy of an earlier text) came to be—either how the poem was originally created and recorded or how it might have been edited or recopied. Because of this lacuna in our knowledge of manuscript history (to be considered in detail in the next chapter), we cannot confidently and justly claim certain orality for *Beowulf*. Nevertheless, more than enough work has been done since Francis P. Magoun's pioneering article of 1953 to certify that we are dealing with at least an oral-derived text.[40] Traditional features of formula, theme, and so forth abound, and the heroic magnitude of the epic depends intimately upon their resonance.

To be sure, *Beowulf* meets most criteria for the epic genre as commonly cited in comparative literature studies. But, this much said, we must look long and carefully for real analogs. Some of the Old Norse material has a closely related mythic content, as do poems from other Germanic language traditions, notably the Middle High German *Nibelungenlied* and the Old High German *Hildebrandslied*; but these works do not match *Beowulf* in genre. Within the Old English poetic canon only the fragmentary *Waldere* and perhaps a verse hagiography like *Andreas* can provide possible comparands, but there are serious problems with text and genre, respectively, even in these instances. Epics in other, unrelated poetic traditions, where we find a match in story pattern and thus in epic subspecies, may hold out another alternative. Whatever the case, it is important to remember the generic singularity of *Beowulf* when comparing it to other works in the same tradition or in closely related Germanic traditions.

Tradition-dependent characteristics abound in the Old English epic. Its prosody and narrative structure bear some resemblance to counterparts in

38. As compared to the epic songs (*epske pjesme*), usually performed by men only and in the decasyllabic meter (*epski deseterac*). For exceptions to this differentiation by sex, see Murko 1951, 189–205. For more on the epic meter, see chapter 3 below.

39. For a discussion of these phenomena, see Foley 1980b.

40. For a history of formulaic and thematic studies on Old English poetry, see Foley 1981b, 60–91, 107–22; Olsen 1986, 1988.

ancient Greek and Serbo-Croatian, particularly in the recurrence of core ideas that underlie repetitive phrasing and narrative structures—but even that resemblance has been much overestimated. As we shall see in later chapters, the "formula" in *Beowulf* is much more a process than a fact, much more a continuum that extends from the level of favored metrical patterns up through their reflection in phraseology than a system of diction alone. From a synchronic point of view, the recurrent kernel of Beowulfian diction will seem to be the root morpheme, a still point surrounded by a looser aggregation of relatively less important words. The cores of themes, then, will often be key words and short phrases of great flexibility, all attracted by an abstract idea-pattern, without the kind of line-for-line verbal correspondence among instances that is typical of many themes in the Serbo-Croatian epic tradition. It is crucial to any aesthetically sound interpretation of *Beowulf* that we recognize these traditional features in their idiosyncratic Old English form, and that we dispense with the often undertaken but pointless search for what amounts to a tradition-dependent form from another tradition (for example, the Homeric Greek formula, the canonical unit). Once recognized, these traditional features can provide the most immediate context for a successful reading of the poem.

As is often the case in dealing with an Old English poem, the diachronic perspective must focus on a Germanic structure overlain by, and often blended with, a Christian sensibility. In *Beowulf* this is a particularly knotty problem, since in this poem the two are so masterfully integrated. Nonetheless, comparative diachronic analysis of the kind suggested by Alain Renoir (esp. 1981b, 1986) can create a traditional context to assist in a faithful reading of a work, particularly in those cases in which, as in *Beowulf*, the conventional contextualizing instruments of literary history are virtually useless because of lack of information. Finally, I would mention the research on Indo-European meter and at least pose the question of the relationship between alliterative verse and a possible ancient precursor (see further chapter 3). We can be sure of one measurement along these lines: the alliterative meter has evolved much farther away from the reconstructed Indo-European syllabic and quantitative line than have corresponding verse forms in ancient Greek and Yugoslav epic, an evolutionary history traceable to the proto-Germanic shift of stress and consequent redefinition of the metrical "prosodeme" from syllable to initial stress. A great deal more work remains to be done in this last area.

5. The final exemplar text to be considered in the light of the reading program for traditional texts is the Old English *Seafarer*. The unique copy of the poem forms part of the Exeter Book manuscript, a miscellany of various kinds of works ranging from folk riddles through short lyric poems to the macaronic Latin and Anglo-Saxon *Phoenix* and variations on the antiphons for Advent in the Roman Breviary. We know that the manuscript as it presently stands is a tenth-century collection donated by Bishop Leofric to Exeter

Cathedral, but we know nothing of the history of the making of *The Seafarer* previous to its inclusion in the codex. Both because of that uncertainty and because of the ample evidence in the poem of the poet's Latin learning, we must ascribe it to the oral-derived category of texts. In fact, the appearance of traditional and non-traditional structures side by side in the same text has led not a few scholars to accuse *The Seafarer* of inconsistency or mixed modes. But as I have argued elsewhere, the presence of two kinds of forms for articulating meaning need not prompt an accusation of interference between the two.[41] Rather, we may understand the traditional and non-traditional as simply two different and complementary ways of evoking meaning, the one through reference to the poetic tradition and the other through reference to religious tradition and the deployment of rhetorical figures borrowed from the Latin *ars rhetorica*.[42] The text is, in modern critical terms, "active"—that is, it calls for a complex, multi-leveled response on the part of the reader, and it offers an aesthetic experience which takes shape along two distinct phenomenological axes.

The hybrid nature of the diction extends to the poem's genre as well. *The Seafarer* has been termed an elegy, an allegory, an ascetic journey of expiation (a *peregrinatio*), and a medieval *planctus*. But we would be most accurate to view each of these labels as apposite rather than as all-inclusive, and to understand that *The Seafarer* is a work *sui generis*. Its truest comparands in Old English are poems which answer some of the same generic criteria and which demonstrate a similarly hybrid phraseology, rhetorical structure, and Christian sophistication; among them would be numbered *The Wanderer*, *The Wife's Lament*, and *The Husband's Message*. Outside the Anglo-Saxon tradition, the shorter Christian poems from Serbo-Croatian oral tradition, which also show traditional forms in the hands of a gifted artist, offer a promising analog (see Foley 1983b). Finally, many of the same tradition-dependent and diachronic considerations may be applied to *The Seafarer* as were applied to *Beowulf*. Again the pagan-Christian blend is most prominent here, and is of course intimately connected with other parts of the reading program.

From this point on I shall turn away from both general issues in contemporary oral literature research and the reading program for traditional texts in order to conduct a more focused examination of epic poems from the ancient Greek, Old English, and Serbo-Croatian traditions. In accordance with the reading program, we shall first look at the comparability of the documents themselves in order to assess as exactly as possible what authority each has in presenting its oral or oral-derived poem.

41. See Foley 1983a,b. The co-existence of oral traditional structure and Latin learning in the same text may be explained in part by the cultural diglossia prevalent in the medieval period; see further Stock 1983 and Ong 1986.

42. For examples of the latter technique, see Campbell 1966, 1967, 1978.

TWO

Comparability
of the Documents

If our comparative analyses of the Homeric *Odyssey*, the Old English *Beowulf*, and the Serbo-Croatian Return Song as exemplified in the recorded repertoires of the Stolac *guslari* are to have real validity, we should start by making an attempt to understand the "gross anatomy" of the different texts, that is, the nature of the actual extant documents. In the past it has been customary to assume equivalent authority among the Homeric texts we find whole only in the medieval period, the Anglo-Saxon insular minuscule manuscript of *Beowulf* from the tenth century, and the Yugoslav epic songs taken down from actual oral performance, whether acoustically or pen in hand by an amanuensis. But quite clearly each of these is a unique medium with a unique history, and before simply erasing their inherent differences and proceeding on to comparative evaluation, it is well to discover what we can about their individuality. The shreds of information about the Homeric and Old English documents are admittedly and frustratingly few, and it will occasionally be necessary to fall back on a best hypothesis where no fact is available; we can, however, learn an appreciable amount merely by struggling toward the sort of full and unambiguous answers that prove so rare in the ancient and medieval periods. And at the same time, not incidentally, we shall be taking another step toward the kind of complex and truly comparative poetics that oral literature studies deserve.

THE JOURNEY OF THE HOMERIC TEXTS

The *Iliad* and the *Odyssey*, as we have them in the Byzantine recensions that are the earliest complete texts of the Homeric epics, have stubbornly resisted the text and transmission models imposed upon them by generations of scholars. Each set of hypotheses, however apposite in some ways, seems to founder on

at least one important stage of the manuscript record: either the con
accepted idea of the "vulgate," the phenomenon of the so-called wild
of the third century B.C., or the elaborate editing undertaken by the Al_.an-
drian scholars escapes the web of overall explanation. This is perhaps no wonder,
for we are dealing with a history of which we know tantalizingly little and one
that stretches from the eighth century B.C. to the tenth century A.D.—that is,
nearly two millennia—without a single surviving complete text to anchor supposition. Notwithstanding these severe problems, by bringing to what we can
learn about the different stages of the transition a model for textual evolution
that suits the likely facts of emergence out of an oral tradition, we can at least
approach a coherent view of what our texts of the *Iliad* and the *Odyssey* are
and how they must relate to Homer's traditional poems.

Although Homer himself is customarily dated to the eighth century B.C., we
have no evidence for a fixed text of his poems until the version assumed to
have been compiled during the Panathenaic Festival of the sixth century B.C.
While we may choose to agree with Albert Lord's (1953) persuasive argument
that the fullness of the poems as we now have them makes it likely that they
were oral-dictated texts, that is, that they were taken down from dictation in
a manner which allowed the singer to proceed relatively slowly and to compose
carefully, we may also imagine the earliest stage of transmission of fixed or
semi-fixed texts as primarily memorial.[1] As Parry contended from his first
writings onward, the tradition epitomized in Homer must have been vigorous
and continuous for centuries before the monumental poet composed the epics
of which some version has survived, and the tradition may be traced back as
far as the Mycenaean era.[2] Likewise, there is no reason to believe that, even
if the *Iliad* and *Odyssey* that have reached us were fixed in the sixth century
B.C., oral composition of the Homeric ilk immediately ceased.[3] More likely,
the Panathenaic Festival simply provided the opportunity and perhaps the
impetus to commit to written and permanent form what Gregory Nagy
(1979, 7) has identified as a Panhellenic "standard" version of Homeric poetry,
one which "synthesizes the diverse traditions of each local city-state into a
unified Panhellenic model that suits most city-states but corresponds exactly
to none." If this is so, then we may assume that the more parochial versions
of Homeric poetry—now at least two centuries removed from the probable
date of composition by Homer—must have continued to disseminate themselves, at first through oral composition and later through memorization and
rhapsodic performance.

For available evidence suggests that both oral composition, the craft of the

1. For discussion of memorial preservation in Middle English literature, see Parks 1986; of
related interest is Opland 1975. For an opinion in opposition to Lord's hypothesis, see Hillers
and McCall 1976 on Near Eastern traditions.

2. Cf. Page 1959, 218–96; and Janko 1982. On Indo-European roots, see G. Nagy 1974, 1979.

3. On the lack of effect of fixed texts on a continuous tradition, see Lord 1967b, 1986c.

aoidos, and a creative brand of memorization, the province of the rhapsode (*rhapsôidos*), contributed to the early transmission of Homer. In ways we do not entirely understand, the sixth-century Homeridae, or "sons of Homer,"[4] seem to have followed the great poet in safekeeping his poems; they claimed to recite Homer *ek diadochês* ("by right of succession"), or almost by a kind of exclusive copyright. Most scholars interpret their relationship to the great poet not as real kinship but as a guild, a cooperative effort to forestall the proliferation of different versions of the poem that must have resulted from the rhapsodes' activities. For alongside the singer of tales, whose primary oral tradition must have begun to recede after Homer, stood the rhapsode, who, in taking as his principal charge the effective oral recitation of Homer from memory or script (often in competition with other rhapsodes), must have felt relatively free to modify the canonical, received work. Indeed, he may well not have realized, or for that matter been prepared to recognize, that such variation was taking place; in the last stages of primary oral tradition, there would be an opportunity for rhapsodes to draw on their own experience of the singer's art to modify phraseology or perhaps even narrative structure. It is telling that references to the Homeridae stem from about the time when, on the one hand, rhapsodic activity and local traditions had produced many variants of what the ancient Greek world knew as "Homer" and, on the other, the Panathenaic text was reputedly being compiled.

This hypothetical first fixed text was apparently a response to what is known as the Panathenaic Rule, a law that governed fidelity to text in rhapsodic competitions from the sixth century B.C. onward, although there also exists a well-known legend that Solon or Hipparchus the son of Peisistratus first "arranged to have all the Homeric poems recited at the Panathenaea in relays of rhapsodes" (Lesky 1966, 73). Whatever the case may actually have been, all of these clues point to the establishment of a fixed text in that time and place. Scholars have explained this text either as a "Peisistratean recension," a hypothesis assembled from reports of interpolations made in the name of local patriotism and from the classical legend (first attested in Cicero) that Peisistratus was himself responsible for the arrangement of the poems,[5] or as a text brought to Athens by Hipparchus, perhaps directly from the Homeridae of Chios.

As mentioned above, however, Nagy's idea of the gradual evolution of fixed Homeric texts as a function of both composition and proliferation best fits both the surviving evidence and what we know of oral tradition. As he puts it,

> composition and proliferation need not necessarily be related as an *event* followed by a *process*: the evolution of the fixed texts that we know as the *Iliad* and *Odyssey*

---

4. For discussion of available evidence on the Homeridae, see Davison 1963a, 235; Davison 1963b, 219.

5. For a review of ancient sources and opinions on this point, see T. Allen [1924] 1969, 226–38; he discounts the theory of a Peisistratean recension, seeing it as a legend without basis in historical fact.

may be envisaged as a cumulative process, entailing countless instances of composition/performance in a tradition that is becoming streamlined into an increasingly rigid form as a result of ever-increasing proliferation. (1979, 8; see also G. Nagy 1986)

Besides taking into account the political aspects of contemporary Panhellenism, this explanation has the advantage of not overlooking the obvious fact that by the sixth century Homeric poetry had already spread from its probable source in Ionia to all parts of the Greek world and, equally important, would continue to be (re-)composed and performed throughout those areas for many years to come. With the hypothesis of a text at this point in history, then, we posit a single epitome: a pair of monumental poems that bear the burden of a long tradition, that represent the Panhellenic fervor of the emerging city-states, and that are spoken (and written down) in a polydialectal Greek no one had ever used for non-poetic purposes. We most assuredly do not posit the immediate demise of the large tradition and the smaller local traditions out of which the poems were fashioned.[6] The Homeric texts are monumental and no doubt the flower of their now-perished tradition, but they did not exist outside of that tradition.

The Athenian texts of the Panathenaea or some version of them then passed into the capable hands of the Alexandrian scholars, most notably Zenodotus of Ephesus (head of the library in the mid-third century B.C.), Aristophanes of Byzantium (head 195-180 B.C.), and Aristarchus of Samothrace (head ca. 180-145 B.C.). There is considerable historical irony in the fact that we know a great deal about the editing procedures employed by each of these men, even the details of their copyediting marks, but almost nothing about the actual texts they produced, if in fact they did produce whole editions of Homer. Further, since their learned observations and opinions seem to have had little effect on the transmitted vulgate text—a surprising turn of events that may have more to do with the lack of anything approaching a contemporary book trade than with lack of attention to their remarks[7]—we are left to infer their role in transmission indirectly. Davison (1963b, 223) and others

6. On this point it is instructive to compare the well-recorded Serbo-Croatian tradition, which consists of the set of all local traditions (among which there is considerable variation), each of which in turn consists of singers' individual or idiolectal traditions. See further the latter part of this chapter, along with chapters 5 and 8.

7. On the basis of Aristarchus's 664 known readings and their influence, T. Allen ([1924] 1969, 304) concludes that "it is plain we possess no 'Aristarchean edition,' and as the papyri (which are all non-Aristarchean) form a catena from 300 B.C. to A.D. 600, it is also plain that no Aristarchean edition was ever put on the market." Allen is not alone in explaining the situation with the general observation that "at all periods of the Greek world the connexion between organized learning and book production seems slight, if not non-existent" (p. 320); cf., e.g., S. West (1967, 16): "the view that Aristarchus published the Vulgate involves an anachronistic conception of the relationship between the scholar and the book trade: the Museum was not a publishing house; there was no Alexandrian University Press."

note that with Aristarchus's rather conservative but well-founded style of editing Homer, the number of so-called wild papyri, those fragments of the *Iliad* and *Odyssey* that vary considerably from the received vulgate, diminishes sharply.

Although silent witness is usually the rule in assessing the contribution of the Alexandrians, we can appreciate the enormity of their task by taking account of the fact that the Library collection of Homeric poetry contained an imposing number and variety of texts. Of the editions current around 300 B.C., just before Zenodotus assumed command, there are records of thirteen that contain readings adopted by men of letters (*kat' andra*), over sixty-six anonymous "city" editions (*kata poleis* or *hai politikai*), and fifty-two vulgate (*koinê*) texts. Added to these variants from all over the Greek world, which most scholars assume were collated by Aristarchus but not in any sense "published," is a group of contemporary papyrus fragments heterogeneous enough to be conventionally designated as the "eccentric" or "wild" papyri. We do not know exactly how the Alexandrians treated these excerpts from the *Iliad* and *Odyssey*, but we can observe, as noted above, that their number seems to fall off rapidly after Aristarchus. Perhaps S. West's (1967, 17) suggestion that "the post-aristarchean tradition underwent the influence of the Aristarchean Text, without being descended from it," best explains the discernible facts without depending on an anachronistic model of transmission.

But what of this mélange of texts, and especially of papyri? How do they relate to the hypothetical Panathenaic text, itself at least two centuries removed from the supposed time of Homer? Even if we assume with most scholars that the sixth-century Athenian Homer became the vulgate, which in turn gave way to the Byzantine codices on which we base our modern editions, we must still deal with those witnesses that are probably not a part of the direct line of descent. To begin with, we should recall the point made above that a Panathenaic epitome, a fixed text made under the rule for rhapsodic competition, does not in any way presuppose the end of the oral tradition. Rather, it is only logical to believe that the art of oral verse-making continued on for some time, albeit from that point on exclusively in the diverse local traditions rather than Panhellenically.[8] The fieldwork and collecting of Parry and Lord have shown that the local tradition is a very important unit in the overall ecology of oral epic composition, and on the basis of evidence gathered firsthand in this living laboratory it is clear that just such a great intersectional and rationalizing force as Panhellenism would be required to mold the disparate local traditions into a pair of national poems. More importantly, the making of such a text—and its use as a standard for rhapsodic competitions—would not in any way

---

8. It is worth noting that, from the point of view of the history of an oral narrative tradition, such an epitomized text is endemically "unnatural"—that is, it is not the characteristic medium of the tradition but rather a neologism created under political influence.

cause the local traditions from which it was drawn to cease their own independent activity, for by its very nature oral tradition does not recognize the
individual text or performance as definitive. At the outset, then, we should
realize that it is only natural that the Alexandrians (and the Greek world as
a whole) were awash in versions of Homer; the continuing oral tradition and
later the "memorization" and "performance" of generations of rhapsodes must
have further parochialized the diversity that the Panhellenic spirit sought to
counter. Even limited (and chiefly memorial) "publication" of the Athenian
epitome through the rhapsodes would lead to variation, since we must expect
that such performers often drew from their own Homeric wordhoards to
embellish and personalize their performances.

The Ptolemaic papyri present a problem of a different but ultimately related
sort. They diverge from the canonical Homeric texts in ways that cannot be
explained as purely mechanical corruption associated with scribal practice,
and S. West (1967, 11) makes the telling point that although we conventionally
refer to them as "wild," "yet there is no evidence that at the date they were
written there was anything abnormal about these texts." Indeed, the early
papyri are characterized by a high proportion not of substituted but of
additional lines,[9] and these additions are not random but of a particular kind:

> The proportion depends partly on the context: passages containing many *versus
> iterati*... or a summary of a typical scene described elsewhere in greater detail...
> attracted plus-verses, while a passage for which there are no close parallels else-
> where in Homer was likely to remain free from them. Concordance interpolation
> exercised a powerful attraction: thus a line or group of lines which follow a
> particular formula in one place are inserted after it in another passage where
> they may be rather less suitable. (pp. 12–13)

This "concordance interpolation," as West calls it, belies the existence of a
still-fluid vestige of oral tradition, perhaps by this point exclusively the possession of rhapsodes (or even schoolmasters)[10] who could read and write but
had committed much of Homer to memory. However far away we may be
from the composing *aoidos*, we have not yet very nearly approached the stage
of a single absolutely fixed, inviolate text. The papyri argue that, even while
Aristarchus and his fellow scholars labored over the editing of their manuscripts, others outside the mainstream of textual transmission—but still very
much a part of the traditional context—were performing and recording versions of Homer faithful to the overarching tradition yet couched, as our three
Yugoslav *guslari* might put it (see below), in slightly different "words."

In fact this particular kind of interpolation, one that adds lines traditionally
associated with other lines or with specific themes or typical scenes, can hardly

---

9. West feels that Homeric style was by its very nature always vulnerable to such additions,
but that there are even more such lines than even that endemic vulnerability would seem to permit.

10. See T. Allen [1924] 1969, 271–306.

have been due to any other cause. To put it proscriptively, only those acquainted with the multiformity of Homeric epic tradition could make "errors" of this sort, just as only singers actively involved in the process of composition—as distinct from this latter-day practice of reinterpreting multiforms, mistakenly thought of only as "interpolation" into an early *editio princeps*—would be able to engender true "narrative inconsistencies."[11] And once one brings to bear the well-documented example of multiformity in the Serbo-Croatian oral epic tradition, the case is complete: what Lord (1960, chaps. 2–3) illustrates as customary variation among instances of formulas and themes in the *epske pjesme* of such singers as Ibro Bašić, Halil Bajgorić, and Mujo Kukuruzović is very similar to the sort of "concordance inter-polation" West identifies as characteristic of the relationship between the papyri and the canonical text of Homer.[12] In a real sense the tradition of Homer was, if not active and "primary-oral," at least fluid and responsive possibly as late as the second century B.C.[13]

From this point on the wild papyri taper off rather suddenly, evidently in part because of Alexandrian scholarship, and perhaps eventually in part because the much more capacious codex, which could entirely contain a long work and thus theoretically help to standardize it, was to replace the papyrus roll, in which little more than a single book of the *Iliad* or *Odyssey* could be recorded. The vulgate text now effectively goes underground until its emergence in the first complete surviving *Iliad*, Venetus Marcianus 454, an early-tenth-century minuscule manuscript that remains the most important source for modern editions because of the famous A Scholia[14] included with the text. Almost in concert with its mysterious past, the A manuscript then underwent textual criticism by generations of Byzantine scholars and

11. On narrative inconsistencies, see esp. Lord 1938; Gunn 1970; Foley 1976a. See further chapter 10 below.

12. It is only fair to note that West (1967, 13), being unfamiliar with the Serbo-Croatian tradition on a philological level, concludes otherwise, namely that "the relatively minor scale of the interpolations argues against the view that there is a connection between the eccentricities of the early texts and the long oral tradition of the poems, except in so far as the rather discursive style suitable for oral technique attracted interpolation." As I have tried to contend, the "relatively minor" differences foregrounded in the papyri are major indicators of oral traditional variation, such variation being marked by its rather conservative limits. Wholesale invention, or even variations that occurred outside of the associations of line or scene that West herself describes, would be counter-evidence against the influence of oral tradition. As Lord puts it (1960, 120), "multiformity is essentially conservative in traditional lore, all outward appearances to the contrary."

13. For descriptions of a parallel kind of oral transmission, Middle English romance, see Baugh 1959, 1967; H. Duggan 1976.

14. These consist of versions of Didymus's *On the Edition of Aristarchus*, Aristonicus's *On the Signs of the Iliad and Odyssey*, Nicanor's *On Punctuation*, and Herodian's *Prosody of the Iliad*; the A manuscripts thus contain more information than any other single source about Aristarchus's principles of edition.

re-emerged with a number of other texts of Homer in the West. As Davison (1963b, 226) notes, it was rediscovered in the Marcian Library in Venice, "to which it came in the fifteenth century from the library of Cardinal Bessarion, only to be forgotten until the late eighteenth century." Although critics have labored long and diligently to establish stemmata for the surviving manuscripts from the Byzantine period, most agree that a definitive genealogy for the extant witnesses is beyond our reach. But even if such a genealogy could be established, we would still be faced with about a millennium during which the complete text of Homer is unattested in any direct way. At any rate, the poems reach their true *editio princeps* in 1488 with the printing of an edition of Homer by Demetrius Damilas. From that point on, and especially after Wolf's *Prolegomena* of 1795,[15] the problem of setting the text and deriving its antecedents has turned on the answers made by various ages and schools of criticism to the Homeric Question itself.

In summary, then, as we enter on textual studies of Homer to be undertaken in a comparative context, it is well to recall the long and circuitous journey of the Homeric poems from the eighth century B.C. forward almost three millennia to our own time. The circumstances of the recording of the great *aoidos* himself remain completely unreported, of course, but we may imagine a written or, more probably, memorial tradition of preservation through the Homeridae[16] down the two centuries to the Panathenaea and what was probably the first full text. Whether this memorial tradition was based on the kind of oral-dictated text described by Lord we shall perhaps never know, but in any case some variation from the performance of Homer would have occurred no matter how pure the intent of the preservers. The singers and rhapsodes who transmitted the poems must have made their own contributions, according to their lights and their usual mode of performance; as noted above, even the inertia provided by a manuscript text did not prevent a rhapsode from "stitching" together episodes of the poems as he performed them. What surfaced at the Panathenaea, whether under the aegis of Peisistratus or not, must have been a text true in its essential nature not only to the fact of the eighth-century performance but also in some measure to the multiform idiom that allowed the poems to live and flourish after their monumental poet was no more.

Gazing along the probable path of the poems as they reached the first

15. See further A. Parry 1971, xiv-xvi, xxiv; Foley 1988, chap. 1.

16. One possibility is that urged by M.W.M. Pope (1963, 6–7): "What we must have then to account for the variant reading is *different dictations* from an originally *single version*. This version one must imagine not as a written text but as a memorised one, learned from the lips of the poet (a possibility envisaged by Parry), and transmitted at first by singers, who would naturally retain for some time their capacity for original composition, and later perhaps by pure reciters." While I prefer Nagy's model of a Panhellenic fixation of the text as sketched above, Pope's comments offer a realistic explanation of the post-sixth-century situation.

professional textual critics in Alexandria, moreover, we realize that nowhere in the ancient records is there incontrovertible evidence that the vulgate and Panathenaic texts were one and the same. It is of course convenient to assume a direct line of descent, since we can then avoid having to deal with problems of "genuine" or "spurious" texts. But by making that assumption we obscure if not forget a crucially important dimension of Homeric art; we push aside as an unnecessary complication the evidence that no less than 131 separate editions of Homer were deposited in the Alexandrian Library, some with commentary, some as part of the vulgate record, and some attributed to various cities. When we add to this evidence the phenomenon of "concordance interpolation" that characterizes the surviving Ptolemaic papyri, the picture comes clearer. The practice of Homeric poetry must have been alive in some form all over the Greek world for centuries after Homer;[17] by insisting on a simple, literary model for transmission of the Homerid, Athenian text directly to Alexandria and beyond we miss that essential point. The *Iliad* and the *Odyssey* began as—indeed were part of—oral epic tradition, and we have no reason to believe that the poems (as distinguished from the extant texts) were entirely cut off from that tradition for many centuries thereafter. "Homer" was known to all, apparently in many different forms, but the essence of the poems is likely to have remained quite intact within the shape-shifting of phraseology and narrative structure that was the very medium of their transmission.

Just as we cannot be sure that the Athenian text held pride of place as the *koinê* that apparently eluded the editorial signature of Aristarchus and his predecessors, so we have even less reason to believe that this same primordial text surfaced whole in the tenth-century Venetus Marcianus 454 and its brethren. In fact, from the very moment when (let us hypothesize) an amanuensis started to commit Homer's words to writing, there began an editing process that continues to the present day.[18] Anyone concerned with mere intelligibility, not to mention aesthetic judgments, would have a hand in rendering the oral performance "acceptable" in grammatical terms at least, and this editing would still be necessary (if less frequent) for an oral-dictated text composed more slowly and carefully than a sung performance. From this beginning memorizers and rhapsodes alike, no matter how meticulous they

17. We may compare the cases of the "literary" imitators of Serbo-Croatian oral epic tradition, such as Bishop Njegoš and Andrija Kačić-Miošić. See further Lord 1986a; Haymes 1980; Miletich 1978a,b.

18. The inevitable editing associated with taking down a song from dictation may be glimpsed in (the amanuensis and *guslar*) Nikola Vujnović's transcriptions of sung performances by the Parry-Lord *guslari* (e.g., text no. 6699 by Halil Bajgorić; see chaps. 5 and 8 below). Lines and parts of lines are omitted, changed, and even added in the process. A second possible stage of editing is exemplified by the nineteenth-century collector Vuk Karadžić's occasional modification of texts collected by others before final publication (see Foley 1983b).

were in pursuit of perfect preservation, would continue to modify the received text and to shape it to their conception of what Homer must have said or meant. These processes, along with the important phenomenon of local traditions mentioned above, go a long way toward explaining both the multiplicity of editions of Homer (in addition to the hypothesized Panhellenic epitome) and the typical variation among papyri. The fact that these papyri start to die out after Aristarchus is perhaps attributable less to his reputation or influence as a textual scholar than to the simple phenomenon that by about the middle of the second century B.C. the last vestiges of a once-vigorous tradition are gone. The poetic tradition, having passed from *aoidos* to rhapsode and beyond, had to all appearances died out completely.

If we cannot be certain that the Byzantine texts look directly back to Homer, indeed if we cannot discover any verifiable connection even to Alexandria, are we then lost in a scholar's nightmare of editorial debris? Not, I propose, if we look at the evidence that actually exists and resist the impulse to impose stemmata and other generalized models that are the literary scholar's stock-in-trade. Consider for a moment the audiences of Homeric poetry in the primary oral phase; like audiences that attend the composition and recitation of oral epic narrative in other cultures, they "knew the story" of what was transpiring (Lord 1960, 99-123). Even the Panhellenic text, after all, had to have an audience, perhaps in that case a rather heterogeneous group accustomed to variations on what they were hearing, and this constituency heard the authoritative Homer against the echoes of the poems as they (no doubt quite differently and individually) knew them from prior experience. There was for them probably nothing especially sacred about this particular text except for its role in rhapsodic competitions, and even those singers and rhapsodes present at the Panathenaic Festival may well have returned to more parochial versions in other milieus.

Editions and papyri from the time of the Alexandrian scholars offer the same impossible problem for the literary critic seeking to confer a literary order on these materials, and present the same opportunity for those willing to seek another answer, one more faithful both to the available facts and to the period in which the texts were made and transmitted. The editions multiplied because the local traditions that began well before the sixth-century epitome continued to develop in their separate ways, dependent on rhapsodic activity and memorial transmission as well as on the written word. The papyri varied in ways that betray some sort of oral traditional transmission; even if we understand their production as exclusively a written process, we must make the minimal assumption that the writers knew and could use the oral traditional style, otherwise we cannot explain their characteristic variation.[19]

In short, the journey of the two Homeric epic *texts* is most fruitfully and

19. Cf. Lord 1986c on transitional texts; see also note 17 above.

faithfully understood as the journey of the Homeric *poems*. Whatever lacunae exist in the manuscript history (and there are many), we may be sure of this much: up to the time of Aristarchus, Homer's poems existed not in one exclusive version but rather in many versions of different but—from the perspective of tradition—equal authority. Held together by what Lord has so felicitously called a "tension of essences" and by an overall conservatism of language and thought possible only in a homeostatic idiom such as the archaic Greek poetic language, Homer's *poems* survived the centuries intact—from Homer's own texts through the Panhellenic standardization and on through the Alexandrian and Byzantine eras. Under these conditions, searching for a textual archetype must be as futile an exercise as searching for the archetypal form of a story. In the end it does not matter which manuscripts the Alexandrian scholars favored or exactly how the rhapsodes stitched in their own contributions; what matters is that the text we have is the result of a concatenation of processes, all of which served to "edit" the oral performance of Homer.

As a negative conclusion, we should thus be hesitant about attributing the term *oral epic* to the surviving *Iliad* and *Odyssey* without qualification. Given the uncertainties of transmission and the inevitable editing that Homer's songs underwent, it would be wiser to understand these texts as "oral-derived" in the sense advocated in chapter 1. Surely the poems' essence has survived the journey of the text, and we would be shortchanging Homeric art to deny its traditional nature; multiformity was an active part of text-making, and then of textual transmission, long after the advent of writing and Panathenaic epitomization of the text, and it remains a crucial aesthetic dimension of our *Iliad* and *Odyssey*, a dimension much in need of further investigation. At the same time, though, it would be at best romantic and at worst misleading to treat these same Homeric texts as if they were the completely unedited songs recited for dictation by a Yugoslav *guslar*. Especially when, as in the present volume, we seek answers to structural questions, we must be aware that while the Serbo-Croatian material is unambiguously oral and presents the welcome opportunity to measure a living oral tradition quantitatively, the Homeric poems as they have come down to us are oral-derived and cannot simply be equated with the *epske pjesme* for the purposes of comparison.[20]

But positive conclusions are also possible and necessary. For example, the mélange of editions and papyri helps us to describe how Homer was transmitted and understood: in effect, his poems must have had an active audience versed in the oral traditional inheritance as late as the mid-second century B.C. Could it be that the poets of some of the medieval—and also oral-derived—

---

20. As Mark Edwards (1986) cautions, we must be careful to consider variant readings when conducting statistical analyses designed to determine the possible orality of the Homeric poems. My purpose in these studies is not to attempt such a quantitative assessment but rather to clarify the tradition-dependent character of formulaic phraseology in each tradition.

epics addressed this same kind of audience?[21] If the Alexandrians seem not to have affected the vulgate text in a major way, we may justifiably conclude that, owing in part to the absence of a book trade, the transmission of Homer was not in any important fashion a scholarly enterprise. Perhaps, like the verse romances of later medieval England, these poems were passed on as a kind of oral palimpsest, to be "erased" and re-"written" in accordance with traditional structure and within the limits of the multiform idiom. Most of all, we should recognize that Homer's poetry was itself a powerful enough medium and a sufficiently finely crafted instrument to assure its own preservation as it wandered through the bewildering historical maze of poets, rhapsodes, and editors. In their essentials, then, these are Homer's, and his tradition's, poems.

THE RIDDLE OF COTTON VITELLIUS A. XV.

If the Homeric texts that survive to our time provide only brief glimpses into a long and uncertain past, at least the evidence permits reasonable hypotheses to be drawn about their probable recording and the first standard texts, as well as about some of the prime historical influences which those or related texts must have undergone. Such is not the case with the *Beowulf* poetry, which comes to us in a single copy and whose date and provenance remain objects of lively debate among paleographers and students of the poem.[22] We know very little even about the circumstances under which such a poem might have been collected, copied, and transmitted; with no real chronology for the verse of this period outside of a few *termini a quo*,[23] scholars have estimated the "date" of this version of the poem at anywhere between the mid-eighth and early eleventh centuries. There was no Alexandrian Library to (theoretically) hone the textual tradition, no set of scholia to provide fodder for readings or textual emendation, and no Byzantine scholarship to keep interest in the poem alive. *Beowulf* surfaces as a unique text in the middle of the sixteenth century, and is treated as a poem rather than an archaeological or paleographical curiosity only well into the twentieth century.[24] All in all, the story of the text reads more like an Anglo-Saxon riddle than a Homeric epic journey.

21. Especially considering the phenomenon of medieval diglossia; see Stock 1983, 30–87.

22. For the older conventional arguments, see Klaeber 1950, cvii–cxx. For a sense of the variety of modern opinion, see Chase 1981a.

23. "The Battle of Maldon," for example, celebrates a historical battle fought on August 11, 991.

24. Notwithstanding, for example, Thomas Jefferson's introduction of Old English into the curriculum of the University of Virginia in 1825 (see Hauer 1983), Jefferson's interest being primarily in the language and law of the Anglo-Saxons. Only with J.R.R. Tolkien's justly famous essay "*Beowulf*: The Monsters and the Critics" (1936) did scholarly attention really turn toward the text as poetry.

The earliest identifiable owner of the manuscript, Laurence Nowell, dean of Lichfield and one of the first students of Anglo-Saxon, is also our earliest witness to the dated existence of the poem, and the date at which he signed his name was 1563. Shortly thereafter it came into the possession of Sir Robert Bruce Cotton (1571-1631), the noted antiquary whose library housed so many precious medieval manuscripts. The designation of the manuscript containing *Beowulf* as Cotton Vitellius A. xv. indicates its physical position in that library—in a case under the bust of the Roman emperor, on shelf A, fifteenth place. In 1731, one hundred years after Cotton's death, a fire at Ashburnham House, the location of the library at that time, destroyed much of the original collection. We are thus perhaps fortunate that the *Beowulf* text was merely singed at the top and sides. Over the years that followed, however, the originally relatively slight damage was worsened by handling of the now-brittle vellum leaves, and invaluable bits of the written record itself began to crumble away. Around 1870 authorities at the British Museum checked the process of deterioration by separating the manuscript book into single folios and installing a paper binding to protect the page edges.

Modern scholarship has benefited enormously from various transcripts made of parts of Cotton Vitellius A. xv. Even before the fire, Humphrey Wanley had recorded part of *Beowulf*, and Franciscus Junius had copied all of the accompanying fragmentary *Judith* that remained (Bodleian MS. Junius 105). But the most important transcripts for *Beowulf* scholarship are those made by the Icelander G. J. Thorkelin:[25] two copies of the complete text written in 1787, about fifty years after the fire, when the manuscript was presumably in much better condition than it is now. The so-called A transcript was apparently made by a scribe whom Thorkelin hired for the purpose, and his errors and omissions reveal that the scribe was not well acquainted with the language in which he was working. Thorkelin himself wrote out the B transcript, however, and the professional knowledge of the philologist of Germanic languages shows through at every turn. Logically enough, this difference in preparation makes the A text usually more trustworthy than the more professional B text; since the amanuensis copied only what he could see with his untrained amateur's eye, he did not make educated guesses about emending crumbling words or filling lacunae.[26] These two transcripts taken together provide an invaluable companion for editing *Beowulf*.

From these materials—the unique text and its transcriptions—scholars have over the last two centuries established a poem epitomized in the edition of Friedrich Klaeber. We also have facsimiles by Zupitza ([1882] 1959) and Malone (1963) to use as evidence of the original manuscript contents, as well

25. For the facsimile edition, see Malone 1963.

26. This is not a universal principle, of course, since A could make errors of his own, especially with interpretation of minims. But when A omits a word or part-line altogether and B restores it in full, a careful editor will suspect the expert's intrusion.

as hundreds of proposals for repairing occasionally disturbed lexicon and syntax in the text.[27] The emendations tend to enter the poem that we read and interpret relatively slowly; in fact, from time to time there have arisen among scholars movements to reverse the tide of emendation and to maintain original manuscript readings wherever possible.[28] Behind questions of manuscript condition, transcription, and emendation, however, stands the seminal problem of the authority of the text as received. Unless we can gain some idea of exactly what Cotton Vitellius A. xv. offers us—and specifically with what authority it presents the poem—our decisions about consequent matters of editing and analysis will not be firmly grounded. And since the question of authority leads directly to dating, or early history, and to provenance, let us inquire first what can be discovered about the genesis of the text.

In an important sense, any attempt we might make to date the poem *Beowulf* would amount, in the words of David P. Henige (1964), to a "quest for a chimera." First and foremost, we are dealing with what is minimally an oral-derived text, a work that emerges from oral tradition along pathways we cannot now retrace and is intimately tied to that oral tradition, even if by the time our version of the poem was made the written word had become the sole textual medium.[29] The formulaic phraseology and narrative multiformity typical of oral narrative composition comprise the very fabric of *Beowulf*;[30] although we may choose to insist on a literate editor or "author" for the surviving text of the poem, we cannot ignore its more than evident roots in an Anglo-Saxon tradition of tale-telling that arose and flourished without the aid of writing.[31] This has been the most significant lesson of the excesses of the oral theory as propounded by Magoun ([1953] 1968), and equally of the intemperate reactions against that first statement. As described above in chapter 1, *Beowulf* need not answer all of the (tradition-dependent) criteria established by comparison with Serbo-Croatian and ancient Greek epic in order to be an oral traditional poem in a meaningful sense. Indeed, this greatest of surviving Old English poems may even have passed through one or more stages of composition or transmission that involved writing and still lay claim to oral traditional provenance. Once the critical dust has settled, the phraseology and narrative structure of the poem remain verifiably oral traditional, and we must confront that reality on its own terms.

27. Especially noteworthy in this regard are the recent observations made by Kevin Kiernan (1981a) after a fresh examination of Cotton Vitellius A. xv.

28. For a recent example, see Tripp 1983. In 1984 at the Modern Language Association, a panel entitled "Subtractive Rectification" pursued exactly this course.

29. Cf. Renoir on oral structures even in later, written texts (e.g. 1976b, 1988); and we do not know that *Beowulf* is not yet closer to the oral tradition than any of the texts Renoir is examining.

30. See the entries under "Old English" in Foley 1985; even Benson (1966) admits the formulaic structure of the poem.

31. Consider the analyses of Niles (1983) and Opland (1980) on this point.

Studies in Homeric archaeology, for example, have illustrated how futile the quest for a uniform date for a traditional work must be: the assortment of weapons and armor in the *Iliad*, to offer a famous illustration, stems variously from Mycenaean through Dark Age times, with the individual elements in the armament never all current at any one time in history.[32] Oral tradition does not recognize the anachronisms that result from our linear, non-recurrent sense of history, any more than we would be content with tradition's customary interpretation of important societal events through pre-existent story-patterns.[33] Thus it is that *Beowulf*'s oral traditional character itself precludes our assigning a single date to the work; even had we been present at the (oral or written) composition of our *Beowulf*, we could not ascribe the poem to that very moment. The phraseology and narrative style that constitute the poetic medium, as well as the story of *Beowulf* that is its content, long predate that moment, and any attempt to compress the diachrony of the tale-telling tradition would amount to a falsification of the poem's structure, and therefore of its aesthetics.

Under such conditions it is only fair to admit necessary uncertainty about the "date of *Beowulf*" and to shift the inquiry to firmer ground, that is, to the nature of our text of *Beowulf* and to its witness in Cotton Vitellius A. xv. Allowing for the undeniably oral traditional roots of the poem, we could comfortably place this text of the poem anywhere in the eighth or ninth century, or perhaps a bit later. While over the years critical opinion has ranged all the way from the fourth to the eleventh centuries (Chase 1981a), moving the text earlier than the eighth or later than the early tenth century entails special problems. One faces either the lack of an appropriate historical or social context or, alternatively, the necessity of explaining too many linguistic or political anachronisms.[34]

If we are to gauge the provenance of the *Beowulf* document, however, we must construct a reasonable hypothesis to cover the most significant ascertainable facts. I start with the minimal assumption of an oral-derived poem—

32. See, e.g., Snodgrass 1974; and on the linguistic parallel, M. Parry 1932.

33. Cf. Lord (1970, 27–28): "There is no reason to suppose that the patterns of ancient Greek epic tradition began with the Trojan War. They seem already to have been long in operation by the time of Homer, whenever one may place him in time. Historical events cannot give to a pattern the intensity and force needed for it to survive all the changes of tradition. These changes are not the corruption of time, but the constant reinterpretation of succeeding generations and societies. Not corruption, but constant renewal and revivification. The patterns must be suprahistorical to have such force."

34. If recent scholarship in this area makes anything clear, it must be that we should keep an open mind on the date of the extant *Beowulf* text. In *The Dating of Beowulf* (Chase 1981b), contributors' opinions range from John C. Pope's argument for the eighth century through Kiernan's preference for the eleventh (see also Kiernan 1981a, together with the responses of, e.g., Boyle [1981] and Chase [1982]). On the dependability of linguistic criteria for dating, see Amos 1980.

that is, a text of demonstrably oral traditional character—and therefore with the tradition that must have preceded and given birth to our text of *Beowulf*. This minimal assumption, backed up by an appreciable amount of scholarship, does not demand positing an "oral poem," but it does entail recognizing that the creation of our text was necessarily more a process than an event. For a start, then, like most reviewers I must doubt the likelihood of Kevin Kiernan's (1981b) explanation of the poem as coeval with the manuscript; in fact, I see no reason to contend that the first text was coeval with the manuscript. Earlier scholarship assumed as a paleographical commonplace that Cotton Vitellius A. xv. represents a copy some generations removed from the "archetype," and I find no incontrovertible proof suggesting that we should desert that position. Most importantly with respect to the eleventh-century dating, if we do accept the argument that Kiernan proposes, we in effect cut the poem off from its oral traditional provenance, and that would be a serious error—just as serious an error, one might add, as would be tacit acceptance of Magoun's first formulation of oral traditional art, a formulation that underestimated the aesthetic dimension of the poem. We need a hypothesis that allows the work both its undeniable roots and at least the possibility of memorial or written "polish."[35]

Placing the origin of our text in the eighth to ninth centuries (or perhaps the very early tenth) violates none of the paleographical, historical, or linguistic data per se and permits us to view the artifact in its oral traditional context. I would designate the beginning of the eighth century, in fact, as a *terminus a quo* for the introduction of the Beowulf story into the written medium. After that point the making of a written *Beowulf*, whether by oral dictation or as an autograph, would be a logical, reasonable enterprise. And although, given that manuscript production was exclusively a monastic enterprise and therefore not as subject to the influence of the political situation as some have suggested, I do not place as much emphasis on historical as on other aspects of available evidence, it can be said that the times were not uniformly inhospitable to the production of what has been called a Danish poem. Copies almost certainly intervened between that first text and Cotton Vitellius A. xv. (in a moment we shall consider the implications of the hypothetical transmission process). But if we settle on the eighth century as the earliest possible dating of this text of the poem, with the added proviso that it had to have emerged before two and one-half centuries had passed, we shall not be far from the truth. Most importantly, we shall not lose contact with the poem's lifeblood, its tradition.[36]

35. Compare what was said above in relation to the Homeric poems about the inevitability of editorial "polishing" during the process of transmission.

36. Compare Pope's (1981, 195) remarks on this point, made as part of his argument for an eighth-century date: "I cannot imagine that the author himself did not have a long period of apprenticeship in the art of poetry before composing such a masterpiece. It would not be surprising

Manuscript Authority

Since we have even fewer clues to the transmission of *Beowulf* than to that of the Homeric poems, and since we are describing a work whose most essential style and content owe so much to a precedent and perhaps contemporary oral tradition, it will be impossible to build much of a case for manuscript authority on grounds acceptable to modern textual criticism. As we have seen, neither an original date for execution of the poem nor a chronicle of its transmission can be established. To these realities we must add the fact that, as Kenneth Sisam ([1946] 1953) has pointed out, the Old English poetic manuscripts generally give us little reason for confidence in their authority. He notes (p. 36) that

> ample evidence from other sources confirms that copyists of Old English texts were not expected to reproduce their originals letter for letter, as they were when copying Latin and especially Biblical texts. Modernization of forms in the course of transmission was allowed and even required by the use for which Old English works were intended, and the practice was obviously dangerous for the wording.

Indeed, one cannot account for errors and changes by ascribing them to visual or aural mistakes, he continues, and "as compared with the variants in classical texts, they show a laxity in reproduction and an aimlessness in variation which are more in keeping with the oral transmission of verse" (p. 34).

An illustration of this last tendency (phrased perhaps too negatively, or at least literarily, by Sisam) may help to clarify the point. One of the few Old English poems to survive in two versions, "Soul and Body," exists in an incomplete Vercelli Book copy of 166 lines (usually called "I") and an ostensibly complete Exeter Book version of 121 lines ("II"). That these two texts are somehow related to a single poem is obvious: in addition to similar overall content, they share a large number of repeated or formulaically related lines.[37] What is more, even the formulaic modifications occur at metrically predictable spots, with substitutions of words following prosodic rules.[38] Further, most of the "unique" lines, those not shared by the two texts as we

---

if he had acquired most of his skill by oral composition. Certainly he had mastered a style well suited to oral delivery. As a pure conjecture I would suggest that the oral poets of the seventh century were largely responsible for the growth of the style and the story, and for pointing the way, in courtly and sometimes monastic surroundings, for the remarkable adjustment of Christian beliefs and pagan story that *Beowulf* represents and the Icelandic poems and sagas (greatly to our present satisfaction) so conspicuously lack."

37. See Alison Jones's two articles on "Soul and Body" (1966, 1969), as well as the *ASPR* Exeter Book version, which marks repetitions and equivalents.

38. We may also observe that the fourth stressed position in a line, the one stress that almost never participates in the alliterative pattern, is the most common locus for modification. Since it is not constrained by alliteration, this position can most easily tolerate the substitution of a synonym.

have them, echo against the larger referent of the Anglo-Saxon corpus as a whole, so that both texts are essentially traditional. What we seem to have in "Soul and Body" I and II, then, amounts to two versions of what was once a single poem, with each version having taken an idiosyncratic textual form best explained as a substantive traditional variant. While it is possible and even likely that these two texts diverged in part through individual histories of manuscript transmission, we should also admit the not exclusive possibility that memorial transmission in an oral context accounted for their formulaic resemblance.

Thus it is that the term *manuscript authority* really constitutes a misnomer in reference to the Old English documents. In addition to the many spelling changes and other typical scribal modifications, the editor and critic must consider the feature of formulaic, and perhaps memorial, transmission as well.[39] Whether such a medium was used both for the shorter, more memorizable poems and for the longer works like *Beowulf* is a question we cannot answer with certainty, a problem in genre-dependence that we do not have the evidence to solve.[40] But in assessing the authority of our received text of *Beowulf*, it is well to keep in mind that what Sisam has called "a laxity in reproduction and an aimlessness in variation" may be signs that the most important manuscript record for Old English poetry—like its Homeric counterpart essentially an oral palimpsest—was the memory.[41]

Implications for Comparative Analysis

At first sight the Homeric and Old English documents may seem quite comparable, both preserving a dead-language poetry about whose history we have little hard information. But there the resemblance ends. The *Beowulf* manuscript is a *unicum*; we cannot collate it with other texts, attempt stemmata, weigh precious bits of historical information, or even solve the minimal problem of the likely date and provenance of the poem it encodes. Much more so than even the Homeric poems, the work we call *Beowulf* is severed from its origins and history by its very uniqueness and lack of ascertainable background. The text can be dated, I have argued, most easily to the period A.D. 700–950, but that assignment does us little good in the face of so many missing facts. Our poem may have descended through one or a dozen scribal reformulations, some more exacting (in our modern sense) than others; it may have experienced, in part or in whole, a memorial transmission that altered its original form considerably. The plain truth is that, unless dramatic new

39. Compare the reconstructions of the memorial process in Fry 1974, 1981; Lord 1986c.

40. See chapter 1 above and Foley 1983b.

41. It is worth adding here that the tradition-dependent nature of Old English prosody would have allowed more variation than would the Homeric hexameter; see further chapters 4 and 6 below.

evidence emerges, we shall never know how far removed from its originative traditional composition this version stands.

As we did with the texts of the *Iliad* and the *Odyssey*, let us consider first the negative conclusions to be drawn from these remarks. First, since the Homeric and Old English manuscript records remain mysterious and idiosyncratic, no scholar interested in precise and sensible analysis can feel justified in quantitative comparison of these two remnants of two great traditions. The documents to be analyzed are vastly different not only in tradition (and therefore in language, prosody, phraseology, and even narrative structure) but also, and most basically, in their very physical make-up. If we cannot establish the primary oral nature of these texts, and if further we cannot certify that the items we are proposing to compare are truly comparable, then how is it possible to draw meaningful conclusions about, for example, formulaic density? The documents cannot be forced into a single category, any more than the languages or prosodies involved can be forced into absolute comparability.

But there are also positive conclusions to be drawn. Just as re-examination of the textual history of the Homeric poems indicates that the *Iliad* and *Odyssey* were but the epitome of an oral tradition that continued in some form well beyond their Panhellenic apotheosis, so the relative isolation of the *Beowulf* manuscript need not mean abandoning the search for poetic context. Although *Beowulf*, like the *Iliad* and *Odyssey*, must not without further proof be termed oral in the unambiguous sense that the Serbo-Croatian material collected by Parry and Lord is oral, neither can it be denied the designation *oral-derived*.[42] Over the past thirty-five to forty years a great deal of evidence has accumulated indicating that *Beowulf* and other Old English poems show the oral traditional features of formulaic phraseology and thematic structure, and no one would argue today that the poem's roots are not planted firmly in an Anglo-Saxon oral tradition. Exactly how far (if at all) *Beowulf* is removed from primary oral tradition is a question we cannot settle, but neither should we "throw the baby out with the bathwater" by ignoring the poem's indisputable oral-derived character. Once that minimal and justifiable assumption is made and accepted, the way is clear to invoke the remainder of the Old English poetic canon as a context (with proper calibration) and to begin to describe the meaning of traditional elements in *Beowulf* by reference to their recurrence in other oral-derived poems.[43] While we should be careful to acknowledge genre-dependence in this endeavor, and while the comparisons made within

42. Although I prefer the connotations of Burton Raffel's term *oral-connected* (1986), since it emphasizes continuity rather than discontinuity, I maintain *oral-derived* in order to stress the difference between texts that are obviously and verifiably oral and those which exhibit oral traditional features but cannot be proven on other grounds to be primary oral texts.

43. Or to expand the context beyond the Old English poetic canon to other Germanic and non-Germanic traditional poems; see, e.g., Renoir 1979b, 1981b, 1986.

the Old English canon cannot be (by definition) comparisons of parallel works from a primary oral tradition, this method of searching the oral-derived wordhoard for information about its constituents takes into account the more-than-literary relationships among surviving works. In short, what we lack in conventional literary-historical background about the document we call *Beowulf* can be in part replaced by the poem's most natural context—what has survived of its poetic tradition.

THE YUGOSLAV *GUSLARI* AND THEIR TRADITION

When in 1928 Milman Parry underwent the *soutenance* associated with the presentation of his two theses on the traditional style of the Homeric poems, he was as yet unaware of the next step he would take in positing that a Homer who composed traditionally must also have composed orally.[44] Parry attributed this conceptual leap to remarks made by his mentor, Antoine Meillet, during the defense and to the presence of Matija Murko, the Slovenian ethnographer who had been recording and studying the oral epic bards of the South Slavs for some years.[45] Although Parry did not at that time recognize the importance of the lectures Murko was presenting in Paris (later to become Murko 1929), he observed in his field notes, "Ćor Huso," that "it was the writings of Professor Murko more than those of any other which in the following years led me to the study of oral poetry in itself and to the heroic poems of the Southslavs" (*SCHS* 1:3). The advances documented in his classic articles on Homer and oral tradition (1930, 1932) had their point of origin in the 1928 *soutenance* and in the influence of Murko that became more significant as the years went on.

After a period of reading about the practice of oral poetry as described by Murko, Gesemann (1926), and Radloff (1885), and after realizing that his thinking on the subject was entirely theoretical, Parry determined to observe the phenomenon of oral composition at first hand.[46] Always foremost in his mind, however, was the applicability of the research to ancient Greek epic; in his own words, "it was least of all for the material itself that I planned the study" (*SCHS* 1:3).[47] Nonetheless, with a characteristic blend of imagination

44. For a full account of Parry's work and its antecedents, see Foley 1988, chaps. 1–2.

45. Murko's seminal but under-appreciated writings on oral epic in the South Slavic territories began as early as 1912; his major works were published in 1929 (the French monograph) and posthumously in 1951 (the two-volume magnum opus in Serbo-Croatian). My translation of these two latter works is in preparation (Foley forthcoming).

46. See *SCHS* 1:3–20; Lord 1951b, Lord 1960, chap. 1; and Bynum 1974.

47. He continues (*SCHS* 1:4): "In other words the study of Southslavic poetry was meant to provide me an exact knowledge of the characteristics of oral style, in the hope that when such characteristics were known exactly their presence or absence could definitely be ascertained in other poetries, and those many large and small ways in which the one oral poetry differed from written poetry for its understanding could be carried over to the Homeric poems."

and assiduousness, he carefully planned and carried out a program of collecting unequaled in any European tradition, before or since. The results of his efforts, including also expeditions undertaken in later years by Albert Lord and David Bynum, constitute the Parry Collection of Oral Literature at Harvard University, an archive of more than two thousand recorded songs, some of the best and most representative of which have been published in the series *Serbo-Croatian Heroic Songs.*

Parry's first trip in 1933 was chiefly an organizational mission, and he returned in 1934-35 to spend fifteen months recording and interviewing *guslari*. With his co-worker Albert Lord and native assistant Nikola Vujnović, Parry visited six principal centers in his search for oral epic comparanda: Novi Pazar, material from which region is published in *SCHS*, vols. 1-2; Bijelo Polje, the homeland of Avdo Medjedović, the finest *guslar* Parry encountered (*SCHS*, vols. 3-4, 6); Kolašin, in Montenegro; Gacko, represented in *SCHS*, vol. 14; Bihać (also represented in *SCHS*, vol. 14); and Stolac, the homeland of the singers whose epic narratives are in part the subject of the present volume.

Among the many songs and versions of songs to be found in the repertoires of *guslari* from these six centers, Parry soon discovered that a particular subgenre of epic would best suit his comparative work. As Lord points out (*SCHS* 1:16): "For his Homeric studies Parry found the songs of the Moslem population of Yugoslavia more significant than those of the Christian tradition, although it should be pointed out immediately that the singing tradition of both the Moslem Southslavs and their Christian brethren is the same." Parry preferred the Moslem songs because of their greater length, the result both of the Moslems having been the ruling class and of the continuous influence of the thirty-day feast of Ramadan, during which a month's worth of nightly entertainment in the coffeehouse was necessary. Under such conditions the singers of Moslem songs naturally developed much longer, more ornamental epic poetry, a poetry not unlike that of Homer.[48] When we add that the Return Song (as described in chapter 1) occurs in both Christian and Moslem traditions but takes a much longer, more elaborate form in the latter, we can see where the most suitable comparand for the Homeric *Odyssey* lies—in the Return Song of the Moslem tradition.

In respect to the actual medium of performance, the songs collected by Parry and Lord are of three major types: *sung* texts, performed at customary speed (varying both by singer and within individual song-texts) to the accompaniment of the *gusle*; *recited* texts, performed without the instrument; and *dictated* texts, taken down in writing at a much slower pace by an amanuensis. Lord's (1953, 132) description of the special nature of this last category of song-text makes clear the major points of divergence:

---

48. We may note that Parry was in effect observing a kind of genre-dependence by trying to suit the Serbo-Croatian comparand as closely as possible to the Homeric poems.

An oral poet who is asked to dictate a song for someone to write finds himself in an unusual and abnormal position. He is accustomed to composing rapidly to the accompaniment of a musical instrument which sets the rhythm and tempo of his performance. For the first time he is without this rhythmic assistance, and at the beginning he finds it difficult to make his lines. He can easily learn to do this, however, and he sets up a certain rhythm in his mind. He is also some-what annoyed by having to wait between lines for the scribe to write. His mind moves ahead more rapidly than does the writer's pen. This technique he can also learn, particularly if the scribe is alert and helpful. The singer is accustomed to the stimulus of an audience, but again an intelligent scribe and a small group of onlookers can provide this stimulus.... The chief advantage to the singer of this manner of composition [oral dictation] is that it affords him time to think of his lines and of his song. His small audience is stable. This is an opportunity for the singer to show his best, not as a performer, but as a storyteller and poet.

In general, the oral-dictated text reveals fewer "errors" of all kinds: fewer "bad" lines (unmetrical or fragmentary verses), slips of the tongue (substitution of words such as near-homophones), nonsensical lines (whether or not these occasion a partial repetition immediately following), divergences in the narrative, and other blemishes in phrasing or plot structure. Such dictated texts are often slightly longer than sung texts, since the *guslar* once accustomed to this medium can compose more carefully, without much of the pressure he otherwise feels in performance. These and other features have led Lord to posit that the Homeric poems as we have them must have originally been oral-dictated texts, and that Homer must have been familiar and comfortable with dictation. Whatever the case may be, I have selected both sung and dictated texts for the Return Song sample analyzed in these studies, in the hope that such an approach will pluralize our findings. The structural profiles of phraseology, narrative structure, and story-pattern, in other words, are not dependent on or limited by the medium of the songs examined.

One more issue must preface a closer look at the singers of Stolac and their songs. We need to recognize from the start a basic limitation on comparability in the case of the Serbo-Croatian witness. Whereas the ancient Greek and Old English texts are (minimally) oral-derived, the two histories of transmission diverge sharply; as noted above, various factors must calibrate any comparison we may wish to make. In the case of the Serbo-Croatian material, however, the problem of document comparability in a sense looms even larger: although our characterization of the work is not handicapped by lacunae in our information about memorial or manuscript transmission, the fact is that in Yugoslav oral epic no "text" exists until it is recorded—after which point its "polishing" by editors is either minimal or non-existent.[49]

---

49. This pertains, of course, to the Parry-Lord texts and not, for example, to the songs collected in the nineteenth century by Vuk Stefanović Karadžić, which did undergo some editing (see Foley 1983b).

The Stolac songs, whether sung, recited, or oral-dictated, constitute oral tradition in its purest form, without the usual deflections inevitable in any transmission process. Yet at the same time, each "version" represents an equal performance variant of the song or "work" that itself remains forever untextualized.[50] Before overall comparisons can be meaningful, they must be contextualized by a meticulous examination of each comparand on its own terms. In the case of the Serbo-Croatian material, this examination includes not only the points developed above but also the three Stolac singers and their repertoires of songs.

The Guslari *of Stolac*

Milman Parry and Albert Lord began their recording of oral traditional epic in the Stolac district of central Hercegovina, a region that in 1933–35 supported a strong and varied Return Song tradition. Songs by twenty-eight Stočani were gathered during the early expeditions, and later trips in the 1950s and 1960s by Lord and David Bynum added substantially to the sample of epic singing from this area. In later chapters we shall be looking both at the local tradition of the Stolac region in general and at three individual *guslari* who in particular help to comprise that tradition. Each has in his recorded repertoire a number of Return Songs, and it is principally to a selection of these works that we shall turn for evidence on phraseological and narrative structure in an unambiguously oral epic tradition.

IBRAHIM BAŠIĆ

Although he spent the greater part of his life in the Stolac area, Ibro Bašić was born in Vranjevići in the district of Mostar. At the age of fourteen he left his father's household to become a servant to Ahmet-efendija, a wealthy landowner from Opijač in Dubrava, with whom he remained for about ten years. He then entered the service of Salihagha Behmen on the occasion of his new master's wedding. After three or four years he himself married and lived for a time with his bride, Djula Džanko, in her village of Ošanjića. Subsequently they left the village and Ibro found work as an attendant in a coffeehouse (*kafana*).[51] During this period Djula became quite ill and her brother took her home to live with him in the hope of improving her health.

---

50. See further Foley 1986a.

51. Although he does not tell Nikola anything further about the coffeehouse experience, it seems safe to speculate that during this time Ibro had an opportunity to hear many singers perform. He may well have learned from them and perhaps even performed there himself. A fragmentary description from Parry text no. *291b* and an elaborate episode from no. *6598* indicate that he had at various times been paid for singing publicly. I employ the standard Parry Collection notation in citing the texts by number (for a digest of material collected through 1951, see *SCHS* 1:21–45); the italicized numbers indicate texts that were recorded from actual oral performance, the Roman numbers those taken down in writing from dictation.

Ibro soon followed her back to Ošanjića but became bedridden himself with a tumor in his leg.[52] He remained in the village for some eleven years after his recovery, living with a Ratkušić family. Djula died shortly thereafter, and a childless remarriage lasted only four years. By 1934–35, when Ibro was about seventy years of age, one son had moved to Belgrade and a second was with his father working at their modest woodcutting trade.

Ibro began to learn to sing at the age of eight or ten,[53] first from his father, a skilled *guslar* who was part of the local tradition in which a singer characteristically performed in villages near his own. While in the service of Ahmet-efendija Ibro also often traveled to nearby villages and heard *guslari* sing. In those years, he recalls, he was able to hear most songs only once and remember them well enough to perform them. Along with his father, Ibro also encountered five more singers of varying age and reputation in his early years. From Sule Tabaković he learned *Djerdelez Alija and the Ban of Karlovo* (Parry nos. 291, *291a*, 6596);[54] from Ibro Ćorić, *Grga Antunić Attacks Raduč* (no. *6692*); from Osman Marijić, *Hrnjičić Mujo and the Ban of Karlovo* (no. 645) and *The Wedding of Smailagić Meho* (no. 12491);[55] and from Selim Bašić and Selim's father, *Alagić Alija and Velagić Selim* (nos. *291b*, 1283, *6597*).[56]

In addition, we hear in conversation no. *6598* of a semi-legendary *guslar* of a previous generation, a certain Isak of Rotimlja by name, who was summoned for only the grandest occasions and was always splendidly rewarded for his performances.[57] Isak's legendary accomplishments include invitations to play before beys and pashas, a paradigmatic triumph in a song contest with a lesser singer named Gačanin, and requests for his presence at weddings of all religious denominations. Ibro seems never to have actually met Isak, and the complete lack of historical context and personal contact as well as the stories of his remarkable feats lead one to believe that this greatest of singers belongs to the same world of folktale inhabited, for example, by the Anglo-Saxon *scop*

52. This illness is a very "heroic" one, reminiscent in its hyperbole of Salih Ugljanin's account of how to behead a man (*SCHS* 1:63–64, 2:5).

53. On the special gift of youth in learning to sing, Ibro says (Parry no. *6598*): "A child of four years naturally remembers more than if he were twenty. The child is a great wonder; he can learn and retain it in his head. It's in the nature of a child." Cf. Lord's description, "Singers: Performance and Training" (1960, 13–29).

54. In text no. *291b* he credits Selim Bašić, his father, as the source of this song; this is the only contradiction about sources, however.

55. This last text, recited without the *gusle* and imbedded in the very lengthy conversation no. *6598*, demonstrates the important pacing function of the instrument. Hypersyllabic lines abound; compare *SCHS* 1:107–16 and 117–26.

56. Ibro explains that he heard the last song first from Selim himself and later from Selim's ninety-year-old father, who claimed to have been a "standard-bearer" (*bajraktar*).

57. In text no. *6598* Ibro says that "Isak was the best singer in Hercegovina" and that he was always paid because, unlike all the other *guslari*, "it [singing] was his profession" ("to je njemu zanat bijo").

Widsith.[58] At any rate, Isak seems to serve for Bašić, and for other singers, as a folk anthropomorphization of the epic singing tradition that they also embody.

Other sections of Ibro's conversations with Parry's native assistant Nikola make it clear that the *guslar* considered his songs "true," and yet that he also had a concept of what has often been called "ornamentation." For example, when asked whether the story had truth (*istina*) in it, Ibro says: "All is true, I believe, yes, even though some things are added (as you know)[59] to make it more fitting [*zgodnije*]; but there were all sorts of things then—there were heroes (and in yet earlier times there was a great number of them), and there were horses and swords and all. It was not then as it is today" (no. *6598*). In other words, in singing he is recalling or re-creating a heroic age when the events that make up his and others' songs actually took place, and although that time is far removed from the present day, he believes in its reality. In order to portray that age and those events in the most "fitting" way possible, he and others "add" the stateliness and grandeur of the epic tradition. This concept of the truth and its embodiment echoes Lord's (1970, 28) memorable observation on the relationship between historical truth as we know it and its representation in oral epic tradition; he notes that the stories are primary because "their matrix is myth and not history; for when history does have an influence on the stories it is, at first at least, history that is changed, not the stories."

Ibro also gives us an insight into the singer's craft in his response to Nikola's probing about the "accuracy" of repeated performances of a song—whether he composes and re-composes "word for word" each time—and about the very nature of a "word" (*riječ* or *reč*) in a song. Consider this excerpt from conversation no. *6598*:

> *Nikola*: What is, let's say, a *riječ* in a song? Give me a *riječ* from a song.
> *Ibro*: Here's one, let's say, this is a *riječ*: "Podranijo od Kladuše Mujo, / Na vrh tanke načinjene kule" ["Mujo of Kladusha arose early, / At the top of the slender, well-made tower"].
> *Nikola*: But these are lines.
> *Ibro*: Well yes, but that's how it is with us; it's otherwise with you, but with us that's how it's said. . . . But here's one, let's say, that is [a *riječ*]: "Podranijo od Kladuše Mujo," let's say, a *riječ* for "podranijo" ["arose early"]; "Prije zore i ogranka sunce" ["Before dawn and the sun's rising"], that's a *riječ* for "podranijo, uranijo, podranijo," so.

Apart from clearing up the confusion over what *guslari* really mean when they claim to perform songs "word for word" (*riječ za riječ*) each time,[60] these observations illustrate how the singer conceives of the units in his songs. Simply

58. See further Foley 1978b.

59. Nikola was also a practicing singer, and Ibro here assumes his knowledge of the role of ornamentation in the making of a song.

60. Compare the very different and limited perspective of G. S. Kirk (1962, 100) on the South Slavic *guslari*: "These particular poets pay lip-service to the ideal of complete accuracy in

put, his words are poetic lines, units that epitomize what Parry called an "essential idea" and which are governed by the metrical structure of the tradition. Ibro is telling us that the idea "arose early" equals, or can be expressed by, a decasyllabic expression in a song, and implicitly that lines, groups of lines, and perhaps metrical segments of lines are his *riječi*. Units of typographic description, demarcated by white spaces that serve as silent reading mnemonics, have no place in his "emic" or "ethnic" grammar of poetic diction. We would do well to keep his quite sophisticated observations in mind as we embark on a study of Serbo-Croatian oral epic phraseology.[61]

HALIL BAJGORIĆ

The second of our three *guslari* from the Stolac region, Halil Bajgorić, lived in Dabrica, a village so remote that he had to travel for three to four hours to reach the town in which Parry and Lord were recording and interviewing singers from that region. At the first encounter in 1934, Bajgorić was only thirty-seven years of age, unusually young for a *guslar* of his accomplishment (Lord was to record more songs from him seventeen years later). Of his personal history this singer says less than most. He relates stories of beys and their descendants in Dabrica and an engaging account of his grandfather's being tricked by a bey into forfeiture of his land over an unpaid loan. This unhappy turn of events in Montenegro led the old man to settle in the village of Blagoja, where both Halil and his father were born. Such family history follows story-patterns well known in the epic songs, such as escape from captivity, and the singer ornaments them with details from the epic tradition, such as lengthy catalogs of items or people. Throughout his conversation with Nikola, Halil time and again summons this kind of traditional idiom to tell legendary stories from his family's and district's past.

Bajgorić began to learn to sing as a young boy, first in emulation of his father and specifically in order to join him in performing in the coffeehouse or at a wedding or other celebration.[62] Although his father was, like himself,

---

reproduction, and are under the impression that they come very close to it. They are, in fact, far too optimistic; and their very confidence and lack of self-criticism prevents them from trying to achieve a higher standard of accuracy, which certainly lies within their power. The truth remains that even within their simple and unsophisticated oral tradition, with its incomplete formular technique, poems—not merely 'substance' or 'technique'—*are* transmitted, though with some variation and contamination."

61. See further chapter 5. On the distinctions between "emic" or "ethnic" categories on the one hand and "etic" or "analytic" categories on the other, see Ben-Amos 1969 and Dundes 1962. In the case of the *guslar*'s description of his compositional units, however, we should take the "emic" perspective especially seriously, since these same units are responsible for the compartmentalization and articulation of traditional meaning. See Foley 1986a.

62. It is typical of Bajgorić that he speaks somewhat romantically of the first stages of this process (no. *6698*): "So I stole the *gusle* from my father. I went into another room, and when he went to sleep I would sing a little."

a farm laborer and not a professional in any sense, he enjoyed a reputation for being the finest *guslar* "in three districts." Bajgorić makes no secret of the fact that he too is held in high esteem by his fellows, nor that he is customarily rewarded generously (albeit in kind) for his performances. While most of the songs in his repertoire came directly from listening to other singers, Halil admits that he did learn one, *Tsar Šćepan's Wedding*, from a songbook by having it read to him. In fact, he might well have learned more from that same source had not the process been so time-consuming and the selection, in his view, so parochial.[63] As it stands, then, he designates his father and one Ilija Bradurić, the latter of whom he says with some approbation was literate and could therefore draw his material directly from songbooks, as the sources for his own songs.

In addition, Bajgorić was among many *guslari* who spoke of a legendary singer from the past, an idealized figure whom they characteristically distinguished from the men who actually taught them their craft. Gifted with special talents and sought after in many quarters, Hasan Ćoso—as Halil called this figure—was a singer of wide experience: "He traveled everywhere throughout the world. And he lived for one hundred twenty years." Despite Halil's efforts to locate Hasan in real time and space (he is said, for example, to have spent most of his life in Dabrica), the nature of the biography reveals that this best of singers, like Bašić's Isak, was more a symbol than a fact: "My God, he died very long ago; from what they say it was probably seventy years ago. He was not even my father's father."[64] While he claims that his father learned to sing from Hasan, Halil himself denies any personal contact with the man. And although he indicates that his father and Hasan lived no more than a kilometer apart, it becomes apparent that this greatest of singers was unique in the community that surrounded him: "It is said that he could still jump twelve paces a half-year before he died. People say he neither dug nor plowed, nor did he ride a horse, but he always carried a rifle and some goods on a beast of burden, and thus traveling lightly he enjoyed himself and played the *gusle*." From these and other indications, it is clear that Bajgorić effectively understood Hasan as a kind of personification of the epic tradition—an anthropomorphic focus for the stories and wisdom of oral epic not unlike Ibro Bašić's Isak.

The songs passed down from such a paragon are of course "true," Bajgorić assures Nikola, and he is prepared to gloss any item or feature of the story as he related it. One of these textual footnotes, most of which concern names or minor events in a given narrative, offers a glimpse of the *guslar*'s own

63. The book in question, which, while never identified, sounds a great deal like some version of the poems collected and published by Vuk Karadžić, contained only Serbian songs and therefore no Moslem songs, particularly no *ličke pjesme* ("songs of the Lika").

64. Further probing established this last expression as an idiomatic way of denoting relative age rather than as an assertion of kin relation.

attitude toward traditional diction. On being asked for the origin of the ubiquitous toponym Markovac, Bajgorić replies that the term designates the mountain village in which the great Serbian hero Marko Kraljević was nursed. This assignment of the toponym naturally means that the village bears a name unsurpassed for its honorific and heroic import. But then Nikola confronts Halil with a problem: if this interpretation is correct, how does he explain the verse formula "Pa eto ga niz Markovac *kleti*" ("There he is below *accursed* Markovac")? His suggestion of Markovac as the revered cradle of Serbia's most significant hero is at odds with a line he has himself sung; Bajgorić therefore falls back on the explanation that *in a song* "mora da se rekne" ("it has to be said [like that]"). As Lord and others have argued, the tradition speaks diachronically in the synchronic performance of the individual *guslar*, and that person need not—and often does not—consciously analyze and understand the nature of the idiom he is employing by right of succession. It is enough for Bajgorić to know that "Pa eto ga niz Markovac kleti" constitutes a *reč*, a traditionally defined and indivisible "word," which he can draw from his compositional lexicon in the making of his song.

Like Ibro Bašić, Halil conceives of the action described in his songs as having actually taken place much earlier, in some sort of "Golden Age," and he offers the observation that most of the heroes involved, such as Aliagha Stočević and Mustajbeg of the Lika, lived at approximately the same unspecified period in history. When he sings of these and other heroes, moreover, they are subject to the same traditional ornamentation used by Bašić. At times this compositional flexibility—that is, the multiformity that is the lifeblood of the oral epic tradition—leads to what we might term an outright error or omission, the kind of narrative blemish that has so often influenced Homeric scholars to picture the great poet "nodding." A case in point is Nikola's calling to Halil's attention the omission of the hero's preparations for travel from a second version of a particular song.

> *Nikola*: Yesterday you sang this song, but today when you sang it you skipped over one whole section that is usually sung—for example, when Marko readies himself and his horse for travel.... So did you shorten [the song]?
> *Halil*: It's possible that I shortened some "words" [*reči*].
> *Nikola*: Yes, yes. Did you do it intentionally?
> *Halil*: No, I didn't; it was only an oversight [in the] heat of performance.[65]

On closer inspection it becomes apparent that the "words" that the *guslar* "skipped over" amounted to the usually paired themes of the hero arming for battle and readying his horse. We may draw two conclusions from these observations. First, Bajgorić understands the omitted section of the song in terms of *reči* or "words," the same unit described by Bašić in reference to a

---

65. Bajgorić speaks here of a *velika vatra* (literally, "great fire") that temporarily addled his thinking and caused him to stray from what he considered the proper story line.

line or group of lines in a song. Second, he not only is aware of the possibility of ornamentation by means of multiforms but also falls victim to the other side of the same process; flexibility of narrative structure means that occasionally a singer will delete one or more elements from what is customarily a sequence. As we shall see again in reference to the works of the next singer, this deletion may take place without the *guslar*'s conscious notice. It is the price one pays for a generative compositional idiom that tolerates substitution and variation within incremental limits.[66]

MUJO KUKURUZOVIĆ

The third of the Stolac *guslari* whose recorded works we shall be examining, Mujo Kukuruzović, lived originally in the village of Grbavica in the district of Mostar and was forty-three at the time of the initial Parry-Lord fieldwork. Like both Bašić and Bajgorić, he could neither read nor write, and like Bajgorić he earned his living farming land he had inherited from his father. Although he seems to have learned the craft of singing in the customary way, Mujo was unique among this group in the variety of sources he claims for his songs: he attributes his repertoire of thirty-eight different items to a long list of singers, eleven in all, none of whom was apparently related to him.[67] He also classified each of these singers into one of two categories, the *narodni* (or "folk") *guslar* who was not for hire but could be rewarded for his services with food and drink, and the coffeehouse singer (*guslar u kafani*) who was paid by the proprietor for his performances according to a pre-arranged agreement. We find both kinds of singers among his putative tutors, although Mujo's own preference is for the less commercial and less professional *narodni guslar*.

Mujo's conversation with Nikola proves him a lively informant, not least because of his willingness to offer an opinion on nearly every aspect of the singer's métier. While we cannot accept everything he says without critical evaluation, especially since like other *guslari* he tends to spice answers to questions about his personal history with the heroic details of his oral epic tradition,[68] his comments on the art and process of singing are without doubt the most perceptive of those made by any of the three Stočani. For example, he knows of songbooks but says he does not use them because as a rule they contain only the newer songs, not the longer Moslem epics to which he feels a special affinity. And he is never slow to affirm his own ability to master the songs he has heard from others or had read to him. During discussion of the

66. On the meaning of such variation and its context, see Foley 1984b.

67. Note, however, that the two accounts of attribution, one in the repertoire (no. 1287) and the other in the conversation (no. *6619*), at points differ on which singer is to be credited as the source for a given song.

68. He claims, for example, to have been imprisoned in Hasan Pasha Tiro's tower! Hasan Pasha Tiro is a character from the epic, most prominent in *The Wedding of Smailagić Meho* (see *SCHS*, vols. 3–4).

Ženidba bega Ljubovića (*The Wedding of Bey Ljubović*), for instance, he tells Nikola how easily he can pick up songs to enlarge his repertoire:

> *Mujo*: So now, brother, you go ahead and find some song I don't know; then, brother, read it to me and give me the *gusle*; if I get confused, I'll give you a finger off my hand.
> *Nikola*: And you'll sing the whole song this way?
> *Mujo*: I'll repeat every single *reč*.
> *Nikola*: Well, that's a wonder to me.
> *Mujo*: It'll be so, I guarantee it.

We might view this exchange as mere bravado on Kukuruzović's part, and perhaps it is just that, at least on one level;[69] but later on in the conversation he glosses the term *reč* memorably by echoing Ibro Bašić's and Halil Bajgorić's concept of the traditional "word." After defining a *reč* as "an utterance [*besjeda*] which comes after another as that [former] one passes forth, as it goes, as it falls out all in order—from beginning to end, as it is ordered and placed and so on," he prescribes one or more lines as the unit *reč*:

> *Nikola*: Let's consider this: "Vino-pije-lički-Mustajbeže" ["Mustajbeg of the Lika was drinking wine"]. Is this a single *reč*?
> *Mujo*: Yes.
> *Nikola*: But how? It can't be *one*: "Vino-pije-lički-Mustajbeže."
> *Mujo*: In writing it can't be one.
> *Nikola*: There are four *reči* here.
> *Mujo*: It can't be one in writing. But here, let's say we're at my house and I pick up the *gusle*—"Pije vino lički Mustajbeže"—that's a single *reč* on the *gusle* for me.[70]
> *Nikola*: And the second *reč*?
> *Mujo*: And the second *reč*—"Na Ribniku u pjanoj mehani" ["At Ribnik in a drinking tavern"]—there.
> *Nikola*: And the third *reč*?
> *Mujo*: Eh, here it is: "Oko njega trides' agalara, / Sve je sijo jaran do jarana" ["Around him thirty chieftains, / All the comrades beamed at one another"].

In fact, not only does Kukuruzović sense what Lord has called the "adding style" of oral epic and manage to communicate to Nikola a rather sophisticated notion of the functional kernel of traditional composition, but he is also able to conceive of the separateness of the four units that we, outside of the traditional idiom, would call "words." Although Mujo's comments on the sources of his songs may be contradictory and his estimate of his own ability as a *guslar* a bit inflated, his analysis of the units of compositional meaning—the *reči* that make up his song—is extremely enlightening. Quite naturally, with-

---

69. See the discussion of his revealing departure from the story line in chapter 10 below.

70. Notice that Kukuruzović has metathesized the words *vino* and *pije* in this second mention of the line. Such flexibility is just one characteristic of the compositional "word" employed and deployed by the *guslar*. See further chapter 5.

out the scholarly precision possible only for an outsider but from a perspective available only to a traditional singer, he is very close to describing formulaic composition.

Kukuruzović is also aware of the possibility for *okitinje*, or ornamentation, of the story as it is performed. In response to Nikola's questions about exactly what such ornamentation consists of, he is less than clear, but he does comment, for example, that he can sing a song that will prove "more harmonious" or "more integrated" than those customarily found in songbooks. He considers the stories basically true, although he retains a pragmatic attitude toward the relative "truth" of versions by various singers: "You know, I count as true that which I've more often heard." As we shall see in chapter 10, the question of multiformity at the narrative level—of ornamentation and different versions of a song—looms large with Kukuruzović. For along with generic song-types of (a) Return and (b) Alliance with the enemy, he includes in his repertoire what we shall call a *song amalgam*, that is, a third type that is an additive combination of (a) and (b). We shall be able to watch the progress of traditional tale combination by tracing the outlines of the two constituent songs in the larger song and by observing the kind of connective tissue provided by the tradition to bind the two into a greater whole. What is more, the suture had not entirely healed at the moment that Mujo's repertoire was recorded, and the "narrative inconsistencies" (this time of major proportions) in one of the composite texts will allow us to follow the logic of *guslar* and tradition in the act of song-making.

THE PARRY COLLECTION TEXTS USED FOR COMPARISON

For phraseological analysis I have chosen a unified group of five Moslem epic songs from the singers of Stolac, as summarized in table 1.[71] These selections, made from a total of twenty-one songs I have edited from the singers of this region, reflect a mixture of media (three dictated and two sung texts) but a near unanimity of subgenre (four Return Songs and one Wedding Song). The sample thus includes both sung and dictated material from two singers and represents a unified local tradition. Taken together, the five songs total 7,287 decasyllabic lines, an extensive textual basis on which to found an analysis of oral traditional phraseology first within the local Stolac tradition and, by example, elsewhere within the Serbo-Croatian epic tradition.

For the major part of the thematic analysis, I have selected a group of eight Stolac songs in the Return subgenre that were sung or dictated by Bašić

71. The titles given here were assigned by Parry and Lord or, if they provided none, by me. Strictly speaking, titles are quite irrelevant to the *guslar*, who remembers a song in relation to its major figures and central action. The code numbers assigned reflect the protocol of the concordance and will be used in chapter 5 on traditional phraseology in Serbo-Croatian. See further chapter 5, note 23.

TABLE 1. Texts for Phraseological Analysis

Singer	Parry no.	Type	Length	Code no.	Subgenre
Kukuruzović	1287a[a]	dictated	1288	1	Return
Kukuruzović	1868[b]	dictated	2152	2	Return
Kukuruzović	6617[c]	sung	2180	6	Return
Bajgorić	6699[d]	sung	1030	3	Wedding
Bajgorić	6703[e]	dictated	637	4	Return

[a] *Ropstvo Ograšćić Alije*
[b] *Ropstvo Alagić Alije*
[c] *Ropstvo Ograšćić Alije*
[d] *Ženidba Bećirbega Mustajbegova*
[e] *Halil izbavlja Bojičić Aliju*

TABLE 2. Texts for Thematic Analysis

Singer	Parry no.	Type	Length	Subgenre
Bašić	6597[a]	sung	1558	Return
Bašić	291b[a]	sung	1360	Return
Bašić	1283[a]	dictated	1403	Return
Kukuruzović	6618[b]	sung	1422	Return
Kukuruzović	1868[b]	dictated	2152	Return
Kukuruzović	6617[b]	sung	2180	Return
Kukuruzović	1287a[b]	dictated	1288	Return
Ugljanin	674[c]	sung	1811	Return

[a] *Alagić Alija i Velagić Selim*
[b] *Ropstvo Alagić Alije/Ograšćić Alije*
[c] *Ropstvo Djulić Ibrahima*

or Kukuruzović (table 2). Near the end of chapter 8 comparisons are also drawn to a single song by Salih Ugljanin of Novi Pazar (*SCHS* 2, no. 4). Once again we have both sung and dictated texts by each of two *guslari* from the same local tradition, all of them in the same subgenre, with the total sample amounting to 11,363 lines.[72] This large and multi-layered inventory of songs and versions will allow exploration of individual, local, and pantraditional features of the narrative theme.

Before these analyses can begin, however, we must turn to an examination of the prosodies that exist in symbiosis with the ancient Greek, Old English, and Serbo-Croatian epic phraseologies, and which thus ultimately figure in the verbal expression of narrative patterns.

72. Line-count per se is of course not as important a consideration in thematic as in phraseological analysis, but it does afford some idea of the extent of the sample used for thematic investigation. See further chapter 8.

THREE

Comparative Prosody

PROLOGUE

Any study of traditional oral phraseology and narrative structure must very early come to terms with the prosody that exists in symbiosis with them. Milman Parry recognized this need when he stipulated (1928a, in 1971, 272) that the Homeric formula must occur "under the same metrical conditions," and Albert Lord (1960, 20) extended the metrical requirement to the formula in Serbo-Croatian epic. Francis P. Magoun, Robert P. Creed, and others were also careful to prescribe prosodic rules for the recurrence and morphology of formulaic phraseology in Old English poems.[1] In more recent scholarship, however, prosodic strictures on the formula have been relaxed, or at least de-emphasized.[2] Although the declared motive behind this drift away from philological rigor—the putative search for "originality" or "creativity" in reaction against the supposedly mechanistic model of Parry and Lord[3]—may at first sight seem laudatory, in fact we cannot hope to gain an informed perspective by abdicating precision and thoroughness. Aesthetics does not emerge by default from the short shrift of incomplete analysis. We need to know as accurately and intimately as possible all dimensions of formulaic structure before we can responsibly begin to criticize a traditional text. And, as the linear and recurrent formant of all phraseology, prosody deserves highest priority as the most basic stylistic feature of formulaic structure.

---

1. For a history of scholarship on the formulaic phrase in Old English, see Foley 1981b, 52–79, 103–16; also Olsen 1986, 1988.

2. E.g., Nagler 1974, 1–63.

3. This type of reaction began with articles such as Calhoun 1933 and 1935, and has manifested itself more recently in works such as Norman Austin's "The Homeric Formula" (1975, 11–80) and Vivante 1982.

With the fundamental nature of prosody established, the next step is to ask how the prosodic rules of the three poetic traditions compare. Since each language fosters an individual, idiosyncratic meter, we should expect the Homeric hexameter, Old English alliterative line, and Serbo-Croatian epic decasyllable to differ in distinct and recognizable ways. Even if it proves possible to trace each line back to a common Indo-European ancestor, the singular character and development of the three language traditions will have impressed a particular stamp on each prosody. Thus, if we mean to enforce the spirit of philological rigor and the letter of tradition-dependence championed in the preceding chapters—that is, if our comparison is to aspire to a sensitive, articulate account of differences as well as similarities—we cannot hold on to the illogical and demonstrably faulty assumption of either an "archetypal prosody" or an "archetypal formula." Because languages differ, the prosodies formed within them differ; thus the formulaic structures interactive with those prosodies must likewise differ. The universal theorem of formulaic style must be tempered by the corollary of tradition-dependence; if our later discussions of phraseology and narrative structure are to have the meaning that only a truly comparative philology can give them, then we must begin the comparison at the fundamental level of prosody.

METHOD

An interpretive essay on comparative prosody in these three epic poetries would, if exhaustively done, constitute a sizable project in itself. A great deal has been written on the hexameter, alliterative line, and decasyllable, and simple review of that scholarship would demand an expenditure of space unwarranted in these studies as a whole. As a methodological premise, then, I concede from the start that my goal is certainly not a full and exhaustive treatment of the subject per se, but rather an examination of those aspects of the subject most crucial to an understanding of oral traditional structure. In other words, I will be concerned primarily with those prosodic factors which determine the shape and texture of formulaic diction and therefore of the more extensive narrative units that also rely, in the last analysis, on structure at the level of the individual line or even line-part. This is not to say that I intend to ignore or intentionally shortchange any particular areas; I wish merely to indicate from the outset that the emphasis is on the *comparison* of prosodies, and especially on *their role in oral traditional structure.*

I advocate three principles of evaluation as an attempt at a single, unified methodology. First, what follows in this chapter will straddle the gap between an exacting description of each epic line in and of itself and an approach that permits productive comparisons in the directions indicated. Second, uniform and consistent recourse to prevailing scholarly opinion on individual prosodies will give way to consideration of minority views only when no clear consensus on a given point can be identified or when we pass beyond the present state of knowledge. Third, I offer the entire exposition as a useful explicative tool, without proclaiming its necessary "rectitude" and without pronouncing it *ex cathedra*.[4] In this manner the available data on the three individual epic lines can be gathered, collated, and presented in a suitable format. In the subsequent process of comparison for the purpose of understanding the traditional verbal structures based on these lines, I hope to return to each prosody as much new comparative knowledge as was taken from each for the preliminary descriptions.

THE INDO-EUROPEAN QUESTION

Any proposal to compare three prosodies from related Indo-European language families—Hellenic, Balto-Slavic, and Germanic—must take account of the extent to which similarities may be due to emergence from a common prototype or prototypes in Indo-European and of the significance that such genetic similarities might have for the present study. To a degree, then, we should address two interlocking problems. First, what does comparative historical metrics have to tell us about the meters involved, and how convincing are the conclusions? Second, does the historical perspective bear importantly on the particular kind of investigation underway in this and subsequent chapters?

The methods of reconstruction originally developed for recovering elements in the Indo-European lexicon were first applied to the study of meter by Antoine Meillet. In his *Les Origines indo-européennes des mètres grecs* (1923, 76), the great French philologist characterized a prehistoric parent meter deduced from ancient Greek and Vedic Sanskrit evidence:

> Le vers indo-européen, fait pour une langue dont le rhythme était purement quantitatif, était caractérisé par des cadences définies au point de vue de la durée.

4. I do not expect in all or most cases to have chosen the "right" path, or for that matter the "wrong" path, since I do not believe that a descriptive prosody is only either right or wrong, elect or damned. Varying perspectives often camouflage deeper correlations; to put it another way, the nature of any approach must assist more than is customarily assumed in determining the nature of the results. As I suggested in "Formula and Theme in Old English Poetry" (1976a, 208), "a method of scansion is only as successful as it is both thorough and exclusive in accounting for what exists in the Old English poetic corpus. A metrical system which can be thorough and exclusive without devolving into a catalog is extremely useful. No *scop* thought in terms of iambs or measures, but if we can develop a way to talk about what a singer intuitively felt and, at the same time, if we do not seriously distort the continuity of his art into our own critical perspective, then we may proceed without doing violence to that art. We may produce a useful idiom." Compare Martin L. West's closing statement to "A New Approach to Greek Prosody" (1970, 194): "In conclusion, I should like to point out that what is sketched in the foregoing pages is not a 'theory' to be accepted or rejected, but a formula for classifying empirical data; it is no more conjectural than the Dewey system of classifying books, it is neither true nor false. It must be judged on its ability to match the complexity of the facts."

Les vers longs, à partir de 11 ou 12 syllabes, avaient de plus une coupe à place légèrement variable, dans la première partie du vers. La partie initiale du vers —dans le vers à coupe, presque tout ce qui précédait la coupe—ne comportait pas une répartition fixe de longues et de brèves.[5]

Testimony from other language families has since been added to Meillet's work: by Roman Jakobson (1952) for Slavic; by Calvert Watkins (1963) for Celtic; by Gregory Nagy (1974, 1975) for ancient Greek and Sanskrit; by Berkley Peabody (1975) for Indic, Iranian, and ancient Greek; by John Vigorita (1976, 1977a,b) for Slavic and Greek; and by M. L. West (1973a,b) for all of these plus Italic, Germanic, and in smaller compass other groups.[6] The imaginative efforts of these scholars have uncovered much that is valuable and extremely suggestive.

At the same time, it is only fair to report that labors in this incipient field have not been universally accepted without reservation. Jerzy Kuryłowicz (1970, 421-22, 429), for example, argues that "the conclusion that the appearance in two Indo-European languages of, e.g., decasyllables or hendecasyllables, with a partially iambic rhythm, catalectic or acatalectic, enlarged or shortened, etc., points to a common origin of such a metrical pattern, is no more justified than the assertion of the common origins of the IE and Semitic plural, genitive, or subjunctive" and further that "as for the question of a common IE origin of Greek and Indic verse, it must remain open." Likewise, in a brief exposition published in 1976, Henry Hoenigswald reminds us (p. 275) of methodological problems associated with the extension of comparative reconstruction from the hard linguistic data of lexical roots to meter. The comparative method as originally conceived, he maintains, was "uniformitarian":

> In denying that some traits are inherently and characteristically innovative, the comparatists believe that their unreconstructed ancestor language is just another language, different from its descendants to be sure, but, typologically speaking, no more so than descendants may be from each other; whatever structural damage changes in time may cause is sure to be repaired by other changes. It must be admitted that the tenets of historical and prehistorical metrics are non-uniformitarian.[7]

5. Note also his statement (p. 61) that "l'épopée homérique est toute faite de formules que se transmettaient les poètes."

6. See also O'Nolan 1969.

7. He concludes: "It seems to be difficult to get away from the notion that in certain metrical histories (say, in that of the hexameter from Homer to Nonnos) the *nature*, and not just the accidental properties, of the verse changes (say, from 'loose' to 'rigid,' although one could in particular cases argue for something different, or even contradictory; or merely from 'simple' to 'complex'). Actually, Meillet's basis is consensus among the comparanda rather than triangulation from them, though his qualitative judgments were admirable" (Hoenigswald 1976, 275). See also the reviews of G. Nagy (1974) by Hoenigswald (1977) and by Brough (1977).

On balance, however, the pursuit of Indo-European meters has received more support than criticism, and it seems prudent to agree with M. West (1973b, 161) that "the assumption that Indo-European prototypes underlie the metrical forms at least of Indian, Iranian, Greek, Slavic, and Celtic poetry is now respectable."

Roman Jakobson's work on the *deseterac*, the Serbo-Croatian epic deca-syllable, to take the next chronological step from Meillet's *Origines*, is thorough and wide-ranging, although his textual sample could be more extensive.[8] He covers all of the Slavic meters cognate to the *deseterac* and, after carefully con-sidering the idiosyncrasies of each separate language tradition, derives a Common Slavic prototype antecedent to and generative of the various descen-dant types. Although the Serbo-Croatian epic line itself is more properly the subject of the latter part of this chapter, we may note in capsule form the congruity that Jakobson demonstrates between Meillet's Indo-European line and the Common Slavic reconstruction. Both have what may be termed *regular syllabicity*, a consistent number of syllables; *anceps*, indifferent quantity in the final syllable; *right justification*, a relative freedom from any pattern of quantities in the earlier part of the line and a correspondingly more regular succession of quantities near the end of the line; and *caesura*, an obligatory word-break at a constant or slightly variable position within the line. Through discovery and delineation of these regularities, Jakobson (1952, 66) relates the Yugoslav epic line and meters from other Slavic traditions to an ancient precursor, complementing the analysis of Meillet: "The testimony of the third witness to the foundations of the Indo-European verse may now join those of Greek and Vedic."[9]

A number of possible historical derivations for the Homeric hexameter have been offered in the years following Jakobson's (1952, 64–65) championing of Bergk's ([1854] 1886) hypothesis of its development from an Aeolic paroemiac. Prominent among these is Gregory Nagy's account (1974), in which he describes ancient Greek and Indic correlations at some length, taking as a point of departure the cognate Homeric and Vedic formulas κλέος ἄφθιτον and *śráva(s) ákṣitam* ("imperishable fame"). In speaking of his two subject meters and their Indo-European parent, he remarks (pp. 30, 36): "The verse is divided into an opening and a closing, which are marked by flexible and rigid rhythms respectively"; accordingly, "the comparative approach, in short, suggests that freedom in the rhythm of the opening is a feature inherited from

8. Jakobson's body of texts included 783 lines performed by the Montenegrin *guslar* T. Vučić and certain unspecified samples from published texts and the Parry Collection. My comments on the heroic decasyllable later on in this chapter are based on computer analysis of more than five thousand lines from the local tradition of Stolac.

9. Vigorita (1976, 209) concurs with Jakobson's analysis of the structure of the *deseterac*, concluding that of all the South Slavic meters "the epic decasyllable . . . has perhaps the strongest claim to antiquity. It is related to the Greek paroemiac and the rare Vedic decasyllable."

the archetypal Indo-European poetic language." He sees the progressive restriction of freedom as a right-to-left process—"the lineal direction is from line-final to line-initial," the same directional movement posited by Jakobson and Meillet which I called "right justification."[10] Nagy derives the hexameter from an Aeolic pherecratic with dactylic expansion; the pattern that he cites (p. 49) from Alkaios and a generalized schema of the hexameter are as follow:

pher³ᵈ $\overset{\smile}{1}$ $\overset{\smile}{2}$ $\overline{3}$ 4 5 $\overline{6}$ 7 8 $\overline{9}$ 10 11 $\overline{12}$ 13 14 $\overline{15}$ $\overline{16}$ (16 syllables)

hexameter $\overline{1}$ 2 2a $\overline{3}$ 4 5 $\overline{6}$ 7 8 $\overline{9}$ 10 11 $\overline{12}$ 13 14 $\overline{15}$ $\overline{16}$ (17 syllables)[11]

To accomplish the transformation he stipulates (1) the optional replacement of the dactyl by the spondee, that is, of _ ˘˘ by _ _; and (2) the replacement of ˘ ˘ by _ _, which in turn is optionally replaced by the dactyl, _˘˘. One particularly attractive aspect of Nagy's theory is how thoroughly it explains the caesuras and diaeresis, the major word-breaks in the hexameter.[12]

Berkley Peabody also sifts the evidence from ancient traditions in the Indo-European family, specifically Vedic Sanskrit and Iranian (the *Avesta*), and comes up with an alternate derivation for the Homeric line (1975, 47-48):

> The hexameter seems to be a hybrid primary combination that resulted from the fusion of dimeter and trimeter verse forms. The fusion of lines into one integrated verse form correlates with the tendencies noted in both the Avestan and Vedic traditions.... The two-against-three structure of the Greek fusion seems to have produced such a tight formal continuum that the verse tended in time to become functionally transformed into a single diploid line form (a single line—not verse—with twice the usual number of parts).

Although the entire demonstration is much too complex to be conveniently summarized here, we may note in passing that, as with Nagy's hypothesis,

10. Cf. O'Nolan 1969, 17: "The hexameter cannot have sprung fully fledged into existence but is likely to have developed (as Watkins shows for the paroemiac) from a prototype which has a fixed tail-end and a free fore-part. One may imagine a sort of creeping paralysis of versification starting at line-end." Compare also Austerlitz (1985, 46) on a similar tendency in the Finnish (and non-Indo-European) *Kalevala*.

11. Nagy notes (1974, 49) that the sixteen-syllable prototype has the same number of syllables as the *śloka*, the basic unit of Indic epic versification. The hexameter is given here in its wholly dactylic form, without spondaic substitution, for convenience of comparison. The equivalence _ = ˘˘ was at any rate a Greek innovation, so that spondaic feet would obscure genetic comparison.

12. As we shall see later on, Nagy argues that phraseology is diachronically precedent to meter, and so he understands (1974, 61) the word-break pattern in the hexameter as the product of an interaction between formula and meter: "the pher³ᵈ pattern of the archetypal epic hexameter had accommodated the formulas of shorter verses, and it is these formulas that eventually led to the attested caesura- and diaeresis-system of the larger verse."

Peabody's theory accounts well for the major word-breaks in the line.[13] What is more, both formulations manifest a deep concern with diachronic roots and with establishing the hexameter as a metrical shape continuously in the process of reshaping itself.

Martin West's synthetic articles (1973a,b) serve as an overview of the subject of Indo-European meter. Following the original tenets of comparative reconstruction, which require evidence from at least three language families for valid triangulation back to Indo-European Ur-forms, he adduces data from the Vedas, the Gathas of the *Avesta*, and the Aeolic meters of ancient Greek. His simple series of prototypes, generalized and compounded later on, are two:

Acatalectic	*Catalectic*
xxυ⏔υ⏔	5(⏐)x⏔υ⏔⏔
xxxυ⏔υ⏔	xxxυ⏔⏔
xxxxυ⏔υ⏔	xxxxυ⏔⏔
	xxxx⏔υ⏔⏔

where x is a syllable of variable or indifferent quantity; 5 is a protasis of five syllables; and (⏐) is a word-break after the protasis. He conceives of the hexameter as the possible product of "a pherecratean and expanded reizianum, ⏔x⏔υυ⏔x⏐x⏔υυ⏔υυ⏔⏔, welded together and regularized in rhythm throughout" (1973b, 169, n. 10), or, in a manner closer to that of Nagy, as an "expanded pherecratean" (1973a, 186).

Besides the Aeolic meters and ultimately the hexameter, West also tests his prototypes against meters in Slavic (Serbo-Croatian, Czech, Polish, and Russian), Celtic (Old Irish), Italic (Latin), Germanic (Old English and Old Norse), Hittite, Lydian, and Tocharian, with various results. In reference to those meters under consideration in the present study, I find his comments on the *deseterac*, parallel to those of Jakobson, especially suggestive. He explains the decasyllable as a four-syllable protasis of variable quantities followed by the same version of the Indo-European prototype that also generates the Greek reizianum and Vedic colon of the triṣṭubh line. In addition, he sees the quantitative regulation of the second portion of the line only, a phenomenon I have termed "right justification," as an argument for the extreme archaism of the Serbo-Croatian decasyllable. West's comments on the Germanic "standard line" are necessarily sketchier and more hypothetical, given the modulation from a quantitative Indo-European line to the stress-

---

13. "It appears, however, that if the central caesura is seen as the relict of a joint between two earlier line forms, each of which already possessed its caesura, not only are all three caesuras accounted for, but the fact that the central caesura moves in a way different from that of the caesuras on either side is also explained" (Peabody 1975, 51; see further pp. 30–65).

based Germanic vernacular meters that were its eventual descendants. None-theless, he offers a plausible explanation of the very developments that obscure the genetic picture.[14]

To sum up, most Indo-European metrists agree on an Ur-meter that was (1) quantitative, (2) of consistent syllabic definition, (3) relatively free in the distribution of quantities early in the line while relatively rigid in the pattern of quantities later in the line (that is, "right-justified"), and (4) marked by a regularly placed caesura, or word-break, within the line. Through combina-tion and recombination of prototypical metrical forms, through linguistic adaptations resulting from the development of language families and of indi-vidual languages within those families, and through the myriad interactions between phraseology and meter, singular verse forms became differentiated and gained identities of their own. It is essential to keep in mind, especially as we continue the discussion by consulting each language tradition separately, that available evidence indicates that the various meters which have emerged and now stand as entities in the extant texts both stem ultimately from one or a series of Indo-European prototypes of unitary and extremely ancient provenance and also exist as integral and dynamic instruments of individual poetries. In linguistic terminology, then, these meters thus have both a *dia-chronic* history and a *synchronic* identity or definition.

It is time now to consider the place and importance of the Indo-European question in these studies as a whole; in doing so it will be convenient to examine each meter separately and then conclude with some more general remarks. First, the hexameter's relation to Indo-European prototypes is far from absolutely clear. Scholars seem to be able to agree on the rough outlines of the Homeric line's prehistory, so that we can avoid having to posit with Meillet (1923, 62-63) an external "Aegean" origin for the hexameter, but there is no consensus on the particulars of that history. More immediately, one can in the light of competing hypotheses about its evolution easily lose sight of the fact that the hexameter in its present form has to have been a

---

14. "The elastic nature of the traditional cola as they appear all over the Germanic area, from Bavaria to Iceland, makes it impossible to deduce *a posteriori* the existence of proto-Germanic cola of definite shape which we could compare with the IE prototypes" (M. West 1973b, 180; see further p. 181). On the differentiation of various dialects, see Lehmann 1956, 64–123. We will have reason to return to West's observations on the Serbo-Croatian and Old English meters below, but for the moment let us quote his most apposite conclusions (1973a, 180): "In IE verse the unit of composition was the line, in which the number of syllables was fixed and the ending scanned either ∪—∪— (acatalectic) or ∪——— (catalectic), the earlier syllables being of unreg-ulated quantity. The primary cola contained from five to eight syllables. These cola could themselves be used as lines; or a longer line could be obtained by adding four extra syllables at the beginning (marked off by a caesura) or by duplicating the acatalectic cadence, xxxx∪— ∪—|∪—∪—. Lines of different lengths could be mixed in irregular sequence, but it was more usual to use equal lines in series (sometimes with a catalectic verse to conclude), or to have a regular alternation of lines of two sorts, or a three-line strophe of the form AAB."

relatively late development. Peabody (1975, 65) makes this case, buttressed with both historical and synchronic arguments:

> While the hexameter is a pattern universal in the epos, it seems not to have been a static, rigid form. Its shape was in slow but constant redefinition. At the same time that it became crystallized forever (apparently through writing and the analytic establishment of canonic norms), it seems to have been emerging from a period of relatively active change.[15]

As far as the Homeric line as a structure in itself is concerned, then, we must temper the virtual certainty of an Indo-European ancestry with an admission of uncertainty about the particulars of the lineage and with a general conception of the line's evolution as an ongoing process that culminated rather late in the line of Homer and Hesiod. If genetic survivals are to enter the picture, they must enter subject to these conditions.[16]

The Serbo-Croatian epic decasyllable, according to all commentators, is surprisingly archaic in structure given that it is still the verse form of the heroic songs sung by *guslari* in this century. Jakobson (1952, 64–66) posits a "gnomic-epic decasyllable" as the Indo-European prototype, finding parallels to the Slavic in Greek, Vedic, Iranian, and Lithuanian (see note 9 above). M. West (1973b, 171–72), arguing that the Slavic situation is "parallel with the Vedic rather than the Greek situation,"[17] proposes another derivation: he compares the opening four-syllable colon of the *deseterac* to the Indo-European protasis of variable quantities, and the second colon of six syllables to the prototype that also resulted in the Greek Aeolic reizianum:

	1	2	3	4		5	6	7	8	9	10
General Structure	s	s	s	s		s	s	s	s	s	s
Quantitative Series	x	x	x	x		x	x	ᴗ	ᴗ	_	x

15. Thus M. West (1973a, 187–88), for example, notes: "We have seen that dactylic verse was a South Mycenaean development dating probably from the second half of the [second] millennium, while the stereotyped stichic hexameter represents a further development in the Ionian branch of the tradition, perhaps late Mycenaean, perhaps post-migration"; as for epic poetry, "by 1100 it may have existed in south Greece in something like hexameters, though I imagine that they might be rather looser in technique than what we are used to." Cf. Hoenigswald 1977, 82–83.

16. I postpone detailed discussion of the interrelationship between formula and meter until later in this chapter and in the individual chapters (4–6) on phraseology in each tradition. It is enough to say at this point that the possible diachronic priority of phraseology over meter, as posited by Nagy, does not confute but only confirms the intimate dependence of metrical shape and structure on natural-language characteristics. Thus the principle of tradition-dependence, introduced in chapters 1 and 2 at the level of general methodology and textual documents, is confirmed at the level of meter and phraseology.

17. The Common Slavic form entailing "quantitative regulation only in the last four syllables" (M. West 1973b, 173) leads him to this conclusion.

	1	2	3	4		5	6	7	8	9	10
Proto-Slavic (catalectic form)	x	x	x	x		x	x	ᴗ	ᴗ	—	—
IE Prototype (before expansion)	x	x	x	x			—	ᴗ	—	—	

What presents itself again, in short, is uncertainty in the particulars of deri-vation, although the existence of some relationship between the decasyllable and an Indo-European precursor is almost beyond question. And while the apparent archaism of the meter seems to relieve us of the problem of late structural fixation that obscures the evolution of the ancient Greek hexameter, we have still to consider the varying assignment of pitch and stress in the various Slavic vernaculars. In sum, the situation as a whole is similar to that of the hexameter: uncertainty about particulars demands caution in composing the prehistory of the *deseterac* (cf. Petrović 1969, 1974). Nevertheless, it is a verse form that can be well studied analytically in the extant texts, particularly since the textual record is so much more extensive than those of the dead-language traditions.

The situation in Old English is at once more complicated conceptually and simpler from a methodological point of view. Since the emergence of stress as the primary metrical determinant has obscured the quantitative roots of Germanic cola, the possibility of confident theorizing about the genetic prehistory of the alliterative line does not present itself. In this case our problem is not an embarrassment of riches but rather an impoverishment of clear, plausible hypotheses. If we suppose the Old English half-line to have been the earlier verse-unit, one that at some later time was doubled and then knit together by alliteration, and if we further understand the stress-accent typical of the Germanic vernaculars to have replaced the long-short quantitative sequence as the distinctive metrical feature of the verse, we can see with West and Lehmann how the relative number of short unstressed syllables in the line could increase. With the modulation from quantity to stress prominence would come a corresponding modulation from dependence on to relative independence of syllabic count. This tendency toward a larger proportion of unstressed syllables must, however, have been offset to a degree in Old English by the maintenance of traditional patterns of phraseology from earlier Ger-manic tradition.[18] At any rate, by the time of the first recorded Old English texts, the modulation to a stress-based meter was complete, and the genetic prehistory of the line—not to mention the relative chronology of fixation of the line in its present form—was largely lost in the transition. For this reason,

18. "Tradition, therefore, played a greater role in the maintenance of the alliterative line in England than in any of the West Germanic dialects. In early Old English, the strict Germanic line was maintained through retention of an old poetic vocabulary and syntax" (Lehmann [1956] 1971, 102).

and also because our surviving sample of texts from the period is so small,[19] I advocate special attention to a descriptive account of the meter of *Beowulf*.

To these specific reasons for concentrating on a descriptive comparison of the three meters may be added some more general considerations. First, the idea of tradition-dependence, developed in theory in the first two chapters, would seem to demand attention at the level both of prosody and of the formula and more complex levels of tradition. As languages and meters evolve away from their common Indo-European prototypes and continuous, variable interaction takes place between phraseology and meter, tradition-dependent systems come more and more to deserve characterization as entities in themselves. Geography, chronology, and the myriad other factors that contribute to their separate developments also generate increasing numbers of peculiarities, such that by the time the ancient and medieval traditions are committed to manuscript, the group of originally similar members has, as we have seen, grown quite dissimilar. The traditions that preserve and evolve phraseology and meter are most certainly of great age and persistence, as Lord, Georges Dumézil, and others have shown,[20] but this prehistory should not obscure the fact that at a later date different traditions take very different forms, evolve in various ways, preserve and discard elements at all levels, and in general behave idiosyncratically. And we should be aware that the fundamental level of prosody—which must be more immediately reactive to linguistic changes than must narrative units such as typical scenes and story-patterns[21]—is perhaps the most tradition-dependent of all structures.

A second observation on the Indo-European question and its pertinence to this comparative inquiry has to do with the real nature of a descriptive account of the three meters. In focusing primarily on the verse structure of the texts as we find them, are we condemned to the thinnest synchronic slice of the tradition? Will we, in other words, ignore important diachronic roots and settle for a superficial view of the subject? Part of the problem, I believe, lies in the very form of such questions, for the history of the hexameter is in a real sense the hexameter itself: if we pay careful attention to its synchronic structure, noting its rules and tendencies and tracking its tangible variants in pursuit of useful generalizations, we are at the same time studying at least

19. The entire Old English poetic corpus contains only slightly more than thirty thousand lines, about 10 percent of which are epic. As indicated in chapter 1, the comparisons made in these studies must for methodological reasons be limited to a single genre, that of epic. The Anglo-Saxon sample is thus only about one-tenth the size of the ancient Greek epic corpus, and both canons are dwarfed by the available Serbo-Croatian material in the Parry Collection and elsewhere.

20. See, e.g., Lord 1960, 158–97; Dumézil 1973.

21. In his Foreword to Peabody 1975 (p. xii), Lord advocates a hybrid approach: "The study of oral and traditional literature must of necessity be both diachronic and synchronic." I would add that any study is and must be to some degree both, that the kind of study depends on an emphasis or focus rather than a total exclusion of one or the other approach.

part of the story of how it came to be. By combining what we know about Indo-European metrics with what is ascertainable from a synchronic study, we can read the history and present reality of a metrical form—for the structures confronted in the frozen moment of the text are nothing less than the products of a diachronic process, a process that has left telltale vestiges of earlier stages in verse evolution. In this way our descriptive accounts of the hexameter, *deseterac*, and alliterative line can mesh with what has been said about Indo-European prosody and reach beyond the synchronic surface of the texts to their diachronic roots.

PROSODY AND PROSODIES

In borrowing W. Sidney Allen's phrase (1966) for the heading of this section, I mean to indicate an emphasis more general than his. As Allen and others have shown, the notion of what is properly designated by the term *prosody* has varied considerably from ancient times to the present. In this chapter and throughout these studies, I use the term in its widest possible application to refer to all of the "elements and structures involved in the rhythmic or dynamic aspect of speech, and the study of these elements and structures as they occur... in the compositions of the literary arts"; this so-called literary prosody thus "studies the rhythmic structure of prose and verse, not as exemplifying linguistic norms but as functioning... as an aspect of poetic form" (La Drière 1974, 669). We may therefore list among our possible interests not only meter per se, but also alliteration, rhyme, assonance and consonance, stress, tone, hiatus, juncture and elision, and, in general, sound patterns of any sort. There will also be reason to touch on allied linguistic phenomena, such as syntax and morphology, as they relate to prosodic features, although most of our discussion of these last two areas belongs in the chapters on formulaic structure.

Within this large field of prosodic possibilities the chief emphasis will continue to be on those particular properties of the verse that are most important to the structure and deployment of phraseology and therefore to traditional narrative design. The first narrowing of focus, then, is from prosody as the set of all possible metrical and euphonic factors to *traditional prosody*, the more restricted set of factors involved in traditional form and dynamics. Additionally, this second and more refined set of characteristics will vary considerably from one poetry to another; in fact, there is evidence within the three traditions treated in these studies that prosody is genre-dependent as well as tradition-dependent.[22] In Old English, for instance, alliteration

---

22. Besides the more obvious differences among the various meters of different genres within a single given tradition (see, e.g., Jakobson's discussion of Serbo-Croatian laments, or *tužbalice* [1952, 33–35], or Vigorita's comments on the Indo-European origins of "short lines" in lament and epic [1976, 208–9]), I would point to the example of prosodic structure in oral charms, or

between paired half-lines is not a desideratum but a requirement: without agreement of these initial sounds bridging the gap, one does not have a viable metrical line. (For example, "B̲eowulf maþelode, / b̲earn Ecgþeowes" ["B̲eowulf spoke, son of Ecgtheow"; *Beowulf* 529 et seq.: alliteration in b̲]; and "G̲rendel g̲ongan, / G̲odes yrre bær" ["G̲rendel going, he bore God's wrath"; *Beowulf* 711: alliteration in g̲].)

But while absence of this prosodic feature in *Beowulf* calls for emendation of the manuscript text, its absence in a Serbo-Croatian or ancient Greek epic line is no violation at all, not even (necessarily) of euphonic propriety. In the latter two traditions, alliteration may constitute a sound-pattern,[23] but it is not in any way required. In contrast, rhyme of the end of the first with the end of the second colon, or leonine rhyme, is a fairly common phraseological feature in Yugoslav epic; perhaps more importantly, lines that manifest this end-colon (as opposed to end-line) rhyme only rarely show variation from one occurrence to the next.[24] (Examples of leonine rhyme in the *deseterac* include, for instance, "I dan*ica* da pomoli l*ice*" ["And the morning star shows its face"] and "U be*ćara* nema hizme*ćara*" ["A bachelor has no helpmate"].) These facts allow us to assign a compositional status to this euphonic feature in the *deseterac*; although obviously not a requirement, leonine rhyme is for our purposes a significant prosodic element because it plays a part in formula-shaping and, apparently, in maintaining formulaic shape over time. Prosodic features other than meter, or at least those usually classed as euphonic, seem less important in Greek, but, as Parry (1928a, in 1971, 68–74) showed long ago and Nagler (1974, 1–63) has illustrated more recently in some detail, agreement in sound provides a basis for analogy in Homer. Nagler gives many examples of what he calls "phonemic corresponsions," among which we may cite the following six, all of which occur in the adonean clausula (or final two metra) of the hexameter (1974, 8):

_____

bajanje, as contrasted to epic within the Serbo-Croatian tradition. Rhyme, both end-line and in-line, and consonance are on balance much more pervasive in the largely octosyllabic charms. Cf. Lord 1960, 54–58; Lord 1956, 1981; Kerewsky Halpern and Foley 1978; Foley 1980a.

23. For examples in Serbo-Croatian, see the articles cited in note 22 above; further illustration is available in chapter 5. For ancient Greek, see Packard 1974; Stanford 1969.

24. As Jakobson emphasizes (1952, 31), "It is noteworthy that as soon as rhymes begin to appear in the normally unrhymed Serbo-Croatian epic decasyllable (in literary productions of the eighteenth century), the quantitative close weakens considerably." See also Stankiewicz 1973.

Both of the example lines that follow occur too often and too widely in Serbo-Croatian epic tradition to be referenced at any single spot. I have drawn them in this instance from the *Ženidba Bećirbega Mustajbegova* (*The Wedding of Mustajbey's Son Bećirbeg*, Parry text no. 6699) of Halil Bajgorić, a *guslar* recorded by Parry and Lord in the Stolac area in 1933–35 and 1950–51. The first example illustrates the partial rhyme often induced by declension of a formula-part or, as here, produced by leonine near-rhyme of nouns from two different declensions (*danica* = nominative singular diminutive, feminine; *lice* = accusative singular, neuter).

$$\pi\acute{\iota}o\nu\iota \ \delta\acute{\eta}\mu\omega \qquad \tau\acute{\iota}\epsilon\tau o \ \delta\acute{\eta}\mu\omega \qquad \ddot{\iota}\kappa\epsilon\tau o \ \delta\hat{\eta}\mu o\nu$$
$$-\pi\hat{\omega} \ \acute{\epsilon}\nu\grave{\iota} \ \delta\acute{\eta}\mu\omega \quad -\tau\omega \ \acute{\epsilon}\nu\grave{\iota} \ \delta\acute{\eta}\mu\omega \quad -\acute{\iota}\kappa\epsilon\tau o \ \delta\hat{\eta}\mu o\nu$$

These acoustically related elements—*pioni dêmôi* ("[amid] the flourishing populace"), together with the others—argue, Nagler feels, for phonemic relationships that operate outside of the usual formulaic context. Again we encounter a prosodic feature that contributes to traditional structure.

The instances cited so far are few, and we shall need to consider many more at length below. But perhaps enough has been said to indicate that when speaking of "prosody" and "prosodies," two avenues of differentiation must be kept in mind. The first is the acknowledged bias of these studies toward analysis of those factors which affect traditional structures. The second has to do with the varying set of pertinent factors for a given individual tradition—with, in short, the tradition-dependence of prosody.

PROSODY AND FORMULAIC STRUCTURE: THEIR INTERRELATIONSHIP

Implicit in my opening discussion of methodology was an assumed relationship between prosody and formulaic phraseology and, by extension, a secondary relationship between prosody and larger narrative units, which, for all their apparent structure as action-patterns or typical scenes, depend finally on phraseology for their expression. In the early stages of development of the oral-formulaic theory, such an assumption would have encountered no resistance whatever, since prosody was a fundamental part of the concept of formula: thus Parry's original definition, as "an expression regularly used, *under the same metrical conditions*, to express an essential idea" (1928a, in 1971, 13; my emphasis).[25] Without those "same metrical conditions," the formula could not exist; prosody was a crucial and limiting factor in the process of definition. This procedure amounts to claiming that formulaic diction is, to use a favorite philological term, *metri causa*, that it arises from the constraints of meter and, the argument would continue, is retained because it fits the meter. In fact, this was precisely the direction Parry took in illustrating the *thrift* of Homer's diction. Observing that almost always only one noun-epithet formula was available to name a given god or hero in a given metrical segment of the line, he maintained that this characteristic was a sign of a traditional diction, a sign that the phraseology was itself a dynamic poetic entity epitomized by generations of individual singers.[26]

25. Later, in "Studies I" (1930, in 1971, 272), Parry defined the formula in slightly different terms as "a group of words which is regularly employed under the same metrical conditions to express a given essential idea" (italics deleted).

26. In discussing the "formulaic system," which he defines (1930, in 1971, 275) as "a group of phrases which have the same metrical value and which are enough alike in thought and words to leave no doubt that the poet who used them knew them not only as single formulas, but also

This fundamental *aperçu* was, like so many of Parry's theses, a uniquely rigorous and characteristically creative extension of the preliminary work of others, in the present case of Ellendt, Düntzer, and other classical linguists of the late nineteenth century.[27] Parry was proceeding, in other words, from a belief in the shaping and determining function of meter, and he would maintain this view throughout his published and unpublished writings on Homer and Serbo-Croatian epic. Some scholars who have followed Parry, upset with the supposed mechanistic operation and suppression of aesthetic choice that they see in *metri causa*, have tended to "soften" the prosodic requirements originally a part of the formula, or at least to redefine or investigate the flexibility of those requirements.[28] But for all except the most subjective of critics,[29] meter has remained an integral part of the formula's definition and of its very identity.

The fact of such a relationship, whatever its exact nature may be, is important. For whether we choose a formula-meter model as reductive as the "Lego-set" or one as complex as the newer generative or formalist-traditional theories (e.g., Devine and Stephens 1984), we are dealing most basically with language indissolubly allied with prosody. Laying aside for the present the many fascinating questions that could be asked about meters other than the Homeric hexameter and concentrating on the ancient Greek texts out of which formulaic theory was born, we must be struck by the overwhelming consensus (not to say observable fact) that Homer's traditional words are metrically defined. That is, rather than being merely lexical, phonological, morphemic, and syntactic entities, they are metrical or prosodic entities as well, and that prosodic character emanates not from lexical features but from verse structure.[30] Moreover, we would do well to remember that this metrical dimension also proclaims unambiguously the identity of these words as traditional sound, as opposed to the printed transcriptions we have trained ourselves to interpret back toward their original form. Perhaps this is why Yugoslav *guslari*, when

---

as formulas of a certain type," Parry makes the following observations: "The *length* of a system consists very obviously in the number of formulas which make it up. The *thrift* of a system lies in the degree in which it is free of phrases which, having the same metrical value and expressing the same idea, could replace one another" (p. 276; emphasis added). Length may well be a reasonable measure of a formulaic system in traditions other than ancient Greek, but the case is not nearly so clear for thrift; see Fry 1968c and Foley 1981d. See further Parry 1932, in 1971, 325–64.

27. See A. Parry 1971, xix–xx; Foley 1988: chap. 1.

28. I borrow the "hard" and "soft" designations from Rosenmeyer 1965.

29. Nagler (1974, 18) would posit "a preverbal Gestalt generating a family of allomorphs" as a model for Homeric formulaic diction. Cf. Ingalls 1972, who illustrates the colonic form of Nagler's allomorphs.

30. Thus Eugene O'Neill, Jr.'s, concerns about "The Localization of Metrical Word-Types in the Greek Hexameter" (1942). See further the section on the "inner metric" of the hexameter below, and also chapter 4.

asked what a "word" (*reč*) in an epic song is, respond with a couplet or a single ten-syllable poetic line rather than with what we might expect—the dictionary denotation of *word* (see chapter 2). For them too, it would seem, *a word is no word unless it is a prosodic word.*

This line of inquiry holds out the promise of productivity, and I shall return to it at the appropriate time. For the moment, however, let us consider a relatively recent development which cannot help but cast some doubt on the doctrine of *metri causa* in the generation of the formula. In his 1974 monograph *Comparative Studies in Greek and Indic Meter*, Nagy proposes three bold new hypotheses, all of them interrelated. First, he traces the Homeric hexameter to a pherecratic[3d] precursor, as illustrated earlier. Second, he dismisses the usual chronology of Greek lyric poetry growing out of epic and argues for independent Indo-European roots of lyric. But most important for the present discussion is Nagy's third and overarching hypothesis, which unites the first two. By taking a diachronic or evolutionary view of Greek meter and collecting comparative evidence from Vedic and Homeric material, he formulates a history of development which seems to reverse the accepted relationship between formula and meter (p. 145):

> At first, the reasoning goes, traditional phraseology simply contains built-in rhythms. Later, the factor of tradition leads to the preference of phrases with some rhythms over phrases with other rhythms. Still later, the preferred rhythms have their own dynamics and become regulators of any incoming non-traditional phraseology. Recent metrical developments may even obliterate aspects of the selfsame traditional phraseology that had engendered them, if these aspects no longer match the meter.

Far from adopting the consensus correlation, then, Nagy posits that "traditional phraseology had generated meter rather than vice versa." Although this is at best a telegraphic restatement of his position, the essentials are clear enough: the new theory threatens to overturn the mechanical-generation theory of Homeric formulaic diction by placing phraseology in the diachronically determinate position.[31]

Without questioning either Nagy's methods or his evidence,[32] which provide imaginative and far-reaching insights into nagging problems in a number of fields, I would make one simple point about his results, for his

---

31. In "Formula and Meter" (1976, 251), Nagy describes the process in this way: "Predictable patterns of rhythm emerge from favorite traditional phrases with favorite rhythms; the eventual regulation of these patterns, combined with regulation of the syllable-count in the traditional phrases, constitutes the essentials of what we know as *meter*. Granted, meter can develop a synchronic system of its own, regulating any incoming phraseology; nevertheless, its origins are from traditional phraseology."

32. But see Jaan Puhvel's response (1976) to Nagy's "Formula and Meter," and the citations in note 7 above.

proposal that *diachronically* formula generates meter[33] may well seem to qualify the present approach to comparative prosody and the tradition-dependence of the formula. As time goes on, what was originally a phraseology-based interaction between formula and meter becomes a meter-based interaction. Another way of explaining the same development is to observe that, over time, the diachronic generation of meter gives way to the synchronic generation of formula. Because my major focus in these studies must remain on the texts that have survived and are the products of the development, I shall be viewing the process from the chronologically later end of the shift and shall thus look to meter as the prosodic "partner" of phraseology in the Homeric and other oral epic poems.[34]

To this distinction may be added an observation that will indicate further the indissoluble link between formula and meter and the necessity for a comparative study of prosody to begin by recognizing that link. If Nagy's description of the earliest stage of formula-meter interaction is correct, then we have in the generation of meter from phraseology perhaps the most direct proof possible of the influence of natural-language characteristics on meter. What is more, we have evidence of a tradition-dependent meter based on the singularity of a given language from a very early time, since a meter must, we can suppose, be as singular as the language from which it arose. Even when, in the latter stages of the process, prosody came to have a life of its own and was therefore able to accept or reject combinations of elements from its parent language, it was originally that very language which gave it birth and to which it still owed its tradition-dependent identity. With this sort of direct link between a formulaic phraseology and an incipient prosody, there can be no question of persisting in philological reductionism: meters must be as different and idiosyncratic as the languages that spawned them.

In the remainder of this chapter I provide short accounts of each prosody assembled according to the principles explained above.

THE HOMERIC HEXAMETER

Outer Metric

Let us turn first to a consideration of what O'Neill (1942) has conveniently designated the "outer metric," that is, the foot-based or podic structure of

---

33. The emphasis is Nagy's own—see 1974, 140–49; 1976, 251–57.

34. A second perspective on the diachronic process should also be briefly mentioned. If Nagy's formulation is correct, and if we someday have enough hard proof of the earliest stage in the process to deem a significant part of Homeric formulaic diction pre- or proto-metrical, then we will still have to deal with the metrical dimension of formulas. For in this case the metrical aspect will become even more important to an understanding of traditional structure than it is now: the foregrounding of certain patterns as proto-metrical will indicate, at least crudely, the relative age of various elements in the diction and the calibration of the hexameter over time. Compare the linguistic archaeology practiced by Hoekstra (1964) and Janko (1982).

the hexameter.[35] After this standard description, we shall address the more complex questions involved with the "inner metric," the internal structure of the line.

The hexameter may be schematized as follows:

$$\_ \ \cup\cup \quad \_ \ \cup\cup \quad \_ \ \cup\cup \quad \_ \ \cup\cup \quad \_ \ \cup\cup \quad \_ \ \underset{\smile}{\_}$$

1	2	3	4	5	6

Ὡς ἐφάμην, ὁ δέ μ' οὐδὲν ἀμείβετο νηλέι θυμῷ,   (*Od.* 9.287)

$$\_ \ \cup\cup \ \_ \ \cup\cup \ \quad \_ \ \cup\cup \ \_ \ \cup\cup \ \_\cup\cup \ \_ \ \_$$

πεσσοῖσι προπάροιθε θυράων θυμὸν ἔτερπον,   (*Od.* 1.107)

$$\_ \ \_ \ \_ \ \quad \cup\cup \ \_\cup\cup \ \_ \ \_ \ \cup\cup \ \_ \ \underset{\smile}{\_}$$

According to conventional notation, the line is here shown to be composed of six "feet," or metra, numbered 1 through 6. Each of the first five metra may be either dactylic (_∪∪) or spondaic (__), although a spondee in position 5 is rare. The sixth metron is always disyllabic, its second element being regarded as long by position if not by nature (*brevis in longo*). The last two metra, the fifth almost always dactylic and the sixth disyllabic and spondaic by necessity, thus sound the closing cadence to the line, a cadence that, as explained above, some metrists have found echoed in other Indo-European meters. From this perspective the hexameter is a so-called quantitative meter, depending for its shape on the distribution of relatively long and short syllables over six podic units. In this sense it is not primarily stress-emphasis but rather phonologically determined quantity that yields the metron structure of the hexameter.[36]

---

35. For a survey of modern metricians to 1950, see Porter 1951, 3–8; on colometry per se, see Barnes 1987.

36. In general, syllables in the hexameter are long either when their vowels or diphthongs are long by nature (ᾱ, η, ῑ, ῡ, ω, and all diphthongs) or when their naturally short vowels (ᾰ, ε, ῐ, ο, ῠ) take on length by position before a cluster of two or more consonants. The major exceptions to these rules are the shortening of a final long vowel or diphthong before the initial vowel or diphthong of the following word (epic correption), the interpretation of a mute and a liquid as a single consonant, and the upgrading of word-initial μ, ν, λ, σ, and ϝ to double consonants (in the manner of ζ, ξ, and ψ). For a discussion of these basic rules of quantity, see Maas 1962, 123–34.

This is not to say, however, that stress is not a functional feature of the line. If, as W. Allen (1964, 6, 10) argues, "the rules of quantity in Greek verse have a basis in the Greek language" and "it is reasonable to suppose that it was precisely the heavy syllables which were liable to receive stress in the rhythmic pattern of the sentence," then "the so-called 'rules of quantity' are simply rules of stressability." Quantity and stress will, however variously we categorize them, also emerge from exactly the same origin—the verse-ictus of the hexameter. Whether there be a tension between the linguistic stress on the word-isolate and that of the word in verse position is of secondary importance: our first concern is with traditional verse structure, and we have seen that in this primarily quantitative meter both quantity and stress-emphasis follow the same set of rules. The fundamental structure of the line, however much or little it may exhibit a stress feature, depends mainly on the succession of quantities across the metra.

Quantities are distributed in a number of ways, the variability represented by the thirty-two possible types arising (from the point of view of outer metric only) from dactylic-spondaic substitution in the five substitutable metra:[37]

(1)	Wholly dactylic	1	D	D	D	D	D							
(2)	Wholly spondaic	1	S	S	S	S	S							
(3)	4D, 1S	5	S	D	D	D	D							
			D	S	D	D	D							
			D	D	S	D	D							
			D	D	D	S	D							
			D	D	D	D	S							
(4)	1D, 4S	5	D	S	S	S	S							
			S	D	S	S	S							
			S	S	D	S	S							
			S	S	S	D	S							
			S	S	S	S	D							
(5)	3D, 2S	10	D	D	D	S	S		S	D	D	S	D	
			D	D	S	D	S		S	D	S	D	D	
			D	S	D	D	S		D	S	D	S	D	
			S	D	D	D	S		D	S	S	D	D	
			S	S	D	D	D		D	D	S	S	D	
(6)	2D, 3S	10	S	S	S	D	D		D	S	S	D	S	
			S	S	D	S	D		D	S	D	S	S	
			S	D	S	S	D		S	D	S	D	S	
			D	S	S	S	D		S	D	D	S	S	
			D	D	S	S	S		S	S	D	D	S	

Total = 32 types

Theoretically, then, the number of syllables in a Homeric line can vary from twelve (wholly spondaic) to seventeen (five dactyls plus the *brevis in longo* or "final anceps"). Table 3 documents the syllabic distribution in the nearly twenty-eight thousand lines of the *Iliad* and *Odyssey*.[38] As these figures make evident, while all six possible syllabic categories are occupied,[39] the great majority of lines are either fifteen or sixteen syllables in length (over 72 percent for both poems) — that is, almost three-quarters of the *Iliad* and *Odyssey* is composed of lines consisting of either three or four dactyls and, correspondingly, either three or two spondees, counting metron 6 as spondaic. This favored con-

37. As noted above, the sixth and final metron is invariably disyllabic, with the last syllable understood as long by convention.

38. I derive statistics on outer metric from LaRoche 1898 and from Jones and Gray 1972.

39. Examples of all six possible patterns exist, but the only statistically important types are those with two to five dactyls, or fourteen to seventeen syllables.

TABLE 3. Dactyls and Spondees in the Hexameter

No. of dactyls/ No. of syllables	5/17	4/16	3/15	2/14	1/13	0/12
Iliad						
Number	3,011	6,680	4,661	1,248	91	2
Percent	19.2	42.6	29.7	8.0	0.6	negl.
Odyssey						
Number	2,255	4,918	3,860	1,011	62	4
Percent	18.6	40.6	31.9	8.3	0.5	negl.

figuration is quantitatively the *longum-breve* rhythm of the hexameter, an illustration of what I call the "syllabicity" of the line. From this point of view, the hexameter, while not absolutely syllabic (as are for example many Latin and Romance meters), demonstrates a relatively focused syllabicity, taking a fifteen- or sixteen-syllable shape 72 percent of the time. If we add in the wholly dactylic seventeen-syllable possibility, the total comes to over 91 percent and the syllabic focus becomes even more apparent.

This statistical profile may be more finely articulated by determining how the dactyls are distributed. In other words, in those hexameter combinations of dactyls and spondees which can take more than a single form, we may profitably inquire about the absolute position of each metron-type. Within the fourteen-, fifteen-, and sixteen-syllable lines, the placement of metra is as shown in table 4.[40] Avoidance of the fifth-metron spondee—very probably the tradition's effort to preserve the Indo-European closing rhythm and, synchronically, the line-ending cadence for the hexameter—may be seen at the root of many of these statistical phenomena. In the sixteen-syllable line, for example, the spondee is conspicuously unusual in metron 5, and this pattern continues through the fifteen- and fourteen-syllable lines. The chart of metron configurations in the hexameter above also shows the spondee to be relatively rare in metron 3, the predominant locus of the mid-line break; again the pattern extends through the shorter lines. Exactly what the significance might be of the third and fifth metrons' strong tendency toward dactylic shape will be developed in the section below on inner metric. For the moment, let us simply notice that this tendency occurs at points of structural closure, marking half- and whole-line segmentation.

40. On the comparison of the *Iliad* and the *Odyssey*, Jones and Gray (1972, 208) remark: "As far, then, as the outer metric is concerned the similarities far outweigh the differences." The Iliadic Catalog of Ships, filled with proper names and other spondaic forms, is apparently an exception to this general rule; see Rudberg 1972, 20–21.

TABLE 4. Metron-Type Position in the Hexameter

Sixteen Syllables

Spondee in metron	Number	Percent
1	3,669	31.6
2	4,116	35.5
3	1,154	9.9
4	2,374	20.5
5	285	2.5

Fifteen Syllables (descending order of frequency)

Spondees in metra	Number	Percent
1 + 2	2,256	26.9
2 + 4	1,795	21.1
1 + 4	1,756	20.7
(other categories less populated)		

Fourteen Syllables (descending order of frequency)

Dactyls in metra	Number	Percent
3 + 5	1,061	46.5
4 + 5	369	16.2
1 + 5	230	10.1

TABLE 5. Hexameter Pattern Occurrence

Pattern						Iliad		Odyssey	
						Number	Percent	Number	Percent
D	D	D	D	D	S	3,034	19.3	2,256	18.6
D	S	D	D	D	S	2,292	14.6	1,820	15.0
S	D	D	D	D	S	2,207	14.1	1,457	12.0
D	D	D	S	D	S	1,346	8.6	1,023	8.4
S	S	D	D	D	S	1,261	8.0	996	8.2
D	S	D	S	D	S	968	6.2	829	6.8
S	D	D	S	D	S	967	6.2	791	6.5
D	D	S	D	D	S	648	4.1	503	4.2
S	S	D	S	D	S	584	3.7	478	3.9
D	S	S	D	D	S	461	2.9	457	3.8

Another perspective on the dactylic-spondaic texture of the hexameter may be gained by noting the frequency of occurrence of various metron configurations. Table 5 documents the ten most common patterns. It is worthy of mention that these configurations, the ten most frequently occurring of the thirty-two possibilities, account for a full 87 to 88 percent of the *Iliad* and *Odyssey*. In fact, the first three alone make up almost half of all lines in the two epics.

These observations on the podic rhythm of the metra provide an initial characterization of structure in the hexameter. It is clear even from these few remarks that the line is not merely a six-part symmetrical unit that repeats over and over again; it should be equally evident that conceiving of a simplistic verse form cannot help but obscure any conceptions of formulaic structure based on it. The possibilities inherent in the hexameter are many, and all are at one time or another realized; from a statistical standpoint, however, relatively few of these multiple possibilities account for most of the actual lines in the Homeric corpus. Speaking generally and from the perspective of outer metric only, we can make the following points about the hexameter: (1) over 90 percent of all lines are composed of between fifteen and seventeen syllables, over 70 percent of either fifteen or sixteen syllables; (2) spondaic substitution is common in metra 1, 2, and (somewhat less frequently) 4, but much rarer in metron 3 and positively avoided in metron 5; (3) the line ends typically with a "quantitative close," consisting of a dactylic fifth metron and the spondaic anceps. A preliminary view of the hexameter must, in short, emphasize its focused syllabicity and tendency toward certain patterns of dactylic-spondaic alternation. These patterns, with the exception of metron 6, favor spondaic substitution in the opening rather than the closure of half-lines or hemistichs. This tendency is an aspect of right justification, in this case of dactylic feet within half-lines. As we move on to a discussion of inner metric, we would do well to bear in mind these features of the hexameter's outer metric: focused syllabicity, favored patterns of dactylic-spondaic substitution, and right justification.

Inner Metric

In this section I shall treat the internal structure of the line, for it is the rhythm of the inner versus the outer metric that gives the hexameter its characteristic texture. Indeed, as Milman Parry discovered, the internal structure is that dimension of the line which bounds or encapsulates the formula and which constitutes the "same metrical conditions" that Parry cited as a necessary condition for formulaic diction.

The first step in this description is to identify the three principal caesuras,[41] or prosodic breaks, in the hexameter. The diagram below, showing the inner metric of the hexameter, indicates these breaks in terms of multiples of three basic positions, A (1–4), B (1 and 2, the masculine [or penthemimeral] and feminine [or trochaic] caesuras), and C (1 and 2, the hepthemimeral caesura and bucolic diaeresis).

41. The term *caesura* is employed here in a strictly metrical sense without any implication of a pause between elements. On ancient theories of the metrical caesura, see esp. Bassett 1919.

$$\_\mid\cup\mid\cup\mid\_\mid\cup\cup\_\mid\cup\mid\cup\_\mid\cup\cup\mid\_\cup\cup\_\underset{\smile}{\_}$$

$$\begin{matrix} 1 & 2 & 3 & 4 & \quad 1 & 2 & \quad 1 & \quad 2 \\ & & A & & & B & & C \end{matrix}$$

ἡμεῖς δὲ | δείσαντες | ἀπεσσύμεθ'. | αὐτὰρ ὁ μοχλὸν   (Od. 9.396)

$$\begin{matrix} \text{A4} & \quad\text{B2} & \quad\quad\text{C2} \end{matrix}$$

ὅπλεον, | ἡμιόνους θ' | ὕπαγον | ζεῦξάν θ' ὑπ' ἀπήνῃ·   (Od. 6.73)

$$\begin{matrix} \text{A3} & \quad\text{B1} & \quad\text{C1} \end{matrix}$$

I take this diagram and the theory it summarizes from Hermann Fränkel's "Der homerische und der kallimachische Hexameter,"[42] in which the author goes on to posit *cola*, those sections of the line delimited by the caesura system, as the basic constituents of the hexameter. He concentrates not on word-breaks per se, that is, but rather on the material that they enclose—the colon-words in the line.[43]

As one might expect, total agreement does not exist among all scholars about the location or meaning of caesura boundaries. Howard Porter (1951) would limit the A break to Fränkel's A3 and A4 and move the C1 to a position after the opening longum of the fifth metron:

$$\begin{matrix} \overset{\_}{1} \cup \cup \mid \underset{\_}{2} \mid \cup \cup \underset{\_}{3} \mid \cup \mid \cup \overset{\_}{4} \cup \cup \mid \overset{\_}{5} \mid \cup \cup \overset{\_}{6} \cup \\ \text{A2A1} \quad \overline{\text{B2}}\ \ \text{B1}^{\_} \quad\ \ \text{C2}^{\_}\ \text{C1}^{\_}{}^{\_} \end{matrix}$$

While this formulation reduces the number of caesuras from eight to a seemingly more workable six, it sacrifices: a full coverage of colon-types, especially in respect to the A and C boundaries; in the case of Porter's reassignment of C1, concurrence with actual observed data and comparative evidence;[44] and a more general descriptive and analytical adequacy, as will be seen below. But if we cannot entirely harmonize Porter's system with observed fact, some of his generalizations about the nature of cola are apposite. For example, he comments (p. 17):

> Positively the colon is an expected sequence of syllables produced by a brief rhythmic impulse. Four, rarely three, such sequences of syllables constitute the complex unit of the line. They vary in length from 4 to 8 morae. Each colon is usually marked off by word-ends. Any word-end can serve this function. In the hexameter a colon is frequently a short unit of meaning but need not be.

42. In H. Fränkel 1955, 100–156. Fränkel's original exposition of this material was in "Der kallimachische und der homerische Hexameter" (1926). For more recent remarks, including comments on G. S. Kirk's criticisms of his original proposals, see Fränkel 1968, 6–19.

43. As a more recent investigator, Berkley Peabody, has put it (1975, 68), "cola properly should be labeled, *not* caesuras; for, to take a Parmenidean position, caesuras are without substance or meaning in themselves."

44. As Peabody (1975, 348 *n*.4) points out; see also Ingalls 1970, 5.

These remarks help to clarify the definition of the colon, with the only qualification being adjustment of the morae, or counts, per colon, depending on the placement and number of caesura-positions.

Another scholar who disagrees with Fränkel's system of breaks, and even with the four-colon structure that they segment, is Geoffrey S. Kirk (1966).[45] To begin with, he seconds Porter's exclusion of Fränkel's A1 and A2 positions but not his relocation of C1. In fact, Kirk (p. 82) rejects the underlying principle behind binary positions: "Alternatively, of course, we can say that there *is* no 'alternate' to the bucolic caesura, and that in the nearly 40% of Homeric verses which do not have that caesura the latter part of the verse does not in practice normally fall into two word-groups." He then proceeds to consideration of Porter's data, attempting to demonstrate that the four-colon theory is statistically inadequate, and later to his own analysis of a sample passage from the *Iliad* for the same purpose. Kirk argues further that the apparent A and C caesuras are the result of "word-length availability" in the Greek language rather than metrical or sense grouping. To summarize, he would explain the hexameter as

> a complex of causes, some obvious and others less so: the B caesura is a structural division of the verse primarily designed to integrate it and prevent it from falling into two equal parts; the C caesura tends to introduce a distinct verse-end sequence; the tendency to caesura around the middle of the first 'half' of the verse is due primarily to the average lengths of Greek words available in the poetical vocabulary.... The inhibitions on word-end at $3\frac{1}{2}$ and $7\frac{1}{2}$ [Meyer's and Hermann's Bridges, respectively] are caused by the desire to avoid any strong possibility of three successive trochaic cuts, that on 4 [between the second and third metra] being due to the desire to avoid a monosyllabic ending, especially after a heavy word, to a major part of the verse. (p. 103)

In addition to the problems of invoking modern criteria and tautologically assuming that Homeric words—which are, after all, embedded in Homeric meter—should serve as unambiguous evidence for available word-length (both of which problems Kirk admits, pp. 103–4), there are other logical flaws in his formulation. The first and most basic is his tacit contention that the half-line break, or B caesura, should be the standard against which we measure the "inadequacies" of the A and C breaks. But if all breaks were of the same frequency and occurred without variation in the same positions, the hexameter would be a much less fluid and subtle instrument than it most obviously is. To deny a four-colon structure on the basis of Kirk's disclaimer is to require a meter to become a pattern without flexibility, a hardened and stylized set of stringencies which could never accommodate the "mighty line" of Homeric epic.

To carry this idea a bit further, the greater stability of the C (as compared

45. See also Kirk's later remarks (1985, 18–24).

to the A) caesura need not be *only* a function of the line-ending closure identified by Kirk and described earlier, though it most certainly is *in part* due to that closing cadence. Instead, we may understand the 60 percent occurrence of the bucolic diaeresis as in part the opening boundary of the fourth colon in the form of the typical adonean rhythm, which is also the familiar final cadence in the line. Indeed, the two concepts seem to be complementary rather than mutually exclusive. Finally, Kirk's notion of "word-length availability" as determining colon extent does not prove out when applied to the line as a whole. If all caesuras are to be held up to the standard of the B break and therefore taken as equal, the assortment of word-lengths that open the line should multiply variabilities at mid-line and further multiply possibilities at the C caesura. At the very least, the A and C breaks should occur in approximately corresponding variability, with the two-position B boundary making the C perhaps more flexible than the A, which takes its departure from the one-position line-beginning. But although Kirk's model would predict these phenomena, they do not occur. Apparently the A and C caesuras must be explained in another way.

The most recent extensive study of the colometric structure of the hexameter is that of Berkley Peabody (1975), who would assign line-breaks in the following positions:

$$1 \smile \smile | 2 | \smile \smile 3 | \smile | \smile 4 | \smile \smile | 5 \smile \smile 6 \smile$$

A1 A2　　B1 B2　C1　C2

His schema thus differs from Fränkel's in the deletion of the first two of the A positions. Peabody's placement of the three breaks covers most of the lines in his object text, Hesiod's *Works and Days* (A1 or A2, 90 percent; B1 or B2, 99 percent; and C1 or C2, 90 percent), and he founds his theory of cola on comparative diachronic studies of Greek, Indic, and Iranian meters. From this caesura-system he derives twelve principal colonic forms that populate the four-part structure (p. 68; some examples with spondaic substitution):

1	*2*	*3*	*4*
$\_\smile\smile$	$\smile\smile\_$	$\smile\_$	$\_\smile\smile\_$x
ὅττι μιν	ὄιες	Ἔριν	ἀγκυλομήτης
$\_\smile\smile\_$	$\smile\smile\_\smile$	$\smile\smile\_$	$\smile\smile\_\smile\smile\_$x
ἀθανάτων	βουλῆσιν	μαλλοῖς	καταβεβρίθασιν
	$\_\smile\smile\_$	$\smile\_\smile\smile$	
	μαρναμένους	Προμηθεύς	
	$\_\smile\smile\_\smile$	$\smile\smile\_\smile\smile$	
	ἐξαπάτησε	μήλων ἕνεκ'	

I find this recension of colometric theory far the most satisfying of the modifications of Fränkel's original proposals, both because of the comparative diachronic evidence on which it stands and also because it best acknowledges the complexity and flexibility of the hexameter. While one cannot expect absolute congruity of every Homeric or Hesiodic line with any abstraction (for as one moves toward that pattern-example congruity, one also moves toward a schema at the expense of a meter), a theory that accounts for variability and subtlety is inherently more useful and appealing than one that does not. Before going any further with Peabody's modifications, however, let us return to Fränkel's original ideas to clarify some issues.

Fränkel's exposition of cola, based ultimately on an earlier study by Eduard Fränkel (1932), was the first to posit the four-part structure of the Homeric lines. Contrary to Porter's and Kirk's later claims, he does not demand an absolute and firm sense-break (*Sinneseinschnitt*) at every point of caesura, but admits throughout that some caesuras are stronger demarcations than others.[46] Rather, he places the colon boundaries at the positions most commonly marked by editors' punctuation. To be fair, this method is not unambiguous, since it tends to isolate an editor's idea of syntactic boundaries over a sample of lines and then to apply that information back to metrical structure.[47] Still, his results do partition the Homeric line effectively and give an excellent first approximation of the dynamics of the inner metric.

Fränkel explains the exceptions to his rules in terms of an occasional "heavy word" (*schweres Wort*), which, because of its length of six morae or more, bridges a colon boundary and makes the given colon overlong.[48] As one of many examples, he offers *Iliad* 9.145, which contains a bridged B caesura (*verschobene B-Zäsur*):

$$\text{Χρυσόθεμις} \mid \text{καὶ-}\Lambda\text{αοδίκη} \mid \text{καὶ-}\text{'Ιφιάνασσα,} \qquad \text{[no B]}$$

A 4   C 1

Without a mid-line break, the result of the eight-morae *schweres Wortbild* καὶ-Λαοδίκη,[49] the line seems to be divided into three rather than four cola. Of course, the bridging of the hemistich boundary occurs, as we know, only

46. E.g., H. Fränkel 1955, 104: "Zwischen beiden Extremen, Satzgrenze und Wortgrenze, gibt es Einschnitte jeden Grades. Ein Mass für die absolute Stärke eines Einschnittes gibt es nicht, aber die relative Stärke der Sinneseinschnitte in einer Wortfolge ist oft unmittelbar ersichtlich."

47. Fränkel's statistics are taken from a table compiled by A. Ludwich in Rossbach and Westphal 1867–68.

48. He remarks (1955, 107): "*Dem verspäteten Einschnitt geht ein Wort oder Wortbild...von mindestens 6 Moren voraus. Unter dem Gewicht eines solchen 'Schweren Wortes' (SW), wie wir es nennen wollen, kann ein Einschnitt um eine oder mehr Stellen zurückgedrückt werden.*"

49. The idea of *Wortbild* includes both compounds and words combined with enclitics or proclitics. Cf. the "accentual groupings" in the Serbo-Croatian *deseterac* as described by Maretić (below).

about once in a hundred Homeric lines. Somewhat more frequent is the bridging of A and C caesuras, as in the following examples:

ἐκ-μὲν-Σιδῶνος | πολυχάλκου | εὔχομαι εἶναι   (*Od.* 15.425 [No A])
      B1   C2

αὐτούς-τ᾽; | ἦ-γὰρ ἔτ᾽ εἰσὶ | καὶ ἀφνειοὶ καλέονται   (*Od.* 15.433 [No C])
  A3   B2

In these two lines the A and C breaks are, respectively, *verschobene*, and the hexameters again appear to divide into three rather than four cola. However, through Fränkel's combination of multiple possibilities for caesura placement with "heavy word" bridges, he is able to account for all the complexities in these and other particular actualizations—including even those places in the line at which word-break is seldom tolerated, Meyer's and Hermann's Bridges. Both of these zeugmata, the former after a second-metron trochee and the latter after a fourth-metron trochee, are explained as interruptions of the colon system and for that reason are avoided.[50]

In sum, Fränkel's original system well suits the protean flexibility of the hexameter, a flexibility which fosters a correspondingly supple formulaic diction, as the author himself recognizes (1955, 116): "Den Sängern war es darum möglich die Inhalts- und Kolongliederung ohne harten Zwang so weitgehend zusammenfallen zu lassen, weil ihnen das Zäsurensystem eine grosse Zahl von legitimen Varianten zur Auswahl stellte—vier für A, und je zwei für B und C."

In a series of articles dating from 1970, Wayne B. Ingalls has championed Fränkel's system and argued against its critics. Using Porter's own data on the *Iliad* and *Odyssey*, he points out (1970, 6) that Porter's displacement of the C caesura is not statistically justified and shows that "even Fränkel's additional alternative A-caesuras at 1 and $1\frac{1}{2}$ [after the longum in metron 1 and after the first trochee, respectively], rare as they are, are more common than Porter's C2, at 9 [after the longum in metron 5]."[51] In dealing with

---

50. I must in part agree with Kirk, especially in the case of Hermann's Bridge, that these zeugmata are avoided on the basis of a general prohibition against "trochaic cuts." The trochee will falsely signal line-end by imitating, in combination with a previous dactyl, the "quantitative close" or final adonean, that portion of the hexameter from the bucolic diaeresis on. But again I see no reason why these aspects of Fränkel's and Kirk's explanations must be viewed as mutually exclusive.

51. O'Neill and Porter refer to various line-positions by means of a schema that counts every two morae as a whole integer and every mora as a half-integer:

$$1 \qquad 3 \qquad 5 \qquad 7 \qquad 9 \qquad 11$$
$$- \; \cup \mid \cup \mid - \mid \cup \cup \; - \; \cup \mid \cup \; - \; \cup \cup \mid - \; \cup \cup - \; \cup$$
$$1\frac{1}{2} \; 2 \qquad\qquad 5\frac{1}{2} \qquad 8$$

1, $1\frac{1}{2}$: Fränkel's additional A caesuras (A1, A2); 2, 3: Common A caesuras (A3, A4); 5: B1; $5\frac{1}{2}$: B2; 7: C1; 8: C2.

Kirk's objections, Ingalls demonstrates the essential subjectivity of arguments that depend on assertion and are not buttressed at all points with statistics. He then turns to a re-evaluation of Kirk's colonic analysis, which is shown to derive from eliminating two of Fränkel's A caesuras and all C breaks except the bucolic diaeresis. As Ingalls reveals, Kirk's methodology is flawed, for one cannot use one set of rules to determine breaks and another set to define cola: "In so doing [Kirk] naturally precludes the possibility of much concurrence between colometric and semantic units" (p. 11). On the basis of this re-analysis, then, Ingalls is able to dismiss Kirk's objections to the original colon-system and argue that, in the meaning Fränkel had intended, each colon is indeed a sense-unit.

In two later studies (1972, 1976) Ingalls widened his perspective to take in the relationship between metrical cola and formulas. Though this relationship is more properly the subject of later chapters, we may look briefly at some of his more important conclusions which have to do with our present concerns about metrical structure. First, he feels that Parry's original definition of the formula is tied too closely to its syntactic identity as noun plus epithet, and that this first approximation cannot be generalized to other kinds of formulas without becoming misleading. This argument bears directly on our understanding of the link between meter and formula and, if accepted, seems to indicate the need for a finer articulation of the blanket phrase "under the same metrical conditions." Second, he prescribes the colon as a metrical rationalization (Ingalls 1972, 122):

> The formulae from Parry's analysis, then, confirm the intimate connection between formular usage and the colometric structure of the hexameter. Just as the formulae are the linguistic building blocks of the verse, so the cola are the metrical blocks. In other words, the metrical shapes of the formulas tend to coincide with those of the cola with which the verse is composed.[52]

As we shall see in chapter 4, the formulaic process is more complicated than a simple one-to-one relationship between formula and colon, but Ingalls's suggestions, based on Fränkel's colometry, are an important step toward a deeper understanding of that process.

As mentioned above, Peabody's discussion of inner metric in the hexameter is in many ways the most productive approach so far advanced. I shall follow the main descriptive outlines of his presentation both in this chapter and later on, but first let us make clear that the difference between the Fränkel-Ingalls and Peabody theories is basically one of statistical and diagrammatic convenience.[53] From a statistical point of view, Peabody's elimination of the

52. Since Parry was of course working with caesura-bound phraseology, this approach is perhaps not as novel as it might seem. What makes it convincing is the impressive colonic analysis of Nagler's traditional phrases (see esp. Ingalls 1972, 115–18).

53. For figures on relative percentage occurrence of the original *Sinneseinschnitte*, see Fränkel 1955, 104–5.

A1 and A2 caesuras, the only difference between the two systems of colon-structure, equalizes the variance among A, B, and C breaks at two apiece and affects only 4 percent of the sample. Further, even the 4 percent affected is not lost entirely, but simply reassigned to the "all others" category. The number of possible cola is greatly reduced by this simplification, since the possibilities for the beginning point of colon 2 and the ending point of colon 1 are cut in half, from four to two each. From a statistical and presentational perspective, then, more is gained than lost by Peabody's simplified view of the A caesura.[54]

Summary of Inner Metric

What is needed at this point is a standard for ranking, a quantitative measure of the importance of each word-break. As Kirk and others have stressed, the B caesura is the most regular, with the B1 and B2 positions providing a mid-line break in 99 percent of Homeric lines. There simply are no other points in the hexameter where word-break is so regularly observed. If Peabody (1975, 45–65) is right about the prehistory of the Homeric line as two shorter verses joined in a single hybrid (cf. G. Nagy 1974, 49-102), then we have a diachronic explanation of why this hemistich boundary should be so prominent in the synchronic sample of Homeric hexameters. But however we conceive of that prehistory, the shape of the hexameter as we know it indicates that the first and primary segmentation of the line is into two parts—two unequal hemistichs or half-lines:

Possibility 1 (B1 caesura):

$$\_ \cup \cup \_ \cup \cup \_ \mid \cup \cup \_ \cup \cup \_ \cup \cup \_ \overset{\cup}{}$$

Possibility 2 (B2 caesura):

$$\_ \cup \cup \_ \cup \cup \_ \cup \mid \cup \_ \cup \cup \_ \cup \cup \_ \overset{\cup}{}$$

Or, in mora-count:

Possibility 1: 10x | 12x + 1
Possibility 2: 11x | 11x + 1

In either case a slightly longer colon follows a shorter one. This is the most consistently observed dimension of the inner metric: a segmentation at the half-line level.

The A and C boundaries operate on another level of segmentation, as their

---

54. While any descriptive model can be more or less useful according to its innate complexity and ability to represent faithfully the empirical facts, any concept of inner metric will remain an abstraction that *names* and *explains* rather than *is* that inner metric. Our task in all areas of this comparative prosody chapter is to choose the abstraction that communicates the most valuable data in the most convenient manner. If by admitting two positions per caesura we can control 96 percent of the sample, then we have, formally speaking, a very workable model.

lower frequency figures make apparent. While this does not mean that they are to be discounted or questioned as caesuras, it does indicate that the cola which they form will have one boundary less consistently marked than the other. The colon system as a whole thus depends on *Schnitte* of at least three different types: (1) the absolutely regular line-beginning and line-end, always separated by twenty-three counts or morae and ending with the typical closing rhythm; (2) the B caesura, or hemistich boundary, which may take one of two positions and thus form two possible pairs of half-line segments; and (3) the A and C caesuras, whose two positions (four in all) account for a somewhat smaller percentage of all Homeric lines, about 90 percent. To look at the same situation in another way, we could say that Fränkel's "heavy words" bridge breaks according to the following schedule: (1) line-beginning and line-end can never be bridged; (2) the two-position B caesura can be bridged only 1 percent of the time; and (3) the two-position A and C caesuras can be bridged about 10 percent of the time. These are three distinct levels of segmentation in the hexameter, coordinated to be sure, but distinct from one another in frequency and variability of position.

Yet there seems also to be a fourth level of segmentation: Fränkel's A1 and A2 and the two word-breaks commonly found within colon 4. These four structure points occur decidedly less regularly than the main caesuras, but they appear often enough to beg the question of whether any or all of them should be classed as caesuras. Because they seem to function at another level of segmentation, I prefer to distinguish these four positions by labeling them *juncture points*, thus preserving the integrity of the colon structure and avoiding ambiguity in terminology. I believe, however, that they must be considered along with the more regular aspects of inner metric if we are to obtain a full description of the hexameter. By recognizing these juncture points as structural markers but not as caesuras, we can, first, encode in our model for the Homeric line important structural details beyond the hemistich and colon which may lead to a better understanding of phraseology and, second, preserve a relatively simple assortment of what I shall call, with Peabody, "principal colonic types." We can, in other words, limit the A, B, and C caesuras to two possibilities each and thereby limit the number of cola that they can bound to twelve. The levels of segmentation can be seen in table 6.[55] The principal colonic types, after Peabody (1975, 68) are as shown in figure 1. If we thus dispense with Fränkel's A1 and A2 caesuras, preferring to interpret these two breaks and the breaks at $9\frac{1}{2}$ and 10 as juncture points within the first and final cola, and adopt with modifications Peabody's statistically more presentable model,

---

55. The percentage occurrences cited for juncture points consist of ranges based on the following individual percentages: α (at 1), $Il = 39$ percent and $Od = 38$ percent; β (at $1\frac{1}{2}$), $Il = 30$ percent and $Od = 34$ percent; γ (at $9\frac{1}{2}$), $Il = 44$ percent and $Od = 51$ percent; and δ (at 10), $Il = 35$ percent and $Od = 32$ percent. Note that these are simply word-end percentages and are not meant to indicate a metrical boundary.

TABLE 6. Levels of Segmentation in the Hexameter

Level	Percent Occurrence	Increment Bound	Position(s)
1. Line-beginning and Line-end	100	23x	1 each
2. Hemistich boundary (B)	99	10x|12x + 1 or 11x|11x + 1	2
3. Colon boundaries (A, C)	90	12 principal colonic forms	2 each
4. Juncture points $(1, 1\frac{1}{2}, 9\frac{1}{2}, 10)$	30–51	colon segmentation in cola 1 and 4	2 each in cola 1 and 4

Figure 1. Principal Colonic Types in the Hexameter

1	2	3	4
— ∪ ∪	∪ ∪ —	∪ —	— ∪ ∪ — x
— ∪ ∪ —	∪ ∪ — ∪	∪ ∪ —	∪ ∪ — ∪ ∪ — x
	— ∪ ∪ —	∪ — ∪ ∪	
	— ∪ ∪ — ∪	∪ ∪ — ∪ ∪	

we shall have at once a more detailed and a more flexible descriptive instrument. The resulting schema for the hexameter is thus as follows:

$$\begin{array}{cc} \alpha \ \beta & \gamma \ \delta \\ 1|\cup|\cup|2|\cup\cup 3|\cup|\cup 4|\cup\cup|\ 5\ \cup|\cup|6\cup \\ \overline{\quad} \quad \text{A1 A2}\ \ \overline{\text{B1}}\ \text{B2 C1 C2} \end{array}$$

The six main caesuras (A1, A2, B1, B2, C1, C2) and the juncture points (α, β, γ, δ) determine the inner metric of the line. In the next chapter I shall study the relationship of this colonic structure to the verbal data of the Homeric epos, stressing Peabody's insight (1975, 74) that "the remarkable statistical coincidence of the forms of the elements used in the epos with the forms of the principal cola is significant. This coincidence goes far toward proving the essential unity of the metrical and linguistic traditions in the epos. It also shows that the colon, both in origin and function, is a linguistic period, a 'word form.'"[56]

For the moment, however, let us conclude this description of inner metric in the hexameter with a consideration of "right justification," the metrical phenomenon mentioned above in relation to Indo-European meter and the outer metric of the Greek epic line. In the case of the podic structure of the hexameter, the evidence of the tendency toward right justification was the relative

56. See Russom 1987 on the coincidence of metrical units and word-forms in the Old English alliterative meter.

frequency in various positions of the dactylic metron, which occurred more regularly toward the end than toward the beginning of each hemistich and most regularly as part of the closing cadence, or adonean clausula, of the line as a whole. Diagrammatically we may represent this two-level function as follows:

Level	*Manifestation*
Whole line	Line closure and dactylic metron 5
Hemistich	Preference for dactylic metra 3 and 5

This characteristic texture means that the syllabically more extensive metra, those which have either a greater number of syllables (or, to put it another way, more short syllables) tend toward the right or end of metrical units within the hexameter. Still from the perspective of outer metric, then, syllabic extent and short syllables tend statistically to migrate toward the end of these units. Conversely, the left-hand or beginning portions of line and half-line will lean statistically in the opposite direction, that is, toward a shorter syllabic extent and the long syllables of spondaic substitution. This characteristic distribution is, of course, a tendency rather than a rule, but it will prove significant for our discussion of formulaic diction, since the texture of metrical units will be affected by right justification. In other words, lexical elements will typically arrange themselves, both over time and synchronically, in a right-justified order, a relative placement which is to a discernible degree overseen by the ending dactylic cadence of line and hemistich. Since the quantitative close or final cadence is more frequently observed than the preference for a dactyl in metron 3, the second hemistich and whole line will, in general, show the effect of right justification more regularly than will the first hemistich. The basic inclination, however, affects all parts of the line.

The same tendency toward situating longer metrical elements with more short syllables toward the end of metrical units in the hexameter is also apparent in the inner metric, although here it is of course the measure of mora-count which determines the "length" of increments. The hemistich patterns of $10x|12x + 1$ and $11x|11x + 1$, determined as they are by the B1 and B2 caesuras in the third metron, divide the hexameter into two unequal parts: in both cases a shorter first half is followed by a longer second half. By using Peabody's method for schematizing cola, we can analyze these hemistichs for the same tendency toward right justification at the level of the colon (1975, 69):[57]

---

57. But at this point the tendency ends; right justification seems not to enter into the internal texture of the first and fourth cola, specifically that texture created by the juncture points examined above. In colon 1, where these points occur at 1 and $1\frac{1}{2}$, two of the four possible segmentations can yield relatively longer colon-parts in the latter section of the unit, measuring by syllables. Measuring by morae, however, the situation is more balanced, with one possibility being right-justified, a second left-justified, and the remaining two symmetrical. The fourth colon operates in a similar manner; in fact, the segments in this last colon tend, if anything, toward left rather than right justification.

1	*2*	*3*	*4*
4x — ∪ ∪	4x ∪ ∪ —	3x ∪ —	8x — ∪ ∪ — x
6x — ∪ ∪ —	5x ∪ ∪ — ∪	4x ∪ ∪ —	10x ∪ ∪ — ∪ ∪ — x
	6x — ∪ ∪ —	5x ∪ — ∪ ∪	
	7x — ∪ ∪ — ∪	6x ∪ ∪ — ∪ ∪	

Computing by morae (symbolized as x)—that is, by assigning a count of 2 to each longum and 1 to each breve—one arrives at the table above. We can point out a number of instances of right justification in this diagram. First, cola 2 and 4 are on the average considerably longer than their half-line partners, cola 1 and 3, respectively. Second, the most spacious colon of the four is the last one, which, it will be recalled, involves the closing cadence to the line. At the levels of both whole line and hemistich, then, the hexameter forms itself in larger metrical units as one moves from left to right, from beginning to end. What is more, this tendency is apparent from the perspective of both inner and outer metric. But the pattern does not extend to segments formed by juncture points; apparently the influence of this Indo-European characteristic ends at the hemistich level.

To summarize these remarks on right justification, then, I would stress its prominent motive force in the formation of both inner and outer metric in the hexameter. To take the latter first, dactyls migrate toward the ends of both lines and half-lines, making these terminal sections more expansive by both syllable- and mora-count and more densely populated by short syllables. For its part, the inner metric manifests right justification in a longer second hemistich and relatively more expansive second and fourth as compared to first and third cola. Although the principle does not extend to the inner texture of cola, it does figure in all units of the line that recur with regularity. In general, the Homeric hexameter locates the more extensive elements to the right, or toward the end, of a given metrical unit.

We recall that the features ascribed by most scholars to the reconstructed Indo-European ancestor of the hexameter and other poetic lines are four: (1) a quantitative basis, (2) consistent syllabic extent, (3) a regularly placed caesura within the line, and (4) right justification. Because all these features are to varying degrees reflected in both the inner and the outer metric of the Homeric line, we may envision a diachronic history underlying the synchronic patterns of the extant texts. Homeric phraseology takes its shape from these prosodic patterns, ancient Greek reflexes of Indo-European compositional habits culminating over time in the hexameter diction we find in the *Iliad* and *Odyssey*. For the moment, however, the important point is that, notwithstanding a seminal ancestry with many interrelated progeny, Homeric prosody is itself a singular prosody, with rules and tendencies very much its own. To put the matter succinctly—however much it may genetically owe to earlier forms, the Homeric hexameter is tradition-dependent.

THE *JUNAČKI DESETERAC*
(HEROIC DECASYLLABLE)

Serbo-Croatian oral epic tradition takes two primary metrical forms, the fifteen-syllable *bugarštica*, also called the "long line," and the ten-syllable *junački deseterac* or "heroic decasyllable."[58] While both have venerable histories in the poetic tradition—the *bugarštica*, for example, serving as the medium for a song in Petar Hektorović's *Ribanje*, the earliest extant recorded folk poetry in the language (published in 1568)—we shall be concerned in these studies strictly with the *deseterac*, the meter of the Stolac Return Songs, our Serbo-Croatian comparand for the ancient Greek *Odyssey* and Old English *Beowulf*. As an organizational procedure, we shall approach the decasyllable as we did the hexameter, from the perspective first of outer metric and then of inner metric, seeking in each case to establish both the lineage and the idiosyncratic form of the *deseterac*. Only when our grasp of the prosody is sure and unambiguous can we productively proceed to study of the phraseology with which it exists in symbiosis.[59]

Outer Metric

The outer or podic structure of the heroic decasyllable seems at first sight more regular than that of the hexameter. While the Homeric line tolerates spondaic-dactylic substitution freely in the first four metra and grudgingly in the usually dactylic fifth metron, the Serbo-Croatian line seems always to conform to a pentameter scheme involving five two-syllable feet:[60]

$$\overset{s\ s}{1\ 2} \mid \overset{s\ s}{3\ 4} \mid \overset{s\ s}{5\ 6} \mid \overset{s\ s}{7\ 8} \mid \overset{s\ s}{9\ 10}$$

In addition to this five-part regularity, we observe a complementary consistency in a syllable count of ten, as the following examples illustrate:[61]

Posle toga dva čifta pušaka

Behind him two paired rifles

58. For a convenient comparison of the two meters, see Stolz 1969.

59. On the importance of prosody in the study of formulaic structure in Serbo-Croatian epic, consider Lord's remark (1960, 31) that "the formula is the offspring of the marriage of thought and sung verse. Whereas thought, in theory at least, may be free, sung verse imposes restrictions, varying in degree of rigidity from culture to culture, that shape the form of thought. Any study of formula must therefore properly begin with a consideration of metrics and music." Cf. Petrović 1969, 178.

60. With, of course, the exception of the relatively rare hyper- and hyposyllabic verses, which are treated below and in chapter 5. I will refer to examples and discussion from Tomislav Maretić's seminal studies of the *deseterac* throughout the discussion of Serbo-Croatian prosody, citing passages according to the following abbreviations: Maretić A = 1907a; B = 1907b; C = 1935; D = 1936. On shortening and lengthening lines to answer the ten-syllable constraint, for example, see Maretić A:80–112, B:76–122, C:218–42, and D:1–27, where he explains with some care the various methods involved.

61. Unless otherwise noted, all examples are taken from the Stolac texts in the Parry Collection.

> Poče pisat' knjigu šarovitu
> [He] began to write a multicolored letter

In these respects, the *deseterac* exhibits the quantitative basis and syllabicity characteristic of both the hexameter and its Indo-European precursor.

When we inquire about the disposition of these quantities in each of the five metra, however, the situation rapidly becomes more complicated and passes from the certainty of dependable rules to the uncertainty of irregularly observed tendencies. Jakobson (1952, 26) has argued that "the verse inclines toward a trochaic pentameter pattern," noting that the great majority of word-accents fall on the odd syllabic positions in the decasyllable. The model toward which he views the *deseterac* as tending is thus

$$\acute{1} \; 2 \; \acute{3} \; 4 \; \acute{5} \; 6 \; \acute{7} \; 8 \; \acute{9} \; 10$$

Of course, absolute coincidence of lexical accent and verse ictus is not often observed in all five positions in the line. The *guslar* may bend individual lexical patterns to the recurrent and generalized influence of his rhythmic vocal and instrumental melody,[62] and as Lord (1960, 37) observes, "there is a tension between the normal accent and the meter." Because we can actually listen to the Stolac songs (as we cannot do with dead-language texts), we know of other performance variables, such as the particular prominence of the ninth or penultimate syllable, but even without these firsthand observations it is plain that the putative trochaic pentameter pattern must remain a tendency, not a rule.

Other scholars who have considered the possibility of regular trochaic ictus include Svetozar Petrović (1969) and Pavle Batinić (1975). Petrović (1969, 183) examines selections from four of the most famous songs collected and published by the Serbian linguist-ethnographer Vuk Karadžić in the nineteenth century, setting his findings alongside Jakobson's figures for coincidence of word-accent and position (table 7).[63] Throughout the five samples, the strongest correlation between lexical accent and position is at syllables 1 and 5, a fact that is in part explained by noting the prevalence of accented monosyllables in those positions[64] and the regular onset of the two cola (1–4 and 5–10). After syllables 1 and 5 only positions 3 and 9 coincide with accent at all regularly, and these two are not much more prominent than some surrounding even-numbered positions. What syllables 3 and 9 do share, however—and this contributes to their relative importance from the point of view

---

62. On the melody of Serbo-Croatian oral epic performance, see Herzog 1951; the transcription by Béla Bartók from song no. 4, *SCHS* 1:435–67; Lord 1960, 37–41; and Bynum, "The Singing," *SCHS* 14:14–43.

63. Note that the use of the Vuk songs violates the principle of genre-dependence, for many of them are quite short and more lyric than epic. On this point, see Foley 1983b.

64. See Maretić A:41 and C:186–96, as well as the description of right justification below.

TABLE 7. Coincidence of Word-Accent and Position in the *Deseterac* (in Percent)

	Position									
	1	*2*	*3*	*4*	*5*	*6*	*7*	*8*	*9*	*10*
A	68	33	57	0	74	23	37	33	42	0
B	51	38	45	0	74	21	28	57	25	0
C	66	39	52	0	69	40	27	35	50	0
D	62	26	58	0	77	18	46	31	48	0
E	81	21	67	0	79	23	38	28	51	0

Note: A = Jakobson's reported figures; B = Tešan Podrugović, *Ženidba Dušanova*; C = Starac Rašak, *Zidanje Skadra*; D = Starac Milija, *Banović Strahinja*; and E = Filip Višnjić, *Smrt Marka Kraljevića*.

of inner metric—is their penultimate spot in each of the cola. To put the matter another way, each precedes a closing syllable that shows a zero correlation with word-accent. As Petrović indicates, position 7 has the weakest correlation of all odd—and supposedly ictus-bearing—syllables in the line, with text B actually suggesting a dactylic shape for syllables 5–7 and text C presenting a sequence (5:69, 6:40, 7:27) that seems unmetrical.

Also working strictly from the perspective of outer metric and on a sample of some 1,274 lines of mixed material,[65] Batinić attempts to solve the rhythm of the *deseterac* by advocating attention not merely to stress-accent but also to two other properties of Serbo-Croatian lexical units: tone and quantity. Instead of assuming an exclusive correlation between accent and metrical position, he widens the search to include a survey of the three possible tones (rising, falling, and unmarked) and two possible quantities (long and short) in his characterization of syllables. The result, displayed in table 8 (from Batinić 1975, 102), is a description of various syllable-types in terms of their suitability for ictus, that is, of their likelihood of coinciding with an odd-numbered metrical position in the decasyllable. In Batinić's view, any syllable with two or more of these expressive features will almost certainly bear metrical ictus, those with either stress (word-accent) or quantitative length prove ambivalent and can occur in either odd- or even-numbered positions, and those lacking all three linguistic features will occupy the off-beats of the verse.

While this graded schedule of suitability for metrical ictus does provide us with a more exacting description of syllable distribution than is elsewhere available, it suffers both from the tautological assumption of binary feet as the sole and necessary metrical foundation of the *deseterac* and from the "catalog" mode of explication. To take the second objection first, note that more refined

65. Of the entire sample, 815 lines are taken from the Karadžić songs, 305 from the Matica Hrvatska collection of Luka Marjanović, and 154 are left unidentified. The relatively small size and internal imbalance of the material call Batinić's results into question.

TABLE 8.   Batinić's Syllabic Theory of the *Deseterac*

	Stress	Length	Fall	Character	Classes	
1	−	−	0	Depression	Depression	1
2	−	+	0	Ambivalent-A ⎫	Ambivalent	2
3	+	−	−	Ambivalent-B ⎭		
4	+	+	−	Ictus-A ⎫		
5	+	−	+	Ictus-B ⎬	Ictus	3
6	+	+	+	Ictus-C ⎭		

description may better characterize whatever synchronic design one finds in a text or group of texts, but unless that description is not only pertinent to the observed data but also revelatory of the structures underlying those data, it cannot explain them. Trochaic pentameter models, however elaborated, do not completely explain the *deseterac* lines of Serbo-Croatian epic because they do not penetrate to the fundamental structures underlying the verse. A pentameter of binary feet may serve as a helpful first approximation of the decasyllable, but the lack of a uniform fit between syllable (whether characterized by one or three expressive features) and metrical position should warn against accepting that model out of hand. Like the hexameter, the *deseterac* also exhibits an inner metric, and, again like the hexameter, it is on this inner metric that traditional phraseology rests.

Before turning to the description of inner metric, it is well to establish the important outer metrical constraints on the *deseterac* as evidenced in the Stolac material used in these studies. In particular, I am interested in the consistency of syllabic count in these Parry Collection songs, and in the reasons behind any variance from the ten-syllable norm. To begin, let us separate out two distinct categories: oral-dictated and sung texts. The former group will be represented by three poems comprising a total of 4,077 lines: Texts A, Mujo Kukuruzović's *Ropstvo Ograšćić Alije* (*The Captivity of Ograšćić Alija*; no. 1287a, 1,288 lines); B, Kukuruzović's *Ropstvo Alagić Alije i izbavinje Turaka* (*The Captivity of Alagić Alija and the Rescue of the Turks*; no. 1868, 2,152 lines); and D, Halil Bajgorić's *Halil izbavi Bojičić Aliju* (*Halil Rescues Bojičić Alija*; no. 6703, 637 lines). Sung texts are represented by text C, Bajgorić's *Ženidba Bećirbega Mustajbegova* (*The Wedding of Mustajbeg's Son Bećirbeg*; no. 6699, 1,030 lines). The raw figures and references for hypersyllabic and hyposyllabic verses in these four songs are as shown in table 9. In all, the oral-dictated texts (A, B, D) show only five hypermetric and seventeen hypometric lines out of 4,077 (0.12 percent and 0.42 percent, respectively), while the sung text (C) contains twelve eleven- or twelve-syllable lines and six of less than ten syllables out of 1,030 lines (1.2 percent and 0.58 percent, respectively).

Clearly, then, analysis of our sample of over five thousand verses yields no substantial evidence for syllabic variation in the decasyllable, and we shall

TABLE 9. Hyper- and Hyposyllabic Verses
in the Stolac Songs

Text	Number of Hypersyllabic Lines	Number of Hyposyllabic Lines
A	2 (0.16%)	3 (0.23%)
B	2 (0.09%)	9 (0.42%)
D	1 (0.16%)	5 (0.78%)
C	12 (1.2%)	6 (0.58%)

discover that even this minuscule percentage of hyper- and hyposyllabic lines consists principally of verses that generally follow the syllabic rule. To put it positively, the *junački deseterac* proves itself a highly consistent verse form from the point of view of syllabicity, with over 98 percent of our extensive sample unambiguously adhering to this first principle of outer metric. Even if we choose to leave the uncertain approximation of podic structure and trochaic rhythm aside, preferring to explain coincidence of phonological features and ictus through principles of inner metric, we can be sure of this much: in the songs that are in part the subject of these studies, the fundamental metrical measure of ten syllables is a precise and limiting feature of the line.

With this information in hand, we may profitably make two inquiries about the 1.8 percent of the sample that seems not to conform to the metrical rule of syllabicity. First, why do twelve of seventeen hypermetrics occur in the sung as opposed to the oral-dictated texts? Second, and more generally, to what kinds of "errors" do we owe the forty variations reported above? To begin with the sung text C, note that six of the twelve eleven-syllable lines owe their incongruity to initial extra-metrical syllables, in the form either of interjections:

> Oj! Rano rani Djerdjelez Alija   (C.1)
>
> *   1 2 3 4   5   6 7 8 9 10
>
> Oj! Djerdjelez Alija arose early

or what I call "performatives":

> hI jednu, dvije, sebi natočijo   (C.12)
>
> * 1   2   3 4 5 6   7 8 9 10
>
> One, two he poured for himself
>
> I jev' ozdala jednog momka mlada   (C.160)
>
> * 1   2   3 4 5   6   7   8   9 10
>
> From below here was a young man

The lines involving interjections are typical at the beginning of songs, at the resumption of a song following a rest break, and at moments of dramatic intensity. Because they have a rhetorical force in performance, interjections are more appropriate to sung than to dictated texts, and the Parry-Lord amanuensis Nikola Vujnović was more likely to transcribe them than other kinds of variations from the decasyllabic norm. Indeed, it is well to remember that Nikola was himself a *guslar* and a member of the tradition he helped to record,[66] so it is only prudent to be aware of the filter he provided between what was performed and what he either took down from dictation or transcribed from acoustic recordings in later years.

The "performatives" offer an avenue for inquiry into the nature of metrical "flaws." Although we may argue that the extra-metrical *I* (or h*I*, with the aspirate [h] customarily acting as a hiatus bridge between the tenth syllable of one line and the onset of the next line) represents the very common conjunction *i*, or "and," not every case will tolerate that interpretation syntactically (cf. Maretić 1935–36, 255:10–16). In listening to the recording of Bajgorić's performance, it becomes apparent that the sound-image itself can vary from a fully pronounced *i*, at times arguably the conjunction, to the simple glide [j], ostensibly a hiatus bridge or continuant between lines. Its function seems on the whole to be phonological rather than syntactical; this is the reason that I have not felt it correct to "translate" the sound in the examples above. All in all, the concept of a performative—that is, a sound that promotes the phonological continuity of the performance without interceding in the syntax or meaning of the contiguous lines—seems closest to the true function of this sound. And we may assume that Nikola tacitly recognized these sounds for what they were, since he regularly left them untranscribed.

Of the remaining six hypermetrics in text C, two involve the insertion of an excrescent vowel, as in this example:

Jedan kal*a*pak, dvan'es' čelinaka   (C.93)

1 2   3 * 4   5 6   7 8 9 10

One fur cap, twelve feathers

Nikola does not transcribe the aberration, resorting instead to the standard form, *kalpak*. At first sight the addition of *a* might seem idiolectal, as if some peculiarity of Bajgorić's performance style generated an occasional excrescent vowel. This supposition gains some support from the unusual assortment of hiatus bridges in Bajgorić's repertoire: [v], [j], [h], and even [m] and [n] can prevent glottal stops and the momentary interruption of vocal continuity both between and within the words.[67] As a counter-example, we may compare

---

66. On the collection process, see Lord, "General Introduction" to *SCHS* 1:1–20; Lord 1951b.

67. This kind of phonological bridging is consistent with the general tendency of the poetic medium to make colonic "words" out of lexical items.

Ibro Bašić's habit of doubling a stem vowel to eke out the ten-syllable norm of his verse.[68] Whatever the case, the excrescent vowels are, like the extra-metricals, phonological variants which do not affect the lexical or syntactic structure of the decasyllable.

Two or more eleven-syllable lines result from Bajgorić's using the longer of two dialectal forms when the shorter one would have suited the metrical environment:

Vet' i gunjinu samu prebacijo   (C.453)

1 2 3 *4 5 6   7 8 9 10

But he threw on just a peasant jacket

Treba sjutra dijeliti mejdane   (C. 592)

1 2 3 4 5*67 8 9 10

Tomorrow [we] must fight a duel

In choosing the diminutive *gunjinu* instead of the simplex noun *gunju*, the singer exceeds the ten-syllable norm; likewise, by selecting the four-syllable ijekavian dialect-form *dijeliti* instead of the three-syllable jekavian bi-form *djeliti*, he makes a hypermetric verse. While this choice amounts to a metrical error, it is only fitting to point out that it is also further evidence of the polymorphism of oral tradition, a characteristic found at all levels of structure. The doublet *gunju/gunjinu*—or, more generally, the simplex/diminutive substitution that can involve many nouns—is evidence of a compositional flexibility: the poet in performance can select either bi-form on the basis of syllabic count in the rest of the line. Of course, many of his "choices" have been made for him by the tradition that he inherits and in the formulas that he employs, and in any case he does not ponder the choice in performance but rather trusts his "ear" to produce a metrical verse. But the very fact that this kind of hyper-syllabicity can and does occur in the synchronic moment of performance proves a degree of flexibility at some points. The *dijeliti/djeliti* doublet reinforces the argument: perhaps under the influence of cognate formulas,[69] Bajgorić uses the metrically "wrong" bi-form in combination with *mejdane* and produces an eleven-syllable line. In both "errors" we detect an important compositional principle: although this sort of flexibility can occasionally lead to metrical infelicities, like other kinds of traditional polymorphism it serves the needs of the composing oral poet and makes possible over time the evolution of a traditional diction. The price one pays for that synchronic flexibility and

---

68. E.g., line 421 from a sung version of his *Alagić Alija and Velagić Selim* (text no. *6597*), second colon: "baniice mlade" instead of the expected (and hyposyllabic) "banice mlade."

69. Compare the following, all examples drawn from Stolac texts: "Da mi, bane, mejdan *dijelimo*" (*6699*.814), "Ve' dvojica mejdan *dijeliše*" (*6699*.857), "*Dijeliše*, pa se rastadoše" (*6699*.858), "Treba nema pravo *dijeliti*" (1868.2062), and "A danak se s noći *dijeljaše*" (1287a.976).

diachronic development is the relatively rare lapse exemplified by *gunjinu* and *dijeliti*.

The last two examples of hypersyllabicity in text C entail five-syllable first hemistichs:

Dok sve *v*odaje bijo zatvorijo   (C.103)

1   2   * 3 4   56 7   8 9 10

When he had locked all the rooms

Bog te *v*uzdrž'o staru ocu tvome   (C.672)

1   2   *   3 4   5 6 7 8   9   10

God has kept you for your old father

More than the other examples cited, these two lines seem to be true hyper-metrics. Their extra length results from neither supernumerary elements nor an unfortunate choice, and all of the words involved have syntactic roles to play; in fact, in assigning the asterisk in each case to the third position, I have made a somewhat arbitrary decision about which is the "offending" syllable. On the other hand, all would have been well had Bajgorić elided *sve* v*odaje* to *sv'odaje* and *te* v*uzdrž'o* to *t'uzdrž'o*. As the lines stand, however, the hiatus bridge [v] precludes elision and memorializes the hypersyllabic construction. Without a thorough search of all of Bajgorić's sung repertoire and comparison with the Stolac community of singers,[70] we cannot begin to describe how this formation came to be (that is, whether the aberration was frozen or caused by the hiatus bridge), and in the end the question may not be as important as noticing the deformation as it occurs in the text.

The twelve hypermetric verses that occur in the sung text C may thus be divided into four groups: (1) extra-metricals (interjections and performatives), (2) words lengthened one syllable by excrescent vowels, (3) faulty choices between metrical bi-forms, and (4) "true" hypermetrics caused by lack of elision. The first two categories, accounting for eight of the lines, may confidently be designated as purely phonological variations affecting neither the syntax nor the sense of the line. They are typical of sung performances and were not transcribed by the Parry-Lord amanuensis Nikola. The two instances in the third category derive from the same traditional polymorphism that makes possible multiforms at all levels of traditional epic; these infrequent errors are mere synchronic blemishes that fade into the background of the continually re-created diachronic text. The last pair of hypermetrics are thus the only lines that qualify as outright violations of the syllabic constraint in the *deseterac*.

Of the six eight- and nine-syllable hypometric lines in the same sung text,

---

70. There is no evidence in the computerized concordance of Stolac songs of any corresponding phraseology.

four are attributable to missing connectives and temporal conjunctions that Bajgorić probably swallowed in the moment of performance. Nikola, demonstrating his singer's ear, fills the short lines out to the usual increment, fashioning common formulas that match the syntax (added elements are italicized in the following examples):

A napade Mujo buljubaša   (C.641)

And commander Mujo came along

A kad svanu i *j*ogranu sunce[71]   (C.745)

And then the sun rose and dawned

The other two hyposyllabic lines result from, in the case of line 854, an unfortunate elision: **Pa odigra ćaćina goluba* to

Pa 'digra ćaćina goluba   (C.854)

1   2 3 4 5 6 7 8 9

Then he danced his father's horse out

—another example of multiformity gone awry; and in line 886, the transformation of the connective or performative *i* to a glide rather than a full morpheme: *I jovako momak progovara to

*j*Ovako momak progovara
                                                    (C.886)
1 2 3 4 5   6 7 8 9

The young man spoke in this way

Nikola silently corrects these last two lines as well, causing them to conform to the usual *deseterac* syllabicity.[72] The message of the hypometric lines is thus the same as that of the hypermetrics: aberrations are in the main phonological mishaps that stem from the exigencies of composition in performance; the syllabic constraint on the *deseterac* proves once again a very strict and important one.

The few lines that vary from the standard ten syllables in the oral-dictated texts, a total of only twenty-two out of 4,077 lines (0.5 percent), stem from the same kinds of causes as underlie those in the sung text C, with the expectable exception that we find no hypermetrics or performatives in the dictated texts. Excrescent vowels, faulty selection of metrical bi-forms, and

---

71. Here the singer also fills the first two syllables with an especially prominent instrumental passage on the *gusle*.

72. Here and elsewhere it may be easy to overestimate Nikola's editing of the received text. To put the matter in proper perspective, it is well to recall that his "emendations" only reaffirm the overwhelmingly consistent syllabicity of the *deseterac*, representing what the singers would commonly (and in fact do commonly) do, and affect only 15 of 1,030 lines (0.5 percent).

problems with elision all contribute to long and short lines,[73] but once again the overwhelming impression is of a highly syllabic verse form—a line that varies from its ten-syllable shape only in the moment of performance, and then only very infrequently. With over 98 percent of our sample answering the syllabic constraint, and, further, with virtually all those rare departures from the norm explained as momentary ornaments or errors, it is safe to pronounce syllabicity a constant and rigorous rule in the *deseterac*. To pursue other regularities in the line, we must turn to its inner metric.

Inner Metric

CAESURA

All commentators on the *deseterac* add to the decasyllabic constraint a regularly recurring caesura between the fourth and fifth syllables, yielding two cola of four and six syllables each:

$$\overset{s}{1}\ \overset{s}{2}\ \overset{s}{3}\ \overset{s}{4}\ |\ \overset{s}{5}\ \overset{s}{6}\ \overset{s}{7}\ \overset{s}{8}\ \overset{s}{9}\ \overset{s}{10}$$

Šta no nešto | u Zadarju cmili?   (B.1)

What was the shouting in Zadar?

As this example illustrates, no matter what the syntactic form of the line, the word-break will come at precisely the same place in each decasyllable.[74] In fact, even when a line is hypermetric or hypometric, one or both of the two cola will be preserved, as in the following instances discussed above:

  Oj! | Rano rani | Djerdjelez Alija   (C.1; both cola intact)

  * | 1 2 3 4| 5 6 7 8 9 10

  Dok sve *vodaje* | bijo zatvorijo   (C.103; colon 2 intact)

  1   2 * 3 4| 5 6 7 8 9 10

From a practical standpoint, the caesura is never bridged in the *deseterac*. Caesura placement and colon formation are constant throughout the sample of more than five thousand lines and show even greater stability, as these two lines help to prove, than syllabicity.

Before moving on to describe the nature of each colon or hemistich, let us make two related theoretical points. First, it will be recalled that the Homeric hexameter exhibited three caesuras, a highly regular mid-line break at two possible positions (B1 and B2, 99 percent) and two somewhat less frequent breaks within the half-line, each of which could also occur at either of two

---

73. We may suppose that some metrical infelicities are due to *lapsus linguae* or *lapsus calami*, but without an aural recording of the dictated texts it is difficult to be sure. See further Maretić A:76–112; B:76–123; C:218–42; and D:1–28.

74. Maretić affirms the same principle for his study of the Karadžić (A:62) and Moslem texts (C:183).

positions (A1 and A2, 90 percent; C1 and C2, 90 percent). Only by allowing two slots for each caesura do we attain such high percentages, but this controlled variation is to be expected in a verse form in which dactylic-spondaic substitution affects metrical shape so strongly. The point is that the hexameter has three movable caesuras and a correspondingly complex assortment of colon-types; the *deseterac*, in contrast, with its more focused syllabicity and the absolutely regular placement of its single caesura, has only two possible colon-types: the four- and six-syllable increments that together constitute a whole stich. Given this idiosyncratic situation (both traditions exhibit colon formation but the repertoire of types in Serbo-Croatian epic is far less elaborate), it behooves us to consider the patterns within the four- and six-syllable increments, for within the remarkable regularity of syllable count, caesura, and colon formation, the *deseterac* allows and even promotes a complicated display of traditional word-craft.

At the foundation of the singer's art, from both an evolutionary and a performance-oriented standpoint, lies the Indo-European principle of right justification. Much as in the hexameter, this increasing metrical (and therefore phraseological) conservatism as the line progresses from the beginning of a unit toward the end governs the shape of prosody and diction. But just as the rule took a tradition-dependent form in the hexameter—one resulting, for example, in varying hemistich and colon lengths—so it takes another series of forms in the *deseterac*. Indeed, right justification emerges as the principle behind the idiosyncratic texture of both cola, each with its own appreciable collection of individual features. We can trace the synchronic designs created by this diachronic pattern in the textual record of the Stolac songs.

COLON 2 AND THE SHAPE OF THE VERSE

Perhaps the most obvious evidence of right justification is the asymmetry of the decasyllable. As in the hexameter, the second hemistich is longer than the first, leading to a correspondingly greater metrical and phraseological stability in the latter part of the line. As a first approximation, we may recall Jakobson's (1952, 25) demonstration of the "quantitative close" over the last four syllables of the *deseterac*: "An accented short is avoided in the penult (ninth) syllable, and an accented long practically never occurs in the two antepenults (eighth and seventh syllables)." Schematically, then, the close follows this sequence:

$$1\ 2\ 3\ 4\ |\ 5\ 6\ \overset{\cup}{7}\ \overset{\cup}{8}\ \overset{-}{9}\ \overset{\cup}{10}$$

Pa propade prosječenu klancu   (C.504)

    1   2 3 4   5 6 7 8   9   10

Then he attacked the hollowed-out ravine

The quantitative close thus governs the placement of words to some extent, especially by inviting a long syllable in position 9, far the heaviest stress in the *deseterac*. So strong is this penultimate ictus that the poet composing in performance will often stress a lexically short syllable in the ninth position, in which case metrical ictus momentarily outweighs the rules of accent.[75] The singer's rhythm and vocal melody emphasize the quantitative close, and the demands of performance override uncontextualized lexical values. The quantitative close and its focus on the ninth-syllable ictus are important features of the *deseterac*, and they offer one example of the operation of right justification in the prosody and its constraints on verse-making in the decasyllable.

Just as the longer second colon becomes firmer in its distribution of quantities toward the end of the unit, so the shorter first colon also reveals a looser-to-firmer progression of quantities from beginning to end. Although the effect of right justification is, logically enough, less pronounced in the shorter hemistich, we still observe the heaviest performance stress on the third syllable,[76] followed by a complete lack of ictus on syllable 4. All in all, the close of the first hemistich is to an extent a mirror of line closure, with syllables 3–4 and 9–10 serving as boundaries:

$$1 \; 2 \; \overset{\prime}{3} \; \overset{x}{4} \; | \; 5 \; 6 \; 7 \; 8 \; \overset{\prime}{9} \; \overset{x}{10}$$

Kak' upádě, *v*aga selam dádě   (C.216)

As he entered, the aga gave him a selam

We may now correlate these observations with Petrović's figures on coincidence of lexical accent and metrical position, and note that the stress on syllables in positions 3 and 9 stems not necessarily from a trochaic pentameter tendency but from the Indo-European rule of right justification as imaged in the tradition-dependent Serbo-Croatian *deseterac*. Absolutely consistently in the rhythm and melody of sung performance (Lord 1960, 37–38), and with reasonable regularity in the verbal component regulated by the prosody (see Petrović figures above, p. 87), the third and ninth syllables bear the strongest performance stress of any positions in the line, while stress is forbidden in the fourth and tenth syllables. We may thus consider each colon, as well as the entire line, to have a recurrent closing cadence of long-short and stressed-unstressed.[77]

Corresponding to these closing cadences, and in accord with the demands of

---

75. The most common instance of this phenomenon is the *guslar*'s stressing the penultimate syllable of verb forms (chiefly past participles, infinitives, or aorists) when they occur in final position; e.g., no. 6699.224: "Tri, četiri, ćejif ugrabíjo" ("Three, four, the feeling seized him").

76. The third-syllable ictus is not nearly as heavy as that involving the ninth syllable, but the two together are performatively much the most prominent in the line.

77. As will be illustrated in more detail below, this 3–4 and 9–10 configuration of ś š and š̄ š̆ also accounts for Jakobson's empirical description (1952, 25) of a bridge, or zeugma, at the end of each colon.

right justification, we find a looser distribution of quantities at the opening of each colon. These beginnings of units provide for rhythmic (and phraseological) variation, and for this as well as additional reasons to be discussed later in this chapter, the first and fifth syllables are thus the primary sites for stressed monosyllables. We may recall, for instance, that Petrović's figures reveal the highest coincidence of word-accent and position at syllables 1 and 5. For the moment, it is enough to remark that the third and ninth syllables do not usually harbor these monosyllables because to do so would violate the bridges at 3–4 and 9–10.[78] Schematically, then, we expect the configuration

$$\acute{1}\ 2\ 3\ 4\ |\ \acute{5}\ 6\ 7\ 8\ 9\ 10$$

Tad zavika careva gazija   (C.278; stressed first syllable)

Then the tsar's hero began to shout

Dobro gledaj *šta* ti knjiga piše   (C.350; stressed fifth syllable)

See well *what* the letter tells you

Likewise, any initially accented word beginning either of the two cola will bear metrical ictus in positions 1 and 5. When we add to these lexical considerations the tendency of the *guslar*'s metrical stress to fall at the onset of units in the *deseterac*, the following overall pattern emerges:

$$\acute{1}\ 2\ \acute{3}\ \overset{x}{4}\ |\ \acute{5}\ 6\ 7\ 8\ \acute{9}\ \overset{x}{10}$$

That is, there exist four primary sites for ictus, both in the prosody and in the phraseology that it helps to determine: positions 1, 3, 5, and 9. Taken as a group, all four sites are important to *deseterac* prosody and, as we shall see, affect phraseology in significant ways; all four also derive from the fundamental principle of right justification.

Before moving on to examine some specific instances of these general rules and to promote further articulation of the rough sketch that they assist in providing, we should consider what remains after these six positions, four stressed and two unstressed, are described. It may come as no surprise that the second syllable, for instance, shows no strong tendency toward a particular prosodic value. Syllables 6 through 8 reveal a similar ambiguity, as Petrović reminded us and as Jakobson in defining his quantitative close in part illustrated. These four positions are not specifically defined in the *deseterac*; to put the same matter another way, they allow for variation much more readily than do the six syllabic positions at either end of the two cola.

Perhaps we can now see how the hypothesis of a trochaic pentameter came to be, and also how oblique such a concept is to the true nature of the verse

78. Other than an accented monosyllable, only an enclitic could occupy the tenth position alone, and then the formation at 9–10 would amount grammatically and prosodically to a disyllable with initial stress.

form. With stress and length tending to fall on syllables 1, 3, 5, and 9, and with off-beats and shortness coinciding absolutely regularly with 4 and 10, metrists were almost able to fit the *deseterac* into a Greco-Latin quantitative mold. If positions 2, 6, 8, and particularly 7 did not agree with the classical model, the "aberrations" at these points could be explained away by terming the rhythmic pattern a tendency instead of a rule. In fact, the notion of trochaic pentameter obscures the quantitative shape of the decasyllable, designating as it does a line of five stressed-unstressed doublets. The *deseterac* consists of ten syllables, to be sure, but they are divided asymmetrically into two cola of four and six syllables each, with each colon characterized by stress placement at particular positions. Right justification has provided each hemistich with a closing cadence, and an initial stress has likewise emerged in the relatively loose sequence of quantities that begins each unit. Greco-Roman models aside, the *deseterac* takes its own tradition-dependent form.

In addition to the closing cadence and initial stress in each hemistich, right justification provides the second colon with two complementary distribution rules. The first entails the sequence of words according to their syllabic length and prescribes that longer words follow shorter ones, the more extensive words characteristically appearing at the ends of cola and lines.[79] The second and interdependent rule calls for initially accented disyllables, of the shape $\acute{s}\,\breve{s}$, to seek the ninth and tenth positions;[80] this sorting, which answers both the penultimate ictus and zeugma requirements, can, but does not necessarily, override the first distribution rule. To illustrate, consider these examples of the shorter-before-longer constraint in colon 2:

> Kad su bili | dobro podranili   (C.550; dòbro)
>
>   2   4
>
> When they were well arisen
>
> Velik me je | trošak osvojijo   (C.704; trȍšak)
>
>   2   4
>
> The cost has been great for me to manage

As long as the disyllable has an initial short vowel, the first rule is the arbiter of placement in the longer hemistich. When a disyllable with a long stem

---

79. Cf. Maretić B:127–29 and D:32–46.

80. By "initially accented" I mean to indicate those initial syllables with lexically defined natural *length*, that is, those which are long rising ('), long falling (^), or simply long by nature (with macron or unmarked). Cf. Maretić A:58 and C:198–200. In the process of description, Maretić presents a table comparing the preference for line-final disyllables with a long initial vowel over those with a short initial vowel in oral versus written material. This table, derived from his figures (C:198–200), shows how strongly the oral singer favors the line-final disyllable with a long initial vowel and, in the process, offers a possible way to distinguish between oral and "imitation oral" texts. On this last point, cf. Haymes 1980.

vowel is involved, however, the shorter-longer order may be reversed under the influence of the ninth syllable and closing cadence.

U Kanidži | bijelome gradu   (C.705; grȁdu)

4 2

In Kanidža the white city

*v*Osta banu | kabanica kleta   (C.713; klȇta)

4 2

The cursed cloak remained with the ban

It is precisely the firmness of the colon- and line-ending cadence that attracts the initially accented disyllable and causes the 4 + 2 distribution. Both the "normal" shorter-longer order and the reversal as a result of the attraction of ninth-syllable ictus are tradition-dependent realizations of the principle of right justification.

To restate this pair of distribution rules in properly ordered sequence, we can say that in the second hemistich a syllabically longer word will always follow a syllabically shorter word unless the shorter word is an initially accented disyllable, in which case the order may be (but is not always) reversed. Instances of non-reversal do occur:

Ka' što mu je | bane nakitijo   (C.768; bȃne)

2 4

As the ban wrote to him

—so it will prove most accurate to conceive of the ninth-syllable exclusion as a possible rather than certain reversal of the customary order. A corollary to these two rules will further illustrate their interdependence and solve the problem of sequence with syllabically equal words. If two three-syllable words constitute the second colon, leaving nothing to choose between them on the basis of extent alone, then the one with an accented medial syllable will be favored in final position:

*h*Izaberi stotinu momaka   (C.736; momáka)

Choose one hundred young men

The penultimate ictus in the *deseterac* attracts the medially accented tri-syllable,[81] just as it does the initially stressed disyllable:

1	2	3	4	5	6	7	8	9́	1̌0
								klȇt-	a
							mo-	má-	ka

81. The trisyllabic genitive plural (especially partitive), which switches accent from the initial position in the disyllabic nominative singular, becomes a syntactically and prosodically appropriate, and therefore frequent, formation at the end of colon 2.

TABLE 10. Frequency of Principal Metrical Types (in Percent)

Type-Colon 2	Text A	B	C	D	Average
2 + 4	45.2	42.5	43.2	33.3	41.1
4 + 2	19.9	20.8	18.7	25.7	21.3
3 + 3	16.1	18.1	18.4	17.1	17.4
TOTALS	81.2	81.4	80.3	76.1	79.8

This combination of distribution rules, both deriving from right justification in the inner metric of the *deseterac*, yields for our 5,107-line sample the frequencies of principal metrical types in the second colon shown in table 10.[82] As a generalization, we can say that shorter-longer sequence is preferred in the second hemistich of the decasyllable, with approximately an equal number of ninth-syllable reversals and symmetrical (3/3) cola. These distributional rules override normal prose word order when the two come into conflict, although in many cases there is no conflict and customary word order is maintained.[83] The major point is that the inner metric of colon 2 reveals a texture ultimately attributable to right justification but also amounts to a tradition-dependent set of constraints.

This characteristic texture becomes ever more apparent as we examine the distribution of elements in colon 2 more finely. Proclitics, such as prepositions, the conjunctions *i* (and), *a* (and, but), and *ni* (neither, nor), and the negative particle *ne*, are unaccented and cannot be treated metrically or grammatically as single words. From a prosodic viewpoint, a proclitic joins with the word that follows to form an accented unit within the colon and line. Thus the following examples of two-element second hemistichs:

Skoči momak | *na* noge lagane   (C.19)

3   +   3

The young man jumped *to* his nimble feet

Svog dorata | *vod* jasala jami   (C.23)

4   +   2

He took his horse *from* the stable

In the syllabically more spacious second colon this *proclitic binding*, as I shall call it, participates most often in noun doublets, noun-adjective pairs, longer (often prefixed) verbs, and prepositional phrases. Since the two-word units formed by this process of amalgamation are metrically equivalent to one-

---

82. For reasons discussed below, I have included in this table those 2/4 and 4/2 cola that form the longer increment by combination with proclitics, as well as those trisyllabic pairs (3/3) of the shape proclitic-disyllable-trisyllable.

83. Cf. Maretić B:123–64 and D:28–64.

TABLE 11.   Principal Metrical Types, Proclitic
Combinations

Single-element Pattern	Proclitic Pattern	Total
2 + 4: 32.3%	2 + π3: 8.8%	41.1%
4 + 2: 10.8%	π3 + 2: 10.5%	21.3%
3 + 3: 10.4%	π2 + 3: 7.0%	17.4%
TOTALS 53.5%	26.3%	79.8%

element units of the same syllabic extent, we may include the proclitic (π) groups with their single-word counterparts in the order shown in table 11.[84] It is worth noting that the proclitic pattern plays a particularly significant role in both the 4 + 2 and the 3 + 3 configurations, accounting in each case for up to half of the examples located, and further that these three sequences taken together make up approximately 80 percent of all second hemistichs in the 5,107-line sample.[85]

After these major colon-patterns are recognized, the remainder of our sample breaks down into sparsely populated and for the most part statistically unimportant categories. The only category worth tabulating here is that involving three two-syllable words (2/2/2), a sequence that follows the expectable rule of initially accented disyllables in final position and in which the pattern distribution is reasonably consistent.[86]

Presjedeše, piju rujno vino   (C.575; víno)

They spent [the night] sitting, they drank red wine

Likewise, *enclitic binding*, by which an unaccented word "inclines" on a preceding accented word to form a grammatical and prosodic group, proves statistically insignificant, not sufficiently affecting any one pattern to merit categorical analysis. Of descriptive importance, however, are the facts that these accentless elements (1) usually follow the word order of the spoken language, (2) almost never occupy the fifth position (at the beginning of the second hemistich), since this placement would amount to a bridged caesura, and (3) are much rarer in the second than in the first colon.[87] Whereas the

84. I include herein only the statistically prominent proclitic patterns.

85. When the word following a proclitic has a falling accent on the first syllable, the grammatical stress shifts to the proclitic, whether or not it is expressed in the medium of the sung line. Since that shift would place grammatical stress on syllables 5 (patterns 4/2 and 3/3) and 7 (a much lower percentage), we may see proclitic binding as acting in concert with right-justification rules.

86. Text A = 3.5 percent, B = 3.6 percent, C = 4.5 percent, and D = 6.0 percent.

87. For further remarks on enclitics in the spoken language, see Browne 1975. On the rarity of an enclitic bridging a caesura, see Maretić A:63 and C:210; similarly, I find only three examples of a fifth-syllable enclitic in 5,107 lines of the Stolac metrical sample. As for relative frequency of occurrence of enclitics, 85.1 percent are found in the first colon.

TABLE 12.   Principal Metrical Types, Colon I
(in Percent)

Colon I Pattern	A	B	C	D
2/2	25.2	25.1	22.6	33.6
π/3	14.6	15.8	19.1	15.4
3/ε	8.4	7.3	3.1	5.5
TOTALS	48.2	48.2	44.8	54.5

process of proclitic binding, the joining of an unaccented word to what follows it, plays a relatively important role in pattern distribution throughout the line, that of enclitic binding is primarily confined to the first hemistich.

COLON I

In general, the role played by proclitic and enclitic binding reflects the relative lack of prosodic and phraseological fixity of the first as opposed to the second colon. Partly because its brevity precludes setting up regular sequences of nouns and noun-adjective combinations, the opening hemistich reveals a much higher degree of pliability, both in its accommodation of unaccented words and in the large number of lightly populated categories or sequences of elements. This flexibility is a typical manifestation of right justification in the line as a whole, the first hemistich being more loosely organized than the second. At the level of the colon, we may expect the first four-syllable unit to manifest some evidence of greater firmness or regularity toward its end, much as the six-syllable segment showed above. And in fact, the prominence of the first- and third-syllable ictus is, as mentioned earlier, a sign of right justification.

As an initial approximation of the most important patterns, consider the distribution of the three most frequently occurring (table 12).[88]

2/2:   Slabo svlači | a dobro oblači.   (C. 52; svláči)

      2 | 2

He undressed weakly but dressed well.

π/3:   vU vavliju | ključe preturijo.   (C. 112)

      π | 3

Into the courtyard he threw the keys.

3/ε: Dizgine mu | na dva rama tura,   (C. 200)

      3 | ε

He thrust the reins over his two shoulders,

88. Below and in table 12, ε = enclitic, just as π = proclitic.

The most common pattern is a balanced one of two disyllables which follows the penultimate ictus rule in its internal arrangement (*svlači*), while the second and third both consist of what Maretić calls *neprave četvorosložnice*, "facsimile tetrasyllables," formed by two words, one of which is unaccented. Neither of these accentual groups owes its formation to right justification, either by the shorter-before-longer or the penultimate ictus constraints that proved so important in the second hemistich. On the basis of these most heavily represented categories, then, we derive very little evidence of right justification apart from the tendency toward penultimate ictus and the very variability of inner metric patterns.

It is important to notice from the start that this flexibility promotes two different but complementary trends in colon formation. The more obvious one will amount to a synchronic freedom for the composing poet, affording him a section of the line that will remain open, for example, to syntactic adjustments.[89] This is not to say that formulaic structure will weaken or lapse at line-beginning, but, in terms widely used in current scholarship, that verbal repetition is likely to be more systemic than verbatim. The less obvious result of first-colon variability, a corollary to the former trend, will be greater differences in prosodic structures from one text to another and from one singer to another. If this initial section of the line is more open to individual or idiolectal habits of composition, in opposition to the greater regularity of the second-colon inner metric as imaged in its dependence on a few well-represented patterns, then the first hemistich must also prove the site for a degree of prosodic chauvinism. We see some evidence of this latter trend toward individual habits of composition in the figure for the 2/2 balanced pattern over the four texts.[90] With the first colon revealing a greater degree of flexibility, we expect and indeed find a correspondingly greater degree of individuality in prosodic structures. As an example of this individuality, consider table 13, which displays word-types that begin the first hemistich. Some of the percentages most divergent from the averages, notably occurring only in texts C and D, are italicized.

Summary: The Deseterac

In gathering together our findings and observations on the decasyllable, it is well to recognize the tenuous nature of outer metric as a true, definitive aspect

---

89. We may contrast the less flexible second colon, for example, by noting the tendency for second-colon noun-epithet or proper name combinations to be inflected only in the final word. The principle is similar to that of the idiom's characteristic formation of colonic "words" from individual lexical items, a process that, as we shall see in chapter 4, is also typical of Homeric phraseology.

90. While the relative frequency of the disyllabic sequence over the A, B, and C texts remains approximately the same (22–25 percent), the corresponding percentage for D is considerably elevated, representing an increase of between 8 and 11 percent or between 51 and 70 lines in a text of 637 lines.

TABLE 13.   First Position in Colon I (in Percent)

	A	B	C	D	Average
monosyllable (01)	15.8	14.4	16.3	13.7	15.0
disyllable (02)	30.2	30.5	*25.1*	*36.7*	30.1
trisyllable (03)	8.6	7.5	*3.5*	5.7	6.7
tetrasyllable (04)	6.1	5.4	4.5	*2.8*	5.1
proclitic (11/12)	39.0	41.2	43.1	40.8	42.3
enclitic (21)	0.4	1.0	0.8	0.3	0.7

of the prosody. At best, the putative podic structure of the *deseterac* remains a descriptive approximation, much as the six-metron model formally characterized the hexameter. But whereas the Homeric line responded in a limited fashion to this approach by yielding a profile of dactylic-spondaic substitution, the decasyllable reveals no such clearly defined podic units. Scholars have labored to impose on the Serbo-Croatian line a regularity at the structural level of the Greco-Latin foot, but the verse resists all such attempts, forcing a retreat to unconvincing portraits of trochaic pentameter tendencies and the like. What remains after a fair examination of outer metric in the *deseterac* is a firm and unambiguous constraint of syllabic count, a constraint that makes the line absolutely regular syllabically, with all but a very few hypermetric and hypometric lines demonstrably the product of phonological ornamentation and traditional "error." And, as we have seen, these apparent exceptions actually prove the ten-syllable rule rather than bringing its consistency into question.

The same exceptions, when added to the overwhelming regularity throughout the 5,107-line sample, assist also in proving the systematic recurrence of the caesura or word-break between syllables 4 and 5. This key to the inner metric of the *deseterac* thus combines with the equally stringent syllabicity rule to mirror the two corresponding principles first found in the reconstructed Indo-European line and also reflected faithfully in the Homeric hexameter. The caesura divides the decasyllable into two hemistichs or cola, the first of four and the second of six syllables, and their regularity as units derives directly from the demonstrated consistencies in syllabic extent and word-break placement. As already mentioned, the *deseterac* thus involves an externally simpler system of cola than does the hexameter, since the Homeric line divides first into two hemistichs and then into four cola by means of multiple A, B, and C caesuras, although the cola of the decasyllable are, as we have seen, correspondingly complex in their inner make-up. We should note in passing that this examination of the Greek and Serbo-Croatian colon formation typifies the kind of comparison-contrast advocated throughout these studies: the two verses are alike in prescribing regularly recurring intralinear units that give each prosody a particular texture, and each is distinctive in prescribing certain tradition-dependent characteristics of that texture.

As for the third Indo-European and ancient Greek principle, that of right justification, the grossest evidence for a trace of its operation in the *deseterac* consists of the very 4 + 6, shorter-before-longer make-up of the composite line. Even more important for our view of the verse form as the foundation of a traditional diction is the contribution of right justification to the placement of ictus. As shown in detail above, each colon, and particularly the second, maintains a penultimate ictus (on syllables 3 and 9) and an initial ictus (on syllables 1 and 5) that derive from the smaller-to-larger, looser-to-firmer patterns of the line as a whole and of each hemistich individually. With ictus on all odd syllables except the seventh, the assumption of a trochaic pentameter—a podic, outer metric structure familiar to metrists intent on viewing the decasyllable in the canonical Greco-Latin context—seems outwardly logical, but in fact it proves diachronically and dynamically impertinent. Viewed on its own terms, the seventh-syllable ambiguity is not a troublesome flaw in the otherwise straightforwardly trochaic base of the line, but rather a syllable position left unemphasized by the relative distribution of ictus in neighboring positions. In the Serbo-Croatian line, right justification prescribes two cola in an asymmetrical arrangement, the shorter preceding the longer, and further provides for recurrent prosodic ictus on syllables 1, 3, 5, and 9 while forbidding ictus at positions 4 and 10.

Within the second and more extensive hemistich, the same archaic principle finds expression in two complementary distribution rules: (1) syllabically shorter words before longer and (2) initially accented disyllables at positions 9–10, which comprise the conclusion of the ending cadence and collectively constitute a zeugma or bridge. That is, shorter words will precede longer words unless the shorter element is an initially accented disyllable, in which case the disyllable may (or may not) seek the line-ending zeugma by virtue of the coincidence between its lexical accent and the penultimate ictus, thus reversing the more usual order and leaving the syllabically longer element in first position. Although the second hemistich might seem to present greater opportunities for variety in internal design than the less spacious opening hemistich, in fact the longer unit shows itself more conservative prosodically: fully 80 percent of the Stolac sample falls into one of three major colonpatterns—2 + 4, 3 + 3, and 4 + 2—with proclitic binding tending to work toward one of these.

Colon 1, in contrast, utilizes both proclitic and enclitic binding in its general tendency to make larger prosodic elements out of shorter ones. This part of the line is characterized by its relative variability, just as were the first and third cola of the hexameter, with that diachronic flexibility providing a site for synchronic fashioning of the verse in a particular textual situation. Under such conditions we would not expect major colon-patterns to emerge, and indeed the assortment of observed sequences is made up largely of a great many statistically insignificant categories. But right justification takes shape in more than the shorter-before-longer, highly variable nature of the unit as a whole; we also observe a marked preference for shorter elements (monosyllables, disyllables, and unaccented monosyllabic proclitics) at the onset of the initial hemistich. Even when a trisyllable opens the first colon, it almost always gives way to an enclitic in position 4 and so forms a prosodic tetrasyllable. Within an overall flexibility, then, we do perceive some manifestations of right justification, although they are by no means as pronounced as in the more conservative second hemistich.

Overall, the *deseterac* takes its prosodic cue from the Indo-European (and Homeric) features of syllabicity, caesura (implying colon formation), and right justification. As a general observation, then, we might logically expect the two epic prosodies—having at least this much in common as well as a respectable number of disparities—to support comparable phraseologies, that is, poetic dictions that will reveal significant similarities alongside inevitable, tradition-dependent differences. In the history of the evolution of Oral Theory, moreover, this is precisely the Hellenic-Slavic linguistic combination out of which Parry and Lord first forged both the methodology and the interpretive theory that were to serve so many other traditions. Whether the ancient Greek–South Slavic synthesis can be called on to bear such a comparative burden without the aid of other comparanda is a vexed question, as is that concerning the role to be played by other poetic traditions. Let us begin an informed and meticulous answer to both questions by asking how the prosodic descriptions so far developed relate to the prosody of the Old English *Beowulf*.

THE OLD ENGLISH ALLITERATIVE LINE

As with the hexameter and *deseterac*, the search for prosodic structure in the Old English line is primarily an investigation into what, in Parry's famous definition, the "same metrical conditions" might mean in the diachronic development and synchronic morphology of the verbal formula. Toward that end I shall once again concentrate on those compositional parameters most influential in the shape of phraseology, seeking where appropriate to distinguish this prosody from each of the others and to ascertain its tradition-dependent nature.

The Beginnings: Sievers and Some Basic Principles

Since before the time of Eduard Sievers's *Altgermanische Metrik* (1893)[91] almost one hundred years ago, the alliterative line of *Beowulf* has occasioned

---

91. See also his earlier article, "Zur Rhythmik des germanischen Alliterationsverses I" (1885). A convenient translation of an article containing the major premises of his system is his "Old Germanic Metrics and Old English Metrics" (1968).

a large number of metrical theories, with almost no consensus among their proponents. On the basis of comparative Germanic evidence and versificational features of stress and alliteration, Sievers sought to rationalize the enormously variable unit of the alliterative line into five archetypal patterns. Each of these patterns was to represent and account for certain of the *half-lines* (or *verses*) in the poetry, and collectively they were to comprise the entire metrical foundation for the poetic canon. To say that Sievers's prescriptions were at first accepted is misleading: in fact they were accorded the status of law, and textual emendations, for example, were founded on a supposedly necessary agreement between the metrical abstraction and the received manuscript text. Later years have seen the certainty about these canonical rules fade somewhat, and yet Sievers's basic conceptions are still deeply ingrained in some much more recent influential work on Old English metrics (e.g., Cable 1974). No scholar who proposes to treat Old English prosody can avoid coming to terms with his theory.

Sievers's "Five Types" consist of verse- (or half-line-)length patterns divided into two "feet." The first three have what he calls equal feet:[92]

double falling	A	æftĕr cénnĕd	(*Bwf* 12b)
double rising	B	ŏn sídnĕ sǽ	(*Bwf* 507a)
rising falling	C	ŏf brýdbúrĕ	(*Bwf* 921a)

and the other two are composed of unequal feet:

	D	héardhícgĕndĕ	(*Bwf* 394a)
		lýt éft bĕcwòm	(*Bwf* 2365b)
	E	wórdhòrd ŏnléac	(*Bwf* 259b)
		mórþŏrbĕd stréd	(*Bwf* 2436b)[93]

Sievers's basic assumptions in assigning prosodic values have become virtually universal among metrists. First, the most fundamental unit of prosody is *stress*, indicated by an acute accent (ś) for primary or strongest stress-emphasis and a grave accent (s̀) for secondary but still major stress; s̆ marks a syllable bearing minimal or no ictus. This is the initial point, and it will prove a crucial one: the atom or "prosodeme" of Old English meter is not the syllable or mora of such quantitative meters as the hexameter and *deseterac*, but rather the stress. Second, Sievers and others reached the hypothesis of the half-line or verse as the most basic metrical unit by observing the other

92. Line numbers with the notations *a* and *b* following the numeral refer, respectively, to the first and second verses in a given line.

93. Klaeber underdots the *o* in the second syllable of *morþorbed* to indicate that he considers the syllable syncopated.

indispensable feature of the meter—alliteration. As mentioned in the first part of this chapter, alliteration is not a desideratum but a requirement in the prosody of *Beowulf* and other Anglo-Saxon poems: unless there exists an agreement of initial stressed sounds between verses, an Old English line simply is not metrical. Alliteration and syntactic units, in fact, furnish the criteria for editing the run-on prose of the Cotton Vitellius A. xv. and other Anglo-Saxon manuscripts into poetic lines and half-lines, yielding a passage such as the following (*Bwf* 2401–2405):

> Gewat þa twelfa sum   torne gebolgen
> dryhten Geata   dracan sceawian;
> hæfde þa gefrunen,   hwanan sio fæhð aras,
> bealonið biorna;   him to bearme cwom
> maðþumfæt mære   þurh ðæs meldan hond.

> Then a certain one of twelve went, bitterly angered,
> Lord of the Geats, to examine the dragon;
> He had heard whence the feud arose,
> The people's pernicious enmity; to his bosom came
> An illustrious treasure-vessel through the informer's hand.

With the alliterating elements (or staves) underlined and space marking half-lines, we can see that the first (a) and second (b) verses alliterate in every case. The a-verse can, optionally, have two staves instead of one, but this property does not extend to the b-verse.

Sievers assigns his stresses systematically to the alliterating elements and other grammatically significant words in the line, such as other nouns, adjectives, adverbs, and verbs.[94] The phonological criteria are straightforward: if a syllable is long by nature (with a long vowel as its core) or by position (its short vowel followed by two or more consonants), it is stressable. Thus, for example, in the passage above we observe a number of stressable words with initial syllables long by nature: *Gēata, scēawian, fæhð, cwōm, māðþumfæt, mǣre*; and others in the same category but with prefixes (*ge-* and *ā-*): *Gewāt, gefrūnen, ārās.* We also notice words long by position: *twelfa, torne, dryhten, hæfde, biorna, bearme, meldan, hond*, and a prefixed counterpart, *gebolgen*, all of which are equally eligible phonologically and grammatically to bear stress on their root syllables. Such are the lexical items of primary importance in the Old English poetic line.

Of course, not all of the half-lines in *Beowulf* or any other Anglo-Saxon poem maintain a one-to-one correspondence between metrical position and syllable. In the unemended text of *Beowulf* a verse may consist of from two to ten syllables and a whole line of from seven to sixteen. Thus it is that Sievers and all metrists after him have had to admit to their prosodic descriptions twin

---

94. Rarely a word of lesser grammatical importance, such as a possessive pronoun, will serve as a stave.

rules which we may label *resolution* and *ramification*. Resolution entails the distribution of stress over two syllables if the first one is short by nature and position and therefore cannot itself bear ictus. For example, *dracan* in line 2402b of the passage quoted above cannot answer the metrical description of a trochee, or śš, because its first syllable is short and cannot by itself bear stress. Since, however, the word occupies the stave position in the b-verse, alliterating with *dryhten* in the opening verse, it must as a significant prosodic item in the line somehow shoulder a major stress. Resolution allows the word to take the prosodic shape *drācān*, with the stress distributed over both syllables rather than localized over the first one, as in *drýhtĕn*, for instance. The second and complementary rule of ramification accounts for the proliferation of short or unstressed syllables in the various minimally stressed positions among the Five Types. The infinitive *scéawĭăn*, with its two unstressed syllables, provides an example of how ramification—like its fellow principle, resolution—can extend a single abstract pattern to a group of related line-occurrences; the syllable count may vary, but the basic type prevails.

The Idiosyncratic Nature of Old English Meter

With only these few broad generalizations about the shape of the meter, it becomes clear that the Old English line is very different from the hexameter and *deseterac*. For one thing, we observe an extremely large variation in syllable count, with no apparent restriction on when a certain length is to be used; this allows the poet to juxtapose such lines as *Beowulf* 51–54:

> secgan to soðe, seleræden*de*,
> hæleð under heofenum, hwa þæm hlæste onfeng.
>   Đa wæs on burgum Beowulf Scyldinga,
> leof leodcyning longe þrage

> To say in truth, hall-counselors,
> Heroes under the heavens, who received the burden.
>   Then was in the strongholds Beowulf of the Scyldings,
> Beloved nation-king for a long time

This sequence includes in succession lines of ten, thirteen, ten, and eight syllables. As for the half-line subdivisions (indicated in the quoted passages by spaces), these verses, like the lines they compose, have little or no syllabic definition. Nor are the half-line units necessarily symmetrical in length or structure; they seem rather to have a semi-independent metrical life of their own.[95] As indicated above, the prosodeme on which the meter is founded proves to be the *stress-position* rather than the syllable or mora, and the rather

---

95. This half-line model of metrical organization accounts for the attempt of most metrists to formulate a theory of rhythm in terms of the verse unit. It also accounts for most investigators' focus on the verse as the length of the Old English formula. The so-called single verses—many of these combine with whole lines to form "triplets"—are evidence of a hybrid line structure that exhibits both a whole-line and half-line identity. See further Bliss 1971; Foley 1980b.

loose paratactic relationship of the two verses is formalized by required alliteration.

Unlike the hexameter and *deseterac*, then, the alliterative line obeys no rule of syllabicity; indeed, the expansion rules of resolution and ramification work directly against syllabic consistency. And since the half-line division is correspondingly variable, we can speak neither of a caesura, which would have to occur in a regular spot in the line, nor of the cola demarcated by a caesura. Obviously, under such conditions the notions of anceps and right justification are totally without meaning. Moreover, this synchronic portrait also indicates that, diachronically, the alliterative line has developed much farther away from a possible Indo-European precursor than have the ancient Greek and Serbo-Croatian verse forms. What intervened in this development was the shift of prosodeme from syllable to stress during the Common Germanic period, the various results of which are described by Winfred Lehmann ([1956] 1971, esp. 23–63). The birth of Germanic alliterative verse, he reminds us, was coincident with the shift of stress from a variable position to the initial syllable of a word. Under these circumstances, the Indo-European characteristics imbedded in a syllabically regular line-type would be lost. The general conclusion to be drawn is that the line of *Beowulf* is a verse form tellingly different from those employed by Homer and the *guslar*, and that the difference manifests itself both synchronically in the evidence of the text and diachronically in the history of versification.

Where does this catalog of idiosyncrasies leave us as we enter on a description of the alliterative line, which we aim to make sufficient both to allow comparison with the hexameter and *deseterac* and later to provide a basis for understanding formulaic structure in *Beowulf*? The approach from Indo-European features is blocked by the linguistic reality of the stress shift and its foregrounding as the functional kernel of Germanic prosody. Indeed, it cannot be overemphasized that this is a stress rather than a quantitative meter, a prosody that depends on the stressed position rather than a sequence of syllables for its identity. It is obviously illegitimate to impose a Greco-Roman podic model; outer metric has already proven a treacherous because finally external and superficial concept, and it surely has no possible application here. Nor does the distinction of inner metric—the foundation of formulaic structure in the other two traditions—succeed in addressing the metrical issues of the *Beowulf* line; without consistent syllabicity and a regular caesura- or diaresis-system and its assortment of cola, there can be no inner metric. And yet, if we are to examine Old English traditional phraseology we must confront the prosodic nature of the formulaic structure on its own terms, just as was done above for the Greek and Serbo-Croatian traditions.

The Metrical Foundation

If the history of the alliterative line precludes an approach similar to that employed in studying the hexameter and *deseterac*, we would do better to shift focus and attempt to determine what it is about the line that *does* remain constant from instance to instance. Besides the alliteration mentioned above, most scholars agree that the verse form requires four heaviest or primary stresses per line, and two per half-line:

$$\acute{s}\ \acute{s}\ |\ \acute{s}\ \acute{s}$$

where *s* is a syllable or syllables bearing primary stress ($\acute{s}$) and the rest of the line consists of a varying number of secondary ($\grave{s}$) and minimal stresses ($\overset{\times}{s}$). In many cases, this much information allows complete and unambiguous scansion, as in this example from the earlier passage:

drýhtĕn Géată   dracan scéawĭăn   (*Bwf* 2402)

All four primary stresses are assigned, two to the alliterating elements and the remaining two to the phonologically stressable core syllables of grammatically significant words; resolution and ramification are active in the second verse, yet the line takes a relatively simple shape with a fundamentally trochaic pattern.

But the issue of line- and verse-types rapidly becomes more complicated. As we pass beyond the recurrence of the four "stress maxima" (or SMs), we must deal with what has proven a bewildering variety of permutations. Not only are the most basic features of the line wholly different from those of the quantitative, colonic Greek and Serbo-Croatian prosodies, but the ways in which these different features—SMs, the variable number of secondary stresses and unstressed syllables, resolution, and ramification—combine and recombine to produce the lines of *Beowulf* are also idiosyncratic. To begin to appreciate this aspect of tradition-dependence, consider that

béalonĭð bíornă   hĭm tŏ béarmĕ cwóm   (*Bwf* 2404)

and

Hráðe wæs gĕrýmĕd,   swă sĕ rícă bĕbéad   (*Bwf* 1975)

are, from a metrical point of view, equivalent phrases. Both answer to the requirements of Sievers categories A plus B, even though their syllable distribution and secondarily stressed positions are unequal:

Basic Pattern   / x / x | x / x /

It becomes clear that any attempt to catalog line structure, to seek its systematic and recurrent sequence, must resort to a series of generative patterns. Sievers recognized this necessity for an expansible system from the start and made it a feature of the Five Types, and all later metrists have in various ways responded to the same obvious need.

Patterns and Systems

Among these scholars, John C. Pope offered in 1942 a sweeping and significant revision of the Five-Type catalog. Claiming four isochronous measures to a line (and two to a half-line), Pope discovered that by beating a regular cadence there emerged an unvocalized stress at the head of the metrically acephalic B and C verses.[96] In other words, he substituted a rest for the "missing" initial stress and thus brought both parts of the line into accord by supplying initial ictus where there was no lexical item to bear it. To use his own example ([1942] 1966, 39) alongside the Sievers reading, consider:

> Sievers B: sȳððán ǽrěst wéarð   Basic Pattern xx/|x/
>
> Pope B: ⁽′⁾sȳððán|ǽrěst wèarð   Basic Pattern (/)xx|/x\

He proceeded to apply the initial stress-rest, marked (′), or stress taken in vocal silence, to ʾall types of B and C verses, using as a leveling device the theory of isochrony among the four measures of a line. In experimenting with various lines in the poem, Pope ([1942] 1966, 247–409) argued that this realignment of stresses expressed the natural rhythm of the alliterative line more faithfully than the Sievers system.

From the hypothesis of initial rests in Types B and C and general isochrony, Pope derived another and more daring theory—that of the use of a harp[97] to accompany the performance and specifically to mark time. Although instrumental accompaniment had certainly been considered before,[98] no one had proposed that the lyre actually bore one of the major stresses in the line during a vocal rest. Whether the Old English *scop* really used an instrument in his performance, and what the musical aspect of his narrative might have been like, are problems probably beyond our ability to solve given the present state of knowledge. And although most metrists now resist the harp hypothesis in an effort to fashion theories with as few ambiguous or uncertain features as possible, it is interesting that Pope was able to suggest the use of the lyre purely on metrical grounds. Once the isochrony and initial rest are accepted, the way is left open to the possible participation of a device to mark rhythm.

It is not difficult to see that Pope's theories consist, from our comparative vantage point, of attempts to supply another kind of regularity to a poetic line ungoverned by the more familiar parameters of syllable count, caesura, and the like. The principle of four isochronous measures provided this consistency and rationalized the apparent near-chaos of syllabic count, stress distribution, resolution, and ramification. In place of six metra or four cola, or of five feet or two hemistichs, one had four recurrent rhythmic units; some may have been different, some may have begun with a stress taken on the

---

96. Pope ([1942] 1966) acknowledges his debt to the work of Sievers and Andreas Heusler throughout; see the latter's *Deutsche Versgeschichte, mit Einschluss des altenglischen und altnordischen Stabreimverses* (1925–29).

97. Called *se hearpa* by the Old English poets, the instrument probably more closely resembled a lyre; see Bruce-Mitford and Bruce-Mitford 1974.

98. E.g., Sievers (1893, 186ff.), who doubted that any accompanied poetry had survived.

harp, but all were rhythmically equivalent in extent. In positing isochrony and in thus changing the internal divisions in the Five Types (for example, Sievers B or x / | x / becomes (/) x | / x \ and Sievers C or x / | / x becomes (/) x | / \ x), Pope did more than modify "feet" to "measures." More importantly, he attempted to formulate not just a description that suited the observable facts, but a metrical theory that would *explain* them. However we judge the value of his innovations, we must admire his sense of an underlying order and of the importance of reaching beyond the metrist's catalog to the aural reality of the poetry.

Some sixteen years after Pope's work first appeared, A. J. Bliss argued for a return to Sievers's major principles in *The Metre of Beowulf* (1967). Having undertaken a thorough re-examination of the poem, he explicitly dismisses the hypothesis of isochrony and derives Types B through D from the various displacements of stress in Type A, the core pattern which he considers the "norm of Old English verse" (p. 108). He also groups half-lines into light, normal, and heavy categories, depending on whether they contain one, two, or three stresses. Apart from his philologically indefensible discussion of the so-called caesura, which as we have seen cannot by definition exist in the Old English poetic line, Bliss succeeds in recataloging the lines of *Beowulf* into the Sieversian scheme; but of course this exercise cannot fail, because the Five Types had already proven themselves an adequate descriptive metaphor, if not an explanatory system.

More successful in evaluating the systematic nature of Old English meter was Robert P. Creed's "A New Approach to the Rhythm of *Beowulf*" (1966). Agreeing with Pope on the issues of isochrony and initial rests, Creed goes a step further in elevating the measure to a metrical unit. This is an important rationalization: while Pope posited measures of equal temporal duration, he still based his morphology of metrical types on the half-line or verse. Creed, in contrast, sees the measure as the kernel of prosody from a functional as well as descriptive point of view. With a few modifications made since the original article was published,[99] he proposes seven basic measure-types:

Type	Symbol	Pattern	Example
alpha	α	/ x	þréatŭm
alpha +	α +	/ \	féascèaft
beta	β	/ x \	héarpăn swèg
gamma	γ	/ \ x	wéorðmỳndŭm
delta	δ	/ (x)	þáh ⁽ˣ⁾
epsilon	ϵ	(/) x	⁽⁾xĭn
eta	η	(/) \ x	⁽⁾lǽtà̆ð

---

99. For a more recent report, see Foley 1976a, 1978a, and Creed 1989.

One can see the roots of this system of units in Pope's catalog of half-line types: the α represents one element of Sievers-Pope A; α + is an augmented version of α; and γ and β consist of the second element of Pope's D1 and D2 respectively. It may not be so obvious, but even Creed's ε is equivalent to the first part of Pope's B or C. The δ measure, which includes a vocal rest and minimal harp stroke, allows Creed to scan single-syllable measures and maintain a basically trochaic rhythm, while the η is a logical development from the initial-stress hypothesis intended to handle unstressed syllables at the head of a verse:

$$\overset{(\prime)}{\text{ŏfĕrflēon}} \mid \text{fótĕs trèm} \qquad\qquad (Bwf\ 2525a)$$
$$\quad\;\; \eta \qquad\qquad \beta$$

In this last measure-type, the two syllables in the prefix *ofer-* are themselves unstressed but coincide temporally with the stress taken on the lyre. Thus the necessity for anacrusis, the assigning of such unimportant syllables to the foregoing metrical unit (in this case to the end of the second verse of the preceding line), is avoided and the prosodic wholeness of the line maintained.[100]

One of the more recent thorough treatments of Old English meter is that by Thomas Cable (1974), who presents a strong argument for a rigorous and systematic scansion of *Beowulf* that harmonizes with and builds on the original work of Sievers.[101] Cable, however, goes far beyond a mere reworking of the Five Types, even proposing a few changes at the level of categorization; his concern (p. 85) is to establish "that *Beowulf* can be scanned with four metrical positions to the verse."[102] If one accepts his revisions, the result, as shown in table 14, is a group of five *contours* that correspond to Sievers's Five Types, each contour denoting either rising (/) or falling (\\) stress between successive positions (p. 88). Cable's most telling point is that the four positions inexorably generate the Five Types or contours, with the meter being fundamentally the

100. On the subject of anacrusis in B and C verse-types (which until his work was the standard method of dealing with prefixed verbs in double-alliterating lines and similar configurations involving metrically isolated initial syllables), Pope remarks ([1942] 1966, 64–65): "When there is only one such syllable, it may be treated either as anacrusis or as the up-beat of the first measure, after a rest, the choice depending mainly on the degree of intimacy with the preceding verse. Since mere prefixes cannot be made to fill half a measure even after a rest, these should always be read as anacrusis.... Two unimportant syllables may be treated as anacrusis if the connection with the preceding verse is so close that the two verses together form a single long phrase." Note that the η measure solves these problems systematically, without having recourse to non-metrical and non-grammatical criteria.

101. Geoffrey Russom's generative study of Old English meter (1987) came to hand just as this volume went to press; there was therefore no opportunity to take it into account in this chapter.

102. For example, he shifts Sievers D2 verses (with the pattern / | / x \\) to the E category. By *position* he means (1974, 85) "not only the main metrical stresses but also the intermediate stresses, if there are any, and the metrically unstressed sequences, of which there are often two and always at least one."

TABLE 14.   Cable's Five Contours for
the Line of *Beowulf*

	Contour	Sievers Pattern
A	1 \ 2 / 3 \ 4	/ x | / x
B	1 / 2 \ 3 / 4	x / | x /
C	1 / 2 \ 3 \ 4	x / | / x
D1	1 \ 2 \ 3 \ 4	/ | / \ x
D2, E	1 \ 2 \ 3 / 4	$\begin{cases} / \| / \text{ x } \\ / \ \text{x} \| / \end{cases}$

underlying four-unit pattern. Instead of wrestling with what I earlier called the descriptive level of the Types, he understands the A through E verses as the inevitable product of the four-position system. With the single qualification that the second of two "clashing stresses" cannot be the heavier,[103] he is able to predict contours and Types from positions: of the eight possible configurations, the only three that are not observed in *Beowulf* are those three in which the clashing stress rule is broken. Cable's system of explanation is satisfying because self-contained and inherently logical, and it deserves serious consideration by any scholar in search of the regularities of Old English prosody.

Prosody and Composition

From the metrical foundations of the alliterative line, on which all scholars agree, and from these various accounts of the systemic structure of Old English meter, we can derive a workable model for comparison with the hexameter and *deseterac*. To begin, we have learned that the quantitative, colonic verse form of the ancient Greek and Serbo-Croatian epic poetries contrasts sharply with the stress-based alliterative line, not only in the synchronic evidence of the *Beowulf* text but also in the diachronic reality of the history and development of Germanic versification. Indo-European features are not to be found in the Old English line because they could not survive the Common Germanic shift of lexical stress to the initial root syllable and consequent generation of a stress-based rather than syllabic meter. Synchronically, this shift of prosodeme from syllable to ictus means a line without syllabic constraint, without a caesura, and so on.

But we have seen that the verse form did evolve its own set of metrical regularities, and if we are to heed the caveat of tradition-dependence, we must follow out these regularities on their own terms. Fortunately, all metrists

103. Clashing stresses are successive major stresses. See especially chapter 5, where Cable claims (1974, 73) that "the evidence of alliteration and syllabic quantity indicates that we should redefine those types with clashing stress, stating explicitly that the first of two consecutive stresses must always be the heavier."

agree on the crucial recurrence of stress and alliteration—the two major characteristics of the Old English line—and also on the consistent half-line dimension of the prosody. Verses, in other words, stand together and they stand alone: they are bound into a whole line by the alliterative constraint, and yet they complementarily maintain—like so many subunits in oral epic tradition—an independent, integral aspect as well. Not unlike the Greek hemistich, the half-line retains a full prosodic and a normative syntactic unity; we need only think of the typical Germanic device of poetic variation to appreciate this unitary character.[104] Of course, each half-line can vary tremendously in count and texture, and so we cannot summon the comparative notion of colon. What can be said is that a tradition-dependent subunit does exist and recurs consistently. We may add to these standard qualities the four major stresses (or SMs) in each line, occurring as they do according to regularly observed phonological rules of placement and extent.

As noted above, with these regularities—a stress-based meter, alliteration between verses, half-line units, and four stress maxima per line—we reach the limit of general consensus among metrists. From this point on, all seem to go their own way, whether to isochrony, reconstruing of Sievers's rules, the measure, or stress contours. Their catalogs reflect the nature of their individual procedures: Sievers's Five Types descriptively rationalize all lines but offer no real explanation; Pope's innovations add the regularity of isochrony (modifying Sievers's B and C verses), show attention to aural characteristics, and move toward explanation; Bliss refines Sievers's system to deal with the variability of types; Creed employs the rationalizing power of the measure to fashion a generative seven-item scansion system; and Cable shifts Sievers's D2 verses to the E category, posits a sequence rule for clashing stress, and explains the five contours as the inevitable development of four metrical positions per verse. All of these methods also represent responses to the twin principles of resolution—by which a stress may be borne by two syllables if the first one is metrically short—and ramification—by which the number of syllables in an unstressed position can increase markedly, to as many as five or six in some verse-initial configurations and very frequently to two or three in almost any position. With these two avenues of variation so open to syllabic traffic, the only possibility for systemic simplicity is through a generative series of patterns. Each metrist fashions his own, and, bearing the stamp of their makers, the resultant patterns seem mutually contradictory, or at least exclusive.

But even though their premises and explicative power may differ, the metrical theories we have summarized do "translate" from one to the next, and some basic correspondences among the ostensibly dissimilar descriptive

104. On variation, see esp. Brodeur 1969, 39–70; Robinson 1985.

TABLE 15. Basic Correspondences Among Metrical Theories

	Sievers	Pope	Cable	Creed
A	/x|/x	as Sievers	1\2/3\4	$\alpha\alpha$
B	x/|x/	(/)x|/x\	1/2\3/4	$\epsilon\beta$
C	x/|/x	(/)x|/\x	1/2\3/4	$\epsilon\gamma$
D1	/|/\x	as Sievers	1\2\3\4	$\delta\gamma$
D2	/|/x\	as Sievers	1\2\3/4	$\delta\beta$
E	/\x|/	as Sievers	1\2\3/4	$\gamma\delta$

systems can be discerned (table 15). These, then, are the allowed half-line patterns, presented in each of the four major theoretical forms.[105] They may be rationalized into measures, redivided into isochronous units with initial lyre strokes, or derived from a four-position series, but they all prescribe roughly the same permitted sequences of stresses for verse-types in *Beowulf*. Compositionally, this collection of verse-types will constitute the metrical foundation for our discussion of formulaic structure in Old English, with, synchronically speaking, the wide variety of actual lines developing from these patterns via the generative rules of resolution and ramification.

If these patterns constitute the prosody of *Beowulf* at the level of the half-line, what of the whole-line unit? On the basis of computer studies undertaken to analyze the meter of a machine-readable text of the poem,[106] I have been able to prescribe three favored line patterns that, taken together, account for over 90 percent of the metrically recoverable lines of the poem.[107] These line-types are the most commonly used combinations of the verse-types listed above, and represent the *Beowulf* poet's "choice" of patterns from among all possible combinations of verses. Table 16 indicates the make-up of each of the three *paradigms* in terms of all four metrical systems.

Paradigm 1, which accounts for 54.7 percent of the metrical text of *Beowulf*, consists essentially of an A verse followed by either a B or a C verse, the equivalent notation in Creed's system being $\alpha\alpha$ followed by $\epsilon\beta$ or $\epsilon\gamma$.[108] Like

105. I do not, of course, mean to imply absolute equivalence among the four theoretical presentations, for there are, as indicated above, important differences in the criteria according to which they were formulated and the kinds of explanations they are intended to provide. But it is well to notice that, at the level of describing permitted verse-types, all four systems agree in their essentials.

106. See note 99 above. I take this opportunity to thank David Woods, George Maiewski, and Dorothy Grannis for their assistance in programming.

107. The metrical edition, prepared from the manuscript facsimile by Robert P. Creed and myself, eliminated about 2.3 percent of the poem on paleographical grounds.

108. A relatively insignificant percentage of η verses (2.2% of the recoverable text) can also figure in the second-verse pattern in place of ϵ.

TABLE 16. Metrical Paradigms in *Beowulf*

	Creed	Sievers	Pope	Cable
Paradigm I				
Verse 1	$\alpha\alpha$	A	A	A
Verse 2	$\epsilon\beta$ or $\epsilon\gamma$	B or C	B or C	B or C
Paradigm II				
Verse 1	$\gamma\delta$, $\delta\gamma$, $\delta\beta$, $\beta\delta$	D1, D2, E	D1, D2, E	D, E
Verse 2	either I.1 or I.2	A or B/C	A or B/C	A or B/C
Paradigm III				
Verse 1	either I.1 or I.2	A or B/C	A or B/C	A or B/C
Verse 2	repeat	repeat	repeat	repeat

all verse-types and line paradigms, this abstract pattern can be filled out with a variety of syllabic complements, such as

$$\text{Gréndlĕs gúþĕ mĭd grýruṁ écgă} \qquad (Bwf\ 483)$$
$$\qquad\quad \text{A} \qquad\qquad\quad \text{C}$$

or

$$\text{áldrĕ þínŭm, gĭf hḗ ŭs gĕúnnăn wile} \qquad (Bwf\ 346)$$
$$\qquad\quad \text{A} \qquad\qquad\quad \text{B}$$

—lines which would of course be scanned slightly differently in the Pope and Creed systems, with the B and C verses beginning with a stress taken on the instrument during a vocal rest and the fourth primary stress lowered to a secondary. Also, because the Old English alliterative line demonstrates a half-line as well as a stichic prosody, the paradigms may be reversed; even with the possibility of reversal, however, the prescriptive nature of the paradigms remains exacting. For paradigm 1, verse metathesis simply means B or C followed by A, or $\epsilon\beta/\epsilon\gamma$ followed by $\alpha\alpha$:

$$\text{þǽt þĕ Sǽ-Géatăs sélrăn nǽbbĕn} \qquad (Bwf\ 1850)$$
$$\qquad\quad \text{C} \qquad\qquad\qquad \text{A}$$

The possibility of inversion argues implicitly for an associative relationship between the two verse-types; although the first and second verses are not interchangeable at the level of phraseology, since the second half-line cannot tolerate double alliteration, *at the level of prosody* the half-lines or verses do seem to be interchangeable parts of the larger whole which combine according to paradigmatic rules.

The second of these line patterns, paradigm 2, combines a D or E verse with either half of paradigm 1, that is, either with an A type or with a B/C type:

sórhwỳlmŭm sēað,   sĭðĕ nĕ trŭwōdĕ   (*Bwf* 1993)

E   A

Once again, the order of half-lines may be reversed, as in

hátŏn héolfrĕ,   hēorōdrĕorĕ wéol   (*Bwf* 849)

A   E

Together these two versions of paradigm 2 cover another 24.7 percent of *Beowulf*. The third paradigm is also a recombinant form of the first line-pattern, consisting of either verse-type from paradigm 1 taken twice, that is, either AA or two successive B/C half-lines. Examples include

þǽttĕ sŭð nĕ nòrð   bĕ sǽm twĕonŭm   (*Bwf* 858)

B   C

and

blácnĕ léomăn   béorhtĕ scínăn   (*Bwf* 1517)

A   A

Half-line reversal naturally does not enter the picture here; paradigm 3 is the pattern on which 14.9 percent of *Beowulf* is founded, for a three-paradigm total of 94.3 percent.

The combination of and interrelationships among the verses comprising these line-patterns or paradigms indicate the specific prosodic texture of the *Beowulf* text that has survived to us.[109] In conducting our investigation of phraseological structure in Old English epic, we shall be able to proceed directly to the metrical underlay by referring to the compositional habits of the *Beowulf* poet in precise and rational terms. But the most significant findings to have emerged from this analysis may well be the most general. First, what we have in Paradigms 1, 2, and 3 is a group of *metrical formulas*;[110] the Old English alliterative line as we have it in *Beowulf* consists not of a colon-based, quantitative meter with tradition-dependent features arising from the partic-ular tradition's expression of right justification, but rather a verse-based, stress meter which figures itself forth in a set of multiforms. Second, the nature of these multiforms—in particular, their quality of reversibility—reveals that the poet composes in whole lines with verse substitution, that, in short, his making of the poem is a two-level process.

---

109. We cannot extend the analysis any further, for example in an attempt to distinguish individual from general tendencies, because we lack the kind of comparative material necessary to the investigation. The 3,182 lines of *Beowulf* unfortunately stand alone as our only real example of epic in Old English.

110. Cf. Cable's notion of "melodic formulas" (1974, 96ff.).

CODA

Over the next three chapters on traditional phraseology I shall be applying the insights gained in this treatment of comparative prosody to the ancient Greek, Serbo-Croatian, and Old English epic traditions. As we proceed it will be well to recall that while numerous parallels can be drawn among the three phraseologies, with productive results, we must also remember their individuality. Milman Parry's theory of the formula was, after all, based firmly on determining the "same metrical conditions" that made possible the recurrence of elements of diction, and we have discovered in the present chapter that each epic tradition has an idiosyncratic, tradition-dependent *prosody* that we may expect to exist in symbiosis with a correspondingly idiosyncratic and tradition-dependent *phraseology*. As noted in earlier chapters, and as will be evident throughout the volume, the double focus of comparison and contrast must inform the study of structure in oral traditional epic.

FOUR

Traditional Phraseology
in the *Odyssey*

In this chapter we shall be concerned with applying the findings of chapter 3 to Homeric phraseology, specifically to the traditional diction of the *Odyssey*. Because so much has been accomplished along these lines since the monumental work of Milman Parry,[1] I shall not attempt even a brief summary of previous scholarship, preferring to leave that aspect of the history of oral literature research to other works devoted largely or exclusively to that topic.[2] I choose rather to treat only a few of the most seminal and suggestive of Parry's works, and then only in the interest of opening up the questions to be considered in the body of this chapter. Thus the first section will review a few of Parry's basic premises and some recent responses to the chain of events he began. In section 2 we shall inquire as to what sort of phraseology can be expected in ancient Greek epos on the basis of the tradition-dependent prosody described in the preceding chapter. In the third section we shall turn from theory to analysis, looking at the phraseology of the *Odyssey* in two test cases: the renowned usage of *epea pteroenta*, or "winged words"; and a passage of twenty-one lines to be analyzed for formulaic density but also, and for our particular purposes more importantly, for various kinds of formulaic diction. In the final section I shall gather together what has been learned from these two different types of analyses and propose a general theory of the traditional structure of the phraseology.

---

1. For the antecedents to Parry's work on formulaic phraseology, see the account by Latacz (1979a); and Foley 1988, chap. 1.

2. For a general account, see Foley 1985, 3–77; Foley 1988; Latacz 1979a. M. Edwards (1986, 1988) surveys scholarship on the ancient Greek formula in exacting detail.

THE FORMULA: ORIGINAL CONCEPTS AND DEVELOPMENTS

As many scholars have noticed, it was not until his "Studies" I (1930) and II (1932) essays that Parry first broached the possibility that his earlier demonstration of the *traditional* character of Homer's epics must also mean that they were composed *orally*.[3] What has not been as clearly noted is that Parry also expanded his claims from the limited arena of the noun-epithet systems in the *Iliad* and *Odyssey* to the whole of Homer's diction, and that he did so without the laudable rigor exhibited in his studies of the "traditional epithet" (1928a). His explanation of the term "formula" in the 1930 essay provides an illustration. After defining this phraseological unit as "a group of words regularly employed under the same metrical conditions to express a given essential idea" (1930, in 1971, 272), he goes on to give three examples (Parry's trans.):

ἦμος δ' ἠριγένεια φάνη ῥοδοδάκτυλος 'Ηώς ("when it was morning")
βῆ δ' ἴμεν ("he went")
τὸν δ' αὖτε προσέειπε ("he said to him")

While all of these phrases can profitably be termed formulas, they are not, like the noun-epithet formulas, of uniform type or structure. The first is a whole-line recurrence, a dependent clause that introduces an action; the second and third are core sentences that combine with subjects that specify their predicates. Moreover, there is a large metrical disparity among the three phrases, which, on the model of the hexameter developed in chapter 3, would be classed as whole-line, colonic, and hemistich formulas, respectively. Parry recognized some of the dimensions of this elaboration in a footnote that precedes his formulaic density analysis (p. 275 *n*.1):

> Formulas, in the strictest sense of the term, may be of any length, but in studying them we are forced to exclude the shorter word-groups, for the following reasons. If we dealt with formulas of all sizes we should have an unwieldy mass of material of varying importance, and it would be impossible to compare the formulaic element in different poets by means of the number of formulas found in their verse. In the second place, we must set a limit which will shut out any groups of words which are repeated merely by chance, or as the result of their natural order in the sentence. Accordingly I have regarded as formulas, or possible formulas, only expressions made up of at least four words or five syllables, with the exception of noun-epithet phrases, which may be shorter.

Parry's first criterion for this typology or distinction is subjective: he believed that five syllables would command the hearer's attention and four would not. But the second justification reveals much more about his method and goals,

---

3. On the role of his teacher Antoine Meillet and of Matija Murko in the evolution of his thought, see Parry's own remarks in "Ćor Huso" (Parry 1933–35, in 1971, 439–40).

for he argues (ibid.) that "by insisting on four words in a shorter phrase one puts aside almost all chance groups of connective words." Here and elsewhere it becomes clear that Parry's goal is a quantitative profile, a numerical measure of "traditionality" and, he contends, therefore of orality. He sought, in other words, to analyze and to illustrate *by example only*, and at no time did he contemplate a complete theory of formulaic structure. He is in fact quite forthright on this point (p. 307):

> A full description of the technique [of formulaic composition] is not to be thought of, since its complexity, which is exactly that of the ideas in Homer, is altogether too great. One must either limit oneself to a certain category of formulas, and describe their more frequent uses, as I have done in my study of the noun-epithet formulas, or one must take a certain number of formulas of different sorts which can be considered typical.

The goal of his analysis, then, is a sample to be used as a litmus test for the whole work in its much greater complexity, and the limits he puts on the size of the formula are intended to facilitate his quantitative measurements.

As one example of his extension of the concept of formula from the noun-epithet combinations to other elements or phrases, let us examine the system he uses to illustrate formulas of a certain type, "But when X had Y," where *X* is the implicit subject of *Y*, a verb (figure 2; I have added English translations of the verbs to Parry's diagram [1930, 276]). While this collection of phrases certainly shows a multiformity, it is far different from the particular

Figure 2. Parry's Formulaic System

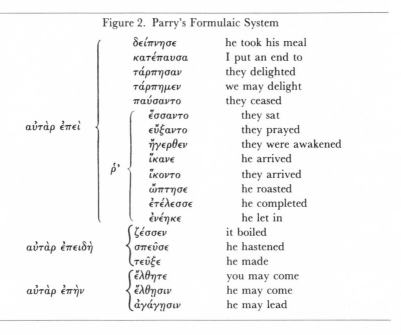

	δείπνησε	he took his meal
	κατέπαυσα	I put an end to
	τάρπησαν	they delighted
	τάρπημεν	we may delight
	παύσαντο	they ceased
	ἔσσαντο	they sat
αὐτὰρ ἐπεί	εὔξαντο	they prayed
	ἤγερθεν	they were awakened
ῥ'	ἵκανε	he arrived
	ἵκοντο	they arrived
	ὤπτησε	he roasted
	ἐτέλεσσε	he completed
	ἐνέηκε	he let in
	ζέσσεν	it boiled
αὐτὰρ ἐπειδὴ	σπεῦσε	he hastened
	τεῦξε	he made
	ἔλθητε	you may come
αὐτὰρ ἐπὴν	ἔλθῃσιν	he may come
	ἀγάγῃσιν	he may lead

systemic character typical of the noun-epithet phrases. Here the emphasis is on the substitutable nature of the verb form, with the only constraint on the actual word chosen being its metrical shape. Each phrase has a clear essential idea, but the group as a whole is too wide-ranging semantically to have one core idea behind it; we cannot treat something as amorphous as "But when X does or did Y" as an element equivalent to the noun-epithet formulas.

Again, Parry was quite aware of the differences among formulas and explicitly addressed that variance in his discussion of the phrase *alge' ethêke* in *Iliad* 1.2. Noting that this phrase, which takes the classic colonic form of the adonean clausula, is not as extensive as some of his other examples, Parry (p. 309) observes that the shorter phrase

> thus belongs to the less obvious part of the technique; yet it would be false to suppose that it is any less helpful to the poet than the longer ones: it is chiefly in the formulas of these shorter types that lie the suppleness and range of the diction, and their usefulness is to be measured by the many different kinds of other short formulas with which they combine.

What emerges from the 1930 analysis, in short, is acceptance of the reality that formulaic diction is in fact a spectrum, that noun-epithet formulas are but one kind of phrase structure within that spectrum, and that the examples summoned are meant to illustrate *pars pro toto* rather than to assist in assembling a comprehensive theory of formulaic structure. By showing what appears to be utility, Parry reasoned, he has shown that traditional Homeric poetry, by analogy to other traditions, is oral.

The reaction to these ideas comprises an epic tale in its own right (see M. Edwards 1986, 1988), but we may point to three quite dissimilar treatments of the Homeric formula that in various ways depended on and reacted to Parry's ground-breaking theories. In 1967 Michael Nagler published an article advocating a generative, synchronic approach to what he called the "traditional phrase" (see also Nagler 1974, 1–63). In his view the locus of "tradition" was in the preconscious gestalt of associations inherited by the singer, associations which were then mapped onto the unique surface structure of the individual performance. One result of this approach is the elimination, welcomed by Nagler and many others, of the dichotomy "traditional versus original" that has gained such currency in a variety of literatures.[4] Another, and for our purposes more significant, corollary consists of enormously multiplying the associative echoes of a given traditional phrase, much as connections between and among ideas can be made in myriad ways, often purely acoustically (Nagler 1974, 8ff.). Since, in Nagler's words (p. 26), "all is traditional on the generative level, all original on the level of performance,"

---

4. This is especially true in Romance language studies, where the terms *traditionalist* and *individualist* (now provided with the prefix *neo-*) denominate fixed and seemingly irresolvable positions. See Faulhaber 1976; Webber 1986.

the phraseological surface of the narrative is of secondary importance to the mythic ideas that underlie it.[5] The surface is infinitely complex because ever shifting, and "a comprehensive systematization of Homer's formulaic syntax can never be accomplished"; he goes on to say (p. 28) that "it now seems more probable that exceptionally simple patterns do not represent the real manner of composition at all, but only appear particularly simple because of secondary factors, complicated by a statistically unjustifiable separation of them from the larger class."

Although Nagler's approach differs considerably from Parry's in his concentration on the preverbal associations that make up the tradition, he too understands the phraseology as an enormously complex instrument that consists of many different types of structures. And, in a departure from more conventional theories, he offers the observation that the most common and most obvious repetitions may not be representative of the diction as a whole, but instead are merely the most immediately obvious sort of patterning discernible. From Nagler's perspective, therefore, "traditionality" cannot be measured quantitatively, since on the generative level all is traditional. In essence, Nagler attempts to detach the notion of tradition from a necessary and one-to-one relationship with formula. While this approach gives a much-needed emphasis to aesthetic considerations and uncovers patterns other investigators had not found, it does not bring us much closer to an appreciation of the actual nature of the phraseology. And unless we are willing to follow Nagler completely in his de-emphasis of the structure of Homeric diction in favor of concentration on the associational web of traditional meaning he sees as its generative matrix, we will lack a philological solution to the problem of the phraseology.

Another model for the origin and deployment of Homeric phraseology was put forth by Gregory Nagy in a book entitled *Comparative Studies in Greek and Indic Meter* (1974; see also 1976 and 1979), which was also discussed in the last chapter. Nagy's theory that from a diachronic point of view formula generated meter and not vice versa, whether or not we accept it in exactly those terms, offers a starting point for a conception of phraseology that takes as its major premise the initial and continuing symbiosis of formula and meter. Certainly, as Nagy himself admits, a metrical norm we abstract from the surviving lines of Homeric epic at some point stabilized and came to serve as a filter for incoming phraseology, but even at that point formula and meter were cooperative and mutually reinforcing. In opening up the diachronic dimension, Nagy also provides a way of understanding how the phraseology is really more like a complicated mix of archaeological strata than a smooth

5. Indeed, he contends (Nagler 1974, 40), "these meanings and the ways in which they are manipulated seem to be, at least in some cases, essentially continuous with the meanings and processes of myth."

surface of substitutable units:[6] his chief example, the Homeric formula *kleos aphthiton*, has roots in Indo-European epic phraseology and is also preserved in Indic verse.

Richard Janko (1982) also furnishes a diachronic view of Homeric style in his analysis of the diction of ancient Greek epos. By testing Homer, Hesiod, and the Hymns for certain kinds of linguistic archaisms and innovations, he is able to assign a relative chronology to the poems involved and to construct a probable "stemma" for the development of the epos from Mycenaean times onward. Janko's study and mathematical analysis are complex, but the unanimity of his findings is impressive: with the exception of the frequency of *n*-mobile used to make position, the percentage shifts of various linguistic features are consistent as one moves from the *Iliad* to the *Odyssey*, then on to the Hesiodic poems and the Hymns (see p. 200). Like Nagy, he emphasizes the evolutionary nature of the diction; while at any one time it may behave synchronically as a substitution system, diachronically it is always developing[7]—maintaining some older elements even as new elements enter the phraseology.

These three conceptions of the formula in Homer open up some questions that need to be addressed by both philological and aesthetic studies. First, as Nagler has shown, the "traditional phrase" can no longer be considered simply a metrical unit that serves a useful purpose in composition. Rather, we should conceive of a spectrum of different sorts of phraseological structures, each redolent with manifold traditional associations that arise as the preverbal gestalt, as Nagler calls it, comes to be realized in the varia of the diction. Nagy leads us away from a purely synchronic and deterministic view of the formation of the phraseology and toward an appreciation of the originative and continuing partnership between formula and meter. And Janko also stresses the diachronic dimension of phrase generation and retention, constructing a realistic model for the ontogeny of the composite diction and its chronologically heterogeneous parts. All three of these studies thus point toward a complication of formulaic theory, a refinement of Parry's original

6. Cf. Peabody 1975; the same concern with diachrony is also apparent in Parry's (1932) discussion of the Homeric poetic language.

7. Of phraseological development Janko writes (1982, 188–89): "In an oral or mainly oral tradition, especially one with a metre as complex as the dactylic hexameter, formulae are preserved over long periods for reasons of convenience, or even necessity, as an aid to composition. Many formulae are handed down through the generations and preserve archaic forms, some extremely ancient indeed. On the other hand, it is clear that there was much scope for flexibility and originality in such traditions. Formulae are modified, where it is metrically possible, in accord with developments in the spoken vernacular, and such modification is an important part of bardic technique. Old formulae, rendered incomprehensible or grossly unmetrical by the passage of time, are replaced by more modern expressions. New formulae are constructed after the analogy of older models, and then there will be totally new elements in the poetry, as new themes are elaborated, and ancient formulae bedded in matrices of new words."

approach (intended, we must remember, only to illustrate by example the extent of schematization of Homeric diction) and a step toward an understanding of the phraseology in its complexity and its richness.

A TRADITION-DEPENDENT
HOMERIC PHRASEOLOGY

Before turning to the series of analyses that will make up the third section of this chapter, let us first weigh the evidence developed about Homeric prosody in the preceding chapter and on that basis inquire what we might reasonably expect of a tradition-dependent Homeric phraseology.

As an initial premise, we recall from earlier discussions that the prosody of the *Iliad* and *Odyssey* is significantly different from those of the Old English *Beowulf* and Serbo-Croatian Return Song (the latter in the *deseterac* meter). Thus, it was argued, the phraseologies in symbiosis with these prosodies cannot be universally comparable; a blanket concept of the formula, for example, fails to take account of the inherent variety of what are finally different natural languages fostering different prosodies. As one manifestation of the principle of tradition-dependence described in general terms in the opening chapter, then, both formula and meter will be tradition-dependent.

The Homeric hexameter, we found, reflected all of the major features of the Indo-European epic verse form, as reconstructed by investigators working in various fields and language families. It demonstrates (1) a quantitative basis, (2) relatively consistent syllabic extent (absolutely consistent in terms of morae), (3) regularly placed caesurae, and (4) what I have called "right justification." Further, this last quality of right justification was seen to be a prominent force in the dynamics of both the inner and the outer metric of the line. To take the latter first, dactyls are favored toward the ends of both lines and half-lines, making these terminal sections more expansive by syllable count and more densely populated by short syllables; this also means that certain metrical shapes will be attracted to these positions and other metrical shapes to other positions. As for the inner metric, it manifests right justification in a longer second hemistich and in relatively more expansive second and fourth as compared to first and third cola. We noted that the principle does not extend to the inner texture of individual cola but that, in general, the hexameter locates the metrically larger elements to the right, or toward the end, of both hemistich and line units.

Let us refer again to the diagram for the inner metric of the Homeric hexameter:

$$\begin{array}{cc} \alpha \ \beta & \gamma \ \delta \\ 1 \mid \cup \mid \cup \mid 2 \mid \cup \ \cup \ 3 \mid \cup \mid \cup \ 4 \mid \cup \cup \mid 5 \cup \mid \cup \mid \ 6 \underset{\smile}{} \\ \text{A1 \ A2} \quad \text{B1 \ B2} \quad \text{C1 \ C2} \end{array}$$

The designations A1 and A2 mark the two possible locations of the first or A caesura, C1 and C2 the two possible locations for the third or C caesura, and B1 and B2 the two possible locations for the mid-line caesura. The *juncture points*, which indicate common positions for word-end but which do not occur with regularity, are designated by the letters *α, β, γ, δ*.

Under such prosodic conditions we may expect first of all a relatively complex phraseology, one that is not easily reduced, for example, to a single kind of formula.[8] One can at least imagine whole-line, hemistich, and colonic phrases, not to mention groups of lines, as recurrent entities. Second, since each of the hemistichs and cola is to an extent idiosyncratic in length and shape, we may also expect a wide variety of formula lengths and shapes, a variety we can start to appreciate by reference to Peabody's "colonic types" as outlined in chapter 3. Third, the degree of complexity and assortment of metrical shapes should also lead us to anticipate a relatively conservative diction as compared to Old English and Serbo-Croatian phraseology. To put it simply, once a phrase passes muster as part of the hexametric traditional vocabulary, it is unlikely to be quickly or easily supplanted. This conservatism is of course cognate to the thrift exhibited by the Homeric line, a feature, let us emphasize, of Homeric verse in particular and not (necessarily) of oral poetry in general.

Finally, we can in general say that the tradition-dependent qualities of the hexameter, as reflected through quantity, syllabic extent, caesura system, and right justification, will exert specific pressures on the formation and dynamics of the phraseology, pressures that are best documented by example (see "Two Phraseological Analyses" below). Taken together, these pressures and the three expectable qualities mentioned above constitute a set of *traditional rules*, that is, a collection of ways in which phraseology becomes Homeric and traditional. Since these rules are by definition tradition-dependent, taking their identity from the idiosyncratic properties of the hexameter prosody, they will be applicable only to Homeric epic. What is more, traditional rules are what

---

8. Cf. Janko 1982, 277 *n*.6: "The hexameter's complexity compared with the simplicity of the stichic metres of other traditions seems to have dictated a higher level of formula rigidity (and also of economy) than is found elsewhere." Contending that these qualities make the Homeric epos seem "more oral" than the comparisons often summoned, he claims that "until a tradition that possesses not only extensive poems covering a considerable period of time, but also a metre as demanding as the hexameter, can be found, the orality of the Homeric tradition will never be approached, though the scop or guslar stand before us and sing. Other epics, be they South Slavic or Saxon, are less formulaic, less thrifty, and less retentive of archaism, and it is the hexameter that makes the difference." While I quite agree with the distinctions he draws and their effect, I must also point out that the absolutism of this statement is somewhat at odds with the principle of tradition-dependence—and thus of pluralism—advocated as the basic theme of the present study. It should also be noted that if one begins by setting up Homer as the unitary example of oral traditional literature, then anything non-Homeric (whether oral traditional or not) will appear, circularly, not to be oral traditional.

differentiate one traditional phraseology from the next; indeed, this is the method we shall use throughout our studies of phraseology, in Old English and Serbo-Croatian as well as ancient Greek epic. From the particular properties of a given prosody we shall be generalizing a set of traditional rules characteristic uniquely of that prosody and therefore of the phraseology with which it is in symbiosis. Analysis of examples from each diction will illustrate the operation of these rules and suggest their importance to formulaic structure. As we turn to that analysis, then, let us keep in mind that on the basis of our investigation of hexameter prosody we may expect to meet a complex and relatively conservative phraseology with units of varying length and internal shape, a diction that responds to and is ordered by a set of traditional rules that are specifically Homeric.

TWO PHRASEOLOGICAL ANALYSES

The purpose of the remainder of the chapter is to fill out the general theoretical statements made above by a series of close analyses of Homeric diction. In an attempt to show how traditional rules operate within a dynamic phraseology, I shall look at a rather large and heterogeneous selection of lines from two different perspectives.[9] The first focus will be provided by the "winged words" formula, long a source of contention among classicists; by examining the occurrences of this phrase in the Homeric epos, we shall determine its status as a formulaic element and try to shed some light on those other elements in the diction with which it combines. In the second part of the analysis, we shall conduct a line-by-line study of a twenty-one-line passage drawn from Book 5 of the *Odyssey* (424-44), with the intention of illustrating the interplay of traditional rules and formulaic structure.

Formulaic Structure and Epea Pteroenta *("Winged Words")*

Ever since George Calhoun's 1935 article, in which he questioned Parry's explanation of Homeric diction according to its usefulness by contending that the "winged words" phrase is employed only when the speaker is in some emotional state, the debate has raged over whether this formula is in fact context sensitive or not. Parry's own rejoinder two years later made the case for a single generic rather than a number of specific meanings, and subsequent

9. In the analyses to follow, the referent against which formulaic density is measured consists of the *Odyssey*, with occasional citations of parallel diction from the *Iliad* and Homeric Hymns (all by reference to Dunbar [Marzullo] [1880] 1962 and Prendergast [Marzullo] [1875] 1971). While I agree with Mark Edwards (1986) that explorations of phraseological multiformity seeking to be exhaustive must take account of variant readings as well, I emphasize that the present study aims not at a determination of orality via formulaic density (if indeed this were possible) or other quantitative goal, but rather at a general demonstration of formulaic structure and the more fundamental role of traditional rules. For this reason I have eliminated variant readings from consideration.

discussion of the matter has neither abated nor reached closure.[10] In a sense the small body of scholarship surrounding this phrase provides a microcosmic survey of some of the most important issues raised by post-Parry studies of the formula in particular and of traditional structure in general.

Our primary interest in this phrase—and it is in my opinion a necessary preliminary to cogent interpretation of the formula as a unit of meaning—is its role in the diction of the epos. How, exactly, is it used? What sorts of phrases combine with it to form longer units? What status does it have as a formula or as a part of a larger unit? How do metrical norms and traditional rules figure in its morphology and deployment? In order to answer these and other questions, we need to search the *Odyssey* for the necessary evidence and interpret that evidence in terms of what we have learned about meter and phraseology from chapter 3.

First, we notice that sixteen of sixty-one occurrences of the phrase consist verbatim of the following line:

$$\kappa\alpha\acute{\iota} \ \mu\iota\nu \ | \ \phi\omega\nu\acute{\eta}\sigma\alpha\varsigma \ | \ \acute{\epsilon}\pi\epsilon\alpha \ | \ \pi\tau\epsilon\rho\acute{o}\epsilon\nu\tau\alpha \ \pi\rho\sigma\eta\acute{\upsilon}\delta\alpha$$
$$\text{A1}\text{B1}\text{C1}$$

On this evidence alone, it looks very much as if *epea pteroenta* comprises part of a larger, whole-line formula that recurs as a single unit. This impression becomes stronger when we take account of the fifteen additional occurrences of "winged words" in lines that vary from the one given above only by insignificant inflections for the gender or person of the speaker. This makes for a total of thirty-one, or slightly over half, of the instances of *epea pteroenta* as recurrences of the same whole-line formula.[11]

But the solution to the question of how the "winged words" phrase is deployed formulaically is not nearly as simple as this large group of lines initially seems to indicate. For alongside evidence for a whole-line formula we find evidence for a second-hemistich system, as in the following examples (partial evidence):

A1
$\kappa\alpha\acute{\iota} \ \mu\iota\nu \ | \ \nu\epsilon\iota\kappa\epsilon\acute{\iota}\omega\nu \ \acute{\epsilon}\pi\epsilon\alpha \ \pi\tau\epsilon\rho\acute{o}\epsilon\nu\tau\alpha \ \pi\rho\sigma\eta\acute{\upsilon}\delta\alpha$ \hfill (18.9)

A1
$\kappa\alpha\acute{\iota} \ \mu\iota\nu \ | \ \lambda\iota\sigma\sigma\acute{o}\mu\epsilon\nu\sigma\varsigma \ \acute{\epsilon}\pi\epsilon\alpha \ \pi\tau\epsilon\rho\acute{o}\epsilon\nu\tau\alpha \ \pi\rho\sigma\eta\acute{\upsilon}\delta\alpha$ \hfill (22.311 plus 2 ×)

$\kappa\alpha\acute{\iota} \ \mu'/\acute{\rho}' \ \acute{o}\lambda\sigma\phi\upsilon\rho\sigma\mu\acute{\epsilon}\nu\text{-} \ \acute{\epsilon}\pi\epsilon\alpha \ \pi\tau\epsilon\rho\acute{o}\epsilon\nu\tau\alpha \ \pi\rho\sigma\eta\acute{\upsilon}\delta\alpha$ \hfill (2.362 plus 8 ×)

$\kappa\alpha\acute{\iota} \ \mu\iota\nu \ \acute{\epsilon}\pi\sigma\tau\rho\acute{\upsilon}\nu\omega\nu \ \acute{\epsilon}\pi\epsilon\alpha \ \pi\tau\epsilon\rho\acute{o}\epsilon\nu\tau\alpha \ \pi\rho\sigma\eta\acute{\upsilon}\delta\alpha$ \hfill (15.208)

$\epsilon\grave{\iota}\varsigma \ \grave{\acute{\epsilon}} \ \kappa\alpha\lambda\epsilon\sigma\sigma\acute{\alpha}\mu\epsilon\nu\sigma\varsigma \ \acute{\epsilon}\pi\epsilon\alpha \ \pi\tau\epsilon\rho\acute{o}\epsilon\nu\tau\alpha \ \pi\rho\sigma\eta\acute{\upsilon}\delta\alpha$ \hfill (22.436)

10. See also Calhoun 1935; M. Parry 1937; Fournier 1946; Combellack 1950; Vivante 1975, 1982.

11. Likewise, in the *Iliad* twenty of the sixty instances of *epea pteroenta* occur in the same whole-line formula.

Quite clearly, *epea pteroenta* also forms part of a hemistich phrase that has a life of its own in the traditional diction; while thirty-one of sixty-one occurrences show one particular, favored combination of hemistichs, this second half-line joins with a variety of partners, some of which are illustrated above. Already we may begin to wonder which identity—the whole-line or hemistich arrangement—is primary.

The picture becomes more complicated when we notice that most of the alternate combinations of *epea pteroenta proseûda* involve a first hemistich composed chiefly of a participle together with one or more function words that help to determine the syntax of the line. In the first two examples cited above, this arrangement echoes the most common whole-line configuration both syntactically and metrically, as the first hemistich is organized by the A1 caesura and the pattern followed is [function wds.] [participle] *e.p.p.* Although we may not wish to accept the idea of a "syntactic formula" (see Russo 1963, 1966; Minton 1965), we must at minimum recognize that the second hemistich has a common association with first hemistich types involving this particular syntax. The association is not as exclusive as that involving a single set of words, but it is well attested, with no fewer than eight different participles found in this position in the *Odyssey* and nine in the *Iliad*.

That this syntactic or structural pattern has some validity of its own is proved by the third and fifth examples cited above. In both of these lines the normal A caesura is blocked by what Fränkel would call a "heavy word," that is, a word of such metrical extent that it overruns one or more of the institutionalized word-breaks in the hexameter. Nonetheless, the pattern of function words plus participle holds, and that unit is joined with *epea pteroenta proseûda* to form one of the series of lines that fit into the general category. Here as elsewhere the evidence points toward the colon as a normative metrical unit but not a phraseological unit, the smallest consistently defined unit of phraseology being the hemistich. The proof in this case is both positive and negative: the hemistich pattern is realized at the expense of blocking the A caesura. Just this much information, especially when suitably expanded by reference to more examples throughout this chapter, should begin to tell us a good deal about whether we can assign contextual meaning to a single colon or hemistich.

The fourth example given above presents a special case of the same pattern being realized through blockage of the A caesura. Here we might propose a slightly different (because more elaborated) whole-line formulaic system:

$$καί \ μιν \ [\text{participle}] \ ἔπεα \ πτερόεντα \ προσηύδα.$$

This model has the advantage—if it is an advantage—of specifying the function words, although it will restrict our idea of the flexibility of the multiform. But apart from these considerations, note that if the participle employed is *epotrunôn*, or for that matter any participle beginning with a naturally short syllable, the A caesura is again blocked. Even though the rest of the line is metrical, and even though other such lines starting with the set of function words *kai min* are also metrical, this particular combination yields a blocked caesura. Such a situation is not unlike the kind of metrical flaws addressed by Parry in his supplementary thesis (1928b), in that a traditional pattern overrides a metrical desideratum. And once again we have evidence that, while the colon is normatively a metrical unit, as far as phraseology is concerned the hemistich is the smallest important unit.

A similar search of the *Iliad* yields comparable results. Of the sixty occurrences of *epea pteroenta*, fully fifty-four combine with *proseuda* to make the second hemistich.[12] Of these hemistich phrases, forty-four are associated with the same [function wds.] [participle] *e.p.p.* first-hemistich pattern as was encountered above. Once again the whole-line and half-line patterns seem to have lives of their own, and once again the rather frequent blockage of the A caesura by a participle that is also a "heavy word" argues the importance of the syntactic pattern as a traditional unit.

Several hypotheses for the traditional structure of the *epea pteroenta* phraseology thus arise. First, we can describe a colonic formula as small as *epea*, which occurs with absolute regularity between the B1 and C1 caesurae; to call this single word a formula, however, would seem quite meaningless, since an "essential idea" is out of the question for a one-word phrase. Here we encounter the initial and most easily resolvable difference between what might legalistically be understood as a phraseological unit and what we might practically interpret as a functional phraseological element.[13] The next possible level of organization would be the noun-epithet phrase *epea pteroenta* as a whole; indeed, its recurrence 121 times in the *Iliad* and *Odyssey* certainly warrants our inquiring whether it might be the compositional kernel of the lines we have examined. But since this phrase is between a colon and a hemistich long, thus having no normative metrical unit to support it, and since it combines (in elided form) with *agoreu-* as well as the much more common *proseuda*, a better hypothesis would be the hemistich system *epea pteroenta* [X], where $X =$ one of these two verbs.

So far, then, we have a choice among colonic formula, hemistich formula (all the occurrences of *epea pteroenta proseuda*, for instance), and hemistich system—but the list must continue. To these possibilities must be added the whole-line formula, e.g.,

$$καί μιν φωνήσας ἔπεα πτερόεντα προσηύδα \quad \text{(1.122 plus 15×)}$$

---

12. The remaining six combine with *agoreu-* (with elision to *pteroent'*).

13. This is not to mention Parry's proscription of any element less than five syllables or four words in length, strictures which, as I tried to show above, were on the one hand subjective and on the other intended to facilitate quantitative explication. It is well to repeat here that Parry excluded noun-epithet formulas like *epea pteroenta* from these requirements.

and the whole-line system, e.g.,

καί μιν [X] ἔπεα πτερόεντα προσηύδα

where *X* can be *phônêsas(')*, *ameibomenos*, and other participles. In fact, we might choose to schematize this system in a structural or syntactic pattern, according to the system [function wds.] [participle] *e.p.p.*

The problem that presents itself, then, is which of these possibilities is the true characterization of the "winged words" formula and its associated diction. On closer examination we find that while each proposal made above has something to recommend it, each is also inadequate by itself to describe some aspect or aspects of the diction involved. The colonic formula, as already mentioned, has no unitary essential idea; furthermore, it breaks the adjective *pteroenta* off from the substantive *epea*. As suggested earlier, and as will be shown throughout this discussion, the colon is a normative *metrical* but not phraseological unit, so this situation is nothing more than could be expected. The hypothesis of *epea pteroenta* as the "atom" around which the diction is constructed also proves disappointing, again for reasons already suggested. The hemistich formula proposition fares no better, since it can account for either *e.p. proseûda* or *e.p. agoreu-*, but not both. Should we select the hemistich system in order to explain both of these phrases, then all of the whole-line patterns will be eliminated from the model. Finally, the whole-line formula hypothesis does not account for the flexibility of the line in its many forms or for other hemistich patterns, and the idea of a whole-line system (which, as we saw, can be conceived as either a semantic or a syntactic pattern) also fails to cover the hemistich patterns. Thus, while conventional explanations do bring us close to the dynamics of the *epea pteroenta* phraseology, none can penetrate completely the complex web of associations surrounding the phrase. What we need is a fresh and complementary perspective that will help to rationalize what seems like a puzzle whose parts cannot be clearly discerned.

Such a perspective is provided by *traditional rules*, which derive, as indicated above, from the tradition-dependent properties of the hexameter prosody. The spectrum of diction observed in association with *epea pteroenta* can be explained by recalling the features of the inner metric as developed in chapter 3, features that stem ultimately from Indo-European verse structure. As a first general principle, we recall that the second hemistich is metrically more spacious and conservative, observing as it does the phenomenon of right justification at the level of the whole line. This general feature accounts for the greater phraseological conservatism of the second hemistich as well, that is, for the fact that there is relatively little variation in the second half as compared to the first half of the line. Thus, it should be no surprise that we observe more variation in the first hemistich, as that part of the line accounts for most of the variation in the whole-line combinations.

At the level of the hemistich as unit, we notice that the metrically more expansive elements—the participles, which are often "heavy words"—are "backed up" against the midline caesura (B1). The force of right justification of this sort, as expressed through the formulaic pattern, is so strong that the participles are located in this spot even if blockage of the A caesura results. Indeed, we have noted above that this caesura is blocked quite often, and we may attribute that phenomenon secondarily to the formulaic pattern and primarily to the right justification that serves as the diachronic foundation for that pattern. Correspondingly, the function words at the opening of the hemistich suit the metrically and grammatically less malleable latter part of the half-line to the narrative and syntactical situation, again following the principle of right justification. And it is well to note that these apparently unimportant and most flexible of words in the line actually adjust the whole line to context as well.

To these general observations on traditional rules we can add more specific measurements based on Eugene O'Neill, Jr.'s, tables of word-type localization (1942).[14] These figures are useful because they reflect the inner metric of the hexameter: against the background of all possible locations for each metrical type are placed the actual percentage occurrences, so that the hexameter's "selection" of favored positions illustrates the influence of the caesura system and right justification.[15] If we examine the figures for the three most commonly occurring words in this group of associated lines, the statistics shown in table 17 emerge. Like all of the shorter metrical word-types, ∪ ∪ __ (the form of *epea*, with *-a* making position) is relatively unrestricted in placement; it occurs with some frequency in four of its five possible positions. The favored position at 7 reflects the fit of this word-type with the colonic form marked by the B1 and C1 caesuras, as well as, from the point of view of the outer metric, the

---

14. My measurements are based on recalculations of word-types made by taking into account the natural quantity of the line-ending *brevis in longo*. Using O'Neill's table 29, then, I have re-figured the percentages for each word-type at line-end; these changes of course meant corresponding shifts in percentage occurrence at other positions in the line.

15. Whereas a full illustration of how the placement of each metrical word-type can be explained on the basis of features described in chapter 3 is beyond the scope of the present study, numerous examples of the correspondence of traditional rules and word-type localization will be given throughout this chapter. In general, colonic forms and placements that do not violate right justification are preferred statistically.

I have adopted O'Neill's system of representing word-type position, now in general use among classicists. He numbers the syllabic elements in the verse consecutively, from 1 through 12, with the arses bearing odd numbers and the theses even numbers. In dactylic metra the two theses are represented as, for example, $1\frac{1}{2}$ and 2. The diagram below will clarify the system:

$$1 \quad 1\frac{1}{2} \, 2 \quad 3 \quad 3\frac{1}{2} \, 4 \quad 5 \quad 5\frac{1}{2} \, 6 \quad 7 \quad 7\frac{1}{2} \, 8 \quad 9 \quad 9\frac{1}{2} \, 10 \quad 11 \quad 12$$

$$— \; ∪ \, ∪ \; — \; ∪ \, ∪ \; — \; ∪ \, ∪ \; — \; ∪ \, ∪ \; — \; ∪ \, ∪ \; — \; \underline{∪}$$

$$\begin{array}{ccccc} 2 & 4 & 6 & 8 & 10 \end{array}$$

TABLE 17. Favored Metrical Positions for
Epea, *Pteroenta*, and *Phônêsas*

Possible positions	Percent occurrence
epea	
7	39.8
5	34.0
3	13.5
9	10.7
11	2.0
pteroenta	
$5\frac{1}{2}$	42.7
12	31.7
$9\frac{1}{2}$	22.6
$3\frac{1}{2}$	2.5
$7\frac{1}{2}$	0.5
phônêsas	
3	52.4
5	33.1
12	7.6
9	6.2
11	0.7
4,6,7,8,10	0.0

consequent certainty of a dactyl in the third metron.[16] It is this position that
epea actually does take, fully in accordance with traditional rules of word
placement.

The metrical type $\cup\cup\_\cup$ (*pteroenta*) also shows some variety in distribution,
with almost all of its occurrences coming at one of three positions. In this
case our example word, *pteroenta*, does not inhabit the most favored position,
but we should also observe both that the three possibilities are statistically
close in percentage occurrence and that the word's actual placement at $9\frac{1}{2}$
hardly constitutes a rare situation. When we add to this reasoning the facts
that placement at $9\frac{1}{2}$ offers the advantages of an initial boundary at C1
and encourages (but does not make certain) the desired dactyl in the fifth
metron, we can start to see that *pteroenta* also follows traditional rules. In fact,
if *epea pteroenta* is taken as the single "word" it seems to be throughout the
diction examined, and therefore is assigned a composite metrical word-type
of its own ($\cup\cup\_\cup\cup\_\cup$), a different and complementary perspective is gained.
For this word-type, rare enough that percentage occurrence figures are insignificant, is found at only three positions in the hexameter: $5\frac{1}{2}$, $9\frac{1}{2}$, and 12.

16. This is also a characteristic of right justification; see chapter 3.

Thus, the noun-epithet phrase as a whole, as a single word, is also well within the operational scope of traditional rules.

The third word, *phônêsas*, belongs to the metrical type ___ ___ ___, which inhabits slot 5 in approximately one-third of its occurrences. This is a common spot for this word-type, particularly because of the colonic form it constitutes, being bounded on one side by the A1 and on the other by the B1 caesura. The only more common position is also a colonic form which reaches from the beginning of the line to the A2 caesura at 3. In the case of *phônêsas*, however, we must take into account the influence of the patterns described above; since most of the configurations associated with *epea pteroenta* favor a participle backed up against the B1 caesura, the pattern—itself based on traditional rules—will to an extent regulate any incoming phraseology and encourage (if not require) placement of all participles in this same position. In this case formulaic phraseology has taken on a life of its own, and, while the birth of the pattern may be traced to traditional rules that are in a sense still operative (if vestigial), it is now apparently the pattern that controls and maintains the diction.

Which, then, is the "truest" characterization of the diction surrounding "winged words"? Is it the colonic formula, the hemistich formula or system, or the whole-line formula or system? The answer offered by traditional rules is clear enough: under their aegis we need not single out any one unit as primary and treat the remainder as derived from that Ur-element. It is quite possible that *epea pteroenta* was the first unit to emerge as a discernible single element, but we cannot be sure. Nor does it matter. Just as Lord (1970; also 1960, 99–123) has warned against seeking a single archetype for a given story or song in oral tradition, so we should beware of treating phrases in isolation—for, long before the Homeric texts that have reached us were recorded, phrases existed not as counters to be shifted about and manipulated algebraically, but rather as parts of larger units (hemistichs and lines), which were in turn parts of ever larger units (themes and songs). Not only did the singers not *conceive of* the kinds of detachable elements we locate by virtue of concordances,[17] but neither was the very phraseology as particle-like as we make it when we analyze the text.

The truest way to conceive of these associated lines is not in terms of either an "atom" of phraseology that attracts various complements or a complex unitary "system" that tolerates variation within its pattern, but rather as a group of lines, hemistichs, and cola associated through traditional rules. This group coheres to the extent that each member was formed first under the

17. See chapter 2 above, and Lord 1960, 30–67. Apropos of Ben-Amos's (1969) distinction between "ethnic" and "analytic" categories, we may note that our analytic category of the *formula* is not only exterior to the ethnic categories of the singer's art but in some ways false to the reality of the phraseology.

aegis of these rules and perhaps secondarily according to a formulaic pattern that, having been formed under the same rules, then assumed a life of its own. The "core" of the phraseology is thus not a particular element or pattern, but the traditional rules themselves. Over time, numerous associations arise between cola, between hemistichs, even between and among whole lines; some of these associations become so institutionalized as to become invariably repeated formulas. Other associations remain at the level of multiform diction, all overseen by the same set of phraseological rules but perhaps developing syntactic or semantic links among phrases as well. Still other associations will drop out of the phraseological inventory altogether, so that overall we are left with some older and some newer combinations (cf. Hainsworth 1978).

This means that the sample of evidence from any one body of material that emerges from any single point in the history of an oral tradition can tell us only a limited amount about the history of the diction. That perspective will be further narrowed by the influence of local tradition, the textual medium, and other matters discussed in chapters 1 and 2. What we should therefore seek, and can seek of course only through analysis of examples, is to understand the dynamics of traditional diction through an understanding of the effect of traditional rules on the expression of ideas. While it will be useful to speak of formulas and systems at both hemistich and whole-line levels, we must remember that our analytic nomenclature does not change the fact that traditional diction consists of a fluid and open-ended set of expressions that follow traditional rules and that can also be related (and even created by analogy) according to patterns built on these rules. If no one hypothesis for the fundamental unit in a series of related lines can rationalize the complex web of similarity and variation, it is simply because no one line or unit is ontologically primary. The phraseology does not merely present the possibility of multiformity; it actively *is* multiform.

Odyssey *5.424–44: Formulaic Structure and Traditional Rules*

In what follows I shall continue to compare the explanations of traditional structure offered by conventional formulaic theory on the one hand and by traditional rules on the other. As a sample passage for this exercise I have chosen *Odyssey* 5.424–44, part of the description of the hero's tribulations at sea after having been advised by the goddess Ino to leave his storm-battered raft. This selection was not made at random, for I wanted the sample passage to fulfill at least two conditions: that it not be an instance of a much-used theme, so that we might avoid too heavy (and unrepresentative) verbatim repetition of formulaic diction;[18] and that it be as far as possible a sample without any special, unusual structure, so that it would be likely to contain a cross-section of phraseology. We are looking, in other words, for an "average"

---

18. Cf. the criteria espoused in Russo 1976.

Homeric passage, one that is neither highly conventional nor (at least apparently) highly idiosyncratic.

The reader will notice that these lines also contain a simile (at 4.432–35), and the question may arise as to whether the analysis of the diction is representative because of the inclusion of such a figure. Again, this choice was quite intentional, since I feel that any theory worth the name should be able to account for all types of phraseology encountered in Homeric narrative, not just this or that subset of the phraseology. While his approach is different from that advocated in this volume, William C. Scott (1974, 136) puts the matter neatly in referring to the similes that occur more than once in Homer: "Consistency in analyzing components of oral poetry demands that the repeated similes be treated as units which were as traditional and autonomous, but also as adaptable, as the basic arming and banquet scenes."[19] However we interpret the similes, we must agree that they are part of Homeric narrative, and so we must deal with their phraseology.[20]

Before presenting my formulaic analysis of 5.424–44, let me set the ground rules for my working notion of *formula* and *formulaic* in Homeric phraseology, remaining quite aware, as indicated in the first two sections of this analysis, that even the most carefully defined units will fall short of uniform interpretation by all investigators.[21] Perhaps the most explicit way of accomplishing this definition of units is first to quote the principles followed by Albert Lord in his widely known article "Homer as Oral Poet" (1967a), and then to comment on each principle before presenting certain modifications or additions of my own. Here, then, are Lord's principles (pp. 25–26):

1. Declension or conjugation of one or more elements in the phrase, providing the metrical length of the phrase remains unchanged.
2. Metathesis, or inversion, or, in general, any change in the order of the

---

19. Scott (1974, 140) conceives of a kind of storehouse of similes from which the poet could draw: "While it is impossible to identify which similes were taken with little or no alteration from the pool of traditional oral units, the examination of the repeated similes demonstrates that the poet did draw upon such a source at the very least seven times." The most recent full study of the similes by Carroll Moulton (1977) agrees in principle with Scott's approach, although Moulton believes that it is not proven that the similes are themselves oral. He feels, in concert with G. S. Kirk (1962) and others, that Homer was the "monumental composer" who put the poems into their present form, and that an oral tradition was certainly involved at some point in their history. Whether the poems as we have them were oral compositions he leaves an open question.

20. As Moulton (1977, 125–26) points out (proceeding from Fenik 1974, 143–44), there are monologues at 408–23 and 465–73 that form a kind of ring or envelope around our sample passage. Both of these monologues are followed and elaborated by similes (432–35 and 488–91, respectively) which signal Odysseus's "endurance in adversity," a major theme of the epic and a quality that "will lead to his ultimate triumph." This conception of structure may account for the texture of the narrative in our sample.

21. Cf. Russo 1976.

words in the phrases as long as the metrical length is preserved and the meaning remains unchanged.

3. Repetition of a formula, even if it be in another part of the line from that of the verse being analyzed.

4. In dividing the hexameter into parts one should consider that there may be lines that should be treated as a whole, that cannot readily be broken into parts. Otherwise there may be normally two or three parts to the verse.

5. When a single word is repeated in the same position in a line, it is conclusive evidence in itself for a formula *only* if the single word occupies the entire part of the line, as happens sometimes with the run-on word or at the end of a line. Otherwise the repetition of a single word in the same position in the line is permissible as evidence only if it is part of a system, which would include the phrase being tested.

To principle number 1 there can hardly be any objection, since morphology is a fact of formulaic life in all three traditions studied in this volume (although they tolerate different kinds and degrees of morphological variation). I would add only the words *and texture* to *length*, since a morphological change that also modifies metrical word-type can affect placement and therefore formulaic structure. The same addition is even more important in principle number 2, since inversion and other changes take place relatively seldom in Homeric phraseology without running afoul of the delicate balance of the inner metric of the hexameter. Once again, the Serbo-Croatian *deseterac* and Old English alliterative line tolerate this kind of change much more readily than the hexameter. The third principle pertains to relatively few cases in Homeric diction, again because of the complex weave of the prosody. Principle 4 proves extremely important, since, as predicted at the outset of this chapter, the prosody allows, or even encourages, the formation and maintenance of units of different sizes. I would add what I consider to be an important modification to this principle, a modification already borne out in our first two analyses: namely, that line and hemistich patterns are not necessarily to be treated exclusively as either the one or the other. We have seen above, for example, that a hemistich formula or system can also participate in a whole-line formula or system, so that in certain cases it is impossible to isolate the "kernel" of a group of related phrases. As for the fifth principle, the idea of making sure that single words have some phraseological context in order to be considered as individual elements in the diction is an excellent one, and we shall have more to say on that score as we go over examples of that phenomenon in the discussion that follows the marked passage below.

Every investigator must make some assumptions about what constitutes valid evidence, and, *pace* those who seek after the chimera of absolute uniformity,[22] scholars will disagree about close cases. In order to make the following

22. Cf. Miletich 1976.

quantitative analysis as uniformly productive of formulas and systems as possible (this goal in turn being an effort to be as open-minded as is practical about the explicative power of conventional formulaic theory), I have resolved the "close cases" in favor of formulas and systems. That is, in those instances which might be better explained by simple word-type localization than by positing formulaic structure, I have for the purpose of the initial quantification called the units "formulaic." In the discussion that follows the analysis, of course, I examine other methods of explanation.

One more assumption should be noted. In concert with what we have learned about prosody and phraseology in chapter 3 and earlier in this chapter, I take the minimal phraseological unit to be the hemistich, not the colon. The latter, we recall, is normatively a unit of meter rather than of phraseology, although the emphasis in that formulation and others must remain on *normatively.* Colonic "words" and phrases do in fact develop, especially in the C1 fourth colon, where, as we have seen, the metrical extent of the line-part is within three morae equal to that of a (B2) second hemistich. There simply is no easy answer to this quandary, no place to draw the line absolutely without mismarking a reasonably large percentage of the diction. The fact that I choose to draw it here does not mean that I do not recognize colonic formulas, particularly noun-epithet formulas like *glaukôpis Athênê.* Even though under my set of assumptions such phrases are taken as parts of formulaic systems and not as formulas in their own right, the final percentages of "formula plus formulaic" will remain the same. What is more, using the hemistich as the minimal unit of phraseology allows a quantitatively defensible scheme of representation, since we can calculate percentages based on hemistichs and whole lines. Otherwise, calculation would either have to proceed by cola or have to place formulas and systems of various lengths against a single standard. Both alternatives are fatally flawed.[23]

What follows, then, is a formulaic analysis of 5.424–44 carried out under the principles established and discussed above. The Greek text is underlined to reflect those words which actually occur elsewhere in what I take (with generous definition) to be formulas or systems, with the minimum unit of phraseology understood to be the hemistich. Wherever the structure of a line is such that one could posit either a hemistich or a whole-line unit, I have consistently marked and counted it as an instance of the larger, whole-line

---

23. One cannot use cola as a base because not only is the colon normatively a metrical unit, but many cola are much too short to provide a site for formulaic structure (consider the three-mora third colon between a B2 and a C1 caesura, which would have to be assessed for formulaic character if cola were used as a basis for calculation). The other alternative, calculating the percentage occurrence of phrases of various lengths against a uniform standard, is logically untenable.

We also recall that the present analysis has as its goal only a diagnostic examination of formulaic theory, and not a determination of orality on the basis of formulaic density.

unit.[24] Likewise, if both an exact repetition and inexact, formulaically related phrases occur, I have taken the line or hemistich as a formula without further notation. My literal translation of the passage is appended, along with a summary of the results and supporting evidence for the judgments made about individual lines (at least one comparand for each unit identified).

ἧος ὁ ταῦθ' ὅρμαινε κατὰ φρένα καὶ κατὰ θυμόν,
τόφρα δέ μιν μέγα κῦμα φέρε τρηχεῖαν ἐπ' ἀκτήν.   425
ἔνθα κ' ἀπὸ ῥινοὺς δρύφθη, σὺν δ' ὀστέ' ἀράχθη,
εἰ μὴ ἐπὶ φρεσὶ θῆκε θεὰ γλαυκῶπις Ἀθήνη·
ἀμφοτέρῃσι δὲ χερσὶν ἐπεσσύμενος λάβε πέτρης,
τῆς ἔχετο στενάχων, ἧος μέγα κῦμα παρῆλθε.
καὶ τὸ μὲν ὣς ὑπάλυξε, παλιρρόθιον δέ μιν αὖτις   430
πλῆξεν ἐπεσσύμενον, τηλοῦ δέ μιν ἔμβαλε πόντῳ.
ὡς δ' ὅτε πουλύποδος θαλάμης ἐξελκομένοιο
πρὸς κοτυληδονόφιν πυκιναὶ λάϊγγες ἔχονται,
ὣς τοῦ πρὸς πέτρῃσι θρασειάων ἀπὸ χειρῶν
ῥινοὶ ἀπέδρυφθεν· τὸν δὲ μέγα κῦμα κάλυψεν.   435
ἔνθα κε δὴ δύστηνος ὑπὲρ μόρον ὤλετ' Ὀδυσσεύς,
εἰ μὴ ἐπιφροσύνην δῶκε γλαυκῶπις Ἀθήνη.
κύματος ἐξαναδύς, τά τ' ἐρεύγεται ἤπειρόνδε,
νῆχε παρέξ, ἐς γαῖαν ὁρώμενος, εἴ που ἐφεύροι
ἠιόνας τε παραπλῆγας λιμένας τε θαλάσσης.   440
ἀλλ' ὅτε δὴ ποταμοῖο κατὰ στόμα καλλιρόοιο
ἷξε νέων, τῇ δή οἱ ἐείσατο χῶρος ἄριστος,
λεῖος πετράων, καὶ ἐπὶ σκέπας ἦν ἀνέμοιο.
ἔγνω δὲ προρέοντα καὶ εὔξατο ὃν κατὰ θυμόν·

While he was turning these things over in his mind and in his heart,
Just then a great wave bore him toward the rugged shore.   425
His skin would have been torn, his bones all battered together
Had not the flashing-eyed goddess Athena inspired him.
As he was rushing on he grasped a rock with both hands
And, groaning, held on while the great wave passed over.
And in this way he escaped the wave at first, but surging back again   430

24. It is important to note that not all lines that show two hemistich systems can support the hypothesis of a whole-line system. Some hemistich patterns are *conjunctive*, in that they form a larger whole as well as two smaller patterns, and others are *disjunctive*, in that they occur together only once in the *Odyssey* and therefore cannot be shown to form a whole-line traditional unit.

It struck him rushing on, and cast him far out into the sea.
As when an octopus is dragged from its lair
And the close-packed stones are held in its suckers,
So the skin was torn from Odysseus' hands
By the rocks. And the great wave covered him over.   435
Then, having reached beyond his measure, Odysseus had surely
    perished, miserable,
If flashing-eyed Athena had not given him presence of mind.
Emerging out of the wave, which belched in to the land,
He swam close by, looking toward land to see whether
He could discover the sloping shores and harbors of the sea.   440
But when indeed, swimming along, he came to the mouth
Of the fair-flowing river, the best place presented itself to him,
Free from rocks, and there was shelter against the wind.
And he saw the river flowing out and prayed in his heart.

The list below summarizes the analysis carried out on *Odyssey* 5.424–44
(see also the formulaic density statistics in table 18).

5.424   whole-line formula (4.120, 5.365)

5.425   hemistich 1 formulaic (3.295 plus 12 × *mega kuma*)
       hem. 2 formulaic (14.1)

5.426   hem. 2 formulaic (12.412)

5.427   whole-line system (16.291 and 4 × add.)

5.428   hem. 1 formula (4.116, 24.316)
       hem. 2 formulaic (22.307, 22.310)

5.429   hem. 1 formulaic (9.415)
       hem. 2 formulaic (see 5.425, hem. 1 above)

5.430   hem. 2 formulaic (9.485)

5.431   hem. 1 formulaic (18.57 and 2 × add.)
       hem. 2 formulaic (1.438 and 6 × add.)

5.432   no related phrases

5.433   hem. 2 formulaic (5.329)

5.434   hem. 1 formulaic (5.156)

5.435   hem. 1 formulaic (14.134, 21.301)
       hem. 2 formulaic (see 5.425, hem. 1 above)

5.436   hem. 1 formulaic (6.206 and 10 × add.)
       hem. 2 formulaic (1.34, 1.35)

5.437   hem. 2 formulaic (1.44 and 48 × add. in nom. case)

5.438   hem. 1 formulaic (5.257)
       hem. 2 formulaic (5.56 and 6 × add.)

5.439   hem. 1 formulaic (5.399)
       hem. 2 formulaic (5.417)

5.440   whole-line formula (5.418)

5.441   hem. 1 formulaic (6.85, 12.1)
       hem. 2 formulaic (18.97)

5.442   hem. 2 formula (7.281)

TABLE 18.   Formulaic Density Statistics for *Odyssey* 5.424-44

Level	Formula	Formulaic System	Formula and Formulaic System
Line	$3/21 = 14.3\%$[a]	$1/21 = 4.8\%$	$4/21 = 19.0\%$
First hemistich[b]	$4/21 = 19.0\%$	$11/21 = 52.4\%$	$15/21 = 71.4\%$
Second hemistich	$4/21 = 19.0\%$	$15/21 = 71.4\%$	$19/21 = 90.5\%$
Both hemistichs (average)	$8/42 = 19.0\%$	$26/42 = 61.9\%$	$34/42 = 81.0\%$

[a] Verbatim formula

[b] For the purposes of quantification only, I have counted each whole-line repeat as a repeat in each hemistich. As explained in note 24, this categorization ignores the difference between conjunctive and disjunctive hemistich patterns. See further the discussion below of 5.424-44.

5.443   whole-line formula (7.282)
5.444   hem. 1 formulaic (11.390 and 4 × add.)
         hem. 2 formulaic (20.59 and 2 × add. *hon kata thumon*; total of 20 × *kata thumon*)

Discussion of the Passage

In general, it is clear that the second hemistich shows more traditional patterning—both of formulas and of formulaic phrases—than does the first. Although we are not attempting to classify the text as oral or written on the basis of these figures, the hemistichs do reveal this obvious reflex of right justification. In what follows, I shall annotate these quantitative measurements, glossing them where necessary with additional information and offering alternative explanations of phraseological structure where appropriate.

5.424. Counting this line as a whole-line formula obscures its component parts and their innate flexibility in combination. First, the second-hemistich formula occurs eleven times in addition to 5.424 and its two verbatim repeats. One could also relate another whole-line formula (24.235), μερμήριξε δ' ἔπειτα κατὰ φρένα καὶ κατὰ θυμόν, which, with allowed morphological variation, occurs three times in the *Odyssey*, but this explanation would likewise not take note of the other first-hemistich partners with which *kata phrena kai kata thumon* joins. Or, alternatively, we might choose to explain this line as one realization of a formulaic pattern [X] ὅρμαινε κατὰ φρένα καὶ κατὰ θυμόν, where X represents either function words or the participial structure *hedzomenos d'* in the other instance at 6.118. While this hypothesis has the advantage of indicating some of the flexibility associated with this group of related phrases, it too falls short of a complete and synthetic description.

To begin with, we may note that while the second hemistich of 5.424 joins with many partners, the first hemistich is found only in this particular combination. This situation then suggests that, although we shall not be able to reduce this collection of lines to a single kernel element and a series of elaborations, we should focus our analytical efforts on the second hemistich in order to determine what makes it so consistently realized as a formula in its own right. The word-type localization of *thumon* offers a clue: the metrical shape __ ∪ generally occurs only 13.8 percent of the time at line-end (position 12), but *thumon* turns up at 12 in fully 34.3 percent of its 102 occurrences. Clearly, then, some process is interfering with the average distribution of this word.

As we have already learned, Homeric phraseology tends toward "larger words" composed of smaller, individual words. Once admitted as larger groupings, such amalgams function as unitary word-types. Although their individual word-types had to be favorable to combination and localization (or at least permissible) in order for the amalgamation to take place, the composite structure then takes on a life of its own. This is precisely the case with the word *thumon*, whose thirty-five occurrences at line-end are broken down as follows:

kai kata thumon	11	C_2+
megalêtora thumon	6	C_1+
hon kata thumon	4	C_2+
kata thumon	4	non-colonic
all others[25]	10	

The first three phrases, all of them colonic forms, are composite "words" that act as larger units and obey traditional rules that apply to those units; thus *kai kata thumon* and *hon kata thumon*, for example, occupy the most favored location for an adonean shape, position 12. Under traditional rules, which designate position and sequence through right justification and the caesura structure of the inner metric, a group of colonic forms has grown up around *thumon*. Various levels of fossilization are apparent: hemistich, colon, and shorter phrase. Some of these possibilities are extremely useful for combination with a variety of less fossilized partners, and so we also encounter 5.424 and its entourage of verbatim repeats and more distant relatives. The point is that none of the lines treated is in any sense "archetypal" or "seminal," and yet the similarities are unmistakable. All of them took shape under traditional rules; whether those rules are active in the formation of the line at hand or to differing degrees vestigial because it was under their guidance that a fossilized element must originally have come into being, we must ascribe the traditional structure of these lines—both individually and as a group—to their influence.

25. Some of the occurrences in this category are likewise to be explained as colonic forms, but none is frequent enough to merit individual consideration. A few also exhibit a blocked C caesura, so that they in effect modulate to hemistich units.

5.425. Although the argument can be made that both of these hemistichs are formulaic, we come nearer the true structure by explaining them as instances of word-type localization. The phrase *mega kuma*, a composite "word" that recurs twice within this very passage (5.429, 5.435), behaves as if it were a ∪∪—∪ shape, with favored positions at $5\frac{1}{2}$, $9\frac{1}{2}$, and 12.[26] The first two of these placements, both of which result in colonic forms, are favored because of their accordance with the inner metric of the hexameter, and are more basic to the formation of the phraseology than the hemistich patterns for which they serve as the foundation.

The evidence for a system in the second hemistich is even flimsier, with the hypothesis resting on the single line 14.1: Αὐτὰρ ὁ ἐκ λιμένος προσέβη τρηχεῖαν ἀταρπόν. Since there is nothing in the syntax that relates this line and 5.425, we must dismiss the notion that calling this hemistich formulaic leads us toward a better understanding of it as traditional phraseology. What is operative in this case is simple localization, with *trecheian* taking one of the two positions ($5\frac{1}{2}$, $9\frac{1}{2}$) that together account for over 90 percent of the occurrences of this word-type. While we must discard the label of formulaic system for this hemistich, then, we can still see traditional rules playing a dynamic role in its formation.[27]

5.426. Here conventional formulaic theory works quite adequately, calling to our attention the existence of the fourth colon in 12.412: πλῆξε κυβερνήτεω κεφαλήν, σὺν δ᾽ ὀστέ᾽ ἄραξε. The only drawback to this explication is its positing of a second hemistich that can, for reasons given above, be understood only as formulaic. This account of the line's structure downplays the integral nature of *sun d' oste' araxe*, which, although only colonic in extent, is a complete syntactic element by itself and from all points of view a unit to which nothing need be added to fill out a larger structure.

In part, this difficulty is due to the stricture we have advocated about the hemistich as the smallest unit of phraseology, and the situation is in part ameliorated by the continuing emphasis of this chapter on the normative—and not absolute—functions of both colon and hemistich. That is, it has been noted that the C1 fourth colon is extensive enough a site to permit the

26. The actual figures for *mega kuma* coincide generally with these word-type (WT) localization figures. Seven instances occur at $5\frac{1}{2}$ (WT = 42.7 percent), five at $9\frac{1}{2}$ (WT = 22.6 percent), and one at 12 (WT = 31.7 percent). We may ascribe the relative paucity of instances at 12 either to the small size of the sample or, more likely, to the second-hemistich system apparent in 5.296, 5.435, and 14.315 (which may have helped to fossilize *mega kuma* in a yet larger structure).

27. Compare the two occurrences of *trecheian* in the *Iliad* (2.633, 2.717), both of which occupy line-end position (at 12). In both cases the adjective has joined with a proper name to form a composite "word" nearly a hemistich in length (preceded by *kai*). The nature of this larger "word" or amalgam is made clearer by the fact that (a) both C caesura positions are blocked by the proper name and (b) the preceding, and presumably optional, *kai* illustrates the malleability typical of right-justified units.

formation of phraseology,[28] and that we should not try to fashion an exclusive and unbending rule from what is actually a strong tendency. In the larger context, we must also remember that the diction forms according to traditional rules of word-type localization and inner metric, and that, other things being equal, the principle of right justification favors patterning (or fossilization) toward the end of the line and intra-linear units. In this case that process of fossilization has satisfied traditional rules that pertain to the C1 fourth colon, and a phrase has been created that becomes useful, or so it appears, in composition.

5.427. This line does not quite as easily yield up its structure to conventional formulaic theory, for behind the convenient approximation of "whole-line system" used for quantitative purposes lies a mélange of interlocking units that do not fall out into additive parts. The second hemistich, for example, can be understood as the full noun-epithet formula *thea glaukôpis Athênê* or as the shorter version *glaukôpis Athênê*; the *Odyssey* contains thirty-two occurrences of the former and eighteen of the latter, and both phrases combine with a wide variety of partners. Nevertheless, in addition to the lines that allow us to posit a whole-line system [X] ἐπὶ φρεσὶ θῆκε θεὰ γλαυκῶπις Ἀθήνη, where X stands for *têi d' ar'* in the two additional occurrences, we also find evidence for a first-hemistich system [X] *phresi thêke*, where X varies widely.

Once again, however, traditional rules help to put the phraseology into perspective. Right justification explains the second-hemistich pair of noun-epithet formulas not simply as bi-forms that fit snugly into the correct spots, but as matched elements that typically allow for flexibility at the opening. Likewise, not only is *phresi thêke* backed up against the mid-line break with the initial part of the first hemistich open to syntactic adjustment, but as a composite "word" this expression also occupies the position most favored for its metrical word-type. Viewing the two hemistichs from this perspective relieves us of the necessity of wrestling with the complex multiformity of the "whole-line system" and points the way toward understanding 5.427 and related phraseology as the partially fluid, partially fossilized medium that it is.

5.428. Since conventional theory offers a satisfactory interpretation of this line, I shall not pause long over its finer points. Suffice it to note that the first-hemistich formula blocks the A caesura, and that the consequent lack of flexibility must have contributed to preserving this phrase as an integral whole. It is entirely detachable from its present partner, which in turn is a classic example of a system (again with a blocked caesura) that is nonetheless formed under traditional rules.[29]

5.429. Since the only other occurrence of *stenachôn* shows no formulaic

---

28. Thus Kirk's claim (1966) that the C1 caesura is an alternate mid-line break. See also Kirk 1985, 24–30.

29. Note that *epessumenos* is at position 9, the most favored locus for its word-type (76.5 percent).

relationship whatever to this line (although it too occupies position 5), this first hemistich must realistically be classed as non-formulaic. This placement does, however, follow traditional rules of localization (second most favored position, 34.0 percent) and right justification. Moreover, as was apparent from the earlier discussion of *epea pteroenta*, participles are especially preferred just before the mid-line caesura. The second hemistich, again involving *mega kuma*, this time shows a truer formulaic system than was discovered in relation to the first-hemistich occurrence of this composite "word" in 5.425. This difference is due immediately to the more extensive C1 fourth colon, and ultimately to the principle of right justification which underlies colon formation.

5.430. Of the first hemistich all that can be said is that it follows right justification in its general ordering of elements and in the placement of *hupaluxe* in its most favored position by word-type. In a sense this sequence of words amounts to the antithesis of, for instance, the noun-epithet formula treated above, *(thea) glaukôpis Athênê*, the former being apparently a "nonce" creation and the latter a fossilized, composite "word." Prior theories would treat these two phrases as diametrically opposed, and there is no doubt of the difference in structure and deployment between the two. But what that dichotomy obscures is the fundamental fact that both obey traditional rules; both phrases take shape under the guidance of word-type localization and other aspects of right justification. The phrases for Athena (really a matched pair as already observed) exemplify the end result of the traditional process, whereby—to put it gnomically—words have jelled into "words" and the rules have become vestigial for individual components, while in the first hemistich of 5.430 those same rules are active and dynamic. Of course, because of its difference in compositional function, the latter sequence is likely to remain ephemeral, and we must always keep in mind that phrases—even if created under the same set of strictures—develop according to their role in the compositional process. Nonetheless, at the source of this development, no matter what its direction or eventual product, we discern the guiding force of traditional rules.

The second part of the line, typically more structured than the first, forms around the placement of *palirrothion* at position 9, the placement of choice for this word-type (76.5 percent, as with *epessumenos* in 5.428). Since the only other occurrence of this word (9.485) is found at position 9 but bears no formulaic resemblance to the present phrase, we must conclude that the governing principle behind the second-hemistich phraseology is once again traditional rules and not a hypothetical system (which would at any rate still be based on those rules).

5.431. On the evidence of three line-initial instances of *plêx-*, one might perhaps insist on maintaining a formulaic system as the best explanation of the first hemistich. However, the colon structure varies over these examples, as does the syntax, and we may more easily interpret this phrase as the product of a compromise in localization. Position 5 is the only other possibility besides 9 (see 5.430, 5.428) for a word of the metrical shape of *epessumenon*, and, as noted earlier, participles are favored just before the mid-line break (cf. 5.314). With this common participial shape backed up against the B1 caesura, the hemistich is in effect open to the typical kind of initial modification we have encountered many times before in the hexameter.

Likewise, parallels can be cited that seem to argue for [X] *embale* [Y] as a system, the most prominent being [X] *embale chersin*, which occurs three times. But this explanation then runs into the complication of the variety of forms in which line-final *chersin* participates. One firm handhold in this sea of related but complexly interwoven phraseology is the regularity with which adonean clausulae form. These C2 fourth cola are, in turn, very often based on the placement of spondaic words at line-end (58.9 percent by word-type alone).[30] To show how *embale pontôi* can be understood as the product of the same process, I adduce the six Odyssean examples of another adonean—*eureï pontôi*:

$$\text{ἀλλ' ἔτι που ζωὸς κατερύκεται εὐρέϊ πόντῳ} \qquad (1.197)$$

$$\text{εἰς δ' ἔτι που ζωὸς κατερύκεται εὐρέϊ πόντῳ} \qquad (4.498)$$

$$\text{ὅς τις ἔτι ζωὸς κατερύκεται εὐρέϊ πόντῳ} \qquad (4.552)$$

$$\text{ὦκα δ' ἐφοπλίσσαντες ἐνήσομεν εὐρέϊ πόντῳ} \qquad (2.295)$$

$$\text{ἠῶθεν δ' ἀναβάντες ἐνήσομεν εὐρέϊ πόντῳ} \qquad (12.293)$$

$$\text{ἡμεῖς δ' αἶψ' ἀναβάντες ἐνήκαμεν εὐρέϊ πόντῳ} \qquad (12.401)$$

While all six lines share the same line-final phrase, which has itself formed under traditional rules, it is deployed in a variety of ways. The first three examples offer an illustration of right justification and the morphology of formulaic diction, as what amounts to a three-colon phrase based on the adonean shows the typical malleable opening that allows for adjustment to syntactic context. Exactly how flexible this first colon is may be understood by noting that this opening part of the hemistich and line varies the position of *eti* according to the other function words, which are in turn dictated by the situation-specific usage. The second group of three examples illustrates another kind of morphology, which involves an alternate B caesura and second-hemistich formula. In all of these cases the present participle is, as might be expected, backed up against the mid-line break, and variation, as in the first group of lines, takes place primarily in colon 1, as prescribed by right justification.

Instead of insisting on a formulaic system for the second hemistich of 5.431, then (and instead of insisting on one or another formula for lines involving *eureï pontôi*), I would advocate explaining both situations via traditional rules,

---

30. A relatively large percentage (in fact the highest) for such a short word-type—that is, for a word-type that can, at least theoretically, take so many different positions in the hexameter.

which favor the formation of an adonean "word" to occupy position 12.[31] Widening the focus to take account of the entire hexameter instrument, in lieu of limiting interpretation to a single word-group produced by that instrument, allows us to credit the poet with a more flexible, multiform linguistic medium, a medium well suited both in its malleability and in its referentiality to the twin goals of compositional aptness and traditional art.

5.432. At first sight there seems to be nothing traditional about this line. The lack of demonstrable formulaic expressions in either hemistich can be attributed at least in part to the fact that this is the first line of the famed "octopus simile." And this in turn means not only that the vocabulary to be employed here and throughout the simile will be far less familiar than in the straight narrative part of the poem, but also that this particular simile, unassociated with any others by Scott (1974), stands alone and unconnected with the rest of the Homeric poems. It is in short no wonder that we find no evidence of patterned diction in the concordance.

But if the words themselves are not repeated, the rules under which they combine to form this and all other lines are ever present, and this unique line thus provides a good test case for seeking traditional structure through the influence of rules rather than through the phraseology which is their issue. We must first acknowledge *hôs d' hote* as one possible realization of the initial multiform partner of the *hôs . . . hôs* frame that marks all similes in Homer, with its opposite number to be found at the beginning of 5.434. From that point on, this line is purely the creation of right justification and traditional rules, as all three word-types take their most favored positions: *poulupodos* at 5, *thalamês* at 7, and *exelkomenoio* at 12.[32] There are no signs of agglomeration of these elements at all; no caesurae are blocked, no formulas or systems disturb the word-type distribution, and each word behaves individually according to its type. In comparison with other lines examined in this section, 5.432 seems to be a line formed according to traditional rules but without much probability of multiformity. It seems, in short, like a simile.

5.433. This line is not much more productive of classically defined formulas or systems than the one preceding, and for many of the same reasons. Nevertheless, we do notice the hapax legomenon *kotulêdonophin* backed up against the mid-line caesura as would be expected; in this case, the blocked A caesura is of no great import because a word of such extent must block

---

31. On adoneans, cf. Nagler 1974, esp. 5–9; and Ingalls 1972. Note also that while by word-type we would expect only 58.9 percent of the occurrences of *pontôi* to be line-final, in actuality fully thirty of thirty-seven, or 81.1 percent, are at position 12. This disparity can be traced to deflection of the normal distribution by the patterned phraseology that we have examined, in which *pontôi* is fossilized as part of a composite "word."

32. By word-type, $\_\cup\cup\_$ occurs 48.6 percent of the time at 5; $\cup\cup\_$ 39.8 percent at 7; and $\_\_\cup\cup\_\cup$ is a rare type exactly equal to a C1 fourth colon.

one of the caesurae no matter where it is located.[33] Of the many examples of *echontai* and its relatives in the *Odyssey*, none really matches the syntax of the second hemistich, and so the interpretation of that section of the line as a formulaic system is legalistic at best. What we can say about the latter part of the line is that *echontai* and its morphological kin (*ech-* plus __ __ or __ᵕ) occur 105 times in the poem, with fully 91.4 percent of them at line-end, in harmony with word-type localization. This placement then associates with numerous other words in different combinations to form a wide variety of patterns, not all of them classically formulaic, that cannot be reduced to sets of units.[34]

5.434. This line also shows signs of being "nonce" diction, that is, phraseology composed according to traditional rules without discernible roots shared by the rest of the *Odyssey* diction. The hypothesis of a first-colon system rests on *petrêisi*'s recurrence at $5\frac{1}{2}$ in 5.156, an interpretation made somewhat more attractive by the fact that it is also preceded by a preposition there, forming an identical accentual grouping. But we must also contend both with the repetition of *pros petrêisi* in line-initial position at 9.284 and with the reality that word-type localization of the composite form (proclitic plus *petrêisi* or __ __ __ ᵕ) is the most basic determinant of position at $5\frac{1}{2}$.

Traditional rules and right justification are even more obviously behind the formation of the second hemistich, which has no possible formulaic relatives whatever. The adjective *thraseiaôn* may block both positions for the C caesura, but it does take the position most favored for its word-type (51.7 percent). And the importance of considering words in their accentual groupings is illustrated by *cheirôn*, which in position 12 seems generally to go against localization rules; although the spondaic word is at 12 fully 58.9 percent of the time, *cheirôn* occurs there in only 12.5 percent of its instances.[35] In the present case we must look to the accentual grouping *apo cheirôn*, or ᵕ ᵕ __ __, which turns up at position 12 every one of the forty-four times it is employed in O'Neill's sample of one thousand lines. Thus both hemistichs show signs of being "nonce" diction, but still diction that depends on traditional rules.[36]

33. In effect, of course, the "word" is a hemistich long because *pros* is proclitic.

34. I note in passing that another word in the second hemistich leads us to an interesting example of Parry's idea of analogy. Under traditional rules the words *pukinon* and *lechos* ("close" or "thick," and "bed," respectively) combine to form a composite "word," a colonic form (B1/C2) of which there are four instances in the *Odyssey*, all localized in the third colon (the prime position for the composite type ᵕᵕ__ᵕᵕ [63.2 percent]). We also find a singular instance of *pukinon lochon* ("close place of ambush"), which may be understood as the product of analogy because *lochon* behaves so differently in its other appearances.

35. Again, as with *pontôi*, the reason for this deflection is fossilization of the individual word within a larger pattern, which then obeys rules appropriate to the larger word-type.

36. It is worth mentioning in passing that a blocked caesura such as the one in 5.434 very often marks phrases that are at one of two extremes, either highly formulaic (usually straight formula; cf. the usage of *trêcheian* in the *Iliad* as documented in note 27) or "nonce" diction.

5.435. The hypothesis of a system underlying the first hemistich is much weaker than the positing of a similar pattern behind the second hemistich. The evidence for the former rests with two other occurrences of *hrinoi*, with different inflections, in line-initial position; in these cases the differing inflection is part of a different syntax, and so the hemistich pattern is not truly systemic. At the same time, however, *hrinoi* occupies the second most favored position for its word-type and, with *apedruphthen*, itself in the most favored placement for ᴗ＿＿＿, shows right justification of the metrically more extensive element. As noted above, the *mega kuma* phrase does seem to form part of a bona fide system (see discussion of 5.429).[37]

5.436. The opening part of this line provides a clear example of how the categories of formula and word-type localization can become blurred. For the first hemistich we can adduce the following comparand (6.206): ἀλλ' ὅδε τις δύστηνος ἀλώμενος ἐνθάδ' ἱκάνει. We can then posit the hemistich system [X] *dustênos*, where *X* may represent a number of function words. Legalistically, this is a formulaic system, but does it really function as such? The same phenomena, which do not include an essential idea, can be accounted for simply by word-type localization (the shape ＿＿ᴗ occurs 54.4 percent of the time at 5). Such a right-justified arrangement would be further favored because of the malleable opening it features. Whether we actually include this hemistich in a list of systems, then, is finally of little consequence; even formulas and systems, as we have seen, are of widely varying types, flexibility, and so on. It is more important to recognize that, on the spectrum of traditional Homeric phraseology, this hemistich pattern falls just at the cusp between a phrase due entirely to traditional rules and a true system.

And while the second hemistich may also seem to have recourse to a system involving *huper moron*, we best construe the half-line by noting the confluence of two localizations: *Odusseus* at line-end (ᴗ＿＿, 92.9 percent at 12) and *huper moron*, a composite "word," as the third colon (ᴗ＿ᴗᴗ, 95.6 percent at 8). One probable method for the construction of the hemistich would be the establishment of this form of Odysseus's metrically variable name at line-end, with a verb forming the adonean clausula and the third-colon "word" filling back to the B2 caesura.

5.437. The noun-epithet phrase *glaukôpis Athênê* (treated above in the discussion of 5.427) is the only true formulaic element in this line, although the rest of the diction naturally follows traditional rules. Word-type localization and right justification order the placement of individual words throughout.

5.438. In an attempt to stretch formulaic theory as far as possible, I counted both hemistichs in this line as formulaic. Of arguably greater significance,

---

37. Cf. *kuma kalupsen* ("wave covered," 5.353) and, by analogy of sound, *kôm' ekalupsen* ("sleep covered," 18.201), which appear to be related to the present phraseology not through formulaic character but rather through traditional rules.

however, is the fact that *kumatos* and *ereugetai* are placed in the most highly favored positions for their respective word-types. Also entering the picture is *êpeironde*, which occurs eight of ten times at 12. Other associations among these words are lacking.

5.439. Comparative evidence yields other examples of *nêche* at line-beginning and of *parex* at the end of an A2 first colon, but not of these two occurrences together. The only replicable part of the first hemistich is the phrase *es gaian*, which functions as a single "word" both linguistically (proclitic plus object) and compositionally; by word-type its preferred position is as a colonic form at $5\frac{1}{2}$, and seven of eight instances are placed in that spot.[38] This positioning is thus traditional, whether we choose to view the hemistich as a system or not.

The participle *horômenos* is found four more times at 8, but this regularity seems to be due more to localization of the generic word-type than to systemic structure involving this particular word. A better possibility for a system is the incomplete phrase *ei/ên pou epheuroi/-ô* at line-end, as also employed in 5.417 with complement in 5.418:

εἰ δέ κ' ἔτι προτέρω παρανήξομαι, ἤν που ἐφεύρω

<u>ἠϊόνας τε παραπλῆγας λιμένας τε θαλάσσης,</u>

I underline to indicate that not only does the last colon of 5.417 match the equivalent part of 5.439, but that the following lines are identically the same (5.418 = 5.440). In other words, what we have in this instance is a formula five cola long—a combination that supersedes the usually formidable line boundary with the aid of an institutionalized (necessary) enjambement. To the spectrum of units of phraseology we now add an element larger than a single line, to accompany the line, hemistich, and colon units.[39]

5.440. For quantitative purposes, and because conventional formulaic theory has no provision for units longer than a single line (unless it be a run of an indeterminate number of lines), I ranked 5.440 in the category of "whole-line formula." As demonstrated above, however, 5.440 is really the latter part of a formula that begins with the adonean clausula of the preceding line.

38. The sole exception occurs at the secondary word-type position ($9\frac{1}{2}$). Since localization figures indicate an expected relative distribution of 52.4 percent for $5\frac{1}{2}$ and 37.8 percent for $9\frac{1}{2}$, we can interpret the deflection of those statistics by *es gaian* as a sign of formulaic structure.

39. Since these two instances of the phrase are only about twenty lines apart in Book 5, and since no other examples are to be found in the *Odyssey*, the issue of proximity and its effect on the formation and maintenance of phraseology must arise. From the point of view of traditional rules, there is nothing to prevent the temporary existence of certain combinations that are not preserved beyond the moment of their immediate usefulness, just as there is no reason to doubt that certain combinations—perhaps by virtue of their wider, more generic application—become fossilized and are employed again and again. Of course, there must be, within a given poem or sample of material, the narrative opportunity for a given phrase to occur and recur, so the element of utility in a given narrative is another dimension to be considered.

The present line also reveals some unusual inner structure that leads to understanding its formation under the aegis of traditional rules. In the first hemistich, the combination of *ēïonas-te* and *paraplēgas*, both metrically heavy elements but both in their second most favored positions according to word-type, leads to blockage of the A caesura and even of the mid-line break. That this metrical infelicity is offset (and from a compositional—that is, synchronic—point of view perhaps caused) by what follows is supported by the C1 phrase at line-end. To this fourth colon we adduce two examples, the first from the *Odyssey* (13.195) and the second from *H. Apoll.* (24):

ἀτραπιτοί τε διηνεκέες λιμένες τε πάνορμοι
ἀκταί τ᾽ εἰς ἅλα κεκλιμέναι λιμένες τε θαλάσσης

These examples establish both line position (including in both cases a blocked mid-line caesura) and the integrity of the C1 phrase as a traditional pattern. Typically, this final unit is the most defined one, the earlier part of the line being constructed according to a compromise between localization tendencies. With the longer formula stretching from 5.439–40, then, we discern one component unit that also exists in other combinations, with the whole set of phraseology governed by traditional rules and right justification.

5.441. The first hemistich may be interpreted as one realization of the system [X] *potamoio*, where X may be any of a number of function words, in the same fashion as the first hemistich of 5.436. But word-type localization explains the situation just as readily without having to resort to a pattern for which no essential idea can be demonstrated. Placing *potamoio* at $5\frac{1}{2}$, up against the B2 caesura, allows a malleable initial section of the hemistich and thus produces an arrangement that has many of the compositional benefits of a formulaic system, short of the word association. The phrase *kata stoma* seeks position 8 (the localization figure is 95.6 percent) in 18.97 as well, but the lack of a match in syntax makes a system a less satisfactory explanation than traditional rules.

5.442. On the basis of 7.281, ἐς ποταμόν, τῇ δή μοι ἐείσατο χῶρος ἄριστος, one can posit a whole-line system underlying 5.442. In order to be cautious and to respect the possibility that the accumulation of function words in the second colon was fortuitous, however, I settled on calling the first hemistich non-formulaic and the second a formula, for the purposes of the quantitative analysis summarized above in table 18. In fact, an investigation of *eeisato* (favored 95.6 percent of the time at position 8) and associated diction reveals that none of the explanations from formulaic theory is entirely correct, for each fails to account for a significant part of the related phraseology.

I choose to represent the interrelatedness of this diction in a kind of stemma, as shown in figure 3. Traditional rules provide for the localization of *eeisato* at 8, either with or without a pattern. Those lines which on available evidence seem to lack further pattern are 2.320 and 22.89:

Figure 3. *Eeisato* Diction

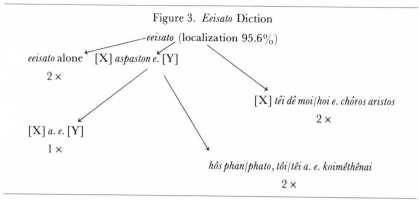

γίγνομαι· ὥς νύ που ὕμμιν ἐείσατο κέρδιον εἶναι
'Αμφίνομος δ' 'Οδυσῆος ἐείσατο κυδαλίμοιο

We also observe a core element *aspaston eeisato* grouped around the mid-line caesura and either unrelated to other elements, as in 5.398, ὥς 'Οδυσῆ' ἀσπαστὸν ἐείσατο γαῖα καὶ ὕλη, or part of a whole-line formula different in some respects from 5.442 (7.343 and 8.295),

ὥς φάν· τῷ δ' ἀσπαστὸν ἐείσατο κοιμηθῆναι
"Ὡς φάτο, τῇ δ' ἀσπαστὸν ἐείσατο κοιμηθῆναι.

Then there is in addition the possibility of the whole-line system mentioned above, which would include 5.442 and 7.281.

This collection of related lines illustrates how formulaic diction of various sorts can evolve from simple word-type localization, or in other words how traditional phraseology can develop from traditional rules. Not only the preferred placement of *eeisato* but also the positioning of the other involved words is governed by localization and right justification, and it is on this basis that formulaic diction takes shape. Establishing formulaic structure is an important, even invaluable part of the study of traditional phraseology, but in order to be fully understood that structure must be interpreted against the background of traditional rules, which govern all Homeric lines.

5.443. According to the program described above for the quantitative analysis, I have counted 5.443 as a whole-line formula, based on the exact recurrence at 7.282. As with 5.439-40, however, we discover that the phraseology reaches beyond a single line:

ἐς ποταμόν, τῇ δή μοι ἐείσατο χῶρος ἄριστος,
λεῖος πετράων, καὶ ἐπὶ σκέπας ἦν ἀνέμοιο.   (7.281-82)

Once again the unit of phraseology is longer than the single hexameter line, and once again enjambement—on this occasion "unnecessary" enjambement —assists in the extension of the phrase. Within this larger pattern, we also find evidence for a second-hemistich system, as suggested by 6.210 and 12.336:

λούσατέ τ᾽ ἐν ποταμῷ, ὅθ᾽ ἐπὶ σκέπας ἔστ᾽ ἀνέμοιο

χεῖρας νιψάμενος, ὅθ᾽ ἐπὶ σκέπας ἦν ἀνέμοιο

Both the longer and the shorter patterns follow traditional rules of word-type localization and right justification, with one exception: the line-final *anemoio*. The expected figures (average occurrence) for words of the shape ∪∪__∪, together with the actual figures for this word, at positions 12, $9\frac{1}{2}$, and $5\frac{1}{2}$, are, respectively, 31.7 and 84.6 percent, 22.6 and 15.4 percent, and 42.7 and 0.0 percent. The preponderance of occurrences at 12 may be explained as the result of a two-step process typical of the development of diction in the epos. First, position 12 is one of the three preferred placements for this word-type, so there is no difficulty with the simple admission of *anemoio* to the position at line-end. From that point on, this particular word has become caught up in a number of traditional phrases, or composite "words," which behave as larger units. In addition to the formulaic patterns already mentioned (which account for four occurrences of *anemoio* at 12), these patterns are *is anemoio* (three occurrences) and *hama/meta pnoieis anemoio* (four occurrences). Thus the deflection of word-type localization stems from formulaic structures in which the given word has been fossilized, structures that are formed in concert with traditional rules governing individual word-types but that later on come to obey the rules appropriate to composite "words."

5.444. Although for the sake of quantitative analysis both hemistichs were counted as systems, the latter one more clearly fits the criteria than does the former. The hypothesis of a first-hemistich system rests on the line-initial position of *egnô* in half of its occurrences, a statistic just as well explained by localization alone, especially since no recurrent essential idea can be discerned for the first hemistich. The second hemistich is formed around the adonean *hon kata thumon* plus a preceding verb, with localization of *euxato* (see the discussion of 5.424).[40]

CONCLUSION

As predicted by the prosodic studies of chapter 3 as extrapolated in the second section of this chapter, the diction of the *Odyssey* cannot fairly be reduced to a single type of phraseological pattern but is most faithfully understood as a *spectrum of phraseology*. In the section just completed we encountered traditional

---

40. We may see ring-composition in the echo of 5.424 (*kai kata thumon*) and 5.444 (*hon kata thumon*).

structure at the levels not only of hemistich and whole line, but also of colon and multi-line unit. The *colon* was shown to be normatively a unit of meter rather than of phraseology, mainly because of its relative shortness but also because of the vagaries of the caesura system; nonetheless, traditional phrases do occasionally form at the colonic level, chiefly in the C1 fourth colon, which is the most extensive metrically and therefore the likeliest site for association of individual words and eventual production of a formula. The smallest normative unit of phraseology was discovered to be the *hemistich*, at least for purposes of quantitative analysis; at this level we had examples of everything from an invariable formula to a system that could barely qualify as such. The *whole line* also proved to be a site for exactly repeated and formulaic diction. And finally, the *multi-line unit*, of which we have had two examples in the passage from Book 5 of the *Odyssey*, illustrated how traditional association could cross the boundary of the line—not as a run of individual lines (the proper subject of chapter 7 on thematic structure) but as a phraseological unit extended by enjambement.

This spectrum of phraseology is the natural result of the Homeric hexameter, and should be confronted in all of its complexity rather than reduced to simplex elements that may be more easily quantifiable but are not true to the reality of the diction. The "common denominator," as it were, of this complexity is furnished by the universally applicable set of *traditional rules* appropriate to (because derived from) the prosody of the hexameter; these are primarily word-type localization and right justification. No matter how intractable phraseology may seem from the point of view of formulaic theory, these rules provide a way to explain the traditional structure of the line without having to resort to the necessarily partial explanation of formulas and systems. In this sense, diction can be understood as traditional even if classically defined formulas and systems cannot be demonstrated, since the rules are the primary laws under which all phraseology—even the formulas and systems themselves —comes into being.

In the end it seems best to conceive of Homeric diction not merely as a patchwork of ready-made phrases (no matter how flexible or ideal)—first since much of the diction simply does not fit that model and second because that model does an injustice to the reality of a phraseology that is developing and dynamic—but rather as an ever-evolving inventory of unequal parts under the dominion of traditional rules. At no time will this diction be "complete" in the sense that all of the parts are somehow contained in the vessel of tradition and ready for deployment. Conversely, at no time will the poet be without a large assortment of ready-made phrases, however different those phrases may be from one another. As recent studies have shown (esp. Janko 1982), there is a good deal of change within traditional diction in the Greek epos, and the Serbo-Croatian comparand (see chapter 5) helps us to imagine how formulaic and thematic repertoires must also have been affected by local traditions and even by the personal habits of individuals in ancient Greece.

Traditional rules offer a way out of this quandary by focusing on the root causes of traditional structure in Homeric diction, rather than exclusively on certain aspects of the diction per se. Under the aegis of these rules, certain cola, hemistichs, lines, and multi-line units fossilize (just as a noun-epithet combination fossilizes), and others do not. Perhaps the frozen bit of phraseology is particularly useful for naming a certain character whose name blocks a caesura even in its most favored localization; perhaps a particular combination proves so useful that not one but many formulas and systems are founded on a single composite "word." Or perhaps, as in the case of the phraseology employed to express the octopus simile, there is no evidence that any parallel units whatsoever exist. In all of these cases, and in the ones situated between these poles on the wide spectrum of Homeric diction, the rationalizing factor is traditional rules. These rules provide the matrix through which all phraseology must pass in order to enter the tradition; they will demand right justification, word-type localization, and observance of the hexameter's inner metric. Having once entered, they may evolve in many different ways—they may form composite phrases, formulas, and systems (which in turn may skew localization figures for individual words, as we have seen); they may remain in their original form, at least for a time; or they may never be used again. The most fundamental point is, however, that whatever the life cycle and growth of such diction, it was formed under traditional rules.

FIVE

Traditional Phraseology
in the Serbo-Croatian Return Song

The foundation of oral epic in Serbo-Croatian is the traditional phraseology employed by the *guslar* as he makes his song. In studying this stylized poetic diction, I shall begin with a review of Albert Lord's theory of the formula and an analysis, based on that theory, of selections from two sample texts of Serbo-Croatian oral epic from the Milman Parry Collection of Oral Literature. With this summary and illustration in hand, I shall then proceed to a discussion of how the traditional prosodic structures examined in chapter 3 underlie the spectrum of formulaic diction and how that diction depends for its function and maintenance on a limited set of traditional rules. Along the way we shall look closely at the lines and cola analyzed in the second section in order to determine the range and morphology of traditional diction and to assess its nature and complexity as a linguistic instrument. As elsewhere, my major concern is the faithful, tradition-dependent explication of structure as a basis for aesthetic inquiry.

ALBERT LORD AND THE CONCEPT OF THE FORMULA
IN SERBO-CROATIAN ORAL EPIC

Just as Milman Parry did for Homeric epos, Lord bases his theory of composition of Serbo-Croatian oral epic on the singer's verbal dexterity in manipulating *formulas*.[1] This phraseological unit, which he defines after Parry as "a group of words which is regularly employed under the same metrical conditions to express a given essential idea" (1960, 30), is construed as the sine qua non of oral style—in the sense not only that it is typical of that style but also, and crucially, that it is necessary to that style. For Lord, as for Parry,

---

1. All references here to *The Singer of Tales* (Lord 1960) come from chapter 3, "The Formula." For other studies of the formula in this tradition, see Foley 1985, s.v. SC [Serbo-Croatian].

the primary quality of the formula is its *utility* to the singer who composes in performance, and throughout his writings he has emphasized the role of usefulness over all other ancillary characteristics.[2]

One telling formulation of the utility argument is Lord's description of formulaic diction as a language, more specifically as a grammar out of which are generated the actual verses in a song.[3] Speaking of the systematic variations as well as the more obvious verbatim repeats, he remarks (pp. 35-36) that "in studying the patterns and systems of oral narrative verse we are in reality observing the 'grammar' of the poetry, a grammar superimposed, as it were, on the grammar of the language concerned." Lines are not simply repeated and memorized, then, but are used by the singer and tradition as patterns, and these patterns give rise to a skein of related phrases.[4] From a functional point of view, the *guslar* has learned not a set of discrete phrases but a *formulaic system* that can be pressed into service in a variety of narrative situations, and that will both retain the fundamental design of the system and take on various situation-specific shapes.[5] Thus, Lord's continuing reference to a grammar of oral poetry explains both straight repetitions and formulaic phrases as the performance products of underlying systemic patterns.[6]

The grammar generates phrases—lines and cola—called *formulas* (defined above) and *formulaic systems*, the latter term referring to units that "follow the same basic patterns of rhythm and syntax and have at least one word in the same position in the line in common with other lines or half lines" (p. 47). Formulaic systems may be unearthed by collecting from a singer's repertoire phrases that satisfy this definition and displaying them as a substitution system. One of Lord's examples of such a group of phrases (p. 48), shown in abbreviated form in figure 4, involves reflexes of a certain verb "to mount" (*zasediti*) and various words for "horse." The essential idea, "to mount a horse," remains the same throughout the series, as do both the syntactic pattern of verb followed by direct object and the metrical pattern of six syllables (3-3, filling the second colon). What changes is the nominal variance in the morphology of the verb[7] and, more importantly because systematically, the specific lexical

2. For a recent example, see Lord 1981.

3. Cf. Ashby 1979 on Old French; and Conner 1972 on Old English.

4. Thus he states (p. 36): "The fundamental element in constructing lines is the basic formula pattern"; he also contends (p. 43) that "there are two ways by which a phrase is produced; one is by remembering it, the other is through creating it by analogy with other phrases; and it may well be impossible to differentiate between the two."

5. See his explanation on p. 43: "New formulas are made by putting new words into the old patterns."

6. He argues (p. 33) that "only the necessity of singing can produce a full-fledged formula. The phenomenon of which it is a manifestation arises from the exigencies of performance. Only in performance can the formula exist and have clear definition."

7. Note that this feature is not formulaic, according to Lord. Formulaic variation at this site in the colon would consist of another lexical choice with the same semantic content.

Figure 4. Lord's *zasediti* Formulaic System

$$
\begin{Bmatrix}
\text{zasednu} \\
\text{zasedem} \\
\text{zasede} \\
\text{zasedi} \\
\text{zaseo}
\end{Bmatrix}
\begin{Bmatrix}
\text{djogata} \\
\text{kočiju} \\
\text{dorata} \\
\text{paripa} \\
\text{hajvana} \\
\text{maljina} \\
\text{binjeka} \\
\text{markova} \\
\text{menzila}
\end{Bmatrix}
$$

designation for "horse." This formulaic system thus answers all of the criteria for a formula except for the exact repetition of the "group of words." Strictly speaking, repetition of any one of the multiple possibilities given above would constitute evidence of a formula, while the multiformity of the group as a whole furnishes evidence of the underlying formulaic system.

These units of traditional phraseology, under the influence of the vocal and instrumental melodies to which the *guslar* learns to sing them,[8] comprise a tissue of ideas to be sorted, adapted, and combined in the composition of Serbo-Croatian oral epic. And in keeping with his and Parry's original focus on utility as the functional reason for such a phraseology, Lord (1960, 34) identifies "the most stable formulas" as "those for the most common ideas of the poetry." Those which recur most often, those which show themselves most useful to the singer in performance will, he indicates, undergo little or no change. Thus formulas having to do with (1) common characters, (2) frequent actions, (3) the time when an action occurs, and (4) the place where an action occurs comprise a significant portion of the traditional staple.

In the first case, the names of characters tend to occupy six syllables and to fill the second colon (e.g., Kraljeviću Marko, beg Mustajbeg lički, etc.), using patronymics, grammatically unwarranted vocative inflections, or descriptive complements to eke out the colonic form; once formed and employed with any frequency, these lexical fossils—like their counterparts the Homeric noun-epithet formulas that Parry used to demonstrate the recurrent nature of that diction—are extremely unlikely to show much deviation. Typical actions, such as speaking to an assembly, mounting a horse, shouting in prison, and the like show somewhat more variation but are relatively constant. Likewise, the time and place involved in an action reveal yet more formulaic variation, since many different times and places must be accommodated in the syntactic and metrical patterns; yet these two latter categories also achieve some stability in the poetry.

8. The dynamic relationship between melody and traditional phraseology is at best only partially understood. For some discussion, see Herzog 1951 (cf. 1940); Traerup 1974; Lord 1960, 37–38; Bynum 1979, 14–43.

Other parameters also assist in shaping and preserving formulaic diction. Besides the little-studied relationship between melody and the poetic line mentioned above, Lord describes the features of word-boundary pattern, syntactic balance, and a variety of acoustic phenomena, among them leonine or end-colon rhyme, colon-initial rhyme, alliteration, and assonance.[9] Although he accords to none of these features (illustrated below) the status of prosodic or formulaic determinant, he shows how they function on an *ad hoc* basis in the composition process.

Word-boundary pattern[10]

Most frequent syllabic patterns in colon 1:
2-2, 1-3, 4
Most frequent syllabic patterns in colon 2:
2-4, 4-2, 3-3

Syntactic parallelism

Kad tatarin *pod Kajnidju dodje,*
Pa eto ga *uz čaršiju prodje,*

When the messenger *came down to Kajnidja,*
Then he *passed along the main street,*

Leonine or End-colon rhyme

U be*ćara* nema hizme*ćara.*

For a *bachelor* there is no *servant.*

Colon-initial rhyme

Zveknu halka a *jeknu* kapija.

The knocker *rang* and the gate *resounded.*

Alliteration

Na *V*isoko *v*iše Sarajeva,

At Visoko above Sarajevo,

Assonance

Još do zore dv*a* pun*a* s*a*h*a*t*a*,

Even two full hours before dawn,

Once more, these morphological, syntactic, and phonological characteristics are active and relatively frequent aids to the *guslar* as he makes his song, and

9. See further Lord 1956.
10. See chapter 3 in this volume for an explanation of word-boundary patterns and their significance. The examples cited here are from the Stolac songs. Throughout this volume I translate the Serbo-Croatian historical present tense as a simple past.

in that way they have a generic identity in the singing tradition. But they are finally only accoutrements of formulaic diction—means by which that diction can achieve and perhaps maintain a certain stability[11]—and are not as regular or as fundamental to traditional phraseology as is its prosody or its formulaic structure. Lord describes the characteristics exemplified above as providing a pathway of sound and structure for the *guslar* as he composes.

Taking account of sound patterns and the like leads Lord to a treatment of the major substructures of the line, the two cola or hemistichs. Understanding the length of the formula as either a whole line or a single colon,[12] he notes that the more spacious six-syllable second colon typically contains most of the noun-epithet combinations, while the initial four-syllable colon very often contains a verb and begins with a conjunction. As for the relationship between the two segments of the line, he remarks (1960, 42) that "the second half of the line is dependent not only syntactically on the first, but is also to some extent suggested by the sound patterns with which the line opens." In this and other ways, the two cola, metrically unequal in both extent and inner structure as we have seen in Chapter 3, tend to parcel out syntactic duties differentially.

Relying on the ideas of a grammar of oral verse-making and of the primary role of utility as the bases of his concept of traditional phraseology, Lord, again following Parry, performs a formulaic analysis of fifteen lines from one version of *The Song of Bagdad* by Salih Ugljanin (*SCHS* 2, no. 1, lines 789–803). The referent for his investigation consists of eleven different songs by Ugljanin, or a total of twelve thousand lines; three of the songs were recorded on phonograph disks, four were recited (not sung) for the records, and four were taken from dictation.[13] Lord's figures indicate that approximately one-quarter of the (whole) lines and one-half of the cola in the passage are repeated verbatim in the referent; these, then, are the formulas. Yet according to the criteria prescribed, there is absolutely nothing that *cannot* be shown to be formulaic; every one of the lines and cola can be traced to a formulaic system by reference to the twelve thousand lines used for comparison. Furthermore, he argues (1960, 47) that had he increased the size of the referent and included within it the songs of other singers, it would have become apparent that

11. Lord puts it this way (p. 57): "A perfectly natural consequence of building passages by syntactic parallelisms and acoustic patterns is that passages so built tend to have a comparative stability, or better, a continuity in time both in the habit of the single singer and, to a lesser degree, in the current of a tradition."

12. He observes (p. 34) that "the length of the action formula is naturally in part determined by whether the subject is expressed in the same line and by the length of the subject." His analyses of formulaic density (pp. 46, 58–59) reflect the same conception.

13. In choosing the sample, he notes that he sought to avoid both the stylized proem or *pripjev* that customarily begins Serbo-Croatian Moslem oral epic and the more frequently recurring themes in order to test a passage that would have no special narrative reason to repeat as a whole and thus skew the analysis.

"almost all, if not all, the lines in the sample passage were formulas and that they consisted of half lines which were also formulas."

This demonstration and the accompanying extrapolation from the observed figures to the conclusion quoted above comprise the locus classicus on which scholars from many disciplines have based the often-emulated analysis of formulaic density as a test for orality.[14] Lord's quantitative investigation of a known oral epic poetry culminated in the proof that this oral epic tradition could be entirely explained in terms of the units Parry had called the "formula" and the "formulaic system." And if one proceeds according to his definitions, there is nothing to gainsay his conclusions for Serbo-Croatian epic: one discovers no exceptions to the rules, no nagging percentage of lines that must be considered "original."[15] It is then a natural step from analyzing colonic and whole-line formulas to interpreting couplets and even runs of lines as traditional multiform units. If, the reasoning goes, unambiguously oral epic is 100 percent formulaic and 25 to 50 percent (and potentially entirely) straight formula, and if the formula is really the essential "word" used by the singer to make his song, then an epic of unknown provenance that reveals a similar formulaic diction should also be oral. This is the basic credo of formulaic theory, as first postulated by Parry in reference to the Homeric texts and as tested by Lord in the living laboratory of Serbo-Croatian oral epic tradition. Thus it is that Lord can say (1960, 65) that "the grammar of oral epic is and must be based on the formula. It is a grammar of parataxis and of frequently used and useful phrases."

Another aspect of traditional parataxis crucial to the shaping and maintenance of formulaic phraseology is that general area encompassing the phenomena of pleonasm (more properly, "terracing"),[16] thrift, and enjambement. All three phenomena are involved in the functional redundancy that operates at all levels of oral poetics, and each will bear brief discussion in relation to the formula. Terracing, to be illustrated at greater length in the third section below, "The Spectrum of Formulaic Diction," consists of the repetition in the following line of a word or words employed in an initial line. For example,

> Kudgodj ide knjiga šarovita,
> Kudgodj ide, do Karlova sidje.
>
> Wherever the multicolored letter went,
> Wherever it went, it came down to Karlovo.

Lord notes that such terracing or pleonasm is related to the "thrift" of formu-

---

14. Some of the most authoritative analyses include Creed 1955 (Old English); J. Duggan 1973 (Old French); Webber 1951 (Spanish ballad).

15. As for "errors," he sees such infelicities as "perfectly normal aberrations" (p. 38) in performance when perceived against the background of tradition; on analogous "errors," see chapters 3 and 10 in this volume.

16. See Austerlitz 1958.

TABLE 19. Enjambement Figures (in Percent, by Singer)

	Salih Ugljanin	Mujo Kukuruzović	Halil Bajgorić
No enjambement	44.5	61.9	54.6
Unnecessary enjambement	40.6	27.2	38.4
TOTAL	85.1	89.1	93.0
Necessary enjambement	14.9	10.9	7.0

laic style (after M. Parry 1928a, in 1971, 83ff.), the principle which demands that a traditional diction harbor few if any metrically equivalent phrases for the same essential idea. His discussion of thrift is complex and I shall not attempt to rehearse it here; it will be sufficient to mark that Lord (1960, 53) recommends interpretation of a given phrase selection by considering "not only its meaning, length, and rhythmic content, but also its sounds, and the sound patterns formed by what precedes and follows it."

As for the implications of enjambement, Lord follows Parry in understanding the bound, integral linear unit as the natural expression of the traditional idea[17] and therefore finds "necessary enjambement," in which the syntactic structure and thought are incomplete in one line, to be the antithesis of the oral style. Complementarily, total lack of enjambement and unnecessary enjambement, the latter of which describes the case wherein syntax and thought are complete at line-end but are optionally continued in the following line, are understood as the hallmarks of oral traditional composition. He finds proof of this connection in a 2,400-line sample (Salih Ugljanin, in table 19); my own figures, based on one thousand lines of Serbo-Croatian oral epic from two Parry-Lord *guslari* from Stolac (Mujo Kukuruzović and Halil Bajgorić in the same table),[18] generally agree with his findings and support his conclusions. Although the three singers vary in their relative percentages of unnecessary versus no enjambement,[19] the totals of these two typical features of oral style in Serbo-Croatian epic are quite close. The primacy of the line as a self-contained unit is secure, at least in Yugoslav and ancient Greek epic.[20]

The final section of Lord's chapter on the formula is devoted to a description

17. Cf. Parry 1929. See also Peabody 1975, 118–67; Clayman and van Nortwick 1977 (and, in response to the latter, Barnes 1979).

18. Kukuruzović 1.1–500; Bajgorić 3.1–500.

19. As a matter of individual style (a subset of traditional style as a whole), Kukuruzović (B) uses many more dependent clauses and vocative phrases than does Bajgorić (C), while Bajgorić employs many more couplets and additive runs. These differences account in part for the variance in unnecessary versus no enjambement figures.

20. But see chapter 6 below on Old English traditional phraseology.

of how the traditional phrase evolved out of ritual into a metrical convenience and compositional device. He views the formula's roots as ultimately religious (1960, 67): "its symbols, its sounds, its patterns were born for magic productivity, not for aesthetic satisfaction." In suggesting this ritualistic origin and in stressing throughout the chapter the compositional utility of the phrase as we encounter it in a *guslar*'s repertoire, Lord echoes Parry's proscriptive emphasis on function and his admonition against interpreting Homer (and by extension his Yugoslav *confrères*) as one would a literary artist fully able to construe his narrative in any style he sees fit to invent for the situation.[21] How tenable such a position is depends, of course, on the fidelity of the description of formulaic phraseology on which it is founded. To assess the fidelity of Lord's description is the burden of the rest of this chapter.

A CLASSICAL FORMULAIC ANALYSIS OF
TWO PARRY-LORD TEXTS

In order to illustrate Lord's analytical technique and to provide supplementary evidence for later discussion, I have conducted a formulaic analysis of two passages of twenty-five lines and twenty-six lines each, or a total of fifty-one *deseterac* verses. The passages are drawn from the performances of Stolac *guslari* Mujo Kukuruzović (text 1, *Ropstvo Ograšćić Alije* [*The Captivity of Ograšćić Alija*], Parry no. 1287a, 1,288 lines, taken from dictation) and Halil Bajgorić (text 2, *Halil izbavlja Bojičić Aliju* [*Halil Rescues Bojičić Alija*], Parry no. 6703, 637 lines, taken from dictation). I selected the first sample virtually at random, the sole criterion being avoidance of major recurrent themes. The second sample, however, was deliberately taken from an occurrence of a common theme in the Return Song, that of "Shouting in Prison,"[22] in order to test the formulaic density and texture of a passage governed by such a typical narrative structure.

The referent for the formulaic analysis consisted of three additional song-texts, two by Kukuruzović[23] and one by Bajgorić.[24] All but the last song

21. See especially M. Parry, "The Meaning of the Epithet in Epic Poetry" (1928a, in 1971, 118–72), and counterpose Parry's own insistence (p. 22) that "it does indeed give a false impression of the character of this language to imply that its creation was, so to speak, a mechanical process" and Lord (1960, 54), on the singer: "The formulaic technique was developed to serve him as a craftsman, not to enslave him." Cf. Foley 1983b.

22. See chapter 8 below for discussion of this typical scene; for its role in the overall story-pattern, see chapter 10.

23. *Ropstvo Alagić Alije* (*The Captivity of Alagić Alija*; Parry no. 1868, 2,152 lines), taken from dictation; *Ograšćić Alija u sužanjstvu* (*Ograšćić Alija in Prison*; Parry no. 6617, 2,180 lines), sung for the records. Here and elsewhere I give standard Parry Collection titles, whether or not they seem strictly grammatical. Suppressed inflections are to be attributed to the singers' (compositional) habit of inflecting only the final element of a noun-epithet phrase, a phenomenon in turn explicable by the composite identity of the phrase as a single *reč*. See further chapter 3.

24. *Ženidba Bećirbega Mustajbegova* (*The Wedding of Mustajbeg's Son Bećirbeg*; Parry no. 6699, 1,030 lines), sung for the records. The analysis was conducted using a computerized con-

mentioned—that is, four of five texts, or 6,246 of 7,287 lines—are Return Songs, so that the selection of sample and referent generally followed the criterion of genre-dependence advocated in Chapter 1. In addition, both *guslari* are from the same "local tradition" of the Stolac area in southern Hercegovina, so we may reasonably expect some congruity in their individual singing styles.[25] In order to put into relief what I shall call the "idiolectal" (individual) and "dialectal" (local tradition) levels of formulaic structure (to be discussed below in the fourth section, "From Prosody to Traditional Rules"), I have purposely limited the Bajgorić sample and referent to these two songs, only one of which is in the epic subgenre of Return; by comparing the density and texture of the two 25-line and 26-line passages from the two singers, we shall to an extent be able to judge the influence of the size and nature of the referent on formulaic analysis and, further, to test which phrases are shared by the two singers and which are (on available evidence) their own. Of course, figures and minor conclusions would change somewhat if the referent were enlarged or differently composed, but since we are pursuing structural principles as a basis for aesthetic inquiry rather than quantitative analysis for its own sake, we may take this configuration of texts as representative.

The first passage, that from Kukuruzović (Parry no. 1287a, lines 1.829–53), details a common enough sequence of events without involving a true theme:[26] a letter is written and delivered, and as a result a speech, preparation, and journey take place. The sample passage is marked after Parry-Lord practice, with solid underlining to indicate a *formula* and broken underlining to indicate a *formulaic system*, according to the definitions quoted above. All lines are analyzed for both whole-line and colonic units, and a literal translation of the text is provided.[27]

---

cordance which I prepared at the Computing Center of the University of Massachusetts/Amherst. I am grateful to the center and to Robert P. Creed and Joel M. Halpern, who helped me to gain access to the system.

25. See Lord (1960, 49), on individuals and their local tradition.

26. Many of these events could be treated thematically by the singer, but he chooses at this point simply to relate their occurrence and not to summon the typical scenes that might be employed to express their essential narrative ideas.

27. Supporting evidence (examples rather than an exhaustive array of related phrases) may be found in the appendix (pp. 393–94). The double underlining in the following passages and discussion indicates formulicity by colon (upper) and by whole line (lower). Although I have tried to keep this formulaic analysis as much in line with that carried out in the *Odyssey* passage in the last chapter as possible, tradition-dependent factors make absolute congruency inachievable. As will be shown in the extended discussion of these two passages from the Parry texts, the cola of the *deseterac* phraseology interact differently from the cola of the Homeric hexameter diction. Nonetheless, I have observed all the formal prescriptions set in chapter 4, counting a given colon (or hemistich) as a formula if a whole-line formula can be demonstrated, or as a system if a whole-line system can be demonstrated (unless, of course, the given colon is a formula in its own right). As we shall see below, the complexity of the diction is better rationalized by *traditional rules* (which are tradition-dependent) than by conventional formulaic analysis. Inevitably, the

Text 1

Kad je Pero knjigu načinijo,

A pod knjigu knjigonošu nadje.   830

Kudgodj ide knjiga šarovita,

Kudgodj ide, do Karlova sidje,

A na ruke banovoj gospoji.

Knjigu gleda, pa se na nju smije.

A ovaku reče lakrdiju: 835

"Ej! Alija, moj na mjestu sine,

Kad se boji beg Mustajbeg lički,

Kad se boji tebe na krajini,

Ako Bog da, kad ovamo dodješ,

Ja ću tebe, sine, darovati."   840

Nek govori i kako mu drago—

Da vidimo šta je bilo 'vamo.

Kad je peto jutro osvanulo,

Tad Alija sigura gavrana.

Pa se krenu do Karlova bila.   845

Njega prati Pero generale,

I do njega Djulić bajraktara,

I hadžibeg Ograšćić Alija.

Kad rekoše da se rastadoše,

Ode Ale u kršne Kotare,   850

Ode Pero do Kara Bogdana,

Ode Djulić Liku i Ribniku,

A Alija u Kotare sidje.

When Pero formulated the letter,
Then he found a messenger for the letter.   830
Wherever the multicolored letter went,
Wherever it went, it came down to Karlovo,
And to the hand of the ban's lady.

---

consequence of my (often legalistic) application of "formula" and "system" will not satisfy all investigators. I stress, however, that this is a shortfall in the method of formulaic analysis itself, a problem that will be with us as long as we fail to take account of the *spectrum* of traditional phraseology.

> She looked over the letter, then she laughed at it,
> And spoke this word: 835
> "Ej! Alija, my foster son,
> Since Mustajbeg of the Lika is afraid,
> Since he is afraid of you in the Krajina,
> If God grants it, when you return here,
> I shall give you gifts, son."   840
> Let him speak as he wishes—
> Let us see what is happening here.
> When the fifth morning dawned,
> Then Alija prepared his raven horse.
> Then he started for white Karlovo.   845
> General Pero followed him,
> And with him Djulić the standard-bearer,
> And hajibeg Ograšćić Alija.
> When they said they would take their leave,
> Alija went to rocky Kotar,   850
> Pero went to Kara Bogdan,
> Djulić went to the Lika and to Ribnik,
> And Alija came down to Kotar.

The second sample passage, that from Bajgorić (Parry no. 6703, lines 4.10–35), consists of the opening part of the ubiquitous "Shouting in Prison" theme.[28] The clamor created by the lamenting captives causes the distraught banica to petition her husband the ban for their release; he responds by entering the prison to discuss matters with the troublemakers. The same analytical procedures as were employed with the first passage are applied here.[29]

Text 2

> Pocmilijo Bojičić Alija   10
> U Kotaru bijelome gradu,
> U djidjije od Kotara bane.
> Oko momka trides' Udbinjana:
> Svi su momci u tamnici cmile,
> A najviše Bojičić Alija.   15
> Cmile Turci za nedjelju dana.
> Polu gradu rezil učinili,
> Učinili i uzabunili.
> Kad deveto jutro osvanulo,
> Dojadilo banici gospodji,   20

28. See chapter 8 for an analysis of this typical scene.

29. The following passage consists of twenty-six (rather than twenty-five) lines because a natural subdivision occurs after 4.35.

Pa i banu na svome čardaku.

Tad banica banu govorila:

"O Boga ti, gospodare bane,

Daj ti Turcim', nakav način traži;

Ne daju mi po noći spavati."   25

Skoči bane, pa srdito viče:

"Čekaj mene, moja gospojice,

Ja ću smicat' Turke sa zindana."

Jami bane ključe na sindžiru—

Jedna halka a četiri ključa.   30

Pa on dodje do svoga zindana.

Na zindanu kapak otvorijo,

Pa zagazi niz mračne skoline.

A dok sadje u dno u zindanu,

A sve Turke na tamnici nadje.   35

Bojičić Alija cried out   10
In the white city of Kotar,
Near the hero the ban of Kotar.
Around the young man thirty men of Udbina:
All the young men cried out in prison,
But most of all Bojičić Alija.   15
The Turks cried out for a week of days.
They shamed themselves before half the city,
Shamed themselves and caused a great commotion.
When the ninth morning dawned,
It became unbearable for the lady banica,   20
And also for the ban on his porch.
Then the banica spoke to the ban:
"O by your God, master ban,
Give in to the Turks, find some way;
They do not let me sleep at night."   25
The ban jumped up, then shouted angrily:
"Await me, my dear lady,
I shall remove the Turks from the prison."
The ban seized the keys on the chain—
One ring and four keys.   30
Then he went to his prison.
He opened the cover on the prison,
Then he went down into the murky depths.
And when he reached the bottom of the prison,
He found all the Turks in the prison.   35

Formulaic analysis of the two sample passages yields the quantitative profile represented in the following list.

	Passage I	*Passage II*
Colon 1 Formula	88%	42%
Colon 1 System	8%	46%
Colon 1 Total	96%	88%
Colon 2 Formula	80%	46%
Colon 2 System	20%	42%
Colon 2 Total	100%	88%
Both Cola Formula	84%	44%
Both Cola System	14%	44%
Both Cola Total	98%	88%
Lines Formula	40%	4%
Lines System	48%	50%
Lines Total	88%	54%

Most important for general purposes is the fact that both passages, the first with a larger and more homogeneous referent, and the second with a much more limited basis for comparison in the work of the singer himself, are 88 to 98 percent formulaic by colon. There are very few cola in either sample (a total of 51 lines or 102 hemistichs) that do not find a formulaic relative elsewhere in the Stolac referent. Furthermore, the Kukuruzović passage reveals a higher density of straight whole-line formulas (40 percent as compared to 25 percent) and colonic formulas (84 percent to 50 percent) than do the fifteen lines from Ugljanin examined by Lord. Even the Bajgorić sample, with a much smaller idiolectal basis for comparison, shows about the same density of colonic formulas (44 percent as compared to 50 percent) as the Ugljanin passage. With virtually universal systemic structure and a high formula count, then, the figures for the Kukuruzović and Bajgorić samples echo Lord's results and support his conclusions.

But there are also some differences between our two passages, and these differences start to indicate how individual styles can exist within more general traditional practice, as well as how referent size and composition can affect analysis. First, the relatively depressed figures for percentage of formulas and the relatively elevated figures for percentage of systems in the Bajgorić sample may be ascribed in part to the disparity in size (1,667 versus 5,619 lines) and generic make-up (two additional Return Songs versus a Wedding Song)[30] of the referent. More significant than the formula-system ratios, however, are the nearly identical sums of these figures; no matter how many or how few cola can be established as formulas in a given context, practically all of them

---

30. On epic subgenres, see chapter 1.

can be proven to be either formulas or systems. Second, the much larger difference in percentages at the whole-line level argues not for the influence of varied referents but rather for differences in individual style. Bajgorić seems, relatively speaking, to eschew composition in recurrent whole lines, and especially in whole-line formulas, in favor of colonic units.[31] While both samples can be shown to be formulaic and traditional at the colonic level, then, the two singers vary widely in the extent to which they depend on whole-line formulaic phraseology. We shall look further into idiolectal characteristics and their significance in the fourth section, but it is well to note here how each *guslar*, while adhering in general to the traditional Stolac dialect of formulas and systems, nonetheless finds his own modus operandi within that verse dialect.

THE SPECTRUM OF FORMULAIC DICTION

The Complexity of the Phraseology

One of the cardinal lessons to be learned from a formulaic analysis such as that just undertaken is an appreciation of the fundamental complexity of the diction under investigation. While it proves possible to categorize each colon and line as a formula, system, or (on the basis of available evidence) neither, one soon comes to realize that this taxonomy inevitably obscures a number of issues and that the sum of these issues amounts to a telling disparity from conventional formulaic theory.[32] For example, a given colon may be repeated both verbatim and with formulaic substitution, but the solid underlining conventionally appropriate to such a situation epitomizes the verbatim repetition and so masks the multiformity of the phrase and, by extension, the suppleness of the diction as a whole. Or, to take another possibility, perhaps the truly formulaic component of a line is only its second colon, with the apparent repetitive phraseology in the opening section of the line merely a circumstance; nonetheless, if we find that opening section of the line repeated—either verbatim or closely enough to resemble a system—we must, perhaps mistakenly, label both it and the whole line as units of traditional diction. For a third instance, consider the fair number of lines that participate in couplets or clusters. In order to represent these elements of phraseology fairly, we should somehow note that their recurrence is overseen by other than purely formulaic (that is, colonic or decasyllabic) constraints.

Examples could be multiplied, and we shall closely examine many

31. Compare Lord's finding (1960, 63), in reference to the 1935 and 1950 versions of *Aliaga Stočević* by this same singer, that "Bajgorić is actually recreating the song with little or no reliance on habitual and frequently sung passages," an example of his general thesis that one can differentiate "individual styles in the epic technique of oral verse-making."

32. See note 27 above.

individual cola and lines in the next section, but for the moment the crucial fact to be confronted is this: *formulaic diction in Serbo-Croatian oral epic does not amount simply to a collection of equivalent units but is most faithfully understood as a complex and responsive spectrum of phraseology.* While Lord's formulaic theory provides an excellent first approximation of this many-sided, multiform phraseology, it does not explain the many different kinds and degrees of patterned diction. As we shall see, the degree of fixity of the various elements of phraseology is not necessarily a function of frequency of use; certain elements simply achieve a more stable form, whether through their compositional role (e.g., proper name), the influence of sound patterns, or merely a happily unique fit of prosody and essential idea that becomes a staple of the *guslar*'s repertoire.[33] Building on the firm foundation of Lord's theory, we shall attempt to glimpse the range and depth of traditional phraseology—both its spectrum of structure and its differential evolution—in the individual styles of two singers from the same region of Stolac.

Synchrony, Diachrony, and the Deseterac

From what, we may ask in beginning our inquiry, does this spectrum of diction evolve? How are we to explain its development to the point at which we observe the range of formulaic structure in, for example, the recorded repertoires of Mujo Kukuruzović and Halil Bajgorić? First, we must observe that Lord's theory, although illuminating certain aspects of the multiformity of the *guslar*'s poetic language, homogenizes its inherent complexity[34] and deemphasizes the fact that phraseology is not a static collection of items but a dynamic inventory ever in a state of flux or evolution. Such a view opens up valuable perspectives on the relationship among elements, but it does so at the cost of certifying these elements' phraseological equivalence. If formulas are understood as generated by patterns, and the patterns are seen as the source of all diction, then each and every element of diction must be functionally equivalent. More significantly for the history and development of oral literature research, the synchronic model of generation from pre-existent patterns seems to validate the determination of orality on the basis of the formulaic-density test. If we construe oral traditional phraseology as atoms of diction which are in turn the issue of formulaic patterns, then proof of a critical density of atoms and patterns should constitute proof of that particular type of phraseology. From a set of definitions proceeds evidence for a mode of composition.

33. This does not mean, of course, that any such element necessarily ever becomes a part of another singer's repertoire.

34. Note that while Lord (1960, 44) contends that formulas "are not all alike either in their genesis or in their intensity of 'formulicity,'" his method of analysis and the conclusions drawn from quantitative evaluation assume the equivalence of phrases. See further his suggestion (p. 43) that "a singer's formulas are not all of the same degree of fixity."

For Lord, .then, the synchronic model provides a way of illustrating multi-formity in the *guslar*'s language, but it blocks the path to further understanding because it does not account for the observable fact that all formulas are not created equal. Likewise, the same discrepancy among units goes a long way toward invalidating the formulaic-density test for orality; if we are testing for identical phraseological units, and if what we actually have in the texts is a spectrum of decidedly unequal elements, then our analysis cannot bear fruit. In addition to the principles of tradition-dependence and genre-dependence discussed in chapter 1, we thus discover another necessary complication which oral literature research must recognize: the natural heterogeneity of traditional phraseology.

Instead of locating the pivot of formulaic structure at a hypothetical point of balance between patterns and the formulas that seem to depend on those patterns, let us take the investigation a step further to the elemental prosody of the *deseterac*, the epic decasyllable that supports the diction we are now examining. We recall from chapter 3 that the outer metric, the usual representation of trochaic pentameter, proved illusory and misleading, the result of a flawed set of assumptions. Prosodic structure in the *deseterac* amounts to the inner metric, the system of cola that comprise the line and the inter- and intra-colonic relationships. In addition to a regular syllable count of ten and a caesura between positions 4 and 5, the *deseterac* exhibits the Indo-European principle of right justification in a number of features: the four-plus-six inner structure of the whole line; the placement of ictus (emphasis on syllables 1, 3, 5, and 9); three complementary distribution rules and a general limitation on allowed configurations in the second colon; and the shorter-before-longer, highly variable make-up of the first colon. All of these prosodic rules are active in the shaping and maintenance of traditional phraseology in Serbo-Croatian epic—not just as a template for one formula or set of formulas, but as the group of rules within which *all* formulaic diction must be made and re-made. Thus these rules, as opposed to the assortment of patterns that the synchronic model uses to rationalize formulas, are the most general parameters, the universal guidelines for an ever-evolving *Kunstsprache* and the supports that assist in preserving phraseology over time.

Apart from the vast disparity between the number of formulaic patterns affected by the two sets of constraints, perhaps the most telling difference between this modest set of prosodic rules and the dictionary of patterns demanded by conventional formulaic theory is that the rules leave the way open for what is *prima facie* observable in Serbo-Croatian oral epic texts: a true spectrum of phraseology. Indeed, it hardly seems possible that they could do anything else: not only would such basic prosodic parameters admit to the *guslar*'s wordhoard initially inequivalent units of diction (verbatim repeats alongside systems and other patterns), but they would also leave room for differential development. Phrases employed by a singer could answer very

Figure 5. Generation of Poetic Phraseology

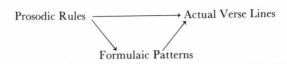

dissimilar descriptions: one might be a six-syllable name-plus-patronymic unlikely ever to change; another might be a verb-direct object phrase "to mount a horse" that admitted a multitude of functional synonyms for "horse" into the system; while a third might amount simply to a particular placement of a given word on the basis of its metrical type. All of these and myriad more kinds of phrases could enter a *guslar*'s repertoire and could evolve toward or away from absolute stability within the range permitted by prosodic rules.

Furthermore, the postulating (and demonstration, see below) of *phraseological rules* to reflect the laws of prosody in the *deseterac* makes the role of obvious formulaic patterns clearer. These patterns are unarguably more exacting, but nonetheless nominal, specifications of prosodic rules; in applying strictly to a small but well-defined group of actual lines or cola, they serve as situation-specific intermediaries between universal prosodic rules and certain groups of related lines. To put the matter schematically (figure 5), we can say that formulaic patterns, the molds that Lord sees as the source of formulas, act as linguistic lenses that focus the more general rules. As the diagram indicates, however, not all verse lines can be derived from such patterns; as we shall see in the discussion that follows, there are lines and cola that reveal the operation of traditional prosodic rules without the interposition of formulaic patterns. This model allows us to explain the variant phraseological structures encountered in the spectrum of Serbo-Croatian epic diction as the natural conclusion of a two-level process: lines and cola are *all* traceable to a few fundamental prosodic rules, and *a certain number* of lines and cola are further structured by a large number of formulaic patterns.

Of course, there are many more factors to be considered in describing the source, shape, and relative stability of the diction. Some of these include sound-patterning in its various types (assonance, alliteration, different kinds of rhyme), syntactic parallelism, terracing, and thematic focus. While each is a significant force in phrase generation and maintenance, we should keep in mind that all are at least as situation-specific as the formulaic pattern. Each, like that pattern, applies to a limited number of lines rather than informing the traditional phraseology as a whole, and therefore none has even a fraction of the overall significance of prosodic rules. With the understanding that more than one situation-specific feature may help to focus the underlying rules, we may picture the process of creation and preservation of formulaic phraseology as in figure 6. Once again we take account of the possibility that diction can

Figure 6. Focusing, or Second-Level, Processes

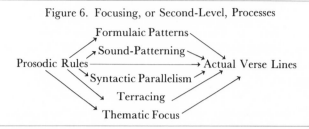

become part of the singer's poetic language without focusing by any of these second-level processes. And while actual lines and cola do appear in Serbo-Croatian oral epic that show no allegiance whatsoever to any of the intermediaries listed above, absolutely none of the 7,286 lines (or their 14,572 cola) examined for the present purpose reveals an important departure from the traditional prosody of the *deseterac* (see chapter 3). Traditional prosodic rules, the idiosyncratic reflex in the *deseterac* of ultimately Indo-European characteristics, constitute the primary basis for traditional composition.

As will be illustrated below, prosodic rules and the various focusing effects collectively produce a diction that cannot fairly and accurately be described as one of equivalent units. Some verse lines and cola take their structure only from phraseological constraints that reflect these primary rules; in such cases one is hard pressed to stretch the definitions of formula and system to accommodate the phrases, and solid or broken underlining seems more misleading than informative or analytical. Only by the most literal application of definitions, one that subverts the whole notion of multiformity by claiming genetic connection between phrases only superficially similar, can the categories hold up. And, more than occasionally, even stretching definitions beyond the limits of credibility will not bring elements of phraseology into the fold. Nevertheless, we shall discover relationships of various sorts—some formulaic, some not —that persist in the singers' repertoires examined and are clearly traditional. This spectrum of relationships, whether dependent on none or on one or more of the focusing features, will all show evidence of the operation of traditional rules. From the invariable noun-patronymic formula secured by sound-patterning to the merest, most nominal phrase without any apparent formulaic identity, all elements of diction in Serbo-Croatian oral epic conform to prosodic and phraseological rules. Their own obvious heterogeneity aside, the singer's phrases are thoroughly and fundamentally traditional.

FROM PROSODY TO TRADITIONAL RULES

In this section we shall selectively re-examine the two passages from Kuku-ruzović and Bajgorić that were analyzed for formulaic density above. For the purpose of conducting an analysis identical in its core assumptions to that made by Lord in *The Singer of Tales*, I employed his definitions of formula and system without qualification. In this way I hoped to present a phraseological profile comparable to his, and in fact the results of my investigation do reinforce his figures. As mentioned above, Lord's notion of formulaic density and all that it implies serve as an excellent first approximation of multiformity in traditional diction. But as I shall document below, we also need to restore a lost complexity to that diction, a complexity that the generic model has eliminated; we need to understand, as explained in the preceding section, that the formula and system are second-level, or focusing, processes and do not represent the most fundamental level of phrase structure. In order to take account of the inherent complexity of the phraseology, then, in what follows I shall forgo automatic categorization of lines and cola as equivalent items in favor of showing just what about a phrase can be considered formulaic. Some elements are manifestly "more formulaic" than others in that they conform to a tighter definition over the sample of related phrases; some are "less formulaic" in that their systemic character is less obvious and more difficult to determine; and some are not meaningfully formulaic at all. Each line or colon drawn from the two samples for commentary and illustration will be examined first on its own terms as a traditional element conforming to phraseological rules and only secondarily as an example of a certain type of traditional diction.

Deseterac *Rules and the Diction*

The three Indo-European metrical characteristics of syllabicity, regular caesura, and right justification give rise to a number of prosodic features in the *deseterac*, as we saw in chapter 3. Syllabic count and caesura (or institutionalized word-break) between positions 4 and 5 are the obvious reflexes of the first two, while right justification manifests itself in an interrelated series of features:

1. an initial four-syllable colon followed by a six-syllable colon, the more extensive unit following the less extensive one;
2. preference for ictus at positions 3 and 9, then 1 and 5;
3. shorter-before-longer words and accentual groupings (SBL) in both cola;
4. initially accented disyllables (IAD) favored at positions 3–4 and 9–10;
5. medially accented trisyllables (MAT) favored at positions 8–10;
6. a generally greater flexibility in colon 1 (accomplished primarily by stressed monosyllables and by accentual groupings that include proclitics and enclitics) and, correspondingly, a generally greater fixity in colon 2.

Rules 1, 2, and 6 are self-evident and have been discussed thoroughly in chapter 3. Rule 3, the most far-reaching of the other three constraints, stipulates that shorter words be placed before longer words[35] in both cola, thus reflecting

---

35. From this point on I use *word* to mean accentual grouping (lexical item plus associated proclitics and/or enclitics) as well as the simplex lexical item.

the same principle of right justification that underlies Rule 1. Rule 4, an exclusion to SBL, may optionally overturn the prescribed sequence, however; IAD mandates that initially accented disyllables can (but need not) migrate to positions 9 and 10,[36] occasionally leaving the second colon with, for example, a four-syllable increment followed by the disyllable. It is important to note that Rules 3 and 4 are ordered: SBL will determine word order unless an IAD intervenes, in which case the order may optionally be reversed.[37] For example,

SBL	A ovaku *rȅče lakrdiju*	(1.835 and 48 add. instances)
IAD	A starac mu *lakrdiju víknu*	(1.648 and 3 add. instances)

Although both lines are used to introduce a speech, and although both second cola have the same syntactic content (verb plus direct object, in whatever order) and functionally the same semantic content ("spoke" versus "shouted" a "word"), the sequence of elements is reversed. In 1.835, SBL (2-4 pattern) reigns unchecked because *rȅče* is initially unaccented (short falling), while in 1.648, IAD causes the accented form *víknu* (long rising) to seek colon-end (4-2 pattern). Thus IAD can supervene SBL, but the exclusion is not required, and we shall encounter many lines in which SBL informs phrase structure despite the presence of IAD.

The third and last of the word constraints, Rule 5 or MAT, pertains to those relatively infrequent situations wherein the second colon has a "balanced" configuration of 3-3. In such cases, when SBL cannot by definition apply, the trisyllables will be sorted by the influence of position 9 in the *deseterac*. Just as with IAD, the word whose lexical accent will coincide with prosodic ictus in the penultimate position will migrate to the final spot in the colon. For example,

MAT   Tad Alija sigùra gavrāna   (1.844)

The length of the medial syllable of *gavrāna*, as opposed to the short medial syllable of *sigùra*, secures the position of *gavrāna* at 8–10. And again, just as does IAD, MAT functions as an optional exclusion to SBL; if traditional placement cannot be determined on the basis of syllabic extent, the next set of criteria has to do with correlation of lexical accent (or length) and prosodic ictus at position 9.

---

36. By *IAD* I mean specifically that the initial syllable is usually accented and long but at least *long in quantity*. Likewise, *MAT* indicates a trisyllable whose second syllable is usually accented and long but at least long in quantity. Thus, in order to qualify for inclusion under the IAD or MAT exclusions, a syllable must be marked with the diacritics ˆ (long falling) or ´ (long rising), or be designated long by a macron; those marked with ˋ (short falling) or ˋ (short rising) do not qualify. For further information on accent in Serbo-Croatian, see Magner and Matejka 1971.

37. Disyllables without initial accent cannot, in other words, assume positions 9–10 and reverse the SBL rule.

As we proceed through examples drawn from the two sample passages, it will become apparent that the normal rules for (prose) word order have a certain force in shaping the sequence of words in oral epic phraseology. But that influence is neither 'as pervasive nor as fundamental as one might expect. The fact that traditional phraseology usually seems to follow conventional prose word-order does not mean that poetic diction takes its cue from that convention, since there are numerous instances—as many as half the lines in some passages—that depart from the supposed prose norm. When we balance this observation with the fact that there are absolutely no important departures in those same samples from the six rules sketched above, we begin to understand the ontology of influences in verse composition. First and most fundamentally, the *guslar* composes according to traditional rules; *then* the influence of conventional word order enters the process. To put it aphoristically, poetic word order tends toward the conventional prose norm within the limitations of traditional rules.

Examples of Traditional Composition from the Stolac Guslari

MUJO KUKURUZOVIĆ

1.829. The opening line of the Kukuruzović passage offers a first insight into the complexity of traditional phraseology:

Kad je Pero knjigu načinijo,

The Parry-Lord notation indicates that (1) the first colon is a formula, (2) the second colon is a formula, and (3) the whole line is a formulaic system. What that notation does not indicate is that both cola are also systemic and that the entire line allows more substitution than the underlining can suggest. We have had to solidly underline the first colon because it appears intact elsewhere in the referent, but, as might be expected, many names and simple nouns other than Pero can appear at positions 3–4, among them Tale, Mujo, Huso, and the nouns *momak* (young man) and *beže* (bey).[38] As for the second colon, it tolerates considerably less variation, but the essential idea remains intact in such phrases as *knjigu preučijo* (he composed the letter) and *knjigu nakitijo* (literally, he decorated the letter).[39] These two colonic systems can occur together, as here, or separately; in the latter case, different whole-line essential ideas are involved.[40] Thus, even a glance at the phraseological context

38. The option *beže* is actually a vocative singular used as a nominative singular subject; this "poetic inflection" allows the word *beg* to take the disyllabic form appropriate to the formulaic system.

39. A usually consequent essential idea, represented by such phrases as *knjigu prifatijo* ("he seized the letter"), may also be construed as related to this system under the narrative aegis of letter-writing and -reading phraseology.

40. E.g., 1.1110: Svakome je *knjigu načinijo* ("he formulated a letter to each one"); 6.1239: *Kad je* Mujo riječ razumijo ("when Mujo understood his words").

reveals a greater multiformity of colonic (and therefore whole-line) structure than is apparent from simple underscoring. Furthermore, we have evidence for two distinct but concurrent levels of organization; each colon can participate in other whole-line phrases and thus has a life of its own outside this particular whole-line system.[41]

This much we can demonstrate without venturing far beyond conventional formulaic analysis. But how do traditional rules come into play? And do they in fact rationalize this more complicated view of formulaic structure in 1.829? In general, we seek to determine the applicability of SBL and the relative fixity of cola 1 and 2, since right justification manifests itself chiefly in these two phraseological characteristics.[42] In colon 2, which permits a narrower range of systemic substitution than colon 1 (the semantic constraint in colon 2 is more limiting than a mere exchange of names), SBL demands the configuration *knjigu načinijo*, or 2-4 by syllable count, and that is the sequence that obtains both in this instance and throughout the system.[43] Although conventional prose word order would be **načinijo knjigu*, SBL prescribes the opposite sequence for traditional poetic diction. Nor can the IAD exclusion reverse SBL to echo the prose convention, since the initial syllable of *knjiga* is unaccented and short.

In turning to colon 1, we notice at once that this phrase behaves differently from the latter part of the line. While it can be said with reason that the range of disyllables seeking positions 3–4 is certainly wider than that of verbs that maintain the essential idea of the second colon,[44] there is more to the difference between phrases than that. The element *Kad je* [name/noun] is simply less fixed in form than *knjigu* [verb "to compose"]; to put it another way, the *Kad je* [name/noun] system is more a nonce formation that recurs because of the confluence of traditional rules and a very generic "When" clause than a formulaic system that is obviously a part of the *guslar*'s repertoire. The proof of this "nonce" character of colon 1 consists of the tremendous variety of line-types that begin with these words. If the colon 1 phrase has any essential idea at all, it is so general and adaptable as to be more a result of traditional constraints producing a generic idea in much the same form than a true formulaic system.

41. The same can be said for narrative themes or typical scenes, some of which occur in different sequences and different subgenres and thus demonstrate lives of their own outside the text under examination. See chapter 8.

42. I set aside the recurrent syllabic and caesural constraints as obvious, and see IAD and MAT as optional exclusions of SBL, as explained above.

43. In fact, the four-syllable verb form (usually in past tense third-person singular or plural) following its direct object becomes an institutionalized feature of *deseterac* verse and shows evidence of existing as a grammatical pattern (based ultimately, of course, on traditional rules).

44. As in many other lines, the greater number of elements in this position are initially accented, so the name/noun tends toward 3-4 by convention.

If we step back a moment and have another look at the whole line, the variegated spectrum of traditional diction begins to come into relief. In essence we have a very focused, tightly organized system (colon 2) combining with the non-systemic issue of traditional rules (colon 1) to form what may be termed a whole-line system. The combination in no way represents the integration of two equivalent elements to synthesize a third. Compositionally, the core of the essential idea behind this line lies in the second colon, and the first colon—quite typically, as we shall see—is the shaping device that suits the core idea to its situation-specific position. Under the influence of right justification, the more flexible first part of the line has adapted the more fixed latter portion to its present purpose.

As we go further and start to gain a sense of what the spectrum of traditional diction actually means, it will become more and more apparent how subtle and dynamic an instrument the *guslar*'s diction is. Conversely, it will become less valuable, as examples multiply and more complexity is introduced into the model, to return to diagrams that are limited in the ways in which they can symbolize different degrees of formulaic character or dependence on other second-level focusing processes. For the moment, however, we can profit from interpreting 1.829 in terms of figure 7. This description of the source and evolution of 1.829 more faithfully represents the singer's (more accurately, the tradition's) task and the nature of the phraseology, first as an essential idea takes shape within the constraints identified as traditional rules and then as it is in part focused by a traditional formulaic system (which itself operates under traditional rules). The singer does not merely mesh two prefabricated units but rather adapts the second-colon "word" to the particular form needed at this juncture in the narrative. The poet is no mere assembler of parts; his compositional task is nothing less than true *poiesis*.

1.831-33. A few lines further on in the Kukuruzović passage we encounter a series of decasyllables best considered as a unit:

> Kudgodj ide knjiga šarovita,
> Kudgodj ide, do Karlova sidje,
> A na ruke banovoj gospoji.

The underscoring indicates that all six cola (actually five, since 831a and 832a are identical) have independent lives of their own outside the whole-line configuration in which we find them, and also that the first two lines exist as combinations of these cola elsewhere in the Stolac referent. The third line is apparently a unique combination of colonic phrases repeated elsewhere verbatim. As an initial profile, then, we have two lines with both colonic and whole-line structure and one with colonic organization only. But the situation proves more complex than that approximation, since the cola themselves are of various sorts. The phrase *knjiga šarovita*, for example, turns out to be a typical second-colon formula in its relative fixity; it tolerates no substitution whatever,

Figure 7. Generation of Line 1.829

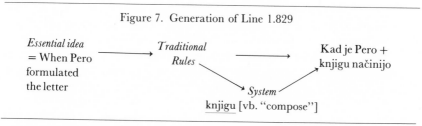

with morphological adjustment the only change observed in seventeen additional occurrences. As a characteristic first-colon formula, *Kudgodj ide* can be modified by occurring either as a phrase complete in itself or as a verb phrase in need of a noun to serve as its subject; the two instances in 831 and 832 make this point. Additionally, *do Karlova sidje* constitutes one specification of a narrowly substitutable system associated with the first colon by the leonine rhyme on *ide/sidje*, and the final line consists of a second-colon formula that itself varies little and a first-colon phrase that always demands a dative complement to fill out its meaning and syntax.[45]

In short, lines 1.831-33 offer us more evidence of how dissimilar cola (and lines) can be in their compositional structure. Although by adhering strictly to Parry-Lord orthodoxy we can posit formulas and systems corresponding to these lines and cola, such labeling takes us only part of the way toward their most fundamental make-up. Once again it is clear that the synchronic model of combinations of equivalent elements will not faithfully describe the compositional process. And added to the complex variety of phraseological units manipulated by the singer is another complication: parallels from elsewhere in the Stolac texts illustrate that these three lines form a "cluster" or "run" that has a unitary dimension of its own, and further that this cluster owes its integrity and stability in part to the institutionalized terrace in 1.831-32. Consider one of the thirteen recurrences of this three-line unit:

> Kudgodj ide Pero generale,
> Kudgodj ide, do Ribnika sidje,
> Svome pobri begu od Ribnika.   (1.1203-5)

> Wherever General Pero went,
> Wherever he went, he came down to Ribnik,
> To his blood brother the bey of Ribnik.

The first line derives from the same system as the opening line of the cluster under examination, only this time the second-colon formula (again one that allows no morphological variance or substitution) names a person instead of

---

45. We may even question the characterization of *A na ruke* as a colonic formula, since without the second colon the essential idea is incomplete.

a letter to be delivered. The second line likewise stems from the system that generates *Kudgodj ide, do Karlova sidje* at 1.832, with the expectable modification of place from Karlovo to Ribnik in order to suit the story's action. The third line, although quite different from the *A na ruke* [person, dat.] system, serves the same general purpose by specifying the person to whom the character or letter mentioned earlier is directed.[46] In this case the idea-sequence of (a) *x* goes, (b) *x* goes generally to a place, and (c) *x* goes specifically to a person takes shape as a single unit expressed over three lines and held together in part by a terraced repetition of *Kudgodj ide*. Since the three lines memorialize and express the idea-sequence traditionally, we would do well to recognize that in this case three lines constitute one unit with a single essential idea. While there can be no doubt that some of the lines and cola that comprise the sequence individually have their own essential ideas, the cluster as a whole takes its noetic shape from the unitary nature of the traditional idea that underlies it.

And in accord with the shape-shifting that consistently characterizes oral traditional phraseology—and which is diachronically the source for its evolution within limits as well as synchronically the source of its usefulness as an idiom—this cluster of three lines can be expressed without the terrace and leonine rhyme contributed by the middle member in the sequence.

> Kudgodj ide knjiga šarovita,
> Ona sidje do Kara Bogdana,
> A u ruke Peri generalu.   (1.957–59)

> Wherever the letter went,
> It came down to Kara Bogdan,
> And to the hand of General Pero.

With reference to the first occurrence analyzed (1.831–33), we can see immediately that lines 1 and 3 of the two clusters derive from the same systems, the only variations consisting of a change of the person to whom the letter is directed and the insignificant substitution of the preposition *u* for *na*. In the second line, however, the poet has adjusted his phraseology to accommodate a syllabically more extensive place-name. But while the actual phraseology has shifted, the essential ideas behind both the second element (*x* goes generally to a place) and the idea-sequence as a whole have not changed in the least. Even the verb *sidje* remains as a traditional specification of the traditional idea.

One more avatar of this same cluster will offer a final perspective on its morphology and suggest the variance between different singers' idiolectal forms of the same unit. This instance is drawn from the Return Song dictated by Halil Bajgorić.

---

46. Note that this person, the beg of Ribnik, occurs here in the dative usage that typifies the system.

Ode momak i knjigu odnese;
Kudgodj ide, na Udbinu sidje,
Pod bijelu Bojičiću kulu. (4.112–14)

The young man went and carried the letter;
Wherever he went, he came down to Udbina,
Below Bojičić's white tower.

The second line in the sequence closely resembles the middle line seen twice above, this time with Udbina substituted as the place-name rather than Karlovo or Ribnik. But there the phraseological comparison ends; lines 1 and 3 bear no formulaic relation whatever to the first and third members of the cluster as examined above. Nevertheless, these same apparently heterodox lines do flesh out—in an idiolectal way—the fundamental sequence of x goes, x goes generally to a place, and x goes specifically to a person. The unitary essential idea persists through the multiformity of the diction and even crosses the border of idiolect; the unit maintains its identity and epitomizes its traditional message.

Beyond the cluster formation, formulaic structure, and other second-level focusing processes singularly applicable to these phrases, lines 1.831–33 reveal the same elemental dependence on traditional rules that characterizes not just certain lines or passages but all *deseterac* phraseology. In 1.831 normal word order obtains in the first colon, but right justification in the form of SBL reverses the expected order in colon 2; just as in 1.829, the initially unaccented *knjiga* is subject to a poetic metathesis. In 1.832 two forces combine to determine phrase configuration and to insure the stability of the whole-line system. The verb *sîdje* will tend toward positions 9–10 via the IAD exclusion, yielding a 4-2 syllabic series (since the proclitic preposition *do* joins its object *Karlova* in a single accentual group). The leonine rhyme on *ide/sidje* helps to maintain the system by providing a phonological bridge between cola. In the final line of the cluster we have SBL reinforcing normal word order in the first colon (1-3 syllabic pattern, with *na* proclitic) and a balanced second colon that may well be the product of analogy to *banova djevōjka*, whose long medial syllable would seek the strong ictus at position 9 (MAT). On these traditional rules are built phrases that exhibit an intricate variety of second-level compositional processes—formulas and systems, leonine rhyme, terracing, and clustering. None of the phrases, however, owes its most fundamental allegiance to these more obvious features; the aegis under which all of them occur and recur is that of traditional rules.

1.836. Another example of the limitations on description imposed by the synchronic model of formulaic structure is provided by this ubiquitous line-type:

Ej! Alija, moj na mjestu sine,

It so happens that this entire line is repeated seven more times in the Stolac corpus, but that fact—and the solid underlining that represents it graphically—turns out to be largely irrelevant. The true nature of the whole-line phrase lies in its systemic properties, which demand that the second colon not change at all while the first colon supplies the name upon which the address is built. Once again colon 1 recurs without colon 2, but *moj na mjestu sine* never occurs outside this whole-line system. So we discover versions of the system, an idio-lectal item that is apparently not a part of Bajgorić's repertoire, with the names Alija (8 ×), Djulić (5 ×), and Ograšćić (1 ×).[47] This combination and shaping of two quite different cola nonetheless rests on the steady foundation of traditional rules: colon 2 is firmer and more limited in scope than the more flexible and adaptive first colon, and SBL orders the first phrase (1-3 or 4), while IAD (*sîne*) causes a modification of normal word order in the second (1-3-2).[48] In short, the line is best and most faithfully interpreted as a right-justified whole-line system that takes shape under traditional rules.[49]

1.840. The multi-leveled process of composition and the rationalizing perspective afforded by traditional rules are again evident in this line, although conventional formulaic analysis does not give the whole picture:

Ja ću tebe, sine, darovati.

At perhaps the most superficial level, this line or one of its relatives serves as the final line in a speech in fourteen of twenty-one occurrences. Beyond that function, however, each colon is much more flexible than the solid underlining would cause us to expect. The phrase *Ja ću tebe* and its morphological variants prove common enough—indeed, inevitable enough given traditional rules—to beg the question of whether it deserves to be considered a formula or system at all; even if we accord it that status, though it has no demonstrable "essential idea," we must recognize that the phrase is by itself incomplete and in general much less stable and tightly defined than many other cola studied above. Alongside this typical initial phrase stands the colon that completes the verb construction (*ću* . . . [infinitive]), and, again typically for a second colon, its variation is more controlled. If the vocative case noun (in this instance *sine*) is understood as comprising part of the system, thus yielding a template like [noun in vocative] *darovati*, we shall find only four recurrences, three with *sine* and one with *beže*. If we are willing to broaden the essential idea to permit

---

47. Another form of the system without the first-colon specification occurs in 6.2064: *Jes', Boga mi, moj na mjestu sine* ("Yes, by God, my foster son").

48. The more customary order would be **moj sine na mjestu* (1-2-3, with *na* proclitic), but *mjestu* is not initially accented.

49. That is, to see 1.836 as the melding of two equivalent units is simply reductive. In fact, I would question the formulaic character of colon 1, since it seems to be merely the inevitable way to fill out the whole-line pattern via traditional rules; see further the initial colon of 1.829.

Figure 8. Traditional Phraseology with *darovati*

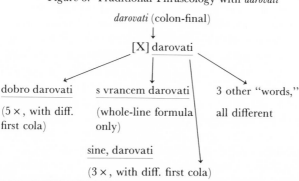

the substitution of adverbs, adverbial phrases, and direct objects at positions 5–6, the list of referents quickly grows in length and complexity.

The clue to a proper perspective on this complexity consists of concentrating on the most fundamental structure of the lines concerned, that is, on traditional rules. Figure 8 represents the source of and genetic similarities among various formulas and systems related to the second colon of 1.840. The infinitive *darovati* tends toward colon-final position via the SBL rule, a clear example of right justification, and into the colonic "word" template thus formed enter a variety of disyllables, including two vocative nouns (*sine*, "son," and *beže*, "bey"), an adverb (*dobro*, "well"), and an adverbial prepositional phrase (*s vrancem*, "with a dark horse"). Although one can argue that the disparity in syntax precludes calling all of these phrases members of the same formulaic system, at least by the classical definition, there is no denying their relationship through traditional rules and the "word" template that results from the application of those rules.[50] Whereas the usual shortcoming of conventional formulaic analysis is the collapsing of phraseology into an oversimplified taxonomy, thus obscuring the differences among elements of diction, in this case the conventional approach does not penetrate far enough to illuminate a highly traditional (if not actually formulaic) association.

1.843. Both Kukuruzović and Bajgorić use variants of the system underlying this line as a diurnal marker to segment the progress of the narrative:

Kad je peto jutro osvanulo,

The underscoring indicates that both cola combine with other partners in otherwise unrelated lines, the former as a system and the latter as a formula.

---

50. Note that SBL takes precedence here, the optional exclusion by IAD (with *sine* and *s vráncem*) not occurring. This situation is due most immediately (that is, synchronically) to the [x] *darovati* frame, but ultimately (that is, diachronically) to the hierarchy of traditional rules: IAD only optionally supersedes SBL.

In fact, as we might expect, the *Kad je* [x] system does not exist in any meaningful sense outside this whole-line system, since its shape is the inevitable issue of traditional rules and not a demonstrable full-fledged pattern in its own right. Equally typically, the second colon turns out to be a stable core idea, "the morning dawned"; there are no other related uses of *jutro* and no other uses at all of the verb *osvanuti* in the entire Stolac referent. Further, since *jutro osvanulo* does not occur in lines wholly unrelated to 1.843,[51] we can best understand the line in question as a whole-line system, or a traditional "word" one verse in length. This line thus exemplifies another principle of traditional composition: units—or, as I prefer to call them, *traditional words*—are of different lengths as well as of different texture and stability. Far from being mere counters simply moved into appropriate position by the poet composing in performance, they comprise a vast and complex network of phraseology that epitomizes essential ideas in forms subject to the dictates of traditional rules.[52]

1.845. The second colon of this line provides another example of an essential idea epitomized optionally in a colonic form (as we shall see below, it can also take a whole-line form):

Pa se krenu do Karlova bila

The phrase *do Karlova bila* recurs verbatim and can thus be labeled a formula by the classical definition, but it is also a member of a colonic system that substitutes other place-names into the middle position; we find instances of Janok and, with a shift of preposition, Ribnik as well. Should it prove useful to the Stolac singer, he also has available a whole-line version of this colonic system, Do [place-name] grada bijeloga, employed in genitive and prepositional inflections with the cities Karlovo, Kanidža, Janok, and Koluto. Depending on the narrative and phraseological situation, the *guslar* may turn to either the colonic or the whole-line form of the essential idea, the only difference between them consisting of the metonymic noun-epithet phrase "the white city." Kukuruzović does just that, using both versions (or lengths) of the idea, while Bajgorić consistently turns to the longer form only, whatever the situation.[53] Thus the two singers' idiolects sort the multiformity of their traditions differently, but still consistently within formulaic patterns and ultimately within traditional rules.[54]

51. Line 1.1157, *Dvades-peto jutro osvanulo* ("The twenty-fifth morning dawned"), is a borderline case and makes the argument for considering *jutro osvanulo* a formula per se.

52. Briefly stated, colon 1 follows normal word order reinforced by IAD (*pȇto*), and colon 2 is organized, again in agreement with conventional order, by SBL (*jȕtro* is initially unaccented).

53. See, for example, line 4.11 of the Bajgorić passage.

54. The adjective *bíla* provides an IAD to override the SBL rule and reverse the normal word order (4-2, with *do* proclitic). The SBL rule orders colon 2, and the IAD (*grȃda*) in this case does not supersede it, again yielding a reversal of customary order.

1.847. Lines 1.846–48 enumerate, in a fashion very common in Serbo-Croatian epic, the characters who will undertake an action, in this and many other instances a journey. The middle member of this short passage well illustrates typical differences between the compositional functions of the first and second cola:

I do njega Djulić bajraktara,

Both cola are apparently formulas in their own right, recurring elsewhere with other partners but combining uniquely in this line. However, an examination of the referent reveals that colon 1 is only one version of a multiform (cf. *A do njega, I kod njega*; with morphological adjustments as well) that is incomplete in itself, a very generically defined system that seeks a complement to perform its enumerative function. For its part, the second-colon complement, here *Djulić bajraktara*, just as characteristically permits no change other than morphology. In other words, the relationship between these cola is of the common type that includes a second colon which fixes on one of various possibilities and tolerates no systemic change and a first colon which tends to vary systematically or, from the point of view of traditional rules, inevitably. Compositionally, colon 1 adjusts the grammar and position of the line to bring into play the semantic and informational focus of colon 2. This kind of combination reflects the effect of right justification at every level, most obviously in its characteristic colon structure and texture and the formative role of traditional rules.[55]

1.849. One final example from the Kukuruzović passage will demonstrate the formative role of traditional rules and of the second-level process of leonine rhyme, as well as furnish an instance of idiolectal phraseology:

Kad rekoše da se rastadoše,

While viewing colon 1 as a formula may be viable according to the classical definition, that perspective leaves unexplained the fact that it can occur either as a colonic clause complete in itself (in which case application of the label *formula* seems more justified) or as an incomplete prelude to a whole-line system. In this example what binds the cola together and contributes a certain degree of stability, in addition of course to the continuous syntax, is the leonine rhyme of the two aorist verbs in colon-final position (in -*oše*). Functionally a feature of the poetic language (since it does not figure to any extent in contemporary standard Serbo-Croatian), the aorist tense is not seldom employed in this way as a syntactic/phonological bridge between cola that tends to help preserve phraseology over time.[56] In addition, then, to the force of SBL in

---

55. Colon 1 forms an accentual group of four syllables (proclitic-enclitic-disyllable) that admits variation most readily at positions 1-2, while colon 2 follows SBL (2-4).

56. Numerous examples could be cited from the Stolac referent, such as *Kad rekoše da pokajitiše* (6.513) or *Kad rekoše da se kumovaše* (1.139). See further Stankiewicz 1973.

both cola and the formulaic pattern that underlies the whole line, the colon-end syntactic balance and rhyme in aorist tenses provides traditional structure. And within this structure, Bajgorić varies slightly but noticeably from Kukuruzović by employing a traditional linear "word" that substitutes a second coordinate phrase for the dependent clause used by Kukuruzović:

To rekoše, pa se rastadoše   (4.445)

They spoke, then they took their leave

Such idiolectal variance within the scope of traditional rules amounts to the individual's signature on the unwritten document of oral traditional style.

HALIL BAJGORIĆ

In looking further at selected phrases in the passage from Halil Bajgorić (4.10–35), we shall again be concerned with description of the complexity of the oral traditional idiom, and specifically with understanding the role of traditional rules and of second-level processes in generating phraseology. At the same time, we shall continue to point out examples of the singer's personal idiolect versus instances of the traditional dialect shared by both *guslari*. By extending the analysis from Kukuruzović to Bajgorić, we not only generalize our results beyond a single poet's repertoire but also offer a more finely articulated perspective on the inherent complexity of the phraseology as a firm basis for the eventual establishment of an aesthetics suited to the art of oral traditional verse-making.[57]

4.12. Early in the Bajgorić passage we encounter a line reminiscent in its typical texture of many verses by Kukuruzović:

U djidjije od Kotara bane.

As the underlining indicates, the colon *od Kotara bane* recurs in other combinations as well as in a whole-line association that we may tentatively call systemic. The evidence for this system is a single comparand found only in this same text:

U komšije od Kotara bane   (4.97)

Near his neighbor the ban of Kotar

In fact, the second colon itself is systemic, with the ban of Janok (*od Janjoka bane*) as its referent, and the whole line seems more the result of traditional rules than of a linear pattern. The situation is thus a familiar one: the core of the linear phrase is a second-colon system of tight definition and limited

---

57. I repeat the caveat that the referent for the Bajgorić Return Song is considerably smaller than that for the three Return Songs by Kukuruzović, for the reasons stated above. This difference will result in fewer comparanda for the elements of diction used by Bajgorić, especially, of course, for those phrases limited to his idiolect.

multiformity which is shaped to fit the narrative and phraseological situation with the aid of a "nonce" first colon based on traditional rules. The SBL constraint marshals the phraseology of both cola—reinforcing the normal word order in colon 1 (1-3, or 4 with *U* proclitic) and causing a reversal in colon 2 (IAD, *bâne*, 4-2 with *od* proclitic)—while the second-level process of a formulaic system assists in maintaining stability in the second part of the line. Right justification forms the basis for the composition of the verse, both in the relationship between cola and in the intra-colonic texture of the phrases.

In contrast to Bajgorić, Kukuruzović develops three additional whole-line patterns using *od* [Janjoka/Kotara] *bane*. As might be expected, one of these consists of a complex of lines introducing speeches, among them the following:

Progovara od Janjoka bane:	(6.764)
The ban of Janok began to talk:	
Tad im reče od Janjoka bane:	(6.873)
The ban of Janok spoke to them:	
Tada reče od Janjoka bane:	(6.1913)
Then the ban of Janok spoke:	

All of these initial cola, the latter two related formulaically, also combine with other noun-epithet formulas, the introduction lines in Serbo-Croatian epic being many and various. A second category involves the opening colon A da vidiš... ("But you should have seen...") or its near-relative, but again this fairly fixed initial phrase finds completion in any number of noun-epithet sequences. A third category, or traditional word, one which happens to include only *od Janjoka bane* and no other colonic name in the present sample, is

Udrijo je od Janjoka bane	(2.726 and 7 ×)
The ban of Janok attacked	

Apart from its usage in 4.12, then, the second-colon system has a life of its own and recurs in three quite different kinds of lines. A smooth-surface, synchronic model for such phraseology will not suffice; the rule of thumb for traditional diction continues to be its heterogeneity and complexity.[58]

4.15. At times the distinction between essential ideas and their expression proves less than absolutely discrete, as this apparently simple line of specification illustrates:

A najviše Bojičić Alija.

---

58. Also worthy of mention is the fact that Kukuruzović evolves an alternate and idiolectal formulaic phrase for the idea expressed in *od Janjoka bane*: the colonic form *mlad janjočki bane* ("the young ban of Janok"), which is not found in Bajgorić's repertoire. As with the *grada bijeloga* expression discussed in reference to 1.845 above, the added concept of *mlad* is metonymic and not to be considered as forming a different essential idea.

The interpretation encoded in the underscoring has broken *najviše* into its two constituent morphemes, the superlative prefix *naj-* and the comparative root *više*, in order to show that multiformity in a traditional word need not respect what we customarily define as a lexical unit.[59] Thus comparanda for 4.15 include such lines as

A najprije Bojičić Alija:	(4.38)
And first of all Bojičić Alija:	
A najprije gaće i košulje,	(3.53)
And first of all pants and shirts,	
A najprvo pade do Otara.	(2.1955)
And very first he came down to Otar.	
A najpotlje vjerenica ljuba	(1.415 and 2 ×)
And finally the beloved fiancée	

Notwithstanding the usually slight differences in connotation of the root word (the final example being equivalent syntactically but semantically exactly opposite), the syntactic pattern is identical throughout, and the general idea of the four colonic phrases is certainly consistent enough to support terming these lines members of a formulaic system. But we come yet closer to the truth when we interpret the whole line as composed of that initial colonic system—incomplete by itself and requiring a focus in a new phrase—and a characteristically more strictly defined second colon. Most often that partner phrase will be a noun or a noun-epithet formula of little or no flexibility.[60] *Bojičić Alija* thus completes the colonic system with the customary invariable phrase, and, while we have little evidence for calling 4.15 a whole-line system by the classical definition, we misinterpret the line if we do not take into account the association of the first-colon formulaic phrase with the more stable focus it requires for completion of its function.

In addition, it is well to note the idiolectal character of Bajgorić's traditional "word," if we may in some way see this line as a unit. For he uses only *najviše* (1 ×) and *najprije* (2 ×) in positions 2–4, while Kukuruzović employs only *najprvo* (1 ×) and *najpotlje* (8 ×). As for the second colon by itself, once again we have an example of a phrase that combines with numerous different partners to form lines otherwise unrelated to this one, and once again some of these lines are integral units in themselves. In effect, then, the colonic element *Bojičić Alija* offers us evidence that traditional words can serve two, or even more, masters: they can exist both as self-contained units to be pressed

59. Of course, there are many examples of multiformity in which a colon is treated as a word—such as noun-epithet sequences that add inflections only to the end of the colon-final lexical unit—but formulaic character of the sort observed in 4.15 is much rarer.

60. In addition to those examples cited above, we find instances of *od Orašca Tale, Pero generale,* and *beg Mustajbeg lički.*

into service in association with phrases such as *A naj*[-više/-prije] and as permanent parts of whole lines repeated verbatim and themselves understood as (larger) units. As in the case of Homeric phraseology, the spectrum of diction as evidenced by the Stolac material contains both cola and whole lines of every description, and it is this richness that is the *guslar's* traditional inheritance.

4.16. The description of the Turks' noisy wailing in prison presents another example of the heterogeneity of traditional phraseology:

Cmile Turci za nedjelju dana.

The Stolac concordance shows that the simplex *cmil-* (from *cmiliti*, "to cry out, lament") occurs in one of three formulaic systems and nowhere else:[61]

1. [x] cmili [za nedjelju dana/tri bijela dana]   (4 ×)

    [x] cried out [for a week of days/three white days]

2. [Kako/Ako] cmili, nevolja [mu/joj] bila   (3 ×)

    [How/If] he cried out, it was [his/her] misfortune

3. [x] u tamnici cmile   (6 ×)

    [x] cried out in prison

System 2 is a well-defined whole-line pattern whose syntax and acoustic patterning *(cmili/bila)* contribute to its stability. System 3, much less tightly organized, admits a wide range of first-colon noun phrases as subjects; while this pattern is surely not the same sort as system 2, it would be shortsighted simply to call it a colonic unit and ignore its connection to the initial colon. As the underlining suggests, the system that lies behind 4.16 takes a variable subject (either *sužanj*, "prisoner," or *Turčin*, "Turk") and one of two second cola, both denoting a period of time. The verse thus has a whole-line identity, a linear pattern. But, as in other examples we have considered, the second colon also has a life of its own in traditional diction; both *za nedjelju dana* and *tri bijela dana* appear in other, unrelated combinations.[62] Once again we have evidence that a phraseological element—typically a relatively more sharply defined and more stable second colon—can exist both as part of a whole-line pattern and as a fully formed unit with an independence signaled by its compositional adaptability.

Of the three systems involving *cmil-*, the first two are employed by Kukuruzović only and the third by Bajgorić only. In addition to these idiolectal categories of phrases, even the choice of numbers in the variable colonic

---

61. The word order in the first colon of system 1 can be reversed, as in 4.16, for reasons discussed below (note 64).

62. Examples include *Od dnev' do dnev' za nedjelju dana* ("From one day to the next for a week of days," 1.1261) and *Ev' imade tri bijela dana* ("There passed three white days," 6.1492).

TABLE 20.   Idiolectal and Dialectal Phrases for Time

Phrase	Kukuruzović	Bajgorić	Provenance
A za nedjelju dana	2	1	dialectal
B nedjelica dana	3	0	idiolectal—K
C tri bijela dana	12	0	idiolectal—K
D dva bijela dana	0	2	idiolectal—B
E sedam godin' dana	7	0	idiolectal—K
F dvanaest godin' dana	3	0	idiolectal—K
G cijo mjesec dana	2	0	idiolectal—K

pattern [x] *bijela dana* helps to characterize the individual singer; for Kukuruzović the number is always three, for Bajgorić always two. In fact, some other analogous phrases for duration of time, all of them second-colon formulas and nearly half of them constituting part of many different linear arrangements, are also idiolectal, as table 20 shows. To further illustrate the heterogeneity and complexity of the phraseology, we note that only examples A and D are strictly colonic and reveal no involvement with whole-line patterns of any sort. These are also the only two formulas of this category in Bajgorić's analyzed repertoire.[63] Formulas F and G, at the other end of the spectrum, occur without exception in whole-line arrangements. The remainder of this category turns out to consist of phrases that can combine with a number of initial cola and, like *za nedjelju dana*, can exist as units complete in themselves or as participants in larger units. This kind of multiformity, with units that comprise one or more different types of traditional phrases, is characteristic of all levels of oral epic structure in Serbo-Croatian.

The fundamental traditional rules that govern the formation of the second-level system underlying 4.16 prove quite simple. As is typical of the more flexible first colon, the word order—here reversed from the conventional prose norm—could go either way: both words are disyllables and both have initial accent.[64] The phrase *za nedjelju dana* (4-2 with *za* proclitic), which follows conventional sequence, is ordered by the IAD *dána*.

4.17. Often a particular phraseological pattern proves dependent on the rules that govern the phraseology of the *deseterac* and, at the same time, looms larger than the classically defined formulaic system. Line 4.17 exemplifies such a pattern:

Polu grada rezil učinili,

---

63. We may recall that figures for different levels of formulaic density as presented in section B also suggested that Bajgorić depended more on colonic and less on whole-line patterns than did Kukuruzović.

64. Both show IAD: *cmíle, Túrci.* In the three additional examples of the same phrase system, *cmíli* (IAD) takes second position at syllables 3-4 in deference to *sužanj* and *Tùrčin,* neither of which is initially accented.

While the first colon has no formulaic relatives anywhere in the Stolac referent, colon 2, with its essential idea of "to bring shame," is repeated elsewhere verbatim and thus qualifies as a formula. But, as in most cases, this first approximation does not penetrate to the functional core of the phrase, and we must look to the multiformity of the second colon in order to understand its compositional structure. The most faithful representation of the pattern on which the latter section of the line is based would be [x] učinijo, -ili, -ila, -iti, etc., where *x*, the direct object of some form of *učiniti* ("to do" or "make"), is a Turkish loan word. Under the influence of the Turkish language, especially during the Ottoman Empire, the poetic idiom admitted many such lexical items and enclosed or fossilized a large number of them in what amounts to a traditional "word." To put it another way, this very system amounts to diachronic evidence of the influence of Turkish vocabulary on Serbo-Croatian *deseterac* diction.[65] What was diachronically an influence has become a synchronic stylistic habit as construed traditionally in a pattern much larger and more pervasive than most formulaic systems; many variant ideas, rather than one essential one, are imaged in this pattern, but the integrity of the phrases as belonging to one "word" is beyond question.

The [x] *učiniti* element presents an interesting morphology, as documented in the following list:[66]

Turkicism	Meaning	Frequency
(h)izmet	service	20 ×
zulum	violence	19 ×
rezil	shame	16 ×
ićram	honor	14 ×
jemin	oath	13 ×
konak	overnight stay, shelter	12 ×
zorba	force	11 ×
hinla	trick	10 ×
pešćeš	gift	6 ×
timar	grooming	5 ×
juriš	attack	5 ×
dževab	response	3 ×
haber	news	2 ×
sejir	vista	2 ×
fidah	sacrifice	2 ×
gajret	attempt	1 ×
takum	service	1 ×
teslim	delivery	1 ×
hisa	share	1 ×
devar	grave-offering	1 ×

65. Cf. Skendi (1953) on the influence of the Albanian language and epic phraseology on Serbo-Croatian epic.

66. The source for the meaning of the Turkicisms is Škaljić (1979), with my English translations.

On this pattern, well attested in the analyzed repertoires of both *guslari*, Kukuruzović idiolectally erects a related "word." In effect, he turns the unit to yet wider usage by including some non-Turkicisms, that is, words of Slavic etymology that did not enter the poetic language during the Ottoman occupation or later but were part of the earlier language stock. As opposed to 145 total occurrences of this colonic "word" with Turkicisms over the whole of the Stolac referent, we find only nineteen instances of the same pattern with a native noun or adverb in the substitutable position:

krivo	falsely, wrong	6 ×
pomoć	help	4 ×
trka	race	3 ×
jad	misery	2 ×
tako	so	1 ×
mjesto	place	1 ×
logor	camp	1 ×
želja	wish	1 ×

Clearly, the phrase pattern was developed for and continues to serve words of Turkish origin, but Kukuruzović has formed phrases by analogy with the older pattern, that is, neologisms that take their structure from a traditional unit.[67]

The influence of traditional rules is manifest in the SBL organization of the second colon of 4.17 and of all its Turkish and Slavic relatives; furthermore, the 2-4 syllabic grouping throughout the 164 examples in the Stolac referent constitutes proof that the phrase pattern and not the individual instance is primary, since none of those instances which feature IAD have changed the already reversed SBL word order. In fact, and significantly, traditional rules also marshal the ostensibly unformulaic phraseology in colon 1. The IAD rule sorts the balanced 2-2 configuration by exerting pressure to align *grâda* with the third and fourth positions at the end of the colon. Thus, even if *Polu grada* cannot be shown to be formulaic, it can still be understood as traditional, for it follows the rules from which all second-level features of phrase generation take their cue.

4.18. The very next line furnishes another example of what amounts to a nonformulaic but still fundamentally traditional phrase:

<u>Učinili</u> i uzabunili.

---

67. I judge the pattern to have arisen from use with Turkicisms because of their much greater number and variety in the repertoires of both singers. On the basis of the Stolac referent, I further posit that Kukuruzović used eight additional phrases constructed on the pattern of the system; although he may have learned these eight phrases elsewhere and thus not have been responsible himself for their "creation," they are nonetheless a feature of his idiolect on the basis of available evidence.

Here again the underlining is misleading, because it depends on a single recurrence of *učini-* in initial position:

> U z'o čas ga trku učinijo,
> <u>Učinijo</u> trku i veselje.   (6.1169–70)
>
> Just now I completed the race,
> Completed the race and my joy.

Moreover, the instance of *učinijo* in 6.1170, just as *učinili* in 4.18, derives not from a formulaic phrase but rather from the second-level process of terracing; in both cases the verb *učini-* repeats the final element of the preceding line. As for the second colon, although *uzabunili* is a hapax legomenon in the Stolac referent, we can see that sound-patterning, another second-level process, also helps to hold the line together. Not only the syntactic balance of two past plural verbs and the consequent leonine rhyme in *-ili*[68] but also the assonance of *uč-* and *uz-* participate in an aural network that binds the cola into a linear whole. In respect to traditional rules, we should remember that leonine rhyme depends on the relative prominence of colon-end positions (3–4 and 9–10), so that the *-ili* sound pattern is finally a reflex of right justification.

4.22. Like many other examples we have considered, this line finds its focus in a relatively well-defined second-colon system tailored to the narrative situation by a first-colon phrase of much more flexible texture:

> <u>Tad banica banu govorila:</u>

The second-colon system, best understood as a noun in the dative singular (indirect object) followed by *govorila* (also including other inflections for gender) that recurs thirteen times in the analyzed referent, has a life of its own outside this particular combination. As a formulaic phrase it also follows SBL, with the syllabic configuration 2-4.[69] At the same time, the apparent system [x] *banica*, where *x* stands for *Tad, A, Pa,* or *Kad,* is more a direct reflex of traditional rules than a systemic unit; according to right justification, it varies only at the beginning of colon 1 and assigns the three-syllable item to positions 2–4. Once more we view the typical difference of pattern and formulaic character between the two cola of the *deseterac*. In this case, however, the whole-line structure is supported by another second-level focusing process, that of function—for 4.22 is one of a number of lines used as introductions to speeches, and, just as in the Old English and Homeric epic traditions, these kinds of verses gain a stability due at least in part to their compositional role.

---

68. Cf. the leonine rhyme and syntactic balance of two aorist-tense verbs in the Kukuruzović passage (line 1.849).

69. Only three of these 13 reverse the 2-4 order, all of the reversals involving IAD or MAT (*Zlâti, mâjci,* and *Halílu*).

4.26. This line also functions as one of introduction to a speech, but in this instance idiolectally:

Skoči bane, pa srdito viče:

Whether the first-colon system is deployed as a sentence complete in itself (four occurrences) or as part of a whole-line phrase (four occurrences), all examples in the referent are from the Bajgorić texts. Characteristically of first-colon formulas, this phrase shows a good deal of flexibility in the length of the "word," in its combinations with second cola, and in its own variability.[70] When Kukuruzović wishes to express the same essential idea as in the first colon of 4.26, he turns to one of two dialectal systems of his own:

Tada skoči Pero generale	(1.794; 2 related exs.)
Then General Pero jumped up	
A Alija na noge skočijo	(11×)
And Alija jumped to his feet	

In their particular ways, all of these cola and lines follow basic traditional rules, but the resulting phraseological variety testifies that these same rules leave room for a singer to develop and maintain individual habits of composition.

The latter portion of 4.26, *pa srdito viče*, contains a middle element that proves a hapax legomenon in the Stolac referent, but we still have sufficient information to declare the colon a traditional phrase. For even if we chose not to define an involved system pa/a/i [adverb/adv. phrase] viče, so that lines like A sve beže pa iz grla viče (6.143) can be viewed as comparanda, traditional rules will govern the formation of the colon; that is, the IAD *viče* seeks colon-final position and reverses the SBL order (4-2, with *pa* proclitic). That IAD is more fundamental than the second-level focus contributed by the proposed formulaic system can readily be seen by observing that, leaving aside the four formulaic comparanda, all eight additional occurrences of *viče* in colon 2 are at positions 9–10 while ten of twelve in colon 1 are at positions 3–4.[71] This line thus offers a clear example of how traditional rules shape second-level processes: underlying the more immediately recognizable systemic patterns of the diction are rules that depend ultimately on the principle of right justification. In a sense, traditional rules are as current as the *guslar*'s most recent performance and yet as ancient as Indo-European versification.

70. Examples of its morphology include *Skoči Djulić, hizmet mu učini* ("Djulić leaped up, he served him," 3.180); *Skoči momak na noge lagane* ("The young man leaped up to his light feet," 3.19); *Skoči Mujo i za glasa viče* ("Mujo leaped up and shouted in a loud voice," 4.333).

71. The two exceptions to the rule are in fact not exceptions. One of them, *A viče mu buljubaša Mujo* ("And commander Mujo called to him," 4.299), uses enclitic binding (and normal enclitic placement) to construct the first colon (SBL, 1–3), while in the other, *Viče bane četiri telala* ("The ban called four criers," 6.806), the initial colon is sorted by the other IAD (*báne*).

SUMMARY

Through the foregoing analyses and examples I have attempted to show that the oral poetic language of Serbo-Croatian epic is a much more complex and sensitive instrument than has heretofore been realized. We have seen, in short, that all elements of phraseology—all traditional "words"—are not created equal. The wide spectrum of diction includes some units that are always repeated exactly, some that undergo only morphological change, some that admit regular substitution and can be meaningfully described as formulaic systems, and some "non-formulaic" cola and lines that are best viewed as the inevitable issue of fundamental traditional rules. Nor does the traditional expression always assume one canonical length: units of colonic, linear, and multilinear dimensions have been shown to populate the Stolac referent. In the face of this heterogeneity and complexity, we have argued, it proves only logical to recognize the limitations of the concepts of formula and formulaic system, and to understand that synchronic approximations that go far toward making evident the characteristic multiformity of the *guslar*'s poetic language can also obscure its variety and richness. Our philological and critical imperative is consequently quite clear: we must come to appreciate this variety and richness as the basic character of the compositional idiom if we are to make informed and faithful aesthetic judgments about the works of art it figures forth.

Specifically, we need to concentrate on *traditional rules* as the most fundamental and pervasive influence on the making and re-making of diction. As illustrated in chapter 3, the *deseterac* verse form preserves the ultimately Indo-European features of syllabic count, caesura, and right justification. This third feature is expressed idiosyncratically in the decasyllable in a variety of ways: the initial shorter colon of four syllables followed by the longer one of six; preference for ictus at positions 3 and 9, then 1 and 5; shorter-before-longer arrangements of words and accentual groups in both cola (SBL); initially accented disyllables favored at positions 3–4 and 9–10 (IAD); medially accented trisyllables favored at positions 8–10 (MAT); and a generally greater flexibility in colon 1 and correspondingly greater fixity in colon 2. This combination of rules (and not simply the poor approximation of a trochaic pentameter and associated patterns) underlies the formation of all *deseterac* phraseology, no matter what more superficial process may aid in its creation and maintenance. In other words, while formulas and systems explain the poetic idiom inexactly as a dictionary of quantitatively equivalent but qualitatively different paradigms, traditional rules account for the entire spectrum of traditional phraseology—every line of every song-text.

And just as we see these rules in action in every line of every text, so we also see their formative influence on the series of second-level processes that further focus the expression of essential ideas in the poetic tradition. To put it hierarchically, none of these focusing features can operate except within traditional rules; since each of the second-level features pertains to a very small percentage of the lines in a given sample, each can affect its limited constituency only if it works within the set of constraints that determines the shape of all lines in the wordhoard. At this second level, the formula and system are the most pervasive structuring devices in the poetry, but we must remember that these two terms refer to an enormous "dictionary" of actual units and that even the most generative of single phraseological patterns oversees a relatively modest number of cola and lines. In fact, even when a *guslar* makes a "new" phrase by analogy to a pattern he already knows and uses, he does so under the immediate influence of that pattern but within the much more far-reaching code of traditional rules. As we have seen, formulaic structure is a significant aspect of diction, and analysis by formula can lead us to understand the multiformity of oral epic phraseology in numerous interesting and valuable ways; nonetheless, formulaic theory is at its most powerful only when we also take into account its basis and continuing context in universally applicable traditional rules.

Other second-level or focusing processes also assist in the creation and maintenance of traditional diction, among the most important of which is sound-patterning. In Serbo-Croatian epic, assonance, consonance, and alliteration play large roles, often stitching together words, cola, phrases, lines, or even extended passages. The primary site for rhyme proves to be colon-end, that is, either at 9–10 in two successive lines (relatively less frequent) or at 3–4 and 9–10 in a single line (also called leonine rhyme and considerably more frequent). Both forms derive from the stress-emphasis at colon-end, which is in turn a reflex of right justification. Thus institutionalized internal rhyme constitutes another example of a synchronic echo of an ancient poetic characteristic.

Added to these focusing processes are the stylistic features of terracing or pleonasm, which actually promotes unnecessary enjambement in Serbo-Croatian, and of syntactic balance or parallelism, which can take myriad forms either within a single line or from one line to another. We may end this list, necessarily incomplete,[72] with the feature of thematic focus, whereby, as in the sample text from Bajgorić, narrative structure to some extent marshals the deployment of certain phraseology.[73] But I must stress that while all of

72. The list is necessarily incomplete because second-level processes are both dialectal and idiolectal. This discussion is intended to cover the major features of traditional diction as a whole and not to treat exhaustively any important features in the analyzed repertoires of these two singers. It remains for future investigators to add to and qualify these beginning (but hopefully fundamental) remarks.

73. I emphasize that this last principle affects only a limited number of phrases, since many lines—formulas and tightly defined systems among them—occur independently of thematic structure. See chapter 8 below; cf. G. Nagy 1979, 2–4 and passim.

these processes, from formulaic structure through the thematic constraint, participate dynamically in the shaping of diction and therefore in the act of oral traditional epic composition, all are decidedly second-level features in that they affect only limited parts of the much larger body of *deseterac* phraseology. All of them operate on traditional diction that takes its archetypal shape from rules that in turn echo the prosody of the epic decasyllable and ultimately that of Indo-European verse.

One more step remains to be taken in our assessment of traditional structure in Serbo-Croatian phraseology, and in taking that step it is well to remember how our investigation has proceeded from establishing the general tenets of Indo-European prosody to a tradition- and genre-dependent view of the *deseterac*[74] and on to the two levels of phraseological organization—traditional rules and a series of second-level focusing processes. Rules and processes as powerful as these, generating at the first level all lines in the Stolac referent and shaping at the second level much smaller but still significant groups of verses, must necessarily be generic enough to order the expression of a vast panorama of traditional ideas. For this very reason, they will also leave space for a *guslar* to place his personal (if largely ephemeral) signature on the wordhoard by making or re-making idiolectal phraseology employed, as far as can be determined, only by him. For the mediocre singer, the more general local dialect of the poetic language shared among the singers in his community will be the phraseological support used to buttress by far the greatest part of his individual performance. But the talented singer will depend somewhat less on the lingua franca of verse dialect and at least slightly more on his own idiolect.[75] From the perspective described and advocated throughout this chapter, a *guslar*'s idiolect consists of expressions unique to an individual and yet constructed in accordance with traditional rules; we shall see more evidence of the individual's signature on his tradition when we study thematic structure in chapter 8. Thus, to the lengthy lists of tradition- and genre-dependent factors that make for complexity and suppleness in the compositional idiom as employed by any given singer, we can add the "singer-dependent" phenomenon of a traditional idiolect.

What do we gain by tracing the *guslar*'s words from Indo-European versification forward through the maze of compositional devices described in this chapter? And what do we make of the result—a complex, heterogeneous, ever-evolving collection of inequivalent elements overseen by rules and processes no singer ever consciously imagined? Briefly stated, what we gain, apart

74. Note that Lord has laid the basis for a tradition-dependent perspective on phraseology: "Whereas thought, in theory at least, may be free, sung verse imposes restrictions, *varying in degree of rigidity from culture to culture*, that shape the form of thought" (1960, 31; emphasis added). See also Lord 1986c.

75. On a similar point, see Bynum 1981, esp. 72–77; cf. Lord 1960, 49.

from a philologically sound profile, is a foundation for aesthetic inquiry that is firm because it is faithful to the language and poetics of Serbo-Croatian epic. By formulating rules for the phraseological events we perceive as lines, we begin to restore a lost complexity to oral traditional diction; in effect, the point of view advocated in this chapter, and for that matter throughout the volume, allows us to "re-complicate" poetic composition, to take it out of the arena of lockstep simplicity and back to the realm of language—the most complex of human abilities and arts. On the basis of the observations made and the examples provided above, it should be more than obvious that the *guslar* is no mere assembler of pre-fabricated parts, no automaton mindlessly spinning lines of verse from a limited selection of movable counters.[76] Rather, the Yugoslav oral singer is fully a poet who has come to be able to speak his native poetic idiom, with a fluency determined by a combination of his own talents and the bequest he has received from tradition. If we can restore this natural quality to traditional diction by understanding it not as a patchwork of remnants but as a highly complex weave accomplished by blending many different colors and textures according to fundamental rules of order and pattern, then we re-admit the possibility—even the necessity—of oral poetic art in its archetypal sense: the individual *poiesis* of tradition.

76. That this mechanism is not what Milman Parry and Albert Lord had in mind is apparent as early as Parry's M.A. thesis (1923), with its remarkable analogy of Greek traditional verse to Greek sculpture.

SIX

Traditional Phraseology
in *Beowulf* and Old English Poetry

The history of scholarship on formulaic phraseology in Old English poetry is long and complex, stretching from the German Higher Criticism of the nineteenth century to the present, and so I shall make no attempt to summarize its evolution here,[1] choosing instead to proceed directly to an analysis of the phraseology. As in the preceding chapters on ancient Greek and Serbo-Croatian epic diction, the object will be an understanding of the phraseology on its own tradition-dependent terms, that is, on the basis of traditional rules particular to Old English poetry. Once again, reference will be made to the findings of chapter 3 on comparative prosody, and distinctions will be drawn among the three phraseologies involved.[2]

FROM PROSODY TO FORMULAIC STRUCTURE

In lieu of attempting to reshape an existing model in order to represent fully the complex structure of Old English poetic phraseology, let us follow the practice established in earlier chapters and begin by asking what we might reasonably expect to find in the way of formulaic structure. In other words, given the idiosyncratic prosody of *Beowulf* and other Anglo-Saxon poetry, what kind of diction is possible and likely?

We recall that, while the ancient Greek and Serbo-Croatian metrical

---

1. For summaries of prior research, see Foley 1981b, 51–79, 103–16; Foley 1985, 3–77. The latter digest will be updated annually in the "Year's Work" bibliographical section of the journal *Oral Tradition*. See also Alexandra Hennessey Olsen's survey (1986, 1988).

2. Because of the relatively modest size of *Beowulf* (3,182 alliterative lines), I shall occasionally make reference to non-epic Old English poems. At the level of phraseology, genre-dependence in the Old English tradition is not as limiting a factor as it is, for example, in the Serbo-Croatian tradition.

lines—the hexameter and *deseterac*, respectively—show at least some similarity in their outward make-up and inner morphology, the Old English alliterative line diverges widely from these two comparands. Not only is the Anglo-Saxon line a stress-based rather than a quantitative meter, but it also varies significantly in syllable count, has no caesura and therefore no colonic structure, and exhibits nothing of the Indo-European tendency toward what we have called "right justification." Under such variant conditions there is, we discovered, no reason to expect the colonic formulaic morphology typical of Homer and the *guslar*. Indeed, this important dissimilarity was what led to our outright rejection of formula-density tests of Old English verse that use the colonic formula as the phraseological model.

Instead of the encapsulated phrase that can vary only in strictly defined ways under the constraints of syllable count, colon configuration, and other features inherited from the symbiosis of Indo-European meter and phraseology, we encounter in Old English poetry a phrase that in its very inscrutability reflects the prosody that supports it. It is perhaps not an accident that no issue in Old English scholarship has been more and longer contested than the definition of the meter, in part because this Germanic line does not fit any familiar, institutionalized Greco-Roman model. And with the understanding of the prosody in a state of uncertainty, the "metrical conditions" of Parry's concept of the formula could not be adequately and fairly set. If investigators adhered too stubbornly to the colonic formula, or searched for too tidily synchronic a model of its morphology, it is at least in part because they had no way to confront the highly idiosyncratic prosodic underpinnings of Old English poetic diction.

In chapter 3 it was demonstrated that most metrical systems proposed for Old English poetry agree in large part that the chief prosodic features of the line are stress emphasis and alliteration. Beyond these regularly occurring characteristics of the meter, we found that the poet used a limited set of stress-patterns; whether we refer to these patterns as Sievers's Five Types or employ the revisions of Pope, Creed, or Cable, the overall picture is approximately the same: four stress maxima (SMs) per line, with a varying number of secondary and minimal stresses. The possibility for variation is greatly enhanced by the further factors of resolution (more than one syllable under a heavy stress) and ramification (multiple minimally stressed syllables), while the restricted set of permitted half-line types counterbalances the tendency toward multiformity. Whatever metrical theory we may select to tabulate line-types and explain their interrelationships, these are the bare metrical facts one must confront in attempting a faithful account of formulaic structure in Old English verse.

A few additional facts can be derived from these first premises, and they will aid us in pursuing the assortment of traditional structures we find in *Beowulf*. First, from the prior scholarship on prosody and from chapter 3 we can readily see that the alliterative line is a hybrid prosody—that is, it reveals both half-line (or verse) and whole-line levels of metrical organization.[3] At the half-line level, as demonstrated earlier, only a limited number of stress patterns are permitted. Furthermore, all of these patterns, however defined, can occur in either the first or the second verse, so that there is an interchangeability among half-line metrical patterns that is restricted only by the prosodic rule that second half-lines (or b-verses) cannot bear double alliteration. Again unlike the Homeric hexameter and Serbo-Croatian *deseterac*, then, the Anglo-Saxon alliterative line is a balanced, symmetrical unit with essentially interchangeable halves.

At the same time, because alliteration binds the two half-lines together and creates a larger unit at another level, the alliterative line also shows a whole-line metrical structure. Although the individual verses are largely interchangeable, this agreement of initial sounds defines the composite structure as an entity in its own right. And, as we saw in chapter 3, there is evidence that the *Beowulf* poet superimposed on this whole-line variety a set of three favored line-types or -patterns which further organized the meter and his phraseology. Although the corpus of comparable poetry in Old English (that is, epic poetry that could serve a comparative role under the criterion of genre-dependence) is far too small to permit determination of whether this kind of *metrical formula* was a general phenomenon[4] or not, the fact of the increased metrical conservatism constitutes further evidence for whole-line metrical organization.

To summarize, then, we should begin our search for the formulaic structure of *Beowulf* by realizing that the Old English alliterative line consists not of a colon-based, quantitative meter with some expression of right justification,[5] but rather of a stress-based meter which figures itself forth in a limited series of multiforms governed by morphological rules. And while we note the importance of the half-line unit in these respects, we should also remember that the ways in which these multiforms combine under the aegis of binding alliteration reveal that the poet also composes in whole lines. The truest explanation of the compositional process, at least from a metrical perspective, is as a two-level or hybrid process. If we choose to reduce it to only the one or the other (probably to concentration on the half-line, as has usually been done), we may simplify the task of description, but we shall at the same time

---

3. See further Foley 1980b.

4. Compare the assortment of vocal melodies used by the Yugoslav *guslar*; see, e.g., Herzog 1951.

5. As we shall see below, there is a marked tendency for many Old English word-types to seek final position within verses, but there seems to be no way to connect this phenomenon with Indo-European prosody. I resist referring to this tendency as "right justification" because it is not nearly as strong or thoroughgoing a feature in Old English as in ancient Greek and Serbo-Croatian.

remove the rich complexity inherent in the process and sabotage any attempt at a faithful account of formulaic structure.

One last feature, uniquely a characteristic of the Old English line, needs to be brought to light before we proceed to an overall description of the kinds of traditional patterns permitted under the alliterative prosody. This feature stems from the balance between verses in any line, and for that matter among all verses. Given such balance, or interchangeability—so different from the "four and six" cola of the *deseterac* or the complex collection of unequal cola in the Homeric hexameter—it is inherently unlikely that lines will be end-stopped as frequently in Old English as in the other two poetries. That is, the balanced line structure may be construed as actually encouraging enjambement; more often than not, that enjambement may well be of the "unnecessary" variety that carries over into the next line to add to an already syntactically complete utterance,[6] but there is nothing metrical to discourage the use of "necessary" enjambement as well. Indeed, since one verse is, with the exception of the alliterative constraint and metrical formula, just like any other, a phrase may be completed at mid-line or end-line as the poet wishes.[7] Or he may "sort" his traditional patterns over more than a single line, since there is little metrical resistance to doing so. We shall soon see in more detail how this feature affects not only enjambement but also traditional patterns larger than a single line, but for the moment it is perhaps enough to observe that the typically Anglo-Saxon poetic figure of *variation* (the accrual of appositives to a noun or verb to form a paratactic string of poetic synonyms)[8] can be traced to this metrical feature.

THE SPECTRUM OF TRADITIONAL
PHRASEOLOGY IN *BEOWULF*

With these tradition-dependent features of Old English prosody in mind, we should be able to predict the shape of traditional expression to be encountered in *Beowulf*. First, because there is a definite half-line structure to the alliterative line, there should arise a collection of *verse formulas and formulaic systems*. To the extent that the half-line is a functional unit in the act of composition, these "classic" phrases, analogous but not directly comparable to colonic formulas in ancient Greek and Serbo-Croatian epic, should constitute some reasonably extensive part of the poet's and tradition's wordhoard. Of course, there will be qualifications, such as the matter of idiolect versus traditional dialect as

6. See Fry 1968c; cf. chapter 4 above.

7. In the Old English *Maxims*, for example, alliteration seems to be employed to link together discrete gnomic sayings. Compare the phenomenon of "terracing" in Vogul and Ostyak as discussed in Austerlitz (1958), as well as Calvert Watkins's remarks (1976) on responsion.

8. See Robinson 1985.

illustrated for the *guslar* in chapter 5,[9] but prior research has shown that a significant number of such verse units actually does exist and that they are functional.

But here the synchronic model of formulaic structure will no doubt require further articulation from a diachronic point of view—for, as we have seen with other traditional phraseologies, not every "formula" or "system" in a given poetic tradition will answer precisely the same definition. To put it more tellingly, not all of the verse-length patterns found in *Beowulf* and Old English poetry are likely to be exactly equivalent in terms of semantic, rhythmic, or syntactic complexity. If Anglo-Saxon phraseology is as multi-leveled as ancient Greek and Serbo-Croatian, then some half-line patterns will be able to be defined rigorously using all of these three criteria, some will depend more on one or another of the measurements, and some will be mere predispositions that nonetheless recur with regularity and must be recognized as traditional. We may wish to reserve the classical term *formula* only for those units that answer a rather strict definition, but we shall still need in some fashion to explain and to take account of those obviously traditional elements that do not fit the imposed definition. In short, we may expect, if prior experience is any guide, a whole spectrum of formulaic diction that has evolved differentially (and was no doubt continuing to do so)[10] under the tradition-dependent rules of Old English verse-making.

In addition to verse-length units, we should expect to find *whole-line formulas and systems*; the whole-line dimension of the alliterative meter, both the linkage made by alliteration between verses and the whole-line metrical formulas, would promote the formation and maintenance of such longer units. Once again, however, we shall have to make allowance for the probability that not all such longer patterns will readily conform to a single synchronic definition. No less than the verse-length units, whole-line patterns are likely to reveal a spectrum of forms, from absolutely constant verbatim repeats such as lines of introduction, through systemic lines in which one verse is regularly associated with, for example, a given alliterating word in the other verse, and on to weaker associations involving metrical predispositions. Positing both half- and whole-line phraseological units does not amount to a contradictory hypothesis; rather it recognizes the hybrid character of the meter and anticipates its reflection in the poetic diction.

Given the tradition-dependent nature of Old English prosody, and especially its emphasis on stressed elements and relative inattention to the unstressed syllables that surround these metrical peaks, it is not difficult to understand

9. While not enough evidence exists to make final judgments about the extent of idiolectal composition in Old English, some example demonstrations are possible; see Butcher 1986.

10. The modified phraseology in the Christian poems in the Anglo-Saxon poetic corpus is perhaps the best evidence of the continuing "flexibility" and evolution of diction and narrative structure.

why recurrent single words play such an important stylistic role in this poetry. If the meter is such that it foregrounds these words—that is, the root syllables of alliterating and other stressed elements—then these are also the words that are likely to be constant as the poet uses and re-uses his traditional diction. Indeed, this is no more than, for example, Fry (1967b, 203) has pointed out by defining his "formulaic system" in terms of "the identical relative placement of two elements, one a variable word or element of a compound usually supplying the alliteration, and the other a constant word or element of a compound, with approximately the same distribution of unstressed elements."

But can *single words or root syllables* also function as traditional elements outside the verse or whole-line formula? It would seem logical that, especially because the Anglo-Saxon metrical filter is so relatively permeable, roots of single words could form traditional complexes of their own, with their half- or whole-line contexts assembled, as it were, at the moment of composition— although under the traditional rules of poetic composition. Two possibilities, with some middle ground in between them, emerge: first, an associative "bundle" of roots might form around some concept or event and bring along with it the formulas and systems in which the words in question are most often found; or, second, the associative package might supersede verse and linear formulaic structure, just as enjambement is in effect encouraged by the balanced structure of the line. If such morphemic bundles can occur in a phraseology as colonic and relatively tightly bound as ancient Greek,[11] then how much more likely are they to surface in Old English poetry? In fact, to look ahead just slightly, it may be that we can trace the origins of the well-known Anglo-Saxon principle of "verbal echo"[12] in this ultimately prosodic feature of emphasis on roots of single words.

This in turn means that we must hold open the possibility of *formulaic structures* not only lesser than but also *greater than a single verse or line*. There may be such things as three- or even four-verse patterns which are not multi-line "runs" so much as integral structures—that is, they are not concatenations of unitary elements but rather elements in and of themselves. Albert Lord (1986b) has suggested that such longer patterns exist in Anglo-Saxon poetry, and the balanced, additive prosody would seem to favor their formation. If they do exist, then we shall have another very clear example of the tradition-dependent character of Old English verse.

To these working hypotheses we must add a caveat. If analysis of a sample from the *Beowulf* text turns up even a portion of what might be expected on the basis of the alliterative prosody, and especially if—as in ancient Greek and Serbo-Croatian epic—not all members in a certain category can be considered equivalent in form and function, then we shall need a further explanation

---

11. See chapter 4 above; also Peabody 1975, 168–215; Hainsworth 1976.
12. See, e.g., Beaty 1934; Hanning 1973.

that somehow rationalizes the variety. That is, if the synchronic model of the half-line system cannot account for the richness of *Beowulf*'s traditional diction, then another, more fundamental solution must be sought. But first let us see what the poem itself has to tell us.

GRENDEL'S APPROACH TO HEOROT
AND TRADITIONAL STRUCTURE

The ritual gesture for formulaic analysis customarily includes either an exhaustive analysis of the entire text or an apology for the chosen sampling and a claim that the sample to be analyzed is representative of the whole. Since, however, we seek not to reduce the complexity of traditional diction in *Beowulf* to any one model or to "prove" its orality, but rather to discover the kinds of traditional structures that underlie the poem and give it meaning, we shall be content with looking closely at a sample of about thirty lines: the famous tripartite passage involving Grendel's approach to Heorot (702b–30a).[13] Yet at the same time, we shall not be content merely to find some evidence of half-line systems, or of any other single type or form of phraseological structure; instead we shall attempt to uncover whatever sort of structure seems to be operative in each verse and line.

First I present the passage in the original Anglo-Saxon, followed by a quite literal translation into modern English:[14]

Com on wanre niht
scriðan sceadugenga.   Sceotend swæfon,
þa þæt hornreced   healdan scoldon,
ealle buton anum.   Þæt wæs yldum cuþ,   705
þæt hie ne moste,   þa Metod nolde,
se s[c]ynscaþa   under sceadu bregdan;—
ac he wæccende   wraþum on andan
bad bolgenmod   beadwa geþinges.

Ða com of more   under misthleoþum   710
Grendel gongan,   Godes yrre bær;
mynte se manscaða   manna cynnes
sumne besyrwan   in sele þam hean.
Wod under wolcnum   to þæs þe he winreced,
goldsele gumena   gearwost wisse   715
fættum fahne.   Ne wæs þæt forma sið,
þæt he Hroþgares   ham gesohte;
næfre he on aldordagum   ær ne siþðan
heardran hæle,   healðegnas fand!

13. See, e.g., Renoir 1962b on the dramatic, even cinematographic, structure of this episode.

14. I quote from the Klaeber edition (1950), without the diacritics; the three-part structure of the passage is emphasized by added spacing.

Com þa to recede   rinc siðian   720
dreamum bedæled.   Duru sona onarn
fyrbendum fæst,   syþðan he hire folmum (æthr)an;
onbræd þa bealohydig,   ða (he ge)bolgen wæs,
recedes muþan.   Raþe æfter þon
on fagne flor   feond treddode,   725
eode yrremod;   him of eagum stod
ligge gelicost   leoht unfæger.
Geseah he in recede   rinca manige,
swefan sibbegedriht   samod ætgædere,
magorinca heap.   730

        In the dark night
the shadow-goer came stalking. The warriors slept,
those whose duty it was to guard the horned building,
all but one. It was known to men that,   705
if the Ruler did not wish it, the injurer
could not draw them into the shadows;—
but [Beowulf], awake and fiercely angry,
awaited the battle's result, enraged in heart.

Then, out of the moor, under the misty cliffs   710
came Grendel, he bore the wrath of God;
the wicked ravager intended to trap
one of the men in that high hall.
He advanced under the clouds until he could most readily see
the wine-building, the gold-hall of men   715
adorned with plates. Nor was that the first time
that he sought Hrothgar's home;
[but] never in earlier days, either before or since,
did he find stronger hero[es], hall-thanes!

Then to the building the warrior came journeying,   720
the one bereft of joys. The door, held fast by fire-forged bonds,
immediately sprang open after he touched it with his hands;
then the baleful-minded one swung open that building's mouth,
when he was enraged. Following this, the fiend
quickly trod over the decorated floor,   725
went along angry in spirit: from his eyes
there stood out a horrible light, most like fire.
In the building he saw many a warrior,
the band of kinsmen sleeping all together,
a troop of young warriors.   730

ANALYSIS

In what follows I shall consider selected examples of the traditional structure
of this passage, proceeding half-line by half-line but remaining aware that

our examination of alliterative prosody has suggested that patterns both larger and smaller than the single verse are to be expected. Once the analysis is complete, it will be possible to propose a single, overarching theory for traditional phraseological structure that will explain the idiosyncratic form of Old English diction.

702b. Com on wanre niht ("Came in the dark night"). Comparative evidence from other Old English poems[15] may at first sight seem to encourage one of two hypotheses about the traditional structure of this phrase:

> #1: <u>Com</u> [x], where *x* is loosely defined
> #2: <u>Com</u> [x], where *x* is defined as a prepositional phrase

With the added proviso that the stable core of the phrase may include the ubiquitous adverb *þa*, we find numerous examples of the first formulaic system and twelve instances of the second, more limited kind of phrase, including line 702b. But while either of these two descriptions adequately symbolizes some of the connections between the half-line under examination and apparently related verses elsewhere in the poetic corpus, neither of them seems rigorous enough—that is, basic enough—to explain line 702b as a traditional element. What of the rest of the phrase? And what of the relative placement of *com* and the prepositional phrase?

Turning then to *on wanre niht*, we have no more satisfying result. The closest phrase, *on sweartre niht* (*Chr* 872a; also translated as "in the dark night"), occupies an entire half-line by itself, and the only other combination of the root *wan* with *niht* in a prepositional phrase likewise fills a verse on its own (*Glc* 1028b). In fact, this problem of varying "size" or "extent" furnishes us with an early glimpse of a general problem: how are we to explain phrases which serve as both half-lines and parts of half-lines in different contexts?[16]

If the system <u>Com</u> [x] in either of its descriptions and the system <u>on</u> [x] <u>niht</u> cannot completely account for line 702b, we might consider further analysis of the verb *cuman* in order to determine whether there could be some semantic basis for the formula in an "essential idea." Once again, however, the search yields no programmatic result, since other forms of *cuman* behave very differently from the preterite third singular *com*.[17] In addition to providing

---

15. Because of space limitations, I shall cite comparative evidence only selectively, and generally in the footnotes. The interested reader may wish to consult my source for these data, Bessinger-Smith 1978; I also employ the title abbreviations advocated in that volume (pp. xiii-xv).

16. This kind of dual function would be impossible in both ancient Greek and Serbo-Croatian epic phraseology.

17. The plural preterite, *c(w)omon* (also *-an*), occurs in verse-initial position 19.0 percent of the time and in verse-final position 78.6 percent, as compared to 38.5 percent and 57.8 percent, respectively, for the preterite singular *c(w)om*. What is more, of the verse-final occurrences, the plural form occupies only Sievers A and C types, the singular only types B and D/E.

evidence that the *Com* system, if that is what this phrase really is, does not allow much morphological variation, this difference in behavior tells us something significant about formulaic dynamics in Old English. It tells us that the metrical form $\acute{s}$ (a single stress) is somehow importantly different from $\acute{s}\overset{x}{s}$ (a single stress plus an unstressed syllable). If we recall the conclusions of chapter 3, we shall remember that the primary aspects of consistency in the Old English line are alliteration and stress patterns. While the extra syllable in *comon* would mean nothing as far as the absolute syllable count of the line is concerned, the addition of even a single unstressed syllable can interrupt the stress pattern and cause it to change. In effect, such a shift of stress pattern would mean that Parry's criterion of "under the same metrical conditions" would be violated.

But while we do not find this or other such Old English systems exhibiting much morphological variety, we can detect a definite patterning having to do with word-type placement.[18] The monosyllabic preterite third-singular verb tends toward either the very beginning or the very end of the half-line; if it occurs at the beginning, as it does in 702b, it almost never alliterates.[19] This phenomenon, chiefly a metrical requirement because it involves a word-type rather than a single word or semantic grouping, bears no necessary connection with what follows in the half-line, and we find a great variety of complements, from the prepositional phrase as we have it in the present example, through adverbs, to subjects of the verb, and so on. And the phrase *on wanre niht*, itself highly variable in that it can occupy an entire verse or part of one, is combined with the central idea, *com*, to comprise the first in a "rhetorical" series of three "comings."[20]

From a traditional perspective, then, the most formulaic aspect of *com* seems to be its placement as a particular word-type at the beginning of the verse. The poet also has at his command a phrase we may profitably construe as <u>on</u> [x] <u>niht</u>, as long as we do not demand that it be a classically defined verse formula. Diachronically, the predisposition toward placing *com* first and in a non-alliterating position is accompanied by the existence of a phrase that can either fill a verse by itself or complement that placement and word-type. From a synchronic point of view, we may see the poet substituting *wanre* to match the alliteration of the preceding half-line. In short, although we cannot define classical systems that satisfactorily describe the structure and dynamics of 702b according to the usual notion of formulaic structure, there is no doubt that this half-line is the product of traditional processes.

703b. sceotend swæfon ("the warriors slept"). The second half of the line has

18. Cf. O'Neill 1942, and the results of analyses of word-type placement in ancient Greek and Serbo-Croatian epic phraseology, chapters 4 and 5 above, respectively.

19. Fully fifty-two of fifty-three instances of verse-initial *com* in the corpus are non-alliterating.

20. This half-line phrase provides an example of the concatenation of traditional phraseology with what we would call rhetorical structure.

enough correspondences to other diction in the corpus to permit two hypotheses regarding its formulaic system:

$$\#1: \text{ sceotend } [x]$$
$$\#2: \overset{\wedge}{[x]} \text{ swæfon}^{21}$$

The second of these possibilities will better serve our needs, since its essential idea ([x] slept) is more focused than that of the first posited system (the warriors [x]). In addition, it turns out that the very act of sleeping in the Beowulfian context is extremely important and rife with overtones—the "sleeping-feasting" theme has been recognized by a number of commentators as a traditional pattern,²² and so we are further justified in locating the traditional core of the phrase in *swæfon*.

But what does this mean for the rest of the line, since *swæfon* is the only word that does *not* alliterate in the entire line (the alliteration being in *sc*, or [š])? For one thing, this situation should warn us away from making any necessary and exclusive connection between the alliterative staves and the fundamental traditional meaning of the phrase; *swæfon* bears the fourth stress in this line and does not participate in the "sc" series, but it is clearly the most significant word thematically. From another point of view, we may note what amounts to the converse of that observation: that is, the poet manages to harmonize all of the "non-essential" words in the same alliteration. From the core idea of "[x] slept," expressed in the second verse, he constructs a whole-line increment without the benefit of another formula or system. Is this first half-line then an example of "nonce" phraseology²³—of diction created for the moment with no life of its own outside this circumstance?

It would be hard to reconcile purely nonce diction with a traditional perspective. And indeed there is no reason to try to do so, for 703a, while it may have no (surviving) formulaic relatives in the sense conveyed by the classical definition, does participate in a pattern larger than the single half-line, and even than the whole line—that is, in a *cluster* of roots that recur together²⁴ and that collectively embody the idea of the onset of night, shadows, and the ending rhythm of the diurnal cycle. To make the point, I reproduce both another occurrence from *Beowulf* and a section of the passage under consideration:

> oþ ðe nipende   *niht* ofer *ealle*,
> *scadu*helma gesceapu   *scriðan* *cwoman*
> *wan* under wolcnum.   Werod eall aras.   (649–51)

21. Here and elsewhere the caret indicates the position of the alliterating element.
22. See De Lavan 1981; Kavros 1981.
23. Cf. Hieatt 1986.
24. Cf. Ritzke-Rutherford 1981b. The "cluster" unit was earlier suggested in Foley 1974; see also, e.g., Foley 1980b.

until *night*, growing dark over *all*,
the shapes of *shadow*-cover *came stalking*
dark under the clouds. The troop all arose.

  Com on *wanre niht*
*scriðan sceadu*genga. Sceotend swæfon,
þa þæt hornreced healdan scoldon,
ealle buton anum.   (702b–5a)

The density of the italicized words and roots of words that recur even in this small sampling argues strongly for a cluster of morphs, a group of elements associated with a particular traditional idea—the onset of darkness and all of the terror and ravaging that it poetically connotes. Just as comparative prosody would predict, the key elements in this association are stressed roots (whether words or elements of compounds), and the particular shape they take in a given instance is (again as predicted) only very loosely controlled. The fact of their co-occurrence is not to be attributed to half-line formulaic structure, which is at a loss to explain certain phrases. But the cluster of morphs, which as indicated above is a structure consonant with the tradition-dependent character of Old English prosody, accounts both for the striking resemblances between the two passages as a whole and for elements as apparently untraditional as the two hapax legomena *sceadugenga* and *scaduhelma*, in this case an association further focused by their mutual alliterative collocation with *scriðan*. Although we could not imagine this sort of structure occurring in ancient Greek or Serbo-Croatian epic, the *cluster* of roots—a sorting of traditionally associated morphs in metrically and formulaically permissible patterns—is in fact a common feature of traditional structure in *Beowulf*.[25]

Diachronically, then, we can ascribe the first half of line 703 and the association with *scriðan* to a cluster of roots which also occurs elsewhere in *Beowulf* and which bears certain connotations. These connotations are catalyzed by the juxtaposition of the "sleeping" idea, which has definite negative implications in each of the three monster-fights in *Beowulf*. The actual phraseology owes something to what we may style the "[x̣] swæfon" system, but this is a half-line structure very much subject to the larger design of the cluster, as the traditional character of the hapax legomenon *sceadugenga* also illustrates. The poet has thus summoned the core idea of "sleeping and feasting" and linked this important mythic and thematic complex with the associative cluster connoting the onset of night and its perils.

704b. healdan scoldon ("had to guard"). The phrase *healdan scoldon* is a highly traditional phrase whose structure is best appreciated on a number of levels. If we posit a very generic system, [x̣] [sculan/willan], where x represents an in-

----

25. Note that the formula and system are in effect subordinate to the cluster from the point of view of expressive structures; the cluster will use formulas and systems to sort the expression of its elements, but the half- and whole-line patterns are in no way determinative of the cluster's structure or meaning.

finitive bearing the alliteration, we find a great many examples of second-verse phrases. In this case I believe it is helpful to postulate such a generic level of structure,[26] even if it has no true essential idea, because the syntax is so widespread and lends itself to so many different sorts of formulaic systems. In addition, a glimpse of different levels of structure reminds us that the synchronic model of the half-line system, summoned to explain all diction, has to be supplemented to reflect the morphological complexity and diachronic nature of the phraseology.[27]

Within this large group, there are thirteen additional instances in which the infinitive is *healdan*, so we may identify a more focused system, healdan [sculan/willan, finite form], to compare with the system described above.[28] This second-verse pattern has clearly become a traditional element in the diction, and serves a useful compositional purpose in widely different situations with a large selection of half-line partners. But while the system in 704b obviously has a diachronic identity, in both the generic and more focused forms, the same cannot be said for 704a, which merely fills a permitted metrical type. We may thus conceive of the poet as working toward a stable core in the second half-line and adjusting the first verse, with the alliterating element *horn*- providing the synchronic solution to the problem of whole-line structure.[29]

706b. þa Metod nolde ("if the Ruler did not wish it"). At first sight this phrase seems to be a classically defined formula, with a verbatim repetition at *Beowulf* line 967b. But we may also posit a system, þa/þæt [x] nolde, where *x* is the subject of *nolde* and the alliterative stave for the half-line. The first possibility is restricted to *Beowulf* and thus seems, on the basis of available evidence, to be an idiolectal formula, while the more generic system also finds expression in two phrases from *The Battle of Maldon*—*þæt se eorl nolde* (6a) and *þæt se cniht nolde* (9b)—and thus is arguably a tradition-wide system.

But once again we gain a full understanding of the phrase only by taking the whole-line pattern into account as well. Consider these two lines from *Beowulf*:

> þæt hie ne moste,   þa Metod nolde,   (706)
>
> that he might not [draw] them, if the Ruler did not wish it,
>
> Ic hine ne mihte,   þa Metod nolde,   (967)
>
> I might not [hinder] him, if the Ruler did not wish it,

---

26. Cf. the Serbo-Croatian pattern of [Turkicism] *učiniti* studied in chapter 5, an element that had no true essential idea but that provided a way to understand the entry of Turkish words into the epic *Kunstsprache* under the aegis of traditional rules.

27. Note also that *sculan* and *willan*, especially in their disyllabic forms, seek line-end; that is, they are regularly positioned as the fourth, and most frequently non-alliterating, stress in the line.

28. It is interesting in this regard how untraditional the uses of *healdan* are in the Psalms, texts which are of course translations from the Latin vulgate; see P104.8.3, P120.4.2, P148.6.2.

29. In addition, *horn*- is closely associated with Heorot, and the line as a whole follows the most common of the metrical formulas discussed in chapter 3.

Clearly, the *Beowulf* poet is employing a whole-line pattern, with just the sort of consistency and also the kind of variability we predicted on the basis of the Anglo-Saxon alliterative meter. The first half-line shows traditional placement of the single stressed item in an a-verse configuration,[30] and the line is filled out by the much more stable formula in the b-verse. In each case the b-verse, though informational, is also a bridge to the next line (and next alliterative pattern), and the bridging is accomplished by use of a ready-made formula. Again in each case, the poet will go on to specify the very general action of this line in a subsequent infinitive dependent on *moste* or *mihte*. One of the aspects of the utility of 706a, then, is its non-specific lead-in to a specific following action.

To summarize, this line exhibits half-line prosody and phrase patterns (placement of *moste/mihte* and the b-verse formula), as well as whole-line prosody and phrase patterns (collocation and the whole-line system). In effect, the entire construction reaches forward to the next line, since *moste/mihte* requires an infinitive to complete its sense. On the basis of available data, the phrase *þa Metod nolde* seems to be an idiolectal reflex of a more generic, tradition-wide formulaic system, while the whole-line pattern is the *Beowulf* poet's own compositional element.[31]

707a. se s[c]ynscaþa ("the injurer"). This half-line, whether construed as the manuscript *synscaða* or as above,[32] has three formulaic relatives in four additional occurrences of the main word:

þa se synscaþa	(*Jln* 671b)
þone synscaðan	(*Bwf* 801b)
þær ðe synsceaðan	(*Chr* 706a)

At least we can define a system—[x] s(c)ynscað-, where *x* represents one or more function words—that could theoretically underlie all of these phrases. But in ascribing the half-lines to this system, we are doing little more than conferring formulaic character on a single word. It would be better, and truer to Old English diction as we have examined it, to recognize in this regularity not a substitutable system but rather consistent placement of a word-type ($\acute{s}\,\widehat{ss}$) at the end of a verse, with flexibility in what precedes the word. The C-Type metrical pattern institutionalizes that flexibility in a particular way, a way that in turn allows for grammatical and syntactic adaptability,

---

30. In a second-verse version, we might have a pattern such as **þæt hie ne þonan moste*.

31. I do not mean that he created that pattern; it is impossible to ascertain who might be personally responsible for phraseology formed according to traditional rules, and even the successful assigning of this or that element to a given individual may be insignificant. I mean only to say that, whether within a local tradition no longer preserved or whatever, the *Beowulf* poet is using an element idiosyncratically, as the unique reflex of a more general system.

32. Emendation to *scynscaða* was suggested in order to match the alliterative pattern in [sc].

as the three phrases cited above demonstrate. The traditional, diachronic character of the verse lies in the placement of *s[c]ynscaþa* and its recurrences (all but once)[33] in the C-Type metrical pattern; synchronically these features make available to the composing poet a good deal of grammatical and syntactic latitude in the opening syllables of the verse.

A further level of structure then derives from this consistent word-type placement in verse-final position. We can describe two formulaic systems involving the same root:

#1: [x] [y]-sceaða-

#2: [a] [y]-sceaða-

where *x* is defined as one or more function words and *y* is a compounding element bearing the alliteration, and *a* is an adjective that alliterates with *y*. System #1 can occur in either half-line and demonstrates great syntactic variability because of the many possibilities for function words (thus a direct object, relative clause, prepositional phrase, and other elements are observed). System #2 is restricted to the first half-line because of the double alliteration it involves, but it in turn yields a number of related phrases, such as

fah feondscaða	(*Bwf* 554a)
faa folcsceaðan	(*And* 1593a)
fah fyrnsceaþa	(*And* 1346a)
lað leodsceaða	(*Gen* 917a)
laðra leodsceaðena	(*And* 80a)
laþum lyftsceaþan	(*FtM* 39a)

The first of the two systems takes a C-Type metrical configuration and occurs twenty-seven times in the corpus, whereas the second is usually a D1-Type in its sixteen instances;[34] more significantly, there are no occurrences of compounded *sceaða* that do not fall into one of these two patterns. At the root of both systems is the word-type placement at verse-end.

708a. ac he wæccende ("but he, watching"). The most well-defined system that could be posited for this and ostensibly related lines is [x] [y] wæccende, where *x* is a function word and *y* a pronoun subject.[35] Once again, this phrase seems as much an example of a traditional rule—namely, that the metrically most

33. The exception is *Gen* 55: *besloh synsceapan sigore and gewealde*. Indeed, even this first verse is very close to a C-type.

34. When the first element is inflected—e.g., *laðra leodsceaðena* (*And* 80a)—the metrical pattern modulates to a heavy A-Type, but this is hardly a major change.

35. Comparative evidence may be found in *þæt he wæccende* (*Jul* 662b), *gif he wæccende* (*Bwf* 2841a).

complex elements seek verse-end except in E-Type arrangements—as the product of a formulaic system.[36]

708b. wrapum on andan ("fiercely angry"). Here the system is [x] on andan, where *x* is defined as the alliterating element and can be either an adverb (including a dative adverb) or a noun in the dative plural. In the line as a whole we may see the *wæccende* phrase as a response to the narrative surroundings, which at this point are emphasizing that all of the men slept, with the sole exception of Beowulf. Matched to that *wæccende* is *wrapum*, the substitutable word in the second-verse system. While its halves are perhaps less closely linked than some of the other half-line pairs we have examined, the line as a whole does follow the favored metrical formula and provides an alliterative bridge to the next line, to which it is also linked semantically.

709a. bad bolgenmod ("he awaited, enraged in heart"). The best hypothesis for a half-line system would be [x] bolgenmod, where *x* is either a verb (alliterating) or function words.[37] But since this configuration lacks a clear essential idea ("[x] enraged in heart" is hardly a well-defined concept) as well as consistent alliteration and syntax, it is difficult to see how it could have been a functional element in the poet's and tradition's working idiom. What these few phrases do have in common is the placement of the metrically extensive and complex element *bolgenmod*, which, like *wæccende* and *s[c]ynscapa* in preceding lines, occurs at verse-end, this time however in a D2 pattern.[38]

As for *bad*, it behaves similarly to *com* as described above (line 702b). That is, this word-type—a third-singular preterite verb—seeks either the beginning or the end of a verse. In the case of *bad*, most instances occur at verse-end (23 of 28). Comparative analyses of *swæf* and *bær*, both examples of the same word-type, confirm this explanation and show that if such a word-type is used as an alliterating item, it must take a D configuration (in the first half-line) or a B configuration (in either verse). If non-alliterating, it will occupy the final position in an E pattern in the second half-line. These patterns of occurrence are thus due not to the formulaic system involving a particular word, or for that matter even to the behavior of a given single word, but rather to the behavior of a word-type.

Even if we cannot demonstrate a clear debt to any one formulaic system, then, line 709a certainly merits being considered a traditional element. Not only is the anger signaled by the root *bolgen-* conventionally associated with the hero's fight against the monster in *Beowulf*,[39] but, more importantly,

36. Explanation of the phraseology in terms of a possible system [x] [y] [present participle] is far too abstract and provides more evidence of traditional rules (metrically extensive word-types seeking verse-end) than it does of a formulaic system.

37. The comparative data are *breat bolgenmod* (*Bwf* 1713a) and *pa him bolgenmod* (*Dan* 209a).

38. We should also note that *bolgenmode*, the same lexical entry but a different word-type because of the ending, behaves entirely differently. Cf. its use as a whole verse in *And* 128a and 1221a, *Glc* 557b.

39. Cf., e.g., *Bwf* 1539b.

traditional rules of word-type placement underlie the construction of the verse.

709b. beadwa geþinges ("the battle's result"). A number of factors converge to form this half-line, among them the system [x] geþinges, where *x* is a noun in the genitive plural (though translated here as singular) bearing the alliteration. But this is not the only aspect of structure in this case; we must also cite an alliterative collocation with *bolgen* (cf. *Bwf* 1539) and, perhaps even more suggestively, an association with the verb *bidan* ("wait") that seems not to depend on alliteration. The comparative evidence makes the latter point:

> on brime *bidan*   beorna *geþinges.*   (*Ele* 253)
> *await* on the sea the *result (fate)* of men.

> lætað hildebord   her on*bidan,*
> wudu wælsceaftas   worda *geþinges.*   (*Bwf* 397–98)

> leave the battle-shields here to *await,*
> the slaughter-spears, the *result* of words.

While the passage from *Elene* links the roots in contiguous verses, in the *Beowulf* passage they occur in separate lines. What apparently underlies all three cases, then, is a sequence bidan . . . [x] geþinges, which the poet may or may not sort into a single line. And although we find a fairly well focused formulaic system in 709b, we miss the complexity of the overall traditional structure if we end the investigation without taking account of the collocative association with *bolgen* and the larger pattern involving *bidan.*

710a. Đa com of more ("Then came out of the moor"). Like 702b, this half-line answers rules of word-type placement better than the hypothesis of an underlying formulaic system. One difference between the two phrases, however, is the prepositional complement that follows *com;* in the former example, that phrase could and did stand by itself as a half-line, while in 710a *of more* is not long enough metrically to do so.

710b. under misthleoþum ("under the misty cliffs"). A system such as under [x] would have no useful meaning or function, so we must posit [x] misthleoþ- or, more generically,

$$[x] \ [y]\text{-hleoþ-,}$$

where *x* is defined as a preposition (usually *under*) and *y* is a compounding word that supplies the alliteration. To this pattern we may add the collocation between *mor-* and *mist-* as further evidence for traditional structure.[40] The variability of the system in the second half-line allows the poet to fill out the opening verse, itself primarily a product of traditional placement rules, with a properly alliterating element. It should also be pointed out that the second-verse system is conventionally associated in the poetic tradition with

---

40. See *Bwf* 162 and, more generally, the association of both roots with the monsters' actions and habitats.

danger and death, that is, with actions performed in liminal areas; this conceptual link helps to account for the system's presence and function in this passage.[41] Once again, then, a line exhibits both half-line and whole-line structure.

711a. Grendel gongan ("Grendel going"). After 710b, which serves in effect as an alliterative bridge to this line (but which in the process brings forth some traditional associations, as we have seen), 711a completes the pattern begun with *com* by supplying the dependent infinitive, just as *scriðan* did in 703a. Indeed, we shall encounter the same pattern again with the *Com* of 720a and the infinitive *siðian* of 720b. This com . . . [infinitive] sequence is a core phrase which, like the bidan . . . [x] *geþinges* sequence examined above, is not necessarily expressed in a simple whole-line form. Nor is it a unique phrase or one peculiar to *Beowulf*, as the following quotations illustrate:

> *Com* þa on uhtan   mid ærdæge
> hæðenra hloð   haliges *neosan*
> leoda weorude;   (*And* 1388–90a)
>
> Came then at dawn with the break of day
> the band of heathen *to seek* the holy one
> with a troop of men;
>
>   gæst yrre *cwom*
> eatol æfengrom   user *neosan*,   (*Bwf* 2073b–74)
>
>   the spirit *came* in anger
> horrible evening-fierce [one] *to seek* us.

This traditional pattern thus furnishes another example of a reasonably common phenomenon in Old English poetic diction: an association of lexical and syntactic items that is functionally independent of single-verse or single-line prosody. It may be realized within one verse or line, but its coherence as a traditional element is not dependent on such a realization. But this is nothing more than our study of the alliterative prosody would lead us to expect—a sequence or pattern of words larger than the single line.

The importance of this pattern becomes obvious when, after examination, we find that (1) no other cases of verse-initial *Grendel* exist (so a system based on that element is out of the question) and (2) any system involving *gangan* as the constant element would be of such generic definition as to be of little use in composition. Nonetheless, the poet does manage to complete the "pending" *com* with *gangan*, to match that completion with Grendel, and to do so in a metrical A-verse.

712a. mynte se manscaða ("the wicked ravager intended"). There are only three instances of the particular form *mynte* in the poetic corpus; all of them occur in *Beowulf*, and the other forms of the same verb, being different word-

---

41. Cf. *Bwf* 820, 1409, 1427; *And* 1233, 1577; *Dan* 61; *WfL* 48; *Ele* 653. See also Fry 1986.

types, behave quite differently. Within this small sample, we can posit a system mynte [x], where *x* represents the alliterating subject of the clause, on the basis of *mynte se mæra* (*Bwf* 762a). The second part of 712a, however, can also serve as a whole verse by itself, on the model of *Bwf* 707a, *se s[c]ynscaþa*, and so the situation turns out to be analogous to 702b, in which *on wanre niht* served to fill out the *Com* phrase even though metrically it could stand by itself. From the point of view of larger patterns, we should also note that *mynte* seeks completion in a dependent infinitive and, as we shall see, 712b provides an alliterative bridge that leads to that infinitive. Synchronically, then, the poet has matched the *mynte* pattern, which involves a verse-initial alliterating item and eventual completion in an infinitive, with the same formulaic system that produces 707a.

712b. manna cynnes ("of mankind"). This is a classically defined formula, a phrase that recurs nineteen times without variation in other Old English poems. As such, it provides a phraseologically sturdy bridge from the essential and incipient action of *mynte* in 712a to its completion in 713a. While not a "tag," this phrase—perhaps best understood as a single word[42]—offers the poet a metrical element that is highly adaptable contextually and therefore useful in any number of compositional situations. As the *mynte . . . besyrwan* idea takes shape over two lines, this formula serves as a stable configuration against which to balance the alliteration.

713b. in sele þam hean ("in that high hall"). As opposed to the first half-line, this verse seems to be an idiolectal formulaic system (virtually a formula), that is, a phrase used exclusively by the *Beowulf* poet. Its pattern is [in/on/to] sele þam hean,[43] and it occurs three additional times in the poem and nowhere else. Like *manna cynnes* in the preceding line, this phrase serves as a functional, adaptable element that fills out the alliteration and, while not adding necessary or crucially important action to the passage, specifies the locale of that action. As in other lines considered above, the best way to understand 713b is to consider it in the context of the two-line sequence 712-13, wherein the poet solves the compositional problem of metrically and traditionally rendering the idea *mynte . . . besyrwan* (itself a traditional syntactic pattern) by an assortment

---

42. See the discussion of the *guslar*'s concept of the "word" in chapter 2 above, as well as the examples of "traditional words" in chapters 4 and 5.

43. Note that two of the four occurrences of this half-line system are also involved in a whole-line system: *swiðhicgende | to sele þam hean* (*Bwf* 919) and *swiðhicgende | on sele þam hean* (*Bwf* 1016). As we have seen in other examples, the alliterative meter supports a diction that includes phrases with more than one metrical identity; for example, the system [x] [y]-*sceaða* can either fill a verse (e.g. 707a) or combine with another element to compose a verse (e.g. 712a). Similarly, the half-line system underlying 713b can also participate in a whole-line formula or system, as indicated in the two examples above. Compare the multiformity of the Homeric "winged words" phrase discussed in chapter 4 and that of narrative elements described in chapter 10.

of formulas, formulaic systems, alliterative bridges, and placement rules. This spectrum of diction, rather than a simple series of half-line systems, constitutes his traditional phraseology.

714a. Wod under wolcnum ("He advanced under the clouds"). Moving on to this much-discussed verse, we must first decide whether in the system postulated as underlying it and its relatives, [x] under wolcnum, we should limit the alliterating element *x* to a verb form (as does Magoun [1953] 1968, 109) or also allow the substitution of adjectives and nouns and even the inclusion of semantically similar but formulaically unrelated phrases (as does Riedinger 1985, 297–304).[44] In order to preserve the integrity of the phraseological unit, I would advocate drawing the line at the formulaically related phrases. But there is another question to ask as well: in short, just what is the usefulness of the system assumed to underlie 714a? Is the essential idea merely "[something] under the clouds"? And if so, how does it compare as a compositional element with phrases like [x] besyrwan (e.g., 713a), where a definite idea is presented in a relatively well focused way?

Perhaps it would be better to begin by pointing out that what *under wolcnum* represents at a minimal level is a consistent occurrence of a phrase in the same metrical position: at verse-end in an A-Type pattern. The fact of its consistency as the core "word" in this phrase allows the tremendous semantic and syntactic flexibility that the multiform as a whole enjoys. If the pattern is employed in the opening half-line, as happens thirty-six of fifty times in the corpus, the initial element will almost always alliterate (thirty-four times) and the second half-line will of course join in the same alliteration in *w*.[45] We may add to these specific observations the much more general fact that the word-type represented by *under wolcnum*—defined as [prep] [x], where *x* is a noun that bears the alliteration and is the object of the preposition—seeks consistent placement either as a complement like *of more* (710a) to fill out a verse after a certain other kind of word-type or, if it is metrically extensive enough, as a verse in itself.

This pattern differs from the *Com* phrases in that it includes double alliteration, and therefore alliteration on the initial element. Its fundamental shape and morphology, although immediately attributable to a formulaic system, are best understood as deriving from traditional rules for placement of word-types. Like some other phrases discussed above, *under wolcnum* seeks verse-end and, from a synchronic point of view, opens up the substitutable

44. This widening of the phraseological definition does indeed weaken the concept of formula and system as functional compositional elements. Although I agree with Riedinger that we should sense what I would term a metonymic link between phraseology and the thematic structure of the poetry, I would stop short of so loosening the idea of formula that it becomes, in effect, an untraditional element in the diction.

45. The phrase *under wolcnum* also demonstrates a life of its own by recurring outside this pattern; see *Chr* 588, and cf. *Exo* 350.

first position in the opening half-line and sets the alliteration for the line as a whole. Since, as the comparative data indicate, this core recurrence has produced a pattern to which so many different metrical solutions have accrued over time, the pattern becomes a very useful compositional device, and also one heavily laden with associative meaning.[46]

716b. Ne wæs þæt forma sið ("Nor was that the first time"). With the onset of the next unit of thought we encounter a true formulaic system, [x] forma sið, where *x* is defined as a group of function words, usually including some form of the verb "to be," and the half-line takes a B-Type metrical configuration. This phrase answers the classical definition of the system precisely, with its stable core and adaptable first section. Because of this adaptability, it is available synchronically for syntactic adjustment; for example, it can begin a new sentence or paratactically continue an already-started one.

Apart from the four additional occurrences of this phrase (three of them in *Beowulf*) we also find a semantically related formula, *forman siðe* ("on the first time or occasion"), which when compared to the system underlying 716b well illustrates the tradition-dependent character of Old English poetic diction. The second phrase, *forman siðe*, takes a different metrical form (an A-Type), never varies, and lacks the special syntactic flexibility of the system. The traditional word-type rule under which *forma sið* seeks verse-end (the word-type $\acute{s}\,\overset{x}{s}\,\grave{s}$) cannot apply to *forman siðe* because of its different stress pattern ($\acute{s}\,\overset{x}{s}\,\acute{s}\,\grave{s}$). Thus traditional rules, based on metrical strictures, are seen to be more fundamental than the lexical elements that make up an expression.

717b. ham gesohte ("he sought the home"). Evidence from the poetic corpus might lead us to consider this phrase a formula, since there are two exact repetitions:

Hreðcyninges *ham gesohte*		(*Wds* 7)
he sought the home of the king of the Hreðgotan		
and mid heofenwarum *ham gesohte*		(*SFt* 33)
and *he sought his home* with the heavenly dwellers		

But if we choose this route, we miss the complexity and truly traditional character of 717b. For of the thirty-three instances of the verb form *gesohte*, fully thirty occur in A-Type metrical patterns of the sort [x] gesohte, where *x* represents a noun bearing the alliteration; furthermore, seventeen of these thirty have *x* as the direct object of *gesohte*. Or we may turn to the possibility ham [x], where *x* represents the verb taking *ham* as a direct object, a well-attested pattern that can involve infinitives as well as finite verb forms.

All of these levels of structure are, however, built on the foundation of traditional word-type placement rules, here chiefly the stricture that calls for

46. See Riedinger 1985, 297ff.

verbs prefixed by *ge-*, and thus of the generic form *ǵe*-RÓOT + ending, to tend strongly toward the end of an A-Type metrical pattern. The element to which such a word-type is joined is, of course, a stressed monosyllable or the equivalent[47]—very often, as we have seen, the direct object of that verb form. Thus the stressed monosyllable or its equivalent comes to bear the alliteration in what is exclusively a second-verse phrase pattern. From a synchronic viewpoint, this and phrases like it provide the poet with a flexible way of handling prefixed verbs, which otherwise, especially in the first verse, can cause rather unwieldy metrical configurations. What is more, this half-line offers a good example of why the "formulaic system" concept is often quite useful and descriptive, but at the same time fundamentally inadequate to the task of demonstrating all aspects of the traditional character of a phrase. Whatever system we choose to nominate as the mold for 717b, it will conceal as much as it reveals about the essential structure of this and related half-lines; for an accurate measure of that structure we must return to the most basic traditional rules and derive levels of patterning from that point.[48]

718a. næfre he on aldordagum ("never he in earlier days"). The fact that *aldordagum* is a hapax legomenon in the Old English poetic corpus may obscure the fact that this half-line belongs to one of the richest, most generative (and therefore most useful and echoic) systems in the poetry. We may define the core of the system as [x] [y]-dagum, where *x* is defined as a preposition and *y* is a compounding element that bears the alliteration.[49] This phrase, one of the first to be studied as a compositional element,[50] proves extremely plastic: it can be employed as a half-line by itself in a wide variety of different situations (in the form schematized above), or it can "add on" function words before the preposition and thus take on another whole selection of syntactic functions. Not only does it recur in both a "core" formation filling a verse and as the stable end of a longer phrase (as in 718a), but it also can take on special functions in either identity. As a whole-verse pattern, the system is perhaps most familiar to us as part of the heroic proem sequence common to a number of Anglo-Saxon poems; for example,

47. Through expansion by resolution or ramification (see chapter 3), the stressed monosyllable may become two or more syllables, as long as the overall metrical pattern is not violated.

48. We may note two further levels of structure involving some examples of this phrase. First, in *Wds* 7, as quoted above, we recognize the same genitive singular construction (*Hreðcyninges*) as in 717a (*Hropgares*), a correspondence that argues for a traditional linkage between the b-verse phrase and the genitive construction in the matched half-line. Second, the *Christ and Satan* poet has extended the *ham* [x] pattern—itself also based on traditional rules, as explained above—into an idiolectal whole-line system peculiar to his poem (see *XSt* 91, 147, 503, 551).

49. Some idea of the extent of this formulaic system may be gained by observing that the prepositions used include *in*, *on*, and *æfter*, and—more tellingly—that thirty-five different compounding elements are used with some form of *dæg-*. Space constraints preclude presenting more than a sample of these copious data here.

50. See Bryan 1929.

Hwæt! We Gardena	in geardagum,	(*Bwf* 1)
	in days of yore	
Hwæt! We gefrunan	on fyrndagum,	(*And* 1)
	in olden days	
Hwæt, me frod wita	on fyrndagum,	(*Vgl* 1)

As part of an enlarged pattern, we can cite the following idiolectal usage:

þe git on ærdagum	oft gespræcon,	(*HbM* 16)
in earlier days		
þe git on ærdagum	oft gespræconn.	(*HbM* 53)

In a real sense the [prep.] [y]-dagum phrase acts as a "word" in the diction, open to additive morphology but not to internal re-arrangement. Few phrases in Old English poetry are as self-contained as this one.[51]

As integral a unit as this system is, however, we should also point out that traditional rules do supersede, or rather govern, its formation. In cases involving the element [y]-*dagum* that do not fit this formulaic system, we observe that the element still regularly seeks verse-end, in these latter cases almost always to constitute a variation on the D1-Type pattern (e.g., *Gen* 1072a: *frod fyrndagum*). What we have, then, is a word-type, specifically [y]-*dagum*, as the verse-final element, which then takes on two separate identities in the tradition—one as the system underlying 718a and so many additional verses and the other underlying a D1-Type verse where the "word" customarily acts as a dative complement.

What the poet manages to accomplish in 718a, from this perspective, is to state the condition "never" (*næfre*) in traditional formulaic language, using an expandable system built on the core [prep.] [y]-dagum and a compounding element that, while it yields a hapax legomenon, matches the alliteration of the second-verse formula.

718b. ær ne siþðan ("before or since"). Although this half-line recurs only once in the corpus, we can safely call it traditional. For besides satisfying the minimum criteria for a formula, it is related to a whole system of diction using the same words with slight variations in form and meaning. We have, for example, eighteen occurrences of the patterns sið [x] ær and ær [x] sið, wherein both cases x stands for and/ond, ne ("nor"), or oþþe ("or"). The difference, of course, lies in word-type: while 718b (and *Chr* 39b) fill a whole verse, the two metrically shorter patterns cited above must comprise only part of a half-line,[52] most often a B-Type in place of the A-Type in the half-line under consideration.

---

51. In contrast, as we saw in chapters 4 and 5, both Serbo-Croatian and ancient Greek epic phraseology have many such "words."

52. The single exception is *Glc* 369a (*ær oþþe sið*), which is unmetrical.

720a. Com þa to recede ("Came then to the building"). This phrase shows the same general structure as 702b and 710a, as discussed above, although it should be pointed out that within this traditional pattern the poet is able to vary the complements to the action of *com* in a way that increases the tension of the approach: Grendel is seen first "in the dark night," then advancing "out of the moor," and finally coming "to the building."

720b. rinc siðian ("the warrior journeying"). Here the poet completes the *com*...[infinitive] pattern within a single line by taking advantage of the alliterative collocation between *reced* and *rinc* (cf. *Bwf* 412 and 728). Although we might posit for this half-line the system [x] siðian, where *x* is defined as an alliterating noun with the semantic value of "man, warrior," some other analogs illustrate the more fundamental structure of the whole line:

þa com ofer foldan fus *siðian*	(*Gen* 154)
Then he came journeying eager over the earth	
þa com ærest Cam in *siðian*,	(*Gen* 1577)
Then first Ham *came journeying* in,	
þa com ellenrof eorl *siðian*,	(*Gen* 1844)
Then the courageous nobleman *came journeying*,	

The pattern *com...siðian*, a more focused version of the *com*...[infinitive] phrase we have encountered twice before, provides the backbone for line 720 and these three additional examples on a whole-line basis, and each verse is adjusted for alliteration with complements—in the case of 720, with a collocative pair.

721a. dreamum bedæled ("bereft of joys"). At first sight we might interpret this half-line as simply an alliterative bridge, a filler that harmonizes syntactically with 720a and allows the poet to proceed on to the next important action. To be sure, it is a highly formulaic phrase, a variation on the system [x] bedæled, where *x* is a noun bearing the alliteration and designating some positive communal value.[53] In fact, it may well be best to consider *dreamum bedæled* a true formula on its own account, since the essential idea of loss of social context is so powerfully and memorably expressed.

But it is a measure of the poet's singular art that, far from being the slave of his traditional diction, he molds that diction toward aesthetic ends. While 721a is clearly meant to serve as a bridge to *Duru* (and thus to Grendel's bursting into Heorot) in the second verse, *dreamum bedæled* is hardly a throw-

---

53. It is also possible to see this half-line as associated with the system *dream-* [verb of deprivation], of which there are numerous examples, but this is probably not the fundamental form, especially since all other such verbs also alliterate in [d].

away; by metonymic reference to the wordhoard, the poet deftly brings out another aspect of Grendel—that of Exile.[54]

721b. Duru sona onarn ("The door immediately sprang open"). There is only one other instance of *onarn* in the poetic corpus, and it turns out to be an exact repetition of this phrase (*And* 999b). On this basis we can certainly call 721b a formula, but stopping the analysis at that point will obscure the traditional depth of the phrase and therefore its metonymic meaning. To pursue the matter in proper perspective, we must quote the passage from *Andreas* in which the formula appears (996b–1003; quoted from Brooks 1961):

> Ða se halga gebæd
> bilwytne fæder,   breostgehygdum
> herede on hehðo   heofoncyninges god,
> dryhten dem[de].   <u>Duru sona onarn</u>
> þurh *han[d]hrine*   haliges gastes,
> ond þær in *eode*,   elnes gemyndig,
> *hæle* hildedeor.   Hæðene *swæfon*,
> dreore druncne,   deaðwang rudon.

> Then the holy one prayed to
> the gentle Father, in his inmost thoughts
> praised the Heaven-king's goodness on high,
> glorified the Lord. <u>The door immediately sprang open</u>
> through the *hand-touch* of the holy spirit,
> and in there he *went*, mindful of valor,
> the battle-brave *hero*. The heathens *slept*,
> drunk in blood, they reddened the death-place.

The italicized words and elements of compounds also occur as a group or cluster in the passage under examination from *Beowulf*. In addition, we may note that this cluster has a narrative basis in the action of a "warrior" invading a sanctuary where his foes are sleeping and wreaking havoc among them. In the case of *Beowulf*, that warrior is Grendel the Exile; in *Andreas* it is St. Andrew bringing revenge on the Mermedonians. Thus this cluster, a traditional unit larger than the verse or line, assists in the composition of this section of the poem through the agency of associated words, and we must likewise take account of the traditional meaning of the cluster in reading both passages.[55]

54. See Greenfield 1955 for the first statement on "Exile" as a traditional narrative structure; a complete tabulation of all identified Anglo-Saxon themes is available below in chapter 9. See also Baird 1966.

55. See further the discussion of *Andreas* in chapter 9, and note the discrepancy between the prose versions of the Andreas story and the traditional narrative poem at this juncture (as reported in Brooks 1961, 96).

722a. fyrbendum fæst ("[held] fast by fire-forged bonds"). Although *fyrbend* proves a hapax legomenon in the poetic corpus, we can describe a common system underlying this verse, [x]-bendum fæst, where *x* represents a compounding element bearing the alliteration. This compound takes a wide variety of forms, from the straightforward *irenbendum* ("iron bonds," *Bwf* 774b and 998b) to the more abstract *hygebendum* ("mind-bonds," *Bwf* 1878b). It occurs once in *Guthlac* and six times in *Beowulf*, with a total of seven different compounding elements. And yet this is not the end of the story, for in addition to these instances we find two related structures. First, the compound [x]-*bendum* can, if the initial element is metrically extensive enough, occupy a whole verse and not just part of one; thus *irenbendum* can either join *fæst* in the system under discussion (*Bwf* 998b) or stand by itself (*Bwf* 774b). Second, there are numerous compounds, many of them closely synonymous to [x]-*bend*-, that behave in very similar ways, some of them even participating in analogous systems with *fæst*. Here are two examples:

fetorwrasnum fæst	(*And* 1107a)
fast in tight bonds	
feondgrapum fæst	(*Bwf* 636a)
fast in the fiend's grips	

With these and other examples, two further perspectives emerge. While this system apparently has a life of its own in the poetic tradition (chiefly in *Beowulf*), its first element may be employed alone—outside the context of the formulaic system. As we saw above in the case of certain prepositional phrases that acted as complements to the *com* series, some traditional elements do have this ability to play different versificational roles, depending on the particular situation. This sort of multiple function is impossible in symbioses of prosody and phraseology such as those associated with the Homeric Greek hexameter and Serbo-Croatian *deseterac*. Interestingly, however, as we shall see in chapter 10, this twofold function is paralleled at the narrative level by story-patterns that can serve either as simplex sequences for an entire poem or as additive elements that can be combined to form longer and more complex poems.

Another insight on the compositional process is afforded by the behavior of words outside of the specific [x]-bendum system which nonetheless match this element in word-type. The similarity in formulaic morphology and the consistent behavior of *fæst* as a monosyllabic adjective seeking verse-end in this and many other situations[56] lead us to understand that the system observed in its many manifestations is also, and fundamentally, a reflection of traditional rules. The system is a highly focused structure built on these rules, a pattern that has apparently proven useful and has developed its own identity in the

56. Cf. *cuð* in 705b.

poetry. While it would be misleading not to recognize 722a as a formulaic system, it would be equally wrong not to place this pattern in the context of the rules under which it has come into prominence and under which it continues to function.[57]

722b. *sypðan he hire folmum [æth]ran* ("after he touched it with his hands"). This is perhaps the most idiosyncratic verse in the passage under examination, for there is nothing in the poetic corpus that could be summoned as evidence for any kind of system. We may, however, juxtapose to that lack of apparent structure two compositional features. The first is specific to this passage and to the cluster that helps to define its structure and meaning: the inclusion of *-hran* ("touched"), one of the words that we noted was also associated with St. Andrew's forced entry, and *folmum* ("with hands"), whose synonym *hand(-)* was also employed in the *Andreas* scene (*handhrine*, "hand-touch"; 1000a). The second feature is more general and typical of many verses in addition to 722b. This amounts to the simple fact that "acephalic" metrical types—that is, Sievers B and C—are much more open to variation than are other types because of their lack of a stressed element in initial position. If one or more function words can occupy first position in a metrical type, with no real restriction on semantics or grammar, then such types will of course exhibit wide variation even if the following stressed elements show regular occurrence. This is an elementary but very significant characteristic; what is more, it provides yet another reason why all half-line phrases cannot be judged equal and why, as a result, we must expect a spectrum of traditional phraseological forms.[58]

To sum up, the central idea of these few lines can be abstracted as "The door sprang open at Grendel's touch," which is expressed by 721b and 722b using a formula and cluster-words traditionally appropriate to the poetic task. Line 722a, a relatively common formulaic system with its roots in traditional rules, acts as an alliterative bridge, not absolutely necessary to the expression of the central action but, thanks to the poet's skill, an artful detail that amplifies Grendel's entry. Thus the sequence 721b–22 contains a formula, a system, a half-line we cannot ascribe to a system, and part of a traditional cluster, and all phraseological and narrative units are meshed to form a finely crafted and

---

57. An interesting glimpse of how fundamental traditional rules really are is afforded by two virtually synonymous Beowulfian half-lines, both of which fulfill the final element in the traditional theme of sea-voyaging (see further chapter 9): *on ancre fæst* ("fast at anchor," 303a) and *oncerbendum fæst* ("fast by anchor-bonds," 1918a). Although these verses may be said to have the same essential idea, and although they perform the same thematic function, their phraseological shapes are entirely different. Nonetheless, note that in both verses we observe consistent placement of *fæst* and, further, that each in its own way follows traditional rules in sorting the repeated elements into metrically permitted form.

58. Although this particular kind of institutionalized inequivalence is of course impossible in the hexameter and *deseterac* dictions, they have, as we have seen, their own tradition-dependent spectra of phraseology.

resonant description; such is the rich inheritance of tradition and such is the art of the *Beowulf* poet.

723b. ða (he ge)bolgen wæs ("since he was enraged"). This verse is clearly a formula, as four verbatim or very nearly verbatim usages illustrate (*Gen* 54b; *Bwf* 1539b, 2220b, 2550b). In each case the formula is associated with a major battle, whether with God's fight against Satan and his company in *Genesis*, Beowulf's battle against Grendel's mother, the dragon's anger over the stolen cup, or Beowulf's fight with the dragon. In other words, this phrase seems to be associated, particularly in *Beowulf*, with the idea and expression of battle; and we would not be far wrong if we considered it thematically associated with the monster-fight scene in *Beowulf*, as a metonymic signal of the magnitude and intensity of the battle. To be *gebolgen* in this way is to possess battle fury, and this phrase encodes that special anger.

When we add to these observations the evidence for a collocation between the root of the verb in 723a and the highly charged word *gebolgen* (not to say its ritual expression in this formula),[59] we perceive another example of a half-line formula which nevertheless has traditional associations outside the single verse. The overall picture then becomes one of the fundamental idea (*-bræd . . . ða he gebolgen wæs*, "drew or swung open . . . since he was enraged"), with the [x]-*hydig* compound filling out the first verse under the aegis of traditional rules. Although one half-line is a true formula and the other not demonstrably formulaic, the line as a whole is once again thoroughly traditional.

724a. recedes muþan ("the building's mouth"). Since this verse is metaphorical, denoting as it does the door of the hall, neither the general pattern recedes [x] nor the literal pattern [x] muð can serve a systemic function; the first possibility is too generic and lacks an essential idea, while the second would need further definition of *muð* in the special metaphorical sense.[60] Thus only two half-lines in the poetic corpus present themselves as possible comparands:

merehuses muð	(*Gen* 1364a)
the sea-house's [ark's] mouth	
rum recedes muð	(*Mx2* 37a)
the building's wide mouth	

The first phrase describes the opening of Noah's ark, and the second serves as a variation on *duru* in the preceding half-line. Both phrases could in a sense be said to participate in a formulaic system with 724a were it not for the fact

59. *Bwf* 1539, *brægd þa beadwe heard, þa he gebolgen wæs*, apparently an idiolectal collocation, but no less powerful for that.

60. Compare the discussions of a possible X *muþ-* system in Fry 1968b, 520; and Niles 1983, 125–26.

that they do not match it metrically. The verse from *Genesis* also uses a synonym for *reced* rather than the word itself.

Still, we may be able to show more of a connection between the *Maxims* and *Beowulf* phrases than is immediately apparent. Both verses amount to virtually the same expression connoting "door" and, apart from metrical differences and the word *rum*, are virtually identical. Consider for a moment the poet's essential idea, in this case one that is highly focused, metaphorical, and ostensibly traditional, and the continuing synchronic problem of metrical versification that he faces. Both phrases are successful renderings of that idea in that they conform to a permitted metrical configuration, and both use the core phrase *recedes muð-*. The major difference between the two is that *Mx2* 37a assumes a strong masculine declension for the main word (nom. *muþ*) while *Bwf* 724a assumes a weak masculine declension (nom. *muþa*); further evidence for both possibilities in the corpus indicates what seems to be a true ambivalence in the lexicon and therefore in the diction. For the *Beowulf* poet, the weak form yields a metrical verse in the accusative singular, *recedes muþan* (724a), while the strong form would result in a short, unmetrical half-line: *recedes muþ. This is precisely the problem faced and solved by the *Maxims* poet, who understands *muþ* as a strong form and adds the adjective *rum* to the core phrase *recedes muþ* to give a metrical phrase, *rum recedes muþ*.[61] Indeed, although these two examples cannot be shown to proceed out of the same formulaic system, they are without doubt related traditional phrases. And the example of their less-than-obvious relation sheds further light on the morphology of Old English poetic diction.

726a. eode yrremod ("[he] went angry in spirit"). Two patterns present themselves as possible systems: [x] [y̲]-mod,[62] where *x* is a verb and *y* is a compounding element usually bearing the alliteration (*x* also alliterates in the more common first-verse pattern), and eo̲d̲e̲ [z̲], where *z* is an alliterating adjective modifying the implied subject of *eode*. If we are willing to term the first possibility a bona fide system in spite of its lack of semantic focus and essential idea, there are numerous examples in the poetic corpus to support interpreting 726a as a product of that system. Meanwhile, phrases like *eode unforht* (*Exo* 335a) and *eode ellenrof* (*Bwf* 358a) can be drawn on to support the second hypothesis.

Since the first pattern is so generic, and since *eode* participates in so many different kinds of phrases (so that it seems not to follow a specific traditional rule), the second hypothesis is a better description of the system underlying 726a. But we should note that [y̲]-mo̲d̲, in obeying the traditional rule of the

---

61. If the *Maxims* poet had understood the word as a weak masculine and tried to apply the same solution, the result would be **rum recedes muþan*, an unmetrical verse.

62. This pattern undergoes frequent metathesis in the double-alliterating form characteristic of first-verse occurrences.

metrically more complex element seeking verse-end, constitutes the more
fundamental structure of the phrase; in effect, this word placement creates
the sequence *eode* [ẓ].

726b. him of eagum stod ("from his eyes stood out"). Phrases like *þæt he on
botme stod* (*XSt* 718b) or *se ðe on greote stod* (*And* 254b) may encourage positing a
system [x] [prep. phrase] stod, where *x* represents one or more function words
and the prepositional phrase, with the object alliterating, is defined only
grammatically. But since such a pattern is much too generic to serve the
composing poet, we would do better to point out that *stod* follows the traditional
rule of monosyllabic preterite verb seeking final position and to see *eode yrremod*
as an alliterative bridge (and partial variation of the preceding half-line, *feond
treddode*) that allows the poet to proceed smoothly from one action to the next.
And while the phrase *of eagum* and the idea it embodies may seem ornamental,
in fact the detail of a mysterious light marks all three monster-fights in
Beowulf.[63] Both the traditional phraseological rule and the "deep structure"
of the monster-fight theme, then, help to shape the second half-line.

727a. ligge gelicost ("most like fire"). Underlying this half-line is the common
system [x] gelicost, where *x* is a noun in the dative singular case bearing the
alliteration and the phrase as a whole constitutes an institutionalized way to
construct a simile. Ten other instances occur in the poetic corpus, in a variety
of poems, so we may safely assume that this system is tradition-wide rather
than idiolectal. To these general comments may be added the more specific
observation that this phraseological element, like many others we have
examined, exists both as a unit in itself and as part of a larger pattern. An
example is furnished by lines drawn from the sea-voyaging passages in *Andreas*
and *Beowulf*:[64]

færeð *famigheals, fugole gelicost*   (*And* 497)

The foamy-necked [one] travels, most like a bird

flota *famiheals fugle gelicost*   (*Bwf* 218)

The foamy-necked ship most like a bird

The Beowulfian version of the simile also provides an alliterative bridge to
the *leoht* of the following half-line, and thus adds a synchronic function to its
traditional, diachronic identity.

728a. Geseah he in recede ("In the building he saw"). Although we may posit
a system Geseah [x], where *x* is a prepositional phrase, this pattern has no
more validity as a compositional construct than does the similar pattern

63. See also the strange light emanating from Grendel's mother's cave (1516b-17) and the
more obvious light of the dragon's fiery breath (2582–83b). I owe the mention of this characteristic
of the monster-fight to Robert P. Creed.

64. See further chapter 9. Since it depends on multiform traditional diction rather than direct
echoing, this example would argue against direct borrowing and in favor of a shared diction.

initially proposed for the half-lines involving *com*. More to the point is the consistent behavior of the verb *geseah*, which in eighty occurrences in the poetic corpus seeks verse-initial position thirty times and verse-final position forty-nine times.[65] This verb form can occupy either slot in either verse and very seldom takes part in the alliterative structure of the line. To put the same matter another way, this word—and word-type—can be and is used outside formulaic systems and the alliterative complications they regularly entail. In so employing this word-type, the poet is beginning a construction that, again like the *Com* pattern, demands closure in an infinitive;[66] he will bridge the gap between *Geseah* and that infinitive with an alliterative collocation and a formulaic system.

728b. rinca manige ("many warriors"). The formulaic system is <u>rinca</u> [x], where *x* is a noun or adjective that specifies the group denoted by the genitive plural *rinca*. The alliterative collocation consists of the pair *rinc* and *reced*, which the poet has matched twice before in *Beowulf*, at lines 412 and 720. We begin to see the whole-line pattern as well as a continuation to the next line through the central action of *Geseah...swefan*. The infinitive *swefan*, of course, will participate in its own alliterative and formulaic series in addition to providing closure for *Geseah*.

729a. swefan sibbegedriht ("the band of kinsmen sleeping"). Just as the relatively independent word and word-type *geseah* took on an alliterative series with a built-in (that is, traditional) collocation in line 728, so the infinitive *swefan* not only completes the action of *Geseah* but also takes on an analogous series of its own. For while we find some support for positing a system [x] <u>sibbegedriht</u>, where *x* is an infinitive, that same evidence (*Bwf* 387) also argues for a more extensive pattern:

> seon *sibbegedriht   samod ætgædere*
>
> to see *the band of kinsmen all together*

To call this correspondence a half-line system overlooks both the second verse and the whole-line pattern. In addition, two other examples, both of them from outside *Beowulf*, demonstrate the central significance of the collocation (as opposed to possible systems) and the pan-traditional character of the alliterative link:

> eal seo *sibgedriht   somod ætgædere*   (*Exo* 214)
>
> all the *band of kinsmen all together*

---

65. The single exception to this traditional rule occurs in the Psalms (*P101*.17.3), which, as we saw earlier, often demonstrate quite untraditional diction.

66. Of the thirty verse-initial occurrences of *geseah*, eighteen are followed by an infinitive; although the selection of infinitives is naturally weighted toward those involving a visual impression, a variety of words are used to close the expression. As for those instances of *geseah* not followed by an infinitive, the favored constructions are a direct object and indirect statement.

mid þa *sibgedriht   somud*eard niman   (*Glc* 1372)

with the *band of kinsmen* to take the *together*-home

The line from *Exodus* shows that the relationship between the alliterating elements is not dependent on the first-verse system, while the example from *Guthlac* illustrates independence of the collocation from the second-verse formula.[67]

729b. samod ætgædere ("all together"). This phrase is of course a common formula in the Old English tradition, occurring seventeen times in a variety of poems. Once again, then, we have an instance of a unit—this time a half-line formula—that has a life of its own in the tradition and yet can also combine with other phraseological elements to produce a larger pattern that has its own identity. In the other direction, we note that *ætgædere* always occurs in either verse- or line-final position,[68] as its metrically extensive word-type would lead us to expect. Thus the formula observed in 729b is erected on the basis of traditional rules.

To sum up, the central action begun in 728a by *Geseah* and completed by *swefan* in 729a is filled out in each line by an alliterative collocation, the latter of these also assuming the form of an idiolectal whole-line system in *Beowulf*. Evidence from outside *Beowulf* helps us to see what the poet's contribution has been to this series, and once more we encounter a hierarchy of structure, from a two-line series through collocations, a whole-line system, a formulaic system, a formula, and traditional rules. It is the poet's achievement to use the materials of his tradition to convey the central action with such power and resonance.

730a. magorinca heap ("a troop of young warriors"). A variation on *rinca manige* and *sibbegedriht*, this half-line may be assigned to a system [x] heap, where *x* is an alliterating noun denoting "warriors, troops" in the genitive plural (partitive construction). This pattern can stand by itself if the noun is sufficiently extensive metrically and can form a part of another system if it is not. While not as well defined as many formulaic systems, the [x] heap phrase does express a focused essential idea and proves useful in many different situations. It is also a more specific example of the general pattern of [partitive gen. pl.] [number/group noun] observed throughout the poetry.[69]

---

67. The hapax legomenon *somudeard* ("together-" or "common land") may be understood as a reflex of the collocation between *sib(be)gedriht* and *somod*, in other words as just the sort of neologism one might expect when certain words or elements of compounds are associated in the context of Old English prosody and then used in a divergent narrative situation.

68. All thirty-one instances are verse- or line-final, twenty-seven occurring at line-end and four at the end of the first half-line.

69. Although further analysis is beyond the scope of this chapter, we may note in passing that the poet employs the [m]-alliterating *magorinca* to harmonize with a half-line system in 730b: system = Đa [x] mod ahlog, giving þa his mod ahlog (*Bwf* 730b) and Đa ure mod ahloh (*And* 454b).

Quantitative Analysis

Table 21 will serve as a reference point for the foregoing discussion, recording the status of each half-line in the passage (whether formula, formulaic system, or neither) and the traditional rules that apply to each verse (abbreviations are explained in the following discussion). Two caveats are necessary: first, my judgment of whether a phrase is a formula or a system is developed from the analysis presented selectively above and may not agree at all points with the definitions of other investigators;[70] second, designating a phrase as belonging to one or another category of diction hardly explains its entire traditional identity and context. As a practical matter, if a phrase can be termed a formula on the basis of available evidence, I have not indicated in this table whether we can also call it formulaic.[71] Nonetheless, it may be instructive to compare the figures we derive with the perspective offered by traditional rules.

In purely quantitative terms, the passage consists of 19.5 percent formulas, 51.8 percent formulaic systems, and 28.6 percent verses that cannot be satisfactorily explained as belonging to either category. As mentioned in chapters 1 and 2 and earlier in this chapter, I cannot accept the premise that such quantitative analysis determines the oral or written provenance of this or any other passage, first because of the criteria of tradition-dependence and text-dependence that are two of the guiding principles of my approach to the study of comparative oral and oral-derived epic. On the basis of the line-by-line investigation and its results, we may add another reason to question the density test: if all systems are not equal in complexity and usefulness, and further if the system hypothesis does not fully explain the traditional character of many of the half-lines, how then can we expect it to serve as an unambiguous measure of a given text's orality?

What should be emphasized about table 21 is the absolute consistency of traditional rules; not a single verse is left unexplained by this more fundamental level of structure, while the formula/formulaic system model leaves more than a quarter of the passage unexplained as traditional phraseology. We shall finish our discussion with a summary and codification of traditional rules, the foundation on which a viable aesthetics can in the future be erected.

TRADITIONAL RULES: A SUMMARY

Earlier in this chapter we attempted to predict the kinds of phraseological structures that might be expected to form under the aegis of the idiosyncratic

---

70. For example, the mere fact that a substitution system can be posited as the structure underlying a given verse is insufficient to count that verse a formulaic system if the pattern is highly generic and no essential idea can be located. As explained by example above, these instances are the issue of traditional rules and not of substitution systems.

71. Of course, some theorists would join Fry (1967b, 1974) in assuming that all formulas are necessarily products of systems, making separation of these categories impossible.

TABLE 21. Formulaic Profile for *Beowulf* 702b-30a

Line	Formula	System	Neither	Traditional Rules
702b		x		WTP[a]
703a			x	WTP, Collocation, Cluster
703b		x		WTP, Theme
704a			x	WTP
704b	x			WTP (*sculan/willan*)
705a		x		WTP (prep. phr.)
705b		x		WTP
706a			x	WTP (single stressed wd.)
706b	x			WTP
707a			x	WTP
707b		x		WTP, Cluster
708a			x	WTP
708b		x		WTP (prep. phr.)
709a			x	WTP
709b		x		WTP (attrib.-spec.)
710a		x		WTP
710b		x		WTP, Collocation, Theme
711a			x	WTP
711b			x	WTP
712a		x		WTP
712b	x			WTP (attrib.-spec.)
713a		x		WTP
713b	x			WTP (b-verse pattern)
714a		x		WTP (prep. phr.)
714b			x	WTP
715a		x		WTP (reversal)
715b	x			WTP (b-verse pattern)
716a		x		WTP (attrib.-spec.)
716b	x			WTP
717a			x	WTP
717b		x		WTP
718a		x		WTP (prep. phr.)
718b	x			WTP
719a		x		WTP, Litotes
719b			x	WTP
720a		x		WTP, Collocation
720b		x		WTP, Collocation
721a	x			WTP (attrib.-spec.)
721b	x			WTP, Cluster
722a		x		WTP
722b			x	WTP, Cluster
723a		x		WTP
723b	x			WTP, Theme

TABLE 21 (*continued*)

Line	Formula	System	Neither	Traditional Rules
724a		x		WTP (attrib.-spec.)
724b		x		WTP (stave & prep. phr.)
725a			x	WTP, metrical rule (B-Type)
725b			x	WTP
726a		x		WTP
726b			x	WTP
727a		x		WTP (attrib.-spec.), Simile
727b		x		WTP
728a			x	WTP, Collocation
728b		x		WTP (attrib.-spec.), Collocation
729a		x		WTP, Collocation
729b	x			WTP, Collocation
730a		x		WTP (attrib.-spec.)

[a] WTP = word-type placement

Old English alliterative meter. As expected, our subsequent analysis revealed not one but a variety of types of diction: alongside the classical half-line phrase stand single words, whole-line patterns, multi-line patterns, collocations, clusters, and themes. Likewise, even within these different categories not all members are equivalent; some formulaic systems are more variable than others, some larger patterns more restrictive than others, and so on. Then too, we found a number of elements that had more than one compositional identity, as when a phrase could serve as a half-line unit by itself or join with another word or words to make up a verse. In most cases, even if we could realistically posit a formulaic system underlying a given phrase, simple reporting of that proposed system proved insufficient to a complete understanding of the phrase as an element of traditional phraseology. In short, the synchronic model of half-line substitution systems, while a valuable first step in assessing the character of Old English poetic diction, does not go far enough; the simplification it offers is purchased at the price of incomplete analysis and therefore of an unsound basis for aesthetic investigation. At the same time, the wide spectrum of traditional forms uncovered in the passage from *Beowulf* analyzed above, while fulfilling what was predicted about the diction, begs the question of how the poet and tradition could have managed to handle so many apparently diverse forms concurrently.

The first response to this question must be a general one, but one that is not often enough appreciated by those involved in the analysis and explanation of oral traditional phraseology. Most simply put, the diction we encounter in

Beowulf and Old English poetry—and in the oral epics of Homer and the Yugoslav *guslar*—is by its very nature not a set of substitution systems. Even if we were to hypothesize (quite unrealistically) that at some point in the distant past of a poetic tradition the *Kunstsprache* was made up entirely of equivalent elements, so that one formulaic system, for example, was always and everywhere equal to all others, the dimension of diachrony that separates us from that Ur-diction would demand a reinterpretation. Over time, some systems and other structures will develop differently from others, and this inherently uneven evolution must produce some structures that permit extensive variation, some that permit none, and many that fall somewhere in between these two poles. Likewise, the same evolution (and the natural-selection model may not be entirely inaccurate for the process) must yield structures of different "sizes" and complexity, with certain phraseological relationships "growing" from one size to another, perhaps retaining the original form, but perhaps not. And we must also introduce into this same equation the dimension of different singers versus the local tradition and the tradition as a whole—what were called idiolect, dialect, and language in relation to the Serbo-Croatian poems. Although we lack the background information and textual records to apply this kind of discrimination to *Beowulf*, we have in fact noticed some structures that seem, on the basis of available information, to be idiolectal.

What the dimension of diachrony indicates is thus another level of complexity in a diction, another reason to analyze carefully *what is really there* instead of settling for a convenient and simple model that partially explains a healthy percentage of the cases we encounter. Of course, evolution of traditional forms will be guided both by the conservatism of tradition in general and by the prosodic filter of the poetry in particular, but we should not expect the text we are interpreting to submit tamely to a synchronic analysis. The language of *Beowulf* is a highly complex and resonant instrument, one that carries with it enormous internal resources of associative meaning and yet is also pliable enough to respond to the poet's individual craft, one that harmonizes well with Yeats's notion of the poet as "both finger and clay."

While we cannot reduce the complexity of this spectrum of traditional phraseology and still hope to provide a firm foundation for aesthetic interpretation, we can nonetheless rationalize the diversity of many forms to a single set of traditional rules that, like the corresponding inventory in the poetic idioms of Serbo-Croatian and ancient Greek epic, are neither as situation-specific as those governing the formula and system nor as general as metrical constraints. Lying in between these two extremes and built, as indicated above, on the logic of the tradition-dependent prosody, traditional rules are inscribed in every half-line and line, whatever category of structure that half-line or line falls into. They serve both as regulators of incoming phraseology and as continuing supports for the morphology of that diction which the poet is accustomed to employing. In a word, these rules supersede the synchronic dimension, for they are not phrase-specific or even category-specific; rather, they connect all phraseological patterns—no matter how small or large, how simple or elaborate—by serving as the group criteria of what is (and becomes) traditional.

The most far-reaching of these rules, *word-type placement*, furnishes a prime example. This set of constraints governs the recurrence of words not on the bases usually prescribed for the formula and system (those of lexicon and semantics "under the same metrical conditions") but on the basis of the word's metrical and grammatical type. Indeed, this is exactly what we would expect in a prosody that emphasizes not the syllable and the colon but rather the sequence of stresses. For example, we found during the earlier analysis that monosyllabic preterite verbs consistently occupied first or last position in a verse; this phenomenon was a result not of any one verb or (primarily) of any particular formulaic system, but of a rule that applies to a metrical-grammatical category of words. To summarize, I list below the various kinds of word-type placement encountered in the passage from *Beowulf*:[72]

1. Monosyllabic preterite verbs are either verse-initial or verse-final
2. Metrically more extensive word-types seek verse-end (suspended by rule #1)
3. *Attributive-specifier*: any sequence involving a specifying word and a dependent attributive (partitive genitive, dative of respect, participle plus instrumental, etc.) will occur in the order attributive followed by specifier
4. Finite verbs in general seek verse-final position
5. Prepositional phrases seek verse-final position (subject to the priority of rules #1–4)
6. Single stressed words seek verse-final position (subject to the priority of rules #1–4)
7. Any sequence rules are subject to inversion in the first half-line if (a) the verse has double alliteration and (b) the inversion corresponds more closely to normal prose word-order
8. WTP at the level of the half-line or verse in general obeys the metrical laws of the alliterative line (as symbolized, e.g., in Sievers's Five Types)
9. WTP at the level of the whole line in general follows the predisposition of the metrical formulas described in chapter 3

These rules are arranged in approximate order of descending importance; that is, #2 is regularly superseded by #1, as in 719b (*healþegnas fand*), and #4 by #2, as in 712a (*mynte se manscaða*). Constraint #3 is a very powerful and general stricture, accounting for phrases as apparently diverse as 721a (*dreamum bedæled*), 722a (*fyrbendum fæst*), and 730a (*magorinca heap*). Prepositional phrases are essentially treated as the single words they linguistically are and positioned

---

72. This list of WTP rules is not intended to be complete, but is offered as a beginning statement of the sorts of constraints one can expect. Further investigation, especially of poems other than *Beowulf*, may suggest the need not only to add more rules, but perhaps to define certain of these nine further and more individualistically as well.

at the ends of units, unless another rule supervenes that localization. Note also that the first verse in any line shows special flexibility in allowing reversal of the usual patterning if conditions are right. Correspondingly, the second verse provides a regular locus for a non-alliterating fourth stressed element, and many second-verse phrases take advantage of this provision. Rules #8 and #9 apply at the prosodic level to virtually all of *Beowulf*; even if no other constraint orders a given phraseological element, the verse meter and whole-line metrical formula will prescribe pattern in the involved diction.

Other rules, compositionally analogous to the second-level "focusing" features discussed in relation to Serbo-Croatian epic phraseology, also contribute to the poet's and tradition's structuring of the phrase and line:[73]

1. Collocation (alliterating pair of words or roots)
2. Cluster (association of words outside of the alliterative constraint)
3. Theme (narrative structure)
4. Special "rhetorical" structures (e.g., litotes)[74]

The *Beowulf* passage has given us examples of all these rules in action, from the quite common pairing of alliterating words through the cluster of morphs and on to the theme and rhetorical figures. These influences are much more telling on the actual phraseology than is usually recognized, especially because the conventional model assumes a simple inventory of formulas and systems for thematic units.[75] These rules, just like the word-type placement rules, contribute both uniformity and variety to traditional phraseology: the most fundamental aspects of structure remain consistent, while the absolute verbal shape of any one instance—or even one set of instances—varies considerably.[76]

Finally, the point needs to be made that the discovery of traditional rules and of their significance at the deepest levels of composition does not in any sense invalidate or call into question the permanently useful research done on the formula and system—for traditional rules do not supersede these structures; they simply rationalize them. Instead of settling for an approximation of phraseological patterning, a convenient explanation that has the

73. See the discussion of Serbo-Croatian traditional phraseology in chapter 5.

74. I call such structures "rhetorical" in that they seem to be native Anglo-Saxon verbal tropes and need not necessarily be ascribed to the Latin rhetorical tradition. There is of course no reason why Latin figures could not have become part of the Old English poetic tradition, but literary history has, I feel, too often jumped to the conclusion of borrowing without considering whether such figures might be of native origin. See Campbell 1966, 1967, 1978; Bonner 1976.

75. In this respect Calvert Watkins's idea that the theme serves as the "deep structure" for the formula (see, e.g., G. Nagy 1979, 3–5) is a liberating first step, but one must also take account of the inequivalence of traditional units and the dimension of diachrony, not to mention variance among idiolect, dialect, and language.

76. One may compare the "tension of essences" that Lord (1960, 98) describes as holding together complexes of themes.

advantage of simplicity, we can now go further and explain what different formulas and systems have in common among themselves and even what they share with ostensibly non-formulaic (but still traditional) diction. We need not be burdened with conflicting definitions of the formula, none of which captures all of the half-lines in *Beowulf* and explains fully their traditional character; indeed, we can see that, given the tradition-dependent nature of Anglo-Saxon prosody, such a definition is an impossibility. Most importantly, by recognizing that formulas and systems have their roots in traditional rules, we are basing our understanding of the poetry on the idiosyncratic reality of the individual poetic tradition, as well as on a comparative perspective on oral epic poetry as a whole. By placing the broadly comparative concept of formulaic structure against the distinctly tradition-dependent background of traditional rules, in other words, we are creating a responsible interpretation of the diction of *Beowulf*, one that will serve faithfully as the foundation for later aesthetic investigation.

SEVEN

Thematic Structure
in the *Odyssey*

In this chapter we shall examine narrative structure in the *Odyssey* at the level of what has been called the *theme* or *typical scene*, seeking to establish the identity and morphology of this traditional unit in ancient Greek epic. A selective review of the most significant scholarship in the area will be followed by a brief section on what our earlier studies of traditional phraseology would lead us to expect of thematic structure in the *Odyssey*. The third part of the chapter will be devoted to example analyses of the Bath, Greeting, and Feasting themes, with special attention to the issues of shared idea-sequence and verbal correspondence among instances. There we shall also have the opportunity to consider the artistic dimensions of Homeric traditional structure by closely examining both the generic and individual qualities of particular occurrences of these themes.

PRIOR SCHOLARSHIP

The history of research on this aspect of traditional structure is a history of studies related by their general concern with narrative patterns but differentiated by their specific definitions and assumptions.[1] Scholars customarily designate Walter Arend's *Die typischen Scenen bei Homer* (1933) as the origin of interest in typical scenes, perhaps as much because of Milman Parry's famous response (1936) as because of the painstaking taxonomic presentation of the study itself.[2] What Arend provided was a first sketch of the narrative morphology behind such scenes as arrival, sacrifice and feast, departure (of ships

---

1. For further bibliographical information, see Foley 1985 (updated annually in *Oral Tradition*).

2. For an earlier study concerned in various ways with typical scenes and narrative structure in Homer, see Rothe 1890, and for Serbo-Croatian epic, Gesemann 1926 (esp. 65–96, "Kompositionsschema und heroisch-epische Stilisierung").

and other vehicles), armor and dressing, sleep, pondering, oath, and bath. Parry praised the philological acumen exhibited by this analysis but, fresh from his fieldwork among the Yugoslav *guslari*, criticized the accompanying explanation of scenic morphology: rather than agree with Arend's "philosophic and almost mystic theory" (1936, in 1971, 405), he ascribes thematic structure to the poetic tradition. But, although post-Parryan scholars have universally concurred with the explanation from oral tradition (whether or not they view the Homeric poems in their surviving form as oral in origin), Arend's sturdy little volume did help to focus attention on the narrative equivalent to formulaic structure, and it still has value today.

Fifteen years after Parry's review proposed a new explanation for what Arend had uncovered, Albert Lord (1951a, 73) described the unit of the theme or typical scene in Homer and Serbo-Croatian epic: "The theme can be identified as a recurrent element of narration or description in traditional oral poetry. It is not restricted, as is the formula, by metrical considerations; hence, it should not be limited to exact word-for-word repetition." Giving examples from Avdo Medjedović's *The Wedding of Smailagić Meho*, he argues (p. 80) that "the singer's themes aid his 'memory' and, what is just as important, leave him free to concentrate on the general complex structure of his story." Later on, in his classic *The Singer of Tales* (1960), Lord would expand on the nature of this narrative structure as documented in Yugoslav epic and extended to the Homeric poems.[3]

With Bernard Fenik's 1968 study of the scenes of battle in the *Iliad*, we come upon the first divergence in nomenclature and therefore the first problem with results. The author himself (p. 2) stresses that the large masses of details and incidents in which he is interested are not typical scenes or themes in the sense employed by Arend and by Parry and Lord, but rather larger narrative patterns that nonetheless show the familiar play of variation within traditional limits.[4] In this and other similar studies,[5] levels of structure above the theme or typical scene, reaching all the way to story-pattern (as discussed in chapter 10), are probed and explained. This kind of research on larger patterns is important, since it extends the principle of multiformity beyond the level of the Parry-Lord theme and illustrates how traditional structure is operative at all levels of the oral and oral-derived epic, from the microcosmic level of

3. Since the next chapter includes a substantial account of the theme as presented in Lord 1960 (esp. pp. 68–98), and since that description pertains chiefly to the Serbo-Croatian theme, I shall not now elaborate any further on *The Singer of Tales*.

4. In his "Summary of Contents," Fenik explains that "the result demonstrates that almost all the Iliad's battle narrative consists of an extensive, but limited, store of 'typical' or repeated details and action-sequences which undergo numerous and repeated combinations."

5. See Thornton 1970, esp. 38–57 on guest-friendship, testing, and omens; Hansen 1972 and 1978, 20–22, on narrative sequence; and Powell 1977, on a single action-pattern for all of Odysseus's adventures.

sound patterning and phraseology up through the mythic sequences embedded in story-patterns or tale-types. Of course, as the unit under consideration becomes larger and more comprehensive, the possibility of a regular, repeating verbal component lessens. Or, to put the same matter differently, while relatively close repetition—within tradition-dependent rules—serves an important function for the smaller traditional units, the larger, more comprehensive units must be more and more abstract in order to fulfill their function of templates for greater and greater multiformity. For our present purposes, then, we shall confine the discussion to the smaller, more tightly knit structures first mentioned by Arend and by Parry and Lord.

Another aspect of the variance of definition of themes and type-scenes in the work of different scholars may be traced to the general attempt to loosen what were felt to be the too confining bonds of compositional technique proposed by Parry and Lord. Symptomatic of this point of view is Joseph Russo's (1968, 281-88) argument for a spectrum of thematic units, which would include four categories of multiforms: (1) the verbatim repetitions, plus or minus varying additional lines; (2) recognizably traditional scenes that are nonetheless handled creatively; (3) "scenes where the stock pattern or type is handled rather loosely, or distorted to such an extent that the poet gives the impression not of *depending* on the existing type scheme to keep his narrative going, but of twisting some traditional elements into quite new meanings under the impulse to innovate" (p. 286); and (4) those which show an almost complete lack of repetition. Whether or not this particular taxonomy fits with our ideas about traditional narrative structure and the role of the individual poet, it is well to note Russo's helpful suggestions toward a spectrum of typical scenes. For in their eagerness to demonstrate thematic structure and continuities, scholars have at times tended to overlook the fact (demonstrated in fine in Arend's seminal work and observed in Lord 1951a as well) that instances of a theme can vary considerably from one occurrence to the next and that, consequently, we should not expect in all cases a simple list of composite motifs or a certain verbal correspondence.[6]

Another step forward in thematics was taken by David M. Gunn a few years later, in his articles on narrative inconsistency (1970) and thematic composition and Homeric authorship (1971). These papers have the advantage of a comparative perspective, with Gunn using the Serbo-Croatian material as an analogy to aid solution of certain long-debated problems in Homeric studies. Employing Lord's definition of the theme, he is able in the former piece to discriminate what he interprets as a singer's inconsistencies in the *Iliad* and *Odyssey* and thus to distinguish Homer from a "memorizer" (p. 202):

---

6. Cf. the spectrum of units described in Serbo-Croatian oral epic tradition (chapter 8 below, and Coote 1980).

For the latter [an oral singer] depends not upon a rather circumscribed ability to string together large memorized slabs of narrative but upon the *versatility*, in the face of the varied circumstances of performance, that comes with his familiarity with, and mastery of, a formulaic diction and the content and patterns of themes (including some which he is able to repeat verbatim or to "modify" at will).

This same notion of a plastic compositional unit, augmented by an appreciation of the differences between the units employed by different singers and in different local traditions, also underlies Gunn's discussion of the likely authorship of the Homeric poems.[7]

The next major theoretical advance was made by Michael Nagler (1974), who described the units of "motif" and "motif sequence." In concert with his view of Homeric phraseology as both traditional and spontaneous—that is, as generated from traditional habits of thought and articulation to suit the needs of the moment—Nagler (p. 82) understands the typical scene not as a fixed sequence of words or ideas but as "an inherited preverbal Gestalt for the spontaneous generation of a 'family' of meaningful details." As to the matter of ideational structure or diction shared among instances of such a unit, he argues that "in practice... not only are no two passages normally the same *verbatim*, they need not be of a pattern (an identical sequence of elements) in order to be recognized as the same motif." The elements Nagler speaks of are in turn quite abstract narrative features (examples include *procedo, non sola*, and *ancillae*) that may be realized in many different expressive forms; far from requiring any particular formulaic content or verbal correspondence, then, he opens up the definition of the motif and typical scene to allow for the widest possible range of association and referentiality.[8] The "motif sequence," in turn, is "a recurring sequence of common motifs—each subdivisible into elements and capable of functioning independently—which seems to acquire a meaning of its own" (p. 112).

7. See chapter 8 below. Also appearing about this time were Lord 1970, which deals with duplication and other traditional narrative devices, and Segal 1971, whose discussion of the theme of the mutilation of the corpse in the *Iliad* assumes a larger, less definite sense of "theme" than that employed here. A few years later Fenik (1974, 153–71) discussed "themes and typical situations" in the *Odyssey* in much the same manner as he studied typical scenes in the *Iliad* (1968); and Shannon (1975, 20–30) considered arming scenes in the *Iliad* as part of a larger study of the arms of Achilles.

8. Of the traditional resonance of the unit defined in this way, Nagler (1974, 85) says: "Despite the paratactic independence of the motif elements, when they occur in the happy synergism of a meaningful pattern an artistic entity is generated (a *sphoṭa*), which is somehow greater than the sum of its parts. It is this flash of meaning upon the mind that the oral poet is really after; it is also, I believe, as close as we may ever come to the true psychological building blocks of his performance, compared to which the factual line of his story is but the foil, a mere allurement which may well lapse from consistency or verisimilitude to an extent that causes such discomfiture to the modern reader."

Whereas Nagler's approach consisted of a search for units that have no necessary sequential structure or verbal identity, contemporary studies by Lord (1975), Peabody (1975), and later G. Nagy (1979) stressed the importance of the phraseological dimension of the theme. In his article "Perspectives on Recent Work on Oral Literature" and in response to Donald K. Fry's research on Old English themes and type-scenes (1968a), Lord (1975, 20) stressed the phraseological part of the concept he had developed in *The Singer of Tales*:

> if by theme one means a repeated narrative element together with its verbal expression, that portion of a poem, an aggregate of specific verses, that tells a certain repeated part of the narrative, measureable in terms of lines and even words and word combinations, then we find ourselves dealing with elements of truly oral traditional narrative style.

Drawing the model for themes from the Serbo-Croatian material, Lord describes self-contained narrative units with semi-independent lives of their own in the tradition, units that depend on both idea-pattern and verbal correspondence for their identity and function.

Peabody's five-level system of traditional structure includes a similar unit, also called a theme, in ancient Greek epos. It exists alongside *song* in the narrative structure of Hesiodic and Homeric poetry, and is understood as the actual expression of traditional ideas (1975, 214):

> One level is generative of the textual fabric itself. It is functionally self-sufficient and requires no additional controls. This level consists of traditional thought and is called theme. The other is a diachronic metalevel, one which cannot generate traditional discourse—for if it generated text, it would produce unstable prose. This level is associated with the feedback of memory and provides the parameters of associational decorum in a bard's composition. This level is called *song*.

Peabody introduces "phonic clumps" as the textual, aural data of his theme, extending the importance of patterns of sound from the level of phraseology to that of thematics.

Starting his investigation with the hard data of formulaic patterns, Nagy projects pre-formulaic themes that regulate the deployment of phraseology. Using the methods of comparative reconstruction, he finds (1979, 2) that

> certain noun + epithet combinations in Homeric diction go back to a time that predates the very existence of the Greek hexameter; further,...the choice of epithet is ultimately determined by themes that can be reconstructed all the way to a period when Greek was not yet differentiated from its sister languages in the Indo-European family.

This reasoning leads him to conclude that while phraseology is certainly regulated by meter from a descriptive or synchronic perspective, it is regulated historically or diachronically by theme.[9] Nagy's explanation of the art of the Homeric poems is thus based first and foremost on their traditional nature.

Some of the most useful recent work on themes or typical scenes has been done by Mark Edwards (esp. 1975, 1980a,b), who insists on a rather strict model for the unit, at least in terms of its narrative structure. Following Arend, Fenik, and Lord, he explains discrepancies in the story as a whole by reference to the unitary, integral nature of type-scenes, which may occur in a variety of contexts and occasionally contain details in conflict with (or at least oblique to) their surroundings. In addition, Edwards (1975, 71-72) sees no conflict between his position and that of scholars who prescribe a more abstract, generative model for the theme:

> I fully accept the possibility of superb artistic skill, of the kind Nagler persuasively identifies, in the design of the epics on both the large and the small scale. Nevertheless, I hold that, just as much of the time the common formulae are used automatically, even if occasionally imperfect adjustment results in a metrical anomaly, so too the regularity of common type-scenes exerts a compelling force on the poet which can sometimes be seen to result in awkward transitions.[10]

Edwards demonstrates the utility of his approach in his study "Convention and Individuality in *Iliad* 1" (1980a), in which each scene in the first book is related to the type-scene that underlies it. Here the emphasis is on the importance of bringing to the individual instance of a thematic unit the richness of traditional association as glimpsed in the rest of the Homeric poems. For Edwards (p. 1) what was once a compositional technique has developed in Homer's hands into an aesthetic instrument, for "the major means of giving dignity, color, and emotional impact to the narrative is by controlled elaboration of details of the type-scenes, by skillful selection of the amount of elaboration in a particular instance and of its nature and relevance to the situation." In his view the traditional techniques apparent in the *Iliad* can and often do show the influence of the individual craftsman at work.[11]

EXPECTABLE PHRASEOLOGICAL MAKEUP

As noted above, we shall be concerned in this chapter with the theme as defined and illustrated by Arend, Lord, and Edwards, that is, as a self-contained

9. In a footnote (4n4) Nagy (1979) adds: "Even from a descriptive point of view, I will consistently argue that Homeric epithets are indeed appropriate to the themes associated with the words that they describe."

10. Cf. the observations of Hansen (1978, 18): "The forms of themes are usually not so fixed that the poet need only insert the appropriate names into the proper slots. It is frequently not possible to classify themes (or formulas) neatly, since the one gradates into the other, and a given passage is often a blend of materials elsewhere appearing independently. Like the verbal formula, the theme is an analytic convenience."

11. See further Edwards 1980a, 27; Edwards 1980b.

unit describing a single event. The more extensive patterns, from Fenik's more heterogeneous "typical scenes" of battle to Hansen's "narrative sequences" and on to the tale-type or "story-pattern," lie beyond the scope of this chapter.[12] Although these other patterns are worthy subjects and, to the extent that they also illustrate the central role of multiformity in oral and oral-derived epic, are certainly relevant to the concerns of the present volume, we shall be concentrating on scenes that are readily comparable to the units found in Serbo-Croatian and Old English epic, and thus shall limit our analysis to the theme in the more restricted sense of the term.

Returning now for a moment to the findings of chapter 4 on Homeric phraseology, let us consider what we might be able to predict about the verbal dimension of these narrative structures. We established that the diction of the *Odyssey*, which developed in symbiosis with the hexameter, was a tradition-dependent diction that took its shape from the idiosyncratic prosody to which it was partner. Thus the phraseology was shown to be based on the inner metric of the hexameter, a complex poetic line with a complicated system of colonic shapes.

While the normative unit of meter turned out to be the colon, the minimal normative unit of phraseology proved to be the hemistich. Nonetheless, our analyses of elements of diction were unanimous in denying primacy to any one "length" for either "the formula" or "the formulaic system." From *epea pteroenta* through the twenty-one-line passage from Book 5, the evidence was the same: the diction simply could not be fairly reduced to a single type of phraseological pattern but had instead to be understood as a spectrum of phraseology. Hemistich, whole-line, and multi-line units were encountered; what is more, in many cases a given line seemed to be related to more than one of these levels in the diction, so that it was impossible to point to any single phrase as the primary unit, the core around which the others were formed.

Since (quite arbitrarily) denominating one level of structure as primary necessarily meant shortchanging the relative importance and the dynamics of other levels, I proposed a new solution to the riddle of the phraseology that avoided giving false prominence to any one proposed configuration and thus avoided reducing the plasticity and vitality of Homeric diction to a collection of mechanical parts. This solution involved the derivation of a number of *traditional rules* for the formation and maintenance of the phraseology from the principles of comparative prosody developed in chapter 3. Along with the Indo-European principle of right justification, we demonstrated the significance of *word-type localization* for the structure of hexameter phraseology. It was observed that these rules allowed us to explain the shape of formulaic

---

12. See chapter 10 for a discussion of story-pattern.

and (on available evidence) non-formulaic lines from the *Odyssey*, and in so doing to reach well beyond conventional formulaic analysis.

Of course, Homeric phraseology, like other traditional phraseologies treated in this volume, was in a constant state of evolution, and we recognized this developmental fluidity by noting cases in which formulaic structure has superseded minimal word-type localization. In these cases, usage has created families of formulaic elements or patterns that in their group coherence deflect the percentage occurrence figures for certain words away from the average percentages for overall word-types. That is, the individual lexical elements that make up these formulas and systems, although admitted to the phraseology on the basis of traditional rules, now skew the average figures because of the utility of the larger phrases in which they are embedded. This phenomenon also contributes to the varied spectrum of traditional phraseology.

Thus, in turning to the three analyses of thematic structure to follow, we may conceive of the verbal data for those narrative units as a spectrum of different kinds of elements rationalized by traditional rules. These rules provide the matrix through which all phraseology must pass in order to enter the tradition; they will call for right justification, word-type localization, and observance of the other features of the hexameter's inner metric.[13] Once having entered, these elements may evolve in virtually countless ways: they may form composite phrases, formulas, and systems; they may remain in their original form, at least for a time; they may disappear from the repertoire of a singer, local tradition, or the tradition at large; or—perhaps—they may come to be marshaled by thematic structure.[14] Whatever the individual case, we may be sure that the general relationship between thematic structure and phraseology will be at least as complex and many-sided as the diction itself, and further that the diction used to express the traditional ideas of themes will be overseen by traditional rules.

THREE THEMATIC ANALYSES

In this section I shall present three examples of thematic morphology in the *Odyssey*: Bath, Greeting, and Feast. In each case the goal will be to determine the extent to which the theme is dependent (a) on a definite grouping of actions or elements and (b) on a recurrent phraseological content. Especially in the third example, that of the feasting scenes, we shall also be concerned with the flexibility of the multiform, and thus with the ways in which Homer manipulates a generic pattern to adapt it logically and aesthetically to the given situation.

13. As G. Nagy (1974, 1976) has brilliantly shown, it was formulaic language that (diachronically) established that inner metric.

14. See, e.g., G. Nagy (1979, 3–5).

The Bath

This theme or typical scene was first noted and analyzed by Arend (1933, 124-26), who in his customary fashion reported the most consistently realized (*feste*) form and then went on to describe related occurrences that shared only a few details or lines. For the purposes of this first illustration, let us consider chiefly the most consistently realized instances of the "Bath"; in this way we can investigate both the structural and phraseological dimensions of a closely knit multiform. Later on we shall look at a multiform whose instances are much less closely or obviously correspondent, so that both ends of the spectrum will be covered.

According to Arend, the action of this theme or typical scene consists of "washing, anointing, and donning new clothes." This is a fair characterization of the general outline of the sequence, which varies from four to eleven lines in the seven instances he cites as the most consistent representations (3.464-69, 4.48-51, 8.449-57, 10.360-67, 17.85-90, 23.153-64, 24.365-71).[15] It proves to be a very adaptable multiform, one that can be used in many different situations. The first example occurs just after the elaborate slaughter and sacrifice at Nestor's palace, the second after Telemachos and Peisistratos arrive at Menelaos's home, the third following the heating of water and laying out of clothes for Odysseus at Alkinoos's palace, and the fourth on Kirke's island after four maids have prepared bed, bath, food, and drink. In Book 17 Telemachos rebukes Penelope before entering the bath, in Book 23 singing and dancing precede Odysseus's cleansing, and in the final book of the *Odyssey* the returned hero and his father Laertes converse before the latter's bath.

Just as telling as the variety of situations in which the Bath theme may be included is the limited set of possibilities to which it leads. In all but one of the seven instances, the Bath serves as an exordium for a feast. Although conversation and, in one example, other actions may intervene, the Bath seems to be conventionally associated with a following feast. Any departure from, or even delay in fulfilling, this sequence thus constitutes a special case; whatever material intercedes between the Bath and the traditionally consequent feast will be foregrounded and will take on special significance.

Before looking at the morphology and dynamics of the theme as a whole, however, let us consider the structure and phraseology that underlie its recur-

---

15. The line numbers given here correspond approximately to those cited in Arend. In defining the passages, I am aware that in some cases another line or two might have been included. As other investigators have observed, thematics is not an exact science, and there will always be some small difference in various scholars' ideas about where a given thematic occurrence begins and ends. The important point with all traditional units is to recognize that these elements are not simply counters mindlessly manipulated by a technician, but phraseological and narrative predispositions governed by traditional rules. Both diachronically and synchronically, plasticity and an internal dynamics are necessary to the survival of a traditional unit. For further discussion, see Foley 1986b.

rence in these seven instances. The first occurrence (3.464-69) demonstrates a core of diction repeated in other instances:

Τόφρα δὲ Τηλέμαχον λοῦσεν καλὴ Πολυκάστη,
Νέστορος ὁπλοτάτη θυγάτηρ Νηληϊάδαο.
αὐτὰρ ἐπεὶ λοῦσέν τε καὶ ἔχρισεν λίπ' ἐλαίῳ,
ἀμφὶ δέ μιν φᾶρος καλὸν βάλεν ἠδὲ χιτῶνα,
ἔκ ῥ' ἀσαμίνθου βῆ δέμας ἀθανάτοισιν ὁμοῖος·
πὰρ δ' ὅ γε Νέστορ' ἰὼν κατ' ἄρ' ἕζετο, ποιμένα λαῶν.

Meanwhile lovely Polykaste, who was the youngest
of the daughters of Nestor, son of Neleus, had bathed Telemachos.
But when she had bathed him and anointed him sleekly with olive oil,
She threw a splendid mantle and a tunic about him,
and he came out from the bath looking like an immortal
and came and sat down beside Nestor, shepherd of the people.[16]

The first of the underlined hexameters describes the washing and anointing, and it recurs verbatim in the Bath sequence in Book 10 (line 364) at Kirke's home. In that situation it is followed by a verbatim repeat of the next line (3.467 = 10.365). But we cannot so easily dismiss the phraseology expressing what Arend terms the "Waschen, Salben" action of this theme, for in the other five instances the same action is expressed in the hemistich λοῦσεν, -αν καὶ χρῖσεν, -αν ἐλαίῳ ("she/they bathed and anointed [him] with olive oil"). Thus either the whole-line formula or the second-hemistich phrase, the latter of which is of course open to variation in the first hemistich, can carry the burden of traditional meaning for the theme.

The second-hemistich phrase, in turn, combines with one of two sorts of partners, either the general expression τοὺς/τὸν δ' ἐπεὶ οὖν δμῳαὶ ("Now when the maidservants...them/him"), which occurs in three of the five examples (4.49, 8.454, and 17.88), or the more specific designation of a particular maidservant who performs the ablutions: Εὐρυνόμη ταμίη ("the house-keeper Eurynome"; 23.154) and ἀμφίπολος Σικελή ("the Sicilian attendant"; 24.366). This selection of expressions for washing and anointing, along with the selection of partners (B1 first hemistichs composed according to traditional rules),[17] gives some idea of the plasticity within limits that characterizes Homeric phraseology. Additionally, the focus on two phrases—the whole-line

16. Translations here and below are taken from Lattimore 1965, with occasional minor modifications.

17. In addition to the right justification of the line as a whole, with the less variable portion being the second hemistich and the first hemistich correspondingly showing less fixity, the first-hemistich partners themselves obey traditional rules. The thrice-repeated general expression locates *dmōiai* at the end of the phrase, in one of the favored positions for its metrical word-type, with the function words in the most variable section of the hemistich. Likewise, the word-types underlying *Eurunomē* and *Sikelē* and their epithets all accord with expectation.

and hemistich versions—begins to indicate the kind of pressure for selection a theme can impose on diction.

Both versions, it should be stressed, depend on traditional rules for their shape and texture. In the case of the whole-line expression αὐτὰρ ἐπεὶ λοῦσέν τε καὶ ἔχρισεν λίπ' ἐλαίῳ, all major elements (the verbs *lousen* and *echrisen*, the nouns *lip'* and *elaiôi*) occupy favored positions for their word-types. But the degree of fossilization of the phrase is more apparent in the localization of what amounts to a single "word": the dative phrase *lip' elaiôi*, which as a composite belongs to the pattern ◡◡＿＿, occurs at 12; and line-end turns out to be the only spot at which metrical words of this kind appear.[18] As for the hemistich version of this expression, λοῦσαν καὶ χρῖσαν ἐλαίῳ, once again the main elements occupy some of the metrically favored positions, and once again a composite "word"—*chrisan elaiôi* in the shape of an adonean (＿◡◡＿＿)—reveals right justification and fixity in its occupation of line-end position.[19] As observed in chapter 4, Homeric phraseology is governed by traditional rules, and even diction that is further focused by a well-defined theme obeys the same strictures.

In the occurrence in Book 3 quoted above, one notices that the whole-line phrase for washing and anointing and the hexameter used to express the donning (of a cloak and tunic) are followed by a third underscored line, ἔκ ῥ' ἀσαμίνθου βῆ δέμας ἀθανάτοισιν ὁμοῖος. Here another dimension of multiformity begins to emerge, for this line does not occur with its two partners in their only other appearance together (10.364-65). Rather, it follows a simile in the instance of the Bath theme in Book 23, the most idiosyncratic of the seven occurrences. True, in Book 23 we also find the "donning" line present in precisely the same form as in Books 3 and 10, but (a) the "donning" and "godlike" phrases are separated by eight lines, none of which are associated with this theme, and (b) in Book 23 the "washing and anointing" are expressed in the hemistich rather than the whole-line version.

The Bath theme in Book 4 (lines 48-51) illustrates some further dimensions of multiformity:

ἔς ῥ' ἀσαμίνθους βάντες ἐϋξέστας λούσαντο.
τοὺς δ' ἐπεὶ οὖν δμῳαὶ λοῦσαν καὶ χρῖσαν ἐλαίῳ,
ἀμφὶ δ' ἄρα χλαίνας οὔλας βάλον ἠδὲ χιτῶνας,
ἔς ῥα θρόνους ἕζοντο παρ' 'Ατρείδην Μενέλαον.

They stepped into the bathtubs smooth-polished and bathed there.
Then when the maids had bathed them and anointed them with oil,
and put cloaks of thick fleece and tunics upon them, they went
and sat on chairs beside Menelaos the son of Atreus.

18. Theoretically, ◡◡＿＿ could also appear at 4, 6, 8, and 10, but all of these would result in metrical infelicities of one sort or another. O'Neill (1942) reports forty-four instances of this word-type in his sample, all occurring at 12.

19. Of the twenty adonean words reported by O'Neill (1942), all occupied the slot at 12.

In the second line we recognize the hemistich version of "washing and anointing," wholly underscored here to indicate its recurrence two additional times with the same partner. The remaining correspondences are not quite as straightforward. Line 4.48 includes a first hemistich that can appear in modified form either at the commencement of the scene (with *es*, "into") or at its close (with *ek*, "from"); in all cases except one it follows the pattern *es/ek hr'/d' asaminthous/-on/-ou/-ón* + some form of *bainô*. To illustrate the wide variety of partners that combine with this phrase, I list below all of its thematic occurrences:

ἔκ ῥ' ἀσαμίνθου βῆ δέμας ἀθανάτοισιν ὁμοῖος	(3.468)
ἔς ῥ' ἀσαμίνθους βάντες ἐϋξέστας λούσαντο	(4.48)
ἔς ῥ' ἀσάμινθον βάνθ'· ὁ δ' ἄρ' ἀσπασίως ἴδε θυμῷ	(8.450)
ἔκ ῥ' ἀσαμίνθου βὰς ἄνδρας μέτα οἰνοποτῆρας	(8.456)
ἔς ῥ' ἀσάμινθον ἔσασα λό' ἐκ τρίποδος μεγάλοιο	(10.361)
ἐς δ' ἀσαμίνθους βάντες ἐϋξέστας λούσαντο	(17.87)
ἔκ ῥ' ἀσαμίνθων βάντες ἐπὶ κλισμοῖσι καθῖζον	(17.90)
ἐκ δ' ἀσαμίνθου βῆ δέμας ἀθανάτοισιν ὁμοῖος	(23.163)
ἐκ δ' ἀσαμίνθου βῆ· θαύμαζε δέ μιν φίλος υἱός	(24.370)

This group of lines exemplifies a familiar phenomenon in Homeric phraseology. The hypothesis of a "core" hemistich cannot explain the two whole-line formulas (3.468 = 23.163 and 4.48 = 17.87) except by extension, while those two whole-line expressions cannot by themselves account for the five other lines that show no mutual pattern past the first hemistich.

By viewing this set of lines, particularly the opening sections, as the product of traditional rules and formulaic association, however, we can rationalize the heterogeneity. First, we can easily see how the *ek/es hr'/d' asaminth-* + *bainô* phrase, once established, would tend to remain stable; the A caesura is blocked by the "heavy word" at position 4 and thus would not be amenable to substitution or other types of variation. The question is how it entered the phraseology initially, since it is so metrically unlikely at 4, its word-type normally occurring only at line-end. The answer seems to be found in the localization of the participle *bantes*, which, while permitted as a word-type in many positions, is as a part of speech consistently "backed up" against the mid-line caesura. While the general pattern $\_\_ \cup$ is of course permitted at many places in the hexameter,[20] this particular word occurs seven of eight

20. Favored placements are $9\frac{1}{2}$ (29.6 percent); $5\frac{1}{2}$ (26.0 percent), as in seven of eight occurrences of *bantes*; $1\frac{1}{2}$ (24.0 percent); 12 (13.8 percent); and so forth. The sole occurrence of the word *asaminthos* in the *Iliad* (10.576) is in a phrase precisely equal to *Odyssey* 4.48 and 17.87. We may compare the frequent blockage of the A caesura with participles backed up against the mid-line caesura in the system of diction associated with the *epea pteroenta* ("winged words") phrase, as discussed in chapter 4.

times at $5\frac{1}{2}$, whether as part of this hemistich phrase or not.[21] Given also that two of the four non-formulaic occurrences of *bantes* are preceded by an adverbial phrase of direction similar to *ek/es asaminth-*, we may conclude that the hemistich phrase entered the diction through the fixation of *bantes* at $5\frac{1}{2}$ and the analogy of the adverbial phrases for direction. With the participle against the mid-line caesura, the proclitic *es* or *ek*, with metrical lengthening via the following particle, combined with *asaminth-* to yield a pattern that fit the hemistich perfectly. Once formed around the right-justified kernel *bantes*, this hemistich then took on a life of its own and, by a second step in analogy—and this time quite clearly under traditional rules—then acquired an identity as a whole-hemistich "word." From that point it was only a small step to changes in the morphology of *bainô* and thus to the selection of B1 and B2 hemistichs listed above.[22]

These hemistich phrases are quite consistently associated with the Bath theme. In five of the seven instances, the *ek* (or "from") version of the phrase occurs at or near the end of the scene. In the two remaining instances of the theme (Books 4 and 10), the *es* (or "to") form introduces the sequence of actions.[23] Additionally, the *es* and *ek* forms of the phrase can bound the theme in an example of the very typical structural pattern of ring-composition.[24]

It would be quite possible to continue with this sort of analysis of the phraseology shared by the seven examples of the Bath scene, but perhaps the foregoing is sufficient to demonstrate that the actual verbal expression of this theme consists not of a completely fossilized run of hexameters but rather of a fluid collection of diction that can take on numerous different forms. Although the thematic "deep structure"—Arend's "washing, anointing, and donning of new clothes" as a first approximation—surely focuses the verbal component and attracts traditional phraseology, it does not exist in a one-to-one relationship with a single inviolate phraseological component. Ideas are expressed in diction that follows traditional rules and exhibits formulaic structure, but that expression can take on a variety of forms.

In order to gain a complementary perspective on this process and its importance for a given narrative situation, let us examine more closely a single instance of the theme. For this purpose I choose Odysseus's bath in Book 23,

21. Thus position $5\frac{1}{2}$ also seems to be a favored one for participles (see note 20). Compare the occurrences of the same participle in other inflections, all three of which are also at $5\frac{1}{2}$: *banta* (4.680, 17.575) and *bante* (8.296).

22. The degree of fossilization of this particular phrase may be indicated by noting that the noun *asaminthos* is used only in this phrase. Considering its traditional (as well as syntactic) integrity as a unit, it is not surprising that two instances show a sentence boundary at the mid-line caesura.

23. In Book 10 it is the anomalous phrase *es hr' asaminthon hesasa* that performs this function.

24. On ring-composition, see the seminal studies of van Otterlo (1944a,b, 1948), as well as later works (e.g., Whitman 1958; Gaisser 1969). For similar studies on *Beowulf*, see Hieatt 1975; Niles 1979. For Serbo-Croatian epic, see Lord 1986a.

which (we note here for later reference) occurs just after a celebration involving singing and dancing and just before the riddle of the olive-tree bed is solved and the rapprochement is complete.

αὐτὰρ Ὀδυσσῆα μεγαλήτορα ᾧ ἐνὶ οἴκῳ
Εὐρυνόμη ταμίη λοῦσεν καὶ χρῖσεν ἐλαίῳ,
ἀμφὶ δέ μιν φᾶρος καλὸν βάλεν ἠδὲ χιτῶνα·   155
αὐτὰρ κὰκ κεφαλῆς χεῦεν πολὺ κάλλος Ἀθήνη
μείζονά τ᾽ ἐσιδέειν καὶ πάσσονα· κὰδ δὲ κάρητος
οὔλας ἧκε κόμας, ὑακινθίνῳ ἄνθει ὁμοίας.
ὡς δ᾽ ὅτε τις χρυσὸν περιχεύεται ἀργύρῳ ἀνὴρ
ἴδρις, ὃν Ἥφαιστος δέδαεν καὶ Παλλὰς Ἀθήνη   160
τέχνην παντοίην, χαρίεντα δὲ ἔργα τελείει,
ὡς μὲν τῷ περίχευε χάριν κεφαλῇ τε καὶ ὤμοις.
ἐκ δ᾽ ἀσαμίνθου βῆ δέμας ἀθανάτοισιν ὁμοῖος·
ἂψ δ᾽ αὖτις κατ᾽ ἄρ᾽ ἕζετ᾽ ἐπὶ θρόνου ἔνθεν ἀνέστη,

Now the housekeeper Eurynome bathed great-hearted
Odysseus in his own house, and anointed him with olive oil,
and threw a beautiful mantle and a tunic about him;   155
and over his head Athene suffused great beauty, to make him
taller to behold and thicker, and on his head she arranged
the curling locks that hung down like hyacinthine petals.
And as when a master craftsman overlays gold on silver,
and he is one who was taught by Hephaistos and Pallas Athene   160
in art complete, and grace is on every work he finishes;
so Athene gilded with grace his head and his shoulders.
Then, looking like an immortal, he strode forth from the bath,
and came back then and sat on the chair from which he had arisen,

Lines 153-54 form a two-line unit that recurs in slightly modified form in Book 24 (lines 365-66):

Τόφρα δὲ Λαέρτην μεγαλήτορα ᾧ ἐνὶ οἴκῳ
ἀμφίπολος Σικελὴ λοῦσεν καὶ χρῖσεν ἐλαίῳ,

Since this combination occurs nowhere else, and in fact since the second hemistich in the first line occurs nowhere else, we may be tempted to think of the couplet as a traditional unit associated with the Bath theme. But our earlier demonstration of the flexibility of the second line stands as evidence against that hypothesis, and we once more see how the phraseology, though focused by the Bath theme, still remains flexible and recombinative.[25]

Line 155 occurs verbatim at 3.467, with related lines in each of the other

25. To be specific, the second hemistich of the second line has now been shown to occur (1) as a unit by itself, (2) in a whole-line formula, (3) in a whole-line system, and (4) in a multi-line system. No one of the identities is "primary" and the rest "derivative"; rather, they are all equally "primary" in their derivation from traditional rules.

instances of the theme.[26] In each case the verse expresses what Arend called "donning new clothes," and the mix of phraseology is similar to that involving 23.154 and its counterparts. *Line 156* shows very little that could be interpreted as formulaic, although it does obey traditional rules for formation (e.g., the placement of *Athênê* at line-end). *Line 157*, however, begins a six-line section that finds a virtually exact counterpart at 6.230-35, the only variation being the prefix in the two verbs *pericheue* and *katecheue*. These six lines in both cases follow a scene of bathing and anointing, although the episode in Book 6 is otherwise different enough in action and phraseology to raise the question of whether it is truly the same or an alternate Bath theme. As is customary, the occurrence in Book 6 leads eventually to a feast, albeit a modest one, for Odysseus has just washed up onto Phaeaecia and his brief scene of grooming prepares the way for a one-man dinner. After this special inset describing Athena's gifts to Odysseus, the Bath theme in Book 23 moves toward closure with *line 163*, which has a verbatim repetition at 3.468 as well as the phraseological relatives discussed above. In accordance with the limits prescribed for the other examples, I have ended the passage at *line 164*, which, although it has three other related occurrences in the *Odyssey*, does not seem to be conventionally associated with the Bath theme.[27]

This closer examination of 23.153-64 gives some idea of the morphology of a theme in the *Odyssey*, even one as brief as the Bath. Certain core ideas that consistently make up the scene (or at least this version of the scene) attract to them a regular means of expression, so that we can demonstrate a verbal correspondence among instances. But that verbal correspondence is not simply a "run" of hexameters; rather, it consists of a collection of phrases that share important aspects of diction without being reducible to one primary means of expression and some variants.

In addition to these regular phraseological dimensions that stem from the repetition of core actions, we notice lines that particularize this instance, that color the generic scene of the Bath in individualized hues and suit it to context. These phrases, like line 156 or the six-line set-piece on Athena's gifts, enrich the scene at hand with details that are not as regular as the central actions of washing, anointing, and donning new clothes. While these lines themselves are demonstrably traditional in that they can be shown to be formulaic or, at minimum, to follow traditional rules, their function in this theme is not traditional.

Scholars will differ over the exact boundaries of the Bath and other themes, and that is no doubt as it should be: no poetry worth the name should be

---

26. The other instances are 4.50, 8.455, 10.365, 17.89, and 24.367.

27. The three additional occurrences include one verbatim comparand involving Amphinomos (18.157) and two related lines involving Odysseus (21.243) and Philoitios (21.392). None of these includes the Bath; apparently this line is one of the many which is not tied to a single theme but available for general use.

too readily dismemberable.[28] Given the scope I have prescribed by making these selections, however, I would add a few details to Arend's "Waschen, Salben, Anlegen reiner Kleidung" core. First, the Bath is embedded in the ritual of hospitality, the common Homeric portrait of *xeiniê*.[29] But although this association exists, it is not totally prescriptive: the theme can occur in a number of different narrative situations and is not confined to following any single scene. Second, the Bath theme customarily leads to a consequent feast scene, whether that feast is expressed through the theme we shall study below or in a shorter, non-conventional form. For example, the Feast theme follows the Bath in Books 4, 10, and 17, while only simple dinner episodes, often merely a few lines long, occur in Books 3, 8, and 24. Although it would be difficult to explain the reason for this variance in the usual terms, since we would be ascribing an intentionality to the poet which comparative oral studies do not universally support,[30] we might note that in Book 3 the abbreviated feast may be a compensatory response to the elaborate slaughter and sacrifice that precede the Bath. Likewise, in Book 8 Demodokos's singing is the more important narrative event following Odysseus's bath, and in Book 24, the occurrence at Laertes' home, one cannot imagine a full feast taking place in the relative poverty of the surroundings.

The Bath-Feast sequence in Book 10 offers an interesting example of how Homer fleshes out a traditional generic structure to suit the specific situation. Here the Bath scene leads, as would be expected, to the preparatory lines of the Feast theme (10.368-72), but no further. The actual feasting, in other words, is apocopated. This delay in fulfillment of the action creates a tension of expectation, and into the breach is inserted the description of Odysseus's seeking and obtaining his men's release from captivity as swine. When Kirke asks the hero why he is not partaking of the sumptuous food and drink set before him (that is, as the narrative asks why the traditional coda has been suspended), he replies that he cannot think of such things while his companions are in such miserable condition. This response prompts Kirke to take pity and to free the companions, an action that allows closure of the Bath-Feast sequence (467-68), albeit with lines other than those conventionally used for the purpose in the Feast theme.

A small but significant action performed by Kirke reinforces the traditional nature of this sequence. After the captives have been changed back from swine

28. Among the Yugoslav poets recorded by Parry and Lord, it is a truism that those whose texts are easiest to analyze in terms of formula and theme are also the least accomplished artists.

29. Studies on the ritual of hospitality in the *Odyssey* include Podlecki 1961 and Levy 1963.

30. To what extent we may ascribe intentionality to Homer is a question that awaits definitive resolution (for the two sides of the argument, see, e.g., Lord 1967a and Amory Parry 1973). As in many matters associated with oral and oral-derived literature, the best approach may well be through more careful attention to tradition- and genre-dependence. See further chapter 1 above and Foley 1983b.

and before the long-delayed feasting takes place, she performs the traditional preparatory ritual for them, just as she did for their leader some lines before.

Τόφρα δὲ τοὺς ἄλλους ἑτάρους ἐν δώμασι Κίρκη
ἐνδυκέως λοῦσέν τε καὶ ἔχρισεν λίπ᾽ ἐλαίῳ,   450
ἀμφὶ δ᾽ ἄρα χλαίνας οὔλας βάλεν ἠδὲ χιτῶνας·
δαινυμένους δ᾽ εὖ πάντας ἐφεύρομεν ἐν μεγάροισιν.

Meanwhile, within the house, Kirke with loving care the rest of
    my companions
attentively bathed and anointed sleekly with olive oil,   450
and threw cloaks of thick fleece and tunics upon them.
We found them all together, feasting well in the halls.

In both a narrative and a traditional sense, this second, more abbreviated occurrence of the Bath theme prepares the way for the feast that has been expected for almost one hundred lines. With this washing, anointing, and donning of new clothes, not only Odysseus but also his companions who have been suffering under Kirke's spell are ritually cleansed and made ready for the culmination of Homeric hospitality—the Feast.[31] Thus the entire scene, from the first Bath through the long-awaited dinner and drink, is opened up to accommodate the story of Odysseus's freeing his men through the agency of his goddess-lover Kirke. The particularizing detail is important, since it allows the story to be told, but the scene would lack tension and power were it not for the traditional underlay that serves as a backdrop and creates the expectation of a conventional series of events.

In addition to these larger dimensions, we may take note of a third narrative detail that seems to be associated with the Bath: the seating of the protagonist among his fellows. Between the Bath and Feast the hero is conveyed to a seat of prominence, where he stays for the duration of the festivities. This is a small detail, and one that is expressed in no special formulaic phrase, but it does assist in moving the action along between the two themes.[32] In five of the seven passages examined, the "seating" takes place immediately after the Bath is complete, and this seems to be the expected configuration. We see another example of Homer's suspension of closure and insertion of particularizing features in the remaining two instances. In Book 8 some fourteen lines elapse before the expected seating, during which time Nausikaa gazes fondly on Odysseus, bids him farewell, and the hero gives her thanks for her role in his deliverance. In the final book, Laertes' moving reminiscence over

31. Note that, given the original bestial condition of the companions, the feast could not have occurred until the Bath ceremony had made them ritually (and traditionally) worthy to take part.

32. In this sense the action is very similar in function to the "boundary lines" or "position change lines" of Serbo-Croatian oral epic (see chapter 8), which, while not part of any given theme, serve to accommodate one narrative element to the next.

his younger days as a proud warrior who could have aided his son and grandson in their battle against the suitors intervenes between Bath and seating.[33]

Finally, we should confront the major discrepancy in the occurrence of the Bath-Feast sequence in Book 23. Put most simply, this is the only one of seven instances that has no feast, whether of the formal thematic variety or the compressed, descriptive sort. After the Bath and seating, and in traditional expectation of the sharing of a meal and all that it implies within the conventions of Homeric hospitality, Penelope poses the riddle of the olive-tree bed, a riddle she knows only her husband can solve. With his careful exposition of the fashioning of the bed,[34] husband and wife are reunited and the *telos*, as the ancients called it, toward which the *Odyssey* has been moving for more than twelve thousand lines, is imminent. It is a measure of Homer's profoundly traditional art, I suggest, that the Feast is this time a celebration not of eating and drinking but of long-sought reunion and fulfillment, not of consuming elaborately prepared foodstuffs but of finding once again the feast of love and tenderness that had been denied for twenty years. For in a vital sense, this instance of the pattern shows not a deviation from expectation but an augmentation of the conventional sequence, and its extraordinary make-up derives directly from the traditional expectation on which Homer, or his poetic tradition, has so brilliantly built.

The Greeting Theme

For a second example of thematic structure in the *Odyssey* I turn to what Edwards has called the "greeting type-scene," the action of which he defines thus (1975, 55): "usually a person hands a cup of wine to another, and with words of welcome, farewell, or honor (often *deidisketo* or some other form of the verb, and *chaire*) makes a prayer or wish for him; sometimes he invites the other to make a libation and pray." Edwards locates five full realizations of this pattern in the *Odyssey*, in Books 3 (lines 41-50), 4 (59-64), 13 (56-62), 15 (150-59), and 18 (119-23, 151-52).[35]

These instances of "Greeting" occur in various narrative contexts. In Book 3 it constitutes Peisistratos's welcoming of "Mentor" (Athena) and asking her to offer a prayer to Poseidon, during whose festival he (she) has arrived. The

---

33. In neither of these situations do we need to posit a literary sensibility, since both amount to variations on a traditional pattern that is used a number of times in the *Odyssey*. Nonetheless, we can appreciate the artistry of Homer, as is evident in the poignant adaptations of a powerfully connotative convention.

34. Reminiscent in its way of the raft-building episode in Book 5, this may well be a set-piece effectively "memorized" by Homer and, like the similes, summoned to narrative present as a composite "word" in itself. Analogs to such units exist in Serbo-Croatian epic, as in the case of the ban's threat to the shouting prisoner (see chapter 8).

35. He also finds "short forms" at 14.112–13 and 447–48 and "greeting without the offer of wine" at 20.197–99.

second instance, in the fourth book, is Menelaos's invitation to Telemachos and Peisistratos to eat; it occurs between Bath and Feast. The next, near the opening of Book 13, is Odysseus's parting salute to Queen Arete as he prepares to leave Phaeaecia. In Book 15 the Feast theme (which we shall examine in the next section) precedes the Greeting theme, which involves Menelaos's libation for the return journey about to be undertaken by Telemachos and Peisistratos; Telemachos's thanks, wish for the homecoming of his father, and an omen indicating the vengeful nature of that homecoming follow. The last of the five full occurrences of the type-scene involves Amphinomos's greeting to the disguised Odysseus, about which variation we shall have more to say later on.

Even from this brief description, it should be clear that, unlike the Bath theme, Greeting has no particular association with other themes in the tradition. Not only is the material preceding it quite different from instance to instance, but it seems to lead not to one but to a wide variety of consequent actions. To be sure, it is associated with the general situations of coming and going, that is, of arriving and taking leave, but there is no traditional link to another theme that would create an expectation of what should precede or follow. Such ubiquitous character is quite at odds with the Bath-Feast linkage, and this difference begs the question of whether we are dealing with the same sort of unit and, further, whether the themes will reveal other divergences as well.

To answer these questions, let us consider the two axes of correspondence among occurrences of Greeting: narrative pattern and verbal correspondence. First, the general nature of Edwards' description of the actions entailed in this theme or type-scene argues a somewhat less specific idea-structure than underlay the Bath. The Greeting scene may involve welcome, farewell, or honor, or a combination of either of the first two with the last; it may comprise a prayer or wish for someone; it may include one person's speech or that speech plus the other's reply.[36] In short, as the two following examples testify, this particular theme is simply not as tightly organized around discrete actions as is the Bath.

$$\text{ἀνὰ δ' ἵστατο δῖος 'Οδυσσεύς,}$$
'Αρήτῃ δ' ἐν χειρὶ τίθει δέπας ἀμφικύπελλον,
καί μιν φωνήσας ἔπεα πτερόεντα προσηύδα·
"Χαῖρέ μοι, ὦ βασίλεια, διαμπερές, εἰς ὅ κε γῆρας
ἔλθῃ καὶ θάνατος, τά τ' ἐπ' ἀνθρώποισι πέλονται.   60
αὐτὰρ ἐγὼ νέομαι· σὺ δὲ τέρπεο τῷδ' ἐνὶ οἴκῳ
παισί τε καὶ λαοῖσι καὶ 'Αλκινόῳ βασιλῆϊ."   (13.56-62)

36. The instances also differ considerably in length, but as we have seen earlier, this is a common enough variation among thematic occurrences. And the fact that the theme is split in Book 18 is likewise not unusual.

But great Odysseus stood up
and put the handled goblet into the hand of Arete,
and spoke to her aloud and addressed her in winged words, saying:
"Farewell to you, O queen, and for all time, until old age
comes to you, and death, which befall all human creatures.   60
Now I am on my way; but have joy here in your household,
in your children and your people, and in your king, Alkinoos."

'Αμφίνομος δὲ
ἄρτους ἐκ κανέοιο δύω παρέθηκεν ἀείρας   120
καὶ δέπαϊ χρυσέῳ δειδίσκετο φώνησέν τε·
"χαῖρε, πάτερ ὦ ξεῖνε· γένοιτό τοι ἔς περ ὀπίσσω
ὄλβος· ἀτὰρ μὲν νῦν γε κακοῖς ἔχεαι πολέεσσι."
. . . .
°Ὡς φάτο, καὶ σπείσας ἔπιεν μελιηδέα οἶνον,
ἂψ δ' ἐν χερσὶν ἔθηκε δέπας κοσμήτορι λαῶν.   (18.119-23, 151-52)

Amphinomos, taking
two loaves of bread out of the basket, set them before him,   120
and drank his health in a golden cup and spoke to him, saying:
"Your health, father and stranger; may prosperous days befall you
hereafter; but now you are held in the grip of many fortunes."
. . . .
So he spoke, and poured, and drank the honey-sweet wine, then
put the cup back into the hands of the lord of the people;

It would be difficult to imagine two more divergent uses of the same type-scene. In Book 13, Odysseus's farewell to Arete is full of respect, admiration, and thanks; she and her husband, Alkinoos, have served an essential function in helping the hero toward his homeland of Ithaka. There is no explicit reply, as occurs in many of the Greetings, although king and queen send escorts and gifts for Odysseus as he strides down to the shore and enters the fleet Phaeaecian craft. The Book 18 exemplar, while following the general pattern of salute, salutation, and wine drinking, reverberates with foreboding. Although Amphinomos is the favored suitor, and perhaps the only honorable one in the lot, his apparently sincere toast of the disguised Odysseus is qualified by his last few words; indeed, more than he knows, the man he salutes is "held in the grip of many fortunes."

Specifically, then, we can agree with Edwards's definition of the Greeting theme: it does involve "words of welcome, farewell, or honor," it does include the speaker "mak[ing] a prayer or wish," and it does (optionally) involve a reply in the form of a libation or prayer. All of the instances cited also feature one person handing a cup of wine to another, or some close variation of that action. But there the definition of this type-scene must end, for we find no series of actions both as differentiated and as integrated into a logical, recurrent series as is the group of "washing, anointing, and donning new clothes" that makes up the body of the Bath theme. Once again, then, is this difference enough to demand separate taxonomies for scenes like Bath on the one hand and Greeting on the other?

Consider first that both patterns serve at least two functions: they are compositionally useful and connotatively dynamic, in that some degree of expectation is created by their appearance in a narrative. While the Bath is more prescriptively conventional and specifically echoic because its structure is tighter and more integrated, in its own way each theme assists the poet and provides him with an instrument that carries with it institutionalized associations. We may add to this comparison the fact that the greater structural flexibility of the Greeting, as well as its lack of definite attachments to other themes or narrative situations, confers on it a kind of utility that is lacking in the Bath theme. In short, on the basis of narrative pattern alone, Bath and Greeting seem both to reveal thematic structure, even if the dimensions and implications of that structure vary somewhat.

This last point may be most clearly made through reference to an example. The instance of Greeting in Book 18, as quoted above, consists of Amphinomos's actions and speech and, after an ellipsis not designated as part of the type-scene by Edwards,[37] the closure in Odysseus's drinking of the wine and passing of the cup back to the suitor. So far the generic form of the pattern is observed. But in between these two sections (lines 124-50) lies what in other occurrences of the same type-scene proves to be the gracious response of the person saluted.[38] Here, however, the disguised stranger offers no simple thanks to his host or server, but rather a praise of the man himself coupled with a warning of what may befall him as part of the troop of suitors:

"Amphinomos, you seem to me very prudent, being   125
the son of such a father, whose excellent fame I have heard of,
Nisos, that is, of Doulichion, both strong and prosperous;
they say you are his son, and you seem like a man well spoken.
So I will tell you, and you in turn understand and listen.
Of all creatures that breathe and walk upon the earth there is nothing   130
more helpless than a man is, of all that the earth fosters;
for he thinks that he will never suffer misfortune in future
days, while the gods grant him courage, and his knees have spring
in them. But when the blessed gods bring sad days upon him,
against his will he must suffer it with enduring spirit.   135

37. With this judgment I must agree, at least on formal grounds; but see below for the modification that lines 124-50 represent.

38. As noted above, not all occurrences have a response; but where some reciprocation does manifest itself in the form of a speech, it is always—that is, traditionally—a gracious and thankful response to the ritual gesture of Greeting. See 15.155-59 for an example.

For the mind in men upon earth goes according to the fortunes
the Father of Gods and Men, day by day, bestows upon them.
For I myself once promised to be a man of prosperity,
but, giving way to force and violence, did many reckless
things, because I relied on my father and brothers. Therefore,   140
let no man be altogether without the sense of righteousness,
but take in silence the gifts of the gods, whatever they give him.
Even so, now, I see the suitors, their reckless devisings,
how they show no respect to the wife, and despoil the possessions
of a man who, I think, will not for long be far from   145
his country and friends. He is very close by. But I hope your destiny
takes you home, out of his way. I hope you will never face him,
at the time he comes back to the beloved land of his fathers.
For I believe that, once he enters his halls, there will be
a reckoning, not without blood, between that man and the suitors."   150

We recall the instance of the Bath theme in Book 10, at Kirke's home, in which the conclusion of the pattern was suspended in favor of the inserted episode of Odysseus's freeing of his men from the witch's magic spell. Once they were freed and suitably washed and anointed, the expected feast could—narratively and traditionally—take place. The situation involving Amphinomos and Odysseus in disguise is not dissimilar in structure and effect, for once again the expected closure is suspended while a unique, non-traditional insert is related. That is, Homer interrupts the pattern and rhythm of the theme, thus creating the same kind of tension described in relation to the Bath on Aiaia, and into this environment places a speech that bears only a formal resemblance to what traditional structure leads us to expect. The praise of Amphinomos seems genuine, but is overshadowed by an excursus on the gods and fate followed by a less than thinly veiled prediction of the slaughter that Odysseus—not yet a real presence—will perpetrate on those whose company the otherwise admirable Amphinomos has been keeping. As in the Kirkean Bath scene, the force of the whole is to foreground that which is unexpected—thematically untraditional, here—so that the philosophizing and dire prediction grate more harshly against the narrative situation than they would if they were spoken outside of the traditional theme of Greeting. Even if Greeting has proved less structurally bound than Bath, it still has thematic pattern, which is useful compositionally, and thematic connotation, which is crucial to the aesthetics of traditional poetry.

As for the phraseological component of these five instances of the Greeting type-scene, they share virtually nothing outside of the *chaire* and *deidisketo* forms cited by Edwards in his definition. That is to say, there seems to be no core of verbal correspondence traditionally associated with the ideas in this pattern, no two- or three-line segment or collection of related phraseology that conventionally expresses Greeting. In those four of five occurrences in which some form of *chaire* or its functional equivalent[39] appears, a vocative phrase follows; but none of these phrases are formulaically related. The remainder of the examples vary widely from one to another, the consistency of the scene being measured almost entirely according to its idea-pattern rather than its phraseology.

Nonetheless, although Greeting does not closely marshal an assigned core of diction, it is composed, as is all of Homeric epic, of traditional phraseology. The difference is that that phraseology is not further focused—in this particular case—by the theme. To illustrate this difference, let us analyze the occurrence of Greeting in Book 15 (lines 150-59).[40]

στῆ δ᾽ ἵππων προπάροιθε, δεδισκόμενος δὲ προσηύδα·   150
"χαίρετον, ὦ κούρω, καὶ Νέστορι ποιμένι λαῶν
εἰπεῖν· ἦ γὰρ ἐμοί γε πατὴρ ὣς ἤπιος ἦεν,
ἧος ἐνὶ Τροίῃ πολεμίζομεν υἷες Ἀχαιῶν."
      Τὸν δ᾽ αὖ Τηλέμαχος πεπνυμένος ἀντίον ηὔδα·
"καὶ λίην κείνῳ γε, διοτρεφές, ὡς ἀγορεύεις,   155
πάντα τάδ᾽ ἐλθόντες καταλέξομεν· αἲ γὰρ ἐγὼν ὣς
νοστήσας Ἰθάκηνδε, κιχὼν Ὀδυσῆ᾽ ἐνὶ οἴκῳ,
εἴποιμ᾽ ὡς παρὰ σεῖο τυχὼν φιλότητος ἁπάσης
ἔρχομαι, αὐτὰρ ἄγω κειμήλια πολλὰ καὶ ἐσθλά."

He stood before the chariot and pledged them: 150
"Farewell, young men; give my greeting to the shepherd of the people,
Nestor, for always he was kind to me like a father,
when we sons of the Achaeans were fighting in Troy land."
      Then the thoughtful Telemachos said to him in answer:
"Surely, illustrious sir, when we arrive we shall tell him   155
All that you say, and I wish that even so I too, arriving
in Ithaka, could find Odysseus there in our palace,
and tell him I was returning from you, having had all loving
treatment, and bringing many excellent treasures given me."

Although we find no formulaic relatives for *line 150*, *proparoithe* consistently seeks position at $5\frac{1}{2}$, thus filling the colon bounded by the A2 and B2 caesuras (in eleven of twelve occurrences in the *Odyssey*), and *proseuda* is found in its regular position at line-end.[41] Traditional rules are observed, in other words, and the participle *dediskomenos*, one of the few verbal signals consistently associated with Greeting, appears. As noted previously, there are no formulaic relatives demonstrable for the various forms of *chaire*, as in *line 151* (*chaireton*), and we may add that the vocative phrase *ô kourô* is similarly without an

---

39. At 3.43 the place of *chaire* is taken by *eucheo nun*.
40. Here I follow Edwards in distinguishing this type-scene from the one that precedes (in miniature) at 15.147–49.
41. See chapter 4, in the section on "winged words."

obvious family of diction. Nevertheless, all instances of *chair-* occur in initial position and are followed by a vocative, and all resultant first hemistichs are governed by traditional rules.[42] The second hemistich is classically formulaic, the adonean formula *poimeni laôn* occurring a total of nine times in the poem.[43] The rule of right justification, which on one level means that the second half of the line is more usually formulaic than the first, also manifests itself in *line 152*. For although there is nothing in the *Odyssey* that seems to be phraseologically associated with the opening hemistich, the latter one is repeated three times verbatim: thus "he was always kind to me like a father" appears in Telemachos's speech to the suitors, in reference to his father (2.47); in "Mentor's" speech about Odysseus (2.234); and in Athena's speech to Zeus and the other gods, again about Odysseus (5.12). We cannot link this hemistich formula to Greeting, to be sure, but there is no denying its traditional structure and deployment.[44]

Right justification is also evident in *line 153*, which belongs to a collection of phrases that include an exact whole-line repetition (13.315),[45] a second-hemistich repetition (14.240), and five additional occurrences of *huies Achaiôn*. The most stable part of the line, in other words, is the ending clausula, with more flexibility as one moves toward the beginning of the hexameter. *Line 154* is a much-repeated line of introduction (forty-three occurrences in the

42. We may compare the flexibility of these initial hemistichs to those involving *asaminth*-phrases in the Bath phraseology. Quite clearly, whereas the former are the result of traditional rules governing phraseology which apparently has not (for whatever reason) coalesced into formulaic diction, the latter is specific enough in its meaning and yet generic enough in its applicability that the fossilization into a hemistich system with a blocked caesura is no compositional handicap.

43. Of these, one is metrically identical to 15.151 (*Mentori poimeni laôn*, 24.456) and two others fill the entire second hemistich (*Agamemnoni, poimeni laôn*, 3.156 and 14.497). Compare also 17.109: *Nestora, poimena laôn*, the accusative form.

44. As we have seen many other times in Homeric phraseology, in this case the traditional associations of the hemistich in question do not end with the verbatim repetition of the phrase. In the last two occurrences cited, it is also part of a five-line passage that recurs word for word (2.230–34 = 5.8–12) and expresses the contrast between the gentle ruler Odysseus and the kind of kingly action that seems to be needed to straighten out the present situation: μή τις ἔτι πρόφρων ἀγανὸς καὶ ἤπιος ἔστω / σκηπτοῦχος βασιλεύς, μηδὲ φρεσὶν αἴσιμα εἰδώς, / ἀλλ' αἰεὶ χαλεπός τ' εἴη καὶ αἴσυλα ῥέζοι, / ὡς οὔ τις μέμνηται Ὀδυσσῆος θείοιο / λαῶν οἷσιν ἄνασσε, πατὴρ δ' ὡς ἤπιος ἦεν ("No longer now let one who is a sceptered king be eager / to be gentle and kind, be one whose thought is schooled in justice, / but let him always rather be harsh, and act severely, / seeing the way no one of the people he was lord over / remembers godlike Odysseus, and he was kind, like a father"). Just as before, we cannot denominate either the hemistich formula or the five-line phrase as the "primary" element of diction; the phraseology forms and re-forms under traditional rules, so that the hemistich formula (or whole-line system) and the "run" of lines exist side by side in the same family of diction.

45. It is worth noting that the line (13.314) which precedes the exact equivalent bears some resemblance to 152, although we would be hard pressed to call the relationship formulaic: τοῦτο δ' ἐγὼν εὖ οἶδ', ὅτι μοι πάρος ἠπίη ἦσθα.

Odyssey; see chapter 4) with no special attachment to any narrative situation. The most consistent element in *line 155* is of course the adonean, *hôs agoreueis*, with six additional instances, but we also find evidence of a second-hemistich structure (24.122)[46] and of patterning in the opening part of the line.[47]

Line 156, like many of the hexameters analyzed in chapter 4, has no formulaic relatives whatever; all of the individual constituents up to the bucolic diaeresis are, however, located in favored word-type positions.[48] The closing phrase of *line 157*, *eni oikôi*, recurs thirty-three additional times, always in the same position, but, given the variety of syntax and vocabulary associated with it, we would no doubt do better to consider it a composite "word" that follows traditional rules rather than the core of an extremely plastic formulaic system.[49] All other elements also occupy the favored positions for their word-types, with the quite explicable exception of the elided form *Odusê'*.[50] The rather loose aggregation that makes up *line 158* likewise has no formulaic relatives, but once again its individual constituents do follow traditional rules. Finally, *line 159* presents a typical collection of phrases that demonstrate some genetic relationship, but it is not possible to show any one of them to be primary; there are five total instances of *polla kai esthla*, involving the clausula as well as an exactly repeated second hemistich (19.272) that could also be interpreted as part of a whole-line system.

In short, what our analysis of the Greeting type-scene reveals is a generic mold or matrix of actions that individually and collectively are less distinct than the discrete actions that compose the Bath theme. Nonetheless, as has

46. Although whether this other line is truly an example of a hemistich formula may be in question, since *diotrephes* itself is localized in all of its seventeen occurrences in this same position (8, the favored position for this word-type, 95.6 percent).

47. The sequence *kai liên kein-* occurs four more times in the *Odyssey*. This is the kind of phrase to which some scholars would assign formulaic status, while others would demur because of the relative unimportance of the words (preferring to think of the sequence as a nonce formation). In the end it may be more significant to observe that, as usual under traditional rules, such relatively insignificant words are consigned to the opening of the line by the rule of right justification.

48. The sentence ends at position 8, so that the adonean is a loosely structured colon more typical of the beginning of a sentence (which normally occurs at the beginning of a line) than at the end of a hexameter.

49. The pattern of which *eni oikôi* is an example, ∪∪__ __, occurs 100 percent of the time at position 12.

50. Of the seven total occurrences of the shortened form in the *Odyssey*, none occupies the most favored position (at 7, normally 39.8 percent); four appear at 3 (normally 12.5 percent), two at 5 (normally 34.0 percent), and one (15.157) at 9 (normally 10.7 percent). While at least two lines from this apparently divergent group can be explained by the formation of a formulaic system (18.326 and 19.65), the overall picture is of *Odusê'* not conforming to expectations based on its word-type localization. I would suggest that such elided forms, which show more synchronic activity or pliability than unelided forms, are at least theoretically more susceptible to such variance.

been discussed, Greeting creates some degree of expectation within its own boundaries (although not as unambiguously as does the Bath, which leads to the feast); and the instance in Book 18 illustrates the power of that expectation and the effect of its frustration. In addition to the narrative structure of the Greeting pattern, we have seen that this theme exerts no special pressure on its expression in the phraseology (other than the inclusion of *chaire* and *deidisketo* or some other form of the same verb), so that the bound diction associated with the Bath, for example, has no counterpart in this other theme. As we would expect, the actual phraseology used shows the usual mix of classically formulaic diction with lines that are simply composed according to traditional rules but that have not, on available evidence, evolved true formulaic structure.

These two themes were not chosen at random but were selected to exemplify the range of brief, compact narrative structure in the *Odyssey*. There exist both more and less obviously stable patterns, as well as the great number that fall somewhere in between these two examples, but our two illustrations make the point that thematic structure is not all of a piece. Like traditional phraseology, traditional thematics cannot be captured or accounted for by one exclusive definition; to prescribe or proscribe too absolutely is to lose the ability to sense the different kinds of multiformity that make up the traditional foundation of the *Odyssey*, and in the end to lose as well the basis for faithful aesthetic inquiry. As we move on to a third example of the Homeric theme, we would do well to keep in mind the range and power of thematics, both as a traditional compositional technique and as a vital force in the art of the *Odyssey*.

The Feast Theme

Feasts in the *Odyssey* can take a number of forms, depending, as we shall see, on the narrative circumstances. For the purposes of the present analysis we shall be concerned not with all scenes of feasting (or of simply eating) in the poem, but with a recurrent theme or type-scene of Feasting that has both a definite (though flexible) narrative structure and an associated phraseological dimension that recurs along with that idea-pattern. In the course of discussing this theme, there will be reason to make reference to non-thematic portrayals of feasting and eating in the *Odyssey*, but these moments are not our primary focus.

Given what we have discovered in the first two sections about the Bath and Greeting themes, we shall be asking three interrelated questions or sets of questions about Feasting. First, what is the narrative structure of this traditional unit? How definite are the actions and how regularly do they occur? Second, to what extent does the thematic pattern marshal or determine phraseology? Is the phraseology bound to this particular theme or is it more generally traditional? Third, how does Feasting compare to Bath and Greeting as a traditional multiform?

To begin, let us specify the occurrences of Feasting in the *Odyssey*. The passage below (1.125-57) represents the first such scene in the poem, and will serve as the point of reference or comparison for the other five instances. As the diagram to the right of the passage indicates, each of the other occurrences shares a certain amount of exactly correspondent phraseology with the Feast in Book 1.

	IV	VII	X	XV	XVII
Ὣς εἰπὼν ἡγεῖθ', ἡ δ' ἕσπετο					
Παλλὰς 'Αθήνη. 125					
οἱ δ' ὅτε δή ῥ' ἔντοσθεν ἔσαν δόμου ὑψηλοῖο,					
ἔγχος μέν ῥ' ἔστησε φέρων πρὸς κίονα μακρὴν					
δουροδόκης ἔντοσθεν ἐϋξόου, ἔνθα περ ἄλλα					
ἔγχε' 'Οδυσσῆος ταλασίφρονος ἵστατο πολλά,					
αὐτὴν δ' ἐς θρόνον εἷσεν ἄγων, ὑπὸ λῖτα πετάσσας,					
καλὸν δαιδάλεον· ὑπὸ δὲ θρῆνυς ποσὶν ἦεν.					
πὰρ δ' αὐτὸς κλισμὸν θέτο ποικίλον, ἔκτοθεν ἄλλων					
μνηστήρων, μὴ ξεῖνος ἀνιηθεὶς ὀρυμαγδῷ					
δείπνῳ ἀδήσειεν, ὑπερφιάλοισι μετελθών,					
ἠδ' ἵνα μιν περὶ πατρὸς ἀποιχομένοιο					
ἔροιτο. 135					
χέρνιβα δ' ἀμφίπολος προχόῳ ἐπέχευε φέρουσα	52	172	368	135	91
καλῇ χρυσείῃ, ὑπὲρ ἀργυρέοιο λέβητος,	53	173	369	136	92
νίψασθαι· παρὰ δὲ ξεστὴν ἐτάνυσσε τράπεζαν.	54	174	370	137	93
σίτον δ' αἰδοίη ταμίη παρέθηκε φέρουσα,	55	175	371	138	94
εἴδατα πόλλ' ἐπιθεῖσα, χαριζομένη παρεόντων·	56	176	372	139	95
δαιτρὸς δὲ κρειῶν πίνακας παρέθηκεν ἀείρας	57				
παντοίων, παρὰ δέ σφι τίθει χρύσεια κύπελλα,	58				
κῆρυξ δ' αὐτοῖσιν θάμ' ἐπῴχετο οἰνοχοεύων.					
'Ες δ' ἦλθον μνηστῆρες ἀγήνορες. οἱ μὲν ἔπειτα					
ἑξείης ἕζοντο κατὰ κλισμούς τε θρόνους τε. 145					
τοῖσι δὲ κήρυκες μὲν ὕδωρ ἐπὶ χεῖρας ἔχευαν,					
σῖτον δὲ δμῳαὶ παρενήνεον ἐν κανέοισι,					
κοῦροι δὲ κρητῆρας ἐπεστέψαντο ποτοῖο.					

	IV	VII	X	XV	XVII
οἱ δ᾽ ἐπ᾽ ὀνείαθ᾽ ἑτοῖμα προκείμενα χεῖρας ἴαλλον.	67			142	98
αὐτὰρ ἐπεὶ πόσιος καὶ ἐδητύος ἐξ ἔρον ἕντο	68			143	99

μνηστῆρες, τοῖσιν μὲν ἐνὶ φρεσὶν ἄλλα
μεμήλει,
μολπή τ᾽ ὀρχηστύς τε· τὰ γάρ τ᾽
ἀναθήματα δαιτός.
κῆρυξ δ᾽ ἐν χερσὶν κίθαριν περικαλλέα
θῆκε
Φημίῳ, ὅς ῥ᾽ ἤειδε παρὰ μνηστῆρσιν
ἀνάγκῃ.
ἦ τοι ὁ φορμίζων ἀνεβάλλετο καλὸν
ἀείδειν,   155
αὐτὰρ Τηλέμαχος προσέφη γλαυκῶπιν
Ἀθήνην,
ἄγχι σχὼν κεφαλήν, ἵνα μὴ πευθοίαθ᾽ οἱ
ἄλλοι·

So speaking he led the way, and Pallas Athene followed him.   125
Now, when the two of them were inside the lofty dwelling,
he took the spear he carried and set it against a tall column
in a rack for spears, of polished wood, where indeed there were other
spears of patient-hearted Odysseus standing in numbers,
and he led her and seated her in a chair, with a cloth to sit on,   130
the chair splendid and elaborate. For her feet there was a footstool.
For himself, he drew a painted bench next to her, apart from the others,
the suitors, for fear the guest, made uneasy by the uproar,
might lose his appetite there among overbearing people,
and so he might also ask him about his absent father.   135
A maidservant brought water for them and poured it from a splendid
and golden pitcher, holding it above a silver basin
for them to wash, and she pulled a polished table before them.
A grave housekeeper brought in the bread and served it to them,
adding many good things to it, generous with her provisions,   140
while a carver lifted platters of all kinds of meat and set them
in front of them, and placed beside them the golden goblets,
and a herald, going back and forth, poured the wine for them.
Then the haughty suitors came in, and all of them straightway
took their places in order on chairs and along the benches,   145
and their heralds poured water over their hands for them to wash with,
and the serving maids brought them bread heaped up in the baskets,
and the young men filled the mixing bowls with wine for their drinking.
They put their hands to the good things that lay ready before them.
But when they had put away their desire for eating and drinking,   150
the suitors found their attention turned to other matters,
the song and the dance; for these things come at the end of the feasting.

A herald put the beautifully wrought lyre in the hands
of Phemios, who sang for the suitors, because they made him.
He played his lyre and struck up a fine song. Meanwhile   155
Telemachos talked to Athene of the gray eyes, leaning
his head close to hers, so that none of the others might hear him:

The idea-pattern for this theme, as opposed to the structure of other expressions of feasting, may be described as a series of discrete actions that collectively embody a sumptuous Homeric feast.[51] After the "seating" (line 131) of the protagonist(s), which as we have seen usually intervenes between the Bath and the Feast, the actions are:

1. A maidservant brings water for washing (136-37)
2. A table is placed before guest(s) and host (138)
3. A housekeeper provides bread and other foodstuffs (139-40)
4. A carver passes out meat and golden cups (141-42)
5. The diners eat (149)
6. The diners are satisfied (150)

An "optional" line (1.145; cf. 15.134) detailing the seating of guest(s) and host on benches and chairs also seems to be associated with the theme, although not as regularly or institutionally as are some other lines. This action may occur either at the beginning of or during the Feast theme, and thus lacks the participation in a definite sequence shown by the other recurrent actions.

Of course, as Lord has shown in respect to the unit of theme in Serbo-Croatian epic, all actions need not occur in every manifestation of this multiform, and the diagram opposite the above passage illustrates the variance among instances. As with the Bath theme, the central actions are mostly repeated verbatim in phraseology associated exclusively with Feasting, but even some of these lines have wider application within the poetic tradition, as we shall see below. And as noted above, there are indeed other ways to express the idea of dining or feasting in Homer. What is more, this traditional and generic cluster of ideas and lines is susceptible to a more particular focus through context-dependent description added to the scene, so that instances of the same theme may look (and actually be) very different.

As an example of this flexibility in the narrative idiom, we may compare the feast in Book 1 with that in Book 4. The earlier scene, quoted above, is filled with the tension created by the suitors' arrogant presumptions. With Odysseus absent and Telemachos only on the verge of manhood, the unwelcome guests abuse the rituals of hospitality with impunity and Penelope and Telemachos are virtually held hostage to their unreasonable demands. The feast at Menelaos's home, however, presents us with the icon of civility and serenity, in stark

---

51. In what follows I provide line numbers for the occurrence of the actions in Book 1. Consult the diagram in the passage above for references within other occurrences.

contrast to the tensions underlying the Ithakan scene. After the Bath and seating of the guest, Telemachos, the Feast appears as follows (4.52-70):

> A maidservant brought water for them and poured it from a splendid
> and golden pitcher, holding it above a silver basin
> for them to wash, and she pulled a polished table before them.
> A grave housekeeper brought in the bread and served it to them,   55
> adding many good things to it, generous with her provisions,
> while a carver lifted platters of all kinds of meat and set them
> in front of them, and placed beside them the golden goblets.
> Then in greeting fair-haired Menelaos said to them:
> "Help yourselves to the food and welcome, and then afterward,   60
> when you have tasted dinner, we shall ask you who among
> men you are, for the stock of your parents can be no lost one,
> but you are of the race of men who are kings, whom Zeus sustains,
> who bear scepters; no mean men could have sons such as you are."
> So he spoke, and taking in his hands the fat beef loin   65
> which had been given as his choice portion, he set it before them.
> They put their hands to the good things that lay ready before them.
> But when they had put away their desire for eating and drinking,
> then Telemachos talked to the son of Nestor, leaning
> his head close to his, so that none of the others might hear him: 70

The underscored lines are those conventionally a part of the Feasting theme, and may be compared with corresponding verses in Book 1 or any of the other instances of Feasting in the poem. But apart from these core actions that identify the pattern as a compositional unit and carry with them larger traditional connotations, numerous context-specific details help to focus this scene and distinguish its singularity against the backdrop of the generic unit. In Book 4 the guests are not merely welcomed but honored, both with Menelaos's cordial greeting fulfilling the ritual of Homeric hospitality and with his gesture of placing the loin section in front of Telemachos and Peisistratos. Even the whispered speech that follows this scene contrasts directly with Telemachos's earlier conversation with Mentor.[52] In Book 1 the talk was of the presumptuousness of the suitors and general disarray of the Ithakan household, while in Book 4 the same Telemachos can only wonder at the magnificence of the household in which he is such an honored guest.

These two instances of the theme serve as an example of the plasticity of a pattern that, although it consists of several discrete actions and not a few precisely repeated lines, can still be shaped not just to fit but to aesthetically embody quite disparate narrative situations. And, as noted above in respect

---

52. Although the lines that introduce the two speeches in question (1.157, 4.70) are identical.

to the Bath and Greeting, the scenes draw their power as much from the generic traditional matrix of ideas and phraseology as from the unassociated actions and lines that individualize them. It is the combination of the generic and particular, the traditional and the context-specific,[53] that underlies the Homeric aesthetic.

Thus the narrative pattern of Feasting proves to consist of a set of discrete, self-contained actions that cohere in a definite series and sequence. Each of these actions is appropriate to a quite elegant feast, and the description as a whole takes on a traditional resonance that can be heard in each occurrence. Nonetheless, each instance also includes a number of actions and lines that, although they are in themselves traditional, are also not conventionally associated with this narrative pattern. As in the examples from Books 1 and 4 discussed above, the combination of the generic mold and the particularizing actions produces an individual, context-sensitive scene that resonates against the timeless pattern of Feasting. The outrages of the suitors are ever more apparent against this traditional background, and the order and hospitality of Menelaos's splendid feast are likewise foregrounded. This is the kind of compositional flexibility and traditional connotation available in the narrative structure of Feasting.

From the idea-pattern we turn now to our second question, that concerning the nature of the phraseology used to express those ideas. For the purposes of this analysis, I have chosen the occurrence of the theme from Book 1. In what follows I shall examine selected lines from the passage quoted above, with special attention to their conventional use and deployment in the *Odyssey*.[54] Thus we shall be looking both at some verses conventionally associated with Feasting and at others that are not so bound, the object being to assess the role of verbal correspondence in the dynamics of this Homeric theme.

Line 125 is a situation-specific rather than a generic line; that is, it serves a narrative purpose unassociated with Feasting. Nonetheless, like others in its category, it reveals a traditional heritage in the highly recurrent phrases *hôs eipôn* (thirty-five instances in the *Odyssey*, all at this position) and *Pallas Athênê* (eighteen instances, all at this position). The clue to *line 127* lies in the fact

---

53. As we shall see below, the actions and diction used to particularize a scene are themselves quite traditional; the distinction is that they are not bound to the theme of Feasting but are more generally applicable elements in the traditional idiom.

54. I shall make no attempt to examine every line from 1.125–57, but only those whose traditional structure offers a good example of some dimension of the relationship between phraseology and thematic structure. During the analysis it will become apparent that the instance of the theme might have been delimited somewhat differently, excluding some lines and including others. I have defined the passage as I have because there seems to be a natural break on either end, but finally the question of etic or analytic definition is less important than the representative illustration of traditional processes; even if my decision does not accord with that of other investigators, I hope the discussion of this passage serves to indicate the compositional and aesthetic nature of Homeric themes.

that all five occurrences of *kiona* are as part of the phrase, or composite "word," *pros kiona makrên/-on*. In the former configuration, the phrase ends with a longum and occurs only at 12 (2 ×), while in the latter it terminates in a breve and occurs only at $9\frac{1}{2}$ (3 ×). As would be expected from our findings in chapter 4, the second of these possibilities, which features a blocked C caesura,[55] participates in the more stable second-hemistich configuration (*pros kiona makron ereisas*, 3 ×). One of these three formulaic occurrences, 17.29, helps to describe Telemachos's standing of his spear by the pillar on his arrival home and might thus be suspected of being associated with the idea of feasting as in Book 1. But, on the evidence of other instances of the thematic pattern and of the detachability of this action from those that follow it, I would argue that the idea and phraseology of 1.127 are not thematically associated with Feasting.[56]

At *line 129* we encounter an example of a formulaic phrase with applicability to a variety of narrative situations. The epithet *talasiphronos* is restricted to Odysseus and to position 8 in the hexameter, where the noun-epithet combination occurs a total of eleven times in the *Odyssey*. This placement blocks the A caesura and creates a following adonean, with the result that a large variety of two-syllable increments precede the formula and a similarly large variety of clausulae follow it. And although there is evidence of one whole-line phrase (1.87 = 5.31), we find no trace of other more extensive phraseological relatives. *Line 131*, in contrast, can boast an interesting range of formulaic kin in the poem. The entire line is repeated verbatim twice in Book 10 (lines 315 and 367), with the only change being one of inflection (gen. s. *kalou daidaleou*). Likewise, the second hemistich recurs in other combinations (4.136; cf. 19.57). But what is most telling about this line is the fact that both 10.315 and 10.367 are preceded by lines that also describe the seating of the protagonist, which, as we have seen, is an action intermediary between Bath and Feast, or at least associated with the one if the other is not part of the story at that point.[57] This correspondence thus serves as an example of optional ways to express a given traditional idea, that is, of partial flexibility of actual diction. While 1.131 cannot be shown to be an integral part of the Feasting pattern, its action, though separate, is traditionally associated with the onset of the theme.[58]

---

55. *Pros* is proclitic and therefore cannot be separated prosodically from the rest of the phrase.

56. This does not mean that an association like that between the Bath and subsequent dining might not be involved, although the available textual sample would not support such a hypothesis. Note also another difference between the two cases: 1.127 is unnecessarily enjambed with the following line, while at 17.29 the sentence is complete at line-end.

57. Thus 10.314–15 = 10.366–67. This seems to be an instance of the poet's remembering a recently employed phrase or phrases in favor of optional ways of expressing the same essential idea.

58. Note that 4.136 and 19.57 are linked with neither Bath nor Feast but rather with the entrances of Helen and Penelope, respectively.

Line 135 is unrelated to the action of the Feasting theme, so its recurrence at 3.77 must be ascribed to the shared feature of Telemachos's asking about his lost father, an inquiry perfectly appropriate to the exchange of information that customarily takes place during such an event (but that is not part of the thematic pattern). Other clues that this near-whole-line formula does not participate in the particular narrative structure under consideration include the fact that in Book 3 it actually follows rather than precedes the main action of the feast. The role of sequence, as illustrated above, is important in Homeric patterns. Additionally, in Book 3 this line is necessarily enjambed with what precedes and unnecessarily enjambed with what follows, while in Book 1 the verse is unnecessarily enjambed with what precedes and not enjambed at all with what follows.

No such variance marks the next five lines, *136-40*, which make up the heart of the feasting theme. As documented above, these lines express discrete actions: a maidservant brings water for washing (136-37), a table is placed before guest(s) and host (138), and a housekeeper provides bread and other foodstuffs (139-40). Each of these actions occurs in all six manifestations of Feasting in the *Odyssey*, in the same order and precisely the same diction. No lines are added to or interspersed in this series, and the group of lines may accurately be termed a unit in itself. *Lines 141-42*, repeated verbatim and in the same position in Book 4, may also be considered a part of the same core. They express an associated action—a carver passes out meat and golden cups[59]—and, in the two cases in which they appear, contribute to the formation of a seven-line version of the core unit in this theme.

The fact that this ordered sequence of discrete but (both socioculturally and traditionally) related actions can take two forms, one of five and the other of seven lines, may at first seem curious. The conventional explanation, of course, would posit a synchronic flexibility in the unit, with a basic kernel and some optional additions. But this kind of explanation misrepresents the traditional character of this multiform. Like the collection of lines whose formulaic "core" cannot be unearthed, this kind of thematic variance cannot be rationalized by a simplex/variation model. All six forms of this inner sequence—whether with five lines or seven—are equally legitimate manifestations of the traditional idea-pattern. Just as formulaic phraseology cannot be reduced to schemata but must be understood in terms of traditional rules that underlie formulaic structure, so the recurrence of these lines must be seen as an aggregation of ideas whose bound, invariant phraseology happens to reflect that aggregation monolithically. If the carver is not a part of any given Feast, the scene

59. Note that the C1 fourth colon *chruseia kupella* also occurs without this formulaic context at 10.357, during the special version of the Bath theme involving the four maidservants. This comparison offers an example of how a phrase, having entered the diction according to traditional rules (here word-type and inner metric), can become fossilized as part of a larger form associated with the feast and yet remain thematically unassociated in its colonic form.

is no less a Feast for his absence. And there is no reason to view the five-line sequence as "lesser" or "apocopated," any more than we would characterize a hemistich (rather than a whole-line) formula as "lesser." No matter which form it takes, this group of ideas remains the kernel of the Feasting theme and thus offers to the poet both its compositional utility and an opportunity for particularized elaboration on a generic and highly resonant multiform.

Line 145 presents an example of an idea that can logically attach itself to scenes of feasting, but that does not seem to be regularly associated with this particular theme.[60] Exact repetitions occur at 3.389, a version of greeting or wine drinking different from that examined above, and at 24.385, an abbreviated feast at Laertes' home. Five additional instances of the second hemistich, *kata klismous te thronous te*, combine with different partners, and their distribution and placement are interesting. Three of these occurrences (17.86, 17.179, and 20.249) take the whole-line form χλαίνας μὲν κατέθεντο κατὰ κλισμούς τε θρόνους τε ("they laid down their mantles along the chairs and benches") and introduce the action of laying down robes before the bath. In 10.233 the hemistich appears just before the fateful, enchanting feast served by Kirke, and at 15.134 it is part of Menelaos's festive meal for Telemachos and Peisistratos. Only in the last of these instances is the hemistich associated with the theme under examination.

Although we may be tempted to include line 145, or at least its second part, in Feasting on the premise that, like 141-42, it plays a role in the traditional group of ideas associated with the event, I would contend that the verse and its parts are more generally (and thus non-thematically) associated with feasts and baths. Their occurrence at 1.145 and 15.134, in other words, may be more accurately traced to the ubiquitousness—and compositional utility—of the "seating" idea that we first encountered during our study of the Bath theme. At this point the major and characteristic actions of the Feast have been carried out for Mentor's benefit, and with this second "seating" line (cf. 1.131) the arrogant suitors enter and begin a second and quite uncharacteristic dinner of their own, the untraditional nature of which stands in marked contrast to the ritual of hospitality and guestship embodied in the Feasting theme.

Other traditional diction not conventionally associated with this theme but with attached structures of its own includes *lines 146* and *148*. In Book 1 only these two lines occur, but in Books 3 (preparatory to a libation being poured

---

60. I pass over more detailed consideration of 1.144, in which the noun-epithet formula *mnêstêres/-as agênores/-as* (occurring a total of seven times and always at position 8) acts as a composite "word" and structures the line. A wide variety of diction takes shape around this phrase, much of it illustrating the common phenomenon of a new syntactic unit beginning at the bucolic diaeresis. Note also the strong attraction between the noun and epithet, which appear separated but in the same line at 18.346, 20.284, and 23.8 (colonic forms at positions 3 and 8, respectively).

before going to bed) and 21 (preparatory to the disguised Odysseus asking for the bow, lines 270-73) a four-line sequence repeats nearly verbatim:[61]

τοῖσι δὲ κήρυκες μὲν ὕδωρ ἐπὶ χεῖρας ἔχευαν,
κοῦροι δὲ κρητῆρας ἐπεστέψαντο ποτοῖο,
νώμησαν δ' ἄρα πᾶσιν ἐπαρξάμενοι δεπάεσσι·

. . . .

αὐτὰρ ἐπεὶ σπεῖσάν τ' ἔπιόν θ' ὅσον ἤθελε θυμός,   (3.338-40, 342)

The heralds poured water over their hands to wash with,
and the young men filled the mixing bowls with wine for their drinking,
and passed to all, after they had offered a drink in the goblets.

. . . .

But when they had poured, and drunk, each as much as he wanted,

Once again we have a typical mix of phraseology, with considerable flexibility in the make-up of the multi-line unit. And although this group of lines is not thematically linked to the Feasting theme, its general applicability to various kinds of ritual events makes it a frequent enough companion of ideas and phraseology that are traditionally bound to Feasting.[62]

The theme comes to a formal close with *lines 149-50*, which appear in four of six instances. First the guest(s) and host lay their hands on the food brought before them; the second line, always a dependent clause that leads into a new section of the narrative, indicates that the diners have "thrown off the eros" of eating and drinking. Quite clearly, because of both the recurrence and the nature of these complementary actions, we must interpret them as part of the Feasting theme. But, as with colonic or hemistich phrases that recur both in their simplex forms and as part of larger combinations, these same lines have an identity outside of Feasting. In addition to the thematic instances, the first line, for example, appears seven times in the *Odyssey*, always verbatim. Six of these are associated with feasting or at least eating of some kind, and range from the meal of the gods offered to Odysseus by Kalypso (5.200) to the much humbler repast in Eumaios's hut (16.54); the seventh (4.218) is preparatory to the washing of hands and pouring of a libation at Menelaos's home.[63] The important point here is that, whether or not the context is that of the theme

---

61. Line 3.341, γλώσσας δ' ἐν πυρὶ βάλλον, ἀνιστάμενοι δ' ἐπέλειβον, illustrates how even a sequence of lines that we might term a unit in itself is open to paratactic amplification. Note also that 1.148 = 3.339 and 21.271; cf. 2.431.

62. This is a distinction which in itself deserves further study. Traditional elements are of differing compositional utility and differing connotative force, and should be assessed in their individuality if we are to promote faithful interpretation of the Homeric (and other traditional) texts. For another example of an action appropriate to inclusion in a feasting scene but not demonstrably a part of the theme under consideration, see *line 155* and its near-equivalent 8.266, both of which are concerned with singing and the feast.

63. The other occurrences are 8.71, 8.484, 14.453, and 20.256.

we have been examining, this line and the action it expresses are associated with feasting scenes of some sort.[64]

Closure of feasting scenes may involve both lines 149 and 150, as in five cases in addition to the thematic occurrences, or it may be accomplished simply by the latter member of the pair, as in six other instances.[65] No matter what the configuration, however, it is important to note that closure of a feast is virtually the sole function of both of these lines and, further, that the Feasting theme proper uses them both in four of six occurrences. This distribution then begs the question of how the thematic occurrences in Books 7 and 10 reach closure, since neither typical line is observed at their terminations. In the former case, Feasting is augmented with Alkinoos's instructions to mix a wine bowl, which in turn leads to the king's speech about helping his guest, Odysseus's reply, and the narrative equivalent of the more familiar closure (7.228). Likewise, in Book 10 the Feast is interrupted, as discussed above, and formulaically unrelated but narratively equivalent lines again end the action (10.469-70).

Line 152 presents another possibility for formulaic irony. Its second hemistich, *ta gar t' anathêmata daitos*, seems quite appropriate to its position in Book 1, although it would be difficult to argue on available evidence that the idea encoded in this hemistich ("these things [singing and dancing] are the glories of the feast") is thematically associated with Feasting. In its only other occurrence (21.430), this same hemistich appears in a related verse with slightly different syntax: μολπῇ καὶ φόρμιγγι· τὰ γάρ τ᾽ ἀναθήματα δαιτός. This latter line and the two that precede it refer, of course, to the "feast" of blood and revenge that Odysseus has planned for his "guests" the suitors. But we need not posit a non-traditional kind of irony in this passage, for once the poetic association of this final feast of the suitors with the traditional idea of the Feast has been made, the association through actual phraseology is natural and institutionalized. The convergence of slaughter and dining, in other words, takes place by means of the poetic melding of ideas that, being associated within the tradition with certain phraseology, then find expression in a particularly poignant and ironic way.

64. The question of possible formulaic irony arises with the one other line in the *Odyssey* that in any way resembles 1.149 and its kin: ἀλλ᾽ ὅ γ᾽ ἀναΐξας ἑτάροις ἐπὶ χεῖρας ἴαλλε. This verse (9.288) of course refers to Polyphemos's "feasting" quite ingloriously and inhospitably on Odysseus's companions. Although some might hear an echo of the Feast closure here, I prefer to interpret the resemblance as at most structural.

65. The former group consists of 8.71–72, 8.484–85, 14.453–54, 16.54–55, and 17.98–99, the latter of 3.67, 3.473, 12.308, 15.303, 15.501, and 16.480. We should also note the alternate closing line used in association with Odysseus's dinner or feast with Dolios (24.489): Οἱ δ᾽ ἐπεὶ οὖν σίτοιο μελίφρονος ἐξ ἔρον ἕντο, which shares a clausula with the more usual verse. This single use of the variant formula, coming as it does in the so-called Continuation of the *Odyssey*, agrees with the evidence brought forward by Postlethwaite (1981) in supporting the possibility of a different composer for this section. See further the discussion of the *guslar*'s own idiolect in chapter 5.

That this association of ideas is more than a momentary turn of phrase is evident from the terrible, and prefigurative, feast of Book 20. In this last sharing of food and drink before the wrath of Odysseus takes over in the next book, the portrait of the arrogant, presumptuous suitors modulates horribly:

> In the suitors Pallas Athene   345
> stirred up uncontrollable laughter, and addled their thinking.
> Now they laughed with jaws that were no longer their own.
> The meat they ate was a mess of blood, their eyes were bursting
> full of tears, and their laughter sounded like lamentation.

The prophet Theoklymenos explicitly makes the traditional connection that Odysseus repeats in capsule form at lines 21.428-30, reading the prefiguration of inescapable carnage and death in the aberrant scene before him. Whatever the source of the linkage, and it may well predate even the Odyssey story, it joins a traditional association to the revenge that the story-pattern would lead one to expect, and does so in a memorable and moving fashion.

In summary, our example analyses of Bath, Greeting, and Feasting have illustrated that thematic structure in the *Odyssey* cannot be forced into a single narrow definition or a restrictive category. Traditional narrative pattern manifests itself in different ways—sometimes in an ordered and tightly knit series of discrete actions (as in parts of the Bath and Feasting multiforms) and sometimes in a looser aggregation of general outlines that leave more room for individualized variation (as in the Greeting). Even when the actions are discrete and ordered, however, there is always the opportunity for shaping the generic commonplace to its context, as the comparison of feasts in Books 1 and 4 has shown. From the point of view of idea-pattern, then, our conclusion about the Homeric theme must be that the consistency with which the narrative superstructure is observed from instance to instance varies with the individual theme. Some units are simply more focused than others, no doubt for compositional reasons. But whether a given theme or type-scene tends more toward the "fixed" or the "flexible" end of the spectrum, it carries with it both compositional utility and aesthetic referentiality.

The other chief aspect of thematic structure, verbal correspondence among instances of a given multiform, also varies from one theme to the next. We have seen that Greeting has no particular phraseological component, the only conventionally associated diction being at the level of two single words.[66] However, the core actions of the Bath are expressed in formulaic language, as are the major ideas of Feasting; of course, in both these latter cases we find many additional, interspersed lines that do not repeat from instance to

---

66. And single words, as shown in chapter 4, are only partial "words" from the point of view of traditional phraseology. See the remarks on "words" by Yugoslav *guslari* in chapter 2 (pp. 44–50).

instance, since the ideas they express are not traditionally associated with Bath and Feasting. In addition, our analyses have also revealed that the "particularizing" verses, those that suit the generic mold to its narrative position, are themselves quite as traditional as any other lines in Homer. In concert with the findings in chapter 4, we discovered that these lines cannot always be shown to be formulaic in the classic sense, but that they are consistently structured in accordance with traditional rules. Indeed, this last point also means that there exists both bound and unbound phraseology in the *Odyssey*, that is, that some diction is exclusively tied to one thematic structure, some is tied to one or more narrative events but not necessarily to a particular theme, and some is largely free of thematic association.

Thus it appears that the best explanation of Homeric thematic structure, and therefore the truest basis for aesthetic inquiry, is the positing not of a single model but of a spectrum of traditional narrative patterning. Themes in the *Odyssey* vary in the consistency of both narrative structure and verbal correspondence; by conceiving of this dimension of traditional structure as a spectrum, it becomes possible to sense the compositional utility and aesthetic power of themes or type-scenes without having either to eliminate certain examples or to erect over-elaborate taxonomies that separate patterns which should be considered together. In the end, such a spectrum will also furnish the key to aesthetic interpretation, because it will rationalize the differences among narrative multiforms in Homeric tradition and refocus our attention on the continuity of traditional narrative structure.

EIGHT

Thematic Structure
in the Serbo-Croatian Return Song

A search for thematic structure in Serbo-Croatian oral epic entails the location and description of narrative units, those integral patterns which the *guslar* knows and follows—although he is of course not consciously aware of doing so—in the making and re-making of his song. These themes constitute the narrative logic of his performance, contributing their individual and associative traditional meanings to the creation of the moment. Since the sample of materials from Stolac is large and various, we certainly have no shortage of unambiguously oral traditional themes on which to found a description and set of generalizations.

Before proceeding, however, we should consider two preliminary matters. The first amounts to a caveat and speaks to the twin criteria of tradition-dependence and genre-dependence, principles worked out earlier (chapters 3-6) at the prosodic and phraseological levels. Since both the prosodic and the formulaic structure of Serbo-Croatian epic differs graphically from those of ancient Greek and especially of Old English epic, we may expect a corresponding disparity in the actual verbal expression of narrative themes in the three traditions. Although a sequence of ideas per se would seem immune to linguistic differences, its verbal data are not; thus the Serbo-Croatian theme, expressed in the idiom of its diction, will take a spectrum of verbal forms or variants that will compare faithfully to ancient Greek and Old English themes only after the requisite adjustments or "translations" have been made. Oral epic structures are tradition-dependent to some degree at every level, and the theme is no exception. As for genre-dependence, I shall be limiting coverage to Return Songs (and all but one from the Stolac region) in order to preserve generic congruity. This constraint will prove a productive strategy at the level of narrative structure, since the subgenre of Return attracts to itself a specific core of themes that permits felicitous comparison.

The second methodological matter concerns the present state of scholarship on thematic structure in Yugoslav epic. Although no more than a brief overview is justified here,[1] we should ballast the analyses to follow with mention of what has already been accomplished. After this short survey, I shall focus on what can be determined about the theme in Serbo-Croatian from the way a *guslar* resumes his performance after a break for rest. The balance of the chapter will be devoted to a demonstration of the various levels of narrative organization—by a single singer (idiolectal), within a local tradition (dialectal), and tradition-wide (language).

PRIOR SCHOLARSHIP

Albert Lord began the description of thematic structure in 1938 with his study of narrative inconsistencies in Homer and South Slavic epic, and thirteen years later he focused on thematics as a compositional process in both poetries (1951a).[2] But while these articles proved influential in the spread of oral theory to other literatures, his major statement on the theme was to be, and remains, the fourth chapter of *The Singer of Tales* (1960). For Lord the most important characteristic of the theme is its *multiformity*: as a protean narrative pattern of consummate utility to the composing oral poet, the theme provides both an outline of related actions balanced from within and a kernel of verbal correspondence among its various instances. Apart from the external profile a scholar assembles to help keep track of elements associated with the pattern, the theme has no "norm" or archetype; it takes shape only in the variety of its instances, with all occurrences being equivalent (if differing) variants of the unit.[3]

The first of Lord's definitions in *Singer* (p. 68) is the most general: themes are "the groups of ideas regularly used in telling a tale in the formulaic style of traditional song." But although this unit of narrative exhibits a formula-like quality, it is most essentially a multiform and can take many (theoretically an unlimited number of) shapes. As he puts it (p. 69), "the theme, even though it be verbal, is not any fixed set of words, but a grouping of ideas." Lord describes and shows how variation can occur and how the degree of phraseological correspondence among instances may differ according to the given theme, singer, song, and circumstances of performance. We learn in addition that the pattern may be broken down into smaller narrative elements, a composite structure of motifs or minor themes that has attracted the attention of other scholars seeking to explain the structure of Serbo-Croatian epic.

---

1. For comparative bibliography, see Foley 1985 (with updates in *Oral Tradition*).

2. Note also Milman Parry's "On Typical Scenes in Homer" (1936), itself a review of Walter Arend's *Die typischen Scenen bei Homer* (1933).

3. Cf. Michael Nagler's idea of the Homeric *motif* (1974, 64–111).

As he did with the formula, Lord emphasizes (p. 86) the usefulness of the theme, noting that "it is always at hand when the singer needs it; it relieves his mind of much remembering, and leaves him free to think of the plan of the song itself or of the moment of the song in which he is involved." By the same token, certain multiforms are termed "ornamental," since they broaden or further articulate a scene or description without necessarily moving the action forward.[4] Whatever the case, however, there exists a discernible order in the theme, and the poet senses or follows that order even if he does so in an idiosyncratic manner, for within the general plan there is much room for individual variation:

> In all these instances one sees also that the singer always has the end of the theme in his mind. He knows where he is going. As in the adding of one line to another, the singer can stop and fondly dwell upon any single item without losing a sense of the whole. The style allows comfortably for digression or for enrichment. (p. 92)

The order and balance so characteristic of the unit may proceed from any number of sources—a question-and-answer series, the logical sequence of events that are comprised in the dressing or arming of a hero or the caparisoning of a horse, and so on. The actual verbal means by which the singer travels these cognitive pathways varies from performance to performance, from singer to singer, and from one local tradition to another.

In their combination with other such units in a song, narrative themes present a double aspect. They have a certain associative attraction to other themes, and yet at the same time they maintain an integrity and completeness of their own. This quality of relative independence allows the kind of ubiquity that constitutes the lifeblood of an oral narrative tradition—without such a general application, any unit would prove of little utility in traditional composition; the same ubiquity, however, can also lead to narrative inconsistencies when two or more juxtaposed themes are not thoroughly adapted by the singer to their role in the given song he is composing.[5] As Lord remarks (p. 94), "the theme in oral poetry exists at one and the same time in and for itself and for the whole song."

Of Lord's studies since *The Singer of Tales*, the most important for the present purpose is "Perspectives on Recent Work on Oral Literature" (1975).[6] In the midst of a survey of scholarship on various traditions, he takes up in a precise manner the question of verbal correspondence among instances of a theme. His aim is to distinguish the more usual literary sense of the term, which implies a subject only, from the special sense in which he means it—as

---

4. Compare Patricia Arant's (1981) description of thematic structure and articulation in Russian *byliny*.

5. In addition to Lord 1938, see Gunn 1970.

6. See also Lord's sequel to "Perspectives," devoted largely to the formula (1986c).

the recognizable narrative unit of oral epic composition that assumes a similar verbal form in every occurrence. He thus argues (p. 20) that the theme as subject has no real bearing on oral literature research, "but if by theme one means a repeated narrative element together with its verbal expression, that portion of a poem, an aggregate of specific verses, that tells a certain repeated part of the narrative, then we find ourselves dealing with elements of truly oral traditional narrative style." Thus, although Lord does not demand a verbatim correlation among instances of a multiform (else the multiform would become a mere literary fossil and cease to be useful to the singer as he composes in the traditional way),[7] he does demand some concrete verbal dimension as a requirement of the unit.

David E. Bynum's complementary studies of the South Slavic epic theme began with his 1964 dissertation, in which he established a directory of recurrent multiforms based on seventy-five Wedding Songs drawn from the Milman Parry Collection and six published sources. In doing so he defined the theme (p. 39) as "a conglomeration of narrative matter in oral epic tradition which recurs in the tradition, and which is discrete because some of its occurrences have no consistent sequential relationship with other such units. Defined internally, it is a conglomeration of narrative the parts of which, if they are present, occur regularly together." It will be noted that Bynum includes no general requirement of verbal correspondence, that his concept of the theme is of a group of ideas that agglutinate and persist as a unit in oral tradition. A few years later, in a study devoted to themes of the young hero in Serbo-Croatian epic (1968), he would reiterate this concept in its essentials and point out that the order of elements or motifs within a multiform is irregular and further that associative clustering rather than sequence seemed to be the ruling force within the theme.

In two later works Bynum emphasized this associative dynamic and turned his model to acts of criticism. A 1970 article on thematic pattern illustrated how the poet and tradition transform a generic character by making him the agent or focal point of certain multiforms. Far the more ambitious project, *The Dæmon in the Wood* (1978) considers a worldwide mélange of oral fable from the point of view of motifs involving trees. Bynum argues persuasively for a single tradition of fable by treating diverse sources with a taxonomy founded on the sort of theme he had been describing in earlier studies. Themes are "the bounded kind of motival clusters," as opposed to an unbounded cluster not under the aegis of narrative pattern; the generic motifs involved in a theme are "like the fibres of a timber or the atoms in a molecule, capable

---

7. Further on (p. 21), he notes: "Although the repeated passages will not be word for word alike, there will be at least a sufficient degree of similarity of wording to show that the singer is using a unit of story that he holds already more or less formed in his mind." On the nature of fixity, see also Lord 1981.

of analytical separation from patterns but incapable of entering into the composition of traditional stories except as integrants of patterns, where they are held indissolubly in their orbits of association with other motifs by the powerful cohesive force of story-telling custom" (pp. 79-80).[8] This last point will prove an important one: as presaged in Lord's phrase "tension of essences" (1960, 97), themes—and the motival elements that comprise them—cohere not by the mechanistic imposition of a narrative latticework but rather through the mutual attraction of the involved units for one another, an attraction memorialized by thematic multiformity and ubiquity within the tradition. It is a cohesion that emerges over time, as the singer and tradition use and re-use a theme, group its parts, and reconstrue its whole; the cohesiveness that appears to us to be synchronic fixity is in reality the associative pull of diachrony.

David M. Gunn also contributed to the study of the theme in Serbo-Croatian epic by comparing selections from volume one of *Serbo-Croatian Heroic Songs* with passages from the *Iliad* and *Odyssey*. In the first of two articles (1970) he argues for rejection of the verbatim memorization theory for ancient Greek epic texts and for adoption of the oral-dictation hypothesis, adducing an inconsistency in a song by Sulejman Fortić as an analog to Homeric compositional practice. His comparison depends on Fortić's apparent attempt to ornament a theme and employs the concepts and definitions developed by Lord.[9] His second and more extensive study (1971) presents more detailed thematic morphologies for the two traditions and works toward a claim of unity of authorship in Homer based on the distinctiveness of narrative design in the *Iliad* and *Odyssey*:

> We find idiosyncrasies in vocabulary, in formulaic expression, in preference for certain elements, and in the particular sequence of elements whether couched in formulaic language or not. Moreover, in the instances of a singer's theme we can discern the degree to which the theme in whole or in part is "fixed" in the singer's mind. (p. 3)[10]

Gunn's emphasis on individually tailored occurrences of a theme thus harmonizes with Lord's ideas on verbal multiformity (although with an unambiguous basic correspondence among instances in terms of repeated phrases and words)

---

8. Cf. the biological analogy as presented in Turner 1986.

9. It is worth pointing out that Gunn's (1970, 194) explanation of *Pa da vidiš, moji sokolovi* ("But you should have seen, my falcons") as a clumsily intrusive filler line is inaccurate. As will be shown below, such "boundary lines" mark the extremities of narrative units and serve as a frequent compositional gloss on the *guslar*'s (and tradition's) sense of thematic structure. Thus understood, the line actually proves strongly supportive of Gunn's larger argument, since in the example he chooses it mediates between the more usual form of the theme and its ornamental, inconsistent continuation.

10. He goes on to note patterns characterized by formulaic expression among its instances and others characterized by lack of such phraseology.

and with Bynum's observation that the sequence of elements within the unit may permute and combine in various orders.

This collective stress on avenues of flexibility within limits was continued by Mary P. Coote in her thoroughgoing analysis of themes in the Parry Collection *guslar* Ćamil Kulenović's *The Captivity of Vrhovac Alaga* (1980). Coote (p. 202) prescribes two aspects for the multiform: the *paradigmatic theme*, "a general narrative idea which the singer restates in performance using specific motifs"; and the *compositional theme*, "a piece of narrative that repeats a set of formulas." Although she finds the Kulenović song-text entirely thematic, not all of its multiforms are compositional—that is, not all of them are appreciably formulaic with respect to other occurrences. The wide variation in density of verbal correspondence leads her to posit not a single type of narrative unit but rather a taxonomy of themes (p. 233): those called *formulaic* demonstrate at least a 75 percent density of formulaic phraseology and consistency in the order of elements or motifs; *marked* multiforms reveal neither significant phraseological stability from instance to instance nor a consistent sequence of motifs but are characterized by certain recognizable phrases or clusters of phrases; *neutral* themes express a paradigm without the features of the marked pattern; *unusual* multiforms also exhibit a common paradigm but include rare motifs; and *rare* themes are those used infrequently by a singer. Coote shows that Kulenović depends chiefly on compositional, or formulaic, themes for his song-making, and that compositional and marked multiforms together constitu.e about 85 percent of the 3,388 lines in the *Vrhovac Alaga*.[11] In other words, the singer employs most often those themes that have a heavy or at least discernible formulaic content. In this respect Coote corroborates Lord's insistence on significant verbal correspondence as a necessary hallmark of the narrative theme.

In sum, research on the theme in Serbo-Croatian oral epic has produced several points of consensus. First, there is general agreement that a "formulaic" narrative unit, multiform and therefore suitable for many different contexts, underlies the *guslar*'s compositional practice. Second, all investigators concur that the traditional quality of this unit—both its integrity as a complete pattern in itself and its associative links to other multiforms—make it a crucially important feature of the singer's craft. As for the actual structural make-up of the theme, however, we find some disagreement. Lord prescribes, most forcefully in his later writings, a necessary aspect of verbal correspondence; without this phraseological core, he stipulates, we have no theme. Bynum defines the multiform somewhat similarly but without the criterion of verbal stability, seeking in his most recent work to relate narrative themes across traditions to a worldwide pattern of fable. Gunn follows Lord's model rather

---

11. Her figures (p. 232) indicate that formulaic themes account for 1,628 lines (48 percent) and marked themes for 1,235 lines (35 percent).

closely in his comparative analyses, but Coote enlarges the concept to include five kinds of themes, a taxonomy founded on differing formulaic content and on adherence to an order of subunits.

Clearly, then, there has been much evidence brought forward for the existence of a narrative multiform and enough unanimity of scholarly opinion registered to make possible more than a rough sketch of the unit and its traditional importance and behavior. Just as clearly, however, we can discover no consensus on its internal structure, specifically on the questions of its phraseological texture, the significance of the order of its constituent parts, and the exact relationship among various occurrences. In pursuing answers to these questions, it will be well to turn to the texts themselves as the primary witness on thematic structure. Let us begin where the Stolac *guslar* Ibro Bašić leaves off—at a narrative seam incised by his pause for rest before resumption of performance and story.

A SINGER'S PAUSE AND THEMATIC STRUCTURE

At times during a lengthy oral performance, a singer breaks off his story to rest before continuing. Much has been hypothesized about the possible consequences of such breaks for the structure and texture of the Homeric poems,[12] for example, and similar suggestions might be made about other ancient and medieval texts that have reached us only in manuscript. In the Yugoslav tradition, however, there is no need to resort to hypothesis, for the collected texts themselves provide hard evidence. Lord (1936, 106) has shown that the *guslar*, "when not interfered with by his audience, will pause at almost any point in the narrative to rest himself or to put off singing to another occasion." But it is demonstrable that the singer will not resume his song at just any point; rather, as we shall see, he "backtracks" to the last traditional boundary and, after a brief proem for continuance, begins anew from there. This usually means reverting to the last thematic or subthematic structure and identifying it as a starting point.

To illustrate, consider Ibro Bašić's rest in his two sung versions of the Return Song *Alagić Alija and Velagić Selim*. Here his break falls during an arming or dressing episode, in which the heroine Fata prepares herself to undertake the journey to Zadar and, eventually, to rescue her betrothed truelove, Alagić Alija (AA). In each version a sequence of subsidiary actions precedes her own preparations: in *291b* AA's mother descends to the kitchen to bake food for Fata's ride, while in *6597* and *1283* Huso readies AA's horse for his mistress.

A da vidiš ostarjele nene—	But you should have seen AA's aged mother—
Dje zagrnu uz ruke rukave.	Well, she rolled up her sleeves.

---

12. See, e.g., Whitman 1958, 249–309; Notopoulos 1964, 7–16.

	A*h* udari kuli niz skaline.		And she dashed down the tower ladder.

Pa dopade, brate, u mrtvake, — Then she entered the kitchen, brothers,
Pa dopade u mrtvake mračne, 955 — Then she entered the dark kitchen,
Pa ona kuha lake brašanice.[13] — Then she baked delicate wheatcakes.

α A da vidiš lijepe djevojke— — But you should have seen the beautiful girl—

β A upade u šikli odaju, — She went into into the gold-adorned room,

γ { Sjede svlačat' žen'ko odijelo, — She began to doff her women's clothes,
   { Ali na se madžarsko odjelo. 960 — Instead she put on Hungarian clothes.

[*Ibro*: Nije kraj; malu ću o*d*počinut'.] — [That isn't the end; I'll rest a little.]

Dje li bismo, dje li ostavismo — Where were we, where did we leave
Malku pjesmu o' duga zemana? — The little song of times long past?

α A da vidiš lijepe djevojke— — But you should have seen the beautiful girl—

β A kad pade u šikli odaju, — And when she went to the gold-adorned room,

γ { Sjede svlačit' žensko odijelo, 965 — She began to doff her women's clothes,
   { A oblačit' madžar' djeisiju. — And to don Hungarian garb.

(*291b*.951–66)

A da vidiš, braćo moja, Huse— — But you should have seen Huso, my brothers—

A Huso je na noge skočijo, — And Huso jumped to his feet,
Do podruma dopade doratu, — He went down to the horse in the cellar,

Čula svali a timar navali. 1075 — Threw off the blanket and fell to grooming.

Pa dorata takum učinijo, — Then he prepared the horse,
Izvede ga na mermer avliju. — Led him to the marble courtyard.

α A da vidiš lijepe djevojke— — But you should have seen the beautiful girl—
β A upade u šikli odaju, —

γ { Sjede svlačit' žensko odijelo,
   { A oblačit' madžar' djeisiju.

(*6597*.1072–81)

Pade Huso u podrume mračne, — Huso went down to the dark cellar,
I sigura konja Alagića, 970 — And secured Alagić's horse,
Izvede ga na mermer avliju. — Led him to the marble courtyard.

α Vid' djevojke Muminove Fate—
β Ona pade u šikli odaju,

γ { Sjede svlačit' žensko odijelo,
   { A oblačit' madžar' djeisiju.

(1283.969–75)

13. A five-syllable first hemistich results in a long line.

When he broke off the performance at *291b*.960, Ibro had completed three lines of the dressing theme. After the boundary line (957), which served characteristically to identify Fata as the agent of the narrative unit to follow, he removed her to the location of the action of the next theme, just as he and other *guslari* often do in preparation for the onset of the succeeding episode.[14] The requisite change of position effected, he then sang the "argument" of the theme in lines 959-60. In resuming his performance, Ibro first sings the standard two-line phrase to introduce continuation (961-62) and then turns to the same cluster of lines with which he began the description of Fata's dressing before the break. Although the fourth line shows incidental variation, the structural sequence of boundary line (a), position change (β), and argument (γ) is repeated exactly. He picks up the song, in short, by retracking to the last thematic boundary. The singer's thinking as he resumes is traditional in that he bases the continuation not simply on "the rest of the story" but rather on the narrative structure of the song. He may indeed stop his performance almost anywhere (here he halts within a theme), but in beginning again he respects the thematic structure of traditional narrative.

Texts *6597* (lines 1078-81) and *1283* (972-75) share with *291b* the same four-line segment in the same initial position, with minor differences in verbalization.[15] From this point on, however, the line-for-line verbal correspondence drops sharply as the primary unit of organization becomes not the formula but the single action, in whatever manner the action is verbalized.[16] At certain junctures, either under the pressure of performance or because he feels he has reached a boundary, Ibro sings a line that may be described as the formulaic system <u>Kad se cura</u> ["When the girl"] plus a verb for "preparing" in the past tense. This line, represented below as XX, tends to occur at the same points in the sung versions, and to demarcate the same clusters of descriptive elements. The overall order of constituents in *291b* and *6597* is as follows:

	291b	*6597*
boundary line	963	1078
position change	964	1079
argument	965-66	1080-81
XX	967	1082
sword	968	1083-84
cap	969	1085-86
coins	970-72	1087-88

14. A change of position line, as discussed below, often coincides with either a thematic boundary or a juncture between elements in a theme.

15. Given the much less frequent occurrence of boundary lines in the oral-dictated text, we may confidently interpret 1283.972, a common variation for Ibro on the conventional "A da vidiš..." line, as marking an important narrative seam.

16. See the next section ("Multiformity Within the Traditional Theme") for more on the variable density of verbal correspondence among instances of a theme.

	291b	*6597*
XX	973	1089
sword	974-76	—
XX	977	—

Text 1283 diverges significantly from the pattern of the two sung versions, and in just the manner we might expect of an oral-dictated text—with greater ornamentation. Besides some of the accoutrements listed above, we hear in 1283 of additional descriptive details: Fata's Hungarian braids, three crosses of gold, *ćelenke*, a leather arms belt with two English and two Venetian pistols, and so forth.[17]

The three versions of the passage taken together offer a glimpse of the internal dynamics of the arming/dressing multiform. The four-line initiatory sequence shows little variation: the boundary line is highly structured, the second colon of the position change is a very stable phrase in Ibro's idiolect, and the argument is in three of four instances based on the sound-and-meaning relationship between "to doff" (*svlačiti*) and "to don" (*oblačiti*). No such constraints order the verbalization of the remainder of the theme, and the singer may be brief or lengthy, sparing or ornamental, in his rendering of the actions and objects involved in dressing/arming before he turns to the thematic coda, the golden coins.

Indeed, this example illustrates more than a singer's method of resuming an interrupted song, of re-starting his narrative: by its revelation of a thematic structure on which the *guslar* depends as he reconstitutes the pattern of the epic, it gives evidence of a traditional underlay, a unit that proves useful to the singer as he finds his way back into the flow of the performance and one that, we can extrapolate, may well prove just as integral to the compositional process in an uninterrupted performance. Ibro's retracking to a thematic boundary reveals the presence and shape of this unit; in this case we need not depend on visual apprehension of patterns of verbal correspondence—the capsular nature of the theme is implicitly identified by the singer himself in his choice of a new starting point. Although there is nothing in conversations with the Stolac *guslari* to indicate that they had even the faintest notion of our concept of narrative theme,[18] Ibro's very dependence on these multiforms in the resumption of the song shows that he and his tradition "know" its nature and texture. As further examples will emphasize, the theme is one of

17. A *ćelenka* is "a kind of plume, made of gold or silver in the shape of feathers joined together, sometimes adorned with precious gems" (Škaljić 1979, s.v. *ćelenka*). Not surprisingly, many of the objects described in text 1283 also occur in other songs recorded from Stolac singers, such as Halil Bajgorić's arming of Djerdjelez Alija in Parry no. *6699, The Wedding of Mustajbey's Son Bećirbeg*.

18. In general, *guslari* seem unable to discuss the nature of their craft; to put it more accurately, they see no need to reconstrue their craft in the abstract, analytical terms we favor. On analytical versus mimetic representation, see esp. Havelock [1963] 1982, 1987.

the singer's "words"; like the formula, or phraseological word, the theme—or narrative word—contributes through its multiformity an important group of entries to the traditional lexicon. And it would be a violation of traditional grammar and semantics for the *guslar* to resume his tale in "mid-word."

MULTIFORMITY WITHIN THE TRADITIONAL THEME: "SHOUTING IN PRISON"

As we shall see in chapter 10, the Return Song begins in a great many cases with a theme we may call "Shouting in Prison."[19] The onset of this multiform prefigures a longer set of actions far beyond its immediate extent, the entire process culminating by tale's end in the *Odyssey*-like re-emergence of the seemingly lost hero and his re-accession to his proper social and familial position through a series of contests and a prolonged rapprochement with his wife or betrothed. In its obvious significance to the story-pattern of Return, as well as in its relatively large compass and complex inner fabric of motifs, the Shouting multiform is an ideal candidate for structural analysis. Following Lord's suggestions on comparative evaluation of parallel passages and song-texts,[20] I shall look first at instances of this theme in the Return Song repertoire of a single *guslar*. After establishing this initial profile, we shall expand the investigation to take in additional examples of the same multiform in the performances of another singer from the Stolac region, and finally in a text by another singer from a widely separated area, that of Novi Pazar.[21]

Mujo Kukuruzović and the Idiolectal Theme

My first set of examples is drawn from Return Songs sung and recited by Mujo Kukuruzović, a *guslar* collected by Parry and Lord in 1933-35, in particular from two songs called by the collectors *The Captivity of Alagić Alija* (*AA*, texts *6618* and 1868) and *The Captivity of Ograšćić Alija* (*OA*, texts *6617* and 1287a). As we shall discover in chapter 10, they are in fact two variants of the same generic song. By collating the four texts, we can to a limited but representative extent gauge thematic variance from performance to performance and song to song within a singer's repertoire and study the variorum identity of the theme.

19. See Lord 1960, 245–47, 260–61.

20. "The reader's impression of repetitions would be closer to the experience of the singer himself and to that of the singer's audience were he to read first the songs in the repertory of a single singer and then those from singers in the same small district" (Lord 1960, 68).

21. Obviously, the amassing of data on a theme could go on almost indefinitely. At a certain point, however, we pass beyond illustration of compositional form and dynamics to the kind of profile more suited to a directory or to an exhaustive study of a single theme or *guslar*. For the sort of data-gathering and -processing instrument necessary to conduct the latter kind of scholarly work, to which these studies cannot aspire if they are to maintain a comparative and structural focus, see the computerized text-processor described in Foley 1981a, 1984a.

To begin, I offer a brief recapitulation of the major action of Shouting in Prison in Kukuruzović's songs and elsewhere. As the story opens, whether with a proem or not,[22] either AA or OA is crying out loudly in lamentation (motif #1). The banica reports his shouting to her husband the ban and, explaining that the noise has kept their son from nursing or sleeping, demands that the prisoner be either released or hanged (motif #2). The ban refuses on the grounds that before his capture AA/OA had wreaked havoc in Christian territory and he fears a repetition; after the hero dies, the ban says, he will grind up his bones for cannon fodder (motif #3). The banica then replies that she will kill their son unless some action is taken, acerbically noting that the ban is too old to father another heir and that failure to obey her demand will thus mean the end of his royal line. When she repeats her threat, he acquiesces, suggesting that she enter the prison herself and personally conduct the bargaining for release (motif #4).

The breakdown into constituent *motifs* is a convenient first step in penetrating the wholeness of the theme.[23] In addition, I note in passing that a great number of themes in Serbo-Croatian epic seem to divide along dialogue axes, and that I have customarily employed this criterion in marking narrative boundaries. Narrowing the focus, then, I intend to examine rather closely all four motifs that make up Shouting in Prison with a view to (a) their narrative sequences, (b) the extent and kind of verbal correspondence among instances, and (c) the consistency and texture of (a) and (b) from motif to motif. Much of this analysis will seek to test the idiosyncratic nature of thematic structure in Serbo-Croatian; I do, however, offer these findings as a basis for comparison with analogous narrative structures in ancient Greek and Old English epic.

MOTIF #1

As a start, consider Kukuruzović's four versions of motif #1, a static portrayal of the prisoner crying out in his misery.

a_1 Pocmilijo sužanj u zindanu—   20 a_1 Pocmilijo sužanj u zindanu—
        Ako cmili, nevolja mu bila.   Ako cmili, nevolja mu bila.

β_1 Čij' l' je sužanj? Čija li tavnica? β_2 Nije lahko ni dvadeset dana,
        To je sužanj Alagić Alija,   Ja kamoli dvadeset godina,   15
        A tavnica bana karlovskoga.   Prez promjene u lednu zindanu;
                                                  Niti znade kad mu ljeto prodje,
                                                  Niti znade kad mu zima dodje.

---

22. On the proem or *pripjev*, see Pantzer 1959; Foley 1977b; Bynum 1981.

23. Following to an extent the scholars whose work was reviewed above, I offer the hypothesis of the *motif* as a regular constituent of the theme, a smaller unit overseen by the larger paradigm. How far this hypothesis holds and how viable the motif may prove as a descriptive distinction will be the burden of the developing discussion.

γ_1 Pa je jadan Turčin pocmilijo,   25
Od dnev' do dnev' za nedjelju
   dana,
Za nedjelju bijelije dana.
Vazda Turčin u ta*v*nici cmili.
   (*AA, 6618*.20-28 [Text A])

γ_1 Pa je jadan Turčin pocmilijo,
Sužanj cmili za nedjelju dana.   20
   (*OA*, 1287a. 12-20 [Text C])

a_1 The captive was shouting in
   prison—   20
If he shouted, he had misfortune.

a_1 The captive was shouting in
   prison—
If he shouted, he had misfortune.

β_1 Whose prisoner was he? Whose
   prison was it?

The prisoner was Alagić Alija,
And the prison was Karlovo ban's.

β_2 It is not easy for twenty days,

Not to mention twenty years,   15
Without change in a cold prison;
One knows neither when spring
   arrives
Nor when winter comes.

γ_1 So the wretched Turk was
   shouting,   25
Day after day for a week of days,

For a week of white days.
The Turk shouted continually in
   prison.

γ_1 So the wretched Turk was
   shouting,
The prisoner shouted for a
   week of days.   20

a_2 Šta no nešto u Zadarju cmili?

a_2 Što no nešto u Janjoku cmili,
U Janjoku u lednu zindanu?

β_3 Da je vila u gori bi bila?
Da je guja u kamen' bi bila?
Nit' je vila, nit' je šar'a guja,
Nego jadan Alagić Alija.   5

β_3 Da je vila u gori bi bila?
Da je guja u kamenu bila?
Nit' je vila, nit' je šarna guja,   5
Nego jadan sužanj nevoljniče,
Nevoljniče Ograšćić Alija.

γ_2 Turčin cmili tri bijela dana.
   (*AA*, 1868.1-6 [Text B])

γ_2 Turčin cmili tri bijela dana.
   (*OA, 6617*.1-8 [Text D])

a_2 What was the shouting in Zadar?

a_2 What was the shouting in Janok,
In Janok in the cold prison?

β_3 Could it be a mountain nymph?
Could it be a snake under a stone?
It was neither a nymph nor a
   striped snake,

β_3 Could it be a mountain nymph?
Could it be a snake under a stone?
It was neither a nymph nor
   a striped snake,   5

But the wretched Alagić Alija.   5

But the wretched unwilling captive,
The unwilling Ograšćić Alija.

γ_2 The Turk shouted for three
white days.

γ_2 The Turk shouted for three
white days.

Motif #1, here subdivided into the three elements labeled a, β, and γ, follows the proem in texts A and C. While the *pripjev* is itself optional for most singers,[24] its appearance apparently does condition what comes afterward at least in Kukuruzović's songs, for the presence of the proem leads to a certain song beginning (a_1) and its absence to another (a_2). Briefly stated, Kukuruzović follows the *pripjev* with a declarative statement about the shouting (A.20-21 and C.12-13); yet when motif #1 starts the song, it takes the form of a rhetorical question (B.1 and D.1-2), the continuation of and answer to which establish the hero's identity. The β section depends directly on a and is thus influenced by the occurrence or non-occurrence of the *pripjev*, but the γ section seems to be an independent unit that lexically echoes a and completes a small ring structure.[25]

The density of verbal correspondence is greatest between texts B and D, where only a place-name substitution (Zadar/Janok) and what Robert Austerlitz has called a "terrace" (*6617*.1-2 and 5-6)[26] keep the motif instances from being identical. Texts A and C, in contrast, diverge widely in element β, where they share not a single formulaic phrase, and also exhibit a good deal of variation in γ along with some formulaic correspondence. All in all, there is enough variance among the four examples to justify the subscript labeling added above: this relatively consistent first motif in the Shouting multiform can take at least two forms for element a, the argument of the scene to follow; three forms for β, always an elaboration on the argument but highly individual in subject and phraseology; and two more closely related forms for γ. The major point is that verbal correspondence, which takes the form of whole-line and colonic repetition in Serbo-Croatian epic tradition, is not uniform in

24. Here, for instance, it precedes one version of *AA* and one of *OA*; it is also lacking in one version of each.

25. The essential idea of element γ is "The Turk shouted for an extraordinary period of time." Whether that idea is expressed with a phrase indicating a week (*za nedelju dana*, texts A and C) or three days (*tri bijela dana*, B and D), the illocutionary force of the element remains the same. See further Bynum 1981.

26. See Austerlitz 1958, esp. 65-69; he defines the "terrace" (p. 65) as "a complex of two lines in which the latter portion of the first line is identical with the former portion of the following line." In the Serbo-Croatian *deseterac*, absolute identity is impossible, since the two hemistichs or cola are of different lengths (four and six syllables); but the principle behind terracing obtains in four-syllable versions of the six-syllable phrases from immediately preceding lines. Inasmuch as the terrace is a pure form of what Parry and Lord called "unnecessary enjambement," it would seem to be an indication of oral traditional style.

density either from instance to instance within parallel motifs or from one part of a motif to another. While the abstract pattern α-β-γ remains constant over the four texts, the actual verbalization of that pattern can take different shapes, in this case depending in part on the way the song begins.

MOTIF #2

Turning to the second motif, we find all four occurrences consisting of a series of discrete elements: δ, a statement of the banica's sadness, optionally including mention of the prisoner's screaming as its cause; ϵ, her complaint to her husband the ban; ζ, an ornamental element that can take two quite disparate and phraseologically unrelated forms (ζ_1 and ζ_2 below); and η, the banica's first alternative or request. Between elements δ and ϵ are interposed boundary lines, much as in Ibro Bašić's performances examined above.

δ	Pa banici jadu ujadijo;		δ	Pa banici jadom ujadijo,	
	E, njezino čedo usplašijo,	30		I njezino čedo usplašijo.	
	Usplašijo Providura sina.				
	Pa banica rano podranila.			Pa banica rano podranila.	
	Pa je eto banu na odaju.			Pa je eto banu u odaju.	
ϵ	Pa mu 'vako govoriti za*jd*e:				
	"E ja, bane, zemlje		ϵ	"Ustaj, bane, zemlji	
	komandare,	35		komandare,	25
	U z'o čas ga zindan namjestijo,			U z'o čas ga zindan namjestijo,	
	Pa si u njeg' Turke naselijo.			Pa si u njeg' naselijo Turke.	
	Eno Turčin' u ta*v*nici cmili—			Eno Turčin' u tamnici cmili—	
ζ_1	Ja t' je Turčin 'ljeba ogladnijo?				
	Ja crvena vina ožednijo?	40			
	Ja t' je Turčin čohe ogolijo?				
	Ja se Turčin majke uželijo,				
	Uželijo svoga zavičaja?—				
η	Ja ga daji, ja ga preprodaji,		η	Ja ga daji, ja ga preprodaji,	
	Ja Turčina turi na vješala."	45		Ja ga pusti na zemlju turćiju."	30
	(*6618*.29-45 [Text A])			(1287a.21-30 [Text C])	

δ	Then he caused the banica untold misery;		δ	Then he caused the banica untold misery,
	Eh, he frightened her infant,	30		And he frightened her infant.
	He frightened her son Providuro.			
	Then the banica arose early,			Then the banica arose early,
	And she went to the ban's chamber.			And she went to the ban's chamber.

ε Then she spoke to him thus:
"Eh, ban, commander of the
 territory, 35
Woe the day you put him in prison,
When you filled it with Turks;
And now a Turk shouts in prison—

ζ₁ Does the Turk hunger after bread?
Or does he thirst after red
 wine? 40
Or is the Turk without clothes?
Or does the Turk long for his
 mother,
Long for his native land?

η Either give in to him, ransom
 him back,
Or send the Turk to the
 gallows." 45

Kad četvrto jutro osvanulo,
Pa banica rano podranila.

δ Njezino je usplašijo čedo,
Ludo čedo Providura sina— 10
Pa ne more sanak boraviti.
U naramak prifatila sina.

Pa je eto banu u odaju.

ε Ona banu dobro jutro viknu,
A bane joj prifatijo zdravlje: 15
"Zdravo, bila moja gospojice."
Banica mu iz grla povika:
"ⱨE ja, bane, zemlji gospodare,
U z'o čas ga zindan namjestijo,
Pa si u njeg' naselijo Turke. 20

ζ₂ Evo ima tri bijela dana
I četiri noći strahovite—
Kako Turčin u tamnici cmili!
Pa je moje čedo usplašijo—
Pa ne more sanak boraviti. 25

η Ja ga daji, ja ga preprodaji,
Ja Turčina turi na vješala."
    (1868.7-27 [Text B])

ε "Get up, ban, commander of the
 territory, 25
Woe the day you put him in prison,
When you filled it with Turks;
And now a Turk shouts in prison—

η Either give in to him, ransom
 him back,
Or release him into Turkish
 territory." 30

δ Pa banici jadu ujadijo.

Pa banica rano podranila. 10
Pa je eto banu na odaju.

ε Ona banu sjede besjediti:

"Čuješ, bane, zemlje komandare,
U z'o čas ga naselijo Turke,
Naselijo u mome zindanu. 15

ζ₁ Ja t' je Turčin 'ljeba ogladnijo?
Ja crvena vina ožednijo?
Ja taʋnica kuća dodijala?
Ja se Turčin majke uželijo,
Uželijo roda i plemena? 20

η Ja ga daji, ja ga preprodaji,
Ja Turčina turi na vješala."
    (6617.9-22 [Text D])

When the fourth morning dawned,
Then the banica arose early.

δ	He frightened her infant,	δ	Then he caused the banica untold misery.

Her hysterical infant son
   Providuro—   10
For he could not sleep in peace.
She clutched her son to her bosom.

Then the banica arose early.   10

And she went to the ban's
   chamber.

And she went to the ban's
   chamber.

ε   She called good morning
      to the ban,
And the ban received her
      greeting: 15
"Your health, my white lady."
The banica called from her throat:
"Eh, ban, lord of the territory,

ε   She began to speak to the ban:

"Listen, ban, commander of the
   territory,

Woe the day you put him
   in prison,
When you filled it with
   Turks.   20

Woe the day you filled it
   with Turks,
Filled up my prison.   15

ζ_2 It has been three white days

And four horrible nights—
How the Turk shouts in prison!

And he frightened my infant—

So he could not sleep in
   peace.   25

ζ_1 Does the Turk hunger after
      bread?
Or does he thirst after red wine?
Or does his prison home
      oppress him?
Or does the Turk long for
      his mother,
Long for his kin and
      countrymen?   20

η   Either give in to him, ransom
      him back,
Or send the Turk to the
      gallows."

η   Either give in to him, ransom
      him back,
Or send the Turk to the
      gallows."

Overall, motif #2 shows more phraseological and sequential stability than motif #1, the only real variability occurring between elements ε and η with the two forms of the optional element ζ. Nevertheless, some sections can vary considerably in length and development, although expansibility is not a characteristic of all elements. The first subunit, δ, for example, has the essential idea of presenting the sorrowful banica, whether her misery is simply stated in a terse, one-line phrase (*6617*.9) or its cause is articulated over a four-line passage (1868.9-12). That very articulation, couched as it is in formulaic language, offers an interesting illustration of multiformity in expression:

A. *6618*.30-31	B. 1868.9-12	C. 1287a.22
E, njezino čedo usplašijo,	Njezino je usplašijo čedo,	I njezino čedo usplašijo.
Usplašijo Providura sina.	Ludo čedo Providura sina—	
	Pa ne more sanak boraviti.	
	U naramak prifatila sina.	

The first line of this expansion on the argument is a classically defined formula, the only variation resulting from metathesis under the penultimate ictus rule (IAD) and from particles: a colon-initial interjection (A), the enclitic *je* that must take final position in the hemistich (B), and the proclitic *I* placed characteristically before the trisyllable (C). All three lines, as we have seen in chapters 3 and 5, must be considered the same formula from a prosodic and compositional point of view. After this identical start, Mujo adds a variation or terrace on text A, repeating the tetrasyllabic verb form *usplašijo* as the opening colon of the next line. In text B he uses the entire second line as an appositive to *čedo*, so that the first hemistich is filled not by the verb but by *ludo čedo*, a partial terrace on the preceding line and an expansion on *Providura sina* in the next colon. From one perspective these passages show a tightly knit structure: they all gloss the banica's misery with a single formula, explaining her grief in the same manner each time and expressing the idea of fright in virtually identical phrases. But from another point of view, each instance embroiders the central fact somewhat differently; text A adds a terrace, B a partial terrace and a two-line expatiation, C nothing at all. This kind of traditional multiformity, of variation within limits, is the most consistent feature of thematic structure.

Immediately after the δ element we find a *position change* line (e.g., A.33), sometimes accompanied by a verse-type I shall call a *diurnal rhythm* marker (e.g., A.32). Throughout the Stolac material, and throughout the songs from Novi Pazar and other published collections, these lines and others like them act as boundaries, signaling the end of one unit and the onset of the next. Compositionally, they mediate both between thematic wholes and between their parts, that is, between the elements and motifs that comprise a theme. Here they have the latter function: they separate elements δ and ε, marking a narrative seam and allowing easy passage from one scene to another. Text B, in fact, well illustrates the bounded extremities and unitary character of element δ by both beginning and ending the four-line passage with marker verses—the diurnal rhythm lines at the opening (7-8) and the position change at the close (13). It seems appropriate to note that we shall discover other such verses in our analysis of multiforms, including the extremely common type I term the *agent line*, which usually takes the form A/Pa da vidiš [character X] ("But/Then you should have seen [character X]"), where the character involved is customarily the agent of the next multiform, motif, or element. All of these marker verses or boundary lines—position change, diurnal rhythm, and agent lines—perform an invaluable service in affording the *guslar* a traditional, generic way to effect transitions between units that, we should recall, also have individual lives of their own in the poetic tradition.

After the marker verses, Mujo turns to the banica's complaint (ε), for which there seems to be a phraseological core including her address of the ban and the present insufficiency of the prison to contain in silence the shouting Turk who is keeping their son from sleep. This core changes only nominally over the four versions, with minor substitutions in colon 1 of the first line[27]—

> A: E ja, <u>bane, zemlji komandare,</u>
>
> Eh! ban, commander of the territory,
>
> B: *h*E ja, <u>bane, zemlje gospodare,</u>
>
> C: Ustaj, <u>bane, zemlji komandare,</u>
>
> Get up, . . .
>
> D: Čuješ, <u>bane, zemlje komandare,</u>
>
> Listen, . . .

—metathesis of words, and the addition in texts A and C of a fourth line to the three-line kernel.[28] The introductory line or lines preceding her speech vary from none at all (C) to a rather elaborate and formal four-line exchange (B), but this flexibility should be expected in introductory expressions, which are highly generic in the tradition, with the essential idea "he/she spoke" existing in a considerable number of compositionally equivalent phrases. Moreover, the formal giving and receiving of greeting in text B has its own status as a floating and remarkably stable "atom" in the tradition, being available for many and diverse occasions, from the meeting of warriors about to engage in a *mejdan* ("single combat") to the long-sought reunion of two lovers; its presence in text B is simply another aspect of the paratactic structure of narrative multiformity.

From the banica's main and recurring statement of her complaint, three of Kukuruzović's song-texts move to an intensification of and enlargement on

27. The passages in question are *6618*.35–38, 1287a.25–28, 1868.18–20, and *6617*.13–15. As discussed in chapters 3 and 5, these kinds of nominal changes occur in that part of the line most vulnerable to modification, and this susceptibility stems ultimately from an Indo-European metrical tendency preserved in the *deseterac*.

28. Text D combines the second- and third-line formulas into a single and somewhat illogical verse—an example of multiformity gone awry. At all levels the traditional method, in permitting and even encouraging variant formations, also must suffer the occasional infelicitous change. See further the example of a story-pattern miscue in chapter 10.

that complaint. What is more, this optional element ζ, missing entirely in text C, takes two very different forms. In ζ_1, of which we have versions in texts A and D, the banica continues her presentation of the problem by asking a series of questions about what might be troubling the prisoner and causing him to raise such a racket. The first two questions and verses are identical, as are the fourth lines concerning the captive's mother, the only variations being the result of a substitution in line 3 of the element and two somewhat divergent terraces in the fifth lines.[29] Neither the substitution nor the terraces constitute serious modifications of what is generally a stable structure with an ability to expand or contract under changing performance conditions, a kind of flexible set-piece that, like the offering and receiving of a greeting, can occur in different narrative situations. In addition, the list of questions itself proves to be a generic kind of passage, one that will recur when the banica enters the prison and interviews the captive at the start of the second major theme, "Bargaining." The ζ_2 passage, on the other hand, for which we have only the single example in text B, conveys the same notion of just how much misery the Turk has wrought, but it has no such traditional integrity as a floating piece of narrative matter suitable for numerous situations. With its exclamatory third line echoing earlier verses in motif #1 and its coda a recombination and repetition of lines 9-11 in element δ, the ζ_2 passage seems more the closure of a ring than a true element in itself.

With the banica's closing demand (η), we reach the stable end of motif #2. In two highly patterned set phrases she presents the ban with three alternatives: grant the prisoner what he wants, "resell" (*preprodati*) him to his people for a ransom, or simply hang him. Text C substitutes releasing the captive into Turkish territory for hanging. There is nothing in the phrase *Ja ga pusti na zemlju turćiju* to indicate metrical or phraseological malfeasance; indeed, the formula derives from a common system of diction in the Stolac tradition.[30] In all four instances of the element, the first line is held together by a common type of sound-patterning, leonine or end-colon rhyme—"Ja ga *daji*, ja ga pre-pr*daji*"—so that the syntactic balance and semantic correspondence between cola is reinforced by repetition of (-)*daji*. Although the second line of the couplet participates as a third alternative in this syntactic series, it is founded on no such sound-patterning and, as text C illustrates, is vulnerable to substitution. In element η, then, we sense both the conservatism and the inherent flexibility of diction and narrative subunit; multiformity means compositional

29. Note (1) that the substitution of the prison-house for the prisoner's clothes maintains the central conceit of the element and (2) that the variant terraces "his native land" and "his kin and countrymen" are equally appropriate correlatives and themselves nearly the same essential idea.

30. Cf. *Pusti njega na zemlju turćiju* (1287a.73 and 1868.58), as well as *Ja ga spremi na zemlju turćiju* (1287a.68) and others less closely related. In addition, our sample of phraseology from Stolac includes some thirteen instances of [preposition] *zemlj- turćij-*, with various inflections.

tendencies in both directions, both toward stability and toward phraseological and thematic neologisms, and the twin tendencies are overseen by the particular, tradition-dependent dynamics of formulaic and thematic structure as informed by traditional rules.

MOTIF #3

As the next textual comparison indicates, motif #3 subdivides into four elements: θ, introduction and address; ι, AA/OA's heroic deeds; κ, the ban's promise; and λ, grinding the bones.

θ A bane joj 'vako progovara:
     "Gospojice meni mila bila,
     Ni dosad mi nisi mrska bila.

ι A znadeš li u z'o čas ti bilo
     Dok j' Alija bijo na Turćiji?   50
     Dosta nam je jada učinijo—
     I majaka jadni' ostavijo,
     I sestara u crno zavijo.
     Stotinu je kula zapalijo,
     Krajem mora i krajem
        limana,   55
     I sad svaka omedjina sama.

κ Kad sam njega ufatijo živa,
     Bacijo ga u moju tamnicu.
     Tad sam Bogu jemin učinijo
     Da mu neću na tavnicu saći   60
     Dok mu duša u kostimam'
        tuče.

λ hA mu duša iz kostiju izidje,[31]
     Njegove ću kosti pokupiti,
     Pa ću kosti ložit' u odžaku.
     Pa ću kosti u dibeku tući,   65
     Palić u i' moru na širinu—
     Nek od vraga ne ostaje
        traga!"
           (*6618*.46-67 [Text A])

θ "Gospojice meni mila bila,
     Ni dosad mi nisi mrska bila.

κ Kad sam njega živa ufatijo,

     Ja sam Bogu jemin učinijo
     Da mu neću na tamnicu sići   35
     Dok mu duša u kostima tuče.

λ Kad mu duša is kostiju podje,
     Njegove ću kosti pokupiti,
     Ložiću i' mome odžaku.[32]
     Pa ću kosti u dibeku tući,   40
     Palić u i' moru na širinu—
     Šemluk činit' iz moji' topova.

ι A znadeš li dugo jadna bila
     Dok j' Alija bijo na Turćiji?
     Dosta nam je jada načinijo—   45

---

31. A seven-syllable second colon yields an eleven-syllable line. The trouble seems to be a recurrent one; see *6617*.34.

32. In omitting the preposition *u* (cf. *6618*.64), Kukuruzović makes a short second colon and line.

I majaka jadni' ostavijo,
I sestara u crno zavijo.
Stotinu je kula zapalijo,
Krajem mora i krajem limana,
I sad svaka omedjina sama."   50
(1287a.31-50 [Text C])

θ But the ban spoke to her thus:
"My dear white lady,   θ   "My dear white lady,
Until now you have not been   Until now you have not been
  hateful.   hateful.

ι But do you recall how
     terrible it was
When Alija was free in
     Turkish lands?   50
He caused us miseries
     enough—
He left mothers wretched,
And dressed sisters in black.
He set fire to a hundred
     towers,
At the edge of the sea and
     the lake,   55
And now all our borders are
     unguarded.

κ When I captured him alive,   κ   When I captured him alive,
I threw him into my prison.
Then I promised God   I promised God
That I will not enter the   That I will not enter the
     prison   60   prison   35
While his spirit enlivens his   While his spirit enlivens his
     bones.[33]   bones.

λ But when his spirit leaves   λ   But when his spirit leaves
     his bones,   his bones,
I will gather the bones up,   I will gather the bones up,
Heat the bones in a chimney,   Heat the bones [in] my chimney,
Grind the bones in a mortar, 65   Grind them in a mortar,   40
And shoot them into the   And shoot them into the
     wide sea—   wide sea—
Let there remain no trace   I will fire a salute from my
     of the devil!"   cannon.

33. This line resists ready translation, and I have settled for an idiomatic recasting. Literally, it means "while his spirit beats (or strikes) in his bones."

ι   But do you recall how long
you were wretched
While Alija was free in
Turkish lands?
He caused us miseries
enough—   45
He left mothers wretched,
And dressed sisters in black.
He set fire to a hundred
towers,
At the edge of the sea and
the lake,
And now all our borders are
unguarded."   50

θ A bane joj reče lakrdiju:
"Gospojice, dugo jadna bila;

θ A bane joj sjede besjediti:
"Gospojice meni mila bila,
Ni dosad mi nisi mrska bila.   25

ι A znadeš li Alagić Aliju   30
Kad je bijo na zemlji turćiji?
Sedam nam je džada
zastavijo—
Tri su s mora, četiri sa suha.
Stotinu je kula zapalijo,
Krajem mora i krajem
limana,   35
I sad svaka omedjina sama.
Dosta nam je jada učinijo—
I majaka jadni' ostavijo,
I sestara u crno zavijo.

ι A znadeš li u z'o čas ti bilo
Dok je Alija bijo na Turćiji?[34]

Dosta nam je jada učinijo—
I majaka jadni' ostavijo,
I sestara u crno zavijo.   30

κ Pa sam Bogu jemin učinijo—   40
Kad sam njega živa ufatijo,
Bacijo ga u moju tamnicu—
Da mu neću u tamnici sići
Dok ja čujem da je u njem'
duša."
(1868.28-44 [Text B])

κ Pa sam Bogu jemin učinijo

Da mu neću u tamnici saći
Dok mu duša u kostimam'
tuče.

λ hA mu duša iz kostiju izidje,
Njegove ću kosti pokupiti,   35
Pa ću kosti ložit' u odžaku,
Pa ću kosti u dibeku tući,
Palić i' moru na širinu—
Nek od vraga ne ostaje traga!"
(6617.23-39 [Text D])

34. The unelided *je Alija* produces a long first hemistich and an eleven-syllable line.

θ   And the ban spoke a word
       to her:
     "Lady, you were long
        wretched;

ι   And do you recall Alagić
       Alija   30
     When he was free in Turkish
        lands?

     He took over seven roads—
     Three from the sea, four
        from the land.
     He set fire to a hundred
        towers,
     At the edge of the sea and
        the lake,   35
     And now all our borders are
        unguarded.
     He caused us miseries
        enough—
     He left mothers wretched,
     And dressed sisters in black.

κ   And so I promised God—   40
     When I captured him alive,
     I threw him into my prison—
     That I will not enter the
        prison
     While I hear his spirit
        lives."

θ   And the ban began to
       address her:
     "My dear white lady,
     Until now you have not been
        hateful.   25

ι   But do you recall how
       terrible it was
     While Alija was free in
        Turkish lands?

     He caused us miseries
        enough—
     He left mothers wretched,
     And dressed sisters in black. 30

κ   And so I promised God

     That I will not enter the
        prison
     While his spirit enlivens his
        bones.

λ   But when his spirit leaves his
        bones,
     I will gather the bones up,   35
     Heat the bones in a chimney,
     Grind the bones in a mortar,
     And shoot them into the
        wide sea—
     Let there remain no trace
        of the devil!"

The first of these units, element θ, remains quite stable over the four instances, with the usual exception of the introductory line, which typically employs three different second-colon formulas to convey the essential idea of "[he/she] spoke":

A. 'vako progovara ("spoke thus")
B. reče lakrdiju ("spoke a word [utterance]")
C. [no introductory line]
D. sjede besjediti ("began to address")

Conversely, the line of address to the banica recurs regularly, held in phraseological check partly by the internal rhyme on *mila/bila*.[35] Element *ι*, which details the destruction caused by the Turkish hero, appears mobile; as a flashback to former events, it can fit in at various points in the logic of the narrative sequence, either as a motivation for the ban's capturing the offender (texts A, B, D) or as a remembrance of those dark days (C) and therefore a posterior justification of the ban's attitude toward him. From a structural point of view, the mobility of this element illustrates the kind of variation in sequence that may take place under the aegis of multiformity; in turn, this particular sort of flexibility reveals an aspect of the associational or paratactic nature of thematic structure and suggests that the theme is composed of a conglomeration of parts with certain associative relationships to other parts, rather than of a hierarchical framework to which constituents are always and everywhere subordinate. As for phraseological stability, variation in the verbalization of *ι* takes the form of added or deleted whole lines rather than of formulaic substitution. This integral or "quantum" variation is typical of narrative passages that enumerate items, such as the hero's accoutrements in an arming theme. In less cataloglike units, formulaic substitution is more common.

Element *κ* consists of an optional condition ("When I captured him alive") and result, usually followed by the ban's pledge to maintain AA/QA's imprisonment until the captive's death.[36] Here again the verbal correspondence is almost complete. The last unit, *λ*, which occurs in all texts except B, is verbalized very consistently, with limited variance in the first, third, and final lines of the sequence. The first two of these lines vary only in the choice and morphology of related or identical verbs, and the last is a whole-line formula often associated with cannon being fired in celebration. All in all, the motif pattern is once again clear and consistent, with the mobility of element *ι* the sign of its generic relationship to the narrative pattern. The degree of verbal correspondence among the four instances is customarily high but, as we have come to expect, varies from one element to the next.

MOTIF #4

The fourth and final motif in the "Shouting in Prison" multiform consists of a mixture of new, situation-specific elements together with some units we have

---

35. The *bila* pairing shows an interesting priority of sound over syntax and morphology; in the opening line of the couplet it means "white," while in the following line it is the feminine past participle of *biti* ("to be").

36. Text 1868 has a variant ending that does not lead into the ban's pledge; such variance is typical of this text.

encountered earlier in the theme's progress. After the banica generally curses
her husband's foolishness in not responding immediately and sensibly to her
urgent demands (μ), she threatens him specifically by noting that he is too
old to father another child and by promising to drown his only son and
thereby snuff out his lineage (ν). In two of the four versions this threat
concludes with a reprise of element η, with the banica demanding the outright
release, ransom, or hanging of the prisoner. The ban's consequent address to
his wife then begins as before (θ) but within a few lines deflects to a new
element (ξ) in which he tells her to visit the prisoner herself and to strike a
bargain for his freedom.

μ	Banica mu 'vako progovara:
	"E ja, bane, lude ti si glave—
	Piješ vina, vazda si ga žedan,
	Hleba jedeš, vazda si ga
	    gladan,
	Glavu imaš, al' pameti nemaš.
		70		μ	Banica mu tiho progovara:
					"Jadan bane, lude ti si glave—
					Piješ vina, vazda si ga žedan,
					Hleba jedeš, vazda si ga
					    gladan,
					Glavu imaš, a pameti nemaš.
						55

ν_1	A tebi je toliko godina, A ti nejmaš od srca evlada Već jedina Providura sina. Ja ću uzet' Providura sina, Pa ću mlada u vodu skočiti, Jedinog ti sina utopiti— Tvoje će se pleme poništiti.	75		ν_1	A tebi je sedandeset ljeta, A meni su trides' i četiri: U glavi ti djavoljega zuba Da prebiješ koru hljeba suha; Ve' ti vjetar na hrbine puha. A ti nemaš od srca evlada Vet' jedinog Nikolicu sina. Ja ću mlada u vodu skočiti, Nejaka ti sina utopiti— Tvoje će se pleme poništiti.	60 65
η	Ja ga daji, ja ga preprodaji, Ja Turčina turi na vješala."	80	η		Ja ga daji, ja ga preprodaji, Ja Turčina turi na vješala, Ja ga spremi na zemlju turćiju."	
θ	A bane joj 'vako progovara: "Gospojice meni mila bila, Ni dosad mi nisi mrska bila.			θ	A bane joj iz grla povika: "Gospojice meni mila bila, Ni dosad mi nisi mrska bila.	70

ξ	Hajde, bona, pogodi se š
	    njime.
	Radi mudro, ne pusti
	    ga ludo;
	
	Pusti njega na zemlju
	    turćiju."
	(*6618*.68-87 [Text A])
		85		ξ	Hajde pa'ni kapku i zindanu.
					
					Pusti njega na zemlju turćiju;
					Radi mudro, ne pusti ga ludo."
					(*1287a*.51-74 [Text C])	

μ   The banica spoke to
     him thus:
  "Eh ban, you're gone in
     the head—
  You drink wine yet thirst
     for it,   70
  You eat bread yet hunger
     for it,
  You have a head but
     no sense.

μ   The banica spoke to him
     softly:
  "Wretched ban, you're gone
     in the head—
  You drink wine yet thirst
     for it,
  You eat bread yet hunger
     for it,
  You have a head but
     no sense.   55

ν_1 And you're so many years old,

ν_1 And you're seventy summers old,
  And I am thirty-four:
  You have not a tooth in
     your head
  To crack the crust of dry
     bread,
  And the wind blows through
     your clothes.   60

  But from your heart's core
     you have no child
  Except your only son
     Providuro.   75
  I will seize your son
     Providuro,
  I will plunge the infant into
     the water,
  Drown your only son—
  Your lineage will come to
     naught.

  But from your heart's core
     you have no child
  Except your only son Nikola.

  I will plunge the infant into
     the water,
  Drown your helpless son—
  Your lineage will come to
     naught.   65

η   Either give in to him,
     ransom him back,   80
  Or send the Turk to the
     gallows."

η   Either give in to him,
     ransom him back,
  Or send the Turk to the
     gallows,
  Or prepare him for Turkish
     lands."[37]

θ   And the ban spoke to
     her thus:
  "My dear white lady,
  Until now you have not been
     hateful.

θ   And the ban called to her
     from his throat:
  "My dear white lady,   70
  Until now you have not been
     hateful.

ξ   Go, lady, and bargain with
     him yourself.   85

ξ   Go down to the prison door.

37. See the discussion of C.30 above.

Work wisely, don't release
  him foolishly;[38]
Release him into Turkish
  lands."

Release him into Turkish
  lands;
Work wisely, don't release
  him foolishly."

μ Banica mu 'vako progovara: 40
"Čuješ, bane, zemlji
  komandare,
Piješ vina, vazda si ga žedan,
Hljeba jedeš, vazda si ga
  gladan,
Glavu imaš, a pameti nemaš.

μ "E ja, bane, zemlji
  komandare,   45

ν_2 Bojiš li se sanka i
  po*t*ljetka?
Misliš svoga podgojiti sina?
A znadeš li, mlad zadarski
  bane,
Da su Turci hatordžije
  v'oma?
A tebi će 'asum ostaviti,   50
Jedinog ti pogubiti sina."

ν_1 A tebi je sedamdeset ljeta,   45

A meni su trides' i četiri:
U glavi ti djavoljega zuba

Da prebiješ koru hljeba suha,

Ve' ti vjetar na hrbine puha.
A ti nemaš od srca evlada,   50
Vet' jedina Nikolicu sina.
Ja ću uzet' tvog Nikolu sina,
Ja ću mlada u vodu skočiti—
Tvoje će se pleme poništiti."

θ A bane joj reče lakrdiju:
"Gospojice meni mila bila,

θ A bane joj sjede besjediti: 55
"Gospojice meni mila bila,

ξ Hajd' pa'ni kapku i
  zindanu;[39]
Pa se, bona, ti pogodi *s*
  njime.   55
Zaišti mu čizmu madžarija,
I goluba bega od Ribnika,
I zekana Tanković Osmana,
I kulaša ličanina Tal*e*,
I dogata buljubaše Muj*e*,   60
Troje toke Velagić Selima,
Dvije puške Mujina Halila.
Kad to primiš obećanje teško,

ξ Hajde, bona, pogodi se
  š njime.

38. That is, "don't let him purchase his freedom cheaply," a reading attested by text B, element ξ.

39. Apocope of the second syllable of *Hajde* yields a nine-syllable line.

Onda njega pušći iz
zindana."

(1868.45-64 [Text B])

Pusti njega na zemlju
turćiju."

(6617.40-58 [Text D])

μ   "Eh, ban, commander of the
territory,   45

ν₂   Do you fear for your dream
and your heir?
Do you intend to raise
your son?
And do you recall, young
Zadar ban,
How very selfish the
Turks are?
They will leave your enemy
alive,   50
And kill your only son."

θ   And the ban spoke a word
to her:
"My dear white lady,

ξ   Go down to the prison door;

Then, lady, bargain with
him yourself.   55
Demand of him a bootful
of coins,
And the bey of Ribnik's
pigeon,

μ   The banica spoke to him
thus: 40
"Listen, ban, commander of
the territory,
You drink wine yet thirst
for it,
You eat bread yet hunger
for it,
You have a head but no
sense.

ν₁   You're seventy summers old,   45

And I am thirty-four:

You have not a tooth in
your head
To crack the crust of dry
bread;
And the wind blows through
your clothes.
But from your heart's core
you have no child   50
Except your only son Nikola.
I will seize your son Nikola,
I will plunge the infant into
the water—
Your lineage will come to
naught."

θ   And the ban began to
address her: 55
"My dear white lady,

ξ   Go, lady, and bargain with
him yourself.

And Tanković Osman's
  hare,[40]
And Tale of the Lika's
  dun horse,
And commander Mujo's
  white steed,   60
Velagić Selim's three silver
  plates,
Mujin Halil's two pistols.
When you secure this firm
  promise,
Then release him from   Release him into Turkish
  prison."   lands."

Of all the elements in motif #4, the initial one (μ) is the most stable phraseologically,[41] and the reasons for that consistency are readily apparent. Apart from the introductory line, which as shown above is but one of the protean forms for the essential idea "she spoke," the stability of the following three to four lines stems from their logical semantic combination and syntactic balance. Texts A and C begin the litany on the ban's foolishness with the straightforward remark on his weak-minded behavior, the variation in phraseology (*E ja/Jadan*) occurring at the opening of the first colon, in the very position where we have come to anticipate variation. The next three lines, shared in all three texts that include μ, are founded on a syntactic pattern that may be construed as [noun] [verb] vazda si ga [adjective], where the object noun, verb, and adjective are closely related semantically, all harmonized by the essential ideas of eating and drinking. The closing verse has a syntactic balance of its own, this time between cola instead of whole lines; in addition, of course, it continues the skein of second person verb forms, matches the verbs *imaš* and *nemaš* in leonine position, and, in texts A and C, forms a ring structure with the opening line (*glave/glavu*). From many different points of view, this element is highly structured internally, and its persistence in familiar phraseological garb is thus to be expected.

Element ν also shows appreciable consistency in verbalization over three of its instances, but for somewhat different reasons. Setting aside momentarily the variant ν_2, note that from about the middle of the element on (*A ti nemaš od srca evlada*), the three other instances correspond virtually word for word, line for line. Variation over this passage takes the form of substitution of particles in the structurally more flexible positions in the line (*Ja/Pa*,

40. Both "pigeon" and "hare" are epithetic names for the fleet horses belonging to these two Turkish heroes.

41. I leave out of account in this estimation the B text, in which the element is for all practical purposes missing, the only vestige being line 45; it may in fact be more accurate to construe this verse as introductory to ν_2, the unusual form of the banica's threat.

A.77/C.63), indefinite versus definite forms for adjectives (*jedina/jedinog*, A.75/C.62), and slightly more involved forms of recombinant diction just before the formula that seals off this unit (A.78 etc.). The earlier section of ν offers a good example of the expansible nature of multiforms and their parts: in text A Mujo covers the idea of the ban's elevated age in a single verse, without specifying either his seventy years or the exact nature of his decrepitude, but in texts C and D the banica's imprecation takes an identical five-line form replete with precise notations of his advancing age, her many fewer years, and his physical demise. These five verses exhibit their own phraseological and acoustic coherence, with the first two lines founded on the same syntactic pattern and the last three sharing a continuous syntax and end-rhyme. The aberrant form of the element, ν_2 (B.46–51), may well be another instance of the price of multiformity. Its opening formula is ubiquitous in the Stolac tradition, being available for application not just in this motif or theme but in a great many narrative situations;[42] given that flexibility and the inexplicit nature of the threat that succeeds it, we may consider ν_2 a manifestation of a momentary lapse in the singer's handling of traditional flexibility.

Next in order come the familiar elements η (texts A and C) and θ, units more generic than many that surround them. We first encountered η in motif #2, where it also formed the coda to the banica's plea to her husband. In two versions of her second and more threatening speech the element recurs, illustrating its traditional adaptability in contrast to the majority of units that are tied to a particular narrative context. Even less situation-specific is element θ, the ban's formal opening address to his wife. Indeed, an argument could be made for considering θ a floating phrase of general meaning and usefulness, not a narrative entity per se, which is available for use as a highly generic and ornamental opening to many sorts of speeches. I have here chosen to treat it as an element in order to simplify description, but we should keep in mind that such lines of address, or equally the introductory verses mentioned above, represent the kind of non-specific traditional phrase that, like the boundary lines, allow the *guslar* passage between more focused narrative units. Their presence at this point in the motif illustrates that the makeup of a motif and thus of a theme depends on a combination of compositionally heterogeneous elements: some tightly organized and bound (μ), some expansible (ν), and some of generic application (η, θ).

After addressing his wife, the elderly ban—now thoroughly apprised of the danger awaiting should he continue to refuse to take steps to silence the

---

42. In this same song, for example, a formulaic variant of this line (*Pobojat' se sanka i potljetka*, line 1939) is used by General Pero as he attempts to persuade the ban of Janok to follow his plan for deceiving the Turks. The two narrative situations are similar enough to suggest what Mujo calls a "skipping over" from one to the next (for further discussion, see chapter 10).

shouting Turk—suggests that she conduct the bargaining. This element, ξ, which most resembles ν_1 in its degree and kind of verbal correspondence from instance to instance, also proves expansible. In text B Mujo begins with two phrases that have verbatim or near equivalents in the other texts, but then opens up the passage to what Lord and others have called ornamentation. The essential idea of ξ—that of sending the banica to bargain with the captive—is expressed even in the tersest version of this element, and so there is no purely compositional reason to include here the list of demands that the ban instructs his wife to present as conditions for the prisoner's release. But the singer does include the demands, and the reason is near at hand: in the next theme, "Bargaining," the banica will as part of the theme's narrative logic actually present those very demands to the Turkish captive, and he will have to promise to fulfill them before he can gain his freedom.[43] By association with that part of the story-pattern—that is, under the influence of the multiformity that pervades every level of the traditional idiom—Mujo puts a version of those demands into the ban's cautionary words to his wife.[44] The associative nature of traditional thematics promotes this sort of paratactic connection; in this particular case, the multiform "works" logically and does not disturb the flow of the narrative.

As the ban relinquishes control of the captive's fate to his wife, motif #4 and the Shouting in Prison theme draw to a close. Others may choose to place the point of thematic division elsewhere, but I would defend my choice on two grounds. First, as mentioned above, this study attempts a descriptive analysis; thus, some of the distinctions it makes are formulated both because the units seem to divide and combine in certain ways and because marking those passages as units facilitates the comparison of texts and the consequent establishment of a narrative morphology. The ontology of narrative units is in any case a vexed question: do they exist in the singer's mind as building blocks, or are they impositions we make on the texts in order to understand them? I believe we can see from the foregoing analysis that the text depends for its articulation on patterns that are undeniably present both in the tradition and in each of its realizations in performance. At the same time, we must be aware that, in the terminology employed by Dan Ben-Amos (1969), whatever categories we denominate must by definition be "analytic" rather than "ethnic." No singer ever pondered the morphology of themes, motifs, and elements; were he able to do so with any of the philological rigor we espouse, he would have removed himself from the oral tradition and lost the ability

43. Sometimes these demands include a promise to return to his imprisonment after he visits his homeland and mother and/or wife. See the examples of Return multiforms below in chapter 10.

44. Another association possibly promoting this transference from one theme to another is that of the ban and the bargaining procedure. In many Stolac Return Songs, such as those of Ibro Bašić examined below, it is the ban himself who enters the prison and presents a list of demands to the captive.

to sing. Yet even though categories and discriminations of pattern must to an extent be *our* assessment of thematic structure rather than the will o' the wisp itself, we can illuminate the dynamics of tradition by proceeding as faithfully as possible in matching our scholarly apparatus to the material we wish to explicate.

Second, and more specifically, there exists hard textual evidence to place a thematic boundary after the ban's abdication of personal responsibility for the Turkish prisoner. This evidence takes the form of *boundary lines*, those common and generic verses of nearly universal applicability that promote transition between units in sequence. Here are the lines that follow motif #4 in each of the four versions:

Kad banica riječ razumila,	Kad banica riječ razumila,
	O' tavnice ključe prifatila,
Ona pade kapku i zindanu.	O' tavnice kapak podignula.
Kapak diže, pa Aliju viče.	Kapak diže, pa Aliju viče.
Alija se sa tavnice javlja.	Alija se sa tavnice javlja.
(*6618*.88-91 [Text A])	(1287a.75-79 [Text C])
When the banica understood his words,[45]	When the banica understood his words,
	She took the keys to the prison,
She went down to the prison door.	She raised the door of the prison,
She raised the door, then called for Alija;	She raised the door, then called for Alija;
Alija called back from the prison.	Alija called back from the prison.
Tad banica riječ otkitila.[46]	Kad banica riječ razumila,
Ona pade kapku i zindanu.	Ona pade kapku i zindanu.
Kapak diže, pa Aliju viče.	Kapak diže, pa Aliju viče.
Alija se sa tamnice javlja.	Alija se sa tavnice javlja.
(1868.65-68 [Text B])	(*6617*.59-62 [Text D])
Then the banica responded to his words,	When the banica understood his words,
She went down to the prison door.	She went down to the prison door.
She raised the door, then called for Alija.	She raised the door, then called for Alija.
Alija called back from the prison.	Alija called back from the prison.

In each case, and with virtually the same formulas, the locus of the song's events passes from the ban's chamber to the prison, and the involved characters become not the ban and his wife but the banica and the Turkish prisoner. In three of the four instances we can trace the transition to what was called above a *position-change* line: *Ona pade kapku i zindanu*. Although the position change perhaps more often employs systems like the one examined above in

---

45. Literally, "understood his word," with *riječ* in the singular denoting an utterance; on the meaning of *riječ* (or *reč*), see chapter 2.

46. Normally this verb, *otkititi*, is used to describe the process of answering a letter with a *kićeno pismo*, an ornamented epistle. Here the term is pressed into service to express a response to a speech.

motif #2, this too is a frequent way of expressing the same idea. In text C the transition remains implicit, but the action still guides us in perceiving a shift from one multiform to the next. The actual "Bargaining" can now begin, with the Turk and the banica at center stage.

As an interim summary of our findings on thematic structure, four general points should be stressed. First, themes have logical subdivisions that remain under the aegis of a unifying narrative idea but that also, like themes themselves, have more or less independent lives of their own. For the sake of descriptive analysis I have formulated a hierarchy of *motifs*, and of *elements* that make up those motifs. Some of the elements studied were found to be generic and therefore mobile, while others proved stationary and more obviously tied to a specific narrative moment or situation. The relationships among subunits, in short, turn out to be many and various, and it would be reductive to attempt a blanket statement on thematic substructure. Simply put, motifs and elements in a given theme are to an extent comparable with their counterparts in other multiforms but are to a greater degree idiosyncratic.

Likewise, and this is the second point, the density of *verbal correspondence* among instances of Shouting in Prison drawn from Kukuruzović's song-texts is, although generally high, quite uneven. Phraseological consistency may be absolute in certain spots and negligible or even absent in others, depending in large part on the patterns and balances within elements and lines. Some of the stability at the level of diction is due to phonological and formulaic structure (and ultimately, of course, to traditional rules); some is attributable to thematic structure, in the sense that the action of the narrative can contribute to holding some verses in a kind of traditional suspension, keeping them immune from changes that might otherwise occur. This verbal correspondence takes precisely the tradition-dependent shape to be expected on the basis of our study of formulaic phraseology in chapter 5—cola, whole verses, and occasional tightly bound runs of lines. Moreover, the patterns of phraseological variation observed in comparing instances of multiforms are exactly those predicted by our examination of *deseterac* prosody in chapter 3. A third and related point is that a highly formulaic group of verses that we have called *boundary lines* accomplish transitions between units as well as mediate between the theme as part of a larger narrative organization on the one hand and as an independent, integral unit on the other.

Fourth—and this observation really amounts to the sum of the preceding three—thematic structure has shown itself to be an active, dynamic, associative, and paratactic force that binds motifs and elements into an inorganically unified whole. As I trust the example of Kukuruzović's Shouting in Prison scene has illustrated, the narrative multiform cannot be faithfully represented as a bound synchronic whole with a neat and efficient assemblage of working parts. To be sure, its elements and motifs cooperate in the shared expression of its central action, but they are not simply equivalent bits of information that add up to a data base for the epic tradition. To an extent each unit is manifestly itself as well as a member of the narrative entourage, and each has its own characteristics of order, associated diction, and mobility or localization. To insist on a uniform texture for thematic structure is to construct an unrealistic model, one that is untrue to the multiformity of oral tradition and reductive of its art. Thematic structure means a complex aggregate of units and phraseology in the service of a traditional idea, and its shape-shifting form extends from the language in which it is expressed to the sequence of actions that defines its role in oral epic tradition.

From Idiolect to Dialect: The Individual Singer's Community

What we have considered in the four Shouting in Prison instances in the songs of Mujo Kukuruzović is a set of features that characterize an exemplary theme as it takes shape in different texts of a single song-type by one *guslar*. This version of the multiform may thus be construed as an example of traditional *idiolect*, that is, of the range of multiformity found in the practice of one singer. In order to better understand the tradition as a whole, I shall now turn from the features of idiolect to the multiformity observable in the larger Stolac tradition of singing—in other words, to the *dialect* of thematic composition in this district. Just as dialectologists intent on recording lexical and phonological habits expect and report more variance among a geographically designated group of speakers than in the personal speech of a single informant, we may anticipate more variation as we move from singer to singer than was evident in the equivalent passages from Kukuruzović's texts. At the same time, however, there should remain distinct regional commonplaces, genetic similarities in the structural or phraseological physiognomy of the theme. Since this analysis is intended to uncover basic principles and not to establish a full thematic morphology, and also since the space for documentation is limited, I shall confine the comparison to three occurrences of Shouting in Prison as sung or dictated by Ibro Bašić in three texts of his Return Song *Alagić Alija and Velagić Selim* (1283, *291b*, and *6597*; hereafter *AAVS*).

MOTIF #1

As above, I present the theme by subunits; instances of its first motif are as shown in figure 9. With these three versions of Bašić's idiolectal theme we begin to gain a perspective on the nature of the dialectal multiform. In the case of this particular song, Shouting in Prison does not start the action; rather it occurs well into the progress of the story, after one prisoner, Velagić Selim (VS), has heard from a recently captured Turk, Alagić Alija (AA), how enemies have raided VS's homeland of Udbina, threatening his residence, possessions, and family. Indeed, the ban has already paid the prisoners an earlier visit in an effort to extort from them the usual unreasonable agreements in exchange for their release. The effort has been in vain, however, and, just as we reach the quoted passages and the onset of the theme, the captor has angrily departed the prison, hurling back a promise to "grind their bones" —the very promise identified above as element λ. The narrative context surrounding these three occurrences of the theme is thus quite different from that in which the examples from Kukuruzović are embedded: one bargaining session has already taken place, and the banica and her discomforted child have not yet figured in the action.

Nonetheless, after the *boundary lines* at the head of the quoted passages, which include agent lines (e.g., 1283.323), position changes (6597.418), and diurnal rhythm lines (*291b*.365), Ibro does enter on his own idiolectal version of Shouting in Prison, and it follows in its general outlines the multiform employed by Kukuruzović. The first divergence is in the order and occurrence of elements: the only instance of the β unit surfaces in text 1283, where it takes the form β_2[47] and precedes rather than follows the statement or argument a. But the boundary lines on either side of β argue for its independence as a unit, and if we realize that a and γ in the Kukuruzović texts can be understood as a single element split (or ornamented) by β, then we can start to assess the permutations ascribable to multiformity and see how the two singers are really using the same theme. To be sure, each is employing an idiolectal variant of the first motif of Shouting in Prison, but it is the kind of variance one expects among dialect samples. To recapitulate, what seems in the Kukuruzović passages to be an a-β-γ progression may, on the comparative evidence of the Bašić material, be reconstrued as a-β-a. How we actually label the subunits is less important than the fair representation of the recombinative nature of thematic structure.

As for the question of verbal correspondence, the Bašić texts exhibit a good deal more flexibility in phraseology than does the set of examples from Kukuruzović in relation to addition, substitution, and outright omission as well as formulaic morphology. Among the kinds of phraseological flexibility observed are terracing (1283.332-33), colon-initial variation (*Neko cmili/A sve cmili*, 1283.332/*291b*.369), and the other techniques typical of oral epic composition in the *deseterac*.

But in addition to providing another view of one singer's compositional habits, the Bašić examples also show by comparison how widely different the verbal components of different singers' themes can be. Although essential ideas may match rather closely at points, we find not one formula shared between the two groups of texts over this first motif: both singers convey the basic information "the Turk shouted," emphasizing in the process how serious a problem the noise had become,[48] and yet not a single line is common to their

---

47. Cf. 1287a.14–18.

48. The emphasis is expressed in two different ways. Kukuruzović notes in each case the length of the period during which the prisoner shouted (see note 25 above), while Bašić closes all three versions of the a element with a verse on the captive's setting the whole city of Zadar into confusion.

Figure 9. Motif #1, *AAVS* (Ibro Bašić)

A da vidiš od Zadarja bana—
Na tavnici kapak priklopijo.
Ode bane na bijelu kulu.   325
Vid' Alije, žalosna mu majka—

β   Jergo nije lasno tavnovati,
Jergo voda medju pleći tuče.
Braćo moja, ženženje jada!

Sunce žarko za planinu zadje.   330
Kad je bilo noći od ponoći,

α   Neko cmili u tavnici tavnoj,
U tavnici zadranina bana.
To ne čuje od Zadarja bane,
Vet' gospoja zadranina bana.   335
Vas je Zadar zabun' učinijo.

(1283.323—36)

Na tamnici kapak priklopijo.

A da vidiš, age moje drage—
A u tome kara akšam sidje.   365

A da vidiš Velagić Selima—
A da vidiš Velagić Selima—
A da vidiš banice vlahinje—

α   A sve cmili sužanj u tamnici.
jA kako je ljuto procmilijo!   370

Vas je Zadar zabun' učinijo.

(291b.363—71)

A da vidiš od Zadarja bana—
A priklopi kapak na tamnici.
Eto njega na bijelu kulu.

A u tome kara akšam sidje.

A da vidiš, djeco moja draga—   420
Vidi gospoje banice mlade—[1]
Čudo je se, brate, opazila:

α   A pocmilje nešto u tamnici.
Kako cmili sužanj u tamnici!

Vas je Zadar zabun' učinijo.   425

(6597.416—25)

1. This line has eleven syllables because of a five-syllable first colon. Ibro makes the second colon metrical by stretching *banice* to *bani-i-ce* with the insertion of a glottal stop, a very common device in his sung texts. Cf. G. Edwards 1971, 104: "Hesiod is not averse to eking out a word artificially with an extra syllable."

But you should have seen Zadar ban—
He fastened the prison door.   325
The ban went to the white tower.
See Alija, his mother would be sad—

β   Because it is not easy to be imprisoned,
Because water struck between
   his shoulders.
Oh my brothers, the burning sorrows!

330
The bright sun sank behind the
   mountain.
When it was midnight,

α   Someone shouted in the dark prison,
In Zadar ban's prison.
The ban of Zadar did not hear it,
335
But the ban of Zadar's lady did.
[The prisoner] had all Zadar in
   confusion.

He fastened the prison door.

But you should have seen, my
   dear agas—
And then dark evening descended.   365

But you should have seen Velagić Selim—
But you should have seen Velagić Selim—
But you should have seen the
   Vlah banica—

α   And the captive shouted out in prison.
Oh how hysterically he began to   370
   shout!

He had all Zadar in confusion.

But you should have seen Zadar ban—
He fastened the prison door.
Then he went to the white tower.

And then dark evening descended.

But you should have seen, my
   dear children—
See the young lady banica—
She perceived a wonder, brothers: 420

δ   And something shouted in prison.
How the captive shouted in prison!

He had all Zadar in confusion.   425

separate renderings. This, then, is a first approximation of the idiolectal and dialectal forms of a theme; even in the face of relatively consistent substructure, the verbal correspondence that typifies one singer's handling of a theme diminishes markedly as one enlarges the textual sample from individual to area or local tradition. Clearly, the criteria for defining thematic structure must therefore vary as we change our focus from idiolect to dialect.

MOTIF #2

Moving on to the second motif in Bašić's versions, we find more evidence for the same conclusions (figure 10). Once again the elemental structure compares relatively closely with that underlying the four instances in Kukuruzović's texts: after the boundary verses, Ibro places, in order, a statement of the banica's problem (δ), her complaint to her husband (ϵ), and in two cases her demand for some ameliorative action (η).[49] Against this background of similarity we do, however, discern some differences. First, there is no true ζ element, that is, no true ornamental passage to develop the ideas of units δ and ϵ; since ornamental elements are by nature ubiquitous, generic, and optional, this represents no real omission but simply compositional expedience and personal habit. Second, as in general with Bašić's songs, many more boundary lines are present, setting off integral narrative units and furnishing transitions from one to the next. It is as if these verses serve for Bašić to mitigate the paratactic relationship of themes and thematic subdivisions; their frequent use amounts to a stylistic trademark, an idiolectal trait.

A third difference, or set of differences, also constitutes a stylistic idiosyncrasy. As with motif #1, the phraseology with which the singer verbalizes these thematic ideas varies more among parallel passages than does Kukuruzović's diction. We thus have two readings on verbal correspondence from instance to instance in the repertoire of a single singer; both show a number of repeated cola, verses, and runs, but the Bašić texts are more prone to addition, omission, and formulaic remaking. In neither case does one doubt the existence of the kind of theme described by Lord, for we have no shortage of the repeated words, lines, and parts of lines that he demands as one aspect of thematic structure. But neither could we apply the strictures of one poet's compositional style to that of the other. Fourth, and complementarily, verbal correspondence among occurrences is not of uniform density throughout the motif and theme; just as with Kukuruzović's texts, certain elements or even parts of elements are more stable than others. Fifth, as would be expected, Bašić and Kukuruzović employ widely variant diction in expressing the elements in motif #2. In part because he concentrates on the problem of nursing the frightened infant, Bašić uses a personalized mode of expression to render the same general ideas.

---

49. In the third case (291b), the η element is delayed until motif #3, where it also occurs in Kukuruzović's songs (customarily in its second usage within the theme).

Figure 10. Motif #2, *AAVS* (Ibro Bašić)

δ Ima ona malog Marijana;

Marijana zabun' učinijo,
Marijan' se strašno prepanuo.

Sve ga ćeši banova gospoja,   340
Ćeši njega medom i šećerom,

Al' se ne da djete učešiti.

Pa banici jadom ujadilo.

Kad se svanu i ogranu sunce,
A da vidiš banice gospoje—   345
Dje zavika banu u odaji:

"Dobro jutro, mladi gospodare."

"Da si zdravo, vjerna moja ljubo.

Što ti tako nevesela, ljuba?"

A da vidiš pa banova sina—

δ Marijana od godinu dana.

A jes' djete, brate, ustrašeno.

Ćešila ga mila svoja majka,   375
A ćeši ga medom i šećerom,
A ćeši ga sa grla djerdana,
Ćešila sa grla djerdana.[1]

Ne da joj se učešiti djete,
Vet' se djete prepanulo, brate.   380

Kad se svanu i ogranu sunce,
Vid' gospoje pa banice, brate—[2]
Dje eto je banu u odaju.

ε Pa mu 'vako dobro jutro viknu,
A bane joj nazdravijo zdravljem: 385
"Da si zdravo, mlada gospojice."
A besjedi od Zadarja bane:
"Što to jesi meni uranila?"

Vidi, brate, pa banice mlade—

δ Ona ima sina Marijana,
Njemu ima četiri godine.

Pa se djete malo usplašilo.
A da vidiš pa gospodje mlade—   430

Sve ga ćeši medom i šećerom,

I, moj' brate, sisom iz njedara.
A ne da se mali Marijane,
Jer se djete, brate, usplašilo,
Usplašilo sužnja nevoljnika.   435

Kad se svanu i ogranu sunce,
A da vidiš gospoje banice—
Dje eto je banu u odaju,
Ona nosi malog Marijana.

ε Pa evako banu besjeđaše: 440
"Dobro jutro, od Zadarja bane."

Figure 10 (*continued*)

"Ču li mene, od Zadarja bane,   350
Kakva jesi sužnja ufatijo?
Vas je Zadar zabun' učinijo,
A cmiljeći u tešku zindanu.
Nikad mira ja imala njesam,[3]
Nisam mogla saspa't' u odaji;   355
Prep'o ti je sina Marijane.

η   Gospodare od Zadarja bane,
Ja ga smiči, ja ga preprodaji,
Ja ga spremi na svoju Krajinu,
Jer se, bane, djete prepanulo."   360
                    (1283.337–60)

"Ču li mene, od Zadarja bane,
Kakva jesi sužnja ufatijo?   390
Noćas ti je zabun' učinijo;

Prep'o ti je malog Marijana,

Vas je Zadar zabun' učinijo.
Ćešila ga medom i šećerom,
A najpošlje sa grla djerdana."   395
                    (291b.372–95)

Kakva jesi sužnja ufatijo?
Pa je Zadar zabun' učinijo;

A vidiš li malog Marijana—
Pa se mali jes' prepanuo.[4]   445

Sve ga ćesila medom i šećerom,[5]
I najpošlje sa grla djerdana.
Pa se ne da učesiti, bogme.

η   O ču li me, od Zadarja bane,
Ja ga smiči, ja ga preprodaji,   450
Ja, bane, spremaj na Krajinu."
                    (6597.426–51)

1. Colon 1 is short one syllable; on the model of 291b.375, we may assume that the "missing" element is the object pronoun *ga*.
2. An example of Ibro's common strategy of using a direct address to his audience (*brate*) to eke out the syllables of his line.
3. I have taken the transcript reading *ima* as lapsus calami and restored the feminine inflection to *imala*.
4. A five-syllable second hemistich produces a short line, but one which could be emended logically by expanding *jes'* to its full form, *jeste*. The use of *jeste* resembles that of *brate* in 291b.382 and elsewhere.
5. A five-syllable initial colon makes for a long line; cf. 6597.431.

δ She had little Marijane;

[The prisoner] had Marijane in confusion,

Marijane was terribly frightened.

The ban's lady tried to comfort him, 340

Comforted him with honey and sugar,

But the child could not be comforted.

So he caused the banica untold misery.

But you should have seen the ban's son—

δ The year-old Marijane.

The child was surely frightened, brothers.

His dear mother comforted him, 375

Comforted him with honey and sugar,

And comforted him with her necklace,

Comforted with her necklace.

She could not comfort the child,

For the child was frightened, brothers. 380

See, brothers, the young banica—

δ She had her son Marijane,

He was four years old.

Then the child was a little frightened.

But you should have seen the young lady— 430

She comforted him with honey and sugar,

And, my brothers, with milk from her breast.

But little Marijane would not [nurse],

Because the child was frightened, brothers,

Frightened of the unwilling captive. 435

Figure 10 (*continued*)

When the sun had dawned and
   risen,
You should have seen the lady
   banica—
Well, she began to speak in the
   ban's chamber:

ε "Good morning, young master."

"Your health, my truelove.

Why are you so unhappy, love?"

"Hear me, ban of Zadar,
What sort of prisoner have you
   captured?
He had all Zadar in confusion,

345

350

When the sun had dawned and
   risen,
See the lady banica, brothers—

Well, she went to the ban's
   chamber.

ε Then she called good morning
      to him,
And the ban wished her good
      health:
"Your health, young lady."
And the ban of Zadar addressed
      her:
"Why have you come to me
      so early?"
"Hear me, ban of Zadar,
What sort of prisoner have you
      captured?
Last night he had you in
      confusion;

385

390

When the sun had dawned and
   risen,
You should have seen the lady
   banica—
Well, she went to the ban's
   chamber,
She bore young Marijane.

ε Then she addressed the ban thus: 440
"Good morning, ban of Zadar.

What sort of prisoner have you
   captured?
Then he had all Zadar in
   confusion;

With his shouting in the
　terrible prison.
I have not had a moment's
　peace,
Nor could I sleep in my
　chamber;　　　　　　355

He frightened your son Marijane.

η　Oh master, ban of Zadar,
Either remove him, or ransom him,

Or prepare him for his Krajina,

Because, ban, your son is
　frightened."　　　　　360

He frightened your little
　Marijane.

He had all·Zadar in confusion.
I comforted [the child] with
　honey and sugar,
And finally with my necklace."　　395

But you should have seen little
　Marijane—
The little one was surely
　frightened.　　　　　445

I tried to comfort him with honey
　and sugar,
And finally with my necklace.
But he could not be comforted,
　by God.

η　Oh hear me, ban of Zadar,
Either remove him, or ransom
　him,　　　　　　　　450

Or prepare him, ban, for the
　Krajina."

While there is a bit more than in motif #1 to cite as phraseology common to the two singers' texts,[50] still the *guslari* diverge greatly at the level of phraseology, even though they once again converge in respect to narrative pattern.

Because the *AAVS* begins, as indicated above, with a long flashback on the condition of VS's homeland and relatives and with the ban's initial unsuccessful attempt at bargaining with his Turkish prisoners, there is no reason for the ban to decry his wife's protestations and insist on AA's and VS's continuing incarceration without appeal. What is more, their captor has just exited the cell in a fury over their recalcitrance in granting him all of the outrageous conditions he has placed on their release; indeed, he has only a few lines earlier expressed that anger in the "grinding the bones" element (λ) employed by Kukuruzović as part of motif #3. From a traditional point of view, then, motif #3—or its equivalent—has already occurred once Bašić begins the Shouting in Prison theme in the *AAVS*; to repeat it here, between motifs #2 and #4 in Bašić's version of the multiform, would be to disrupt the narrative flow of the story and to pervert its compositional structure. To put the same matter differently, the λ element is another example of a mobile, generic unit that can answer a number of purposes, one that can participate in different ways in different narrative designs. That we do not find the unit in this particular theme in the *AAVS* simply illustrates the protean nature of thematic structure: its fabric of motifs and elements is seldom so impervious to change as to fail to adapt to the demands of divergent story-patterns. Multiformity means the potential for adaptation, and thematic structure depends in definite, observed ways on that multiformity.

MOTIF #4

With the fourth motif we reach the end of Shouting in Prison in these three texts, the actual coda once again marked by boundary lines and followed by the "Bargaining for Release" theme, but this time with the ban rather than his wife as the bargaining agent. (There is no occurrence in 1283.361ff.)

		v "Ako nećeš, od Zadarja bane,
v "A tako mi Boga gospodara,		A tako mi Boga jedinoga,
		Ja ću bacit' malog Marijana,
Bacićú ga niz bijelu kulu;		Bacićú ga niz bijelu kulu; 455
Nek ti slomi ja nogu ja ruku.		Nek ti slomi i nogu i ruku.
Više jesi ostarijo, bane,		Jesi, bane, više ostarijo,

---

50. We may compare, for example, "Ja ga smiči, ja ga preprodaji, / Ja ga spremi na svoju Krajinu" (1283.58–59) with Kukuruzović's "Ja ga daji, ja ga preprodaji, / Ja ga pusti na zemlju turčiju" (1287a.29–30). It may well be that these particular phrases, and others like them, exhibit a degree of stability because of the syntactic balance and sound-patterning evident in their structure.

Govno ćeš ga drugog
   načiniti.   400

Govno ćeš ga drugo'
   načiniti."

            (*6597*.452–58)

η Ve' ču li me, o' Zadarja
    bane,
  Onog sužnja iz tamnice
    tamne—
  Ja ga smiči, ja ga preprodaji,
  Ja ga spremaj na svoju
    Krajinu."

        (*291b*.396–404)

ν "I swear by the master God

  I will cast him down from
    the white tower,
  Let him break either arm
    or leg.
  You have aged too much,
    ban,
  You won't ever father
    another child.   400

ν "If you will not, ban of
    Zadar,
  I swear by the one God
  I will cast young Marijane,
  I will cast him down from
    the white tower,   455
  Let him break both arm
    and leg.
  You have aged too much,
    ban,
  You won't ever father
    another child."

η But hear me, ban of Zadar,
  This captive from the
    dark prison—
  Either remove him, or
    ransom him,
  Or prepare him for his
    Krajina."

Within this motif, essentially an intensification of the banica's complaint, we again encounter the ν element, the threat to kill the infant, and in one instance the η closure used consistently in Kukuruzović's versions. But although these features are shared by the two singers in their idiolectal forms of motif #4, we should note the omission of elements μ and ξ in the Bašić passages, as well as the general lack of verbal correspondence between the two sets of occurrences. Element μ seems to be a stylistic feature of Kukuruzović's texts; strictly speaking, it is not absolutely necessary to the action of the motif and theme, so we may expect its absence in the repertoires of this or that *guslar*. Element ξ, in contrast, depends on the story-pattern for its raison d'être: if the ban himself goes to conduct the bargaining, he obviously will not need to send his wife. The essential ideas of the motif are thus preserved, as Bašić, employing his own idiolectal language and elemental structure, tailors the traditional action of the unit to its place in the story at hand, which is also the Return Song at large.

From Dialect to Language: The Stolac singers and the Epic Tradition

The foregoing examples from the song-texts of Mujo Kukuruzović and Ibro Bašić illustrate the nature and extent of multiformity in a theme shared by two *guslari* from the same local tradition. Let us now broaden the scope of examination once more by comparing a final instance of Shouting in Prison from outside the Stolac region, one from a version of the *Ropstvo Djulić Ibrahima* (*Captivity of Djulić Ibrahim*) by Salih Ugljanin, also a Return Song and text no. 4 in the second volume of *Serbo-Croatian Heroic Songs*.[51] As with Bašić's *AAVS*, the theme occurs well into the story, after a conversation with the servant Rako on the devastation in Djulić's homeland, a flashback on his capture, and the ban's curse have set the scene for his screaming out in misery. There is thus reason to expect a motif sequence not unlike that which Bašić employed, that is, the succession of motifs #1, #2, and #4, with the narrative necessity for #3—the ban's adamant refusal to do anything about the captive's shouting—having been eliminated.

1-α/γ	Ljuto Djulić pisnu ju zindanu.	Djulić screamed hysterically in prison.	
	Sve se kula sa temelja ljulja.	The whole tower rocked on its foundations.	
2-δ	Pisnu banu dva sina bliznaka;	The ban's twin sons cried out;	
	Djeci mu je stravu naturijo.	He had struck terror into the children.	
	Banica hi hrani ju odaju;	The banica was nursing them in her chamber;	230
	Drži decu te hi zataškava:	She held the children and quieted them:	
	"Stan'te, deco, dva sina bliznaka!	"Quiet, children, my twin sons!	
	Eto Turčin vrišti ju zindanu."	That is a Turk screaming in prison."	
	On Djulić sad mišljaš' u zindanu,	Djulić thought now in the prison,	
	Djulić mljaše, niko ne čujaše;	Djulić thought that no one heard;	235

51. Cf. song no. 6 in *SCHS*, another version of the same tale, lines 230–68. I have examined only a single version here because the immediate purpose is to illustrate some parameters of multiformity at the level of pantraditional "language" rather than to offer more examples of idiolectal variation. The translation here is based on that of Lord (*SCHS* 1:93), with a few concessions to formulaic agreement with my translations of earlier passages.

No plaćuju dva sina bliznaka,	But the twin sons cried,
Pa banica decu *j*ostavila.	And then the banica left the children.
Dodje k banu *j*u šikli *j*odaju,	She went to the ban in his ornate chamber,
A kod bana do tri djenerala,	And with the ban were three generals,
A trideset i dva kapetana,	And thirty-two captains, 240
A vojvoda dvades i dva više.	And twenty-two dukes.

2-ε

Ona dodje pa *h*im pomoj dade,	She entered and gave them greeting,
I svi jojzi zdravljem prifatili.	And all returned it to her.
Ta put reće baneva banica:	Then the ban's wife said:
"Dobro jutro, ni će dobro biti!	"Good morning, but it will not be good! 245
Jadan bane sa Zadara grada,	Oh unfortunate ban of the city of Zadar,
Što zatvori Turke *j*u zindanu?	Why did you lock up the Turks in prison?
Ima doba dvanajes godina	For a period of twelve years
Kako lježu ljedenoj tamnici,	They have lain in the cold prison,
Nikad nijesu niko procviljeli,	And not one has ever screamed, 250
Ni se čuju za života svoga.	Nor have they made any sound they were alive.
Ljuto cvilji Djulić bajraktare,	Now Djulić the standard-bearer screams hysterically,
Ljuto cvilji, sve tamnica vrišti,	Screams hysterically, the whole prison resounds,
Sve se kula sa temelja ljulja.	The whole tower rocks on its foundations.

3-ν

Deci mi je stravu naturijo.	He has struck terror into my children. 255
Dece dvoje pofata groznica;	A fever seized both children;
*j*Od groznice more bit' žutica.	Jaundice can develop from fever.
S dece dvoje hajra bit' ne more.	This bodes ill for the two boys.

2/4-η

Kupi, bane, ključe *j*od zindana.	Oh ban, gather up the keys to the prison.
Sljegni brže ljedenu zindanu,	Go quickly to the cold prison, 260

Pa ti vikni Djulić bajraktara,	Then call out to Djulić the standard-bearer,
Koja mu je goljema nevolja.	And ask him what his great sorrow is.
Jalj' ga pušći, jalj' ga posijeći;	Either release him or behead him;
Jedan derman učini Djuliću.	Dispose of Djulić in some way.
Kad je poćeo vriskat' po zindanu,	Since he has begun to cry out in prison, 265
Djecu će mi pamet ostaviti."	The children will lose their minds."

(*SCHS* 2, no. 4.226–66)

In the opening two lines we recognize the essential ideas of elements α, the argument of the theme, and γ, the notation on the seriousness or intensity of the situation. Both units are much abbreviated in comparison to their counterparts in the Kukuruzović material, and we can recognize no formulaic correspondence with the other α and γ elements,[52] but still the narrative logic inherent in the two units and the first motif is preserved and functional. Likewise, Ugljanin follows these three lines with element δ, the onset of motif #2 that furnishes a statement of the cause for the banica's sadness: once again, the Turk's noise has frightened her progeny, this time twin sons instead of the single infant of the other versions. Ugljanin's text is at this point more elaborate than any of those treated above; it includes a full description of not only the boys' inability to eat but also their mother's attempt to soothe them, a palliative entirely absent from the other versions. And as we would by now expect, there exists no verbal correspondence between this instance of the motif and the other passages.

After the boundary lines—at this particular juncture a position change (238) and some ornamentation (239-41)—Salih proceeds to element ε, the banica's complaint to her husband. The verses of formal greeting are familiar (cf. text 1868), and certain features, such as her inquiry as to what sort of Turk the ban has imprisoned, also recall similar ideas in earlier examples, but in general the verbal correspondence with other instances is negligible. After the closure of another ring at lines 252-54 (echoing 226-27), we come upon a kind of ν element from motif #3. True enough, it does not entail the banica's direct threat to drown the infant(s) and end her husband's lineage, but it does entail the indirect threat of fever, jaundice, and eventual death, and in bringing out that danger explicitly it corresponds in principle to the more straightforward challenge.[53] Ugljanin's version of Shouting in Prison

52. Even the verb used to denote shouting is different: a form of *pisnuti* rather than of *cmiliti*.

53. From the perspective of the continuing narrative, the threat of sickness and death is just as effective as that of child murder: the ban is forced to make arrangements to ameliorate the situation.

then closes with an elaborate rendering of the η element found at the close of motifs #2 and/or #4, with the alternative—this time the release, beheading, or some other disposal of the offensive Turk—surrounded by directions on going to the jail and calling to the prisoner, and also by yet another annular reference to his screaming as the source of the problem. In general, these last two elements recall some of the ideas presented in versions from Kukuruzović and Bašić but use virtually none of the same phraseology to express them.

CONCLUSION

As we have discovered in earlier chapters with regard to both traditional phraseology and the ancient Greek typical scene, thematic structure in the Serbo-Croatian Return Song cannot fairly be reduced to a single, one-dimensional commonplace but must be appreciated as a spectrum of traditional forms. The instance of Ibro Bašić's pause for rest and subsequent continuance of his song from a traditionally logical spot illustrated the compositional importance of the narrative unit for his performance. Analysis of such units in terms of constituent motifs and elements established the internal texture of variation within limits that is so typical of the *guslar*'s craft. In addition to this *idiolectal* level of the Shouting in Prison theme, examples drawn from Bašić and Mujo Kukuruzović, his fellow participant in the local tradition of Stolac, showed how there also exists a *dialectal* level for narrative multiformity. With respect to the individual, we found that the ideational structure of the theme remained largely constant, with some concessions to the specific story situation, but that verbal correspondence varied in kind and density from one section to the next. Generalizations proved less trustworthy at the dialect level, with idiosyncratic variance making structural differences more frequent (especially in the case of non-essential motifs or elements) and phraseological correspondence much less likely. This increasing divergence reached its apex at the pantraditional level of *language*: while the same general outline and most important events also characterize the Shouting in Prison theme in the Return Song by Salih Ugljanin from the Novi Pazar district, that passage shares almost no diction with the examples from Stolac.

What these findings indicate, then, is the impossibility of capturing the protean reality of thematic structure in the net of a single model or definition. Rather, we must be aware that themes and their parts, although held in suspension by the recurrent patterns of story that comprise the epic tradition, are, as Lord has emphasized, malleable and multiform. As we look past the foreground of idiolect and dialect toward the deeper background of pantraditional narrative language, the theme appears to exist most essentially in its grouping of ideas—that is, in its association of events to form a coherent, generic whole. This traditional narrative "word," as it were, can be spoken in one's own idiolect, in which case it will customarily sound quite similar with each utterance; or in the local dialect, in which case it will vary somewhat more; or in the larger traditional language, in which case it will sound quite different with each speaking. The actual articulation may thus vary considerably both within the unit and from instance to instance, but there is no doubt that each occurrence is indeed the same "word."

NINE

Thematic Structure
in *Beowulf* and Old English Poetry

In concert with the method used in earlier chapters, I propose to examine the Old English narrative theme as a tradition-dependent entity, that is, as a compositional unit that depends for its structure not only on the general oral-derived nature of Old English poetry but also and equally on the idiosyncratic features of the Anglo-Saxon language and the specialized formulaic diction that serves as its expressive medium. Toward that end we shall first review the scholarship on the Old English theme before turning to analysis of sample passages from *Beowulf* and another long narrative poem from the canon in order to determine precisely how we should view and define the unit. The themes to be analyzed will include the sea voyage and the scourging of the hero. In considering the last of these, drawn from the verse hagiography *Andreas*, we are reaching beyond the poem *Beowulf*, and indeed beyond its genre of heroic epic, to the ubiquitous saint's life. But in doing so we are at least turning to a long narrative poem that may safely be considered oral-derived,[1] thus maintaining a reasonable degree of congruency in the comparison. Were the surviving Anglo-Saxon poetic canon larger, the comparison could be made more exact.

PRIOR RESEARCH

Origins

As with so many other aspects of research on oral traditional structure, scholarship on the Old English theme began with Albert Lord's 1949 disser-

---

1. On the traditional nature of the phraseology, see, e.g., Peters 1951; note also the poet's interruption of his narrative at 1478–91, in which he discusses the compositional problem of making his poem *lytlum sticcum* ("in little pieces"). The major part of this chapter ("Two Example Themes") will provide additional evidence of the oral-derived nature of the poem at the thematic level.

tation, eleven years later to become *The Singer of Tales*.[2] Defining the general, cross-traditional unit as a "group of ideas regularly used in telling a tale in the formulaic style of traditional song" (1960, 68), he went on to illustrate the dynamics of the theme in Serbo-Croatian, ancient Greek, Byzantine Greek, Old French, and Old English. Moreover, because the published version of his account appeared some five years after thematic analysis in Old English poetry had formally been begun by Francis P. Magoun and Stanley B. Green-field, Lord was able to distinguish his concept of the unit from theirs. With typical care and precision he remarks (pp. 198-99):

> I should prefer to designate as motifs what they call themes and to reserve the term theme for a structural unit that has a semantic essence but can never be divorced from its form, even if its form be constantly variable and multiform. It is not difficult to see that even from this point of view there are themes in *Beowulf*: repeated assemblies with speeches, repetition of journeying from one place to another, and on the larger canvas the repeated multiform scenes of the slaying of monsters.

He goes on to give additional examples, such as the arrival of the hero, which along with the assembly is also common in Serbo-Croatian epic, and in general to limit the conception of the theme to an integral narrative unit whose beginning, middle, and end are well defined.

In the meantime, between the submission of Lord's dissertation and its publication, Magoun had isolated what he took to be an oral-formulaic theme: "the mention of the wolf, eagle, and/or raven as beasts attendant on a scene of carnage" (1955, 83).[3] Finding twelve occurrences of this multiform in the canon, he then subjected them to a phraseological analysis, concluding (p. 90) that "the formulas and formulaic systems will be seen to divide up in two ways, those potentially relevant to the subject matter of the theme and those of general usefulness." While this concatenation of narrative details may represent a theme for Magoun, it is clear why Lord would rather consider it a motif: there is no repeated, specific set of actions involved in the "Beasts of Battle," no narrative process preserved from one instance to the next. This is, by comparison to "assembly" or "readying a hero's horse" in the Serbo-Croatian epic tradition, a somewhat static collection of details uncatalyzed by a network of recurrent and associated actions.

Greenfield's (1955) theme of "Exile,"[4] more like Magoun's than Lord's

2. For a fuller account of the background scholarship than is possible here, see Foley 1981b, 1985, 1988; Olsen 1986, 1988. A discussion of Lord's specific proposals may be found above in chapter 8.

3. It is well to recall that in 1953 Magoun (p. 84) had pronounced *Beowulf* and other Old English poetry to be certainly oral, by virtue of the dictum that "oral poetry, it may be safely said, is composed entirely of formulas, while lettered poetry is never formulaic."

4. See also his two earlier articles (1953a,b), which adumbrate thematic analysis without associating the structure with oral tradition.

unit, consists of the four elements status, deprivation, state of mind, and movement in or into exile. Again we encounter a collection of details without a clear narrative matrix, a recurrence of what Greenfield calls exile "images" without a specific network of actions. And once more it is apparent why Lord would choose to call such a unit a "motif" rather than a theme.

The question that these early studies presage is essentially the burden of the present chapter: are all Old English themes really oral traditional units, and how does the principle of tradition-dependence affect the definition? While typologies constructed for their own sake (too often against the empirical evidence) are certainly of limited usefulness, it is equally misleading to dissolve all distinctions in search of an overarching generalization. What we shall seek in the analytical section of this chapter is a workable, tradition-dependent idea of the Old English theme, one that recognizes both the distinctions made by Lord and the discoveries reported by Magoun, Greenfield, and others—for the lesson of the earliest scholarship in this area is that we must be willing to undertake a true comparison, one that can draw on findings in other oral traditional literatures but must nevertheless be rigorously grounded in the philology of its own tradition.

A Brief Summary of Scholarship

Building on the foundations erected by Lord, Magoun, and Greenfield, later scholars have uncovered numerous themes in the narrative poetry of the Old English canon. In lieu of extended discussions of these contributions, I present below a digest of the twenty-four themes or type-scenes reported to date, together with references to the articles devoted to each. A general overview of the most frequent or most often cited themes follows.

Theme	Sources
Beasts of Battle	Magoun 1955; Bonjour 1957; Renoir 1962a, 1976a, 1988; Metcalf 1963
Hero on the Beach	Crowne 1960; Renoir 1964, 1977, 1979a, 1979c, 1981b, 1986, 1988; Fry 1966, 1967a; Thormann 1970; Wolf 1970; Johnson 1975 (Middle English); Olsen 1980, 1981, 1982; Dane 1982
Sea Voyage	Diamond 1961; Ramsey 1971
Approach to Battle	Heinemann 1970; Wolf 1970; Fry 1972
Exile	Greenfield 1955; Rissanen 1969; Renoir 1981a, 1988
Traveler Recognizes His Goal	G. Clark 1965b
War	Diamond 1961
Comitatus	Diamond 1961
Cold Weather	Diamond 1961
Boast	Renoir 1963; Conquergood 1981

Theme	*Sources*
Singer	Creed 1962; Renoir 1981b, 1988
Impact of a Weapon	G. Clark 1965a
Advancing Army	G. Clark 1965a
Feast	De Lavan 1981; Kavros 1981
Cliff of Death	Fry 1986
Grateful Recipient	Magoun 1961
Gesture of Raised Shield	Magoun 1961
Joy in the Hall	Opland 1976
Death	Taylor 1967
Scourging	Foley 1976a
Traditional Knowledge	Foley 1976a
Speaking Wood	Renoir 1976b, 1988
Flyting	F. Clark 1981; Anderson 1980

Far the best-documented thematic unit (fifteen citations), the "Hero on the Beach" was first reported by David Crowne in 1960 and has since been shown to recur not only throughout the Anglo-Saxon poetic corpus but also in Middle English and Old High German.[5] Crowne (p. 368) defined this compositional pattern as "a stereotyped way of describing (1) a hero on the beach (2) with his retainers (3) in the presence of a flashing light (4) as a journey is completed (or begun)." This account of the content approaches Lord's concept of the theme more closely than does Magoun's "Beasts of Battle" or Greenfield's "Exile," since the repeated action is more clearly delineated. But if narrative sequence is part of Crowne's idea of the unit, verbal correspondence among instances most certainly is not. In fact, he goes to some length to demonstrate that the theme in Homer as well as in Old English amounts to a grouping of ideas rather than a critical mass of phraseological items, concluding (p. 364) that the theme "does not depend upon a fixed content of specific formulas for its mnemonic usefulness to the singer." This concentration on narrative fabric as the stuff of which the compositional theme is made—and the abandoning of verbal correspondence among instances as a criterion for identification of the unit—marked a point of departure for studies of the theme or typical scene in Old English poetry. No longer did investigators search for repeated verses as the telltale sign of the recurrent scene; in practical terms, they assumed an unlimited variety of situation-specific instances, with a variety of diction to match. The theme in Old English became purely a sequence of ideas for those following Crowne's lead, and scholars were virtually unanimous in doing so.

Magoun's "Beasts of Battle" has also proved important in the development of thematics in Anglo-Saxon verse. Assuming that the *Beowulf* poet was lettered but composed formulaically, Adrien Bonjour contended in 1957 that this poet,

---

5. For a complete survey of oral-formulaic scholarship in Middle English, see Parks 1986. For Old High German, see Renoir's analysis of the *Hildebrandslied* (e.g., 1979b).

unlike his lesser contemporaries, shows artistic originality in the handling of the "Beasts" pattern. This general notion of the theme as a structural entity that could be shaped according to individual aesthetic design found apparent support in, for example, Robert P. Creed's 1961 article on oral poetics, in which he argued that a given theme should be understood not simply in relation to other instances within a given poem, but also against the larger traditional background.[6] Thus arose the concept of aesthetic manipulation of traditional themes, just as it had for the formula some years earlier. As time went on, specialists in Old English, it is fair to say, were quite willing to accept a narrative unit such as the theme as long as the theory allowed for the poet's conscious artistic control of his traditional medium.

A third significant step in the study of Old English themes is that taken by Alain Renoir in his contextual analyses of various medieval texts.[7] Although one cannot tie his method uniquely to one particular multiform, his efforts have concentrated on elucidating the expressive content (and this means audience expectation as well as textual structure) of the "Hero on the Beach," "Beasts of Battle," and "Speaking Wood" patterns. Renoir's method entails establishing an inter-textual and often cross-traditional directory for a given oral-formulaic theme, even if it occurs in a written text (e.g., 1976b), and interpreting each instance in the context of what is collectively known about the thematic pattern. In the case of poems whose authorship or provenance is uncertain—and this is often the case with medieval works—this approach provides otherwise unavailable insights into a great range of critical issues as various as manuscript authority and rhetorical structure.

CURRENT ISSUES

At the moment the most pressing issues in Old English thematics are (1) the distinction proposed by Donald Fry between "theme" and "type-scene" and its implications, (2) the role of verbal correspondence among instances in the definition of the unit, and (3) more generally, the question of whether we really have a "theme" in Old English verse—and if so, how it is to be reconciled with the obviously quite different comparands in ancient Greek and Serbo-Croatian. While I shall depend on the analyses below to furnish answers for these questions, let me first present each issue in sharper focus.

In 1968 Fry proposed a typology of narrative units since advocated by many scholars. He differentiated (p. 53) between the *type-scene*, or "recurring stereotyped presentation of conventional details used to describe a certain narrative

---

6. With reference to the Serbo-Croatian analog as discussed in chapter 8 of this volume, we may note that the *guslar* possesses an idiosyncratic, idiolectal form for themes that are in general use throughout his local tradition and in the poetic tradition at large.

7. See, e.g., Renoir 1976a, 1976b, 1977, 1979a, 1981b, and esp. 1988.

event, requiring neither verbatim repetition nor a specific formula content,"
and the *theme*, or "recurring concatenation of details and ideas, not restricted
to a specific event, verbatim repetition, or certain formulas, which forms an
underlying structure for an action or description." While both derive from
Crowne's (1960) conception of a unit undefined by verbal correspondence
among instances, Fry's two units seem to diverge sharply, and their divergence
is precisely the presence or absence of a narrative context. If the repeated
collection of details is imbedded in an action-pattern, it is an example of Fry's
type-scene; if it lacks such a narrative matrix, it is his theme. We may recall
the distinction made by Lord at this point and note that Greenfield's "Exile"
(and perhaps Magoun's "Beasts of Battle" as well) would be classed by Fry
as themes, while Lord's examples of Assembly and so forth would be termed
type-scenes. This distinction thus made, one may ask how useful it proves in
analyzing and interpreting Old English poetry.[8]

Our second issue concerns the phraseological aspect, if any, of the Old
English theme. In opposition to the preponderance of critical opinion, which
following Crowne holds that themes in Anglo-Saxon verse are narrative sequences without any particular formulaic content, Lord has argued that a true
theme must exhibit not only a characteristic grouping of ideas but also a
definite verbal consistency. It is primarily on these grounds that he distin-
guishes between the literary concept of theme and the oral traditional unit
(1975, 20):

> If, however, by theme one means *subject*, a narrative element, such as a catalogue,
> or a message, or equipping, or gathering an army, then our definition is inade-
> quate; for clearly we can find gatherings of armies, equippings, messages, and
> catalogues in written as well as in oral literature. The theme as *subject* alone
> is too general for our very special purposes. But if by theme one means a repeated
> narrative element together with its verbal expression, that portion of a poem,
> an aggregate of specific verses, that tells a certain repeated part of the narrative,
> measureable in terms of lines and even words and word combinations, then we
> find ourselves dealing with elements of truly oral traditional narrative style.

As we enter the analytical section of this chapter, this issue of verbal correspondence will continue to be a concern: namely, do we demand an aspect of
verbal recurrence for the theme and, if so, what do we make of the patterns
that show no such verbal recurrence?

This question leads directly to the last of the issues to be kept in mind as we
examine narrative patterns from *Beowulf* and the Old English poetic canon.
Whatever conclusions are reached about what an Old English theme is or is
not, we shall have to confront a real discrepancy between the structure and
texture of narrative units in Old English on the one hand and in ancient
Greek and Serbo-Croatian on the other. That is, even if we were to so tighten

---

8. As illustration, see Fry 1969.

the definition of theme in Anglo-Saxon verse that it admitted only a small number of the twenty-four patterns summarized above, we would still be left with a question more important than the matter of definition. In short, just what function do these other, "non-thematic" units perform, and more specifically, what is their role in *Beowulf* and other poems? Are they traditional and (at least) oral-derived, or do they represent some sort of literate extrapolation of bona fide oral traditional units? These questions have clear implications for the aesthetic study of the poems as well.

THE TRADITION-DEPENDENT NATURE OF OLD ENGLISH THEMES

From a practical point of view, the concept and definition of the theme as developed by Albert Lord in respect to Serbo-Croatian oral epic translated more easily to ancient Greek than to Old English oral-derived poetry. To appreciate why, we need only remember the two aspects of the compositional unit so carefully defined by Lord in 1974: narrative sequence and verbal correspondence. While a sequence of narrative ideas may, unlike phraseology, be free from the idiosyncratic shaping exerted by language and prosody, so that an action-pattern should be able to be defined in approximately the same terms whatever the language of the given tradition, the necessarily varying phraseologies that express those action-patterns will not submit to a single universal concept or definition. And as we have seen from earlier chapters, the phraseological leap from Serbo-Croatian to Homeric Greek is much shorter than from either of those epic poetries to Old English. *Beowulf* and other Anglo-Saxon poems reveal a formulaic diction, to be sure, but it does not follow the prosodic rules observed by Homer or the Yugoslav *guslar*. If this tradition-dependent phraseology serves as the idiom for the actual verbal expression of thematic units (as opposed to their identity as groups of ideas only), then as a first approximation we should expect that verbal correspondence among occurrences of the Old English narrative unit will prove similarly tradition-dependent.

Along with this predictable difference, it is well to recall the nature of multiformity revealed in our close examination of the Serbo-Croatian epic theme in chapter 8. Instead of simple overlays of units, we found that the Yugoslav tradition can be faithfully described only by distinguishing among idiolectal, dialectal, and tradition-wide versions of a given theme. In other words, the theme exists as a replicating unit—one that recurs preserving both the overall grouping of ideas and a significant amount of diction associated with those ideas—most obviously within the repertoire of the individual singer, who has his own "version" of the typical scene. More variation is observed at what has been termed the level of "dialect," that version of a theme employed not by the individual but by his local traditional community, the

singers in his geographically defined district. Still greater variation characterizes the narrative multiform at the tradition-wide level, as one compares
versions of a theme from singers in different, extensively separated regions.
It must be emphasized that such distinctions, possible in such a well-recorded
epic tradition as the Serbo-Croatian, cannot be recovered in dead-language,
manuscript-based poetries like ancient Greek and Old English.[9] Our uncertainty as to the "authorship" of various poems in the Old English canon, not
to mention our probably irresolvable doubt about the actual role of writing
in their composition and transmission, limits the extent to which we can
compare structural details on a one-to-one basis. It will be most prudent first
to attempt a careful characterization of the Old English theme as a tradition-
dependent entity, realizing that a philologically sound definition may vary
considerably from those formulated for ancient Greek and Serbo-Croatian,
and then to collate those observations with earlier discoveries.

One more caveat is in order before beginning analysis. As earlier chapters
have attempted to show, the assumption that all parts of even a verifiably oral
epic are uniformly formulaic is untenable. Likewise, even the Serbo-Croatian
theme (as observed in the work of a single singer and in a single community
of singers) does not prove uniformly dense in verbal correspondence; certain
parts of the unit are, for one reason or another, repeated more exactly than
others from one occurrence to the next. These variations are traceable to a
number of sources, among them the singer's deployment of sound patterns
and his familiarity with a given theme. The point here is that an interactive,
purely synchronic model for formulaic diction and for narrative multiformity
in Serbo-Croatian oversimplifies the real situation. And if we should be prepared for variation in formulaic density and degree of verbal correspondence
in this ascertainably oral tradition with its treasury of recorded performances,
then we should also anticipate similar fluctuations and variations in the manuscript texts of finally uncertain provenance.

TWO EXAMPLE THEMES

In order to determine the tradition-dependent shape of the thematic unit in
Beowulf and Old English poetry, let us consider two narrative multiforms, the
"Sea Voyage" and the "Scourging" scene, the first from *Beowulf* and the
second from the verse hagiography *Andreas*. In each case the focus will be on
measuring the importance of idea-structure on the one hand and of verbal
correspondence on the other.

The Sea Voyage in Beowulf

In examining this multiform in *Beowulf*, it is well to recall four basic properties of the Serbo-Croatian epic theme as a comparative background. First,

9. On this point cf. Gunn 1971.

as would be expected given the colon structure underlying formulaic phraseology in this epic tradition, any verbal agreement among instances of a narrative multiform is expressed largely in terms of whole lines or cola, as in Homeric epic. The entire line and caesura-bound hemistich are thus the "lexical" data of the theme. Second, although narrative sequence seems in all cases to remain almost absolutely constant and to oversee the thematic progress of the story, in rare cases a unit can be transposed, provided that the narrative logic is maintained. Third, verbal correspondence is not of uniform density throughout the theme or from instance to instance; certain motifs are much more stable formulaically than others. Fourth, variation in verbalization of the theme can take a number of forms, among them what may be termed "formulaic variance," in which lines and parts of lines recombine according to systemic principles, and "ornamentation," in which a non-narrative, paratactic gloss not necessary in itself but rather complementary to a necessary element is included.[10]

The Old English theme is equally dynamic, though in its own tradition-dependent way. Its texture is also uneven, with certain sections exhibiting one level of verbal correspondence and others differing. Although we do not have the luxury of multiple texts provided by the well-collected Serbo-Croatian tradition, the typical scene of the Sea Voyage will help to make this point. The two occurrences of the sea voyage in *Beowulf* may be rationalized by the motif structure given below.[11]

Occurrence #1 (205-303a)	*Occurrence #2* (1880b-1919)
A. Beowulf leads his men to the ship (205-9)	A$_1$. Beowulf [leads his men] to the ship (1880b-82a)
B. The ship waits, moored (210-11a)	B. The ship waits, moored (1882b-83)
	A$_2$. [Beowulf] leads his men to the ship (1888-89a)
	W. Armor (1889b-90a)
	X$_1$. The coast-guard approaches (1890b-95)
C. His men board the ship, carrying treasure (211b-15a)	C. His men board the ship, carrying treasure (1896-99; cf. 1884-87)
	X$_2$. The boat-guard is rewarded (1900-03a)[12]

10. See chapters 5 and 8. On other sorts of patterns, such as phonemic series, end-colon rhyme, and semantic association, which also characterize other oral genres in the Serbo-Croatian tradition, see, e.g., Kerewsky Halpern and Foley 1978.

11. On the texts of the following passages, I follow Klaeber (1950) except for his proposed emendation to *naca* in line 1903b (nom. sing. and subject), for which I see no clear justification. I choose to return to the manuscript reading *nacan*, ostensibly a dative singular taking its inflection from the preceding *on*.

12. The *batweard* ("boat-guard") I take to be the same person as the *landweard* ("land-guard,"

Occurrence #1 (205-303a) *(Cont.)*

D. Departure, voyage on
  the sea, arrival (215b-25)

E_1. Mooring the ship (226a)
  W. Armor (226b-27a)
  Z. Prayer of thanks (227b-28)
  X. The coast-guard
    approaches; he and Beowulf
    confer (229-300)
E_2. Mooring the ship (301b-3a)

Occurrence #2 (1880b-1919) *(Cont.)*

D. Departure, voyage on
  the sea, arrival (1903b-13)
  X*. Beowulf and his men
    approach the harbor-guard
    (1914-16)[13]
E. Mooring the ship (1917-19)

The basic narrative structure of the Sea Voyage may thus be represented as a sequence of five elements:

A. Beowulf leads his men to the ship
B. The ship waits, moored
C. His men board the ship, carrying treasure
D. Departure, voyage on the sea, arrival
E. They moor the ship

Within this regular structure are interwoven elements that help to particularize the generic action, to suit the theme to its narrative context. The W motif, "Armor," variable in position, seems to serve as the prerequisite for the X motif, "The coast-guard approaches"; where the latter first occurs, the former closely precedes it. In occurrence #1 above, W introduces X within the E element, and in #2 W is followed by X before the C element. In narrative terms, this means that "Armor" and its consequent can be developed during the mooring of the ship (as in #1) or before Beowulf's men carry the treasure on board (as in #2), in concert with the demands of the situation.

The X motif, most protean of any of the elements, deserves close attention. It concerns an encounter with the guard of whatever coast one lands on or is in the process of leaving, and is applied to at least two distinct characters and situations in *Beowulf*.[14] In occurrence #1 the story line calls for an expansion of X into a lengthy exchange between the coast-guard and Beowulf. Working within the traditional idiom, the poet thus accomplishes two things concurrently: he both fulfills the generic thematic conditions and suits the

---

1890b), since it is the *landweard* who promises to guard Beowulf's ship until he returns (see lines 293–98).

13. Although the Geatish *hyðweard* is certainly not the same person as the Scylding figure involved in X_1 and X_2, he performs the same generic function and can thus be seen as the agent of the thematic variant.

14. See notes 12 and 13.

structure to its narrative environment. Beowulf is forced to identify both his people and his purpose, points of information that are of course vital to what follows, and the identification proceeds naturally (that is, traditionally) out of the Sea Voyage multiform. This same potential for modification or variation shows up in a different way in occurrence #2, where X occurs three times (X_1, X_2, X^*; the symbol X^* is used to denote a reversal of the more usual action of this motif). In all other instances, the coast-guard approaches the Geats; in occurrence #1 he comes to challenge their disembarkation, and in occurrence #2 (X_1–X_2) he again moves to greet them, though this time in a friendly manner, as the *litotes* (1892–95) indicates. The harbor-guard of X^*, in contrast, has been watching for Beowulf and his men for a long time. He has remained on the shore, waiting for the returning heroes to approach him. While this constitutes a reversal of the encounter, it springs from the same traditional form, the X motif, as do the other cited instances.

The major motifs within this theme, that is, elements A-E, also reveal a certain amount of adaptation to context, although they vary in structural stability. Element A, for example, splits in occurrence #2, enclosing a number of details within a narrative capsule.[15] One dimension of this division is clear: A_1 mentions nothing about Beowulf's companions, while in occurrence #1 this motif includes both the hero and his men. A_2 thus fills out the element by describing the embarkation of Beowulf's men. Motifs B, C, and D are quite stable within the Sea Voyage sequence, especially the last of them, which is tightly organized around a three-part series of departure, voyage, and arrival. Two specific features further structure the action of the D motif: (1) the "go until one sees the destination" commonplace[16] and (2) the notation of wind and the ship's sail. The splitting of E in occurrence #1, like that of A in #2, presents evidence of the pliability of traditional elements, as once again the recurrent generic structure is adapted to the narrative situation.

Taken together, the two instances of the Sea Voyage in *Beowulf* collectively exhibit a discernible and dynamic *narrative sequence*, an action-pattern not dissimilar in nature to that found in Serbo-Croatian themes. In applying the first of Lord's criteria to what we have in *Beowulf*, we seem to have a close fit: with the exception of the Old English poet's somewhat greater flexibility in motif development,[17] there is considerable similarity between the Old English and Serbo-Croatian themes in terms of narrative sequence. But what of the second criterion, *verbal correspondence*? Are we likely to observe the same close fit across traditions along the axis of phraseology?

15. Such capsules or envelopes, often understood as elements in ring composition, have themselves been the object of a number of studies. See Bartlett 1935; Hieatt 1975; Niles 1979.

16. On this common pattern, see Irving 1968, 31–42; G. Clark 1965b, 647–48; Gruber 1974.

17. This difference may well stem from the limited textual sample in Old English, from the greater freedom in expression that is characteristic of Old English traditional phraseology, or from both.

To answer this question we must recall what was discovered earlier (chapter 6) about the tradition-dependent character of the formula in *Beowulf*, for with that latter principle in mind it is possible to predict another directly related tradition-dependency—the nature of thematic data. First, we cannot expect a large proportion of classically defined whole-line or half-line formulas as verbal correspondence in Old English poetry, since such an expectation pre-supposes a colonic formula and, as demonstrated earlier, Old English prosody and phraseology are not colonic. Second, what we can logically expect as thematic data are highly variable half-lines that may have in common only their stressed cores. What verbal correspondence exists will thus appear to take the form of single morphs, that is, of roots of words whose systemic context is metrically (and therefore lexically and syntactically) highly variable. This does not preclude formulaic content, as we shall see below, but simply makes it more likely that single words will constitute whatever thematic resonance obtains in the actual phraseology.[18] Following is a tabulation of the morphs and the few phrases that help to define the Sea Voyage multiform in *Beowulf*.

A:A$_1$, A$_2$—none

B:B—none

C:C—sande/sande (213a/1896a), nacan/naca (214a/1896b), stefn/-stefna (212a/1897b)

D:D—Gewat/Gewat (217a/1903b), wæg-/weg- (217a/1907a), winde/wind (217b/1907b), wudu/-wudu (216b/1906b), -sið/siðes (216a/1908a), sæ-/sæ- (223a/1908b), bundenne/bunden- (216b/1910a), brim-/brim- (222a/1910b), sund/sund- (223b/1906b), flota famiheals/fleat famigheals (218a/1909a), -clifu/clifu (222a/1911a), -næssas/næssas (223a/1912a), up/up (224b/1912b)

E$_1$, E$_2$:E—sældon/sale/sale/sælde (226a/302a/1906a/1917a), sidfæþmed scip/sidfæþme scip (302b/1917b), on ancre fæst/oncerbendum fæst (303a/1918a), -wudu/wudu (226a/1919a)

W:W—syrcan/-syrcan (226b/1890a)

X:X—weard/-weard/-wearde/-weard (229b/1890b/1900a/1914b)

In addition to items of verbal correspondence among instances of a theme, there exists in *Beowulf* and other Old English poetry a tradition-dependent, local resonance of morphs that may be called *responsion*.[19] Rather than being attached to a certain narrative event or pattern and echoing traditionally against other occurrences of that same event or pattern, these words respond to proximate partners, lexical relatives usually no more than about twenty

18. I might add that these data cannot be easily explained away as words that are most likely to occur in a given description. Lexical items at positions of metrical stress are the products of a process, and that process, which does not characteristically yield colonic phraseology, should be understood on its own tradition-dependent terms. Compare the grouping of morphs in the Joy in the Hall theme described by Opland (1976).

19. This kind of local verbal echo has received attention as a compositional and artistic feature in Old English poetry. See, e.g., Beaty 1934; Kintgen 1977; Hanning 1973; Foley 1980b.

lines away, and often much closer.[20] Although there is no opportunity in the present discussion to do more than suggest the presence of responsion and to list the occurrences in the Sea Voyage theme (see below), I would emphasize its importance to the poetics of *Beowulf*. For example, many rhetorical figures attributed by some critics to direct borrowing from Latin authors can be derived from the interaction between responsion and other aspects of Germanic verse form.[21]

Occurrence #1

sund-/sund/sund	208a/213a/223b
secg/secgas	208b/213b
leoda/leode	205b/225a
land-/land	209b/221b
-wudu/-wudu	208a/226a
beorge/beorgas	211a/222b
gewat/Gewat/Gewiton	210a/217a/301a
flota/flota	210b/301b
yðum/yþ-	210b/228a
stefn/-stefna	212a/220a
stigon/stigon	212a/225b
wundon/wunden-	212b/220a
guð-/guð-	215a/227a
-searo/-searu	215a/232a
bæron/beran	213b/231a
beorhte/beorhte	214b/231b
liðende/liden/-lade	221a/223b/228a
gesawon/geseah	221b/229a
-fysed/fus-	217b/232a
-holm/holm-	217a/230a
-clifu/-clifu	222a/230a
sældon/sale	226a/302a

Occurrence #2

gold-/golde	1881a/1900b
Cwom/-cuman	1888a/1894a
sæ-/sæ-/sæ-	1882b/1896b/1908b
ancre/oncer-	1883b/1918a
-genga/gange/-genga	1882b/1884a/1908b
rad/rad	1883b/1893b

20. Of course, if a motif is split, as is the case with E_1–E_2 in Occurrence #1, a greater distance between responsions can result.

21. Cf. Campbell 1966, 1967, 1978. Even some of the figures that Campbell cites frequently as examples of borrowed techniques (anaphora, polysyndeton, hypozeuxis, etc.) can be so explained. The subject deserves much fuller treatment than is possible here, and I must for the moment leave the argument at the level of suggestion.

Occurrence #2 (Cont.)

naca/nacan	1896b/1903b
-stefna/-stefna	1897b/1910a
mæst/mæste	1898b/1905a
sande/sande	1896a/1917a
maðmum/maþm*e*	1898a/1902b
Land-/land/lande	1890b/1904b/1913b
yðum/yðe/yþa	1907b/1909b/1918b
sale/sælde	1906a/1917a
fæst/fæst	1906a/1918a
Hroðgares/Hroðgares	1884b/1899a
gifu/ofgeaf	1884b/1904b
wynnum/wyn-	1887a/1919a
hring-/hringed-	1889b/1897b
foron/for	1895b/1908b
scipe/scip	1895b/1917b
-weard/-wearde/-weard	1890b/1900a/1914b
bunden/bunden-/-bendum	1900b/1910a/1918a

If the Beowulfian Sea Voyage and the Serbo-Croatian and ancient Greek themes resemble one another quite closely at the level of narrative sequence, they diverge considerably with respect to verbal correspondence. To be sure, there are some hard lexical data (of similarly uneven distribution) for all traditional themes, but these data take quite different, tradition-dependent forms. The Old English correspondence manifests itself chiefly in morphs in positions of metrical stress, with a less strictly defined, more variable phraseological environment. Occasionally a half-line formula—understood in the classical colonic sense—occurs, but this is relatively rare. What correspondence exists in Serbo-Croatian and Greek, in contrast, consists of lines and cola—that is, of the bound, encapsulated phrases that form in symbiosis with a syllabic and consistently demarcated metric. Neither the Sea Voyage nor either of the other two units is less a theme for its similarity to or divergence from its counterparts, rather, each theme takes shape in a form governed by the prosody of the tradition involved.[22]

22. Of the three additional occurrences of this theme cited by Ramsey (1971, 56)—*Andreas* 230–53, 349–81, and *Elene* 212–75—I would include only the last as a true instance of the Sea Voyage. The *Andreas* passages contain little of the same narrative pattern examined above and none of the phraseology; perhaps because of the influence of the *Praxeis* source, which calls for an extended conversation among the principals during the voyage as an important part of the story to be told, the five-part structure was not useful and did not occur. The *Elene* passage, in contrast, if abbreviated to its core (lines 225–55), does exhibit the characteristic narrative sequence: A—The hero(ine) leads her men to the ship (225–26a, 229–32a); B—The ship waits, moored (226b-28); C—The men board the ship, carrying treasure/armor (232b-36); D—Departure, voyage on the sea, arrival (237–50a); and E—They moor the ship (250b-55). There is enough variation from the *Beowulf* occurrences to suggest the influence of a source, a different poet or local tradition (as in the Serbo-Croatian examples in chapter 8), or both.

One further example of the Sea Voyage in *Beowulf* may help both to broaden our understanding of the unit and to point the way toward the aesthetic implications of traditional structures.[23] Early in the poem, long before Beowulf appears, the archetypal hero Scyld Scefing embarks on a sea voyage, albeit of a significantly different sort. For Scyld the journey is his funeral, the ritual marking his passage from this world to the next. At the appointed time, we are told, Scyld "led his men to the ship" (A, 26-31), with the surviving retainers bearing him according to his previous order. In the next few lines we hear that "the ship waits, moored" (B, 32-33), and that he and his men "board the ship, carrying treasure and armor" (C, 34-48a), the hero being laid by the mast with his grave-gifts and appropriately eulogized by the poet with a litotes. Just as the C element is elaborated with descriptions of the treasure and the hero, so the D element, "Departure, voyage on the sea, arrival" (48b-50a), is correspondingly foreshortened; this is after all no customary Sea Voyage but a ship burial. Finally, instead of the expected form of element E ("They moor the ship"), we hear the agnostic profession of ignorance over Scyld's destination (50b-52):

> Men ne cunnon
> secgan to soðe,   selerædend*e*,
> hæleð under heofenum,   hwa þæm hlæste onfeng.

> Men do not know
> [how] to say in truth, hall-counselors,
> heroes under the heavens, who received that burden.

Whether this particular usage of the Sea Voyage theme was a widely traditional one we shall probably never know, but the recognition of its existence at the root of Scyld's funeral enlarges our notion of thematic morphology and offers a perspective on the poet's art. First, because this narrative structure can be employed in such an (apparently) unusual way, we have more evidence of the Old English theme's consistent narrative pattern and extremely variable phraseology. Complementarily, the referential meaning of the thematic structure—Sea Voyage—imbues the funeral with a significance far beyond the actual event. Not only are the poet and his tradition conceiving of the great hero's departure as a sort of ultimate Sea Voyage,[24] but the conspicuous absence of the traditional closure in the mooring of the ship powerfully evokes

---

23. Although I happened on the thematic correspondences independently, the outward focus of the following analysis harmonizes with that of Ramsey (1971). Much of what his article presents seems sound, but I would advocate going beyond a conception of the relationships as merely habitual and convenient to understanding the referential power of the Sea Voyage multiform as an idiomatic way of describing the funeral.

24. Cf. the extrapolation of the Storm Giant mythologem to Apocalypse in Exeter Riddle I (Foley 1976b), as well as the metonymic import of the unfaithful wife and the consequent lack of the traditional closing to the Serbo-Croatian Return Song (chapter 10).

the cosmic overtones of this last and special journey as well. This view of Scyld's passage from the world is made possible through the metonymic poetics of oral tradition, without whose associative dynamics such a perspective could not be achieved.

The Scourging Scene in Andreas

For a second example of the Old English theme I turn outside *Beowulf* to another long narrative poem, the apocryphal story of St. Andrew among the Mermedonians. Scholars have long recognized similarities of diction and narrative structure in these two narratives, and prevailing opinion ascribes these similarities to their shared roots in the Anglo-Saxon poetic tradition rather than having recourse to the once current literary explanation of common authorship.[25] In extending the analysis beyond *Beowulf* we shall be seeking to test the concept of the theme developed in this chapter on a text in the "religious" tradition of Anglo-Saxon poetry, and therefore very likely an oral-derived rather than a primary oral text, one perhaps further removed from the native Germanic oral tradition than the less patently Christian *Beowulf*.

In the process we must also consider Albert Lord's judgment (1975, 23) on the Old English Christian poems and their relationship to oral composition: "If the religious poems were truly oral traditional songs, I would expect to find a higher degree of verbal correspondence among the various instances of a theme within a given poem, after making due allowance for adjustment to the specific position in the poem which it occupies." In light of what we have so far learned about the Old English theme, can we demand verbal correspondence (implicitly of the ancient Greek or Serbo-Croatian sort) as a sine qua non in this oral-derived hagiography? While there is little doubt that poems like *Andreas* are "transitional" or "mixed," in Lord's terms,[26] I would urge two preliminary caveats: first, it is impossible to determine such transitional character on the basis of criteria shown to be inapplicable to Old English poetry, and second, we cannot assume without testing that even such supposedly mixed poems will not preserve the basic thematic structure we find in *Beowulf*, that is, the tradition-dependent thematic structure of Old English verse.

In one sense *Andreas* provides an ideal opportunity for such a test, since in addition to being composed in the traditional idiom it derives in some fashion from an original and surviving Greek text, the Πράξεις Ἀνδρέου καὶ Ματθεία εἰς τὴν πόλιν τῶν ἀνθρωποφάγων.[27] Although critics have

---

25. Compare Sarrazin 1897 with Peters 1951 and Crowne 1960.

26. See his further remarks on "transitional texts" in Lord 1986c.

27. Brooks (in the standard edition of the Old English poem: 1961, xv-xviii) and Schaar ([1949] 1967, 12–24, esp. 20) concur that the closest source is the Greek *Praxeis*; see their accounts for descriptions of other texts of the same story. Quotations of the *Praxeis* are taken from Bonnet 1898.

sought to explain the divergences between the Greek version of the story and the Old English poem by invoking a lost Latin intermediary, this explanation cannot account for the larger, institutionalized (and recurrent) variations between the two. That is, while the poem's mention of Bishop Platan and Andrew's departure (both examples cited by Brooks [1961, xv]) may be the result of the poet's consultation or knowledge of other versions of the legend, the Old English poet's demonstrably traditional embroidery on the bare fabric of the Greek narrative must be understood as the contribution not of a lost manuscript but of the poetic wordhoard. As long as we stipulate, then, that divergences between the Greek and Old English texts must be institutionalized and recurrent in order to merit interpretation as traditional structures, the way is open to test *Andreas* for thematic patterns by superimposing the details of its story against the usually close source, the *Praxeis*.

For this purpose I have chosen a narrative pattern that recurs in both the Greek and the Old English texts, although, as we shall see, the actual mode of recurrency is quite different.[28] This is the three-day scourging of St. Andrew by the Mermedonians, in both versions a thrice-repeated incident that causes the holy man much suffering as he is dragged about the city until his body is broken and bloody. The cannibalistic heathen, urged on by Satan, are attempting to break his spirit and his faith in God, but the ever-worsening punishment and torture seem only to strengthen Andrew. He survives each scourging and in the end defeats his enemies; after the third incident, God looses a torrent of water on the Mermedonians in answer to Andrew's prayer. Thus, what begins as a threat to the saint's life and faith ends in an affirmation of God's power and of human perseverance through earthly travail.

What is more, each day is a microcosm of the three-day torture of Andrew. In both versions the Scourging process begins with the onset of day and continues until sunset, at which time the still faithful saint is returned to his cell for a night of mental anguish. Whether he is assailed at night by his own doubts or by the direct attack of Satan and seven demons, the diurnal cycle marks the stages in his constant trial, which goes on for three days in basically the same fashion until the divinely retributive flood ends the scourging cycle.

Against this consistency underlying the three successive scenes in the Greek *Praxeis* we may profitably juxtapose the equivalent passages from the Anglo-Saxon *Andreas*, and the result is enlightening: in addition to the consistency attributable to the source, the Old English text reveals further, complementary recurrency of its own—a recurrency that may confidently be labeled "traditional" because it closely resembles the structure of the Old English theme

28. The material to be analyzed is found between lines 1219 and 1462a in the Old English poem and in Chapters 25–28 of the Greek prose. See further Table 22.

as discussed above. Above and beyond the patterning that derives from the *Praxeis*, then, we observe a narrative patterning typical of thematic structure in Anglo-Saxon verse.

The Scourging theme in *Andreas* can be described as a definite series of actions, only some of which are found in the Greek source. These actions or motifs are:

A. The enemy arrives with a large troop
B. They lead the prisoner from his cell and drag him about the city
C. The prisoner's wounds are described
D. They lead the prisoner back to his cell
E. The prisoner confronts night and mental torture

The fact that these five motifs recur in each of the three Scourging scenes, regardless of what the Greek text has at the same point, indicates that this sequence had an independent existence as a narrative unit,[29] one that could be adapted to context, to be sure, but also one that had a certain integrity as a traditional unit. Although, as already mentioned, it is only prudent to view *Andreas* as an oral-derived work necessarily further removed from primary oral tradition than *Beowulf*, with it we can begin to understand the power and longevity of oral-formulaic themes.[30]

One example of the Scourging theme's independence is the modification it forces in the story at the very beginning of the three-day trial. In chapter 25 of the *Praxeis*, following God's exhortation of a few lines earlier, Andrew rises up and boldly reveals himself to the heathen multitudes: in effect, he ends their search for him by giving himself up.[31] This brave act leads directly to the first day of torture, as a diabolically inspired cannibal suggests fastening a rope around Andrew's neck and dragging him through the streets. In the Old English poem God also instills Andrew with courage and counsels him not to hide (1208–18), but no mention is made of the saint actually delivering himself up to his enemies. Instead, what immediately follows God's encouraging and comforting speech is precisely motif A, the onset of the Scourging theme. In place of surrender to the enemy the Old English poet summons a (contextually quite inappropriately) large troop to seize the less-than-threatening saint:

29. Cf. Lord 1960, 69–98. It may have been that the Scourging theme was used only in this one oral-derived text and had no wider currency in the tradition; nonetheless, the structure of the recurrent scene marks it as traditional. Whether a given unit was a functioning oral traditional element, as in the case of the Serbo-Croatian epic, or the result of the traditional method of composition in a transitional text, patterned recurrency of this sort argues its traditional nature and suggests certain avenues for interpretation.

30. Cf. Ong 1965; Renoir, esp. 1964, 1976b, 1986, 1988.

31. "Τότε ἀναστὰς ᾿Ανδρέας ἐνώπιον πάντων εἶπεν· ᾿Ιδοὺ ἐγώ εἰμι ᾿Ανδρέας ὃν ζητεῖτε" (Chapter 25).

Occurrence #1

Æfter þam wordum com werod unmæte,
lyswe larsmeoðas mid lindgecrode,
bolgenmode;

(*Andreas*, 1219–21a)

After these words came an immense company,
false counsellors with a shield-bearing troop,
enraged in spirit;[32]

There is, of course, no equivalent in the Greek; the deployment of the narrative sequence—a traditional deployment of an oral-formulaic unit in this oral-derived text—supervenes fidelity to source.

In fact, as we move on to the second and third instances of this sequence, we find no equivalent for motif A ("The enemy arrives with a large troop") at any point in the *Praxeis*. Occurrences #2 and #3 begin with the equivalent of (or source for) motif B, "They lead the prisoner from his cell and drag him about the city":[33]

Occurrence #2

Πρωΐας δὲ γενομένης πάλιν
ἐξήνεγκαν αὐτὸν καὶ περιάψαντες
σχοινίον περὶ τὸν τράχηλον αὐτοῦ
διέσυρον αὐτόν,

(*Praxeis*, chap. 26)

Occurrence #3

Πρωΐας δὲ γενομένης ἐξήνεγκαν τὸν
Ἀνδρέαν πάλιν καὶ περιάψαντες
σχοινίον περὶ τὸν τράχηλον αὐτοῦ
ἔσυρον αὐτόν,

(*Praxeis*, chap. 28)

Occurrence #2

And in the morning they carried him
out again and, having fastened a rope
around his neck, they dragged him about.

This amounts to further evidence that the Old English scourging theme has a life of its own, even if only within *Andreas*, and that at times this independent structure supersedes the narrative detail of the source. Here are the Old English passages in question, those which constitute motif A in the theme and which have no equivalent in the *Praxeis*:

Occurrence #2

Ða com hæleða þreat
to ðære dimman ding, duguð unlytel,
wadan wælgifre weorodes brehtme;

(*Andreas*, 1269b–71)

32. On the traditional character of *bolgenmode* ("enraged in spirit"), which names the customary battle-rage that precedes the actual fight, see the analysis of Grendel's approach in chapter 6.

33. *Praxeis*, Occurrence #1: "καὶ περιάψαντες σχοινίον περὶ τὸν τράχηλον αὐτοῦ διέσυρον αὐτὸν ἐν πάσαις ταῖς πλατείαις καὶ ῥύμαις τῆς πόλεως" (Chapter 25).

> Then came a multitude of warriors
> to that dark prison, not a small company,
> traveling slaughter-greedy with the clamor of a troop;

Occurrence #3

> Com þa on uhtan   mid ærdæge
> hæðenra hloð   haliges neosan
> leoda weorude;   (*Andreas*, 1388–90a)

> Came then at dawn with day's beginning
> the throng of heathens to seek the holy one
> with a troop of men;

With the exception of a few words like *weorud* ("troop") that we would expect to find in such a description, these three occurrences of motif A do not reveal much in the way of verbal correspondence. In fact, as but a cursory glance at the Greek versions of motif B shows, even the certainly written and untraditional prose of the *Praxeis* reveals more word-for-word and phrase-for-phrase correspondence than do these three equivalent passages from *Andreas*. Thus, while the *narrative pattern* is without doubt thematic—consistently departing from the source to invoke a traditional motif—this section of the Scourging theme reveals no real *verbal consistency*.

Before examining certain of the other motifs in this theme in order to determine whether adherence to narrative pattern and lack of verbal consistency prove characteristic of the Scourging scene as a whole, it may be well to provide an overview of the motif-by-motif relationship between the Greek and Old English texts over all three occurrences of the scene. Table 22 makes the correspondence appear more regular than it actually is. In general, the Greek source is much more telegraphic, much less descriptive; furthermore, it couches each motif in about the same language in each occurrence. But its agreement with the Old English text is often no more than nominal, with mere suggestions in the *Praxeis* giving way to more fully developed motifs in *Andreas*. In addition, as the line numbers indicate, the Old English poet can

TABLE 22.   Relationship of *Andreas* to *Praxeis* by Motif

	And 1	*P* 1	*And* 2	*P* 2	*And* 3	*P* 3
A	1219-28	*	1269b-71	*	1388-90a	*
B	1229-38a	Chap. 25	1272-73	Chap. 26	1390b-91	Chap. 28
C	1238b-48	Chap. 25	1274-80	Chap. 26	1394-97	Chap. 28
			1302-5a			
D	1249-50a	Chap. 25	1307-8	Chap. 26	1458-60a	Chap. 28
E	1253-69a	Chap. 25	1305b-10	Chap. 26	1456b-62a	Chap. 28

Note: Line and chapter numbers are for equivalent passages in the Old English and Greek versions, respectively; an asterisk indicates no equivalent in the *Praxeis* text.

interrupt his narrative pattern to insert details apparently of his own creation, as he does during the first scourging scene with a non-narrative excursus ostensibly meant to mark Andrew as a type of Christ (1250b–52). Nonetheless, the Old English poem typically shows a greater regularity of narrative pattern than does the *Praxeis*, although verbal correspondence among successive scourgings remains as a rule much higher in the source.

As an example of this set of qualities, we may consider the Old English versions of motif B, whose Greek source was shown above to be almost absolutely consistent. Before examining the passages in question, however, there are two general observations to be made about their relationship to equivalents in the *Praxeis*. First, the Greek passages, though terse, are not obviously self-contained; while the fact that they open a chapter makes for a clear point of beginning, in the *Praxeis* motif B flows right into C without a discernible break in narrative structure. Second, this same motif B ("They lead the prisoner from his cell and drag him about the city"), in taking virtually the same phraseological form each time, does not expand, contract, or divide. In short, it does not participate paratactically in a sequence of actions—as the Old English counterpart most surely does—but seems to be a detail with no particular identity of its own. In contrast, not only is the *Andreas* motif a self-contained, discrete member of a sequence, but as a structure with some individual identity it can expand, contract, and divide. But although the B motif exhibits this morphology—a morphology typical of Old English themes, unbound as they are by the phraseological constraints that shape thematic structure in ancient Greek and Serbo-Croatian—it nevertheless recurs consistently as a necessary part of the oral-formulaic pattern.

The occurrences of motif B from the *Andreas* poem are as shown in figure 11. As the parallel passages reveal, aside from the words *heton* ("they ordered") and *lædan* ("lead"), once again the narrative element does not take a consistent verbal form. There seems to be room for much variation in the actual diction of the element, just as with motif A. In addition, the poet can tack on an expatiation on the basic action, as he does in lines 1232-38 of the first occurrence; these verses further specify the action of dragging the prisoner through the streets of the city and have no equivalent either in the *Praxeis* or in the other two occurrences from *Andreas*. Just as with the Serbo-Croatian theme, apparently, a paratactic addition may be made to the fundamental action of a unit, much in the manner of what Lord terms "ornamentation." We should note that this expansion does not change the traditional structure here (as it did not in the Serbo-Croatian examples in chapter 8), since it simply reinforces and elaborates a traditional idea. In short, what we have in element B is another instance of this Old English theme's consistency of narrative pattern and virtual lack of verbal correspondence.

In lieu of exhaustive analysis of all motifs in the Scourging theme, I shall simply report general results for the remaining motifs (C, D, and E) and men-

Figure 11. Motif B in *Andreas*

Occurrence #1

Heton þa lædan   ofer landsceare,
teon ðragmælum   torngeniðlan,
swa hie hit frecnost   findan meahton;
drogon deormode   æfter dunscræfum,
ymb stanhleoðo   stærcedferþþe,
efne swa wide   swa wegas tolagon,
enta ærgeweorc,   innan burgum,
stræte stanfage.   Storm upp aras
æfter ceasterhofum,   cirm unlytel
hæðnes heriges.   (*Andreas*, 1229–38a)

Then they ordered him led out over the countryside, / dragged incessantly, the bitter enemies, / in the most terrible way they could discover; / the savage-minded ones dragged him along mountain caves, / the hard-hearted ones around the rocky slopes, / just as far as the ways extended, / the old work of giants, into the the towns, / the stone-paved streets. A tempest rose up / among the city dwellings, no little noise / of the heathen troop.

Occurrence #2

heton ut hræðe   æðeling lædan
in wraðra geweald,   wærfæstne hæleð.
(*Andreas*, 1272–73)

they ordered the noble one quickly led out / into the power of the wrathful ones, the warrior firm in his faith.

Occurrence #3

heton lædan ut
prohtheardne þegn   þriddan siðe.
(*Andreas*, 1390b–91)

they ordered led out / the much-tried thane for the third time.

tion one telling departure from thematic structure that further illustrates the poet's method. Motif C, "The prisoner's wounds are described," takes (like the unit just examined) a more elaborate form in the first occurrence than in either of the last two. In the second instance it splits into a ring that surrounds Andreas's prayer and the Devil's reply, non-thematic actions from the Greek source that the poet accommodates by enclosing them in a traditional envelope.[34] This is not an unusual technique in Old English poetry, wherein the pressure toward absolute, one-to-one conformity between thematic idea and phraseological expression is not nearly so great as in Serbo-Croatian or ancient Greek epic. For all of its variations over the three occurrences, however, this section shows a surprising though not overwhelming amount of verbal correspondence. This quality, which by now we must see as uncustomary in Old English, probably results from the greater narrative focus of element C, the actual description of the body wounds suffered by the prisoner; since the action is less generic and more highly specialized, we may conclude that even on a purely semantic (that is, extra-traditional) basis, we could expect more repetition of morphs than in, for example, motif A or B.

Motifs D ("They lead the prisoner back to his cell") and E ("The prisoner confronts night and mental torture") return to the model of the first two substructures, regularly representing essential narrative ideas but having little or no verbal correspondence among instances.[35] As such, they typify the Old English theme as a whole. But there seems to be one glaring problem; to the essential action of motif E in the first scourging scene (1253-55a)—

> [Þ]a se halga wæs under heolstorscuwan,
> eorl ellenheard, ondlangne niht
> searoþancum beseted.

> Thus the holy one was under the shadow of darkness,
> the courageous earl, all night long,
> surrounded by cunning thoughts.

—is attached a rather long, apparently unrelated excursus (1255b-69a):

> Snaw eorðan band   1255
> wintergeworpum; weder coledon
> heardum hægelscurum, swylce hrim ond forst,
> hare hildstapan, hæleða eðel
> lucon, leoda gesetu. Land wæron freorig;
> cealdum cylegicelum clang wæteres þrym,   1260
> ofer eastreamas is brycgade,
> blæce brimrade. Bliðheort wunode
> eorl unforcuð, elnes gemyndig,

---

34. On ring composition, see van Otterlo 1944a, 1944b, 1948; Whitman 1958; Lord 1986a. On the related issue of envelope patterns, see note 15 above.

35. Note the enclosure of D within E in occurrences #2 and #3.

þrist ond þrohtheard,   in þreanedum
wintercealdan niht.   No on gewitte blon,   1265
acol for þy egesan,   þæs þe he ær ongann,
þæt he a domlicost   dryhten herede,
weorðade wordum,   oððæt wuldres gim
heofontorht onhlad.

           Snow bound up the earth   1255
in winter-drifts; the weather grew cold
with hard hail-showers, likewise rime and frost,
gray warriors stalking, locked up men's homeland,
the people's dwellings. Lands were frozen;
water's power hardened into cold icicles,   1260
ice bridged over the ocean-streams,
a shining sea-road. Happy in heart dwelled
the blameless earl, mindful of valor,
bold and patient, in great affliction
through the winter-cold night. Never did he cease
    from reason,   1265
stricken by fear, from what he had formerly begun,
but he ever most gloriously praised his Lord,
honored Him with words, until glory's gem
appeared heaven-bright.

At first sight this second passage seems supernumerary, an unnecessary and perhaps illogical addition to the core action expected in motif E. And while there is a nominal equivalent in the *Praxeis* for E, it is merely the briefest of phrases (καὶ ἦν παραλελυμένος σφόδρα, or "and he was sorely distressed") and has absolutely nothing to do with what follows in 1255b–69. We are left to ask whether this second passage can be viewed as a paratactic expansion of the core action, even though it seems in its lyrical and exacting description of winter's locking up the seaways to go well beyond intensification or ornamentation of motif E. Simply put, what has the quite unexpected onset of winter to do with the prisoner's dark night of the soul? Are we then to see the excursus as a flaw, an unwarranted expatiation rather clumsily tacked on to a motif by virtue of prior association or some other cause? For even if the passage appears quite beautifully evocative in its own right, is it not a departure from the narrative business at hand?

    The answer to these questions lies in understanding exactly what the passage represents, and here we penetrate to the innermost layer of the *Andreas* poet's compositional technique. For the "winter" and "sea" imagery that makes up this cluster of lines is associated in the poetic tradition with the theme of "Exile" first discovered and commented on by Stanley B. Greenfield (1953a,b, and esp. 1955). Although this brief passage, subordinate as it is to another theme, does not develop what Greenfield has identified as the four aspects that collectively typify the Exile pattern in Old English verse, all of the lyric imagery used in the *Andreas* instance belongs to (and therefore summons up) the traditional idea of Exile. We need only recall elegies like the *The Wanderer*, *The Seafarer*, *The Wife's Lament*, and more to hear the resonance of the thematic pattern: the isolated, solitary man or woman, deprived of all kinship and social ties, struggles weary-minded to overcome the mental and physical ravages of his or her earthly condition. There is no more powerful or ubiquitous traditional pattern in the Anglo-Saxon poetic corpus, and it comes very near the surface of things as the poet works traditionally to express the tribulations of Andrew's first night in a meaningful way.

That these powerful overtones associated with implicit reference to the theme of Exile are really part of the poetics of this passage can be proved in another way as well. Later on, during the second night of mental anguish, Satan's followers, having first fled Andrew's ready responses, plan to return with their leader to taunt him again. In urging Satan to the task, they say (1358a):

> oðwitan him his *wræc*sið
>
> Let us mock his [Andrew's] *exile*-journey

The use of the morph *wræc*-, "exile"[36]—the key word in all instances of the Exile theme—shows how closely the poet identifies the much-persecuted Andreas with the Old English *peregrinus* figure; the attribution of associated qualities is reinforced when, in the midst of the third scourging, God confronts the holy man with these words (1431-33):

> "Ne wep þone *wræc*sið,   wine leofesta,
> nis þe to frecne;   ic þe friðe healde,
> minre mundbyrde   mægene besette."

> "Do not bewail this *exile*-journey, dearest friend,
> it is not too fearsome for you; I shall keep you in safety,
> in my protection I shall surround you with might."

Not only the use of the key morph *wræc*-, for which there is again no equivalent in the *Praxeis*, but also the following lines that, like *The Seafarer* or *The Wanderer*, promise or hint at a new, divine context for the lost earthly context, indicate how the *Andreas* poet conceives of his hero as an exile.[37] In short, although

---

36. From the verb *wrecan*, "to drive out."

37. To these two occurrences of *wræcsið* at 1358a and 1431a we may add other clues that support the identification of the hero with the Exile figure. At 491–92 Andreas speaks of former journeys (that is, trials) using Exile imagery common to the *The Wanderer* and *The Seafarer*; at 889a another instance of *wræcsið* helps to describe the sinners' journey away from the reward of heaven; at 1283b Andreas describes his tribulations as *earfeðsiðas*; at 1351a a demon frustrated by his and his fellows' lack of success in seducing Andreas calls the holy man an *anhaga* (cf. *Wdr* 1a, e.g.); at 1380a and 1383a Andreas tells the devil that God could easily cause him everlasting *wræc*. Even Mattheus refers to himself, the suffering martyr, as an exile (*eðelleasum*) at 74b.

the poet may seem to depart from the logical succession of the narrative and to tack on a lyric to a motif already functionally complete (and all this without any prompting from the source), in fact he only turns from one theme to another—from the Scourging pattern to the details associated conventionally with Exile, and back again. In relation both to compositional technique and to aesthetics, this is a consummately traditional shift of narrative structure.

THE RELATIONSHIP BETWEEN
PHRASEOLOGY AND NARRATIVE STRUCTURE

The two examples of the Old English theme examined in this chapter illustrate, each in its own way, the tradition-dependent character of the multiform unit. While thematic structure in *Beowulf* and *Andreas* resembles what we have found in ancient Greek and Serbo-Croatian in terms of *narrative pattern*, the Old English unit lacks the density of *verbal correspondence* typical of Homer and the epic *guslar*. There may be a group of morphs associated with certain parts of the Anglo-Saxon theme or occasionally even a classically defined formula, as in the Beowulfian Sea Voyage, but nowhere do we encounter the line- and colon-based correspondence characteristic of instances of themes in the other two traditions. As was remarked above, this lack of regularity in diction is only to be expected in a poetry whose formulaic structure is so divergent from the Homeric and Serbo-Croatian models—that is, whose phraseology operates on such idiosyncratic rules. But, these observations having been made, we must go a step further and inquire how the Old English theme actually does express itself in what has long been known to be a traditional diction. To put the matter directly, given the tradition-dependent nature of the Anglo-Saxon narrative unit, what is the relationship between theme and phraseology?

To begin, we know that this relationship differs from the synergistic but relatively less flexible dynamics of formula and theme in ancient Greek and Yugoslav epic, for in Homer's and the *guslar*'s craft we discern a number of factors that closely marshal the expression of narrative ideas. As Milman Parry long ago observed of Homer, and as Albert Lord has argued is true (to a slightly lesser degree) for the *guslar*,[38] poets in these two traditions have fashioned a phraseology remarkably free of synonymous, metrically equivalent formulas. These dictions are characterized, in other words, by a high degree of *thrift*. In practical terms, thrift means that the essential ideas of a traditional poetry approach a one-to-one relationship with their epitomized expressions, so that a poet wishing to express a given essential idea will, in a given metrical format, turn most often to a single expression.[39] This emphasis on thrift does

---

38. See, e.g., Lord 1960, 49–53.

39. This formulation must of course take into account the poet's use of the formulaic language as an idiom. He does not proceed colon by colon, but "fluently," as it were. Thrift applies most clearly and regularly to noun-epithet formulas.

not of course indenture the poet as slave to the limited resources of his tradition; as Parry began to point out, and as has since been shown at greater length (Foley 1984b, 1986a,b), these expressions are in effect metonymic of the great resources of tradition as a whole. But, the echoic riches of the diction aside, a thrifty phraseology means that a single traditional idea will necessarily lead regularly (even inevitably) to a single expression in the Homeric or Serbo-Croatian *Kunstsprache*.

Thriftiness stems from the inherent morphological conservatism of ancient Greek and Serbo-Croatian formulaic structure. Were it not that these two phraseologies existed symbiotically with two meters that, as was demonstrated in earlier chapters, encouraged the formation and maintenance of encapsulated, right-justified formulas with regular syllabic definition and internal structure, thrift would be impossible. For thrift depends directly on consistency of diction over time, and such diachronic consistency can obtain only when the institutionalized constraints on diction establish—and prevent the collapse of—well-defined metrical categories. If Homeric formulas, for example, could expand grossly in syllabic count, operate without true caesuras and diareses, and ignore the Indo-European rule of right justification, they would quickly lose their ability to recur regularly and predictably. And this change in metrical constraints would in time lead to a lack of (classical) definition as formulaic units. Furthermore, because uniqueness would perish along with definition, the same process would lead to lack of a simple one-to-one correspondence between essential idea and phraseological unit. In short, what we call thrift would be impossible to maintain.

But in fact that is precisely the case in Old English. While we have no reason to believe that the Anglo-Saxon compositional idiom was ever structured more like its Homeric counterpart,[40] it is quite clear that nothing like thrift characterizes Old English as it stands.[41] It would be more accurate to say that both the nature of phraseology and the paratactic, adding style called "variation"[42] that typify Old English poetic style actively discourage thrift and promote *a one-to-many relationship between an essential traditional idea and its verbal expression.*

In chapter 6 it was shown that Old English poetic phraseology is much more flexible than either of its comparands: lacking the metrical requirements of syllabic count, regular caesura, and right justification, it manifests instead a formulaic structure that depends on stressed positions and alliteration between half-lines. This arrangement results not in the highly regular (because encapsulated and internally regulated) diction of Homer and the *guslar* but rather in a far more flexible idiom that permits much more extensive variation around a relatively fixed core of one or more words or morphs. Such a tradition-

---

40. On the prehistory of the Old English alliterative line, see chapter 3.
41. See further Fry 1968c.
42. For discussions of variation, see, e.g., Brodeur 1969, 39–70; Robinson 1985.

dependent phraseology naturally exhibits a less rigidly governed morphology: formulas as elements do not recur verbatim or with only a strictly limited number of variations; instead, they change significantly from one instance to the next. Indeed, with variability as relatively unregulated as it seems to be, even the concept of "recurrence" itself may not be precise enough to describe the protean adaptability of Old English diction. To sum up, with stress position, sequence of stresses, and alliteration as the primary prosodic features of the Old English line, we cannot expect the kind of recurrence found in Homeric and Serbo-Croatian epic.

If, in turn, that sort of recurrence is impossible under the constraints of Anglo-Saxon prosody, then the tradition could never develop anything approaching a one-to-one correspondence of phrase and essential idea.[43] And if that correspondence could not evolve, neither could thrift. Under Old English metrical conditions, one idea may have many phraseological correlates rather than a single epitomized expression, for that is the nature of the idiosyncratic prosody that supports phrase-making and -retention. Correspondingly, we have long known that Old English style leans heavily on the poetic device of *variation*, the terracing of subjects, verbs, or other elements in an additive series. The celebrated short lyric "Cædmon's Hymn" provides an expedient example of this common technique (West Saxon version, *ASPR*, 6:106):

> Nu sculon herigean   *heofonrices weard,*
> *meotodes* meahte   and his modgeþanc,
> weorc *wuldorfæder,*   swa he wundra gehwæs,
> *ece drihten,*   or onstealde.
> He ærest sceop   eorðan bearnum
> heofon to hrofe,   *halig scyppend;*
> þa middangeard   *moncynnes weard,*
> *ece drihten,*   æfter teode
> firum foldan,   *frea ælmihtig.*

> Now we must praise the *heavenly kingdom's guardian,*
> the *measurer's* might and his spirit-thought,
> the *glory-father's* work, as he of each wonder,
> *eternal lord,* established the beginning.
> He first made for the children of earth
> heaven as a roof, *holy creator;*
> then the middle-earth *mankind's guardian,*
> *eternal lord,* afterward appointed
> for the people of earth, *lord almighty.*

The italicized words and phrases (all of which, except in lines 2 and 3, are exactly one half-line in length) all name God, the creator of the universe, in

---

43. The situation should not be phrased only negatively; compositionally, this dynamic also allows for a useful flexibility in verse-making.

his many and diverse aspects, and part of the poem's power derives from the panegyric series of these epithets, one after the other. In the second part of the hymn, four different phrases—"holy creator," "mankind's guardian," "eternal lord," and "lord almighty"—comprise an extended figure of variation. These four epithets, formulaically unrelated, have an additive or aggregate force greater than the sum of their individual contributions because they occur in what may meaningfully be called a rhetorical series, with the last three in direct apposition to one another. Stylistically, the fact that *ece drihten* ("eternal lord") occurs twice in this poem and many other times in the poetic tradition at large, or that *mancynnes weard* ("mankind's guardian," 7b) can be construed as sharing a formulaic system with *heofonrices weard* ("heavenly kingdom's guardian," 1a),[44] is not so significant as the fact of their co-occurrence in the typically Anglo-Saxon figure of variation.[45]

Taken together, these observations about (a) the inherent flexibility of the Old English poetic *Kunstsprache* and (b) the marked stylistic preference for the rhetorical figure of variation lead us to expect exactly what seems to characterize themes in the Old English tradition: they reveal a definite, consistent narrative pattern but little or no verbal correspondence. If the essential ideas embodied in the narrative design have no consistently focused, one-to-one relationship with the elements of traditional diction that serve as their expressive medium, then the theme simply cannot recur with formulaic repetition marking its various instances. Rather, we find the "deep structure" of narrative pattern, to use Calvert Watkins's formulation,[46] imaged in an unbound, non-specialized set of traditional phrases—that is, in a surface structure of diction that can shift widely in its formulaic and morphemic make-up while staying within the theme's ideational boundaries. The flexibility of Old English poetic phraseology—a multiform surface that is not subject to the law of thrift—makes for not simply a single characteristic rendering of a narrative idea but rather for many equivalent possibilities for expression of the theme. If by "traditional" we mean a phraseology that, no matter how repetitive it may be, provides the poet with a language both sufficiently plastic and sufficiently structured to serve his needs as a compositional tool, then the Old English poetic idiom is fully as traditional as its Homeric and Serbo-Croatian counterparts.

Thus it is that tradition-dependence becomes most crucial as one confronts the relationship between formulaic phraseology and narrative structure. Since

---

44. See Fry 1974 for a thorough formulaic analysis of "Cædmon's Hymn." I should add here that I chose the hymn as a convenient example of the figure of variation, not as a comparand for *Beowulf* and *Andreas*.

45. Indeed, it becomes clear that the versificational and stylistic figure of variation actually promotes unperiodic enjambement. As we discovered in chapter 6, the solution to compositional problems often extends over more than one line, supported by the alliteration of half-lines.

46. As articulated in G. Nagy 1979, 2–6.

we have found in earlier chapters that comparison of formulas or themes across traditions is misleading unless we first take into account the inevitable differences that spring ultimately from discrepancies among natural languages themselves, so we should expect corresponding differences in this important relationship. The following list displays schematically two general models for this interaction.

Homeric and Serbo-Croatian	*Old English*
Theme (deep structure)	Theme (deep structure)
↓	↓
Bundles of formulas	Unbound selection of formulas
(surface structure)	(surface structure)

The phraseology and prosody of ancient Greek and Yugoslav epic are such that a one-to-one, bound relationship between the narrative pattern and its formulaic expression can survive over time as—within limits—the single way to capture the traditional wisdom of the theme. Of course, as we have seen, the Homeric and Serbo-Croatian multiforms can also vary in myriad ways on a nominal scale, with addition, deletion, splitting of motifs, and so on; in addition, we have discovered that both of these other epic traditions also include thematic patterns, and parts of patterns, with no firm core of verbal correspondence among their instances. But the phraseology and prosody of Old English are such that the relationship between narrative pattern and phraseological expression is always and everywhere unbound and one-to-many. All phraseology used to express the theme will still be traditional (in terms of the special meaning of that term for Old English verse), but the deep thematic structure will not exert as constraining and deterministic an influence on choice of diction as it can in ancient Greek and Serbo-Croatian epic. It is no accident, in other words, that we do not find occurrences of the "Hero on the Beach," "Exile," or any other Old English multiforms sharing a common fund of formulaic diction, nor is that "lack" a sign that these narrative patterns are not "true themes." The solution to the quandary is once again found in the principle of tradition-dependence, in this case specifically in the idiosyncratic relationship in Old English poetry between the traditional ideas embodied in the narrative pattern of the theme and their actual verbal expression in traditional phraseology.

TEN

Story-Pattern in the
Serbo-Croatian Return Song

A SINGER'S ERROR

At line 677 of his *Captivity of Alagić Alija* (Parry no. *6618*), the *guslar* Mujo Kukuruzović makes what seems to be an error. Instead of sending the hero Alija to a spring near Jezero, as we would expect, he has him set out for Kara Bogdan, the stronghold of General Pero. This turn of events does not bode well for the song that Kukuruzović is at this point only one-third of the way through, for the subsequent action of the tale depends crucially on what happens at Jezero. For the moment it is enough to say that such an error, were it left uncorrected, would lead to a sequence involving the enemy-turned-blood brother Pero in a rather complex battle, rescue, and winning of a maiden. A meeting at the spring, on the other hand, would set in motion a plot moving eventually toward Halil's rescue of his sister, Aikuna. On the face of it, there is no reason for Mujo's misdirection, and he seems headed for a flawed performance.

We know from two sources that the singer recognized his error. The first source is the text itself, which Kukuruzović adjusts after the fact to alter his direction. Since as an oral singer composing his song extemporaneously he cannot go back and erase the mistake, he corrects his text in the traditional way by simply changing the journey's destination with an added series of formulaic phrases.[1] In other words, he follows Alagić Alija's announced intention to seek General Pero in Kara Bogdan (the error) with a cluster of lines customarily devoted to travel, only now specified for the correct location:

> Kudgod ide i goni dorata,
> Kada spade u Jaboku pustu,
> U Jaboku do Jezera hladna—
> Tuka ima bunar voda 'ladna.
> (*6618*.691–94)

---

1. Cf. Lord's account of an uncorrected inconsistency (1960, 94–95); and Peabody's notions of "accident, correction, and retrogression" in Hesiod's *Works and Days* (1975, esp. 231–36).

> Wherever he went and drove the bay horse,
> Then he came to empty Jaboka,
> Into Jaboka and up to cold Jezero—
> Here was a spring of cold water.

At this juncture Kukuruzović has found his way back to the story line, and he has done so in a traditional manner.[2]

In addition to this observable in-progress adjustment, the singer made evident his knowledge of the error in a conversation with Parry and Lord's native assistant, Nikola Vujnović. The context for their discussion is filled out by text no. 1868, a second and this time dictated version of *The Captivity of Alagić Alija* recorded the day before.

> *N*: When we wrote down this song [no. 1868], you told me that when Alija killed his wife, he went off seeking some ban and general. *M*: Uh-huh. *N*: And that they attacked the Lika. *M*: Uh-huh. *N*: But this morning you sang that he killed his wife and then met some harambasha [no. 6618]. *M*: That's right— Päun harambasha. *N*: And that he directed Alija to seize Halil's sister and afterwards Halil set her free. *M*: Uh-huh. *N*: There's a difference here, Mujo, I'd say, and I'd say it's an important difference. *M*: Then it's possible that I skipped over [*Onda može bit' da sam ja preletijo*]. *N*: What's that? *M*: It's possible that I skipped over. *N*: I'd say, by God, that there's some sort of important difference. *M*: Yes, it's possible; I began to set it straight [*popravit'*] immediately, so it's possible. *N*: Then which is the true story? Tell me. *M*: I consider [no. 6618] the true one. *N*: The one this morning? *M*: The one this morning, because, you know, I've heard it done that way more times.[3]

Evidently there looms in this pair of texts an error much more extensive than we originally supposed: no. 1868 stands as an uncorrected mistake of some 1,603 lines, and there are only 2,152 lines in the entire poem. What amounts to nearly the final three-quarters of the epic, then, the singer later terms *kriv* ("false, crooked"). In the case of no. 1868, Kukuruzović did not, for whatever reason, return to his intended story line at all; rather, he continued on to the end of an avowedly "untrue" tale. To recapitulate, we can identify two problems in narrative organization: (1) in no. 6618 the *guslar* has committed an error of place and character which he is able to correct, while (2) in no. 1868 he has committed the same error but does nothing to correct it. This situation begs a number of questions. For example, why does Kukuruzović depart from the "proper" story line? In particular, why does he do so at exactly the same point in both performances? Is there any reason why he strays to the General

---

2. Cf. Ibro Bašić's resumption of the narrative after a pause for rest, as described in chapter 8; in continuing the story he re-tracks to the last thematic boundary and, after a *pripjev* for continuation, begins anew from that point.

3. This and later excerpts are taken from Parry text no. 6619, a conversation with Kukuruzović; translation is mine.

Pero tale both times, and what can be said about its structure and content in relation to the story involving Päun harambasha?

The *guslar* offers an insight into some of these questions further on in his conversation with Nikola:

> *N*: Do you sing other songs, for example, with the same kind of variation as this song? The question really comes to this—do you know these other songs better, or do you know them only as well as this one? *M*: Well, brother, whatever songs I learned from singers, those I know, do you understand? But the songs about Ograšćić Alija and Alagić Alija are enough alike, one to the next, that the verses [*stihovi*] carry over. *N*: Yes, yes. *M*: So it was in this way that I skipped over, so to speak, and leaned in another direction. And then I saw that I was mistaken, but I didn't stop to tell you.

Apparently the singer perceives some kind of congruency between the song under consideration and the tale of Ograšćić Alija, a similarity he describes in terms of "verses."[4] At this stage it is difficult to say exactly what he means by this observation, but he clearly understands the congruency as the precondition for his "skipping over" from one song to the other. Fortunately, the Milman Parry Collection includes two versions of a narrative by Kukuruzović which may be titled *The Captivity of Ograšćić Alija*, one of them sung (no. *6617*) and the other dictated (no. *1287a*). A comparison of story lines will yield additional information about the *guslar*'s error and will document the multiformity of story patterns that fosters both the evolution of story cycles and the production of mixed texts. But first we need to develop a simple and straightforward way of looking at narrative pattern, a "common denominator" that will rationalize individual details to generic outlines. With this methodology and the information it makes available in hand, I will return to Mujo's "skipping over" later in the chapter.

THE RETURN SONG

As Albert Lord has shown, there exists throughout the long history of Balkan oral epic song a widespread and recurrent mythic pattern which he calls the "Return Song."[5] This narrative sequence, which Lord believes to have arisen from "the vegetation pattern of death and resurrection, the dying god who returns," follows a consistent order: "The god or hero disappears for a relatively long period of time and is seemingly dead, but eventually he returns,

---

4. Singers use the term *stihovi* ("stichs") and *reči* ("words") to describe units of utterance, some as small as a single line and others as large as a section of a story. Kukuruzović seems at this point to mean something larger than lines by his use of *stihovi*, perhaps a unit similar to that called an "element" in the analysis below. See also chapter 2.

5. See esp. Lord 1969; also Lord 1951a, 1967a, 1970, 1976; Lord 1960, 186–97. Of related interest are M. Lord 1967; Nagler 1974, 131–66; Peabody 1975, 216–72; Foley 1984b, 1986b.

or is sought after and brought back. During his absence there has been devastation, but upon his reestablishment, which is performed ceremonially, order is restored, prosperity returns, and frequently he re-marries" (1972, 31). Of course, we recognize the story of Odysseus, whose twenty-year absence and triumphant return follow this pattern very closely,[6] but the pattern also resolves a great number of Return Songs in the Serbo-Croatian tradition, such as the many examples preserved in the Parry Collection. As Lord has put it (1962, 320), "I like to think that in 'The Captivity of Šarac Mehmedagha' and in other similar songs in the Yugoslav tradition one is hearing the *Odyssey* or the other similar songs, still alive on the lips of men, ever new, yet ever the same." To posit so direct a connection between Homer and the Yugoslav *guslar* is to claim a good deal, but the Return Song structure does seem to inform both the *Odyssey* and its proposed epic relatives. For the purposes of the present analysis, it will be enough simply to recognize similarities between the Greek and Serbo-Croatian texts. Our most immediate interest will be the way in which the Return Song pattern manifests itself within the Yugoslav oral epic tradition.

The basic Return schema is a "story-pattern"[7] that consists of five elements: Absence (A), Devastation (D), Return (R), Retribution (Rt), and Wedding (W). Certain themes tend to cluster around each of the five elements, providing a characteristic texture to the narrative at the level of the typical scene. The themes are the protean units of verbalization which express the abstract elements of story-patterns, the narrative "words" by means of which the *guslar* fleshes out the traditional sequence of ideas in concrete form. Many such Return epics begin, for example, with three introductory themes: "Shouting in Prison," "Bargaining for Release," and "Preparation for Journey Home" (Lord 1960, appendix 3, 245-49).[8]

Whether these introductory multiforms occur or not, almost all Return Songs open with some evidence of a withdrawn or absent hero (A) and of the hero's suffering at the hands of a captor while a rival strives to take his place at home (D). These stages entail the capture of one or more Turkish heroes and their imprisonment in a Christian ban's *tamnica* ("prison"), a hateful place of confinement often garnished with scorpions and snakes. After striking a bargain for release with the ban or his wife the banica, the captive returns to his homeland (R). Once there he passes the test(s) of the suitor, either implicitly or explicitly defeating his rival (Rt), and claims the wife or bride whom he left behind at the time of his capture (W). Themes of single combat and recognition can fill out the Rt and W elements, as in the *Odyssey*; in fact, vari-

---

6. See also Lord 1960, 158–85; Lord 1965, 1971.

7. A story-pattern is one of those "narrative patterns that, no matter how much the stories built around them may seem to vary, have great vitality and function as organizing elements in the composition and transmission of oral story texts" (Lord 1969, 18).

8. See the examination of "Shouting in Prison" in chapter 8.

ations in thematic articulation take place throughout the Return Song structure. But the overall story-pattern directs the narrative progress of all its variants, with the five-element schema underlying all superficial variations. I turn now to a close examination of Return Songs by Kukuruzović and Ibro Bašić to illustrate the interplay between story-pattern and the individual tale.

THE SINGERS AND THEIR SONGS

In tracking the Return Song structure through a body of material or, for that matter, conducting any kind of investigation into oral poetic techniques, it is important to control as far as possible the variables involved. The conclusions quoted above are based on surveys of a great many texts and thus provide the background essential to more focused research. In order to understand story-pattern dynamics more exactly, I now narrow the sample of material in two ways: by designating for close study exclusively texts from a single geographical area or local tradition, and by further limiting this textual basis to the Return Song repertoires of two singers from within that area.[9] The analysis will cover the local tradition of the region of Stolac, a subset of the Moslem epic tradition as a whole, through its manifestation in the Return Songs of the *guslari* Ibro Bašić and Mujo Kukuruzović, the singer whose "error" began this chapter. While the results cannot have as general applicability to the larger Serbo-Croatian and South Slavic epic tradition as do Lord's summaries, they will illustrate in some detail how an individual singer responds to and within his tradition. And since the investigation will range over seven epic texts—a total of some 11,000 lines[10]—there will be ample opportunity to demonstrate the generative multiformity of story-patterns.

Ibro Bašić and the Alagić Alija and Velagić Selim

The Return Songs of Ibro Bašić are the subject of the first stage of investigation; three versions of his *Alagić Alija and Velagić Selim* (hereafter *AAVS*) will serve as the textual foundation for the opening analysis of story-pattern variation. Two of these are sung texts (nos. *291b* and *6597*) and one is dictated (no. *1283*). The song is in Lord's terminology a "return-rescue" epic, with the Return schema described above forming the first part of the plot structure.[11] The major action may be summarized as follows.

9. Thus the texts are taken from two "idiolects" within the same "dialect" area; see chapters 5 and 8.

10. Texts to be considered are: (1) three versions of Ibro Bašić's *Alagić Alija and Velagić Selim* (no. *291b*, 1,360 lines; no. *6597*, 1,558 lines; no. *1283*, 1,403 lines); (2) two versions of *The Captivity of Ograšćić Alija* (no. *6617*, 2,180 lines; no. *1287a*, 1,288 lines) by Mujo Kukuruzović; and (3) two versions of *The Captivity of Alagić Alija* (no. *6618*, 1,422 lines; no. *1868*, 2,152 lines), also by Kukuruzović, for a total of 11,363 lines.

11. See Lord 1960, 120–23 and 260–65, on the "return-rescue" pattern; see also *SCHS* 1:339–50 for further examples and commentary.

THE GENERAL PLOT OF *AAVS*

The *pripjev* ("proem"), which begins the song in versions *291b* and *6597*, typically does not form part of the main narrative frame but addresses itself to the rhetorical "we" of the singer's audience. The narrative actually commences with cannon thundering in celebration of the ban's capture of Alagić Alija (AA), a young Turkish hero whom he casts into an underground prison. There AA encounters Velagić Selim (VS), who has been incarcerated for twelve years.[12] VS identifies himself and poses a long list of questions about their common homeland, Udbina. He is encouraged by all of AA's answers except the final four: VS's white tower is now overgrown with ivy, his mother has declined with age, his wife is in the process of being re-married, and his horse has been stolen. As VS bemoans his fate, AA interrupts and narrates a long flashback that details his journey to Zadar and subsequent capture. On the eve of his marriage to Muminova Fata, an urgent message begging his immediate aid arrived from Mustajbeg of the Lika. At first he refused to leave his bride in order to rescue Mustajbeg from the siege of General Pero, but an anonymous voice from a window high above the courtyard reminded him of his heroic duty. AA capitulated, rallied the gathered wedding guests to his purpose, and undertook the journey to the Lika. Although AA enjoyed initial success against the malevolent Christian forces, Mustajbeg deceived him by failing to unlock the gates to his tower at the appropriate moment. As the result of this treachery, AA was overcome, seized alive, and imprisoned in Zadar.

The ban of Zadar now overhears the flashback account and offers AA his freedom for a price: a great many valuable gifts, together with his sister, Aikuna. When AA agrees to all but the last condition, the ban angrily threatens him with a gruesome death and departs. On his return to the tower, his wife the banica approaches her husband with an ultimatum. Since the shouting of the captives has so frightened her infant, Marija, that he will not nurse, the banica declares that she will throw the baby to his death unless the ban immediately releases the person responsible for the disturbance. He thus has no choice but to re-enter the prison to confer with VS, and the result is one month's freedom for the prisoner to return to his homeland and attend to his mother and wife.

VS arrives in Udbina to find the wedding party of his wife's suitor encamped below his tower. With hair to his waist and nails grown out *kano u krilaša*

---

12. Lord (1972, 313) reminds us of the mythic significance of this detail: "The number [of years of the hero's absence]—which should, of course, be translated into months—is twelve, nine, twenty, twenty-four; these represent an annual event, or the period of gestation of the human, or a play on words between '*dvanaest*' and '*dvadeset*' ['twelve' and 'twenty,' respectively], or a doubling of twelve." It is also worth mentioning in this regard that the prisoner's speech of lamentation very often includes a notation of the change of seasons, usually a complaint that the coming of spring and winter cannot be distinguished from within the place of confinement.

("like [those] on a winged horse")—that is, in disguise[13]—he passes himself off as an anonymous twelve-year captive begging alms. After an initial encounter with Mustajbeg, who earlier deceived AA, VS next approaches Halil, suitor to his wife. The prisoner is permitted to join the athletic contests and so soundly defeats his rival, Halil, that the outraged suitor challenges him to the martial equivalent of their games—single combat. The ragged captive accepts the challenge, slyly suggesting that it take place near VS's tower and that each of them wager heavily on the outcome. Finally, VS, still in disguise and spinning his Odyssean tale, meets his wife. Far from recognizing him, she is terribly frightened by his appearance and begins to flee. To test her fidelity, he then claims to have known VS as a fellow prisoner and to have buried him. When his wife responds with a reward, VS asks whom she honors in doing so: her dead husband or her present suitor. Tearfully exclaiming her loyalty to VS, whom she now recognizes, she runs to their tower and snatches a sword from the wall, pleading with her husband to behead her and end her misery. Much impassioned weeping ensues, while the returned hero inwardly rejoices over his wife's faithfulness. Mustajbeg overhears the recognition scene and, gathering up the wedding party and the suitor Halil, quickly flees to escape VS's wrath.

The month of freedom comes to an end, and VS keeps his promise to come back to Zadar. The ban's attention now focuses on AA, who has also begun to shout and create a disturbance. AA complains that his life is almost over and requests writing materials to prepare a last letter to his mother. In it he directs her to distribute his arms and armor among their standard-bearers and to allow Fata, his betrothed, to make a new marriage contract. The young girl, however, decides to join her lover in Zadar alone, and she sends their servant, Huso, with a plea for assistance to her father, Muminagha. But Muminagha threatens both Huso and his daughter with death over the shame she has caused him, so she readies herself to leave for Zadar disguised as a Christian warrior. During the journey she spends a night encamped in a mountain pass, with wild animals all about; she speaks to each one in turn, asking that she be allowed to proceed in safety. After entering the city, Fata questions her horse (really AA's war charger) as to where she might gain information about AA and soon finds herself at a tavern, where Mara, the innkeeper, guesses her identity. Because of a kindness once done her by Muminagha, Mara pledges her support. After a change of dress they consult Andjelija, who promises to help with the escape of the Turkish heroes. The next day sees their plan in action, though AA and VS do not at first realize what is happening. Fata heroically fights her way through the hostile ranks until

---

13. The winning of a maiden or wife, as well as the more generalized rescue action, usually entails a hero in disguise. We shall see below a variation of the same collocation of disguise and winning a wife/rescuing a captive in the songs of Kukuruzović.

she reaches the captives; she then frees them and furnishes them with horses and weapons while Muminagha's troops arrive to aid her. In the aftermath, Fata and Andjelija reveal their true identities and later marry AA and the suitor Halil, respectively.

THE STORY-PATTERN OF *AAVS*

Ibro's *AAVS*, one of many similarly structured epics preserved in the Parry Collection, follows the Return Song schema. At the most basic level it consists of a double cycle of the five elements, one cycle for each hero.[14] VS has been absent from Udbina for twelve years (A_{vs}), suffering as a prisoner of the ban of Zadar while Halil strives to usurp his place at home (D_{vs}).[15] He is released for one month and allowed to return (R_{vs}).[16] By defeating his rival in the throwing and jumping competitions, winning their proposed single combat by default, and causing Mustajbeg and the wedding party to flee his wrath, he achieves retribution (Rt_{vs}). In addition, note that in terms of the story-pattern VS's wife is a marriageable maiden, since she is courted by a suitor and, for the period of VS's absence, is without a husband. The successful trial of her fidelity thus culminates in the (re-)establishment of her husband's position, that is, in $*W_{vs}$ (marked with an asterisk to indicate its ephemerality). At this point, then, the first Return Song cycle is complete; a song which we might call *The Captivity of Velagić Selim* has run its narrative course.

But *AAVS* as a whole has not. AA is also absent from their common home-

---

14. At various points in the analysis to follow, the footnotes will gloss the story-pattern in the thematic notation developed by David E. Bynum (1964), who bases his directory of multiforms on seventy-five Wedding Songs drawn from the Parry Collection and six published sources.

15. Although the narrative presents no explicit background information on the imprisonment of VS, we may assume that his treacherous countryman Mustajbeg, the leader of Halil's wedding party who recognizes VS and immediately flees, is largely responsible. Mustajbeg also deceives AA during the fight with General Pero and thus causes his detention by the ban of Zadar. The treason at the root of the heroes' common plight is embedded in Bynum's "Absence" theme, which "concerns the removal of a character, usually a hero or marriageable maiden, from his or her dwelling-place through the machinations of a hostile power, usually in league with those who ought to defend the victim against such ills" (1964, 168). We may also mention that Mustajbeg appears in the epic tradition as a very ambiguous figure; although he commands the Krajina, he is also known as a drunkard and wencher (see, for example, Avdo Medjedović's *Death of Mustajbeg* [nos. 6804, 6807], in which the heroic figure Mujo warns the great leader of the consequences attendant on his excesses).

16. Four of Bynum's themes appear in this section: (1) "A Hero Laments in Prison," (2) "A Woman Intercedes to Obtain a Hero's Release," (3) "A Prisoner Seeks Release in Audience with Captor," and (4) "Captor Releases an Imprisoned Hero." The last theme in this series customarily includes a degree of rehabilitation by the captor (Bynum 1964, 182); but since VS's freedom is temporary and he must in one month re-enter prison, that feature of the theme is suppressed.

land Udbina (A_{aa}).[17] He finds himself a helpless captive in the same prison and in despair writes a last letter to his mother in which he abandons all hope of rescue (D_{aa}). From this element on, Fata serves as the substitute hero by securing AA's release and thereby making possible his return (R_{aa}). She fights bravely, killing many of the ban's army and revenging AA's incarceration (Rt_{aa}). The epic closes with a series of recognitions and the long-deferred marriage (W_{aa}).

We need to appreciate the significance of this second Return cycle fully. The latter section of *AAVS*, which might be termed either *The Rescue of Alagić Alija and Velagić Selim* or *The Return of Alagić Alija*, is both a rescue sequence that concludes the overall "return-rescue" pattern and a Return pattern in its own right. This dual identity of the second section reveals a fundamental symmetry in the structure of Ibro's "return-rescue" song, a symmetry which suggests that the more complex type of epic developed from the simpler, five-element schema. While we cannot go much further with the present evidence than the demonstration of this relationship between story-types and a logical hypothesis about the derivation of one from the other, the essential point of the demonstration is secure: a double-cycle, "return-rescue" epic such as *AAVS* is *genetically*—one might say formulaically—related to the basic Return Song schema. To put it another way, the return pattern is a *multiform* capable of theme-like variation both as a simplex and as a multiple of itself. We should detect something distinctly traditional about this situation.

The narrative pattern of *AAVS* as a whole can thus be described as a recombination of the Return sequence along the lines indicated above. Within the song, $A_{vs} - D_{vs}$ and $A_{aa} - D_{aa}$ are roughly co-extensive: while the personal histories of the two heroes vary slightly, their initial situations of absence and detention in Zadar are comparable.[18] But from this point on the pattern splits. Upon his release VS follows out the Return Song cycle to its logical conclusion $(R_{vs}, Rt_{vs},$ and $*W_{vs})$. But because his freedom is temporary, he regresses to D_{vs} on re-entering prison.[19] Meanwhile, AA languishes in Zadar, managing only to resign himself to death (D_{aa}). In schematic terms the progress of the narrative may be represented as in figure 12. In the rescue section of the song, Fata's surrogate heroics accomplish R_{aa} and Rt_{aa} and clear the way

17. AA postpones his marriage, an event at once the exordium and the coda to the epic, in order to answer Mustajbeg's plea for assistance. This action matches in substance Bynum's theme "A Hero Refuses to Consummate a Marriage Immediately," in which "the business which the hero puts before his marriage is often the rescue or liberation of his elders" (1964, 134).

18. We hear in different ways and to different extents of the heroes' capture, but their misfortunes have in common the evil of Mustajbeg, the problem of a wife/betrothed maiden left behind, and the pain of their present suffering at the hands of the ban.

19. As far as the overall story-pattern is concerned, this regression—or rather the earlier bargain which makes it inevitable—is the crucial link between the two cycles of the song.

Figure 12. *AAVS*, Through Devastation Element

$$A_{vs,aa} \longrightarrow D_{vs,aa} \longrightarrow D_{aa} \longrightarrow D_{vs,aa}$$
$$R_{vs} \longrightarrow Rt_{vs} \longrightarrow *W_{vs}$$

for W_{aa}, thus completing the cycle for AA. But, one may ask, what of VS? Is he not also rescued? And why does he not marry at the close of the epic, as the story-pattern would seem to demand?

One answer is that VS has already married—or re-married, to be exact ($*W_{vs}$). More than a frivolous solution, this line of argument suggests the vitality and integrity of the story-pattern that structures this and so many cognate epic narratives. Another answer—and one perhaps truer to the symbolic nature of the pattern—is that VS does in fact marry again. For just as Fata has taken on AA's heroic identity, a second female substitute, Andjelija, adopts VS's function; thus the paired heroes are freed by paired surrogates. In this way R_{aa} and Rt_{aa} are also R_{vs} and Rt_{vs}. The culmination in double marriage unites Fata (AA's substitute) and Andjelija (VS's substitute) with, respectively, AA and Halil (VS's former rival). At one structural remove, then, VS marries Andjelija and the story-pattern obtains. The narrative as a whole may thus be schematized as in figure 13, in which the section in parentheses is the rescue sequence, itself a Return pattern, while the bracketed section is that part of the cycle undertaken and achieved by the surrogates, Fata and Andjelija.

However the question posed above is answered, it rapidly becomes even clearer just how fundamental the A–D–R–Rt–W schema is to $AAVS$ and yet how complex the narrative that results from combination and permutation of simple story elements can be. As noted above, this particular kind of "return-rescue" epic bears a genetic relationship to the five-element, single-cycle Return Song. The first departure from the basic pattern, VS's conditional release, prepares the way for a second departure, the unconditional release of the heroes. Yet the second event conforms to the same R–Rt–W sequence identically, with the single qualification that the agents of the actions involved are substitutes. In short, the evidence examined so far justifies the following hypothesis: the Return Song story-pattern (the five-element simplex) is more than a narrative latticework; not only does it have considerable potential for variation, but it is also dynamic and process-directing and it lies at the foundation of more complex story-types.

In turning to the second example of variational capacity in the Return Song,

Figure 13. *AAVS*, Entire Pattern

$$A_{vs,aa} \longrightarrow D_{vs,aa} \longrightarrow D_{aa} \longrightarrow (D_{vs,aa} \longrightarrow [R_{vs,aa} \longrightarrow Rt_{vs,aa}] \longrightarrow W_{vs,aa})$$
$$R_{vs} \rightarrow Rt_{vs} \rightarrow *W_{vs}$$

it will thus be well to keep in mind the dual nature of the story-pattern: as a series of abstract potentials, these five elements both *generate* and *control* narrative structure. By marshaling thematic content, story-pattern gives both life and direction to the song; within a context of multiple possibilities, it provides parameters and determines the overall shape of the text. This kind of variation characterizes the largest and most abstract of traditional multiforms, making possible formularity at the level of narrative sequence. But although story-pattern resembles formula and theme in its generative potential, an important difference must be taken into account: at the highest level of structure, a level not directly affected by prosody, consistency of occurrence from one instance to another must depend not on meter and associated phenomena, but rather on the idea-pattern of Return. To state the converse, a small change in story-pattern can mean a very significant change in the epic as a whole.

Mujo Kukuruzović and the Extended Return Song

As noted in chapter 2, Mujo's repertoire was quite large, consisting of a total of thirty-eight *pjesme* on a variety of subjects and apparently learned from a variety of singers. Parry, Lord, and Nikola recorded nine of these songs either on aluminum disks or from dictation, making a total of twelve texts when variants are included. Among those not recorded, *The Young Ban of Janok*[20] seems especially relevant, as will be seen below. Our main focus, however, will be on the four complete texts of Mujo's captivity songs, those about Ograšćić Alija (*OA₁* and *OA₂*, nos. 6617 and 1287a) and Alagić Alija (*AA₁* and *AA₂*, nos. 6618 and 1868).[21]

THE *OA* AND *AA* SONGS

Texts OA_1 and OA_2 are, as is shown below, variant versions of *The Captivity of Ograšćić Alija*, the former sung and the latter oral-dictated.

The Captivity of Ograšćić Alija	OA_1	2,180 lines	6617
		OA throughout	
	OA_2	1,288 lines	1287a
		OA throughout	
The Captivity of Alagić Alija	AA_1	1,422 lines	6618
		AA→OA→AA	
	AA_2	2,152 lines	1868
		AA→OA	

20. This is an abbreviated title. Kukuruzović actually called the song "Pije vino mlad janjočki ban[e] / A do njega Takulija bane" ("The young ban of Janok was drinking wine, / And with him Takulija ban"). The lineation added here illustrates the decasyllabic format of the title, the lines themselves constituting a characteristic opening for a song of attack (as well as for other kinds of songs).

21. Text no. 6616 is what Nikola called a *proba*, a series of beginnings of the same song elicited by Parry for comparative purposes. Since it is an incomplete version of *OA*, I shall not treat it here.

The discrepancy in length—almost 900 lines—will bear explanation as the analysis progresses, since the shorter performance (OA_2) excludes a major section of the narrative which is part of OA_1. Song AA_1 contains the momentary confusion described near the beginning of this chapter; that is, Mujo "skips over" from AA to OA in mid-song, but manages to realign himself within thirty lines and to finish out the AA story. The oral-dictated version AA_2, on the other hand, is really one-fourth AA and three-fourths OA. Losing his song at exactly the same point as in AA_1, Mujo never returns to AA. In reconstructing the story lines of these four closely interrelated performances, I will describe OA and AA concurrently up to the point of divergence,[22] which we shall then need to examine carefully before proceeding to individual accounts of the later sections of the epics.

THE GENERAL PLOT OF AA/OA, SECTION I

After the optional *pripjev*, both songs begin typically with the hero crying out from prison.[23] As in Ibro Bašić's *AAVS*, the Turkish hero's wailing so upsets the ban's infant son that he will not nurse. But when the banica reports this situation to her husband in AA/OA, he refuses to bargain with or to release the hero, citing the havoc caused by the prisoner before his capture as sufficient grounds for maintaining the status quo. The banica is thus forced to become the bargaining agent herself. She descends into the *tamnica* and is greeted as *nerodjena majka* ("unrelated, or foster, mother") by the captive, who then tells her one of two stories. In OA_1 and OA_2 a letter to the imprisoned hero has informed him of his son's imminent marriage. He laments the fact that he has not seen the young man since he was an infant, and that now he will not be able to take part in the wedding ceremony. AA's letter carries a somewhat different but similarly dispiriting message: his wife, having given him up for lost, is about to remarry. Moved by the tale of woe, the banica then opens negotiations with AA/OA. In return for his release, she requires either the prisoner's *pobratimstvo* ("blood-brotherhood") or his *kumstvo* ("godfather-hood," specifically of her son), or both. These synthetic kin relationships establish ritual bonds between two enemies, a Turkish hero and a Christian ban (through his wife, the banica).

When the bargain has been completed, the hero is released and he heads for his home in the Turkish Krajina. Here the story lines again diverge slightly, just as in the case of the letters. During his journey OA encounters the wedding

---

22. The four texts are, for reasons to be shown below, almost identical in story line up to this point, so that describing any one of them would serve the purpose of summary. Small variations will, however, be noted.

23. Here and elsewhere the locale is uncertain; sometimes the hero is said to be imprisoned in Janok, sometimes in Karlovo. The name of the city is finally unimportant, for what matters is that the generic description is of a Christian ban's prison. See further Bynum 1969, 1970; also the analysis of the Shouting in Prison theme in chapter 8 above.

party of his son, Hadžibeg. A series of "Questioning the Captive" themes proves Hadžibeg's loyalty to his father beyond doubt, for the news of OA's death brought by the disguised captive so saddens the young man that he immediately orders a stop to the wedding celebration. At the family *kula* ("tower") OA confronts his wife. Although she does not yet recognize her long-lost husband, she quickly reveals her unfaithfulness by rejoicing over the report of his death. OA then wins a race against the suitor Halil and other members of the wedding party, and later passes the Odyssean test set by Hadžibeg's intended bride—he successfully saddles and rides OA's horse, a feat no one else has been able to accomplish.[24] Finally his wife, mother, and the treacherous Mustajbeg recognize him from his distinctive tamburitza-playing. This group recognition leads up to the close of the first section: Mustajbeg gathers the wedding party and flees to escape OA's revenge, OA's wife dies or is slain by her husband,[25] and his mother discusses with her son the advisability of seeking an alliance with the enemy.

The story of AA from the point of bifurcation to the end of the first section (the locus for "skipping over") is not very different from that of OA. The "Questioning the Captive" theme again precedes the contest with the suitor Halil, only in the AA story the contest divides into two parts: the first, a throwing competition, is vestigial in that AA looks on but does not join in, while the second is very real indeed, consisting as it does of single combat (*mejdan*) between AA and his rival, Halil. Again the preparation of the hero's horse serves an important catalytic function; while in the stable, AA meets and enlists the aid of his sister, who recognizes him by the scar (*biljeg*) he received as a child from being bitten by a horse.[26] Since the wedding procession has left for Halil's home in Kladuša—led, as in so many other instances, by the untrustworthy Mustajbeg—it is up to AA to ride after them. At first he refuses to do so, but after much urging by his mother, he accedes and promises to recoup her "maidservant," his wife. Once in Kladuša, AA fights the *mejdan* and, having defeated his rival, claims his wife. He cuts off her hands, carries her back to his *kula*, and dispatches her in the presence of his mother. The same discussion with his mother then ensues; nothing explicit is mentioned about Mustajbeg, but in the second section plans will soon take shape to work revenge on Mujo, brother to his wife's suitor Halil.

24. This achievement, a common motif in Serbo-Croatian epic song, is reminiscent in narrative form and importance of Odysseus's stringing of the bow.

25. Whatever the actual verbalization of this episode, it is clear that OA's presence is the cause of her death. In text no. 1287a, for example, where he is not as elsewhere said to be the explicit agent of her death, it is OA's tamburitza-playing that causes her demise: "When his truelove heard him, / She shouted what came out of her throat: / 'That's my Ograšćić Alija!' / Three times she spoke it, 'Ograšćić Alija'— / On the fourth she gave up her spirit" (lines 597–601).

26. The parallel between the narrative function of this mark and that of Eurykleia's recognition of Odysseus's scar is striking.

THE STORY-PATTERN OF *AA/OA*, SECTION I

Section I follows the familiar five-element pattern of Return. Each song opens with an imprisoned hero in an enemy *tamnica* crying out in misery. In the course of the conversation between the ban and banica, during which the ban explains why he has no intention of releasing AA/OA, the heroic deeds and capture of the prisoner are rehearsed in a kind of flashback $(A_{aa/oa})$.[27] The Devastation element finds expression in the incarceration and letter (whatever message applies), for AA/OA's demonstrative lamenting is a response to these painful realities $(D_{aa/oa})$. Bargaining with the banica produces the desired results, however; the ritual kinship ties prove an effective means of certifying continued goodwill, and she agrees to release the hero. As is typical of the story-pattern, it is again a female figure who catalyzes the Return $(R_{aa/oa})$.[28] Whether the hero meets his family and adversary on the way back (OA) or in his homeland (AA), he soon ascertains his wife's infidelity and enters into competition—both actual and, with respect to the story-pattern, symbolic—with his rival. All of his actions, undertaken and completed in the "disguise" of a captive claiming to have buried AA/OA, culminate in a twofold revenge $(Rt_{aa/oa})$: he defeats his adversary, Halil, and causes the death of his unfaithful wife. What he accomplishes, in other words, in place of the expected marriage (W), is an "anti-Wedding" $(W-)$ that fulfills the schema symbolically but leaves the overall pattern with a reversed or occluded ending.

This ambivalent character of the fifth and final element is crucial to the structure of the tale as a whole: without the ambivalence of $W-$, the song ends here; with it, the song goes on. It is as if the reversal of W inherent in $W-$ postponed the expected closure and demanded another kind of fulfillment, just as $*W$ in *AAVS* called for continuation in a second cycle. In schematic terms, the progression of *AA/OA*, Section I, may be compared as shown in figure 14. There is thus a clear symbolic logic to the continuation or termination of the song after the Wedding element. If W is either conditional $(*W$ in *AAVS*) or negatively fulfilled in what I have called the "anti-Wedding" $(W-$ in *AA/OA*), it cannot be a final W. Rather, the song will go on, seeking, as it were, an unconditional, positive W to close out the narrative.

To summarize, then, what I have identified as Section I of *AA/OA* is a complete song in itself, a song which we could call *The Captivity of Alagić Alija*

---

27. The elements A_{aa} and A_{oa} are also, of course, implied in the corresponding D elements that follow; many such songs have no flashback and assume the A element without actual description. This kind of flashback is common in oral and oral-derived traditional epic, as both the *Odyssey* and *Beowulf* testify.

28. The female intermediary, often introduced as synthetic kin to the hero, is ubiquitous in Serbo-Croatian epic; cf., for example, *Marko Kraljević Recognizes His Father's Sword* (Karadžić [1845] 1969, no. 56). Such a figure serves the narrative function of promoting a temporary alliance between parties normally separated by institutionalized enmity.

Figure 14. Comparison of Story Lines

Basic
Pattern $A \longrightarrow D \longrightarrow R \longrightarrow Rt \longrightarrow W$ (end of song)

AAVS $A_{vs,aa} \longrightarrow D_{vs,aa} \longrightarrow D_{aa} \longrightarrow (D_{vs,aa} \longrightarrow [R_{vs,aa} \longrightarrow Rt_{vs,aa}] \longrightarrow W_{vs,aa})$ (end

$\searrow R_{vs} \longrightarrow Rt_{vs} \longrightarrow {}^{*}W_{vs} \nearrow$ (*not* end of song) of song)

AA/OA, I $A_{aa/oa} \longrightarrow D_{aa/oa} \longrightarrow R_{aa/oa} \longrightarrow Rt_{aa/oa} \longrightarrow W-_{aa/oa}$ (*not* end of song)

/*Ograščić Alija*, with one crucial difference: the $A–W$ Return Song cycle is left open-ended by frustration of the W element. We should now recall that it is precisely at this point—when the "Return Song within a Return Song" ends—that the singer Mujo Kukuruzović makes his error in texts AA_1 and AA_2. Alagić Alija has dispatched his unfaithful wife and, as the *guslar* himself said, should be headed for the spring at Jezero to make plans for a retaliatory raid. The apparent motivation is AA's disillusionment over his wife's infidelity and his countrymen's lack of fealty; he has already revenged himself once upon Halil in their single combat and will now complete his retribution by attacking Halil's brother. Instead, we remember, he starts out in AA_1 for Kara Bogdan, seat of the Christian enemy General Pero, whom he hopes will join forces with him in making war on the treacherous Mustajbeg and his narrative double, the ubiquitous bey of Ribnik.[29] And while Kukuruzović manages in that performance to correct his "skipping over," in AA_2 he follows the "wrong" story line through to its final W.

KUKURUZOVIĆ'S ERROR: A FIRST APPROXIMATION

A number of explanations for the error now present themselves. We shall need to re-examine the possible solutions later on when analysis of Section II is complete, but we can at least introduce them here. To begin with, an important unit closes with $W-$, so that whatever might follow the death or slaying of the unfaithful wife occurs outside the first Return Song cycle. On the face of it, if variation is to appear, even variation in the form of a "mistake," we would expect it to appear outside of a five-element sequence rather than within it. That is, Kukuruzović's error occurs outside the pattern of themes associated with the story-pattern; it happens, in short, at a vulnerable spot in the narrative. When we add to this observation the demonstrated near-identity of AA, Section I, and OA, Section I, Mujo's "skipping over" becomes a quite understandable phenomenon. To offer a first approximation, then, I would interpret the slip as an instance of what might be called *generic override*, a faulty

29. Kukuruzović interchanges these two characters throughout all four texts of AA/OA. More than just a slip, this substitution results from a narrative equivalence: both are important Turkish heroes who command large armies, and either would be likely to lead a wedding party and therefore to incur OA's wrath.

choice between alternatives that are equivalent in terms of story-pattern but not in terms of actual narrative content—for in both cases, the hero rides off to join an enemy for the purpose of making war on his own countrymen; the particulars vary, but the pattern does not. The singer makes a mistake on the particularized level of the story, but the generic level of AA/OA remains the same, undisturbed and in proper sequence. The source of the error is multiformity, the same multiformity that defines and gives life to the *guslar*'s oral epic tradition.

In order to measure the correspondence between variant texts more exactly, and to understand the basis of generic override in analogy, let us consider Kukuruzović's "skipping over" more closely. Immediately below are the relevant passages from texts AA_1 and OA_1; further evidence from AA_2 and OA_2 will be added as appropriate.

Pa je baci sa konja dorina
A svojom sabljom ispratijo— [30]
U dvije je pole prestavijo.

                                 Vjerna ljuba svijet mijenila.
                                 Vidi, vidi Ograšćić Alije—
                                 Pa ovako iz grla povika: 730

"Čuješ, majko, mili roditelju?
Ja ti vjeru i Boga zadavam: 675   "O tako mi Boga već nikoga,
Ja se idem odmetnuti, majko,   Sad ću moga posjesti gavrana,
Eto tamo do Kara Bogdana,   Idem ići do Kara Bogdana,
Do stolice Pere generala.   Do stolice Pere generala.
Njemu ću se, majko, pridvoriti,   Pa se hoću njemu zamoliti,   735
Pridvoriti, njemu zamoliti.   680   Pa se hoću njemu pridvoriti,
Pa ću begu zulum učiniti,
Njegovom se curom oženiti,
jAli njome jali zemljom crnom."

                                   Da mi dade topove i vojsku.
                                 Pa ću ići begu na Ribniku,
                                 Pa ću begu zulum učiniti—
                                 Sjeći momke, vodiću djevojke,   740
                                 Goniću krave od telaca [31]
                                 I bijele ovce od janjaca—
                                 Sjeći momke, vodiću djevojke,
                                   A ženiti plaćene soldate."

Majka sinu iz grla povika:
"Ej! Alija, moj jedini sine,   685
Nikad nište izdajice bili. [32]

    30. The first colon of line 672 is short one syllable.
    31. The first colon of line 741 is short one syllable.
    32. The noun *ništa*, here part of the emphatic idiom *nikad ništa* ("never anything," or "nothing at all"), seems to take its curious inflection from phonological agreement with the nearby *izdajice* ("traitors").

Kud ćeš ići, nemoj s'odmetati."
"Hoću, majko, današnjeg mi dana."
Pa svojega oturi dorata.
Kudgod ide i goni dorata,   690
Kada spade u Jaboku pustu,
U Jaboku do Jezera hladna—
Tuka ima bunar voda 'ladna.

$$(AA_1. \ 671-93)$$

To izreče, posjede gavrana.   745
Ode Ale do krši Kotara.
Kada spade do Kara Bogdana,
Do stolice Pere generala.

$$(OA_1. \ 728-48)$$

Then he threw [his wife] off the
   bay horse,
And he followed with his sword—
He cut her into two halves.

His truelove passed away.[33]
See, see Ograšćić Alija—
Then he shouted from his
   throat thus: 730

"O mother, gentle parent, do you
   hear me?
I swear to you by my faith in God: 675
I am going to desert, mother,
To that place Kara Bogdan,
To the seat of General Pero.
Him will I serve, mother,
Serve him and seek his favor.   680
Then I will attack the bey,
Take his daughter in marriage,
Either her or the black earth."

"O by my God and by no other,
Now I will mount my horse,
I am going to Kara Bogdan,
To the seat of General Pero.
Then I will seek his favor,   735
Then I will serve him,

That he might grant me cannon
   and an army.
Then I will go to the bey of Ribnik,
Then I will attack the bey—
Having beheaded the young men,
   I will lead away the young
     women,   740
I will drive the cows from their
   calves,
And the white sheep from their
   lambs—
Having beheaded the young men,
   I will lead away the young
   women,
And marry off my mercenaries."

The mother shouted at her son
   from her throat:
"Ej! Alija, my only son,   685

33. Literally, she "changed worlds."

Traitors always come to nothing.
Wherever you go, don't desert."
"But I will, mother, so help me."[34]
Then he turned his bay horse
    away.

Wherever he went and drove
    the bay horse,   690
Then he came into empty Jaboka,
Into Jaboka and up to cold Jezero—
Here was a spring of cold water.

He said this and mounted his
    horse.   745
Alija went to red Kotar.

Then he came into Kara Bogdan,
To the seat of General Pero.

The generic situation is this: AA/OA dispatches his unfaithful wife in the presence of his mother (and sister) and, swearing to revenge Mustajbeg's (or the bey of Ribnik's) disloyalty by attacking his own countrymen (in alliance with the Christian enemy, General Pero), rides away from his homeland. Of those elements parenthesized in this description, the first two are variable in both OA and AA, while the third is found only in the OA story line. Thus the narrative problem posed for the singer consists of bridging the gap from $W-$ to one of two Journey (J) destinations, either Jezero or Kara Bogdan. In symbolic terms the situation may be represented as in figure 15.

Collating all four texts of the $W-$ to J sequence, we can say with certainty that the OA "skipping over" runs at least through line 689 of AA_1. The sequence contains five discrete units: (1) the oath ($AA_1.675$, $OA_1.731$), (2) the announcement of desertion to General Pero ($AA_1.676-78$, $OA_1.732-34$), (3) the plan of revenge ($AA_1.679-83$, $OA_1.735-44$), (4) the mother's distress and caution ($AA_1.684-88$, not present in OA_1),[35] and (5) the actual setting out and journey ($AA_1.689-93$, $OA_1.745-48$). Note that the third unit, the plan of revenge, always carries with it some indication of a W to be fulfilled as the result of AA/OA's continued retribution. In the case of AA_1, the hero promises to take the bey's daughter in marriage, to wed "either her or the black earth." In OA_1 he boasts that he will decimate the bey's troops and take the women as booty, to be married off to his mercenaries. Whether explicitly or not, both the AA and OA story lines somehow include in the plan the capture of the

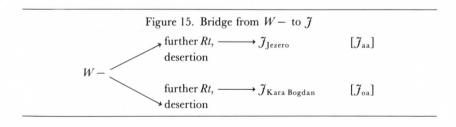

Figure 15. Bridge from $W-$ to J

34. Literally, *današnjeg mi dana* means "by this my day."
35. Text 1287a contains a version of this unit, so it is clear that it appears in the OA story line.

bey's daughter; in other words, the rite of bride-stealing is understood as the culmination of heroic vengeance. It is two units later, during the setting out and journey, that Kukuruzović manages to correct himself by singing a common formulaic series of lines associated with traveling. He has followed the *form* of $W-$ to J all the way through its five units; his only "error" is that he sings $W-$ to J_{oa} instead of to J_{aa}. Generic override, the result of story-pattern congruency and the *guslar*'s traditional impulse toward analogy,[36] has caused the "skipping over." As indicated above, the very vitality of traditional thought has in this case been the downfall of superficial story sequence. Still, in the narrative logic unique to oral traditional song, the form is preserved and, whether or not the "correction" is made, the tale goes on.

But to what does it go on? With the Return Song having run its course, what follows? I remarked earlier that the first parts of AA and OA were enough alike that a single story line summary would adequately render them both. This was indeed the case; Section I of AA/OA is a unit complete in itself except for the modulation entailed in $W-$. But as Kukuruzović indicated in his conversation with Nikola, the second sections of AA and OA are quite different. We shall therefore need to ask a number of questions. Is there any story-pattern underlying the rest of these four texts, either by song (AA vs. OA) or by generalized sequence (all four performances)? If so, what is that pattern, does it function in a manner similar to that underlying the Return Song, and how does it affect the role of Section II in the *guslar*'s "skipping over"? Finally, we should ask whether an overall sequence of elements can be distilled out of AA/OA, an overarching series of abstractions which, as a compound story-pattern in its own right, both limits and generates the narrative substance of the song as a whole. In order to develop answers to these questions, we first need the story lines for Section II of AA and OA; they follow immediately below, together with pattern analysis in a running commentary.

OA, SECTION II: STORY AND STORY-PATTERN

After the $W-$ to J_{kb} section is complete, Kukuruzović moves OA and General Pero along to Janok, where the hero overhears the ban of Janok urging his chieftains to attack the Lika, the territory under the sway of Mustaj-beg.[37] Pero advises raising a force to attack the bey of Ribnik, specifically to steal the bey's daughter and marry her off to one of the captains. OA_1 varies somewhat from OA_2 in that OA overhears both the ban of Janok and Takulija

36. Milman Parry saw the importance of analogy as early as the first *thèse*; see esp. 1928a, in 1971, 68–75.

37. I have assembled this summary primarily from texts *6617* and *1868*, with notations of the few differences that occur. The third performance of OA (*1287a*), a variant in which the hero's plan for revenge terminates rather abruptly with the imposition of a W not found in the other texts of the OA, will not be treated here.

ban planning offensive action. In fact, that particular passage (OA_2.562-66) comprises a common opening to what may be called an "Attack Song," wherein a hero and his army make war on a given city.[38] This clue, along with the fact that Kukuruzović lists a song he refers to as "The young ban of Janok was drinking wine / And next to him Takulija ban"[39] as part of his repertoire in both the conversation with Nikola (no. *6619*) and the listing of his songs (no. 1287), argues strongly for the possibility of a "compound song." When we add to these observations the unitary character of Section I, it seems safe to understand *OA* as an *amalgam of songs*, perhaps a relatively recent amalgam, since the transition between its parts is so unstable. Whatever its actual status, however, the evidence shows that what Kukuruzović knows and sings as one tale was at some point two tales. In fact, in a manner of speaking, it seems still to exist as two songs, since Section II is individually a part of the singer's repertoire.

To continue the sketch of the *OA* narrative, the force which Pero recommends is raised and the ban of Janok enlists the aid of the Knežević twins to spy on the city of Ribnik. These twinned figures have, as it were, a double identity; since their father remained in Ribnik when they joined the service of the enemy ban, they maintain a unique right of passage between Turkish and Christian dominions. Just as they depart Janok to begin their espionage in OA_1, the hero also leaves, but with a different purpose. His original loyalty having re-emerged, OA goes to Ribnik to tell Zlatija, the bey's daughter, of the impending Christian attack.[40] At the same time the Knežević twins, having won their father over, secure important information from him: the bey has left Ribnik and the city is therefore vulnerable to attack. Ruža Knežević, the boys' sister, who has also remained in Ribnik, overhears her father's treasonous disclosure and, after castigating all three of them, runs off to report the news of imminent danger to the same Zlatija lately in conversation with OA. This kind of structural redundancy is not a customary feature of Serbo-Croatian oral epic song, and it makes for a narrative "loop" which stalls the progression of the story. For each time that Zlatija reacts by approaching a Turkish stalwart, Gojenović Ilija (GI), in order to pass on to him what is supposed to be new and startling information, she is accused of dreaming and

38. "Tuka sjedi mlad janjočki bane / I pobro mu Takulija bane, / I kod njega trides' generala / I trideset mladi' kapetana. / Vino piju oko šadrvana." ("Here sat the young ban of Janok / And his blood brother Takulija ban, / And with him thirty generals / And thirty young captains. / They were drinking wine around a fountain.")

39. See note 20.

40. OA does not go to Ribnik at all in text no. 1868, and so the following argument does not pertain to the sequence of events in that text. The variance indicates an instability in the combination of the two songs (Sections I and II), an instability that may well be another sign of the relative newness of the amalgam. In addition, we should consider the possibility that the avoidance of redundancy in no. 1868 may derive from its being an oral-dictated text.

not taken seriously. Another sign that the loop is an unusual feature is the imposition of "boundary line" sequences to maneuver the story line from the Knežević twins to OA and back again. This awkward shifting of narrative direction underlines the redundancy and contrasts sharply with the fluidity of the rest of the song.[41]

The redundancy, loop, and boundary sequences indicate an in-progress adaptation, an interface between the two sections of Kukuruzović's song created under the pressure of composition in performance. Two further signals point to the same conclusion. First, in OA_2 the receiver of Zlatija's news, GI, is in obvious confusion referred to as AA! Not only is the singer uncertain about whether the hero of Section I has exited Section II, but generic override prompts the insinuation of the "wrong" hero, OA's counterpart, AA. Second, after OA's supernumerary report to Zlatija in OA_1, he simply vanishes from the song; he is last heard from, to be precise, at line 895 of a song 2,180 lines in length. We may recall that he leaves the scene even earlier in OA_2. All of this evidence points unmistakably toward OA's actions in Section II of the song as a kind of overflow from the Return Song pattern of Section I. To summarize the pattern symbolically from $W-$ on, then, we have

$$W-_{\text{oa}} \longrightarrow \mathfrak{J}_{\text{kb}} \longrightarrow P \longrightarrow Rp,$$

where P represents the plan hatched by the ban to attack Ribnik[42] and Rp the report of that plan in the place to be attacked. As we have seen, while there is only incidental variation in the forms taken by P, the Rp element absorbs the narrative spillover from Section I of the story amalgam.

The Rp element gives way to the attack (At) and GI's eventual heroic action. When it becomes apparent that Ribnik is indeed under siege, he bravely rides out through the hostile Christian ranks, intending to reach Jaboka, an intermediate locus in the epic geography where the unsuspecting bey of Ribnik is presently encamped. Though mortally wounded, he succeeds with his dying breath in relaying the news of the attack to the bey. At this juncture the enraged Turkish leader takes over, marshaling his force and calling upon the trickster-hero Tale to join him.[43] Undertaking a reconnaissance mission structurally symmetrical to that of the Knežević twins, the bey's ally Mujo rides out from Jaboka toward Ribnik to have a look at the ban's force. His mission may, in terms of narrative pattern, be both the logical counterpart of the earlier spying and a thematic preliminary to offensive

41. Nowhere else in his recorded repertoire does Kukuruzović interpose so many or such bulky phrases to alter the narrative direction.

42. This element (P) should be generalized to accommodate variance in the aggressor and the place besieged; I have left it specified here for the sake of simplicity of explication.

43. Whatever else Tale may be, he is, according to Albert Lord (conversation), a "saint." Despite his almost comic reversal of heroic dignity and appearance, he is essential to wedding parties and armies: as the singers say time and again, one cannot do without him.

action. In any case, Mujo's report moves Tale to urge immediate attack. But before the attack can commence, Kukuruzović inserts the theme of the brothers Mujo and Halil arguing over use of the horse left jointly to them by their grandfather. Halil wishes to use the animal to initiate the battle plan, but his request is denied. This refusal brings about his threat to destroy "his half" of the horse, and Mujo, seeing his brother's rage, finally accedes. As we will note in Section II of AA, this argument (hereafter symbolized M/H) constitutes a theme associated for Kukuruzović with that of Counter-attack (Ct). Thus far the symbolic logic for Section II is

$$W - \to \mathcal{J}_{kb} \to P \to Rp \to At \to M/H \to Ct.$$

From here on the story moves rather fast, with the bey of Ribnik surveying the carnage and determining that the victory is his, with one qualification. He catches sight of General Pero absconding with his daughter Zlatija, and of his allies Halil and Velagić Selim in hot pursuit. Pero reaches Janok and casts his prize into the ban's *tamnica*; when Halil and VS later follow him into an inn, he orders them seized and incarcerated along with the girl. Here the three are left, ostensibly helpless, while their captor rejoices over his *coup*.

We may detect a double structure in the imprisonment of the heroes and the bey's daughter, a rescue pattern which, as we saw above in $AAVS$, is a reflex of the Return Song sequence. For soon after the capture of the prisoners (A) and their suffering in jail (D), Mujo arrives at the inn and begins to plan their release—that is to say, their Return (R)—with Mara the innkeeper, whom we recall as the intermediary in $AAVS$.[44] Mujo dons a Christian female disguise, just as in $AAVS$ the female surrogate hero Fata put on Christian male dress, and gains admittance to the ban's *kula*. Here the narrative begins its double resonance: generally, it follows the rescue (really the Return) pattern and, specifically, it echoes the very opening of the song by closely adhering to not simply a generic pattern but also a series of more particularized events. Mujo bargains for release not with the ban of Janok, but with his wife, the banica. The condition for release is again *pobratimstvo*, blood-brotherhood; once the banica has put to rest her concerns about the safety of her land and people by securing the treaty, she agrees to let all three captives go. After stopping to pick up the same horse over which Mujo and Halil earlier argued,[45] the heroes and the girl proceed to the Turkish border (R) and the tale ends.

44. More important than the identity of name, of course, is the congruency of narrative function; these two "female intermediary" figures mirror other characters as well, such as the banica who bargains with the captive.

45. Note the symmetry, often called "ring composition," between the original occurrence of M/H prior to the attack and its recurrence (in much diminished form) here, after the attack and its consequences have run their course. Another way to put it, one perhaps truer to the *guslar*'s real concern with the spatial dimensions of his story, is that the "horse frame" surrounds the Turks' experience in Janok, marking initial entry and final exit. On ring composition in Serbo-Croatian epic, see Lord 1986a.

To emphasize the dual structure of this section of the story and to summarize the pattern of Section II as a whole, I symbolize below the entire narrative action in two ways: by continuing the progression of elements used so far in describing Section II (*Code 1*) and by juxtaposing to the last part of this progression the same elements in Lord's original notation (*Code 2*).

$$Code\ 1 \quad W - \to \mathcal{J}_{kb} \to P \to Rp \to At \to Rp \to M/H \to Ct \to Cp \to I \to \underbrace{Rl \to H}$$
$$Code\ 2 \qquad\qquad\qquad\qquad\qquad\qquad\qquad\qquad A \to D \ \to R$$

In *Code 1* I have added the elements *Capture (Cp)*, *Imprisonment (I)*, *Release (Rl)*, and *Homecoming (H)* to represent the end of the *OA* song. It is left understood that *Cp* and *I* apply to all three captives, although the bey of Ribnik's daughter is captured and imprisoned earlier than Halil and VS. These four designations adequately account for the action entailed, and they clearly follow the same narrative scheme as the *A*, *D*, and *R* elements immediately below them.

We may draw some interesting conclusions from this comparison. Not only is the rescue, like that of *AAVS*, structurally a reflex of the basic *A-W* sequence; the major differentiation between the two patterns in both Kukuruzović's and Ibro Bašić's songs is at the thematic level. To put it another way, *"Return" and "Rescue" are equivalent at the level of story-pattern and differ only at the level of theme*. This observation in turn argues the primacy of the *A–W* series both synchronically (in the generation of the song during performance) and diachronically (in the generation of song types over time). When we recall the various avatars of the Return Song pattern either studied at length or at least briefly mentioned in this chapter, we can begin to appreciate how fundamental this network of abstractions is to the history and "dialectology" of Serbo-Croatian oral narrative song.

The comparative analysis of Codes 1 and 2 also affords insight into the cyclic shape of the song as a whole. The opening *A–D–R* joins with the ending *A–D–R* to frame the narrative, to yield a ring similar to the Homeric paradigm in general and to the *Iliad* in particular.[46] One problem plagues the near-symmetry of *OA*, however: Section II (and therefore the epic) ends with the Turks' return (*R*) to their homeland. Nothing is said about their possible retribution (*Rt*) for imprisonment or about a wedding (*W*) involving any of them. We might well have expected these last two elements to occur here, largely because of the frustrated *W −* in Section I and the apparent progression toward such a coda throughout most of Section II. Does their absence suggest a flawed song, an imperfect performance which was perhaps cut short for whatever reason?

I would argue against such a conclusion. First, we must recall that there has

46. The tale of Achilles, of course, closes with the Trojan king Priam's approaching the Achaean hero to ransom the body of his beloved Hector, just as it began with Chryses petitioning the Greek ruler Agamemnon for the release of his daughter Chryseis. The paradigm of ransoming one's child informs both scenes.

already been an instance of Turkish retribution against the Christian forces in what has been designated as the Counter-attack (*Ct*). Zlatija was captured earlier in the story, sometime between her report to GI and Pero's ride to Janok, and so the *Ct* can be understood as consequent to her capture. Of course, Halil and VS are seized later still and the final release does not take place until some time afterward, but this splitting of elements is hardly unusual.[47] So *Rt* does indeed appear—as *Ct*—but out of proper sequence.

The *W* element, however, takes no part in the epic's closure; no wedding forms the coda to the action of *OA* in Section II. In fact, what the ban of Janok plans to do, and succeeds in carrying out, is precisely the reverse of the true wedding ritual: he enters on the sacred rite of "bride-stealing,"[48] (1) without proper arrangements, (2) without the appropriate Turkish retinue, (3) in time of war, and (4) as an enemy, a Christian ban intending to take as his prize a Turkish maiden. These are not simply qualifications; they amount to absolute abrogations of custom, actions diametrically opposed to conventional, socially sanctioned behavior. In effect, this bride-stealing, which would usually serve as the ceremonial preliminary to a wedding, constitutes a motif reversed. Order is restored only when Zlatija is rescued and returned to her homeland—when, that is, the insult done her and the Turkish people by the ban of Janok and his forces has been atoned for.

In reality, then, the story-pattern unity of Section II and of the epic overall depends not on a final wedding scene per se but rather on a symbolic equivalent, a reversal of the unlawful bride-stealing that began Section II. Just as the Return Song pattern reached a qualified conclusion with the death of OA's wife ($W-_1$), an event and element paralleled by Pero's rupture of the marriage rite in stealing Zlatija ($W-_2$), so the return of the girl ($W+$) answers both actions and restores order to the story and its elemental structure. In this way Kukuruzović, or the tradition, has solved the problem of ending the story in a deeply traditional manner: the coda completes both "songs within the song" and the larger, composite narrative. Once again story-pattern has both limited and generated the internal logic of the song.

AA, SECTION II: STORY AND STORY-PATTERN

As we have seen, Kukuruzović felt that the correct sequel to the first part of *AA* was the story line that commenced with AA's journey to the spring at Jezero, where he met Päun harambasha and planned a retaliatory raid on Halil's brother Mujo. Their plans are ambitious: in revenge for Halil's wooing of his wife, AA will attack Mujo's *kula*, steal his sister, Aikuna, and attempt to take Mujo himself prisoner. After raising an army for the purpose and

47. On splitting of thematic structures, see the various examples in chapters 7–9.

48. According to the traditional pattern, the ritual seizure can proceed only after proper arrangements have been completed between the families and the requisite honorary force has been assembled; of course, both bride and bridegroom are assumed to be Turks.

gaining entrance to the tower by tricking Aikuna, they accomplish all but the last of their intentions. At this point, we soon discover, Aikuna is spirited off to captivity by the ban of Koluto, a natural (because Christian) enemy. Mujo, far from his home, dreams that just such destruction and capture have taken place, and later hears that his dream is only too true. The ruse perpetrated by AA turns out to be his last narrative gasp; after that, we see him no more.

A few details and larger structures should seem familiar. After the journey, this time to Jezero (J_j), the hero makes his plan for revenge (P) and proceeds to the attack on Mujo's *kula* (At). Even a Report element (Rp) appears, this time *after* the attack has begun. To compare the story-pattern sequences of *OA* and *AA* thus far, consider the two series of elements juxtaposed:[49]

$$OA: \quad W-_1 \longrightarrow J_{kb} \longrightarrow P \longrightarrow Rp \longrightarrow At$$
$$AA: \quad W-_1 \longrightarrow J_j \quad \longrightarrow P \longrightarrow At \longrightarrow Rp$$

The general sequences are identical. In fact, *OA* and *AA* share many details at levels of structure more particularized than that of story-pattern. One of these is the theme of raising an army associated with *P*, though this connection is a generally traditional one not limited to these two songs; almost any attack or journey of a wedding party encountered in the tradition presupposes the occurrence of this theme. Another such similarity lies in the dreams that surround the *Rp* element in both songs. The horrors of war present themselves to GI (in *OA*) and Mujo (in *AA*) as too frightening to be real; the second part of this motif then consists of the hero's discovery that what he faces is more than a dream, that attack (*At*) has really begun and he must therefore take some action. With the impetus thus passing away from the original hero of the song (OA/AA) to a kind of narrative surrogate (GI/Halil), the report is a logical spot for the disappearance of OA/AA. And, in both epics, this is precisely where that disappearance takes place. The transition from the opening Return Song through the revenging attack to the rescue song is complete, and in both *OA* and *AA* we arrive at this point and have no more need of the original hero. From now on the song is to tell of Halil's or Mujo's rescue either of Mujo's sister (AA_1) or of Zlatija, Halil, and VS (OA_1, AA_2).

Before the counter-offensive (the version of *Ct* found in *AA*) can begin, Kukuruzović again interposes the theme of Mujo and Halil arguing over the rights to their horse (M/H). Once more the outcome is crucial to the shape of what follows: Halil's threat to do away with the animal elicits Mujo's permission to use the horse and, what is more, his advice to proceed with a certain course of action in liberating Aikuna. He recommends seeking a series

---

49. It is important to note that $W-_1$ is also continued to $W-_2$ in AA_1, since the capture of Aikuna and her subsequent experience as a prisoner of the ban also constitute a perversion of the conventional bride-stealing ritual.

of heroes including Toša harambasha in Janok, Pop Milovan in Požun, and the familiar figure of Mara the innkeeper in Koluto itself. As Halil goes from one to the next, the first two balk at the prospect of challenging the ban but are shamed into a promise of aid. Once they all reach Mara's inn, the story line returns to a sequence very near that of OA. Mara instructs Halil to disguise himself in the priest Milovan's clothes, a disguise that, like Mujo's in OA, contrasts diametrically with his real identity: it indicates a Christian member of a religious order rather than a secular Turk. Halil manages to enter the ban's *kula* by claiming that he has come to marry the captive to Milić harambasha, but soon takes advantage of the situation by stealing the ban's only son, the infant Marijane. His intent is to exchange the boy for Aikuna, and there ensues a bargaining scene conducted through a messenger bearing letters between Mujo and the banica. And though the ceremony is not explicitly described, it becomes clear by the end that the condition for release (in this case a trade) is again a Turkish-Christian peace treaty in the form of blood-brotherhood. The epic closes with an exchange of prisoners at the border between the territories.

Section II of AA thus follows a symbolic pattern nearly identical to that of OA, Section II, as the diagram below illustrates:

$$OA: \quad W-_{\scriptscriptstyle 1} \to \mathcal{J}_{kb} \to P \to Rp \to At \to M/H \to Ct \;\; \to A \to D \to R$$
$$AA: \quad W-_{\scriptscriptstyle 1} \to \mathcal{J}_{j} \;\; \to P \to At \to Rp \to M/H \to Ct^{*} \to A \to D \to R$$

The only difference in the narratives at the level of story-pattern is that indicated by the asterisked element, Ct^{*}. For in AA there occurs not a martial answer to At, but a plan that nonetheless entails enlisting the aid of a number of people.[50] This plan is, in terms of the overall paradigm, no less a Ct, for it comes after (and is the narrative consequent of) M/H, responds to At, and will serve as the transposed Rt for the rescue sequence to follow. Halil's deception of the ban and stealing of his son constitute payment in kind for the capture of Aikuna and her impending forced marriage to Milić. Indeed, this payment is not so different structurally from VS's Rt in $AAVS$. For in all three cases—$AAVS$, OA, and now AA—the rite of bride-stealing has been perverted by an outside agent, and the hero's task is to restore the normal order. One way or another, the hero accomplishes this restoration, adhering to the fundamental traditional logic of the Return Song pattern, whatever the thematic component and story line of the particular song as a whole. Section II of AA ends with the removal of the stigma that began it, that is, with the transfor-

---

50. Two additional aspects of this plan should be noted. First, like a battle it demands the gathering of leaders and a collective effort. Second, the Stolac tradition as recorded in the Milman Parry Collection contains many examples of the passage of either a character or a letter from one hero in a certain geographical area to a second hero in another, and so on. The experiences at each stop are iterative; that is, they are realizations of the same multiform attenuated to particular situations.

mation of $W-_{1,2}$ to $W+$ in the return of Aikuna. Just as in OA, the A–D–R sequence is explicit, the Rt element is transposed and appears as Ct (here $Ct*$), and the $W+$ obviates the earlier $W-_{1,2}$.

THE AA/OA: ITS FUNDAMENTAL FORM

It is perhaps time to step back and take a wide-angle view of the whole AA/OA. By summarizing the foregoing analysis in symbolic terms, we can see that the epic texts depend finally, for all their apparent dissimilarities, on a single compound story-pattern, as depicted in figure 16. This single pattern, as we observed above and as is also clear from the diagram, is really an amalgam composed of two distinct parts, here called Sections I and II. I have already noted that the first part is in most respects complete in itself, with the conditional $W-$ element leading to continuation. It is now possible to see that the second part contains a similar structure, one that extends at least from Ct through the end of the tale. It too derives from the A–W sequence and forms a unit symmetrically opposed to the opening section.

In fact, having come this far we can now demonstrate an even simpler foundation for the whole song. The original P and its issue At are really extensions of Rt in Section I: in both songs, they represent the continuation of OA/AA's revenge. Likewise, Ct (or $Ct*$) is in both instances the transposed Rt of the rescue, which, as indicated, is also a Return. Making these substitutions $(At = Rt$, Section I; $Ct = Rt$, Section II) and eliminating elements of lesser importance, we have the following pattern:

$$OA: \quad (A \to D \to R \to Rt_1 \to W- \to Rt_1) \longrightarrow (Rt_2 \to A \to D \to R \to W+)$$
$$AA: \quad (A \to D \to R \to Rt_1 \to W- \to Rt_1) \longrightarrow (Rt_2 \to A \to D \to R \to W+)$$

Placing the parentheses in these positions helps to illustrate further the basic symmetry of the story-pattern. Two Return Song sequences are joined, in short, by the foregrounding and opposition of their Rt elements; one act of aggression $(At = Rt_1)$ demands another $(Ct/Ct* = Rt_2)$, and a logical bridge between narratives is constructed by the juxtaposition. Of course, a few inconsistencies arise from the blending of the songs, but we must remember that Section II exists as a song by itself in Kukuruzović's repertoire and therefore has some status as a narrative complete in itself. The important point is that

---

Figure 16. Comparison of OA and AA, Entire Pattern

OA: $A \to D \to R \to Rt \to W- \longrightarrow J_{kb} \to P \to Rp \to At \to Rp \to M/H \to Ct \longrightarrow A \to D \to R \to W+$

AA: $A \to D \to R \to Rt \to W- \longrightarrow J_j \to P \longrightarrow At \to Rp \to M/H \to Ct* \to A \to D \to R \to W+$

Section I   Section II

AA/OA proves to be another example of a "new" pattern composed of familiar elements, another instance of the generativity of the Return Song.

CONCLUSION

What the *AA/OA* song texts offer us is evidence of a song amalgam and a perspective on the evolution of narrative form in oral epic tradition. We have seen that what might be taken as an "error"—perhaps the *guslar* "nodding"— is a flaw only if the song is treated as a detachable literary text, as an artifact without a traditional context. In other words, Kukuruzović's "skipping over" is merely a synchronic flaw, a blemish which fades in significance when placed against the background of story-pattern and the principle I have termed "generic override." If stories depend on particularized elaborations of generic structures, then the same multiformity which is the lifeblood of the tradition can also be a source of apparent confusion. Names of heroes and places change within a song; why should larger, more abstractly based substitutions not occasionally take place? In fact, from the point of view of tradition, both kinds of substitutions are inherently as logical as the mutability observable in the adaptation of formula and theme to various narrative contexts. Particu-larization of the generic is the dynamic process behind oral traditional epic composition, whatever the level of structure. Kukuruzović's own explanation, quoted at the beginning of this chapter, turns out to be quite accurate; he maintained that "the songs about Ograšćić Alija and Alagić Alija are enough alike, one to the next, that the verses carry over."

To take the argument thus construed a step further, we can view the text of any performance as the intersection of two lines of development: one the his-torical or diachronic (what has been called "generic"), the other performance-centered or synchronic (what has been called "particularized"). Both the history of a song—of its singing by various singers at various times in various places—and its momentary shape—in the hands of a single singer at one time in one place—contribute to its text and context. Without tradition such an epic song cannot exist, much less be interpreted; each performance takes its meaning from the multiformity that it momentarily rationalizes.[51] Likewise, we must pay sufficient attention to the single text, which, in representing one possible realization of narrative potential, reveals the singer's and the tradi-tion's response to the exigencies of composition. So it is that text-making involves both the historical and the momentary, the diachronic and the syn-

---

51. As Lord puts it in his foreword to Peabody 1975 (p. xii), "At a time when the emphasis in scholarship and in criticism alike has gone too heavily in the direction of synchronic structuralism, it is well to be reminded of the springs of language and of verbal art in oral traditional literature, because tradition's point of view is by definition diachronic, or, to avoid scientific terminology, is conscious of the past and of the present's debt to that past. The study of oral traditional literature must of necessity be both diachronic and synchronic."

chronic, and in resolving multiple possibilities to a single solution it does not lose the richness of the traditional context. Since the song exists at once as a single performance and as an avatar of a more generic, less particularized structure, it carries with it the resonance of its other possibilities. The synchronic text implies the diachronic context at all points, and the meaning of what we encounter in any one performance text depends directly on the multiformity from which it derives.

Only in a very limited sense, then, can Kukuruzović be said to have committed an "error" in "skipping over." For our concept of "error," based as it is on experience strictly with non-traditional texts, is finally oblique to the situation we find in these tales of Alagić Alija and Ograšćić Alija. What we must recognize as central to that situation is the traditional context formed by the aggregate of these texts, the multiformity that both generates and limits them all. Serbo-Croatian oral epic song has its own logic: it is the logic of tradition.

ELEVEN

Conclusion

Whether for good or for ill, the present studies do not easily submit to a general, encyclopedic summary. But perhaps that is only to be expected, given their comparative nature and the current state of affairs in the field of studies in oral tradition. A pessimist might well be disappointed that the past few years have seen the partial crumbling of certain orthodoxies, the questioning of many of the initial premises put forth by Milman Parry, Albert Lord, and others, and the call for a rethinking of positions that were once considered unassailable. While far the greater part of the early research stands firm, certain areas have been shown to be in need of modification or even wholesale recasting.

However, as not only an optimist in these matters but also one who believes that we shall continue to progress in oral literature studies only when we confront the richness and complexity of the heterogeneous mass of materials we too often force into a single category, I welcome the call for new perspectives, and in fact welcome the chance to take part in their fashioning. It is my hope that the ideas presented in this volume contribute to the ongoing dialogue and debate over the multiform nature of oral poetry (and particularly oral epic poetry), for only if the conversation both continues and continues to develop can we move toward the kind of understanding that this vast subject deserves. Thus it is that these studies are offered equally as a response to what has gone before and as an exordium to future research.

In this spirit, chapter 1 is intended as a kind of map for the volume's explorations. With attention to the differentiating qualities of tradition-dependence, genre-dependence, and text-dependence, it points the way toward an informed comparison that takes account of divergences as well as convergences, that places observed similarities between and among traditions against the background of individual profiles of those traditions. This chapter also makes the case for proceeding from the best tenable hypothesis about a text's orality; if, in short, a demonstrably traditional text cannot be shown unambiguously to have been oral, then with proper care and caution we should assign it to the "oral-derived" category. This conservative approach not only avoids an unsupportable hypothesis of orality for many of our manuscript texts, but it also saves them from being treated as written (and non-traditional) texts by default. Through a series of examples from the three traditions considered in these studies, I have tried to illustrate how the generalization "oral literature" requires further articulation—or, in effect, complication—in order to differentiate among the myriad forms we presently group together. Just as "written literature" would not serve well as a blanket concept for a canon that included Shakespeare's sonnets, the novels of Proust, and the Japanese Noh drama, so we need to enlarge and complicate our conception of "oral literature."

The remainder of the book has thus considered the similarities and differences among texts from what I take to be a single genre, that of oral or oral-derived epic as represented in three traditions: the ancient Greek *Odyssey*, the Old English *Beowulf*, and the Serbo-Croatian "Return Song." The first calibration to be set was that of the documents themselves, an aspect of comparison that, somewhat curiously, has heretofore been largely ignored. We found that the tenth-century Codex Marcianus 454 and its fellows were quite different sorts of witnesses than either the unique Cotton Vitellius A. xv. or the actual Return Song performance-texts collected from Yugoslav *guslari*, and that these incongruencies translated into basic differences in how we approach comparison of the works that the documents encode. For example, the formulaic-density test cannot prove orality if without further qualification we implicitly equate the Homeric texts, some two millennia and many stages of editing removed from their proposed date of creation in that form, and the Serbo-Croatian texts recorded directly from singers by Parry and Lord. And this, of course, is to say nothing about the problems that tradition- and genre-dependence present for such analysis.

Since scholars have shown that the phraseology of these texts was formed in symbiosis with their various meters and general prosodies, I turned next to a discussion of comparative prosody in the three epic traditions. By measuring the Homeric hexameter, alliterative line, and *epski deseterac* against the reconstructed Indo-European precursor, it was possible to illustrate how each prosody diverged from that source into its own identity as a partner in the formation and maintenance of traditional diction. In the course of this investigation we discovered not only that the three prosodies cannot be simplistically equated, but also that one must look most closely at the "inner metric" of each line in order to understand its structure and its contribution to the compositional process.

Chapters 4–6 then applied the lessons learned about tradition-dependent prosody to the study of tradition-dependent phraseology in each tradition.

We found that the most fundamental level of structure in the diction was to be attributed to individual sets of *traditional rules*, unique to each tradition, which formed the basis for formulaic language. Additionally, it soon became apparent that, even within the same epic tradition, no single model would suit the entire phraseological spectrum encountered during analysis, and that the best, most faithful characterization of the diction had to be as a heterogeneous collection of both formulaic and not demonstrably formulaic language —all overseen by traditional rules. In the case of the *Odyssey*, for example, the investigations of *epea pteroenta* and Book 5.424-44 led us to recognize phraseological units as short as a single colon and as long as a number of hexameters, with variability at all levels; since no one single length or form could be understood as primary, we advocated viewing the diction as a collection of unequal parts rationalized by traditional rules.

Many of the same observations were made about traditional phraseology in Serbo-Croatian in chapter 5. The *guslar*'s diction resembles that of Homer in a number of ways (colonic "words," for instance), and it too shows a spectrum of phraseological units that co-exist under the aegis of a separate set of traditional rules. Analyses of material from recorded Return Songs ballasted the argument. In contrast, we discovered that the diction of *Beowulf* shares very few of the features that characterize the language of the other two poetries: the Old English alliterative line relies for its structure not on cola and caesuras but rather on stress and alliteration. While there is thus little compositional pressure for the encapsulated phrases typical of Homeric and Serbo-Croatian epic, Anglo-Saxon does follow its own set of traditional rules. And, as the analysis of Grendel's approach to Heorot helped to illustrate, what results is once again a spectrum of phraseology that resists reduction to a single formulaic model.

The natural heterogeneity of traditional structure was studied at the level of the narrative unit of "theme" or "typical scene" in chapters 7 through 9. Analysis of the *Odyssey* focused on instances of three such units—Bath, Greeting, and Feast—in an effort to determine the role of narrative pattern and verbal correspondence. We found that the theme can consist of a tightly knit series of discrete actions or of a looser aggregation that leaves more room for individual, situation-specific variation, and likewise that the amount of verbal correspondence among instances varies from one theme to the next.

Chapter 8, on narrative themes in Yugoslav epic, showed how the definition of thematic structure rests not only on tradition-dependent features but also on the analytical perspective employed. There will be closer agreement among instances of a unit within a single *guslar*'s recorded repertoire (idiolect) than within his local tradition (dialect) or the larger tradition as a synchronic and diachronic whole (language). While the discussion of the Serbo-Croatian theme rested on the Shouting in Prison multiform so typical of the Return Song, that of the Old English theme drew on analyses of Sea Voyage in

Beowulf and of Scourging in the poetic hagiography *Andreas*. In Anglo-Saxon, it was discovered, the kind of verbal correspondence typical of some themes in ancient Greek and Yugoslav epic is quite rare, the principal reason being the Old English tradition's lack of colonic phraseology. In the process of treating the Scourging multiform in *Andreas*, it proved possible to illustrate how another theme, that of Exile, was employed by the poet to explain his foreign source to an audience steeped in the native tradition.

Chapter 10 offered an analysis of the most extensive of traditional structures—the "story-pattern" that governs the action of the tale as a whole. By taking advantage of the well-collected Serbo-Croatian tradition of Return Songs, it proved possible to observe the multiformity of this ubiquitous taletype in simplex patterns (Absence through Wedding), in double-cycle forms (two heroes, with conditional elements and substitution), and in composite songs (with a final conditional element leading to a sequel story). The most telling part of the demonstration was the observation of wide and yet limited variation on this fundamental pattern, the same sort of controlled multiformity one finds in both phraseology and thematics. Additionally, examination of the songs of Mujo Kukuruzović afforded an example of the creation of a "new," composite song or "amalgam"; one of the two songs was in fact shown to exist separately and individually within his repertoire.

Studies such as these, which concentrate on establishing the structure of oral (or oral-derived) epic poetry, hopefully provide a first step toward a faithful poetics. In the end, the question must be one of contextualization: to what extent are the *Odyssey*, *Beowulf*, and the Serbo-Croatian Return Song really comparable? The last two decades have seen this and similar questions prove increasingly complex, and if the scholarship has been unanimous on any one point, it is that such questions cannot be answered without taking the many dimensions of comparability into account and considering each issue carefully. To the extent that these studies have prompted that kind of consideration, and thus assisted in clearing the way for an aesthetics that recognizes the full measure of the role of oral tradition in these great epic poetries, they have accomplished their purpose.

APPENDIX

Supporting Evidence for Analysis of Text I (examples only)

1.829 Kad je Pero (2.1679), knjigu načinijo (2.1527), Kad je Pero knjigu preučijo (1.1064)

1.830 A pod kulu (2.683), A pod knjigu knjigonošu nadje (1.1040)

1.831 Kudgodj ide (4.329), knjiga šarovita (1.98), Kudgodj ide knjiga šarovita (1.957)

1.832 Kudgodj ide (see 1.831 refs.), do Ribnika sidje (6.884), Kudgodj ide, do Ribnika sidje (2.1442)

1.833 A na ruke (3.330), banova gospoja (1.950)

1.834 Knjigu gleda (1.960), Knjigu gleda, pa se na nju smije (1.1055)

1.835 reče lakrdiju (1.686), A ovaku reče lakrdiju (2.1881)

1.836 Ej! Alija (1.764), moj na mjestu sine (6.2064), Ej! Alija, moj na mjestu sine (1.689)

1.837 Kad se boji (1.838), beg Mustajbeg lički (3.225), Pa se boji beg Mustajbeg lički (1.722)

1.838 Kad se boji (1.837), knjigu na krajinu (4.83)

1.839 Ako Bog da (2.1626)

1.840 Ja ću tebe (6.1831), sine, darovati (6.1985), Ja ću tebe, sine, darovati (1.197)

1.841 Nek halali (6.1676), Nek govori i kako mu drago (1.1100)

1.842 Da vidimo (4.141), Da vidimo šta je bilo 'vamo (2.1266)

1.843 Kad je žarko (2.1775), jutro osvanulo (1.1157), Kad je peto jutro osvanulo (1.1211)

1.844 Tad Alija (6.605), sigura mrkalja (6.2073)

1.845 Tad se krenu (2.1712), do Karlova bila (1.1037)

1.846 Pero generale (6.2061)

1.847 I do njega (2.1991), Djulić bajraktara (6.1498)

1.848 A hadžibeg (1.277), Ograšćić Alije (6.316)

1.849 Kad rekoše (2.160), pa se rastadoše (4.445), Kad rekoše da se pozdraviše (1.146)

1.850 Ode Ale (1.147), u kršnu Kotaru (6.2143), Ode Ale do kršli Kotara (6.745)

1.851 Ode Pero (2.1441), do Kara Bogdana (2.1683), Ode Pero do Kara Bogdana (2.1435)
1.852 Ode Djulić (2.1589), Liki i Ribniku (6.933), Ode Huso Liki i Ribniku (1.1076)
1.853 A Alija (4.623), u tamnicu sidje (1.117)

Supporting Evidence for Analysis of Text II (examples only)

4.10 Pocmilijo (1.12), Bojičić Alija (4.15)
4.11 U Kotaru (4.440), U Kanidži bijelome gradu (3.705)
4.12 od Kotara bana (4.58), U komšije od Kotara bana (4.97)
4.13 Oko bega (3.195), trides' kapetana (6.1876)
4.14 u tamnici cmile (1.28)
4.15 A najprije (3.53), Bojičić Alija (4.10), A najprije Bojičić Alija
4.16 Turčin cmili (2.6, with metathesis), za nedjelju dana (1.1261), Sužanj cmili za nedjelju dana (1.20)
4.17 rezil učinijo (6.1345)
4.18 Učinijo (6.1170)
4.19 Kad je žarko (2.1775), jutro osvanulo (1.1157), Kad deveto jutro osvanulo (1.1268)
4.20 banici gospodji (1.898)
4.21 Ona banu (6.12), na svoga čardaka (4.75)
4.22 Tad banica (6.2152), majci govorila (2.369), A banica 'vako govorila (6.106)
4.23 O Boga ti (6.1015), gospodare bane (4.51)
4.24 Daj ti meni (1.1223), tebe majk*a* traži (2.381)
4.25 Ne dade mi (1.918), pa onda spavati (3.517)
4.26 Skoči Djulić (3.413), pa iz grla viče (6.1463), Skoči Mujo i za glasa viče (4.333)
4.27 Čekaj mene (3.852), moja gospojice (2.16)
4.28 Ja ću pušćat' (4.579), Turke iz zindane (4.589)
4.29 Jami bane (3.982)
4.30 Jedna glava (4.181), a četiri zlata (4.382)
4.31 Pa on dodje (1.426), iz tvoga zindana (2.139)
4.32 U zindanu (6.1721), vrata otvorijo (6.916)
4.33 Pa zagazi (6.1162)
4.34 A dok poče (4.282), u dno polja ravña (2.1139)
4.35 A sve zrno (6.1026), na tamnicu sadje (6.118)

REFERENCES

Allen, Thomas W. [1924] 1969. *Homer: The Origins and the Transmission.* Oxford: Clarendon Press.

Allen, W. Sidney. 1964. "On Quantity and Quantitative Verse." In *In Honour of Daniel Jones,* edited by David Abercrombie, P.A.D. MacCarthy, N.C. Scott, and J.L.M. Trim, 3-15. London: Longmans, Green.

————. 1966. "Prosody and Prosodies in Greek." *Transactions of the Philological Society* 107-48.

————. 1967. "Correlations of Tone and Stress in Ancient Greek." In *To Honor Roman Jakobson: Essays on the Occasion of His Seventieth Birthday,* 1:46-62. The Hague: Mouton.

————. 1973. *Accent and Rhythm (Prosodic Features of Latin and Greek: A Study in Theory and Reconstruction).* Cambridge Studies in Linguistics, no. 12. Cambridge: Cambridge University Press.

Amory Parry, Anne. 1973. *Blameless Aegisthus: A Study of AMYMΩN and Other Homeric Epithets.* Mnemosyne, Bibliotheca Classica Batava, supplement no. 26. Leiden: E. J. Brill.

Amos, Ashley Crandell. 1980. *Linguistic Means of Determining the Dates of Old English Literary Texts.* Cambridge, Mass.: Mediaeval Academy of America.

Anderson, Earl R. 1980. "Formulaic Typescene Survival: Finn, Ingeld, and the *Nibelungenlied.*" *English Studies* 61: 293-301.

The Anglo-Saxon Poetic Records. 1931-53. Edited by George Philip Krapp and E.V.K. Dobbie. 6 vols. New York: Columbia University Press.

Arant, Patricia. 1981. "The Intricate Web: Thematic Cohesion in Russian Oral Traditional Verse Narrative." In *Oral Traditional Literature,* 123-41. *See* Foley 1981d.

Arend, Walter. 1933. *Die typischen Scenen bei Homer.* Problemata, Forschungen zur classischen Philologie, no. 7. Berlin: Weidmann.

Ashby, Genette. 1979. "A Generative Model of the Formula in the *Chanson de Roland.*" *Olifant* 7: 39-65.

ASPR. See The Anglo-Saxon Poetic Records.

Austerlitz, Robert. 1958. *Ob-Ugric Metrics: The Metrical Structure of Ostyak and Vogul Folk-Poetry*. Folklore Fellows communications, no. 174. Helsinki: Suomalainen Tiede-akatemia.

———. 1985. "The Poetics of the *Kalevala*." *Books from Finland* 19: 44-47.

Austin, Norman. 1975. *Archery at the Dark of the Moon: Poetic Problems in Homer's Odyssey*. Berkeley and Los Angeles: University of California Press.

Baird, Joseph L. 1966. "Grendel the Exile." *Neuphilologische Mitteilungen* 67: 375-81.

Barnes, Harry R. 1979. "Enjambement and Oral Composition." *Transactions of the American Philological Association* 109: 1-10.

———. 1986. "The Colometric Structure of Homeric Hexameter." *Greek, Roman, and Byzantine Studies* 27: 125-50.

Bartlett, Adeline C. [1935] 1966. *The Larger Rhetorical Patterns in Anglo-Saxon Poetry*. New York: AMS Press.

Bassett, Samuel E. 1919. "The Theory of the Homeric Caesura According to the Extant Remains of the Ancient Doctrine." *American Journal of Philology* 40: 343-72.

Batinić, Pavle. 1975. "The Meter of the Serbo-Croatian Oral Epic Decasyllable." Ph.D. diss., Columbia University.

Baugh, Albert C. 1959. "Improvisation in the Middle English Romance." *Proceedings of the American Philosophical Society* 103: 418-54.

———. 1967. "The Middle English Romance: Some Questions of Creation, Presentation, and Preservation." *Speculum* 42: 1-31.

Beaty, John O. 1934. "The Echo-Word in *Beowulf* with a Note on the *Finnsburh Fragment*." *Publications of the Modern Language Association* 49: 365-73.

Ben-Amos, Daniel. 1969. "Analytical Categories and Ethnic Genres." *Genre* 2: 275-301.

Benson, Larry D. 1966. "The Literary Character of Anglo-Saxon Formulaic Poetry." *Publications of the Modern Language Association* 81: 334-41.

Bergk, Theodor. [1854] 1886. "Über das älteste Versmass der Griechen." In *Opuscula philologica*, 2:392-408. Halle: Buchhandlung des Waisenhauses.

Bessinger, Jess B., ed. 1978. *A Concordance to the Anglo-Saxon Poetic Records*. Programmed by Philip H. Smith. Ithaca, N.Y.: Cornell University Press.

Bliss, A. J. 1967. *The Metre of Beowulf*. Rev. ed. Oxford: Basil Blackwell.

———. 1971. "Single Half-lines in Old English Poetry." *Notes and Queries*, n.s. 18: 442-49.

Bonjour, Adrien. 1957. "*Beowulf* and the Beasts of Battle." *Publications of the Modern Language Association* 72: 563-73.

Bonner, Joshua H. 1976. "Toward a Unified Critical Approach to Old English Poetic Composition." *Modern Philology* 73: 219-28.

Bonnet, M., ed. 1898. *Praxeis Andreou kai Mattheia....* In *Acta Apostolorum Apocrypha...*, vol. 2, pt. 1. Leipzig: Hermann Mendelssohn.

Bowra, Cecil Maurice. 1952. *Heroic Poetry*. London: Macmillan; New York: St. Martin's Press.

Boyle, Leonard E. 1981. "The Nowell Codex and the Poem of *Beowulf*." In *The Dating of Beowulf*, 23-32. See Chase 1981b.

Brodeur, Arthur G. [1959] 1969. *The Art of Beowulf*. Berkeley and Los Angeles: University of California Press.

Brooks, Kenneth R., ed. 1961. *Andreas and the Fates of the Apostles*. Oxford: Clarendon Press.

Brough, J. 1977. Review of *Comparative Studies in Greek and Indic Meter*, by Gregory Nagy. *Classical Review*, n.s. 27: 297-98.

Browne, Wayles. 1975. "Serbo-Croatian Enclitics for English-speaking Learners." In *Kontrastivna analiza engleskog i hrvatskog ili srpskog jezika* (Contrastive Analysis of English and Serbo-Croatian), edited by Rudolf Filipović. 1:105-34. Zagreb: Institut za Lingvistiku.

Bruce-Mitford, Rupert, and Myrtle Bruce-Mitford. 1974. "The Sutton Hoo Lyre, *Beowulf*, and the Origins of the Frame Harp." In *Aspects of Anglo-Saxon Archaeology: Sutton Hoo and Other Discoveries*, edited by Rupert Bruce-Mitford, 188-97. New York: Harper and Row.

Bryan, W. F. 1929. "Epithetic Compound Folk-Names in Beowulf." In *Studies in English Philology: A Miscellany in Honor of Frederick Klaeber*, edited by Kemp Malone and Martin B. Ruud, 120-34. Minneapolis: University of Minnesota Press.

Butcher, John W. 1986. "Formulaic Invention in the Genealogies of the Old English *Genesis A*." In *Comparative Research on Oral Traditions*, 73-92. See Foley 1986c.

Bynum, David E. 1964. "A Taxonomy of Oral Narrative Song: The Isolation and Description of Invariables." Ph.D. diss., Harvard University.

———. 1968. "Themes of the Young Hero in Serbocroatian Oral Epic Tradition." *Publications of the Modern Language Association* 83: 1296-1303.

———. 1969. "The Generic Nature of Oral Epic Poetry." *Genre* 2: 236-58.

———. 1970. "Thematic Sequences and Transformation of Character in Oral Narrative Tradition." *Filološki pregled* 8: 1-21.

———. 1974. "Child's Legacy Enlarged: Oral Literary Studies at Harvard Since 1856." *Harvard Library Bulletin* 22: 237-67.

———. 1978. *The Dæmon in the Wood: A Study of Oral Narrative Patterns*. Cambridge, Mass.: Center for Study of Oral Literature.

———, ed. 1979. *Bihaćka krajina: Epics from Bihać, Cazin, and Kulen Vakuf*. Vol. 14 of *Serbo-Croatian Heroic Songs*. Cambridge, Mass.: Harvard University Press.

———. 1981. "Formula, Theme, and Critical Method." *Canadian-American Slavic Studies* 15 (1): 61-77.

Cable, Thomas. 1974. *The Meter and Melody of Beowulf*. Urbana: University of Illinois Press.

Calhoun, George M. 1933. "Homeric Repetitions." *University of California Publications in Classical Philology* 12: 1-25.

———. 1935. "The Art of Formula in Homer—*ΕΠΕΑ ΠΤΕΡΟΕΝΤΑ*." *Classical Philology* 30: 215-27.

Calin, William. 1981a. "L'Epopée dite vivante: Réflexions sur le prétendu caractère oral des chansons de geste." *Olifant* 8: 227-37.

———. 1981b. "Littérature médiévale et hypothèse orale: une divergence de méthode et de philosophie." *Olifant* 8: 256-85.

Campbell, Jackson J. 1966. "Learned Rhetoric in Old English Poetry." *Modern Philology* 63: 189-201.

———. 1967. "Knowledge of Rhetorical Figures in Anglo-Saxon England." *Journal of English and Germanic Philology* 66: 1-20.

———. 1978. "Adaptation of Classical Rhetoric in Old English Literature." In *Medieval Eloquence: Studies in the Theory and Practice of Medieval Rhetoric*, edited by James J. Murphy, 173-97. Berkeley and Los Angeles: University of California Press.

Chase, Colin. 1981a. "Opinions on the Date of *Beowulf*." In *The Dating of Beowulf*, 3-8. *See* Chase 1981b.

————, ed. 1981b. *The Dating of Beowulf*. Toronto: University of Toronto Press.

————. 1982. Review of *Beowulf and the Beowulf Manuscript*, by Kevin S. Kiernan. *Old English Newsletter* 16 (1): 73-76.

Clark, Francelia. 1981. "Flyting in *Beowulf* and Rebuke in *The Song of Bagdad*: The Question of Theme." In *Oral Traditional Literature*, 164-93. *See* Foley 1981f.

Clark, George. 1965a. "Beowulf's Armor." *English Literary History* 32: 409-41.

————. 1965b. "The Traveler Recognizes His Goal: A Theme in Anglo-Saxon Poetry." *Journal of English and Germanic Philology* 64: 645-59.

Claus, David B. 1975. "*Aidôs* in the Language of Achilles." *Transactions of the American Philological Association* 105: 13-28.

Clayman, Dee L., and Thomas van Nortwick. 1977. "Enjambement in Greek Hexameter Poetry." *Transactions of the American Philological Association* 107: 85-92.

Combellack, Frederick M. 1950. "Words That Die." *Classical Journal* 46: 21-26.

Conner, Patrick W. 1972. "Schematization of Oral-Formulaic Processes in Old English Poetry." *Language and Style* 5: 204-20.

Conquergood, Dwight. 1981. "Boasting in Anglo-Saxon England: Performance and the Heroic Ethos." *Literature in Performance* 1 (2): 24-35.

Coote, Mary P. 1969. "The Singer's Use of Theme in Composing Oral Narrative Song in the Serbocroatian Tradition." Ph.D. diss., Harvard University.

————. 1978. "Serbo-Croatian Heroic Songs." In *Heroic Epic and Saga: An Introduction to the World's Great Folk Epics*, edited by Felix J. Oinas, 257-85. Bloomington: Indiana University Press.

————. 1980. "The Singer's Themes in Serbocroatian Heroic Song." *California Slavic Studies* 11: 201-35.

————. 1981. "Lying in Passages." *Canadian-American Slavic Studies* 15 (1): 5-23.

Creed, Robert P. 1955. "Studies in the Techniques of Composition of the *Beowulf* Poetry in British Museum MS. Cotton Vitellius A. xv." Ph.D. diss., Harvard University.

————. 1962. "The Singer Looks at His Sources." *Comparative Literature* 14: 44-52.

————. 1966. "A New Approach to the Rhythm of *Beowulf*." *Publications of the Modern Language Association* 81: 23-33.

————. 1989. *Reconstructing the Rhythm of Beowulf*. Columbia: University of Missouri Press.

Crowne, David K. 1960. "The Hero on the Beach: An Example of Composition by Theme in Anglo-Saxon Poetry." *Neuphilologische Mitteilungen* 61: 362-72.

Dale, A. M. 1969. "Observations on Dactylic." In *Collected Papers*, 185-209. Cambridge: Cambridge University Press.

Dane, Joseph A. 1982. "Finnsburh and *Iliad* IX: A Greek Survival of the Medieval Germanic Oral-Formulaic Theme, The Hero on the Beach." *Neophilologus* 66: 443-49.

Davison, J. A. 1963a. "The Homeric Question." In *A Companion to Homer*, edited by Alan J. B. Wace and Frank H. Stubbings, 234-66. London: Macmillan.

————. 1963b. "The Transmission of the Text." In *A Companion to Homer*, 215-33. *See* Davison 1963a.

De Lavan, Joanne. 1981. "Feasts and Anti-Feasts in *Beowulf* and the *Odyssey*." In *Oral Traditional Literature*, 235-61. *See* Foley 1981f.

Devine, A. M., and L. D. Stephens. 1984. *Language and Metre: Resolution, Porson's Bridge, and Their Prosodic Basis.* American Classical Studies, no. 12. Chico, Calif.: Scholars Press.

Diamond, Robert E. 1961. "Theme as Ornament in Anglo-Saxon Poetry." *Publications of the Modern Language Association* 76: 461-68.

Donlan, Walter. 1971. "Homer's Agamemnon." *Classical World* 65: 109-15.

Duban, Jeffrey M. 1981. "Les Duels majeurs de l'Iliade et le langage d'Hector." *Les Etudes classiques* 49: 97-124.

Duggan, Hoyt N. 1976. "The Role of Formulas in the Dissemination of a Middle English Alliterative Romance." *Studies in Bibliography* 29: 265-88.

Duggan, Joseph J. 1973. *The Song of Roland: Formulaic Style and Poetic Craft.* Berkeley and Los Angeles: University of California Press.

———, ed. 1975. *Oral Literature: Seven Essays.* Edinburgh: Scottish Academic Press; New York: Barnes and Noble. (Also published in *Forum for Modern Language Studies* 10, no. 3 [1974].)

———. 1981a. "Le Mode de composition des chansons de geste: Analyse statistique, jugement esthétique, modèles de transmission." *Olifant* 8: 286-316.

———. 1981b. "La Théorie de la composition orale des chansons de geste: les faits et les interprétations." *Olifant* 8: 238-55.

Dumézil, Georges. 1973. *Gods of the Ancient Northmen.* Berkeley and Los Angeles: University of California Press.

Dunbar, Henry, comp. [1880] 1962. *A Complete Concordance to the Odyssey and Hymns of Homer.* Revised and edited by Benedetto Marzullo. Hildesheim: Georg Olms.

Dundes, Alan. 1962. "From Emic to Etic Units in the Structural Study of Folktales." *Journal of American Folklore* 75: 95-105.

Edwards, G. Patrick. 1971. *The Language of Hesiod in its Traditional Context.* Oxford: Basil Blackwell.

Edwards, Mark W. 1975. "Type-Scenes and Homeric Hospitality." *Transactions of the American Philological Association* 105: 51-72.

———. 1980a. "Convention and Individuality in *Iliad* 1." *Harvard Studies in Classical Philology* 84: 1-28.

———. 1980b. "The Structure of Homeric Catalogues." *Transactions of the American Philological Association* 110: 81-105.

———. 1986. "Homer and Oral Tradition: The Formula, Part I." *Oral Tradition* 1: 171-230.

———. 1988. "Homer and Oral Tradition: The Formula, Part II." *Oral Tradition* 3: 11-60.

Faulhaber, Charles B. 1976. "Neo-traditionalism, Formulism, Individualism, and Recent Studies on the Spanish Epic." *Romance Philology* 30: 83-101.

Fenik, Bernard C. 1968. *Typical Battle Scenes in the Iliad: Studies in the Narrative Techniques of Homeric Battle Description.* Hermes Einzelschriften, no. 21. Wiesbaden: Steiner.

———. 1974. *Studies in the Odyssey.* Hermes Einzelschriften, no. 30. Wiesbaden: Steiner.

Fine, Elizabeth C. 1984. *The Folklore Text: From Performance to Print.* Bloomington: Indiana University Press.

Finnegan, Ruth. 1977. *Oral Poetry: Its Nature, Significance, and Social Context.* Cambridge: Cambridge University Press.

Foley, John Miles. 1974. "The Ritual Nature of Traditional Oral Poetry: Metrics, Music, and Matter in the Anglo-Saxon, Homeric Greek, and Serbo-Croatian Traditions." Ph.D. diss., University of Massachusetts, Amherst.

————. 1976a. "Formula and Theme in Old English Poetry." In *Oral Literature and the Formula*, 207-32. See Stolz and Shannon 1976.

————. 1976b. "'Riddle I' of the *Exeter Book*: The Apocalyptical Storm." *Neuphilologische Mitteilungen* 77: 347-57.

————. 1977a. "Research on Oral Traditional Expression in Šumadija and Its Relevance to the Study of Other Oral Traditions." In *Selected Papers on a Serbian Village*, 199-236. See Kerewsky Halpern and Halpern 1977.

————. 1977b. "The Traditional Oral Audience." *Balkan Studies* 18: 145-54.

————. 1978a. "A Computer Analysis of Metrical Patterns in *Beowulf*." *Computers and the Humanities* 12: 71-80.

————. 1978b. "The Oral Singer in Context: Halil Bajgorić, *Guslar*." *Canadian-American Slavic Studies* 12: 230-46.

————. 1978c. "The Traditional Structure of Ibro Bašić's 'Alagić Alija and Velagić Selim.'" *Slavic and East European Journal* 22: 1-14.

————. 1980a. "Epic and Charm in Old English and Serbo-Croatian Oral Tradition." *Comparative Criticism* 2: 71-92.

————. 1980b. "Hybrid Prosody and Single Half-lines in Old English and Serbo-Croatian Poetry." *Neophilologus* 64: 284-89.

————. 1981a. "Computerized Editions of Oral Epic Poetry: The Evolution of the Text-Processor Heuro-1." In *Actes du Congrès international informatique et sciences humaines*, edited by Louis Delatte, 377-85. Liège: Laboratoire d'Analyse Statistique des Langues Anciennes.

————. 1981b. "Introduction: The Oral Theory in Context." In *Oral Traditional Literature*, 27-122. See Foley 1981f.

————. 1981c. "*Laecdom* and *Bajanje*: A Comparative Study of Old English and Serbo-Croatian Charms." *Centerpoint* 4 (3): 33-40.

————. 1981d. "Tradition-dependent and -independent Features in Oral Literature: A Comparative View of the Formula." In *Oral Traditional Literature*, 262-81. See Foley 1981f.

————, ed. 1981e. (special issue). *Canadian-American Slavic Studies*, 15 (1).

————, ed. 1981f. *Oral Traditional Literature: A Festschrift for Albert Bates Lord*. Columbus, Ohio: Slavica.

————. 1982. "Field Research on Oral Literature and Culture in Serbia." *Pacific Quarterly* 7 (2): 47-59.

————. 1983a. "Genre(s) in the Making: Diction, Audience, and Text in the Old English *Seafarer*." *Poetics Today* 4: 683-706.

————. 1983b. "Literary Art and Oral Tradition in Old English and Serbian Poetry." *Anglo-Saxon England* 12: 183-214.

————. 1984a. "Editing Oral Epic Texts: Theory and Practice." *Text: Transactions of the Society for Textual Scholarship* 1: 75-94.

————. 1984b. "The Price of Narrative Fiction: Genre, Myth, and Meaning in *Moby-Dick* and the *Odyssey*." *Thought* 59: 432-48.

————. 1985. *Oral-Formulaic Theory and Research: An Introduction and Annotated Bibliography*. New York: Garland.

————. 1986a. "Reading the Oral Traditional Text: Aesthetics of Creation and Response." In *Comparative Research on Oral Traditions*, 185-212. See Foley 1986c.

————. 1986b. "Tradition and the Individual Talent: Oral Epic, Textual Meaning, and Receptionalist Theory." *Cultural Anthropology* 1: 203-22.

————, ed. 1986c. *Comparative Research on Oral Traditions: A Memorial for Milman Parry.* Columbus, Ohio: Slavica.

————, ed. 1986d. *Oral Tradition in Literature: Interpretation in Context.* Columbia: University of Missouri Press.

————. 1988. *The Theory of Oral Composition: History and Methodology.* Bloomington: Indiana University Press.

————. Forthcoming. *Matija Murko: A Translation of His Writings on Oral Epic Tradition in Yugoslavia.* Irvine, Calif.: Charles Schlacks.

Fournier, H. 1946. "Formules homériques de référence avec verbe 'dire.'" *Revue de philologie, de littérature, et d'histoire anciennes*, 3d ser., 20: 29-68.

Fränkel, Eduard. 1932. "Kolon und Satz: Beobachtungen zur Gliederung des antiken Satzes, II." *Nachrichten von der Gesellschaft der Wissenschaften zu Göttingen*: 319-54.

Fränkel, Hermann. 1926. "Der kallimachische und der homerische Hexameter." *Nachrichten von der Gesellschaft der Wissenschaften zu Göttingen* (phil.-hist. Klasse): 197-229.

————. 1955. *Wege und Formen frühgriechischen Denkens: Literarische und philosophiegeschichtliche Studien.* Edited by Franz Tietze. Munich: C. H. Beck.

————. 1968. *Noten zu den Argonautika des Apollonios.* Munich: C. H. Beck.

Friedrich, Paul, and James Redfield. 1978. "Speech as a Personality Symbol: The Case of Achilles." *Language* 54: 263-88.

————. 1981. "Contra Messing." *Language* 57: 901-3.

Fry, Donald K., Jr. 1966. "The Hero on the Beach in *Finnsburh*." *Neuphilologische Mitteilungen* 67: 27-31.

————. 1967a. "The Heroine on the Beach in *Judith*." *Neuphilologische Mitteilungen* 68: 168-84.

————. 1967b. "Old English Formulas and Systems." *English Studies* 48: 193-204.

————. 1968a. "Old English Formulaic Themes and Type-Scenes." *Neophilologus* 52: 48-54.

————. 1968b. "Some Aesthetic Implications of a New Definition of the Formula." *Neuphilologische Mitteilungen* 69: 516-22.

————. 1968c. "Variation and Economy in *Beowulf*." *Modern Philology* 65: 353-56.

————. 1969. "Themes and Type-Scenes in *Elene* 1-113." *Speculum* 44: 35-45.

————. 1972. "Type-Scene Composition in *Judith*." *Annuale Mediaevale* 12: 100-119.

————. 1975. "Cædmon as a Formulaic Poet." In *Oral Literature*, 41-61. See J. Duggan 1975. (Originally published in *Forum for Modern Language Studies* 10 [1974].)

————. 1981. "The Memory of Cædmon." In *Oral Traditional Literature*, 282-93. See Foley 1981f.

————. 1986. "The Cliff of Death in Old English Poetry." In *Comparative Research on Oral Traditions*, 213-33. See Foley 1986c.

Gaisser, Julia H. 1969. "A Structural Analysis of the Digressions in the *Iliad* and the *Odyssey*." *Harvard Studies in Classical Philology* 73: 1-43.

Gesemann, Gerhard. 1926. *Studien zur südslavischen Volksepik.* Veröffentlichungen der Slavistischen Arbeitsgemeinschaft (Prague), 1. Reihe, Heft 3. Reichenberg: Stiepel.

Greenfield, Stanley B. 1953a. "The Theme of Spiritual Exile in *Christ I.*" *Philological Quarterly* 32: 321-28.

———. 1953b. "*The Wife's Lament* Reconsidered." *Publications of the Modern Language Association* 68: 907-12.

———. 1955. "The Formulaic Expression of the Theme of 'Exile' in Anglo-Saxon Poetry." *Speculum* 30: 200-206.

Grendon, Felix, ed. 1909. "The Anglo-Saxon Charms." *Journal of American Folklore* 22: 105-237.

Gruber, Loren C. 1974. "Motion, Perception, and *oppæt* in *Beowulf.*" In *In Geardagum: Essays on Old English Language and Literature,* edited by Loren C. Gruber and Dean Loganbill, 1:31-37. Denver: Society for New Language Study.

Gunn, David M. 1970. "Narrative Inconsistency and the Oral Dictated Text in the Homeric Epic." *American Journal of Philology* 91: 192-203.

———. 1971. "Thematic Composition and Homeric Authorship." *Harvard Studies in Classical Philology* 75: 1-31.

Hainsworth, J. B. 1968. *The Flexibility of the Homeric Formula.* Oxford: Clarendon Press.

———. 1976. "Phrase-Clusters in Homer." In *Studies in Greek, Italic, and Indo-European Linguistics Offered to Leonard R. Palmer on the Occasion of His Seventieth Birthday, June 5, 1976,* edited by Anna M. Davies and Wolfgang Meid, 83-86. Innsbrucker Beiträge zur Sprachwissenschaft, no. 16. Vienna: Ernst Becvar.

———. 1978. "Good and Bad Formulae." In *Homer: Tradition and Invention,* edited by Bernard C. Fenik, 41-50. Leiden: Brill.

Hanning, Robert W. 1973. "Sharing, Dividing, Depriving—The Verbal Ironies of Grendel's Last Visit to Heorot." *Texas Studies in Literature and Linguistics* 15: 203-13.

Hansen, William F. 1972. *The Conference Sequence: Patterned Narration and Narrative Inconsistency in the Odyssey.* Berkeley and Los Angeles: University of California Press.

———. 1978. "The Homeric Epics and Oral Poetry." In *Heroic Epic and Saga,* edited by Felix J. Oinas, 7-26. Bloomington: Indiana University Press.

Hauer, Stanley R. 1983. "Thomas Jefferson and the Anglo-Saxon Language." *Publications of the Modern Language Association* 98: 879-98.

Havelock, Eric A. [1963] 1982. *Preface to Plato.* Cambridge, Mass.: Belknap Press.

———. 1982. *The Literate Revolution in Greece and Its Cultural Consequences.* Princeton: Princeton University Press.

Haymes, Edward R. 1980. "Formulaic Density and Bishop Njegoš." *Comparative Literature* 32: 390-401.

Heinemann, Fredrik J. 1970. "*Judith* 236-291a: A Mock Heroic Approach-to-Battle Type Scene." *Neuphilologische Mitteilungen* 71: 83-96.

Henige, David P. 1974. *The Chronology of Oral Tradition: Quest for a Chimera.* Oxford: Clarendon Press.

Herzog, George. 1940. "Stability of Form in Traditional and Cultivated Music." In *Papers Read by Members of the American Musicological Society at the Annual Meeting (Washington, D.C., December 29th and 30th, 1938),* 69-73. (Also in *The Study of Folklore,* edited by Alan Dundes, 169-74. Englewood Cliffs, N.J.: Prentice-Hall, 1965.)

———. 1951. "The Music of Yugoslav Heroic Epic Folk Poetry." *International Folk Music Journal* 3: 62-64.

Heusler, Andreas. 1925-29. *Deutsche Versgeschichte mit Einschluss des altenglischen und altnordischen Stabreimverses.* Berlin: de Gruyter.

Hieatt, Constance B. 1975. "Envelope Patterns and the Structure of *Beowulf*." *English Studies in Canada* 1: 250-65.

———. 1986. "On Envelope Patterns (Ancient and—Relatively—Modern) and Nonce Formulas." In *Comparative Research on Oral Traditions*, 245-58. *See* Foley 1986c.

Hillers, Delbert R. and Marsh H. McCall, Jr. 1976. "Homeric Dictated Texts: A Reexamination of Some Near Eastern Evidence." *Harvard Studies in Classical Philology* 80: 19-23.

Hoekstra, A. 1964. *Homeric Modifications of Formulaic Prototypes: Studies in the Development of Greek Epic Diction*. Amsterdam: Noord-Hollandsche Uitgevers.

———. 1969. *The Sub-Epic Stage of the Formulaic Tradition: Studies in the Homeric Hymns to Apollo, to Aphrodite, and to Demeter*. Amsterdam: Noord-Hollandsche Uitgevers.

Hoenigswald, Henry M. 1976. "Summary Commentary." In *Oral Literature and the Formula*, 273-78. *See* Stolz and Shannon 1976.

———. 1977. Review of *Comparative Studies in Greek and Indic Meter*, by Gregory Nagy. *American Journal of Philology* 98: 82-88.

Hogan, James C. 1976. "Double *prin* and the Language of Achilles." *Classical Journal* 71: 305-10.

Holoka, James P. 1973. "Homeric Originality: A Survey." *Classical World* 66: 257-93.

———. 1979. "Homer Studies 1971-1977." *Classical World* 73: 65-150.

Ingalls, Wayne B. 1970. "The Structure of the Homeric Hexameter: A Review." *Phoenix* 24: 1-12.

———. 1972. "Another Dimension of the Homeric Formula." *Phoenix* 26: 111-22.

———. 1976. "The Analogical Formula in Homer." *Transactions of the American Philological Association* 106: 211-26.

Irving, Edward B., Jr. 1968. *A Reading of Beowulf*. New Haven: Yale University Press.

Jakobson, Roman. 1952. "Studies in Comparative Slavic Metrics." *Oxford Slavonic Papers* 3: 21-66.

Janko, Richard. 1982. *Homer, Hesiod, and the Hymns: Diachronic Development in Epic Diction*. Cambridge: Cambridge University Press.

Johnson, James D. 1975. "The 'Hero on the Beach' in the Alliterative *Morte Arthure*." *Neuphilologische Mitteilungen* 76: 271-81.

Jones, Alison G. 1966. "*Daniel* and *Azarias* as Evidence for the Oral-Formulaic Character of Old English Poetry." *Medium Ævum* 35: 95-102.

———. 1969. "The Old English *Soul and Body* as an Example of Oral Transmission." *Medium Ævum* 38: 239-44.

Jones, Frank P., and Florence E. Gray. 1972. "Hexameter Patterns, Statistical Inference, and the Homeric Question: An Analysis of the LaRoche Data." *Transactions of the American Philological Association* 103: 187-209.

Karadžić, Vuk Stefanović, ed. [1845] 1969. *Srpske narodne pjesme*. Vol. 2. Belgrade. Nolit.

Kavros, Harry E. 1981. "*Swefan æfter symble*: The Feast-Sleep Theme in *Beowulf*." *Neophilologus* 65: 120-28.

Kerewsky Halpern, Barbara, and John Miles Foley. 1978. "The Power of the Word: Healing Charms as an Oral Genre." *Journal of American Folklore* 91: 903-24.

Kerewsky Halpern, Barbara, and Joel M. Halpern, eds. 1977. *Selected Papers on a Serbian Village*. Research Report no. 17. Amherst: Department of Anthropology, University of Massachusetts, Amherst.

Kiernan, Kevin S. 1981a. *Beowulf and the Beowulf Manuscript*. New Brunswick, N.J.: Rutgers University Press.

———. 1981b. "The Eleventh-Century Origin of *Beowulf* and the *Beowulf* Manuscript." In *The Dating of Beowulf*, 9-21. See Chase 1981b.

Kintgen, Eugene R. 1977. "'Lif,' 'Lof,' 'Leof,' 'Lufu,' and 'Geleafa' in Old English Poetry." *Neuphilologische Mitteilungen* 78: 309-16.

Kiparsky, Paul. 1976. "Oral Poetry: Some Linguistic and Typological Considerations." In *Oral Literature and the Formula*, 73-106. See Stolz and Shannon 1976.

Kirk, Geoffrey S. 1962. *The Songs of Homer*. Cambridge: Cambridge University Press. (Published in abridged form as *Homer and the Epic*, 1965.)

———. 1966. "Studies in Some Technical Aspects of Homeric Style." *Yale Classical Studies* 20: 73-152.

———. 1985. *The Iliad: A Commentary, Volume I: Books 1-4*. Cambridge: Cambridge University Press.

Klaeber, Friedrich, ed. 1950. *Beowulf and the Fight at Finnsburg*. 3d ed., with 1st and 2d supplements. Boston: D. C. Heath.

Kuryłowicz, Jerzy. 1970. "The Quantitative Meter of Indo-European." In *Indo-European and Indo-Europeans*, edited by George Cardona, Henry M. Hoenigswald, and Alfred Senn, 421-30. Philadelphia: University of Pennsylvania Press.

La Drière, J. Craig. 1959. "The Comparative Method in the Study of Prosody." In *Comparative Literature: Proceedings of the Second Congress of the International Comparative Literature Association*, edited by Werner P. Friedrich, 160-75. Chapel Hill: University of North Carolina Press.

———. 1974. "Prosody." In *Princeton Encyclopedia of Poetry and Poetics*, edited by Alex Preminger, Frank J. Warnke, and O. B. Hardison, Jr., 669-77. Enlarged ed. Princeton: Princeton University Press.

La Roche, J. [1898] 1962. "Zahlenverhältnisse im homerischen Vers." *Wiener Studien: Zeitschrift für classische Philologie* 20: 1-69. New York: Kraus Reprint.

Latacz, Joachim. 1979a. "Tradition und Neuerung in der Homerforschung: Zur Geschichte der Oral poetry-Theorie." In *Homer*, 25-44. See Latacz 1979b.

———, ed. 1979b. *Homer: Tradition und Neuerung*. Wege der Forschung, no. 463. Darmstadt: Wissenschaftliche Buchgesellschaft.

Lattimore, Richmond, trans. 1965. *The Iliad of Homer*. Chicago: University of Chicago Press.

Lehmann, Winfred P. [1956] 1971. *The Development of Germanic Verse Form*. New York: Gordian Press.

Lesky, Albin. 1966. *A History of Greek Literature*. Translated by James Willis and Cornelis de Heer. New York: Thomas Y. Crowell.

Levy, Harry L. 1963. "The Odyssean Suitors and the Host-Guest Relationship." *Transactions of the American Philological Association* 94: 143-53.

Lord, Albert Bates. 1938. "Homer and Huso II: Narrative Inconsistencies in Homer and Oral Poetry." *Transactions of the American Philological Association* 69: 439-45.

———. 1951a. "Composition by Theme in Homer and Southslavic Epos." *Transactions of the American Philological Association* 82: 71-80.

———. 1951b. "Yugoslav Epic Folk Poetry." *International Folk Music Journal* 3: 57-61.

———. 1953. "Homer's Originality: Oral Dictated Texts." *Transactions of the American Philological Association* 84: 124-34.

————. 1956. "The Role of Sound Patterns in Serbo-Croatian Epic." In *For Roman Jakobson*, 301-5. The Hague: Mouton.

————. 1959. "The Poetics of Oral Creation." In *Comparative Literature: Proceedings of the Second Congress of the International Comparative Literature Association*, edited by Werner P. Friedrich, 1-6. Chapel Hill: University of North Carolina Press.

————. 1960. *The Singer of Tales*. Cambridge, Mass.: Harvard University Press.

————. 1962. "Homeric Echoes in Bihać." *Zbornik za narodni život i običaje južnih slavena* 40: 313-20.

————. 1965. "Beowulf and Odysseus." In *Franciplegius: Medieval and Linguistic Studies in Honor of Francis Peabody Magoun, Jr.*, edited by Jess B. Bessinger and Robert P. Creed, 86-91. New York: New York University Press.

————. 1967a. "Homer as Oral Poet." *Harvard Studies in Classical Philology* 72: 1-46.

————. 1967b. "The Influence of a Fixed Text." In *To Honor Roman Jakobson: Essays on the Occasion of His Seventieth Birthday (11 October 1966)*, 1199-1206. Janua Linguarum, Series Maior, no. 32, vol. 2 (of 3-vol. set). The Hague: Mouton.

————. 1969. "The Theme of the Withdrawn Hero in Serbo-Croatian Oral Epic." *Prilozi za književnost, jezik, istoriju i folklor* 35: 18-30.

————. 1970. "Tradition and the Oral Poet: Homer, Huso, and Avdo Medjedović." In *Atti del convegno internazionale sul tema: La poesia epica e la sua formazione*, edited by Enrico Cerulli et al., 13-28. Problemi Attuali di Scienza e di Cultura, no. 139. Rome: Accademia Nazionale dei Lincei.

————. 1971. "An Example of Homeric Qualities of Repetition in Medjedović's 'Smailagić Meho.'" In *Serta Slavica In Memoriam Aloisii Schmaus: Gedenkschrift für Alois Schmaus*, edited by Wolfgang Gesemann, Johannes Holthusen, Erwin Koschmieder, Ilse Kunert, Peter Rehder, and Erwin Wedel, 458-64. Munich: Rudolf Trofenik.

————. 1972. "The Effect of the Turkish Conquest on Balkan Epic Tradition." In *Aspects of the Balkans: Continuity and Change*, edited by Henrik Birnbaum and Speros Vryonis, Jr., 298-318. The Hague: Mouton.

————. 1975. "Perspectives on Recent Work on Oral Literature." In *Oral Literature*, 41-61. *See* J. Duggan 1975. (Originally published in *Forum for Modern Language Studies* 10 [1974]: 1-21.)

————. 1976. "The Traditional Song." In *Oral Literature and the Formula*, 1-15. *See* Stolz and Shannon 1976.

————. 1981. "Memory, Fixity, and Genre in Oral Traditional Poetries." In *Oral Traditional Literature*, 451-61. *See* Foley 1981f.

————. 1986a. "The Merging of Two Worlds: Oral and Written Poetry as Carriers of Ancient Values." In *Oral Tradition in Literature*, 19-64. *See* Foley 1986d.

————. 1986b. "The Nature of Oral Poetry." In *Comparative Research on Oral Traditions*, 313-49. *See* Foley 1986c.

————. 1986c. "Perspectives on Recent Work on the Oral Traditional Formula." *Oral Tradition* 1: 467-503.

Lord, Mary Louise. 1967. "Withdrawal and Return: An Epic Story Pattern in the Homeric Hymn to Demeter and in the Homeric Poems." *Classical Journal* 62: 241-48.

Maas, Paul. 1962. *Greek Metre*. Translated by Hugh Lloyd-Jones. Oxford: Clarendon Press.

Magner, Thomas F., and Ladislav Matejka. 1971. *Word Accent in Modern Serbo-Croatian*. University Park: Pennsylvania State University Press.

Magoun, Francis P., Jr. [1953] 1968. "The Oral-Formulaic Character of Anglo-Saxon Narrative Poetry." In *The Beowulf Poet*, edited by Donald K. Fry, Jr., 83-113. Englewood Cliffs, N.J.: Prentice-Hall, 1968. (Originally published in *Speculum* 28: 446-67.)

————. 1955. "The Theme of the Beasts of Battle in Anglo-Saxon Poetry." *Neuphilologische Mitteilungen* 56: 81-90.

————. 1961. "Some Notes on Anglo-Saxon Poetry." In *Studies in Medieval Literature in Honor of Albert Croll Baugh*, edited by MacEdward Leach, 272-83. Philadelphia: University of Pennsylvania Press.

Malone, Kemp, ed. 1963. *The Nowell Codex*. Early English Manuscripts in Facsimile, no. 12. Copenhagen: Rosenkilde and Bagger.

Maretić, Tomislav. 1907a-b. "Metrika narodnih naših pjesama." *Rad Jugoslavenske Akademije Znanosti i Umjetnosti* 168: 1-112; 170: 76-200.

————. 1935-36. "Metrika muslimanske narodne epike." *Rad Jugoslavenske Akademije Znanosti i Umjetnosti* 253: 181-242; 255: 1-76.

Meillet, Antoine. 1923. *Les Origines indo-européennes des mètres grecs*. Paris: Presses Universitaires de France.

Messing, Gordon M. 1981. "On Weighing Achilles' Winged Words." *Language* 57: 888-900.

Metcalf, Allan A. 1963. "Ten Natural Animals in *Beowulf*." *Neuphilologische Mitteilungen* 64: 378-89.

Miletich, John S. 1976. "The Quest for the 'Formula': A Comparative Reappraisal." *Modern Philology* 74: 111-23.

————. 1978a. "Elaborate Style in South Slavic Oral Narrative and in Kačić Miošić's *Razgovor*." In *American Contributions to the Eighth International Congress of Slavists (Zagreb and Ljubljana, September 3-9, 1978)*, edited by Henrik Birnbaum, 1:522-31. Columbus, Ohio: Slavica.

————. 1978b. "Oral-traditional Style and Learned Literature: A New Perspective." *Poetics and the Theory of Literature* 3: 345-56.

Minton, William W. 1965. "The Fallacy of the Structural Formula." *Transactions of the American Philological Association* 96: 241-53.

Moulton, Carroll. 1977. *Similes in the Homeric Poems*. Hypomnemata, no. 49. Göttingen: Vandenhoeck and Ruprecht.

Murko, Matija. 1929. *La Poésie populaire épique en Yougoslavie au début du XXe siècle*. Travaux publiés par l'Institut d'Etudes Slaves, no. 10. Paris: Librairie Ancienne Honoré Champion.

————. 1951. *Tragom srpsko-hrvatske narodne epike: Putovanja u godinama 1930-32*, 2 vols. Zagreb: Jugoslavenska Akademija Znanosti i Umjetnosti.

Nagler, Michael N. 1967. "Towards a Generative View of the Oral Formula." *Transactions of the American Philological Association* 98: 269-311.

————. 1974. *Spontaneity and Tradition: A Study in the Oral Art of Homer*. Berkeley and Los Angeles: University of California Press.

Nagy, Gregory. 1974. *Comparative Studies in Greek and Indic Meter*. Cambridge, Mass.: Harvard University Press.

————. 1976. "Formula and Meter." In *Oral Literature and the Formula*, 239-60. See Stolz and Shannon 1976.

————. 1979. *The Best of the Achaeans: Concepts of the Hero in Archaic Greek Poetry.* Baltimore: Johns Hopkins University Press.

————. 1986. "Ancient Greek Epic and Praise Poetry: Some Typological Considerations." In *Oral Tradition in Literature,* 89-102. *See* Foley 1986d.

Nagy, Joseph Falaky. 1985. *The Wisdom of the Outlaw: The Boyhood Deeds of Finn in Gaelic Narrative Tradition.* Berkeley and Los Angeles: University of California Press.

Newton, B. E. 1969. "Metre and Stress in Greek." *Phoenix* 23: 359-71.

Niles, John D. 1979. "Ring Composition and the Structure of *Beowulf.*" *Publications of the Modern Language Association* 94: 924-35.

————. 1983. *Beowulf: The Poem and Its Tradition.* Cambridge, Mass.: Harvard University Press.

Nimis, Steve. 1986. "The Language of Achilles: Construction vs. Representation." *Classical World* 79: 217-25.

Notopoulos, James A. 1949. "Parataxis in Homer: A New Approach to Homeric Literary Criticism." *Transactions of the American Philological Association* 80: 1-23.

————. 1964. "Studies in Early Greek Oral Poetry." *Harvard Studies in Classical Philology* 68: 1-77.

Olsen, Alexandra Hennessey. 1980. "Guthlac on the Beach." *Neophilologus* 64: 290-96.

————. 1981. *Guthlac of Croyland: A Study of Heroic Hagiography.* Washington, D.C.: University Press of America.

————. 1982. "Inversion and Political Purpose in the Old English *Judith.*" *English Studies* 63: 289-93.

————. 1984. *Speech, Song, and Poetic Craft: The Artistry of the Cynewulf Canon.* Bern: Peter Lang.

————. 1986. "Oral-Formulaic Research in Old English Studies: Part I." *Oral Tradition* 1: 548-606.

————. 1988. "Oral-Formulaic Research in Old English Studies: Part II." *Oral Tradition* 3: 138-90.

O'Neill, Eugene, Jr. 1942. "The Localization of Metrical Word-Types in the Greek Hexameter." *Yale Classical Studies* 8: 103-78.

Ong, Walter J. 1965. "Oral Residue in Tudor Prose Style." *Publications of the Modern Language Association* 80: 145-54.

————. 1967. *The Presence of the Word: Some Prolegomena for Cultural and Religious History.* New Haven: Yale University Press.

————. 1977. *Interfaces of the Word: Studies in the Evolution of Consciousness and Culture.* Ithaca, N.Y.: Cornell University Press.

————. 1982. *Orality and Literacy: The Technologizing of the Word.* London: Methuen.

————. 1986. "Text as Interpretation: Mark and After." In *Oral Tradition in Literature,* 147-69. *See* Foley 1986d.

O'Nolan, Kevin. 1969. "Homer and Irish Heroic Narrative." *Classical Quarterly,* n.s. 19: 1-19.

Opland, Jeff. 1975. "*Imbongi Nezibongo*: The Xhosa Tribal Poet and the Contemporary Poetic Tradition." *Publications of the Modern Language Association* 90: 185-208.

————. 1976. "*Beowulf* on the Poet." *Mediaeval Studies* 38: 442-67.

————. 1980. *Anglo-Saxon Oral Poetry: A Study of the Traditions.* New Haven: Yale University Press.

————. 1983. *Xhosa Oral Poetry: Aspects of a Black South African Tradition.* Cambridge: Cambridge University Press.

Oral Tradition. A journal devoted exclusively to studies of the world's oral traditions and their influence on written literature and culture. 1986-.

Packard, David W. 1974. "Sound-Patterns in Homer." *Transactions of the American Philological Association* 104: 239-60.

Page, Denys. 1959. *History and the Homeric Iliad.* Sather Classical Lectures, no. 31. Berkeley and Los Angeles: University of California Press.

Pantzer, Eugene E. 1959. "Yugoslav Epic Preambles." *Slavic and East European Journal* 3: 372-81.

Parks, Walter Ward. 1981. "Generic Identity and the Guest-Host Exchange: A Study of Return Songs in the Homeric and Serbo-Croatian Traditions." *Canadian-American Slavic Studies* 15: 24-41.

————. 1986. "The Oral-Formulaic Theory in Middle English Studies." *Oral Tradition* 1: 636-94.

Parry, Adam. 1956. "The Language of Achilles." *Transactions of the American Philological Association* 87: 1-7.

————. 1971. "Introduction" to *The Making of Homeric Verse*, ix-lxii. *See* M. Parry 1971.

Parry, Milman. 1923. "A Comparative Study of Diction as One of the Elements of Style in Early Greek Epic Poetry." M.A. thesis, University of California, Berkeley. (Published in *The Making of Homeric Verse*, 421-36. *See* M. Parry 1971.)

————. 1928a. *L'Epithète traditionnelle dans Homère: Essai sur un problème de style homérique.* Paris: Société Editrice "Les Belles Lettres." (Reprinted as "The Traditional Epithet in Homer." In *The Making of Homeric Verse*, 1-190. *See* M. Parry 1971.)

————. 1928b. *Les Formules et la métrique d'Homère.* Paris: Société Editrice "Les Belles Lettres." (Reprinted as "Homeric Formulae and Homeric Metre." In *The Making of Homeric Verse*, 191-239. *See* M. Parry 1971.)

————. 1929. "The Distinctive Character of Enjambement in Homeric Verse." *Transactions of the American Philological Association* 60: 200-220. (Reprinted in *The Making of Homeric Verse*, 251-65. *See* M. Parry 1971.)

————. 1930. "Studies in the Epic Technique of Oral Verse-Making. I. Homer and Homeric Style." *Harvard Studies in Classical Philology* 41: 73-147. (Reprinted in *The Making of Homeric Verse*, 266-324. *See* M. Parry 1971.)

————. 1932. "Studies in the Epic Technique of Oral Verse-Making. II. The Homeric Language as the Language of an Oral Poetry." *Harvard Studies in Classical Philology* 43: 1-50. (Reprinted in *The Making of Homeric Verse*, 325-64. *See* M. Parry 1971.)

————. 1933-35. "Cor Huso: A Study of Southslavic Song." Field notes, expedition to Yugoslavia. (Extracts published in *The Making of Homeric Verse*, 437-64. *See* M. Parry 1971.)

————. 1936. "On Typical Scenes in Homer." *Classical Philology* 31: 357-60. (Reprinted in *The Making of Homeric Verse*, 404-7. *See* M. Parry 1971.)

————. 1937. "About Winged Words." *Classical Philology* 32: 59-63. (Reprinted in *The Making of Homeric Verse*, 414-18. *See* M. Parry 1971.)

————. 1971. *The Making of Homeric Verse: The Collected Papers of Milman Parry.* Edited by Adam Parry. Oxford: Clarendon Press.

Peabody, Berkley. 1975. *The Winged Word: A Study in the Technique of Ancient Greek Oral Composition as Seen Principally through Hesiod's "Works and Days."* Albany: State University of New York Press.

Peters, Leonard J. 1951. "The Relationship of the Old English *Andreas* to *Beowulf*." *Publications of the Modern Language Association* 66: 844-63.

Petrović, Svetozar. 1969. "Poredbeno proučavanje srpskohrvatskoga epskog deseterca i sporna pitanja njegovoga opisa." *Zbornik matice srpske za književnost i jezik* 17: 173-203.

————. 1974. "Jakobsonov opis srpskohrvatskog epskog deseterca." *Naučni sastanak slavista u Vukove dane* 4: 159-66.

Podlecki, Anthony J. 1961. "Guest-Gifts and Nobodies in *Odyssey 9*." *Phoenix* 15: 125-33.

Pope, John C. [1942] 1966. *The Rhythm of Beowulf: An Interpretation of the Normal and Hypermetric Verse-Forms in Old English Poetry*. Rev. ed. New Haven: Yale University Press.

————. 1981. "On the Composition of *Beowulf*." In *The Dating of Beowulf*, 188-95. *See* Chase 1981b.

Pope, M. W. M. 1963. "The Parry-Lord Theory of Homeric Composition." *Acta Classica* 6: 1-21.

Porter, Howard N. 1951. "The Early Greek Hexameter." *Yale Classical Studies* 12: 1-63.

Postlethwaite, N. 1981. "The Continuation of the *Odyssey*: Some Formulaic Evidence." *Classical Philology* 76: 177-87.

Powell, Barry B. 1977. *Composition by Theme in the Odyssey*. Beiträge zur classischen Philologie, no. 81. Meisenheim am Glan: Hain.

Prendergast, Guy L., comp. [1875] 1971. *A Complete Concordance to the Iliad of Homer*. Revised and edited by Benedetto Marzullo. Hildesheim: Georg Olms.

Puhvel, Jaan. 1976. "Response" [to "Formula and Meter," G. Nagy 1976]. In *Oral Literature and the Formula*, 261-63. *See* Stolz and Shannon 1976.

Radlov, Vasilii V. 1885. *Proben der Volksitteratur der nördlichen türkischen Stämme*. Vol. 5: *Der Dialect der Kara-Kirgisen*. St. Petersburg: Commissionäre der Kaiserlichen Akademie der Wissenschaften.

Raffel, Burton. 1986. "The Manner of Boyan: Translating Oral Literature." *Oral Tradition* 1: 11-29.

Ramsey, Lee C. 1971. "The Sea Voyages in *Beowulf*." *Neuphilologische Mitteilungen* 72: 51-59.

Reeve, M. D. 1973. "The Language of Achilles." *Classical Quarterly*, n.s. 23: 193-95.

Renoir, Alain. 1962a. "*Judith* and the Limits of Poetry." *English Studies* 43: 145-55.

————. 1962b. "Point of View and Design for Terror in *Beowulf*." *Neuphilologische Mitteilungen* 63: 154-67.

————. 1963. "The Heroic Oath in *Beowulf*, the *Chanson de Roland*, and the *Nibelungenlied*." In *Studies in Old English Literature in Honor of Arthur G. Brodeur*, edited by Stanley B. Greenfield, 237-66. Eugene: University of Oregon Press.

————. 1964. "Oral-Formulaic Theme Survival: A Possible Instance in the *Nibelungenlied*." *Neuphilologische Mitteilungen* 65: 70-75.

————. 1976a. "Crist Ihesu's Beasts of Battle: A Note on Oral-Formulaic Theme Survival." *Neophilologus* 60: 455-59.

————. 1976b. "Oral Theme and Written Texts." *Neuphilologische Mitteilungen* 77: 337-46.

————. 1977. "The Armor of the *Hildebrandslied*: An Oral-Formulaic Point of View." *Neuphilologische Mitteilungen* 78: 389-95.

————. 1979a. "The English Connection Revisited: A Reading Context for the *Hildebrandslied*." *Neophilologus* 63: 84-87.

————. 1979b. "Germanic Quintessence: The Theme of Isolation in the *Hildebrands-lied*." In *Saints, Scholars, and Heroes: Studies in Medieval Culture in Honour of Charles W. Jones*, edited by Margot King and Wesley M. Stevens, 2:143-78. Collegeville, Minn.: Hill Monastic Manuscript Library / St. John's Abbey and University.

————. 1979c. "The Kassel Manuscript and the Conclusion of the *Hildebrandslied*." *Manuscripta* 23: 104-8.

————. 1981a. "The Least Elegiac of the Elegies: A Contextual Glance at *The Husband's Message*." *Studia Neophilologica* 53: 69-76.

————. 1981b. "Oral-Formulaic Context: Implications for the Comparative Criticism of Mediaeval Texts." In *Oral Traditional Literature*, 416-39. See Foley 1981f.

————. 1986. "Oral-Formulaic Rhetoric and the Interpretation of Literary Texts." In *Oral Tradition in Literature*, 103-35. See Foley 1986d.

————. 1988. *A Key to Old Poems: The Oral-Formulaic Approach to the Interpretation of West-Germanic Verse*. University Park: Pennsylvania State University Press.

Riedinger, Anita. 1985. "The Old English Formula in Context." *Speculum* 60: 294-317.

Rissanen, Matti. 1969. "The Theme of 'Exile' in *The Wife's Lament*." *Neuphilologische Mitteilungen* 70: 90-104.

Ritzke-Rutherford, Jean. 1981a. "Formulaic Macrostructure: The Theme of Battle." In *The Alliterative Morte Arthure: A Reassessment of the Poem*, edited by Karl H. Göller, 83-95, 169-71. Arthurian Studies, no. 3. London: D. S. Brewer; Totowa, N.J.: Rowman and Littlefield.

————. 1981b. "Formulaic Microstructure: The Cluster." In *The Alliterative Morte Arthure*, 70-82, 167-69. See Ritzke-Rutherford 1981a.

Robinson, Fred C. 1985. *Beowulf and the Appositive Style*. Knoxville: University of Tennessee Press.

Rosenmeyer, Thomas G. 1965. "The Formula in Early Greek Poetry." *Arion* 4: 295-311.

Rossbach, A., and R. Westphal. 1867-68. *Metrik der Griechen im Vereine mit den übrigen musischen Künsten*. Vol. 2. Leipzig: Teubner.

Rothe, C. 1890. *Die Bedeutung der Wiederholungen für die homerische Frage*. Berlin: A. Haack.

Rudberg, Stig Y. 1972. "Etudes sur l'hexamètre homérique." In *Studi classici in onore di Quintino Cataudella*, 1:9-23. Catania: University of Catania.

Russo, Joseph A. 1963. "A Closer Look at Homeric Formulas." *Transactions of the American Philological Association* 94: 235-47.

————. 1966. "The Structural Formula in Homeric Verse." *Yale Classical Studies* 20: 217-40.

————. 1968. "Homer Against His Tradition." *Arion* 7: 275-95.

————. 1976. "Is 'Oral' or 'Aural' Composition the Cause of Homer's Formulaic Style?" In *Oral Literature and the Formula*, 31-54. See Stolz and Shannon 1976.

Russom, Geoffrey R. 1987. *Old English Meter and Linguistic Theory*. Cambridge: Cambridge University Press.

Sarrazin, Gregor. 1897. "Neue Beowulf-Studien." *Englische Studien* 23: 221-67.

Schaar, Claes. [1949] 1967. *Critical Studies in the Cynewulf Group*. New York: Haskell House.

SCHS. See Serbo-Croatian Heroic Songs.

Scott, William C. 1974. *The Oral Nature of the Homeric Simile*. Mnemosyne, Bibliotheca Classica Batava, supplement no. 28. Leiden: E. J. Brill.

Segal, Charles P. 1971. *The Theme of the Mutilation of the Corpse in the Iliad.* Mnemosyne, Bibliotheca Classica Batava, supplement no. 17. Leiden: E. J. Brill.

Serbo-Croatian Heroic Songs (Srpskohrvatske junačke pjesme), 1953-. Collected, edited, and translated by Milman Parry, Albert B. Lord, and David E. Bynum. Vols. 1-4, 6, 8, 14. Cambridge, Mass.: Harvard University Press / Center for the Study of Oral Literature. (Vols. 1-2 co-published with the Serbian Academy of Sciences.)

Shannon, Richard S. 1975. *The Arms of Achilles and Homeric Compositional Technique.* Mnemosyne, Bibliotheca Classica Batava, supplement no. 36. Leiden: E.J. Brill.

Sievers, Eduard. 1885. "Zur Rhythmik des germanischen Alliterationsverses I." *Beiträge zur Geschichte der deutschen Sprache und Literatur* 10: 209-314.

————. 1893. *Altgermanische Metrik.* Halle: Niemeyer.

————. 1968. "Old Germanic Metrics and Old English Metrics." Translated by Gawaina D. Luster. In *Essential Articles for the Study of Old English Poetry*, edited by Jess B. Bessinger, Jr., and Stanley J. Kahrl, 267-88. Hamden, Conn.: Archon.

Sisam, Kenneth. [1946] 1953. "The Authority of Old English Poetical Manuscripts." In *Studies in the History of Old English Literature*, 29-44. Oxford: Clarendon Press. (Originally published in *Review of English Studies* 22: 256-68.)

Škaljić, Abdulah. 1979. *Turcizmi u srpskohrvatskom jeziku.* 4th ed. Sarajevo: Svjetlost.

Skendi, Stavro. 1953. "The South Slavic Decasyllable in Albanian Oral Epic Poetry." *Word* 9: 339-48.

Snodgrass, A. M. 1971. *The Dark Age of Greece: An Archaeological Survey of the Eleventh to the Eighth Centuries B.C.* Edinburgh: Edinburgh University Press.

————. 1974. "An Historical Homeric Society?" *Journal of Hellenic Studies* 94: 114-25.

Stanford, W. B. 1969. "Euphonic Reasons for the Choice of Homeric Formulae?" *Hermathena* 108: 14-17.

Stankiewicz, Edward. 1973. "The Rhyming Formula in Serbo-Croatian Heroic Poetry." In *Slavic Poetics: Essays in Honor of Kiril Taranovsky*, edited by Roman Jakobson, C. H. van Schooneveld, and Dean S. Worth, 417-31. The Hague: Mouton.

Stock, Brian. 1983. *The Implications of Literacy: Written Language and Models of Interpretation in the Eleventh and Twelfth Centuries.* Princeton: Princeton University Press.

Stolz, Benjamin A. 1969. "On Two Serbo-Croatian Oral Epic Verses: The *Bugarštica* and the *Deseterac.*" In *Poetic Theory / Poetic Practice*, edited by Robert Scholes, 153-64. Iowa City: Midwest Modern Language Association.

Stolz, Benjamin A., and Richard S. Shannon, eds. 1976. *Oral Literature and the Formula.* Ann Arbor: Center for Coordination of Ancient and Modern Studies.

Taylor, Paul B. 1967. "Themes of Death in *Beowulf.*" In *Old English Poetry: Fifteen Essays*, edited by Robert P. Creed, 249-74. Providence, R.I.: Brown University Press.

Tedlock, Dennis. 1983. *The Spoken Word and the Work of Interpretation.* Philadelphia: University of Pennsylvania Press.

Thormann, Janet. 1970. "Variations on the Theme of 'The Hero on the Beach' in *The Phoenix.*" *Neuphilologische Mitteilungen* 71: 187-90.

Thornton, Agathe. 1970. *People and Themes in Homer's Odyssey.* London: Methuen; Dunedin, N.Z.: University of Otago Press.

Tolkien, J. R. R. 1936. "*Beowulf*: The Monsters and the Critics." *Proceedings of the British Academy* 22: 245-95.

Traerup, Birthe. 1974. "Albanian Singers in Kosovo." Translated by John Bergsagel. In *Festschrift Ernst Emsheimer*, edited by Gustav Hilleström, 244-51, 300. Musikhistoriska Museets Skrifter, no. 5; Studia Instrumentorum Musicae Popularis, no. 3. Stockholm: Musikhistoriska Museet.

Tripp, Raymond P. 1983. *More About the Fight with the Dragon: Beowulf 2208b-3182.* Lanham, Md.: University Press of America.

Turner, Frederick. 1986. "Performed Being: Word Art as a Human Inheritance." *Oral Tradition* 1: 66-109.

Tyler, Lee Edgar. In preparation. "Traditional Structure in the Heroic Oaths in *Beowulf.*"

van Otterlo, Willem A. A. 1944a. "Eine merkwürdige Kompositionsform der älteren griechischen Literatur." *Mnemosyne,* 3d ser., 12: 192-207.

————. 1944b. *Untersuchungen über Begriff, Anwendung, und Entstehung der griechischen Ringkomposition.* Mededeelingen der Nederlandsche Akademie van Wetenschappen, Afdeeling Letterkunde, n.s. 7, no. 3. Amsterdam: Noord-Hollandsche Uitgevers.

————. 1948. *De ringcompositie als opbouwprincipe in de epische gedichten van Homerus.* Verhandelingen der Koninklijke Nederlandsche Akademie van Wetenschappen, Afdeeling Letterkunde, n.s. 51, no. 1. Amsterdam: Noord-Hollandsche Uitgevers.

Vigorita, John F. 1976. "The Antiquity of Serbo-Croatian Verse." *Južnoslovenski filolog* 32: 205-11.

————. 1977a. "The Indo-European Origins of the Greek Hexameter and Distich." *Zeitschrift für vergleichende Sprachforschung* 91: 288-99.

————. 1977b. "The Indo-European 12-Syllable Line." *Zeitschrift für vergleichende Sprachforschung* 90: 37-46.

Vivante, Paolo. 1975. "On Homer's Winged Words." *Classical Quarterly* n.s. 25: 1-12.

————. 1982. *The Epithets in Homer: A Study in Poetic Values.* New Haven: Yale University Press.

Watkins, Calvert W. 1963. "Indo-European Metrics and Archaic Irish Verse." *Celtica* 6: 194-249.

————. 1976. "Response" [to "Oral Poetry," Kiparsky 1976]. In *Oral Literature and the Formula,* 107-11. See Stolz and Shannon 1976.

Webber, Ruth House. 1951. *Formulistic Diction in the Spanish Ballad.* University of California Publications in Modern Philology 34, no. 2: 175-277.

————. 1986. "The *Cantar de Mio Cid*: Problems of Interpretation." In *Oral Tradition in Literature,* 65-88. See Foley 1986d.

West, Martin L. 1970. "A New Approach to Greek Prosody." *Glotta* 48: 185-94.

————. 1973a. "Greek Poetry 2000-700 B.C." *Classical Quarterly,* n.s. 23: 179-92.

————. 1973b. "Indo-European Metre." *Glotta* 51: 161-87.

West, Stephanie, ed. 1967. *The Ptolemaic Papyri of Homer.* Wissenschaftliche Abhandlungen der Arbeitsgemeinschaft für Forschung des Landes Nordrhein-Westfalen, Papyrologica Coloniensia, no. 3. Cologne: Westdeutscher Verlag.

Whitman, Cedric H. 1958. *Homer and the Heroic Tradition.* Cambridge, Mass.: Harvard University Press. (Reprint New York: W. W. Norton, 1965.)

Wolf, Carol J. 1970. "Christ as Hero in *The Dream of the Rood.*" *Neuphilologische Mitteilungen* 71: 202-10.

Zupitza, Julius, ed. [1882] 1959. *Beowulf* [ms. facsimile]. Revised by Norman Davis. Early English Text Society, no. 245. London: Oxford University Press.

INDEX

Adonean clausula, 64–65, 83, 124, 149, 149n31, 152, 250n19, 263, 264. *See also* Hexameter, Homeric
Advent Lyrics, 18
Aesthetics, question of, 1n1, 2, 2n4, 200, 235, 239, 265, 269–70, 276, 335, 391
Alagić Alija and Velagić Selim, 43, 51 (table 2), 91n68, 284–88, 312–24, 363–69
Albanian oral epic, 193n65
Alexandrian scholars, 21, 23, 25, 26, 28, 29, 30, 31. *See also* Homeric texts
Aliaga Stočević, 47, 171n31
Allen, Thomas W., 25n10
Allen, W. Sidney, 63, 69n36
Alliterative line (of Anglo-Saxon poetry): alliteration as feature of, 108, 116; anacrusis in, 114, 114n100; in charms, 17; and *deseterac*, contrasted, 13; general structure of, 53, 82n56, 106–19, 214, 355n40, 389, 390; half-lines (verses) as units in, 107–19; hybrid prosody, 202–3; idiosyncratic nature of, 109–10; lack of inner or outer metric, 110; lack of syllabicity, 109–10, 112, 202; metrical formulas, 117–19, 203, 203n4, 204, 213n29, 216; question of Indo-European background, 18, 53, 58–59, 61–62, 110, 115, 202, 203n5, 389; ramification, principle of, 109–11, 112, 116, 117; resolution, principle of, 109–11, 112, 116, 117; Sievers's Five Types, 106–9, 111, 114, 202; "single verses," 109n95; stress, grades of, 111; stress-patterns in, 36n38, 61, 107–19; stress-position as prosodeme in, 109, 202; symmetry of verse structure, 204; systems of scansion, 111–15, 116–17, 117 (table 15)
Amory Parry, Anne, 255n30
Amos, Ashley Crandell, 34n34
Analytic categories. *See* Ethnic (emic) vs. analytic (etic) categories
Andreas, 17, 225, 225n55, 329, 336, 342n22, 344–54, 391
Aoidos (ancient Greek bard), 22, 25, 27, 29
Arant, Patricia, 280n4
Arend, Walter, 240–41, 242, 245, 248, 248n15, 252, 254, 255, 279n2
Aristarchus of Samothrace, 23, 23n7, 24, 25, 28, 29
Aristophanes of Byzantium, 23
A Scholia, 26, 26n14
Ashby, Genette, 159n3
Austerlitz, Robert, 57n10, 163n16, 204n7, 291, 291n26

Compositor: Thomson Press (India) Limited, New Delhi
       Text: 10/12 Baskerville
    Display: Baskerville
    Printer: Braun-Brumfield, Inc.
     Binder: Braun-Brumfield, Inc.